ARKANSAS

A Guide to the State

ARKANSAS

A GUIDE TO THE STATE

*Compiled by Workers of the Writers' Program
of the Work Projects Administration
in the State of Arkansas*

AMERICAN GUIDE SERIES

ILLUSTRATED

Sponsored by C. G. Hall, Secretary of State, Arkansas

HASTINGS HOUSE · Publishers · NEW YORK

MCMXLI

FIRST PUBLISHED IN 1941

ARKANSAS STATE PLANNING BOARD
State-wide Sponsor of the
Arkansas Writers' Project

FEDERAL WORKS AGENCY
JOHN M. CARMODY, *Administrator*

WORK PROJECTS ADMINISTRATION
HOWARD O. HUNTER, *Commissioner*
FLORENCE KERR, *Assistant Commissioner*
FLOYD SHARP, *State Administrator*

This book, Arkansas' contribution to the American Guide Series, portrays the state from a viewpoint broader than is ordinarily chosen by a writer or group of writers. Arkansas: A Guide to the State performs several major services: it describes present-day Arkansas and assembles historic details of the past four centuries. It pictures the myriad activities of the region, setting forth the characteristics that give the state unusual variety and interest. It is a source of information for visitors exploring our towns and landmarks and for residents who would know more of their own communities.

Because of its faithful representation of the state and the skill and industry that went into its creation, this guidebook is destined, in my opinion, to serve as a fund of knowledge and understanding of Arkansas for years to come.

C. G. Hall
Secretary of State

79762

Preface

Arkansas: A Guide to the State is the work of a group of research assistants, writers, and editors, who have been aided by scores of volunteer consultants. Because the economic patterns and the folkways of the State have changed greatly in a decade, it has been especially necessary in Arkansas to add to the material obtained from official agencies facts and ideas acquired from the man in the street. Whether questions were asked of apple growers or archeologists, highway engineers or historians, postmasters or professors, the answers were invariably courteous and informative.

To obtain information for the guide, workers of the Arkansas Writers' Project have haunted libraries, handled countless faded documents in archives, and read hundreds of books, magazines, and newspapers. They have driven thousands of miles over highways that crisscross the Delta, slice through deep pine forests, follow river valleys, and ride the ridges of the Ozarks and Ouachitas. It is hoped that out of this collective effort has come an account that represents fairly the yesterday and today of Arkansas.

The editors are deeply grateful to all of the persons named in the List of Consultants appearing in the Appendix. Appreciation for exceptionally valuable assistance is due M. C. Blackman, W. J. Lemke, and L. A. Henry, all of whom read the entire manuscript. Most of the drawings are by Clifton King. Fletcher Miller and H. A. Thomas each contributed two drawings.

The several quotations from Thomas Nuttall's *Journal of Travels into the Arkansa Territory, 1819* are reprinted from Volume XIII of Thwaites' *Early Western Travels,* by permission of the publishers, The Arthur H. Clark Company.

Mrs. Bernie Babcock, Assistant Supervisor of the Arkansas Writers' Project, and the late Charles J. Finger, former State Editor, supervised the early stages of the work. Jean Winkler, Walter E. Rowland, Miss Faye Webber, and Richard F. McCue were members of the editorial staff while the final manuscript was being prepared.

DALLAS McKOWN, State Supervisor

Contents

Part I. Arkansas: Past and Present

Part II. Cities and Towns

Part III. Tours

Page

Part IV. Appendices

Illustrations

xiii

Maps

General Information

Railroads: Principal lines include Missouri Pacific R.R. (MOP); St. Louis-San Francisco Ry. (Frisco); Chicago, Rock Island & Pacific Ry. (Rock Island); St. Louis Southwestern Ry. (Cotton Belt); Missouri & Arkansas Ry. (M&A); Kansas City Southern Ry. (KCS); Louisiana & Arkansas Ry. (L&A); Texas & Pacific Ry. (T&P). There are 34 railroads in Arkansas (of which 15 are interstate), with a total length of 4,711 miles.

Highways: Thirteen Federal highways; principal through routes are US 64, 65, 67, 70, 71, and 82. Total Federal mileage is 5,284; State mileage, 9,280. State gasoline tax is 6½¢.

Bus Lines: Approximately 55 bus lines, of which about 40 are intrastate. Chief interstate lines are: Missouri Pacific Trailways; Southwestern Greyhound Lines, Inc.; Santa Fe Trailways; Tri-State Trailways; Crown Coach Co.; and Arkansas Motor Coaches.

Air Lines: American Airlines, Inc. (transcontinental by way of Memphis and Dallas) stop at Little Rock. Charter airplanes available at several airports, including those at Little Rock, Fort Smith, Hot Springs, Pine Bluff, Texarkana, Stuttgart, and West Memphis.

Waterways: No regular passenger service. Limited freight service furnished by steamboats and barge lines operating on Mississippi, Ouachita, and White Rivers.

Motor Vehicle Laws: Maximum speed for passenger cars, 60 m.p.h.; busses and half-ton trucks 55 m.p.h. For larger trucks the speed limit ranges downward to a maximum of 35 m.p.h. according to tonnage. Residents required to carry driver's license; minimum age for drivers, 16 years. Nonresidents may operate motor vehicles 90 days without Arkansas license, provided they obtain a permit within 30 days. Trucks may be halted by officers and their loads weighed at any time and place. Personal injury or property damage of $50 or more must be reported in writing to Arkansas State Police Department within 24 hours after an accident occurs. Hand signals required by law. A digest of traffic laws may be obtained from Arkansas State Highway Department, Little Rock, or from any American Automobile Association affiliate.

Prohibited: Passing streetcars on L. or while they are loading or un-loading (except at safety zones); passing, in excess of 10 m.p.h., a school bus while loading or unloading children; parking on highways; coasting with gears in neutral; hitch-hiking.

Warning: Since most counties do not require fencing of livestock, mo-torists should drive carefully to avoid striking animals.

Arkansas State Police Headquarters: State headquarters at Little Rock; district offices at Fort Smith, Hope, El Dorado, and Newport.

Accommodations: Good hotels in principal towns and cities. Tourist camps, many with modern conveniences, are numerous along heavily traveled highways and near large towns. Housekeeping cabins are available in most State parks and at several points in the national forests. Mountain resorts offer accommodations varying from elaborate hotel service to sleeping rooms or cabins.

Open seasons for hunting (dates inclusive): Deer (bucks), second Tuesday in Nov. to following Saturday, and second Tuesday in Dec. to following Saturday. Squirrels, May 15-June 15 and Oct. 1-Jan. 1 (no closed season on squirrels in Marion County, but the bag limit is 6 daily; open season on squirrels in Baxter County May 15-June 15 and Sept. 1-Dec. 31; Stone County June 1-Jan. 1). Fur-bearing animals (such as opossum, raccoon, fox, skunk), Dec. 1-Jan. 31. Fox may be chased at any time for pleasure but (except during open sea-son) must be released if caught. Turkey, Apr. 1-Apr. 15. Quail, Dec. 1-Jan. 31. Duck and geese (except wood duck and Ross' geese), Nov. 15-Dec. 29. Rails and gallinules (except coot), Sept. 1-Nov. 30. Doves, Sept. 15-Nov. 30. Woodcock, Nov. 15-Dec. 15. Seasons on all migratory birds subject to change by U. S. Fish and Wildlife Service. No open season until 1943 on beaver, bear, otter, elk, prairie chicken, pheasant, and Hungarian partridge. Bag limits: deer, 1 buck each season; squirrel, 8 daily; duck, 10 daily; geese and brant, 4 daily; quail, 12 daily; doves, 15 daily; rails and gallinules (except sora and coot), 15 daily; coot, 25 daily; woodcock, 4 daily; Wilson's snipe and jacksnipe, 15 daily; turkey, 2 gobblers each season. In the case of quail, duck, geese, or squirrel hunters may possess not more than two days' bag limit, and in the case of rails, gallinules, coot, snipe, wood-cock, or doves only one day's limit.

Hunting Licenses: Nonresident, $25 for all game except fur-bearing animals, or $15 for all game except deer, turkey, and fur-bearing animals. Resident (16 years of age or older), all game $1.50; no license required for squirrel or rabbit. Dogs for hunting deer and game birds, $1.50 each. Nonresident license has three tags, each good for shipment of one day's bag. Not more than one bag a day or two a week may be shipped or carried out of the State. Chicot and Desha Counties require county license in addition to State license for all game except rabbit.

Prohibited: Use of live decoys in taking any species of waterfowl; transporting or exporting game from State, except under nonresident license; shooting migratory birds with repeating shotgun holding more than three shells, or from an automobile, boat, or airplane; taking waterfowl at any time other than between 7 a.m. and 4 p.m.; hunting deer or game birds at night with headlight or torch; trapping deer, turkey, or game birds; buying or selling any protected game bird or animal except for propagation purposes under game breeder's permit.

Fishing: Game fish include bass, trout, jack salmon, pike, bream, crappie, and perch. Open season for taking game fish (except trout) with artificial lures, May 16-Mar. 15; trout, May 1-Oct. 31. All game fish (except bass and trout during completely closed season) may be taken with live bait (minnows, worms, etc.) throughout the year. Daily limit of game fish: trout, pike, and jack salmon, 6; bream and perch, 25; bass and crappie, 15. No more than 25 game fish of all species may be taken in one day, and fishermen may not possess more than two days' catch. Minimum in inches: largemouthed and smallmouthed bass, 10; crappie and calico bass, 8; walleyed pike, 14; trout, 12.

Fishing Licenses: Nonresident (annual), $5; 10-day trip, $2; resident (using artificial bait), $1.50 (no fee if live bait used); trotlines up to 1,000 feet, $5; for each additional 1,000 feet, $2.50; mussel gathering, resident, $1; nonresident, $25.

Prohibited: Use, possession or sale of artificial bait having more than nine hooks; gigging (in most counties), except July 1-Aug. 31; use of wire net or trap; grabbing or grabbling (with hands or hooks) of game fish; shooting fish; dynamiting waters; selling buffalo fish less than 16 inches in length; transporting or exporting game fish from State except under nonresident license; placing any intoxicating or stupefying substances or poisonous chemical in water; taking minnows Mar. 16-May 1.

Liquor Regulations: Beer served in most restaurants and hotels. Spirituous liquors may be sold in licensed liquor stores, in original package. Bottles must bear Federal and State stamps and may not be opened and consumed where purchased nor in any public place. No liquor sales are permitted on Sundays or until after closing of the polls on election days.

National Parks and Forests: Hot Springs National Park, Hot Springs; Ouachita National Forest, western Arkansas; Ozark National Forest, northwestern Arkansas.

State Parks: Crowley's Ridge State Park, 9.7 m. W. of Paragould on State 25; Petit Jean State Park, 14.7 m. SW. of Morrilton on State 154; Mount Nebo State Park, 6.7 m. W. of Dardanelle on State 155; Devil's Den State Park, 11.3 m. SW. of Winslow on State 170; Lake Catherine State Park, 12.5 m. NW. of Malvern on US 270; Buffalo River State Park, 16.9 m. S. of Yellville on State 14; Arkansas Post State Park, 10.2 m. S. of Gillett on State 1 (interest chiefly historical); Watson State Park (for Negroes), 8.9 m. NW. of Pine Bluff on US 270.

Prohibited: Making fires within the limits of any State park or game refuge except under rules of the State Parks Commission or State Game and Fish Commission.

Golf: Approximately 50 golf courses in Arkansas. Outstanding links are those of the Little Rock Country Club, the Hot Springs Country Club, and the Texarkana Country Club. Courses open to the public on payment of a greens fee include Riverside, Concordia, and Fair Park courses in Little Rock, the three 18-hole links of the Hot Springs Country Club, three courses at Fort Smith, and others.

Other Games and Sports: Day and night professional baseball games played by the Little Rock Travelers, of the Southern Baseball Association (Class A-1). University of Arkansas Homecoming game marks the peak of the football season. Water carnivals are staged at Batesville and elsewhere; bird dog and foxhound field trials at various points in the State; rodeos at Fort Smith, Harrison, and North Little Rock; horse racing in Hot Springs for 30 days beginning in February; greyhound racing at West Memphis for 80 days beginning in May; an annual 'possum hunt and banquet at Mena in December.

Poisonous Snakes and Plants: Rattlesnakes and copperheads are occasionally found in the woods, especially in the hill country; cottonmouth moccasins are infrequently encountered in swamps. Poison oak and poison ivy grow throughout the State.

Information Service: American Automobile Association affiliates throughout the State; Arkansas Highway Department, State Capitol,

Little Rock; Arkansas Publicity Department, State Capitol, Little Rock; Arkansas State Chamber of Commerce, 120 E. 2nd St., Little Rock.

Miscellany of Facts: State flag: a blue-bordered white diamond on a rectangular field of red; the border contains 25 stars, the diamond 4 stars.   State flower: apple blossom.   State tree: pine.   State bird: mockingbird.   State nickname: the Wonder State, because of a wide variety of natural resources.   Population: 1,949,387 (1940 census).

Calendar of Events

FEBRUARY

Last week	at Hot Springs	Opening Horse Races at Oaklawn Park (30 days)
No fixed date	Hot Springs	Opening Major League Baseball School

MARCH

No fixed date	at Nashville	Peach Blossom Pilgrimage
No fixed date	no fixed place	All-State High School Choral Festival

MARCH OR APRIL

Easter	at Hot Springs	Community Easter Service

APRIL

First week	at Pine Bluff	Spring Livestock Show
Last week	no fixed place	State High School Band Contest
No fixed date	at Rogers, Bentonville, Siloam Springs, Fayetteville, and Springdale	Apple Blossom Pilgrimage

MAY

Second week	West Memphis	Opening Greyhound Races (80 days)
Last week	at Fort Smith	Arkansas-Oklahoma Rodeo
No fixed date	at El Dorado	South Arkansas Music Festival

MAY OR JUNE

No fixed date	no fixed place	State Amateur Golf Tournament

JUNE OR JULY

No fixed date	at Monticello	Tomato Festival

JULY

Fourth	at Hot Springs	Outboard Speedboat Regatta
Second week	at Pine Bluff	State Tennis Tournament (open to Arkansans only)
Third week	at Nashville	Peach Festival
No fixed date	at Clarksville	Johnson County Peach Festival

AUGUST

First week	at Little Rock	State Open Tennis Tournament
Second week	at Batesville	White River Water Carnival
No fixed date	at Tontitown	Grape Festival
No fixed date	State-wide	County Singing Conventions

SEPTEMBER

Last week	at Texarkana	Bowie County (Texas) Fair
No fixed date	at Blytheville	Mississippi County Fair

SEPTEMBER OR OCTOBER

No fixed date	at West Helena	Phillips County Fair

OCTOBER

First week	at Arkadelphia	Livestock Show
No fixed date	no fixed place	Arkansas State Singing Convention
No fixed date	at Blytheville	Cotton Picking Contest
No fixed date	at Heber Springs	North Arkansas Fox Hunters Meet
No fixed date	at Newport	American Legion Horse Show
No fixed date	at Fort Smith	Livestock Exposition
No fixed date	at North Little Rock	Arkansas Livestock Show and Rodeo
No fixed date	at Pine Bluff	Fall Livestock Show
No fixed date	at Jonesboro	Fall Festival
No fixed date	at El Dorado	Union County Fair

NOVEMBER

First Saturday	at Fayetteville	University of Arkansas Homecoming Day
Fourteenth	at Stuttgart	Duck Calling Contest
No fixed date	at Roe	Bird Dog Field Trials
No fixed date	no fixed place	Arkansas State Fox Hunters Bench and Field Trials

DECEMBER

Eighth	at Texarkana	Founders' Day
No fixed date	at Mena	Polk County 'Possum Hunt and Banquet

PART I

Arkansas: Past and Present

Arkansas Today

NOT long ago a traveler said that Arkansas is "between the South of the piazza and the West of the pony." That is a pretty good characterization, although it would pin the truth down a bit better if it included in "the South of the piazza" some of the plantation country between Little Rock and the Mississippi River. At any rate, the traveler noticed that there is a world of difference between a level, black cottonfield bordered by a levee near Helena, and a loamy pasture where Herefords graze alongside the Texas Line, about two hundred miles west. He saw that Arkansas is where two contrasting regions meet, and that their ways of life sometimes blend, especially in towns scattered through the center of the State. The topography itself has no shadings. East of the mountain-plains line that runs down from Pocahontas to the neighborhood of Texarkana, the land sweeps flat. West of the line the Ozarks and Ouachitas rise abruptly, and there is no gradual transition from lowland to upland.

Probably the best way to sample the impressions Arkansas offers would be to come in through each of the four corners. If you enter through Benton County, in the northwest corner, you will see apple orchards, strawberries, level grainfields, and new farmhouses; you will think you are in the Midwest, in Indiana or Illinois.

But if you drive down from St. Louis, entering at Blytheville, you will see cottonfields to the most distant horizon. Much of the land around here is in new plantations, cleared of timber and crossed with drainage ditches only two generations ago. Over Colonial plantation homes, sharecropper cabins, and barns plastered with signs advertising patent medicines is the feel of the Mississippi. Although you can't see the river, you can get to it by taking side roads, and you'll never fail to be impressed by its majestic sweep. Perhaps in the distance a tugboat thrashes behind a string of barges, so slowly that it seems to stand still. Then a cloud of white steam spurts up and threatens to vanish before the blast of the whistle reaches your ears. You may run across an old-timer who knows where one gaudy packet after another ripped out its bottom trying to compete with the railroads.

Coming from Louisiana into Chicot County, a long way downriver from Blytheville, the traveler sees gray Spanish moss hanging from the trees, and recalls that Creoles and sugar cane are not far to the south.

The journal of an early nineteenth-century expedition commented on this Spanish moss that barely comes into the southeast tip of Arkansas: "It appears that nature has marked with a distinguishing feature [a boundary] line established by Congress."

It's a "fur piece" across from the bayou country to Texarkana's corner, but there you will find the wide-brimmed Stetsons and stockmen's boots that symbolize the nearness of grasslands extending to the Rio Grande and New Mexico.

No matter where you go in Arkansas you discover that its people are close to the soil. In a Little Rock hotel lobby, where legislators stand around in a fog of tobacco smoke, a moderately good ear can distinguish the drawled "heahs" and "theahs" of a cotton-county representative from the slightly nasal burr of a hillman—who is likely to pronounce "put" as "putt" and "where" as "whir." Both men, however, probably know from boyhood experience the kick of a plow when it strikes a root, how hard it is to stalk a crow, and the disheartening length of a field when viewed over a hoe handle. And there is a chance that both are pestering their tenants and hired men by insisting that the green of cover crops, such as oats, vetch, and clover, is really a vernal economic promise.

The cotton planter today may have lines of worry on his face and spend many an evening making out reports, instead of being one of "that lordly race of men" described by Opie Read. But he still swears in the loud, clear tones of a man who feels that his nearest equal lives a long distance away, and, like a Western cattleman, he drives automobiles where they weren't meant to be driven. In an expensive suit he splashes across muddy fields, with a fine disregard that awes the Negroes.

The hillman is usually more reserved and cautious. One of his ancestors may have floated a wagon across the Mississippi by lashing logs alongside. From a town like Batesville, where the Ozarks become steep, the pioneer set out in search of a homestead. He held a rifle under one arm, and from the creaking wagon peered a tired wife and a bevy of wide-eyed children. He built a dogtrot cabin, haggled the timber off a hillside, and plowed shallow furrows around the stumps in this "miniature Appalachia."

The settler from Tennessee took hardships in his stride, but London and New York journalists who wandered through often found fault with wilderness ways. Salt-meat diets, noisy taverns, and saddle sores were always getting into print, and soon a linsey-woolsey mantle had been thrown over Arkansas, to remain there a long time. Just why they picked on Arkansas is still a mystery, made deeper by the fact that Arkansans themselves have created some of the most widely circulated myths. Colonel "Sandy" Faulkner, an Arkansan, concocted the fiddle tune and dialogue known as "The Arkansaw Traveler." A celebrated picture based on the dialogue was painted by another Arkansan, Edward Payson Washburn. One of the State's most prominent political figures was Charles Fenton Mercer Noland ("Pete Whetstone"), who wrote broad humor for a New York paper a hundred years before Bob Burns of Van Buren stood in front of a microphone and began to immortalize imaginary relatives.

Arkansas is not like that at all, of course. In its cottonfields the Diesel tractor is displacing the bobbing mule, while low overhead an airplane lays down a smoke-screen of boll-weevil poison at a hundred miles an hour. There is a promise of new industries and the further development of resources, such as mercury-bearing cinnabar, coal, bauxite, and manganese.

Part of the wealth of Arkansas today is not in its minerals and forests, but in the sights and sounds encountered by a visitor. It may be the small thunder of a covey of quail that he will remember longest, or a flight of mallards wheeling down into a swamp because of a hunter's expertly rendered call, or the bright glow of strawstacks burning in the ricefields after threshing time. The zigzag rail fences overgrown with honeysuckle, the clear smokeless air in the cities, the tumbling of the mountains eastward from Winslow, the smell of woodsmoke from a great stone chimney at the end of a cabin, the pungency of pine sawdust and the whine of the saw biting into a log, the clumps of mistletoe in leafless trees. You won't forget those things soon, even though they are not the important aspects of Arkansas, where the politeness of the South and the friendliness of the West are both responsible for that personal tone in "Y'awl hurry back."

Natural Setting

ARKANSAS is bounded on the north by Missouri; on the east it is separated from Mississippi and Tennessee by the Mississippi River; to the south is Louisiana; and stretching away to the west are the plains of Oklahoma and Texas. In size it stands twenty-sixth among the States, with an area of 53,335 square miles; of these, 810 are water.

From the point where the Mississippi first touches Arkansas, lowlands sweep in a constantly widening arc until they run all the way across the State to Oklahoma and Texas. To the northwest rise the Ozark and Ouachita Mountains, reaching an altitude of nearly 3,000 feet. With adjacent elevations that spill over into neighboring States, the Arkansas uplands (classified as the Interior Highland Province) constitute the only mountains between the Appalachians and the Rockies. The line between the lowland and hill sections is remarkably distinct, particularly at the eastern edge of the Ozarks, where the lift from plain to upland is forecast by only a few mound-shaped sentinel hills.

The level eastern and southern parts of the State comprise the Mississippi Alluvial Plain and the West Gulf Coastal Plain. The Alluvial Plain reaches from the river to the edge of the mountains near Little Rock, then narrows southward. The tablelike surface is broken only by a long, narrow strip of hills called Crowley's Ridge, which runs from the Missouri Line some 150 miles to Helena. Varying in width from half a mile to 12 miles and reaching an altitude of 550 feet near its northern extremity, the Ridge is a notable landmark, its yellow wind-deposited loess topsoil contrasting with the black alluvial earth of the Delta through which it strikes.

In 1889 Dr. John C. Branner, then State Geologist, surmised that the Ridge resulted from two gigantic shifts in the channel of the Mississippi. The river, he held, originally ran west of the Ridge, clearing a broad valley there; then it broke through the hills at Chalk Bluff (*see Tour 4a*), followed the present channel of the St. Francis, and flowed east of the Ridge to Helena. Eventually, it cut farther north, to Cairo, the present confluence of the Ohio and Mississippi. Thus the Ridge represents, according to this explanation, the uneroded strip between the two old channels of the Mississippi. While Branner's view is usually accepted, dissenters claim that the Ridge was uplifted by a folding of the earth's crust, and that it is still being raised. For proof they point to a difference of 13.4 feet in elevation readings at the Piggott courthouse over a 41-year period.

Travelers coming from the Mississippi Delta to the West Gulf Coastal Plain notice not so much the slight rise in elevation as a considerable change in the country's appearance. Near the river vast tracts of the rich land have been cleared and are cultivated in cotton plantations. The clay and sandstone soils farther west, however, are heavily forested, and the occasional farms are of the small, self-sufficient type. The West Gulf Coastal Plain is the great timber belt of Arkansas.

The hill section of the State, like the lowland, is divided into two areas of nearly equal size. To the north are the Ozark plateaus, and to the south is the Ouachita province; between them flows the Arkansas River, through a wide valley which is included in the Ouachita subdivision.

The Ozarks rise from the eastern lowlands in a succession of rolling, tree-covered hills that gradually gain altitude as they continue west and south. The lower portion is known as the Salem and the higher as the Springfield Plateau, but the casual observer will see no particular difference in them. In the extreme northwestern corner of Arkansas the Springfield Plateau is fairly level except where it is cut by deep valleys; here is some of the State's best land for general farming. On the south the plateaus give way to the Boston Mountains, most rugged of the Ozarks. "Gorges 500 to 1,400 feet deep, which lie between steep ridges and jagged spurs, are common enough to warrant the application of the term 'mountainous' to this highland region," says the State Planning Board's *Progress Report* (1936).

By a paradox of topographical classification the Arkansas Valley contains the highest and most impressive peaks of the State. Among these elevations are Nebo, for generations a resort spot; Petit Jean, cleft by a canyon which includes a 75-foot waterfall; and Magazine, which rears its vast bulk 2,300 feet abruptly from the valley floor, and stands 2,823 feet above sea level. South of the Arkansas Valley are the Ouachita Mountains proper, which are subdivided into the Fourche Mountains, the Novaculite Uplift (so called because it is ringed by ridges of this rock, used for whetstones), and the Athens Piedmont Plateau, which dwindles gradually into the West Gulf Coastal Plain. Near Oklahoma, the Ouachitas attain considerable height, and a peak of Rich Mountain just across the border tops even Magazine. Pine-clad, jumbled, and even less inhabited than the Ozarks, the Ouachitas run from Little Rock's back door across the western half of the State, and (especially in the Novaculite Uplift) contain a number of rare and valuable minerals.

All of Arkansas drains southeast into the Mississippi River. Even the White River, which heads into Missouri from the north side of the Boston Mountains, makes a great loop and returns to enter the Mississippi only a few miles from the mouth of the Arkansas. The latter stream, flowing nearly 1,500 miles from its source high in the Colorado Rockies, is the State's principal waterway. The strip between the outlets of the White and Arkansas Rivers is so narrow that a cutoff channel has developed between them, through which water sometimes flows in one direction, sometimes in the opposite. Other major rivers of Arkansas are the St. Francis, which drains the upper Mississippi Delta; the Black, once a heavily traveled tributary of the White; the Ouachita, with its branches, the Little Missouri and the Saline; and the Red, which forms part of the Arkansas-Texas boundary.

In the mountain country the rivers are swift, clear, and cold. When they emerge into the lowlands they meander in lazy bends during dry seasons. Under pressure of floodwaters they swell and sometimes straighten their channels, leaving the abandoned bends as oxbow lakes. Crescent-shaped Lake Chicot, alongside the Mississippi near the Louisiana border, is the most extensive of these riverbed lagoons.

In many parts of the State countless springs pour from the soil. Mammoth Spring, in the Ozarks just below the Missouri Line, is one of the largest in North America, and the hot springs in the Ouachitas have been nationally known for 100 years.

CLIMATE

The climate of Arkansas "is mild, healthful, and very favorable for agricultural and other pursuits" (United States Weather Bureau, *Climatic Summary,* 1930). Most residents of the State greet snow as an infrequent but welcome visitor. In the mountains, of course, it falls more often than elsewhere, and lies longer on the ground, but the average annual depth over a 40-year period for even the Ozark Mountain section is only 10.4 inches. The yearly fall for the State is 5.6 inches. At the Ozark towns of Harrison and Winslow the figure is 14.9 inches. Icy streets are seldom seen in Little Rock, where the average winter temperature is 44° F.

Warm, bright days are common even in December and January. The spring is long and genial, and hot weather usually does not begin until June. Temperatures of 100° or more are reported in some southern counties nearly every summer, but mountain dwellers keep blankets handy the year around, for nights in the highlands are almost invariably cool. Summers extend through September, and the first killing frost does not ordinarily come until late October or November.

The average annual temperature of the State since 1891 has been 61.4° F.

Together with a long growing season, ranging from extremes of 176 days in the northwestern hills to 241 days in the southern lowlands and averaging 211 days, Arkansas receives an abundance of rain. The average fall for the State is 48.25 inches. This is far higher than the national figure of 34 inches, and is exceeded by only 7 States, all of them in the Southeast. In 1936, the driest year on record, the average was 34.75 inches. Most of the rain occurs during the winter and spring months, but even in late summer droughts are rare and usually local. During the warm season more rain falls in the lowlands than in the mountains, but the situation is reversed in winter. The explanation lies in the fact that the prevailing winds in summer are from the south and southwest, and in winter they are from the north or northwest.

Humidity ranges from 55-60 per cent in the eastern two-thirds of the State to 50-55 per cent in the western third. In Little Rock the average relative humidity at 7 a.m. is 80; by noon it drops to 57, and by 7 p.m. it rises to 62.

GEOLOGY AND PALEONTOLOGY

All except about 15 square miles of the exposed rock in Arkansas is of sedimentary origin. In other words, geological evidence indicates that during many millions of years the State was covered by encroaching and receding seas. In these waters accumulated the sediments that make up today's land surface of limestones, sandstones, dolomites, shales, clays, sands, and chalks.

The mountain country in the northwest is the State's oldest land area. Strata overlying both the Ozarks and the Ouachitas were laid down during the Ordovician, Silurian, Devonian, and Carboniferous periods of the Paleozoic era. An outcrop of even greater age, the Collier shale of the Cambrian period, appears in the Ouachitas between Mount Ida and Norman.

Geologists ascribe dissimilar histories to the two ranges. Rock layers in the Ozarks lie nearly flat, except that the entire region is tipped slightly to the south. The Ouachita area, on the other hand, underwent tremendous pressure from the south during the Pennsylvanian period, and the strata were pushed into folds that have now weathered out into long east-west ridges. The central part of the section thus raised is known as the Novaculite Uplift because of its extensive whetstone deposits, some of which, wrote David Dale Owen, are "equal in whiteness, closeness of texture, and subdued waxy luster to the most compact forms and white varieties of Carrara marble . . . though of an entirely different composition."

By the close of the Paleozoic era the seas had receded from the two sets of mountains and from the Arkansas Valley trough, which divides them. This highland region thereafter remained above water and its subsequent history is one of erosion by water, wind, and temperature changes. Shorelines continued to advance and retreat over the lowlands of southern and eastern Arkansas, however, during the Mesozoic and part of the Cenozoic eras. Deposits of clay, sand, marl, and calcareous muds laid down during the Mesozoic era appear today in a roughly triangular section of southwestern Arkansas lying between Arkadelphia, De Queen, and Fulton. Most of the other surface formations in the Coastal Plain, along with those of Crowley's Ridge, date from the Tertiary period of the Cenozoic era. The alluvium which makes the Mississippi Delta unexcelled cotton country was laid down during the Recent period.

Glacial ice sheets that covered the northern part of the United States during the first part of the Quaternary period pushed across northern Missouri but did not reach Arkansas. The State, therefore, does not exhibit the moraine lakes, reversed watercourses, and other topographical changes that characterize the glaciated surface of land farther north. As recently as 1811-12, however, northeast Arkansas was affected by an extensive and severe geological disturbance—the New Madrid earthquake (*see Tour 7*). The quakes continued for more than a year and transformed hundreds of square miles in the St. Francis Valley into swamps and lakes.

Igneous rocks, which well up at molten heat from the earth's interior, occupy less than 0.1 per cent of the State's surface, in outcrops along the mountain-plains line southwest of Little Rock. The rocks are intrusive—that is, they cooled and solidified before reaching the surface—and are placed in either the late Lower or early Upper Cretaceous period.

Despite their small representation, these igneous intrusions contain many rare and several valuable minerals. Among the latter are aluminum and titanium ores and peridotite in which diamonds have been found. Most of the State's commercial minerals, however, are associated with rocks of sedimentary origin. Manganese, mercury, lead, zinc, and antimony, as well as the principal building stones (sandstone, limestone, dolomite, marble), appear only in the Paleozoic deposits of the highland region. The coal beds of the western Arkansas Valley were formed during the Pennsylvanian period of the same epoch. South Arkansas' underground reservoirs of oil are of considerably later (Mesozoic) origin.

Because Arkansas is in a region which for eons contained the shorelines of primeval seas it possesses a wealth of fossil remains, both plant and animal. No comprehensive survey of these survivals has ever been undertaken, but several discoveries have proved of interest to paleontologists. Cretaceous deposits in southwestern Arkansas contain numerous amphibian and reptilian fossils, particularly in the Marlbrook marl of Hempstead County. Here the remains of plesiosaurs, mosasaurs, and other giant lizards have been found, as well as those of turtles and fish. Still more interesting specimens have been discovered in the unconsolidated soils of eastern and southern Arkansas.

When the great ice sheets descended from the North, bringing with them Arctic temperatures, land life of every kind fled southward— flocks of birds as well as primitive deer, tapirs, rodents, giant wolves, elephants, sloths. Their migration halted by the sea, the refugees lived as best they could in the strip between the water and the glaciers. The land that is now Arkansas was, during part of this time, a coastal region and hence sheltered an unusually heavy population of land animals. Sometimes these animals wandered into peat bogs, became mired, and perished. The mud and sand deposited over them preserved their skeletons. Others may have been caught in the floods that swept down from the North when the glaciers began to melt. Some years ago a steam shovel unearthed a mastodon in Craighead County at a depth of 20 feet.

Caves and rock fissures are another source of fossils. Carnivorous beasts dragged their prey into such lairs, devoured them, and left the bones. Other animals, seeking refuge from cold or floods, starved to death or were killed. The most notable find of this nature in Arkansas is the Conard fissure, discovered in 1903 by Waldo Conard while he was searching for lead near Buffalo River in Newton County. Dr. Barnum Brown of the American Museum of Natural History in New York explored the crevice during the following year and removed several thousand bones. These remains, now exhibited in the museum, belong to the Pleistocene period; they include, according to Dr. Brown's report, "two new genera and twenty new species of mammals."

Crowley's Ridge is exceptionally rich in fossilized animals and plants. Near Wittsburg a silicified conifer stump weighing several tons has been unearthed, and petrified tree trunks are so common in the neighborhood of Piggott that they are used as tombstones in the town cemetery. Mastodon bones now in the Smithsonian Institution, Washington, D. C., were found within the city limits of Helena, at the southern end of the Ridge. The bed of Crow Creek, which flows through the Ridge near Forrest City, contains a deposit of oyster shells estimated to be nearly 7,000,000 cubic yards in extent.

PLANT LIFE

Plants grow luxuriantly in Arkansas. Nurtured by heavy rains and a benign climate, they leap impatiently from the soil early in spring, mature with almost tropical rapidity, resist the late summer dry weather, and yield only with reluctance to frost in October and November. Even through the winter many plants flourish. A walk through the woods in February will reveal, beside the conifers, many mosses, ferns, and grasses, hollies with green leaves and red berries reminiscent of Christmas, mistletoe clumps high in the oaks, and in sheltered spots perhaps a few venturesome blue-eyes and violets.

Since Arkansas is situated where the Mississippi Alluvial Plain and Gulf Coastal Plain rise into the mountains, its boundaries cut across botanical divisions determined by climate and elevation. Consequently the State is the habitat of several different types of vegetation. At least 2,600 plants are native, and to the list could be added many naturalized exotics. Among the woody plants are 47 kinds of oak, probably 60 of hawthorn, 21 of hickory, 11 of maple, 11 of wild cherry and plum, 7 of hackberry, at least 8 of willow, 6 each of buckeye and elm, and 5 each of holly, ash, and basswood.

The alluvial plains of the Mississippi Valley bear plants typical of the deep South. Cypresses grow in the bayous and lakes, their "knees" (projections from the roots) rising out of the water perhaps 20 feet away from the main conical trunk. Water oaks and hickories are also found in the bottoms, as well as tupelo gums, ashes, and hollies. In the St. Francis Valley is one of the rarest and most interesting smaller species of American flora, the exotic cork tree, marked by leathery leaves. Shaggy Spanish moss droops from overhanging branches in the moist hollows of Chicot County, in the southeast corner of the State. Palmettoes lift their sharp spears or broad fans in the lower part of the Delta. Ladyslippers, a form of orchid, blossom profusely from May and June to October. Among the lovelier of the other 26 varieties of orchids that grow in the State are the Yellow Fringed and the Purple Fringeless, the latter large and of a rich red-purple color. Yoncopins (of the Chinese lotus family) and other water lilies float on quiet ponds or in the water-filled pits along roadsides where earth has been excavated. The passion flower is so abundant that the legislature once considered making it the State flower, but finally chose the apple blossom.

Crowley's Ridge bestows upon the region a range in species surpassed by few areas east of the Rockies. Almost by the side of plants of the deep South are trees and flowers characteristic of forests in the East and North. Nowhere else in Arkansas grows the stately tulip tree (yellow poplar), a variety most often found in the Appalachians. The

American beech is common on the Ridge and here also grow oaks, hickories, pecans. In the shade of the forests are ferns and flowers, among the more striking of which are the American bell flower, crimson or royal catchfly, butterfly weed, cardinal flower, blue lobelia, phlox, verbena, wild hydrangea, hibiscus, aster, and yellow jasmine. The entire Ridge must have been a natural park before it was cleared for planting crops. Large sections now being taken out of cultivation under the direction of the U. S. Soil Conservation Service, in time may revert to a condition resembling their primitive character.

Most of the Delta wild plant life appears in bottomlands near creeks and lakes or in low areas so frequently flooded as to make raising crops unprofitable. South-central and southwestern Arkansas, however, belong to the forests and are populated largely by plants that are common to the oak-hickory-pine belt along the Gulf Coastal Plain. The two native pines in this area, shortleaf and loblolly, are more numerous than the hardwoods, accounting for about two-thirds of the total cut in the lumber mills. Although a considerable part of this great forest was felled for timber in the interval between the beginning of large-scale lumbering activity (1870-80) and the World War, seedlings and saplings grew so rapidly that trees again stretch almost without a break from the Delta to Texas. Many species of shrubs, flowers, and trees native to the Western and Southwestern plains occur in the southwestern corner of Arkansas.

The Ozarks and Ouachitas are almost as thickly wooded as the coastal plain, but their vegetation is more nearly akin to the oak-hickory forests of the Eastern and Central States. Varying conditions of soil and exposure account for many differences among the species which cover their slopes. The only pine native to the area, the shortleaf, is not nearly so frequent in the Ozarks as in the Ouachitas and on the flats farther south. The green needles of cedars brighten the landscape in winter, particularly in the vicinity of the White River. Along the bluffs of the White grows an immigrant Mexican juniper, called here the Ozark white cedar.

Showy flowering trees, many of them flaunting their blossoms on bare branches in early spring, are dogwood, redbud, red haw, wild plum and crab apple, locust, tree huckleberry, silver bell, service berry, smoke tree, fringe tree, and wax myrtle. Through the summer the mountain forests become a cool green retreat, but in the fall there is a brief, brilliant spectacle when sumacs splash their scarlet against the yellowing hickories and oaks.

Arkansas' two highest peaks, Mount Magazine and Rich Mountain, are particularly notable for the variety and interest of their botanical display. Both are prolific of ferns; and the *Woodsia scopulina,* occurring on Magazine, has been found nowhere else between the Rockies and the Alleghenies. Other species appearing on the mountain are the purple cliff brake, maidenhair, maidenhair spleenwort, marginal shield, and (only on Magazine's north slope) the spiny shield. Spiderwort makes a fine showing in May, flowering in tints from purple to pale pink and almost pure white. Delphiniums add their blue clouds; columbines are on some of the more inaccessible ledges. Among the less common trees are the white fringe, several varieties of mock orange, and the unusual maple-leaved oak (*Quercus shumardii,* var. *acerifolia*).

On Rich Mountain, at the Oklahoma border, hepatica peers out from among the rocks as early as February, shortly before the starry white flowers of bloodroot. Woody plants include the umbrella magnolia, silver bell, witch hazel, and azalea. Here, as on Magazine, rare flowers, ferns, and shrubs mix so democratically with the ordinary plants of the hills that they are frequently overlooked.

Back yards in cities can be turned into gardens with a minimum of effort. Four-o'clocks, cape jasmines, and arbor roses give the night air a heady perfume in many parts of Little Rock. The bright blooms of cannas nod beneath windows, and blue larkspur sweeps over vacant lots. Stretches of Midland Avenue, running from downtown Fort Smith toward Van Buren, are bordered in summer with the flowers of crape myrtle. Specimens of plants ordinarily considered tropical thrive in several cities: a banana tree goes through its strange life cycle on the lawn of the Helena public library, and several lime trees bear fruit on the State Hospital grounds in Little Rock.

Many uncultivated plants have a place in Arkansas kitchens and pantries. Farm wives seek out watercress, lambsquarters, curly dock, dandelion, poke, and other greens. Wild yams, Jerusalem artichokes, and Indian bread vary the menu. Mint is useful for flavoring. Blackberries, blueberries, muscadines, wild grapes, persimmons, mulberries, red haws, and wild cherries are all picked in season. Nuts are gathered from pecan, hickory, walnut, and chinquapin trees. For the medicine shelf the woods and fields yield horehound, spearmint, Seneca-snakeroot, catnip, pennyroyal, ginseng, yellow-root or golden seal, sweet flag, dittany, and sassafras.

ANIMAL LIFE

The first settlers found wild animals so plentiful in Arkansas that they had little difficulty in killing enough game to keep them until they could clear and plant their land. Though agricultural and industrial development has diminished the amount of game, many farmers still consider rabbit, squirrel, and fish as supplies for the family larder rather than as objects of sport.

There are few pastures in the State that one can cross without sending a frightened cottontail bounding for cover, and in the lowlands the swamp rabbit also appears. Red and gray squirrel and opossum are very common. Deer, once almost exterminated, are now multiplying rapidly, especially in the State and Federal game refuges. Raccoon, together with some opossum, skunk, and mink, furnish the basis of a sizable fur trade in the hill section, where the winters are cold enough to produce good pelts.

Hunting has eliminated some species of animals altogether, and reduced others so drastically that their killing is now legally forbidden. The bison, of course, are long since gone. Arkansas was once called the Bear State, but the brown bear that were so abundant have largely disappeared, although a few still lumber through the eastern Arkansas river bottoms, and now and then their unmistakable heavy tracks are seen in the mountain snow of the western Ouachita Forest. Beaver are scarce, and only a few otter now play on mud banks or streak through the water after fish. Enough red and gray fox remain to make the chase a favorite sport, but, except during a brief open season, the fox, if caught, must be released. Wolves, now seldom seen, commanded a bounty until 1929. Another predatory animal whose passing has caused no regret is the panther, variously known as the puma, cougar, mountain lion, or painter; only a few remain, and these in the most remote sections.

The panther's smaller relative, the bobcat or wildcat, is common enough to be hunted frequently by farmers aroused by its widespread destruction of turkey and quail. Other animals of dubious value from the country-dweller's standpoint include the gopher, chipmunk, and several varieties of mice and rats. The mole annoys the housewife by tunneling vegetable gardens. Common in the mountains are the wood-chuck or ground hog, weasel, and muskrat. The small brown bat appears in the uplands, the evening bat on the prairies.

In game birds Arkansas is richer than most States. While old-timers complain that duck-shooting is not what it once was, most Eastern hunters are delighted at the ease with which they can reach the bag limit in wild duck or geese. Thousands of flocks of migrant waterfowl pass down the Mississippi flyway each fall and winter. The sloughs and lakes of the Arkansas, White, and St. Francis River bottoms afford the birds resting places at night. On the Grand Prairie the ricefields are such rich feeding grounds that the Federal Government has established a large refuge on the lower White River for the dual purpose of sheltering the birds and protecting the rice.

Many small game birds also feed in the ricefields, among them woodcock, pheasant, and quail. Quail are found in brush patches all over the State, and in some hill counties a hunter can walk within 10 feet of them before they break. Under protection of refuges, wild turkey are increasing, both in the lowlands and in the Ozarks and Ouachitas. The Arkansas Game and Fish Commission has been highly successful in propagating and stocking wild turkey.

Of the 312 species of birds which observers have counted in Arkansas, songbirds are in the majority. The call of the cardinal and the jeering scream of the blue jay may be heard in the woods all the year around. On spring and summer mornings city people are charmed by the mockingbird's endless repertory. Mountain folk recognize the songs of the whippoorwill, the phoebe, the goldfinch, the robin, and the brown thrasher. In the level country the farmers are more accustomed to the several varieties of warblers, the painted bunting, and the brown-headed nuthatch, along with the mockingbird.

The climatic differences between the mountain and plains regions bring about variations in bird life. Such fish-eating species as the little blue heron and the crane wade the lowland streams, and occasionally one of the few remaining eagles plunges after a luckless rabbit. Other birds of prey in the level land include the Florida barred owl and screech owl, the black vulture, and the turkey vulture. The Mississippi kite, Southern hairy and red-cockaded woodpeckers, Bachman sparrow, blue grosbeak, and chuck-will's-widow appear in the Delta.

Because of its altitude, the Ozark-Ouachita region is a breeding ground for such Northern species as the scarlet tanager, ovenbird, black-billed cuckoo, hairy woodpecker, Carolina wren, and towhee. The junco, chickadee, nuthatch, and several kinds of woodpeckers winter in the mountains. The red-headed woodpecker, now protected by law because his crimson poll was so tempting a target for small-bore rifles, appears frequently in the Ouachitas in January.

Birds are usually valued for sport, food, or the songs they sing, not for their most important service—the destruction of insects. The moist climate and lush vegetation of Arkansas breed insects so rapidly that men are hard put to cope with them.

The hordes of locusts that occasionally range the Western plains and devour everything in their path seldom come as far south as Arkansas, although old residents in the northern counties remember such a visit in the 1870's. Cotton planters, however, carry on incessant warfare against the cotton boll weevil and the army worm. Fruit growers in the higher country dread the codling moth. Termites undermine the foundations of houses, destroy fence posts, and damage furniture, books, and occasionally pecan and other trees. Flooded regions sometimes breed swarms of buffalo gnats numerous enough to kill livestock.

The most serious disease-bearing insect of Arkansas is the anopheles mosquito, which in hot weather spreads malaria throughout the lowland sections and sometimes reaches the lesser Ouachitas. Either the sickness is not so virulent in the State as it is farther north, or else

Arkansans have unusual resistance. They take malaria calmly, dose themselves with quinine, and ordinarily continue their work. The housefly is numerous in summer but dies off in winter, as in most sections of the United States. Spiders appear in great variety, as anyone knows who has ever lifted the last of a winter woodpile; none are venomous except the black widow, whose deadliness has been greatly exaggerated. Chiggers and woodticks sometimes annoy hikers, campers, and berry pickers. Wild bees, one of few insects useful to man, were once plentiful in the State, and still build hives in hollow trees.

In farmyards and fields small boys fondle the beautiful and harmless king snake, but their mothers are not so kindly inclined toward the nonpoisonous blacksnake, which sometimes invades the henhouses, swallows the eggs, and curls up in the nest to sleep while digesting the stolen meal. The garter snake and blue racer are familiar. Less well known varieties include the bull, spotted, Graham's queen, Emory's, keeled green, grass, regal ringnecked, western ground, watersnake, and tantilla. There are four poisonous snakes: the water moccasin, the copperhead, the rattlesnake (timber, ground, and diamondback varieties), and the rare coral or harlequin. Reptiles other than snakes are the turtles—mud, snapping, box and musk (or stinkpot)—and the lizards (skinks and swifts) which sun themselves lazily on rocks and scuttle away with incredible speed if anyone reaches for them.

Frogs and toads, each occurring in several species, are the amphibians most often seen. The newt, the congo eel or snake, the water-dog or mud puppy, and several varieties of salamanders are also common, if more secretive in their habits. Rarely seen, and always astonishing to visitors, are the few alligators which still inhabit the swamps of the Red River Valley. Despite his ferocious appearance, the 'gator will not attack a man or any large animal. Usually he lives on fish, or small land creatures that wander too near the bank.

Despite generations of seining and other wholesale methods of catching, fish are still plentiful. In the mountain waters are smallmouthed bass, Eastern pickerel, and perch. The rivers and lakes of the Delta teem with catfish, sturgeon, buffalo, perch, drum, crappie, bream, and largemouthed bass. In these waters also dwells the gar, detested by sportsmen. A tabulation made in 1890 listed 137 species and subspecies of fish in Arkansas waters, including, besides those already mentioned, minnow, pike, eel, sunfish and shad. Trout have since been introduced in Spring River, the outlet of Mammoth Spring. Commercial fishing for buffalo, cat, and drum is a considerable local industry along the lower White River. The White and its tributaries, the Black, Current, and Buffalo, also contain several varieties of freshwater mussels, which are dredged and sold to button factories in near-by towns.

Resources and Conservation

WHEN the finger of smoke poked its way above the tree tops a ranger in a fire tower squinted expertly through sights mounted over a map. Picking up the telephone, he called a dispatcher many miles away: "This is Blue Mountain Tower reporting. There's a small fire at alidade reading one ninety." The ranger dropped his official tone to add: "John, it looks like it's in that little glade where Ferguson killed the wildcat last winter."

The dispatcher pulled a button from the Blue Mountain location on a map and stretched a string through the number 190 on a graduated scale. Just then a second tower reported the wisp of smoke and gave an alidade reading. After a moment's calculation the dispatcher telephoned a Civilian Conservation Corps camp, told the fire warden where the blaze was, what roads and trails to follow, and how many men were needed. In less than eight minutes after the ranger in the first tower had reported, a pick-up truck with a "hotshot" crew aboard was racing toward the fire. The pick-up, which skidded around curves in a manner that would have delighted a motion picture director, was followed by a slower and larger truck filled with youthful fire fighters. In two hours the blaze was out.

Except for the soil, timber is the most valuable resource of Arkansas, and the protection of more than 22,000,000 acres of trees is a major conservation task in the State. Fire fighting, however, is but one duty of the men who guard the timber.

In the two national forests (Ouachita and Ozark), Federal rangers select the mature and defective trees that are to be logged by privately owned lumber companies. As a timber marker approaches a tree he glances at the top. If the highest branches are dead he blazes two faces shoulder-high on the bole and cuts a nick near the ground. With the back of his ax he stamps "US" above and below the cutting line, so that both the log and the stump can be checked after cutting. If a tree fails to give a sound, clear ring when smacked with the flat of an ax, the forester mentally labels it "redheart" and marks it for felling. In testing a tree's "ripeness" the ranger uses an increment borer to extract a small core from the trunk. As a tree nears maturity it adds less wood to its girth. Thus, by studying the narrowness of the outside annual-growth rings, a forester can determine the suitability of the trunk for lumber. Twenty-five per cent of the receipts from timber sold goes to the county where it was cut, ten per cent is used for roads and trails in the forest, and the rest accrues to the U.S. Treasury.

Practical Federal interest in the conservation of Arkansas timber was first demonstrated in 1907, when President Theodore Roosevelt defined the boundaries of the Arkansas National Forest, later renamed the Ouachita. Since 1907 the original tract has been greatly expanded, until it now includes more than 1,300,000 acres extending from about 20 miles west of Little Rock into Oklahoma. Quick-growing shortleaf pine predominates in the area. The Ozark National Forest, which comprises more than 800,000 acres of hardwood and pine in northwest Arkansas, was created in 1908.

The setting aside of the national forests was a timely act. Much of the 32,000,000 acres of virgin timber that had blanketed the State had been cut as rapidly as railroad tracks could be laid into the woods. Countless sawmill towns had boomed for a few years and then faded into ghosts. Much of the cutover land had become a tangle of brush and second growth, fit for little but game preserves, by the time the State repossessed it for unpaid taxes. Heavy rains swept over the deforested acres, washing soil away and raising the crest of floods.

Several large lumber and pulp mills in the south Arkansas pine belt have followed approved conservation practices for more than a decade, and since 1933 their efforts have been supplemented by the work of the Arkansas Forestry Commission. This agency, among other activities, enters into fire-control agreements with private landowners. In 1939 more than 10,000,000 acres were covered by the Commission's contracts. A network of towers, linked with the Louisiana towers on the south and with the towers of the Ouachita National Forest to the north, guards the entire southern timber belt.

"Pine-tree banking," a practice that has attracted considerable attention from lumbermen, is said to have originated in south Arkansas. A "depositor" agrees to sell a mill all the timber cut from his woodlands, and the company, in return, manages the land on a "sustained yield" basis, logging off at a rate no greater than the rate of growth of new timber. The small timber-owners for whom this arrangement was devised had long presented the State's most difficult forest conservation problem, since most of the large companies learned some years ago that a "perpetual forest" is desirable. As a result of the various approaches to the problem, *American Forests* noted in its December 1939 issue that "The southern Arkansas pine belt . . . is a bright spot on the American lumbering map. In many other parts of the nation, from four to five times as much saw timber is consumed as is grown; yet in southern Arkansas the annual growth exceeds the commodity drain by almost twenty per cent."

Until recently Arkansans talked less of their forests than of the State's underground resources, following, in this attitude, an example that goes back to the time of De Soto's expedition. Gold, silver, and precious stones had been found in Mexico and surely existed to the north, thought the Spanish *conquistadores*. Many of the Frenchmen who came to the region after La Salle's exploration thought likewise. If the engineer Dumont is to be credited, La Harpe came far up the Arkansas River in 1722 looking for a fabulous emerald rock. "I have no doubt there are gold mines in the country," wrote Dumont, "as we discovered a little stream which rolled gold dust in its waters."

The rumors of gold and silver strikes did not vanish with the Frenchmen, but continued at intervals throughout the nineteenth century. As late as the 1880's western Arkansas saw a gold rush that was ended only when the State geologist dashed the miners' hopes. North Little Rock was originally called "Argenta," because a silver mine was supposed to exist near the town.

Although gold and silver have never been discovered in commercial quantities in the State, the list of minerals is so impressively long that, in 1923, the general assembly officially subtitled Arkansas the "Wonder State." If variety is a criterion, the nickname is well deserved: in the mountain counties alone the minerals run an alphabetical gamut—asphalt, barite, calcite, dolomite, eleolite, franklinite, galena, hematite, iolite, jasper, kaolinite, limonite, malachite, novaculite, opal, psilomelane, quartz, rutile, smithsonite, tripoli, uranium, vesuvianite, wavellite, and zinc. Not all of these are commercially important, of course; but, on the other hand, the alphabetical list contains only a few of the State's many minerals.

Three giants among Arkansas resources are the mineral fuels—coal, natural gas, and petroleum.

Beneath approximately 1,620 square miles of the Arkansas River Valley in the western part of the State are beds of semi-anthracite and bituminous coal. Mining began at Spadra (near Clarksville) in 1840, but extensive operations did not get under way until the arrival of railroads in the last quarter of the nineteenth century. Since there is no coal of comparable quality within hundreds of miles, except for small deposits in Oklahoma, the Arkansas mines are important sources of fuel for the five railroads that tap the district. Because it is relatively smokeless and has a rather high heat value, Arkansas coal is now sold in St. Louis and other cities faced with the problem of smoke abatement. In 1939 the tonnage mined was 1,162,329, valued at more than $4,000,000. Sebastian County was the largest producer.

Considerable deposits of lignite are known to exist in Ouachita County and along Crowley's Ridge, but it is unlikely that development will take place until the State's large supplies of petroleum, natural gas, and wood have been depleted.

Although natural gas was discovered near Fort Smith as early as 1888, the State's first commercial well was drilled in 1901. This well, near Mansfield, is still producing at about one-half its original rate. Gas from the Mansfield area and from a field at Massard Prairie (opened in 1904) has been partly responsible for the industrial growth of Fort Smith, and wells at Clarksville and Alma, north of the Arkansas River, also pipe gas for commercial use. Gas flows in great volume from oil wells in southwestern Arkansas but it is not of a kind suitable for burning without processing; therefore most of it is converted into gasoline or is used to "re-pressure" depleted oil wells.

Conservation has been the rule in the older gas fields since the Mansfield well was drilled in 1901, and gas in the oil district has been the subject of much protective petroleum legislation. In 1917, however, before the discovery of oil, the general assembly passed its first "Act to Conserve the Natural Gas Resources."

On January 10, 1921 a torrent of oil from the Busey well, a mile west of El Dorado, marked the entrance of Arkansas into the ranks of the petroleum-producing States. The next year a gusher opened the great Smackover field, a few miles to the north. Since then new fields have been discovered west and south of the city, which had been named El Dorado nearly a century before oil was struck. The several hundred wells, spread through half a dozen southwestern counties, yielded more than 400,000,000 barrels of crude oil between 1923 and 1939 (*see Tours 8 and 14*). In the peak year, 1925, the production was slightly over 77,000,000 barrels, a figure that has gradually dwindled, to become stabilized recently at around 20,000,000 barrels; the flow for 1938 was just below 20,000,000, and that for 1939 was just above.

In the excitement that followed the roar of the first gushers, petroleum conservation received little thought. A State official later reported that "millions of barrels of oil escaped from hastily constructed earthen pits and found its way over the terrain and into the streams. . . . Many wells caught fire and burned for weeks, wells cratered . . . dissipating untold amounts of native reservoir energy." Legal technicalities prevented effective enforcement in the petroleum fields of the 1917 natural-gas legislation, and the general assembly's 1923 enactment making it unlawful for "crude oil, or petroleum to be produced . . . in any manner . . . as to constitute waste" was also difficult to enforce. The need for control was becoming more widely recognized, however, and in 1933 the Arkansas Board of Conservation was created, composed of five men "experienced in, and having a fair knowledge of, the oil and gas industry." Despite scattered opposition to its work, the original board so successfully urged the regulation of output that the cost of production was steadily lowered. The present seven-man control commission operates in accordance with the provisions of the general assembly's 1939 conservation law, a measure that reflects the experience of many other oil-producing States.

Aside from fuel minerals, the most important nonmetallic deposits in Arkansas are the various types of building stone, the gravel and sand used for construction, chalks and marls ground into cement, and clay used for making bricks and pottery. Building stone quarried in 1939 was valued at $450,000; this included sandstone and limestone from the Ozarks and Ouachitas, syenite from near Little Rock, and marble from the vicinity of Batesville. The clay dug in southwestern Arkansas in 1939 was worth almost $1,000,000, and the sand and gravel scooped from pits and streambeds throughout the State was valued at well over that amount. Cement production for the year exceeded $800,000.

Among the minerals are a number which, while not put to any extensive commercial use, are interesting because of their rarity or their possibilities. The best known are the diamonds of Pike County. Discovered in a peridotite deposit in 1906, they were mined and sold for more than a decade in both the gem and industrial markets. In recent years the mine has not been in operation (see Tour 2b).

Novaculite found near Hot Springs was used by the Indians for arrowheads, by white men for whetstones, and by early-day millers, many of whom declared the Ouachita millstones were superior to those imported from France (see Tour 2b).

The geological melting pot of Magnet Cove (which has furnished specimens to museums throughout the world) contains several minerals in commercial quantities; among them are barite, of which about $16,000 worth was extracted in 1939, and titanium-bearing rutile valued at slightly more than $18,000.

One of the largest and most stable mining ventures in the State is the digging of aluminum-bearing bauxite, a few miles southwest of Little Rock. Fields in the neighborhood of the town of Bauxite yield about 95 per cent of the ore mined in the United States (see Tour 2b). In 1939 the output of more than 400,000 long tons was valued at $2,293,000.

Early nineteenth-century geologists discovered lead-bearing galena on the White River ridges. Settlers dug chunks of it from the richest outcrops, smelted it in roaring log fires, and sifted lumps of lead from the ashes. Confederate soldiers worked several mines near Bull Mountain in Marion County, shipping the lead bars down the White and Mississippi Rivers to New Orleans to be moulded into rifle balls. Zinc was mined and smelted at Calamine in Sharp County as early as 1857, and shipments were made to Europe during the Franco-Prussian War of 1871. Small quantities of both zinc and lead are still taken from the Arkansas Ozark deposits, but high transportation costs and other factors keep production down, except when prices are stimulated by unusual conditions.

The manganese that lies near the surface of the hills at Cushman, in Independence County, was first mined about 1850, but regular shipments of ore awaited the building of a railroad from Batesville in 1886. Since that time the tonnage has varied with the market price, the 1939 dig amounting to about 7,000 tons worth $90,000 (*see Tour 17*).

Cinnabar, discovered in southwest Arkansas in 1930, has steadily risen in importance because of a shortage of quicksilver imported from Europe. In 1937 the mercury extracted from Pike County ore was valued at some $7,000. Two years later the tempo of expansion was reflected in an output worth $128,000 (*see Tour 2b*).

Deposits of antimony, iron, silver, and many other minerals exist in Arkansas, but their extent and quality are not fully known. It has been estimated that only about 35 per cent of the State's area has been adequately mapped for geological purposes, a situation that brought about the establishment in 1938 of a mineralogical survey, financed in part with Work Projects Administration funds.

Several large rivers (such as the White, Arkansas, and Ouachita) flow from mountains into lowlands within the limits of the State, and a number of smaller streams have considerable volume and fall. The potential hydroelectric power contained in these drainage systems has been estimated at upwards of 500,000 horsepower. At the present time (1941) about 11 per cent of it is being utilized, the principal development consisting of generating plants at Carpenter and Remmel dams on the Ouachita. A series of flood control dams on the White River and its tributaries has been authorized by Congress, and Arkansas Representatives are making efforts to obtain power facilities at the sites, in order to turn the White River country into a multiple-use area similar to that developed by the Tennessee Valley Authority.

Geographically speaking, there are five major types of soil in Arkansas: the flat alluvial lands of the Delta, the fine silt and wind-deposited loess of Crowley's Ridge, the sandy loam of the forested Coastal Plain, the residual shale and sandstone of the Ouachitas, and the residual limestone of the Ozarks. A hundred years of farming and several decades of spectacular timber cutting have eroded parts of all areas except the Delta. Conservationists have estimated that enough topsoil to cover 13 average-size counties (out of a total of 75) has been washed away in a century. A photographer looking for erosion pictures would be most likely to notice the gullies and torn fields of Crowley's Ridge, but farms on the slopes of the Ozarks and Ouachitas have been more widely, if less violently, damaged.

County agricultural agents and "schoolbook farmers" were advocating terraced fields and strip cropping as early as 1920, but large-scale conservation did not come until the 1930's, when the national conscience was focused on the problem of soil depletion throughout the United States.   Once the seriousness of the situation was realized, Arkansans were quick to respond.   In 1937 Arkansas became the first State to adopt model legislation providing for the organization of voluntary soil-conservation districts.   By 1940 more than 15,000,000 acres (nearly half the State's area) had been embraced in 28 such districts.   Since most of the acreage in the program is outside the Delta, it can now be said that steps have been taken to protect virtually all the threatened land in Arkansas.

Archeology and Indians

T HE Bluff Dwellers, a mysterious people of small stature, were
the first aborigines known to have lived in what is now Arkansas.
No one knows where the race came from, or why it disappeared,
but archeologists digging into burial grounds and refuse heaps have
pieced together a few facts about the Bluff Dwellers. They are usually
assumed to have dwelled here before 500 A.D., though it is possible that
they survived for several centuries later. As their name implies, they
made their homes in caves and under overhanging rock shelves, mostly
along the upper White River. They obtained their food by farming,
hunting, and fishing. The bow and arrow was unknown to them, but
they killed deer, turkey, and other game with darts thrown from a
grooved stick very much like the Aztec *atlatl*. An abundance of fish
bones and scales in their kitchen middens indicates that they were successful fishermen, and it is probable that they used traps and nets.
Stone axes and chisels were fashioned from the flint nodules that occur
in the Ozark limestone.

On level hilltops and in creek bottoms the Bluff Dwellers planted
corn, squash, gourds, pumpkins, beans, and sunflowers. They also ate
wild plants—seeds, bulbs, and fruit. The sedge grass and canes that
grew in abundance provided raw material for much of their household
equipment, for at least during the earlier period of their culture they
did not know how to make pottery. Their baskets, however, were so
tightly woven that the squaws could boil food in them by dropping hot
stones in the mush or stew. Grass was twisted into strings which were
made into shawls, breech clouts, and sandals. When the Bluff Dweller
became sleepy he crawled behind a rock and stretched himself on a
bed of this same grass; after death his body was placed in a pit lined
with grass and leaves.

As with most primitive peoples, the dead were equipped with tools
and other furnishings that relatives thought would be needed in a future
life. In dry caves, some corpses became mummified, and present-day
scientists have studied them in detail. One of the most complete burials,
found at Brown's Bluff in Washington County and now in the University of Arkansas museum, had a bundle of pawpaw bark in front of
the legs and a woven bag, containing a brush and a bone awl, just behind the shoulders. The body had been placed in a flexed position

(lying on one side, curled up) on a piece of deer hide and a mat of cane; near it was the mummy of a small dog.

Ingenious though they were in adapting themselves to their environment, the Bluff Dwellers fell far short of the cultural levels attained by the pre-Columbian inhabitants of the Mississippi Delta and southern Arkansas forests. The lowland groups made pottery and ornaments of notable artistry, and they must have traded with tribes in widely distant parts of the country. Arrowheads chipped from Hot Springs novaculite have been found hundreds of miles away, and many artifacts unearthed in Arkansas are decorated with copper that apparently came from the Lake Superior area. The most obvious relics of the lowland aborigines, however, are the hundreds of mounds scattered along valleys from the St. Francis River to the Red.

From the time of De Soto the mounds that appear throughout the Mississippi Valley and southeastward to Florida excited great curiosity among Europeans. Some scholars believed that the hillocks were the architectural remains of a great vanished empire, but others asserted that they were unimportant early monuments of known Indian tribes. The present general scientific conclusion about the Mound Builders is presented by H. C. Shetrone (*The Mound Builders,* D. Appleton-Century Co., 1930): "To state that they were cultural groups of the native American race, along with the Indians and all other native American peoples; that in many instances they were the racial ancestors of the Indian tribes of historic times; but that as peoples, nations, and tribes, each with its distinctive cultural attainments, they were distinct and different from the historic Indians, would not be far from the truth."

A great many of the mounds in Arkansas are of the flat-topped "platform" variety, presumably once used as ceremonial sites or dwelling-places for tribal leaders. Such mounds ordinarily occupy the highest points in the low Delta country, where they will not be reached by floods. In some cases they seem to have been built as refuges from high water, since no burials or other remains occur except near the top. White settlers have used a few of the mounds as cemeteries and as camping places during floods; it is not a remote assumption to imagine that the mound builders intended the elevations for the same purpose. Other mounds seem to have been sites of houses, which were built of timbers, lathed with cane and plastered with mud.

Among the more important earthworks are the Knapp group, locally known as the "Toltec" (*see Tour 2a*), about 20 miles down the Arkansas River from Little Rock. In 1890 there were 15 mounds here, surrounded by an earth wall on three sides, with a lake on the fourth. The group, seemingly, had constituted a fortification. Near the mouth of White River is Menard Mound, 34 feet high and 167 feet in diameter. A cemetery near this structure yielded many earthenware vessels, including a graceful long-necked water bottle decorated in terra cotta with a star motif. Other outstanding groups of mounds are found on and near Crowley's Ridge from Clay County all the way down to Helena.

The first extensive study of Arkansas mounds was made by Cyrus Thomas in 1890, for the Bureau of American Ethnology. A more complete study, however, was made by Clarence B. Moore between 1908 and 1911, under the auspices of Philadelphia's Academy of Natural Sciences. Using a steamboat as headquarters, and employing a crew of men for excavation, Moore traveled the entire Arkansas shore of the Mississippi, went up the Arkansas River past Little Rock, ascended the Ouachita to Camden, traveled 58 miles of the Saline, and followed the Red River through the State.

Moore divided the State into regions north and south of the Arkansas River according to differences in the pottery his expedition discovered. Artifacts found in the mounds and burial places south of the Arkansas were decorated chiefly with incised figures and designs and were seldom painted in more than one color. Utensils unearthed north of the river were more heavily painted and less skillfully carved. Along the river the two techniques are found in forms having both incised and painted decorations. The ornamentation was apparently found so pleasing that the potters were stimulated to create a third type of decoration —cameo design. Pottery of this type, which has been found in abundance in Pope and Yell Counties, was covered with a thick coat of red pigment and fired. Parts of the vessel were then scraped, leaving the patterns in bas-relief.

North of the Arkansas River, and especially in the northeast corner of the State, archeologists have made rich discoveries of "effigy" vessels—jugs, pots, and tobacco pipes made in realistic or conventionalized likeness of humans and animals. Quantities of these "effigies," seldom seen elsewhere except in adjacent sections of Missouri, have been found at Pecan Point, a deep curve of the Mississippi below Wilson. One example is a water jug shaped like an almost-comic human head, with ears as handles. Another bottle uses human bones in relief as a decorative pattern, while other vessels are designed in the shapes of birds and animals. The potters, evidently desiring that all parts of their vessels be functional, would turn the head of a turtle-effigy, for example, into a spout and the tail into a handle, thus producing a "teapot."

The valleys of the upper Ouachita and its tributaries received little attention from archeologists before M. R. Harrington examined remnants of Caddo culture in 1920 for the Heye Museum of the American Indian. Since then the region has been studied carefully by Arkansas investigators, including S. D. Dickinson and Harry J. Lemley. The two archeologists' discovery of evidence of civilizations preceding the Caddo led to the publication of several monographs. The Lemley collection of Caddo and other artifacts, in Hope, is the most important private archeological museum in the State.

The order of prehistoric cultures in Arkansas, so far as it can be determined at present, is tentatively summarized by Dickinson as follows:

The earliest civilization observed in the Gulf Coastal Plain is the Marksville, named after the Louisiana site where it was first discovered. Apparently, it evolved originally somewhere near the joining of the Ouachita, Red, and Black Rivers in Louisiana, and spread northward, establishing itself in the fertile plains. Its highest, and probably last, pure expression was the Hopewell culture of Ohio. The Marksville people in Arkansas seem to have maintained contact with the clans in other parts of the lower Mississippi Valley, for their remains are generally similar to those found in Louisiana, Mississippi, and Ohio. In the neighborhood of the Ouachita Mountains they used novaculite for many purposes, although at the same time they worked with clay and with bone. There is some evidence that the Marksville culture disintegrated to form the Deasonville and Coles Creek complexes. Deasonville was restricted to certain sections of the Delta, but the latter spread over the entire eastern and southern lowland area of the State.

In northeastern Arkansas arose the Mid-Mississippian civilization, which was apparently influenced not only by Marksville, Deasonville, and Coles Creek patterns, but by some strong foreign element as well. The "effigy" vessels of this section so closely resemble Mexican, Central American, and even Peruvian forms that some students have suggested an actual migration from Mexico to the Mississippi. If any such movement occurred, however, it must have been at a very early period, because the more advanced manifestations of Mexican civilization, such as written characters and astronomical calendars, do not appear. The Mid-Mississippian was not inferior to other late cultures in the United States, and its plastic sculpture was the equal of any in the country. The race has not been positively identified, but its remains are related to those of southeast Missouri, Tennessee, and Alabama, and presumably it belonged to the Muskhogean family, of which the Creek, Choctaw, and Chickasaw were later branches.

The rise of the Caddo culture in southwestern Arkansas was parallel to that of the Mid-Mississippian. Possibly the Caddo, a round-headed people, came from the western Texas coast, since they seem to have had a Mexican origin. They merged with the Coles Creek culture, occupied the deserted sites, enlarged the old mounds, and cultivated the same crops—maize, pumpkins, and tobacco. They bound the heads of some members of the tribe to produce flattened skulls. It is believed that this practice was a mark of aristocratic distinction, since the deformed skulls usually appear in graves holding unusual quantities of pottery and shell work.

Although the Caddo spread as far north as the Arkansas Valley and came into contact with Mid-Mississippian peoples (thereby improving the patterns of Caddoan artifacts), their centers of civilization were in the Ouachita and Red River basins. Here they built large villages, mined Ouachita novaculite for trade with the lowland tribes, and nourished a civilization that continued into historic times.

INDIANS

"By the Way, we saw several Cottages at certain Distances, stragling up and down, as the Ground happens to be fit for Tillage. The Field lies about the Cottage, and at other Distances there are other large Huts, not inhabited, but only serving for publick Assemblies, either upon Occasion of Rejoycing, or to consult about Peace and War. The Cottages that are inhabited, are not each of them for a private Family, for in some of them are fifteen or twenty, each of which has its Nook or Corner, Bed and other Utensils to its self . . . they have Nothing in Common besides the Fire, which is in the Midst of the Hut, and never goes out. . . . The Cottages are round at the Top, after the manner of a Bee-Hive." In this way Joutel, La Salle's follower, described a Caddo village on the Red River as it appeared in 1687 (reprinted from Bulletin 77 of the Smithsonian Institution). The Tula, whom De Soto had battled less than a hundred miles to the north in 1541, were probably a Caddo tribe. The chroniclers of the Spanish party, however, had said little of the Tula except to note that these warriors were "the best fighting people" the expedition had encountered.

The French who pushed up the Red River from New Orleans during the eighteenth century found the friendship of the Caddo useful, for the tribe had close racial and linguistic ties with such Western Indians as the Arikara, Pawnee, and Wichita. Even at the time of the Louisiana Purchase, according to John Sibley, the Caddo exercised "great influence" over nearly a dozen tribes in the same neighborhood "who all speak the Caddo language, look up to them . . . and join them in all their wars." Sibley's report, sent by President Jefferson to Congress in 1805, painted a melancholy picture of a diminishing nation. "They have lived where they now do [120 miles northwest of Natchitoches, La.] only five years. The first year they moved there the small-pox got amongst them and destroyed nearly one half of them. . . . Two years ago they had the measles. . . . The whole number of what they call warriors of the ancient Caddo nation, is now reduced to about one hundred, who are looked upon somewhat like Knights of Malta, or some distinguished military order." In 1835 the Caddo moved to Texas, and in the 1850's they went on to the Washita River in what is now Oklahoma.

Better known to the earliest explorers were the Quapaw, or Arkansas, who lived near the mouth of the Arkansas River. The tribe gave Marquette and Joliet a cordial reception in 1673, performed the ceremonial dance of the calumet, and warned the priest and the fur trader not to descend the Mississippi farther—advice which the French heeded. "These Indians do not resemble those at the north, who are all of a morose and stern disposition," wrote Father Membré, historian of La Salle's expedition. "These are better made, civil, liberal, and of a gay humor."

The Quapaw were of Siouian stock, belonging to a group that once lived on the Ohio and Wabash Rivers. Sometime before 1500, the entire nation migrated westward, probably because of Iroquois pressure. When they reached the Mississippi, four of the tribes (Omaha, Ponca, Osage, and Kansa) went upstream. The Quapaw moved down toward the Arkansas and thus received their name, which is translated as "downstream people." The original form, *Ugakhpah,* is considered the parent word of both Quapaw and Arkansas.

Some early writers contended that the Quapaw once numbered many thousands, but Joutel in 1687 reported only four "Accancea" villages. Apparently four towns also existed in 1722, the year La Harpe ascended the Arkansas. When Jacobo Dubreuil, commandant of Arkansas Post, took a census of the Quapaw in 1784 for Spain, he listed three villages, with a total population of 708.

The Quapaw, whatever their number, continued to live at the mouth of the Arkansas through the French and Spanish occupation of Louisiana. They brought corn, beans, and game to the garrison of Arkansas Post and fought off the Chickasaw, who lived east of the Mississippi. Thomas Nuttall in 1819 narrated an "extraordinary action" of the Quapaw during a battle that had taken place a few years previously. "The Chicasaws, instead of standing their ground, were retreating before the Quapaws . . . in consequence of the want of ammunition. The latter understanding the occasion . . . desired the Chicasaws to land on an adjoining sand-beach of the Mississippi. . . . The chief of the Quapaws then ordered all his men to empty their powder-horns into a blanket, after which, he divided the whole with a spoon, and gave the half to the Chicasaws. They then proceeded to the combat."

Traditionally, the Quapaw had long been recognized as owners of a vast territory bounded on the south by the Red River, on the north by the Arkansas, and extending indefinitely westward from the Mississippi. In 1818 they ceded this region to the United States, retaining only a small reservation on the lower Arkansas. Six years later they sold their remaining land and joined the Caddo along the Red River. They found themselves unwelcome and were given farms that were frequently flooded. Discouraged and starving, they appealed to white authorities for help. In transmitting their plea, Territorial Governor John Pope wrote: "They are a kind of inoffensive people and aid the Whites in picking out their cotton and furnishing them with game. I have heard but one sentiment expressed in this territory with regard to this tribe, that of kindness and a desire that they should be permitted to live among us; I would be particularly gratified to be authorized to assign them a township on this [the Arkansas] river" (reprinted from *Indians and Pioneers,* Grant Foreman, by permission of the University of Oklahoma Press). Apparently nothing came of Pope's suggestion, and the Quapaw eventually settled with the Osage and Choctaw nations in Indian Territory.

The Osage, related to the Quapaw and coming originally from the same Ohio Valley region, were known as a reckless and warlike tribe. Their home territory, as shown on Marquette's 1673 map, was along the river named for them in central Missouri, but they periodically swept southwestward to hunt and fight through territory now included in Arkansas and Oklahoma. Raiding parties robbed and murdered white hunters, burned the villages of other Indians, and disappeared again into the mountains. French and Spanish authorities tried in vain to stop the Osage depredations.

After the Louisiana Purchase the United States Government lost little time in pushing the Osage westward. In 1808 the tribal leaders signed a treaty agreeing to move beyond a line approximating the present western borders of Missouri and Arkansas. Clashes soon occurred, however, between the Osage and the Cherokee who were settling to the southeast in the Arkansas Valley. In 1816 an agent to the Cherokee, Major William L. Lovely, attempted to set up a buffer area by buying from the Osage a large part of northwestern Arkansas and northeastern Oklahoma. This transaction was confirmed by treaty two years later. Meanwhile Fort Smith was established in 1817, partly for the purpose of keeping peace between the two nations.

Shortly after 1800 various Government officials began to plan the removal of Georgia, Florida, Tennessee, Alabama, and Mississippi Indians to the West, a policy finally embodied in the Removal Act of 1830. Long before that date, however, some tribes had been persuaded or forced to exchange their Eastern holdings for land west of the Mississippi. Several of these groups were temporarily given homes within the present limits of Arkansas.

Though a handful of Delaware and Shawnee had migrated to the banks of the White and St. Francis Rivers during the Spanish occupation of Louisiana, the largest band to come in consisted of Cherokee who feared vengeance for the Muscle Shoals (Tennessee) "massacre" of 1794. At President Jefferson's suggestion, Chief Tahlonteskee in 1809 brought 300 Cherokee to the Arkansas River, where they took possession of a tract given up by the Osage. After the building of Fort Smith, several thousand more relinquished their Georgia and Tennessee holdings for land along the Arkansas. Despite intermittent warfare with the Osage, the newcomers cleared farms and planted orchards. In 1822 Reverend Cephas Washburn and his fellow missionaries opened Dwight Mission near the site of Russellville.

Among the Cherokee chiefs was Takatoka, who dreamed of a vast Indian confederation west of the Mississippi which would control the troublesome Osage and the prairie nomads, stop the white man's encroachments, and unite all the immigrant tribes in a strong nation. Takatoka worked tirelessly toward this end, traveling extensively and using his eloquence to win chiefs and warriors to the alliance. Federal authorities encouraged the idea, since it fitted into their plan for removing the Indians from the East, and would give protection against the reckless Western tribes and the Mexicans. Takatoka died in 1824, his dream of a confederation unrealized.

Between the 1790's, when the first Cherokee came to Arkansas as a result of the Muscle Shoals affair, and 1829, when the last of the tribe moved on into what is now Oklahoma, the State was the temporary home of well-known Indian leaders. Sequoyah (George Guess, or Gist), inventor of the Cherokee alphabet, was a familiar figure at Dwight Mission. John Jolly, friend of Sam Houston, was prominent in the western Arkansas councils and was called "a Franklin amongst his countrymen."

During the 1830's long, miserable processions of Indians passed westward through Arkansas on their way to Indian Territory. Most of these were members of the "five civilized tribes" (Choctaw, Chickasaw, Cherokee, Creek, and Seminole) who were forced by the terms of the Indian Removal Act of 1830 to give up their land in the southern Appalachians, along the South Atlantic seaboard, and in the Mississippi Valley. Under the eyes of Government contractors, Indian families were assembled at Arkansas Post and carried up the Arkansas River. Hundreds were taken by steamer up the Ouachita to Écore á Fabre (now Camden) and marched overland to their reservations. Other unhappy caravans, straggling afoot through swamps and canebrakes, gave the name "Trail of Tears" to wilderness roads.

Though the removal of nearly all the Eastern tribesmen into what is now Oklahoma was completed by 1840, residents of Fort Smith and other towns along the border for many years afterward were familiar with the sight of Indians on the streets. During the War between the

States, Albert Pike recruited a brigade of Cherokee for service with the Confederacy. After the war the United States District Court at Fort Smith handled hundreds of criminal cases arising in Indian Territory. It was not until the settlement of Oklahoma by white men at the end of the nineteenth century that Indian affairs began to lose their importance for western Arkansas, which today shares with the whole State a heritage of place names and legends.

History

ON A spring day in 1541, Hernando de Soto, *conquistador* who had been with Pizarro in Peru, crossed the Mississippi and set foot on Arkansas soil. There has been much conjecture as to the spot on the west bank where the Spaniard and his followers landed, but the United States De Soto Expedition Commission decided in 1939 that it was probably about 20 miles below Helena. The expedition is believed to have then made its way northward to the mouth of the St. Francis River, dropped south to the Arkansas, and followed this stream up to where Little Rock now stands. From this point the men wandered through the hills to Hot Springs and Caddo Gap, went down the Ouachita River, and wintered at Camden or at Calion. In the spring of 1542 the band (now reduced to about 300 fighting men and 40 horses) descended the Ouachita into Louisiana. De Soto died in May and the survivors traveled subsequently in Louisiana, Texas, and Mexico.

Despite its arduous and extensive journey west of the Mississippi, the expedition left no records of particular value to later Europeans. The chronicles and maps that soon related the adventures of these ill-fated *conquistadores* were ambiguous and contradictory, destined to become historical puzzles rather than guides. One hundred and thirty-two years passed before white men again came to Arkansas.

In 1673 Jacques Marquette, a Jesuit missionary, and Louis Joliet, a fur trader, set out from Mackinaw, at the head of Lake Michigan, with five companions in two pirogues. After crossing the lake they ascended Fox River, portaged to the Wisconsin River, and floated down to the Mississippi. In July they reached the mouth of the Arkansas. Believing themselves near the Gulf of Mexico, and warned by the friendly Quapaw of hostile tribes to the south, the Frenchmen after a short visit turned upstream and began the journey back to Canada. Thus they left for René Robert Cavelier, Sieur de la Salle, the exploration of the full length of the Mississippi.

La Salle, who had spent more than a decade blazing paths through the forests of the Great Lakes country, obtained in 1678 a patent from Louis XIV of France to extend his travels. His goal was the mouth of the Mississippi, and one of his purposes was to control the fur trade

34

The Setting

WHITE RIVER, IN OZARK NATIONAL FOREST

SAM'S THRONE, AN OZARK PEAK IN NEWTON COUNTY

PETIT JEAN VALLEY FROM THE TOP OF MOUNT MAGAZINE, THE HIGHEST ELEVATION IN ARKANSAS

FALLS OF THE LITTLE MISSOURI,
IN OUACHITA NATIONAL FOREST

Lange: F. S. A.

DELTA COTTONFIELD, MISSISSIPPI COUNTY

RIVERBEND PROTECTION

St. Francis Levee Board

ST. FRANCIS RIVER LEVEE

BUFFALO RIVER NEAR HARRISON

G. R. Case

TRAIL IN OUACHITA NATIONAL FOREST

WATER HYACINTHS

F. M. Blake: U. S. Forest Service

VIRGIN STAND OF SHORTLEAF
PINE, OUACHITA NATIONAL FOREST

REVETMENT WORK AT LELAND NECK, NEAR LAKE VILLAGE

A SWINGING BRIDGE

of the entire valley.   On February 13, 1682, he began his descent of the river and on March 13 he came to the mouth of the Arkansas.

"In the fog, from the right bank, we heard Indian war cries and beat of drums," wrote La Salle's lieutenant, Henri de Tonti.   "M. de la Salle did not doubt there was a village.   We came upon it . . . and . . . during the friendly visit . . . we were well treated and given a cabin for our stay.   M. de la Salle took possession of the land in the name of his Christian Majesty.   It can be said these savages [the Quapaw] were the best of all we had ever seen. . . . They had fish in abundance, roosters and chickens, and several kinds of unknown fruits."

In another month La Salle reached the Gulf of Mexico, claimed the Mississippi Valley for France, and named the region Louisiana.   Enthusiastic over his new province, he returned to Paris to recruit colonists and finance another expedition.   In 1684 he sailed for the West Indies and the Mississippi.   The navigation was faulty, however, and 280 members of the party landed on the Texas coast in February 1685. Troubles quickly arose: one of the ships sailed for France, the others were sunk, men died of exposure and disease or were killed by Indians. After two years of hardship La Salle was murdered in Texas by mutinous followers.

Meanwhile De Tonti (also spelled De Tonty), whom La Salle had left in the Illinois country, descended the Mississippi to meet his chief. Finding no trace of the colonists, he returned northward.   At the mouth of the Arkansas, several of De Tonti's men, perhaps because of Quapaw hospitality, asked permission to build a camp and remain.   He "granted the request to some of them."   This was the origin, in 1686, of the village that became known as Arkansas Post, first permanent white settlement in the lower Mississippi Valley.

During the following summer the residents of the post were startled by the arrival of six haggard Frenchmen, survivors of La Salle's expedition.   This group, led by Joutel, had come from the Texas coast through the forests in a desperate effort to reach Canada.   "We discovered a great cross," wrote Joutel, "and at a small distance from it a house built after the French fashion.   We knelt down . . . to give thanks to the Divine Goodness for having conducted us so happily."   During its first few years Arkansas Post was considered an extension of the French activities in Illinois, but, after settlements had been made on the Gulf (Biloxi, 1699; New Orleans, 1718), the handful of soldiers, trappers, priests, and hunters in Arkansas looked toward the Governor General of Louisiana for supplies and instructions.   The one attempt at large-scale colonization failed, in 1721, with the collapse of John Law's project (*see Tour 12B*).

Louisiana became Spanish by treaty in 1763 and by possession, despite some resistance at New Orleans, in 1769.   In the Arkansas region, the only noticeable effect of the transfer was that the Post was renamed Fort Charles III. French commandants continued to issue orders, although now in the name of Spain, and French soldiers still formed the garrison.

Toward the end of the eighteenth century, cabins began to appear up and down the Mississippi and along the Arkansas and White Rivers. As early as 1766, François d'Armand opened a fur-trading establishment at the mouth of White River, a commercially strategic spot that was later the site of a town, Montgomery's Point. In 1797 Sylvanus Phillips founded Helena at the boat landing where Crowley's Ridge runs into the Mississippi. During the same year, Benjamin Foy and a group of Spanish soldiers gave up their efforts to obtain a foothold on the site of Memphis. Moving to the west bank of the river, they built a fort and village that became Hopefield. Spanish commandants, in order to encourage settlement, made lavish land grants in the eastern half of what is now Arkansas.

Although Louisiana became French territory again in 1800, its inhabitants knew nothing officially of the exchange between Spain and France until after the Louisiana Purchase in 1803. Arkansas Post was formally taken over by a United States detachment under Lieutenant James B. Many in 1804. All of the land that is now in the State was governed as a part of the New Madrid District of Louisiana Territory until 1806, when the larger part of it was organized separately, with headquarters at Arkansas Post. In 1812, after Louisiana became a State, the Arkansas District was attached to the Territory of Missouri.

Immediately after the Purchase, President Jefferson took steps to ascertain just what he had bought for $15,000,000. All sorts of romantic speculations were in circulation: one report, given the House of Representatives in 1804 by its Committee on Commerce and Manufactures, referred to "the masses of virgin silver and gold that glitter in the veins of the rocks which underlay the Arkansas." Whether or not it believed the rumors, Congress appropriated money for several exploratory journeys into the West and Southwest. One of these expeditions was led by William Dunbar and Dr. George Hunter, who began their voyage up the Ouachita River in October 1804. The party ascended to the neighborhood of Hot Springs, where it spent a month examining the waters and reconnoitering the area. A company of 24 men under Thomas Freeman went 600 miles up the Red River in 1806. During the same year Lieutenant Zebulon M. Pike crossed the Western plains from St. Louis to the point where Great Bend, Kansas, now lies. Before Pike went on up the Arkansas River into the Rocky Mountains, he sent Lieutenant James B. Wilkinson with two canoes to descend the stream to the Mississippi.

Wilkinson, in the course of his long voyage southeastward, saw thousands of buffalo, deer, and elk.   He encountered a fur trader, Joseph Bogy, near the Verdigris, and met French hunters near the sites of Little Rock and Pine Bluff.   The first settlement he came upon, however, was Arkansas Post, which he reached in January 1807.   For some years the region remained almost uninhabited.   The population of the Arkansas District, given as 368 by the Spanish commandant in 1799, had grown to only 1,062 by 1810.   East of the Mississippi plenty of free land remained, and, for a short time, the flag had outrun the frontier.

It seemed to President Jefferson that some of the unoccupied territory of Louisiana might well be used by the Indians as a permanent home, leaving the eastern United States open to white settlement. States with large Indian populations favored this idea, which became an official policy under President Monroe.   Congress, however, complicated the plan by rewarding veterans of the War of 1812 with land grants in Missouri and Arkansas.   Although no great number of veterans actually came to live on their land, many of them sold their claims to settlers who did take possession.

At that time most of eastern Arkansas was densely timbered and much of it was periodically flooded.   Therefore, hundreds of pioneers built houses and planted crops as far west as present-day Oklahoma. These frontiersmen protested strongly when Government treaties with the Cherokee in 1817 and with the Choctaw in 1820 gave the Indians large areas in western Arkansas.   The tribes, on the other hand, resented the intrusion of white men into reservations that had been received in exchange for Indian land east of the Mississippi.   Petitions, resolutions, and memorials rose to a peak when soldiers removed white settlers from their farms on Indian-reserved soil.   Boundaries were juggled backward and forward until the Choctaw treaty of 1825 finally established the present border from Fort Smith to the Red River.   Three years later the Cherokee agreed to move west of a line running from Fort Smith northward to the southwest corner of Missouri.

After seven years of existence as a part of Missouri Territory, Arkansas was created a separate Territory by Congress in 1819.   The jog at the eastern end of the Arkansas-Missouri border was, according to most historians, placed there because a wealthy planter wished his land to be in Missouri.   The notch-like southwestern corner of the State's boundary was the subject of disputes inherited from the French rulers of Louisiana and finally settled in 1841.

Settlements in the new Territory were scattered along the main travel routes.   Cabins were most frequent in the wide valley of the Arkansas, where the traveler might find a roof to sleep under nearly every night, at New Gascony, Pine Bluff (first called Mount Marie), Pyeattstown, Cadron, Dardanelle, Mulberry, and Fort Smith.   Near the Missouri border, along the Southwest Trail, was another group of villages, on the Current, Spring, Strawberry, Black, and White Rivers. Pioneers living at a series of Mississippi landings sold firewood, poultry, and fruit to the river boats. Ouachita Valley communities included Blakeleytown and Écore á Fabre (now Camden). There were plantations on both sides of the Red River.

In 1818, because of the wide distribution of settlers, five Arkansas counties existed. Although Arkansas Post in 1819 was the leading town of the Territory, with several merchants, a number of lawyers, and a weekly newspaper, it was too inconveniently situated to remain the seat of government. Accordingly the second session of the Territorial legislature made Little Rock the capital in 1820.

A "salute from the Steam-Boat EAGLE" on March 16, 1822, heralded the arrival of the first paddle-wheeler at Little Rock. Other steamers soon thrashed on to Fort Smith and Fort Gibson (now in Oklahoma). In 1828 the *Facility* began making regularly scheduled runs between New Orleans and Fort Gibson, the round trip requiring a month. The Territory's delegates to Congress obtained appropriations to improve the Arkansas River channel and to clear the "great raft," a 100-mile accumulation of driftwood, from the Red River. During the same period other Federal appropriations were made to improve the Southwest Trail and build a road between Memphis and Little Rock.

Democrats ordinarily swept Arkansas elections, as they did elsewhere along the frontier, although the opposing Whigs were ably led by such men as Territorial Secretary Robert Crittenden and Albert Pike. The price of cotton and hides at New Orleans determined the prosperity of town and country people alike, although no one went hungry in a land full of game. In 1826 a half-dozen workmen at Helena built a sawmill acclaimed for having the first manufacturing equipment in the Territory to be "propelled by the power of steam."

Meanwhile homesteaders streamed into the virgin country by oxcart, keelboat, and steamer. The population jumped from 14,273 in 1820 to more than 50,000 by 1835. Merchants and planters were demanding a government that could make credit easier. Governor John Pope was pushing construction of a magnificent Capitol in Little Rock. The question of applying for admission to the Union became the leading issue of the 1835 elections. In January 1836 a convention framed a State constitution without awaiting Federal authorization. Delayed by anti-slavery opposition, the bill to admit Arkansas as the twenty-fifth State passed Congress in June.

While the first set of State officials were still in office, the Nation plunged into the panic of 1837. Thousands of farmers from east of the

Mississippi poured into Arkansas, almost doubling the population in 5 years; by 1840 there were 97,574 people in the State.

In the 1830's the struggle of Texas against Mexico aroused wide interest, and the town of Washington became a gathering place for men who came to take part in the fight for independence. When the United States declared war on Mexico in 1846, Archibald Yell resigned from Congress to lead a regiment of Arkansas cavalry, and was killed at Buena Vista. One of Arkansas' Senators, Chester Ashley, made a noted speech in 1844 urging annexation of the Republic of Texas; the other Senator, Ambrose H. Sevier, was one of the commissioners who negotiated the peace treaty that followed the war.

Stagecoach travel became common and taverns were opened along the routes to give passengers lodging and food. The new steamers that went up and down the rivers were faster and more luxurious than the original packets. Coal seams were discovered at Spadra in 1840, and a year later the first boatload of coal was shipped down to Little Rock. Seminaries in all parts of the State began to advertise for pupils. In the capital a theater presented melodrama and comedy. A celebrated group of attorneys rode from town to town for court sittings, embellishing their legal addresses with Ciceronian quotations and flaying opponents with measured rhetoric.

In 1849 Fort Smith became a concentration point for the great wave of gold hunters that swept toward California. In 1853 the legislature chartered railroads that were to run from Little Rock to Fort Smith and to Memphis, but little track was laid prior to the War between the States. However, the California traffic encouraged the establishment of the Butterfield stage line through western Arkansas in 1858. The State's first telegraph line followed the Butterfield route from St. Louis to Fayetteville in 1860, a year before wires were strung from Memphis to Little Rock.

Although most Arkansans were still farmers on a small scale, a good many large plantations had been cleared in the Mississippi Delta below Helena, in the Arkansas Valley, and in the bottomlands of smaller rivers. In these sections slave labor rapidly replaced yeomanry. The number of Negro slaves rose from 4,576 in 1830 to 47,100 by 1850.

As sectional tension over the slavery issue grew in the Nation, Arkansas aligned itself with the South. State authorities took over the Federal arsenal at Little Rock in February 1861. Nevertheless, a convention met in March and voted against secession, although it also opposed coercion of the seceding States.

The first actual fighting, in April, crystallized opinion in Arkansas. "In answer to your requisition for troops . . . I have to say that none will be furnished," replied Governor Henry M. Rector to Lincoln's call for volunteers. Fort Smith was seized by State troops on April

23. Early in May a second convention passed a secession ordinance with only one adverse vote, and Arkansas formally joined the Confederacy.

At the opening of the war the battlefront extended through Virginia, Kentucky, and Missouri. Arkansas troops were sent to all three States. In March 1862 the bloody battle of Pea Ridge (Elkhorn Tavern) was fought in northwest Arkansas. The Confederates carried the field, but their commanding general, Van Dorn, withdrew and soon afterward took his army to the defense of Corinth, Mississippi. Meanwhile the troops of Federal General Samuel R. Curtis made their way through the Ozarks to Batesville, with the intention of marching down White River and advancing on Little Rock from the east. General Thomas C. Hindman had been successful in organizing an army to hold the capital, and after some skirmishes, Curtis went on southeastward to Helena.

In 1863 Federal troops gained their principal objective in the West, the control of the Mississippi River. One step in this campaign was the capture of Arkansas Post on January 11. Grant besieged Vicksburg, the last Confederate stronghold on the river, in May. On July 4, in a final desperate attempt to divert part of Grant's troops, Southern regiments launched a costly attack on Helena. They were driven off and Vicksburg surrendered on the same day. The Federal army in Helena, now commanded by General Frederick Steele, began a drive toward Little Rock in August. Outnumbering and outflanking the defenders under General Sterling Price, Steele took the capital on September 10.

In the spring of 1864, Steele and General N. P. Banks, then Federal commander in New Orleans, attempted a pincers movement to trap the Confederate armies in southern Arkansas and northern Louisiana. Banks moved up the Red River toward Shreveport, while Steele marched southwest from Little Rock and occupied Camden. Banks was repulsed in Louisiana, and Steele found his position at Camden precarious because Confederate detachments were capturing his supply trains. He retreated northward until the Confederates overtook him at Jenkins Ferry on the Saline River. In the battle that ensued both sides suffered serious losses, but Steele eventually reached Little Rock. The only other important action in the region during 1864 was Sterling Price's spectacular September dash, which carried him north as far as the Missouri River and then west to the Kansas border before he was forced to retire.

The surrender of General Kirby Smith on May 26, 1865, officially ended the fighting in Arkansas. Soldiers who had been at Manassas, Shiloh, Gettysburg, Chickamauga, Vicksburg, Lookout Mountain, and Appomattox straggled back to their ruined farms and tried to borrow mules and plows with which to plant their cotton and corn. The war left Arkansas destitute of resources and faced by countless problems of readjustment.

In 1863 the State government of the Confederates had moved southwest to Washington, where the executive officials, the general assembly, and the supreme court continued to function. Early in 1864, delegates from 23 counties met at Little Rock and drew up a Unionist constitution, under which State and local officials were elected. Thus there were two civil governments in Arkansas during the later years of the war, one giving allegiance to the Confederacy and the other to the Federals; the dividing line roughly followed the Arkansas River.

After the surrender the Washington government disappeared, and Arkansans generally accepted the administration of Governor Isaac Murphy. Every county in the State sent representatives to the 1866 legislature. However, Arkansas had not been readmitted to the Union, and the Senators it elected through 1866 were refused seats by Congress.

A Federal act of March 1867 declared the governments of Arkansas and nine other former Confederate States illegal. These areas were placed under military rule until they should adopt new constitutions and ratify the Fourteenth (Negro suffrage) Amendment. This Congressional action put the Republican party in firm control and launched the period known as Reconstruction.

The first Governor elected after the adoption of the 1868 constitution was Powell Clayton, a resident of Kansas until he came to the South as a Federal army officer. Clayton, who has been called "the most astute and stern of the carpetbaggers," was elected to the United States Senate in 1871, but the chaos he had helped to create in Arkansas did not abate for several years. Reconstruction reached a climax in the "Brooks-Baxter War" of 1874, when armed forces of two claimants to the governorship faced each other across Main Street in Little Rock. Clashes also occurred up and down the Arkansas River. Elisha Baxter, the successful candidate by President Grant's proclamation, had the support of the Democrats in the dispute, and he thereafter worked with them to obtain remedial legislation and a new constitution. Democrats carried the election of 1874 and have won every balloting since that year.

Despite the clashes of carpetbaggers and Ku Klux Klansmen, the looting of public funds, and the resentment of citizens denied participation in politics, Arkansas slowly rose to its feet after the war. Freed slaves worked the fields on a crop-sharing basis. National banks began business at Little Rock and Fort Smith in 1866. Public schools were opened for Negro children, State institutions for the blind and deaf were established, and Arkansas Industrial University (now the University of Arkansas) held its first classes in 1872. Finally, the State was linked with the rest of the Nation by railroads.

In 1871 the Little Rock and Fort Smith Railroad (now the Missouri Pacific) advertised that its trains were running as far west as Lewisburg, near the site of present-day Morrilton. Tracks between the capital and the Mississippi River were also completed in 1871. The greatest mileage was laid between 1880 and 1890; significantly, in this decade the State's population made its most decided numerical gain, growing from 802,525 to 1,128,211. With the railroads came the sawmills that gave Arkansas its largest industry. The coal that had been mined in the Arkansas Valley since 1840 now found ready sale. Farmers began to choose their crops with an eye for distant markets; Arkansas apples took first prize at exhibitions in New Orleans, Boston, and San Francisco.

During the same period the protest of farmers against near-monopoly control of money and transportation gave rise to a new political party which challenged Democratic rule of the State. Organized into the Agricultural Wheel, which had originated in Prairie County in 1882, the farmers joined forces with labor groups and came within 15,000 votes of electing their candidate for Governor in 1888. Fearing the strength of this coalition, the Democrats took over the Wheel platform piece by piece. The same sentiment, on a national scale, brought about the nomination of William Jennings Bryan on a free-silver ticket in 1896. Populist voters in Arkansas returned to the Democratic Party in 1900 to elect Jeff Davis as Governor; the insurgent movement then died away.

Until the railroads came in the 1870's the life and wealth of Arkansas had been most in evidence along the rivers and, particularly, in the Arkansas Valley. The stream itself was the main artery of transportation, and planters who grew cotton on its fertile lowlands were among the most influential citizens. However, in the last quarter of the nineteenth century, and afterward, the new railroads swept farming and industry to inland counties. The forests of southern Arkansas were dotted with lumber mills. Tourists began coming into the Ozarks and Ouachitas. The northern part of the Delta, between West Memphis and Blytheville, heard the whine of large sawmills about 1900. When the land cleared by lumbermen here was drained, it grew cotton in undreamed-of quantities. In southwest Arkansas farmers found that the sandy soil would grow peaches, watermelons, and other fruits. The northwest plateau became well known for its diversified crops and apples. Successful cultivation of rice rejuvenated farm life on the Grand Prairie, long considered unsuitable for good farming.

The new State Capitol, commenced in 1899, had been completed about a year when the United States entered the World War in 1917.

A total of 63,632 Arkansans were in the Nation's military services by November 1918. The scale of the war preparations was brought home to civilians by the presence at Camp Pike, near Little Rock, of some 100,000 recruits, more soldiers than the capital had residents. An aviation training field was laid out near Lonoke.

Discovery of oil near El Dorado in the early 1920's caused a fever of excitement, and a new industry arose in several south Arkansas counties. As the decade advanced business optimism became strong in the State. Tall new office buildings and hotels changed the appearance of the cities. Public schools were vastly improved in standards and equipment. Automobile roads were built to remote towns. Pipe lines for natural gas and high-tension electric lines penetrated many sections. In 1924 the State's first large hydroelectric dam was constructed across the Ouachita River near Malvern.

In 1927 the Mississippi rose to a record height and Arkansas suffered its worst flood. So vast was the yellow tide rushing down the Mississippi Valley that it seemed the Great Lakes were emptying themselves into the Gulf of Mexico. The State's own rivers, unable to discharge their swollen waters, backed up and submerged millions of acres in the Delta. One-fifth of the entire area of Arkansas was inundated. "It is the greatest peace-time disaster in our history," said Herbert Hoover. A Federal program of river control, authorized by Congress in 1928, kept the Mississippi within its banks during the high water of 1935 and 1937, although backwater floods indicated the need of additional protection along the Arkansas, White, and St. Francis Rivers.

During the 1930's agriculture, industry, communications, and social services marked out new paths. Livestock shows in a number of towns and cities reflected the increasing interest in cattle raising. Improvement of dairy cattle breeds heightened milk and cream production, so that cream-buying stations began to dot the countryside. Cotton began to retreat from the mountain counties. Arkansas led the Nation in the proportion of farm land voluntarily included in soil-conservation districts. Raising broiler-size poultry became an art and an industry in northwest Arkansas. Discovery of cinnabar ore at the southern edge of the Ouachitas led to the refining of mercury. Sawmills intensified their experiments in selective cutting and reforestation. Tolls on highway bridges were abolished. A transcontinental airline angled across the State from Texarkana to Memphis. Sales and liquor taxes brought in additional revenue for social services. Hundreds of new schools, courthouses, and other public buildings were erected. In 1941, looking into the future, the State saw its cotton kingdom growing smaller, its agriculture becoming more diversified, and a promise of increased industrialization.

Government

A LOOSELY knit and poorly-manned government ruled the Indians, trappers, and traders in Arkansas for nearly a hundred years before the Louisiana Purchase. Though a small French garrison had been stationed at Arkansas Post since 1686, the first formal arrangement for governing the area was made in 1721, when Arkansas became one of the nine commands of Louisiana. The command extended indefinitely to the west, but the north, south, and east borders were about the same as the lines that now bound the State.

From 1721 until Spain assumed active control of Louisiana in 1769, a succession of French commandants at Arkansas Post wielded full military and civil authority; their decisions were subject to review by the governor and superior council at New Orleans. Under Spanish rule (1769-1800), Frenchmen in the service of Spain were usually chosen to command the wilderness outpost and administer the law.

In the possession of the United States after 1803, Arkansas was first a part of Louisiana Territory, and from 1812 a district of Missouri Territory. Arkansas Territory was created in 1819, and the first legislature declared that all laws of the Territory of Missouri were in force. The legislators in later sessions enacted additional laws to meet the needs of the new Territory.

Five constitutions have provided foundations for government since Arkansas was admitted to the Union. The first, adopted in 1836, was coincident with its rise to statehood. Four later instruments, including the one under which the State now functions, were outgrowths of Secession, the War between the States, and the turbulent period of Reconstruction.

All of the State constitutions have provided for three departments of government—legislative, executive, and judicial. Outstanding differences in the earlier documents involved the questions of slavery and suffrage. The constitution of 1836 recognized slavery and denied to the general assembly the power to emancipate slaves without the consent of owners. On the other hand, it granted the legislature the right of preventing slaves from being brought into the State as merchandise, and empowered that body to pass laws "to oblige the owners of slaves to treat them with humanity."

In 1861 Arkansas withdrew from the Union, and the Secession convention adopted a new constitution. Declaring Arkansas to be a free and independent State, the Secession constitution recognized slavery, and in several clauses setting out the rights of citizens, confined the privilege of slave-owning to "free white men, and Indians."

Shortly before Federal troops occupied Little Rock in September 1863, Governor Harris Flanagin ordered official records removed from the town and established a temporary capital at Washington, in Hempstead County. Soon afterward a movement was started in north Arkansas for the formation of a State government sympathetic to the invaders. In January 1864 delegates from 23 counties met in Little Rock and wrote a pro-Federal document which abolished slavery, repudiated secession, and declared that the constitution of 1861 was "null and void, and is not now, and never has been binding and obligatory upon the people." On the whole, the new document was a restatement of the constitution of 1836, aside from its prohibition of slavery.

In March 1864 voters north of the Arkansas River ratified the new constitution and elected as Governor, Isaac Murphy, who held the office four years, but Governor Flanagin continued as chief executive for the Confederate-controlled part of the State until the close of the war.

In 1868 another convention assembled in Little Rock and adopted a constitution which granted the franchise to Negroes. It reaffirmed allegiance to the Government of the United States and recognized the Federal right to employ armed force to compel such allegiance. Because of the extension of privileges to freed slaves, and restrictions upon former citizens of the Confederacy, this instrument of 1868 has often been referred to as the "Carpetbag Constitution."

In the interim between 1868 and 1872 dissension developed within the Republican Party, then in control of the State administration, with the result that a new party developed. Called the Liberal Republican Party, it represented a coalition of a number of Democrats and dissatisfied Republicans. In convention the Liberal Republicans nominated the Reverend Joseph Brooks for Governor; the Democratic Party endorsed this ticket, while the Republicans nominated Elisha Baxter. On the face of the returns, Baxter was elected. His victory was promulgated by the legislature of 1873, but the Brooks faction, charging the returns were fraudulent, took the issue to court. In early legal efforts Brooks was unsuccessful, but in April 1874 he obtained a Pulaski County circuit court order adjudging him entitled to the office. A friendly supreme court justice administered the oath. Brooks forcibly ousted Baxter from the Governor's office and entrenched himself in the Capitol. Baxter immediately set up offices outside the Statehouse and what is known in Arkansas history as the Brooks-Baxter War ensued. There were troublous times in Little Rock and elsewhere, several armed skirmishes, and a few casualties. The strife was ended when President Grant proclaimed Baxter Governor.

While the conflict with Brooks continued, Baxter summoned a special session of the general assembly, which in turn called a constitutional convention. The latter body drafted the document of 1874. With its amendments, this constitution is still in force.

Regarded as one of the most important additions is an amendment adopted in 1910, giving voters the right, by petition, of initiating laws and amendments to be passed upon at general elections. This alteration also removed the limit of three amendments to be voted upon during one election, a restriction imposed when changes could be submitted only by the general assembly.

Under the constitution now in force the legislative branch of the State government consists of a house of representatives of 100 members, and a senate of 35 members. Each county has one or more representatives in the lower house, while senators are elected by districts. The lieutenant governor is the presiding officer of the senate. The house chooses one of its members to preside as speaker. Representatives are elected for terms of two years and senators for four years. Regular sessions of the general assembly are held biennially, in odd-numbered years, beginning the second Monday in January. Though sessions are limited to 60 days, they may be extended 15 days by a two-thirds vote of each house. The Governor is empowered to call special sessions in emergencies and may in effect prolong regular sittings through such action.

Constitutional State officers are: Governor, lieutenant governor, secretary of state, treasurer, auditor, attorney general, land commissioner and seven supreme court justices. The office of lieutenant governor was created by constitutional amendment, and the first elective official with this title took office in January 1927. Officers appointed by the Governor include the heads of the highway and revenue departments, members of the corporation commission, state comptroller, public utilities commissioners, and many others. Appointments of practically all these officials are subject to approval of the senate.

One of the more recent and important bodies created by the legislature is the State Planning Board. The Governor is *ex officio* chairman, and the board includes in its membership one representative from each of the following State offices or departments: highway commission, office of geologist, corporation commission, parks commission, forestry commission, board of education, board of health; also one representative from the College of Agriculture of the University of Arkansas and six members who are not regularly employed by the State. None of the members receives remuneration, but the board employs an engineer-director, an assistant engineer-director, and other necessary employees.

Duties of the Planning Board, as set out in the act creating it, include the formation of a plan for the physical development of Arkansas. Specific mention is made of highway location and improvement, waterway and water-front development, railroad and motor transportation routes, aviation fields, power transmission facilities, flood control, prevention of stream pollution, forest reservations, State parks, wildlife refuges, conservation projects, public buildings, and land utilization programs for agricultural, mineral, forestry, industrial, or other purposes. Since its creation in 1935 the board has made steady progress and has been especially effective in planning orderly development of State institutions. Typical of its comprehensive and valuable reports is the board's *Arkansas Water Resources* (1939).

The highest judicial power of the State is vested in a supreme court composed of a chief justice and six associate justices, all elected. Terms of chief and associate justices are eight years. Except in rare instances, the supreme court confines its deliberations to appellate matters.

The constitution of 1874 also makes provision for the following kinds of courts: circuit, chancery, county, corporation (municipal), and justice of the peace. Circuit courts have jurisdiction in all civil and criminal cases which cannot be disposed of by lower bodies, except suits in equity. Chancery courts, which like circuit courts are set up by districts, handle all cases involving matters of equity, including mortgage foreclosures, probate matters, and divorce and domestic relations cases. There are 18 judicial circuits and 14 chancery circuits.

The county judge presides at county court sessions, and, in effect, is also county manager. He passes upon all bills and claims against the county, has charge of road work, the county hospital, the jail, and the county farm, and heads the quorum court which, in fact, is not a court but a county directorial group. The quorum court is composed of all the justices of the peace in a county. This body can legally function only when a majority of the justices are in attendance. Chief duties of the quorum court are the levying of taxes and appropriation of funds for county offices and agencies. It is within the discretion of this group to say whether the county shall carry on such programs as farm and home demonstration work, health education, cattle-tick eradication, and testing of livestock for diseases. The plan of county government also includes a sheriff (who in most instances is tax collector), a tax assessor, treasurer, and county clerk.

Prosecuting attorneys are elected by districts which coincide with judicial circuits. It is customary for these officials to appoint deputies in each of the counties in their districts, particularly to represent the State in justice of the peace and municipal courts.

In the larger cities municipal courts have been created by statute. Here elected judges handle minor civil litigation and misdemeanor cases. In the smaller towns, however, mayors sit as magistrates or police judges. Justices of the peace have original jurisdiction in misdemeanor cases and in civil suits of a contractual nature involving not more than $100. City affairs ordinarily are handled by a mayor, city council, and department heads.

Arkansas is represented in the U. S. Congress by two Senators and by seven members of the House of Representatives. The Congressional districts have been made the basis for appointment or election to many State boards or commissions.

In Arkansas, as in many other Southern States, nomination by a Democratic primary election is usually equivalent to election. The primaries themselves are a check against the building up of long-lived political machines, and the Corrupt Practices Act of 1913 has proved a deterrent to election frauds.

As a Territory, Arkansas in 1819 was divided into five counties— Arkansas, Lawrence, Clark, Hempstead, and Pulaski. The legislature of the Territory of Missouri had fixed the boundaries of Arkansas County in 1813, and had created Lawrence County in 1815. Clark, Hempstead, and Pulaski were formed from the first two subdivisions. As settlement was extended and the population increased, additional counties were created at frequent intervals by a process of division. With the formation of Cleburne County in 1883 the present number of 75 was reached. Twelve of the counties have courthouses at two towns instead of one. This peculiarity dates back to early days, when roads were few and centers of population were separated by such natural obstacles as unbridged rivers and impassable mountains.

In recent years a few students of government, several of the larger newspapers, and some State department heads have unsuccessfully urged a reduction in the number of counties. Proponents of consolidation contend that improved roads and rapid transportation have made once distant points now easily accessible, and that the number of units might be reduced to a third or fourth of the present total, with an increase in efficiency and a saving in the expense of county government.

The State in 1939 employed some 13,000 persons. Of these, 3,215 were specifically authorized by the constitution or by legislation, and the remainder were employed by departments. Expenditures and revenues for the year were about $30,000,000. Of the total revenue, more than a third was raised by a gasoline tax, while property taxation brought in little more than a tenth of the State's income.

Recent controversial issues in affairs of government include the questions of poll tax repeal and civil service. Arkansas is one of seven States, all Southern, which require a fee for registration on the voting lists, the tax here being $1 a year. Payment of the tax as a prerequisite for voting was prescribed by a constitutional amendment passed in 1892.

The amendment was declared inoperative by the State supreme court in 1904; it passed again in 1908, and subsequent campaigns to repeal it have been unsuccessful.

In 1937 the general assembly placed most of the appointive employees of the State under a classified civil service plan. The act aroused protest from persons both in and out of office, and was repealed by the legislators during the 1939 session.

Transidation

Transportation

IN an old French print, *La Concession de Monseigneur Law*, a carpenter is shown waving a hammer with negligent grace at the ribs of an unfinished 20-foot boat. Though it is unlikely that the half-starved residents of John Law's colony at Arkansas Post (1719-21) constructed craft as elaborate as the one in the print, the artist was correct in assuming that boats were important in the early days of the Post. The only convenient transportation for Arkansas' first white inhabitants was by water.

The usual vessel was the pirogue, of Indian invention. In Southern forests the pirogue was usually made by hollowing out a log. This simple, but large-capacity canoe took French explorers and hunters up the Arkansas, the White, the Black, the St. Francis, the Ouachita, and the Red Rivers. The same craft took the trappers' cargoes of furs down river.

The pioneers who came to Arkansas after the Louisiana Purchase were looking not for peltries, but for land to clear and cultivate. They brought with them their families, household goods, tools, and supplies. They brought also the keelboats that had carried them down the Ohio, the Tennessee, and Mississippi. Keelboats were big, heavy-timbered affairs, from 40 to 75 feet long and 8 to 12 feet wide, with a cabin for shelter, laid on a keel thick enough to withstand scraping over sand bars or bumping into snags. Useful, even comfortable, for floating downstream, the unwieldy craft drew many a frontier curse from the men who tried to navigate them up the Arkansas rivers. Sails were of little use in these tree-lined channels, and the boats had to be rowed, towed, or poled—sometimes all three at once—against the current at the rate of six or eight miles a day.

None the less it was the keelboat that brought in most of Arkansas' earliest settlers; that took merchandise to the traders of Arkansas Post; that carried the Territory's first Governor, James I. Miller, in state from Pittsburgh to the Post; that transported the soldiers who built Fort Smith and Fort Gibson.

The years that saw settlers come to Arkansas in keelboats and flatboats also marked the beginning of vehicular travel in the Territory. Countless generations of Indians on foot and horseback had followed the Southwest Trail (*see Tour 1*) along the eastern edge of the Ozarks and Ouachitas from Missouri down into Texas and Mexico. But the white immigrants who lashed their oxen through the wilderness frequently had to stop and cut trees to permit passage of their wagons. Most of the trails were little more than general routes which became impassable when the rivers went out of their banks.

Among the most heavily traveled of the traces was the route that cut westward from Memphis to intersect the Southwest Trail (see Tour 3a). Jungle-grown and swampy, it involved difficult crossings through the bottoms of three considerable rivers, but it was the only way of getting through the Delta to Little Rock without traveling hundreds of extra miles. At right angles to this road a trail ran down the top of Crowley's Ridge, high and dry from Missouri all the way to Helena, and a favorite route for incoming homeseekers. From Little Rock a trail soon followed the north bank of the Arkansas southeast to Arkansas Post and west to Fort Smith. Paths spread out from the first towns on the river banks into the surrounding areas, some of them for long distances. Many of the pioneers in southwest Missouri, for instance, came up the White River by keelboat to Norfork, then reloaded their belongings into wagons for the trek through the Ozark hills into the level country around Springfield. Northwest Arkansas, on the other hand, cut off by mountains from the rest of the State, was most easily reached from Missouri, and many early Arkansans came down the route successively known as the State Road, the Wire Road, and US 71.

Travel in Arkansas during the first quarter of the nineteenth century involved hard, back-breaking work, whether it was hauling at a keelboat towrope (cordelle) or prying a wagon out of axle-deep mud. There were panthers in the woods, snags and sand bars in the rivers, and outlaws ready to turn their hands either to highway robbery or piracy as the chance offered. Anyone who spoke of a "pleasure trip" would have been considered a humorist or a madman. For that reason the appearance of the steamboat constituted a revolution in Arkansas transportation.

Steamboats meant that a man could lounge on deck, surrounded by a cosmopolitan company, while he traveled in a few days distances that would have taken as many weeks by keelboat. Isolated communities like Batesville on the White River or Van Buren on the Arkansas could have such luxuries as store whisky, dressed leather shoes, and wheat flour. Still more important for the future social structure of the State, steamboats meant that planters could immigrate there. So long as travel had been by keelboat, no large landowner in Georgia or South Carolina would have considered selling his household furnishings and slaves to battle the Arkansas wilderness. But with steamboat transportation slaves could be shipped ahead to clear land and build houses, so that the wealthy man's family could come to the new country with a minimum of frontier hardship.

The steamer *Comet* visited Arkansas Post as early as 1820, but the first steam-propelled boat to reach Little Rock was the *Eagle*, which arrived March 16, 1822, on her way to Dwight Mission, near present-day Russellville. The *Eagle* went aground above Little Rock, but less than a month later the *Robert Thompson* successfully negotiated the river to Fort Smith with provisions for the garrison.

Supply boats for Dwight Mission, Fort Smith, and Fort Gibson accounted for most of the Arkansas River traffic during the next few years. In 1828 Captain Pennywit brought the *Facility* up the river on his way to the Verdigris, and descended with a cargo of hides, furs, and 500 barrels of pecans. He found the run profitable and put his boat into regular service between Fort Gibson and New Orleans, thereby providing the first regular schedules on the Arkansas.

The *Facility* on its upstream voyage in 1828 had carried several hundred Creek to their reservation in Indian Territory. Large-scale movements of various tribes in the next few years led to the appearance of numerous new boats on the upper Arkansas. Some 10,000 Choctaw were brought up from Memphis and Vicksburg in 1831-2, and they were followed by about 14,000 Creek shortly thereafter. Cherokee also passed through the State by thousands in the 1830's and early 1840's. Without this tremendous upstream passenger business it is unlikely that the thinly settled country would have witnessed so rapid a development of steamboat traffic.

Operating a steamboat line, though it brought considerable profits, was a hazardous enterprise. Boiler explosions, fires, snags, and sand bars were so numerous that the average life of a boat was four years. However, no dangers could outweigh the advantages of steamboat transportation. Captain Pennywit took the *Waverly* up White River to Batesville as early as 1831, and in ensuing decades other boats managed to scrape over the shallows all the way up to Forsythe and Branson, Missouri. Packets reached the old towns on Black River—Powhatan, Clover Bend, Pocahontas—and Madison and Wittsburg on the St. Francis. Cargoes of cotton were shipped down the Ouachita and the Red. Steamers even churned the waters of such small streams as the Petit Jean and Fourche la Fave. On the western bank of the Mississippi a series of towns grew up, of which Napoleon (now part of the river's bed) and Helena were the most important.

The War between the States interrupted steamboat traffic just as it was reaching its peak, Federal gunboats and ironclads almost completely closing the rivers. After the war, during the decades 1870-90, occurred the greatest development of water transportation. It was in this period, when the railroads were laying tracks throughout the cotton-growing areas of the State, that passenger luxury and freight capacity achieved their climax. In 1870 the *Pat Cleburne,* a 4-boiler boat with accommodations for 125 passengers and space for 2,000 bales of cotton, astonished Arkansans with her magnificence. The *Jas. Howard,* built the following year, had a 350-foot hull and an extreme width of 96 feet.

Land transportation during the steamboat era definitely occupied a secondary place. Swollen rivers and swamps in the lowlands made the roads exasperating and frequently impassable, while narrow valleys and steep pulls in the hills were difficult for mules or even slow oxen. Stagecoach lines established in the 1830's usually supplemented steamboat routes. A line from Little Rock to Rock Roe (near present-day Clarendon) connected with White River packets and enabled travelers to reach the Mississippi without winding the endless curves of the Arkansas.

The route between Little Rock and Van Buren, although it competed with the steamers, was probably the best patronized in the State. Along this rough-hewn road taverns and coach houses were built, post offices were established, and villages prospered.

The California gold rush of 1849 put a heavy strain on both land and water transportation systems in Arkansas, since Fort Smith and Van Buren were taking-off points for thousands. One result of the westward rush was the establishment of the Butterfield stage route from St. Louis to the coast in 1858. Coming down from Springfield, Missouri, the route passed over the northwest Arkansas plateau, touched Fayetteville, and then threaded the Boston Mountains to Fort Smith. A letter written by a traveler in 1860 contains a fervent description of a journey over the mountains:

> No one who has never passed over this road can form any idea of its bold and rugged aspect. . . . Over such a route as this the coaches of the mail company are driven with fearful rapidity. The horses are seldom permitted to walk, even when traversing the steepest and most tortuous hills, and when drove at their utmost speed, which is generally the case, the stage reels from side to side like a storm tossed bark, and the din of the heavily ironed wheels in constant contact with the flinty rock, is truly appalling. . . . Yet, with all these indications of danger and recklessness, accidents rarely occur. . . . The coaches are built expressly with reference to rough service—and none but the most reliable and experienced drivers are placed upon the mountain district. The horses are of the most powerful description to be found, and when once thoroughly trained to the service, perform the laborious run with apparent pleasure and delight.

"The Butterfield business," wrote Grant Foreman (*Chronicles of Oklahoma,* Sept. 1931), "employed more than 100 Concord coaches carrying from five to six passengers each, 1000 horses and 500 mules and nearly 800 men. . . . The stages made two trips weekly each way, and the fare from San Francisco to St. Louis, 2391 miles, was

$200.00 in gold." Until it suspended service in the confusion of marching armies the Butterfield line gave northwest Arkansas direct and speedy passenger and mail service to the Atlantic and Pacific coasts.

In the 1850's the national excitement over railroads reached Arkansas. A planter whose slave-woman bore quadruplets named the infants Mississippi, Ouachita, Red River, and Railroad, after a pioneer line. Numerous companies were formed, routes discussed, and land grants obtained. The only actual construction prior to the War between the States was by the Memphis & Little Rock Railroad, and by the Mississippi, Ouachita & Red River, which built a few miles of track inland from the Mississippi ports of Chicot and Arkansas City.

The Memphis & Little Rock route was of foremost importance to the State because the swamps of eastern Arkansas made Memphis, only 133 miles from Little Rock, virtually inaccessible by land, and the water route wound far to the southeast. Building proceeded eastward from Little Rock and westward from Hopefield (opposite Memphis) in 1857, and was fairly rapid until the eastern section, laid mostly on trestles, had reached Madison on the St. Francis. By 1862 the western section extended to De Valls Bluff on White River. The war, and the engineering problem of constructing a roadbed through the morasses bordering the St. Francis, Cache, and White, stopped track laying for several years. Meanwhile passengers covered the distance between Madison and Clarendon by coach, and traveled from Clarendon to De Valls Bluff by steamboat. The two sections were completed in 1871, and the line was opened amid general celebration.

A veteran engineer on some of the earliest trains in Arkansas recalls that "Wood yards were placed from 15 to 30 miles apart. . . . There was a crew of men at each wood pile that kept the wood piled up on temporary platforms by the side of the track. . . . We would go to this wood pile and stop and everybody on the train assisted in piling the wood up on the tender. . . . Firemen in that day and time were experts in handling wood. Some of them could stand in the back of the tender and throw a stick of wood in the firebox door, a hole about 18 inches in diameter."

The war delayed railroad building in Arkansas for a decade. By 1870, however, ambitious promoters of the St. Louis, Iron Mountain & Southern had pushed a line south from St. Louis to the Arkansas border and were looking toward Texas. They bought up the Cairo & Fulton, which had secured rights-of-way before the war but had done no building, and constructed the first railroad that crossed the entire State. These tracks followed the general route of the old Southwest Trail to Fulton on the Red River. In 1872 the road reached Little Rock. Its terminal on the Texas border, where the new city of Texarkana was to grow, was completed in 1874. At the same time the

State's other major highway, between Little Rock and Fort Smith, was being paralleled by the Little Rock & Fort Smith Railroad. Construction stopped at the coal fields of Clarksville in 1874, and the route was not extended to Fort Smith until 1879.

Jay Gould, who had acquired the Iron Mountain lines, visited Arkansas in 1882 to inspect his roads and investigate the possibilities of extending his transportation empire in the Southwest. The same year he bought the Little Rock & Fort Smith and added it to the Iron Mountain system, which continued to grow until it became the largest in the State.

Gould and other entrepreneurs realized that only railroads could tap the wealth in 30,000,000 acres of virgin timber, and thereafter Arkansas railroads and lumbering developed together. Section camps became lumber camps, and frequently grew into mill towns. Spurs built solely to haul timber were occasionally linked together to form a through railroad line. Conversely, lines built to reach a good timber section were sometimes abandoned after the forest had been exhausted. Throughout the rest of the nineteenth century and until the World War, steel tracks were urged on through swamps and jungles by lumbermen eager for more cypress, pine, and oak.

Quite as striking as the feverish boom in railroads and lumbering was the shift in population from the old river towns to sites along the new steel highways. Dozens of communities that had based their prosperity on steamboat traffic disappeared completely. Other trading centers, more firmly held together by tradition and sentiment, maintained their existence but languished. Most of Arkansas' leading cities date their founding or the beginning of their growth from the building of their railroad, and very few besides Helena and Batesville have prospered without a major interstate rail route.

The Missouri Pacific system, which in 1917 formally absorbed the Iron Mountain, is today the most important railroad in the State. The company's main lines to the Southwest and to Mexico cross Arkansas, still following the old Southwest Trail route of the Cairo & Fulton. Other principal sections of the system branch to Memphis, to Fort Smith, down the Arkansas Valley toward New Orleans, through the Ozarks to Joplin, Missouri, and along Crowley's Ridge to Helena; a network of lines covers the southeast corner of the State. The Chicago, Rock Island, & Pacific, which eventually acquired the old Memphis & Little Rock, now continues westward into Oklahoma, with two branches running south through the timber and oil country. The St. Louis-San Francisco has several lines across the northeast corner of the State to Memphis, and also follows the old Butterfield stage route across the northwest counties to Fort Smith; additional tracks run from Hope into southern Oklahoma. Commonly known as the Cotton Belt, the St. Louis Southwestern swings in a great arc through the cotton, rice, and timber land of eastern and southern Arkansas, and goes on into Texas. The Missouri & Arkansas cuts from Joplin, Missouri, through the Ozarks southeast to Helena. The Kansas City Southern follows the western boundary of the State, crossing and recrossing the border on its way to Port Arthur on the Gulf. The Louisiana & Arkansas, which runs from Hope to a Louisiana connection with New Orleans, is controlled by the Kansas City Southern. There are now approximately 4,700 miles of track in Arkansas.

As the importance of railroad transportation increased, that of waterways waned, though there was a sizable traffic even after the turn of the century. But the gleaming packets with their towering super-structures and broad decks have already become romanticized in the haze of memory, and most Arkansas children have never seen a steamboat. Silt and sand, much of it loosened by deforestation, have washed into the principal rivers until most of the channels are all but impassable.

Where dredges have cleared away the sand bars, and revetments have held the currents to a steady course, barge trains carry a surprising volume of freight. Docks on the Ouachita at Camden and Calion handle large shipments of oil, sugar, cotton, and miscellaneous goods. Helena, with its Mississippi barge terminal, finds river commerce profitable. From time to time businessmen request the Federal Government to deepen the Arkansas River, and War Department Engineers are engaged in a survey of navigation possibilities and potential tonnage.

Construction of good vehicular roads in Arkansas, as elsewhere, awaited the perfection of the automobile. Until 1913, when a State Highway Commission was established, road building was in the hands of the counties, and highways formed no coherent pattern. In 1915 local communities were empowered to organize road improvement districts which could issue bonds and levy property taxes to retire the bonds. This experiment had unfortunate results. By 1921 the districts had piled up a debt of $60,000,000 and had no money to maintain the roads they had built. Legislation in 1923 imposed a 4¢ gasoline tax in order to put the burden of road building on the user rather than on the property-owner. In 1927 the tax was raised to 5¢, the indebtedness of the districts was assumed by the State, and a program of new construction was launched. Heavy bond charges caused an increase of the gasoline tax to 6½¢ in 1934.

Today (1941) the Arkansas highway system compares well with that of other States. Concrete highways run from Memphis to Fort Smith, and from Missouri to the Texas border. Other major roads are integrated into a plan, are graveled or paved with blacktop, and maintained in good condition. New steel and concrete bridges span many of the rivers; fills and trestles carry the highways through flooded bottoms; well-graded roads pass through thinly settled sections. All State-owned bridges were made toll-free in 1938, and the last two privately-owned toll bridges were acquired by the State and were thrown open to the public in 1940.

Acquainted with aviation through the wartime Eberts Field near Lonoke, Arkansans eagerly welcomed travel by plane. In 1917 Little Rock established an airport which was made an intermediate air depot by Federal authorities. Facilities built at this landing-ground made the city a stop on the transcontinental route of American Airlines. Various other air lines have been projected for the State and several have operated for brief periods. Carrying mail and passengers, American at present offers the only regular service, planes jumping east to Memphis and west to Dallas. Fort Smith, Texarkana, Hot Springs, Pine Bluff, and other larger towns maintain airports, and landing fields are scattered widely throughout the State.

Agriculture

A VISITOR in those counties that lie just west of the Mississippi River knows he is in the cotton belt, regardless of the season. In spring the lacy green of trees along bayous and creeks is sobered by vast fields of brown earth. Some of these have just been planted in corn, but the most familiar pattern is one of low, washboard-like ridges left by the cotton planter. In summer, leaves and stalks cover the flat land with a rich green mat. Later, when each boll has burst into a fistful of white lint, there is a stir in the villages. Pickers invade the fields, and cotton that has fallen from wagons lies along the road like melting snow. Even after dark, in the autumn, a traveler is aware of the cotton harvest, because the electrically lighted gins keep up a vibrant hum until nearly midnight. In winter, the gins alongside the railroad tracks and the compress warehouses in larger towns stand as architectural symbols of the State's leading crop.

Cotton was introduced into Arkansas about 1800, just prior to the Louisiana Purchase. Before that time agriculture had been less important in the region than hunting and fishing. The Indians had planted only small patches of beans, melons, and corn, sufficient for their own use. The Frenchmen who garrisoned Arkansas Post at intervals for more than a century had relied on New Orleans for much of their foodstuff.

After the Purchase, however, a tide of cotton began to creep up the river valleys. As early as 1808 Fortescue Cuming saw fields north of Helena and wrote that settlers there would go in largely for the crop if they had enough capital for a gin. The gins were soon installed, and in a few decades the tide had splashed even the rugged hill country to the northwest.

The first cotton growers in Arkansas were small homesteaders, but they were followed by slave-holding planters from older States. If the plantation owner's land touched a water front, he usually built his own wharf. River traffic was increasing each year, and the stern-wheelers that rode heavily down the current toward New Orleans were almost swamped with their cargoes of lint. In 1860 the yield reached 367,000 bales.

After the destructive years of the War between the States, cotton again began to spread along the narrowest creek valleys and over the ridges, sometimes in patches so small there was barely room to turn a mule. It was here the "shoetop cotton" grew, and here it got its name from pickers who had to stoop nearly to the ground to gather the lint from scrubby plants.

In the early 1900's lumber companies began the deforestation of northeast Arkansas, opening vast tracts of alluvial soil to the plow. Because this newly cleared earth was almost incredibly fertile, cotton began trickling down from the hills. The tide receded slowly, but by 1939 nearly half the State's crop was being grown in nine northeastern counties. The extent to which cotton has shifted toward the Mississippi is shown in a newspaper article from a mountain area (1940): "In Marion, Boone, Newton and Searcy counties there were in all about 20 well-equipped gins 20 years ago. . . . Now there is only one modern gin in the whole territory."

Although cotton is giving way to diversified farming in the highlands, and the acreage has declined since 1930 even in the lowlands, Arkansas still stands near the top among States producing the staple. Ordinarily its rank is either third or second. In 1939 the yield was 1,410,000 bales; this, together with the seed, was worth $75,458,-000—about half the total cash farm income for the year. Cotton was grown on about one third of the 6,066,000 acres planted in field crops.

Improved varieties, new cultivation methods, and retirement of the poorest land under the Government crop-curtailment program have brought about a larger yield on each acre. The average crop for the years 1936-9 was a fraction under 300 pounds to the acre, as compared with an average of 209 pounds for 1931-5 and only 178 pounds for the preceding 5 years.

Growing good cotton is not as simple an art as it sometimes seems to tourists from the North. The farmer must contend with boll weevils and army worms. Plant breeders strive for drought-resistant, long-staple varieties and for cotton with a high "gin turn-out"—that is, a boll with few seeds and much lint. The weather, too, is important and has been the cause of more profanity than all the mules in Arkansas. Good cotton weather must begin in the winter, with a hard freeze to kill hibernating insects. There must be plenty of rain or snow to store moisture in the soil. Spring should come early and be moderately wet. The summer must be fairly dry, and the nights hot. If it is cool enough for a farmer to sleep comfortably, his cotton is suffering. On the Delta when nights are stifling, the cotton shoots up like tropical bamboo, and the farmer steams contentedly in his bedroom. A dry, bright autumn and late frost would complete a round of perfect seasons.

Mules, though their number has declined since tractors took over much of the level land, are still preferred to horses in cottonfields. The mule is tough, stubborn, and wiry. He drinks water so muddy that a self-respecting horse would snort at it. He humps his back to a wintry wind and nibbles forage a mustang would scorn. It would seem that a mule has a governor to control his speed, just as a steam engine has. Most horses show an eagerness in their work and, if careless hands are on the lines, will sometimes kill themselves on the gumbo soil under a blazing sun. But if a teamster peppered his mules with a shotgun, they would go just so fast, and no faster. Unfortunately, a mule generally becomes most evil-eyed and active when you try to hem him up so you can slip the bridle on. In such a situation, planters agree, the average Negro farm hand is supreme, artfully supplementing his barrage of threats with enough coaxing to leave the mule uncertain whether to bolt or submit. And if the mule kicks, it is not with the intensity of hate that a high-strung horse directs at an enemy. The mule's cussedness is merely genial and rough, as impartial as the cockleburs in his tail.

Ranking next to cotton in value is corn, which is grown on about one third of the field-crop land and was worth $21,330,000 in 1939. Very little corn is exported, since most of the yield is used on the farm as stock feed. Although the crop is grown in all parts of the State, its cultivation is on the largest scale in northeast Arkansas. In Mississippi, Crittenden, and several adjoining counties, mechanical harvesters that snap the ear from the stalk are becoming common. Small gristmills, some of them water-powered, are still to be found in the hills; here locally-grown white corn is ground into meal. Occasionally an old water mill will have in its attic the sifting and bolting apparatus made obsolete when farmers abandoned soft wheat several decades ago. Before the door may be found the old wheat burs that have been replaced by stones set for corn. Wheat was once a crop that regularly passed the 2,000,000-bushel mark, but it has shrunk greatly in importance. Only 41,000 acres were sown in 1939, and the grain was worth $285,000.

Another crop that has almost disappeared is tobacco, which once competed with the "shoetop cotton" of the mountain districts. In 1860 nearly 1,000,000 pounds were grown in Arkansas, Izard County alone producing about 200,000 pounds. When farming was resumed after the War between the States, tobacco cultivation shifted to the level land of Washington, Benton, and Boone Counties. Today there are only a few small fields in isolated sections, and the leaf is consumed at home.

Rising in acreage, and now third in cash value, is tame hay. Like corn, most of the crop is fed to livestock on Arkansas farms. The earliest cultivated hay in the State was the cowpea, which arrived with the first settlers from the Old South. Alfalfa was introduced about 1900. Although it is a superior grass under good conditions, and may be cut as often as four times a year, alfalfa has rather definite soil requirements and can be hurt by ill-timed pasturing. Partly for this reason, Asiatic varieties of lespedeza have become popular in the last few years. Sericea, a Korean variety, has won wide favor as "poor land alfalfa." Soybeans appeared shortly before 1920 and since that time have taken increased acreages. Mills in Mississippi County, North Little Rock, and other places now extract oil from the beans, and some varieties are canned as food in Blytheville. The remarkable increase in legume-hay production is largely the result of Federal agricultural and conservation programs that have taken land out of cotton and encouraged the planting of soil-building crops. Between 1932 and 1939 the lespedeza acreage jumped from 26,000 to 236,000. During the same period soybean acreage rose from 84,000 to 180,000. Cowpeas (still grown on more than a half-million acres), clover, timothy, sweet sorghum, and other hays brought the total planting to 991,000 acres. The tonnage harvested in 1939 was worth $8,532,000.

In 1808 Fortescue Cuming suggested that a small lake in the neighborhood of Helena would make "a fine situation for rice grounds," since it was flooded each spring by the rise of the Mississippi but became "a luxuriant meadow" after the water drained away. It was nearly 100 years later, however, and about 60 miles west of the location mentioned by Cuming, that a commercial rice crop was grown in the State. In 1904 William H. Fuller reaped a successful stand near Carlisle. Five years later the harvest had passed the 1,000,000-bushel mark, and since 1919 it has ranged from 6,000,000 to 10,000,000 bushels. Arkansas is one of the 4 leading States in production, growing about a fifth of the Nation's crop. From the field where Fuller harvested his grain, rice spread southeastward across the Grand Prairie, a region well adapted to rice growing because of a tight subsoil that prevents water from seeping away (*see Tour 12*). Soil suitable for rice is also found to the northeast of the older area, and in recent years the cereal has been planted in L'Anguille, Bayou de View, and Cache River bottoms west of Crowley's Ridge. The water that gushes from irrigation pumps is clear and cold but, in the fields, becomes warm and brackish, making a perfect habitat for frogs. Thousands lay their jelly-like eggs among the rice plants, and during summer nights the croaking of frogs almost drowns out the steady chugging of pumps.

Before a railroad reached Boone County and the surrounding Ozarks in the early 1900's, much freight was brought southward from Missouri in wagons. Teamsters, so that they might have a payload on their return trip to Springfield, encouraged the production of eggs, thereby giving an incentive for poultry raising on a commercial scale. The eggs were hauled northward uncrated, between layers of straw in the wagon bed. Chickens for home use had been raised in the region from the earliest time, even before 1758, when a priest at Arkansas

Post reported that "A hen, flying over the altar overthrew the chalice, which had been left there at the end of Mass."

The State has become important as a poultry producer since 1920, when the first carload shipment of Wyandotte broilers was made from Springdale, in Washington County. Since 1934 the incubating and fattening of broiler-size chickens for sale in distant markets has increased rapidly, and now nearly 10,000,000 broilers are shipped from northwest Arkansas each year. Hatcheries in Benton and Washington Counties have a capacity of 1,500,000 eggs. In 1939 the value of all chickens sold from farms was $4,816,000; eggs brought an additional cash income of $3,988,000.

Peaches, grown in pre-Territorial Arkansas by the Cherokee Indians, became a commercial crop about 1900. Elbertas were introduced into the Clarksville region and the Ozarks of Crawford County shortly before the turn of the century, and into southwest Arkansas shortly afterward. From seedlings planted in 1924 grew the orchards of a third major district, along Crowley's Ridge between Wynne and Forrest City. In 1939 the 2,709,000-bushel peach crop was worth $2,438,000, and Arkansas ranked fourth in the Nation among peach-growing States.

As early as 1885 the Shannon apple of Washington County was taking prizes in world expositions. In 1887 the first carload shipments were made from Benton County. Orchardists in the northwest corner of the State set out millions of trees during the next 20 years. A crop of 7,000,000 bushels was picked, and 4,574 carloads were shipped, in 1919. Two years later, drought and parasites damaged the orchards heavily, and the 1919 peak has never been regained. Ada Red, Transparent, Jonathan, and Delicious were the most common varieties in the 625,000 bushels marketed in 1939.

Northwest Arkansas, the leading apple area, also has more vineyards than any other part of the State. The concentration of grape growing in Washington and Benton Counties was inspired in part by the success of vineyards cultivated at Tontitown by Italian settlers prior to the World War. Another pioneering group of vineyardists was composed of Germans who settled at Altus in the latter part of the nineteenth century. In 1932 a bumper crop of 13,600 tons was picked. Since then the yield has zigzagged, amounting in 1939 to 8,200 tons valued at $287,000.

Strawberries have been grown commercially in the central and western parts of Arkansas since 1900, although the greatest increase in acreage took place after the World War. The 8,324 acres of 1919 rose to 29,978 by 1934. Nearly 800 carloads were shipped to Northern and Eastern markets in 1939 as a part of a $2,066,000 crop, which was exceeded in only 3 other States. White County, with 587 carloads, was the largest producer (*see Tour 1a*).

Watermelon patches appear on nearly every farm, but the huge melons of Hempstead County have drawn national comment. The champion to date, looking like a Bob Burns fabrication, weighed 195 pounds (*see Tour 1b*).

Vegetables to be canned or sold fresh are grown in widely separated parts of the State, although rarely in large fields. The upper Arkansas Valley and the southwestern foothill counties have always been the most productive sections. Spinach for canning in both the spring and fall is grown in the Van Buren area. Tomatoes are harvested and canned at a number of points in Carroll, Madison, and adjoining counties, as well as in the opposite corner of the State, around Monticello. Canneries, in 1939, processed snap beans from about 1,500 acres.

Sweet potatoes and Irish potatoes grow well nearly everywhere except in the Delta, where care must be taken to select the proper soil. The best crops of Irish potatoes are those of the upper Arkansas Valley, while yams usually do better in the southern tiers of counties. Out of the 1939 crop of Irish potatoes (more than 3,000,000 bushels), 291 carloads were exported.

Since 1920 there has been a strong trend toward dairying and live-stock raising. Between 1924 and 1934 the number of cows milked and the amount of milk obtained each rose 34 per cent. National dairy companies opened cream-buying stations and built cheese factories at several points. Northwest Arkansas and the Arkansas Valley lead in milk production, but pick-up trucks tour cream routes daily or twice a week in many counties. Cash sales of milk in 1939 totalled $8,852,000.

More striking than the increase in the number of dairy and beef cattle and other livestock is the improved quality of the stock. In 1938 alone more than 1,000 purebred bulls, about two-thirds that many boars, and a third as many rams were added to the herds. Perhaps the most profitable branch of the cattle business during the past few years has been the raising of "feeder calves." A mild climate brings up the grasses early in spring, and calves born in February and March can be put on the range quickly. At the end of summer, the young animals are sold to Midwestern corn growers for fattening and sale as "baby beeves."

As a result of the new emphasis on livestock, auction barns dot many parts of the State. Visitors find the weekly sales entertaining, if only for the good-natured raillery of the proceedings and the energy of the auctioneer. Usually he is a red-complexioned, leather-lunged fellow who can drown out the various brays, bleats, and bellowings at his back with a roar that is almost as unintelligible as that of a tobacco auctioneer on a radio program. Without slackening the speed of his talk, he stamps and puffs and mops perspiration from his brow. As a particularly dramatic gesture, he throws wide his arms and whacks the side of the barn with the heavy cane he uses to stab at contesting bidders. With more vehemence than grammatical elegance, he calls upon the great god Caveat Emptor to witness with what niggardly stinginess these flinty sons of Scotland make cautious offers for what is beyond any question the finest animal he ever beheld. While pleading, he peers shrewdly from under his eyebrows at the faces in the amphitheater about him, knowing to a split second when to interpose some humor, or when to burst out upon the more likely of two bidders he has been playing against each other. When an especially well-built calf wobbles into the pit, he hammers violently upon an old locomotive bell and threatens impressively to purchase the animal himself.

The liveliness of the weekly stock auctions is but a reflection of the production statistics. In 1940 there were 1,174,000 head of cattle in Arkansas, almost a third more than in 1930. During the same decade, the value of the average cow sold for beef rose from $19.20 to $24.60, although the national average came up only $1.58 a head. The number of hogs almost doubled between 1930 and 1940, rising in the latter year to 1,374,000 head. Sheep, which had declined in number for several decades, increased from 61,000 in 1930 to 75,000 in 1940. The income from all meat animals in 1939 was $21,815,000.

Figures do not tell the entire story of agriculture. One has to see inside the smokehouses and pantries. Within the past few years, Arkansas farm wives have learned more about preserving foods than six generations of their ancestors knew. In the not far distant past, killing a beef animal on the farm was unusual, because the meat could not be preserved. Today one may see in hundreds of farm homes glass jars and tins filled with roasts, fried chicken, sausage, soup stocks, vegetables, and fruits. This growing and preserving of foods for home use is especially important in Arkansas, because this is primarily an agricultural State, with nearly 80 per cent of its people living on farms or in towns classed as rural.

Since 1888, when the University of Arkansas College of Agriculture plowed the test fields at its first experiment station (Fayetteville), farmers have been given technical advice by a growing number of State and Federal agencies. Branch experiment stations have been established by the College of Agriculture, since 1925, at Marianna, Stuttgart, Hope, and Batesville; these specialize respectively in cotton, rice, fruits and vegetables, and livestock and forestry. Working with the University's Extension Service are county agricultural agents and home demonstration agents. There are four district agricultural colleges (*see Education*).

Of the new Federal agricultural agencies working throughout the State, the ones that have had the most far-reaching effects are the Soil

Conservation Service (*see Resources and Conservation*) and the Farm Security Administration. Dyess Colony, established in 1934 (*see Tour 10*), was an early attempt to reestablish impoverished farmers under conditions that would give them a reasonable chance of success. At Lake Dick, Plum Bayou (*see Tour 12*), Lakeview (*see Tour 12A*), and other places Farm Security Administration projects have been set up since 1934. On a street corner in Pine Bluff a converted skeptic was once heard to remark:

> Well, it's this way. The Government spends a million dollars or so to buy a forty-acre farm for a down-and-out sharecropper. They give him a mule, a bathtub, and an electric shoelacer. They lay a railroad track to his house to carry the tons of forms he has to fill in. A bunch of experts figure out his milking I.Q. Lo and behold, they teach his wife how to hook rugs and can beef and spinach, and they show the feller how to plant soybeans and prune an orchard—and, by darn, Luke, them Government people can actually do it! After we poke fun at their red tape for a year or two they ups and proves their experiment is self-liquidatin'—that the feller is making his payments and raising a family, too. And I don't know who's more surprised, me or the 'cropper.

The Arkansas tenant farmer has figured so often in sociological studies and fiction that many tourists believe anyone seen between plow handles is a "sharecropper." The name, however, is correctly applied only to those tenants who have their seed supplied by the landowner, and who use his work animals and implements. In return the sharecropper gives the landlord half the crop. A little higher on the economic scale are the renters, who either pay in cash or a portion of the crop; a third of the cotton and a fourth of the corn is a standard rate. About one third of the farms in Arkansas were being handled by sharecroppers, and another third by renters, in 1930. During the next 5 depression-years more than 50,000 townspeople moved to farms, 8,782 to become sharecroppers, and 18,752 renters. Despite the expanded rural population the total number of sharecropper-operated farms declined 12.5 per cent, as mechanized cultivation methods spread—to create a new agricultural class, the wage laborers.

Sharecroppers and wage laborers formed the nucleus of the highly publicized Southern Tenant Farmers' Union, organized in 1934 (*see Tour 3a*). The union, after spreading into Missouri, Oklahoma, and other States in 1937 affiliated with the United Cannery, Agricultural, Packing, and Allied Workers (CIO). The connection was dissolved in 1939, and the State now has two unions of tenant farmers, both drawing their memberships largely from the Delta country.

Arkansas farm organization began in 1872, when a unit of the National Grange was formed at Helena. Three years later the State Master, John T. Jones, was elected head of the national group. The Grange took part in politics and set up co-operatives, which were unsuccessful; one of its innovations was the admitting of women to its meetings.   More militant than the Grange was the Agricultural Wheel, organized in Prairie County in 1882 as the Wattensas Farmers Club. "We hold to the principle," wrote the founders, "that all farmers should save their own meat and bread; raise more corn, wheat, oats, and the grasses, and less cotton, so as to increase [the] demand."   After a rapid growth through the South and Southwest, the Wheel became a national organization in 1886 and added free coinage of silver and other reforms to its platform.   Many of the Arkansas members joined the Knights of Labor in forming the Union Labor Party.   The party polled nearly 85,000 votes in the 1888 Arkansas gubernatorial election.   After William Jennings Bryan's defeat as Presidential candidate in 1896, the Wheel faded from sight.   About 1904 a few of its most active members organized the Arkansas Farmers Union, which today has a membership of some 5,000 and conducts a mutual insurance company.

Industry, Commerce, and Labor

IN 1818 Henry Schoolcraft and a companion, after wandering through the Ozarks for twenty days without seeing a human habitation, came at last to a clearing on the North Fork of White River. "The first object worthy of remark which presented itself on [our] emerging from the forest," Schoolcraft wrote, "was the innumerable quantity of deer, bear, and other skins, which had been . . . stretched out, and hung up to dry on poles and trees around the house."

Peltries and animal fats were the earliest commercially valuable products of Arkansas, and the search for them took French trappers and hunters up the rivers of the region as early as the middle of the eighteenth century.

"The hunters count much on their profits from the oil drawn from the bear's fat, which, at New Orleans, is always of ready sale," reported William Dunbar and George Hunter, who explored the Ouachita River in 1804: "[it is] much esteemed for its wholesomeness in cooking, being preferred to butter or hog's lard. It is found to keep longer than any other animal oil without becoming rancid, and boiling it, from time to time, upon sweet bay leaves, restores its sweetness."

Aside from furs and animal oil, the early settlers had little to sell and needed to buy little except guns and powder. They raised their food, made their clothing, shoes, and furniture. They built their own houses and, when necessary, could turn blacksmith to repair their wagons. Bullets could be cast from the lead mined at various Ozark diggings. Salt, a major item of local trade, was boiled down from the water of saline springs. John Hemphill, in 1811, bought from the Indians a salt works on the Ouachita River. Early in the 1820's, Sequoyah, inventor of the Cherokee alphabet, operated a salt refinery near Dwight Mission. Along the streams and in small towns appeared other processing establishments: gristmills, sawmills, harness shops.

The growth of Little Rock as a commercial center began after 1836. In 1840 a small "hat manufactory" was opened. Shortly afterward two German brewers began making ale and beer in the capital. Announcing that he had "at length got his cast-iron foundry in full blast," S. J. Bennett advertised in 1847 that he would take orders for "steamboat shafts, cranks, gudgeons, gin and mill irons."

The lack of large industries in the early days of statehood aroused the attention of merchant and farmer alike. In 1843 a newspaper correspondent, interested in a proposed plant to make pottery, asked: "Is it not better that we should have this article produced at home, than to send out money abroad for it, and then to pay freight and merchant's profits? . . . Do you expect the people will obtain the means to support the State so long as we manufacture nothing for our domestic consumption—nothing for exportation?"

A lack of credit, made worse by an experiment in State banking, to some extent retarded the growth of industry. Authorized by the constitution of 1836, a State bank was organized the same year, and the Real Estate Bank was opened in 1838. Like many State banks throughout the United States, the depositories responded to a popular demand for currency by issuing more notes than they could redeem. Some of the bank managers and stockholders took their own loans and salaries in the form of specie instead of in currency. A tight money market and the national panic of 1837 led to the sale of bonds at heavy discounts. Governor Archibald Yell began to denounce banking and credit in general, warning that "the safest reliance is upon our own frugality and industrious habits."

The Real Estate Bank forfeited its charter in 1844 and the State bank ceased operations shortly afterward. In 1846 the general assembly, without a dissenting vote, ratified a constitutional amendment declaring that "no bank or banking institution shall be hereafter incorporated, or established in this State." What little banking existed for many years after this drastic amendment was carried on by individuals. Money was extremely scarce, and small change brought a premium. "Merchants going to New Orleans to buy their spring stocks," wrote a Delta storekeeper, "would bring back what amount of money they would need for purposes of trade requirements for the year." In some parts of the State, bills of exchange and drafts could not be cashed. When currency was shipped, a banknote was sometimes torn into halves and the two pieces sent by different mails, as a precaution against theft.

In 1881 W. B. Worthen finally completed liquidation of the Real Estate Bank. This institution, he wrote in 1906, "transacted business for the limited period of three years, three months, and twenty days, and it required nearly thirty-nine years of tedious and expensive litigation to wind up its affairs . . . the slow development of this State, due to disinclination of outside capital to invest here, is in a great measure chargeable to the gross mismanagement of these two banking corporations."

Whatever the cause, Arkansas remained an agricultural State, with fewer than 0.5 per cent of its people engaged in industry in 1860. For that year the Census of Manufactures listed 518 establishments, many of them one- or two-man shops.

Railroads plunged into the forests in the last quarter of the nineteenth century, bringing capital and a rapid expansion of lumbering, the State's greatest industry. A steam sawmill had been built at Helena in 1826. In 1860 there were 177 in operation, employing about 5 men each, and with an average annual milling valued at $6,530. Lumber production reached 500,000,000 board feet in 1890 and 1,600,000,000 in 1899. The peak year was 1909, when the timber cut amounted to 2,111,000,000 board feet and Arkansas ranked fifth among the States in lumber output. Because some of the more valuable hardwoods of the Delta were cut later, however, the peak production in terms of dollars was reached in 1919, when the production was valued at $84,008,309. In 1937 there were 17,322 workers who made a year's cut of 1,400,000,000 board feet. At the turn of the century the average sawmill was employing 26 men; the number, in 1937, had risen to nearly 60.

Methods of lumbering vary widely in different parts of the State. In southern Arkansas, where the forests stretch for miles across level land, huge mills operate with impressive efficiency. The felled trees are snaked to narrow-gauge railroad spurs and hauled to logging camps; here they are loaded on flat cars, shipped to the plant, and processed so that every possible inch of wood is used. In the hills and other areas where timber patches are scattered, boards are usually cut by small mills that range down to four- or five-man crews working a portable plant powered by a gasoline engine.

After railroad lines linked the State with distant markets, woodworking plants began to appear. Most of the establishments that made carriages, wheels, coffins, sashes, and doors disposed of their products locally. Other plants, however, have long used tough hickory and oak to make tool handles sold throughout the world. Several large Arkansas mills specialize in the manufacture of hardwood flooring made from red and white oak. Barrel head and barrel stave factories made the Ozarks known as "the home of the white oak cask." The market for cooperage practically disappeared during the years of national prohibition but revived after 1934.

Wooden parts for automobile bodies first appeared on the list of Arkansas products in 1919; the value of the production was then $253,654, and rose to $3,551,359 in 1929. During the 1930's the industry declined sharply as automobile makers turned to all-steel bodies and wheels.

The manufacture of furniture, ranking fourth among Arkansas industries in 1937, first became a sizable enterprise during the 1890's. Beds, tables, chairs, and other furniture made in 1937 had a value of $6,827,435. Fort Smith, with more than a half-dozen plants, is the leading producer but there are also factories in Benton, Little Rock,

Camden, and several smaller communities. One of the most successful devices to help overcome the handicap of high freight rates and long distances from markets is the production of unassembled furniture. The parts are shipped to assembly plants in States to the East and North.

A wood-product industry of great potential importance is the manufacture of kraft paper from the fast-growing yellow pine of southern Arkansas. Two such pulp mills are now in operation, near Camden and at Crossett.

Oil was discovered in the heart of the southern Arkansas timber belt in 1920, and the trickle became a river a year later. By 1925 eight refineries had been built and products for the year were worth $11,807,-192; the processing of petroleum had become, and remains, the State's third largest industry. Five refineries, two of them in El Dorado and the others near by, operated in 1937 to produce gasoline, lubricating oil, and by-products valued at $14,383,526.

Outranking petroleum in value is another kind of oil—that pressed from cottonseed. The seeds, combed out of lint by hundreds of gins, yield products of such value as to rank their extraction second among the State's industries. Vegetable oil and cooking compounds, fertilizer and cattle feed head the long list of items made in the oil mills. Indeed, some specialists in the utilization of by-products feel that much cotton may eventually be grown for the seed rather than for the fiber. The general assembly in 1861 incorporated the first cottonseed-oil mill, which was to be built at Pine Bluff. In 1899 there were 20 mills in the State, with a production valued at $3,189,000. Peak activity was reached in 1919, when the output of 35 plants was worth $25,304,034. Twenty-five mills, the largest of which are in Little Rock, Pine Bluff, and Texarkana, reported a 1937 production valued at $21,320,560.

While some industries were rising in importance, others were declining or disappearing. With the advent of the automobile, the saddle makers, leather and harness shops, and wagon-builders of earlier years were doomed. Flourmilling and gristmilling, which led Arkansas industries in 1870 and 1880, have declined steadily. In 1937 only 6 flour mills were reported, with a total of 10 employees. The disappearance of flour mills is partly attributable to the extension of good roads, which made available to every crossroads store the hard-wheat flour from Western States.

Ranking eighth among the State's industries in 1937 was the canning of fruits and vegetables, including such products as grape juice pressed at Springdale and vinegar fermented at Rogers. Eighty-two establishments employed 2,315 workers to process food valued at $3,-859,656. The heaviest concentration of canneries is in the northwestern corner of the State. Small tomato canneries flourish in the western half of the Ozarks.

In North Little Rock, Pine Bluff, McGehee, Cotter, and Harrison, railroad shops have long been an economic backlog. Feed mills, newspaper publishing houses, and creameries also stand high on the list of the State's industries. Meat-packing products in 1937 were worth $1,217,614, and have probably risen somewhat since that year.

In 1880 there were 2 cotton-goods and 25 woolen-goods factories in the State. These early enterprises, however, did not survive competition with Northern mills, after railroads had made the imported products available. The 1899 census shows no spinning activity of any sort. In 1937 there were four cotton mills (at Magnolia, Monticello, Morrilton, and Malvern), with 819 employees and a total production of $2,435,546.

When Territorial Governor Pope's persistence forced the adoption of Gideon Shryock's plans for the magnificent Statehouse in 1833, the first step in construction was setting up a brickyard. In 1860 there were 6 brickyards in the State, and by the twentieth century 55 kilns were making brick or tile. In 1921 terra cotta and fire clay had been added to the list of products. Peak production came in 1929 with a total of $1,961,283, then fell sharply as building virtually ceased. By 1937 it was back up to $793,244. Brick plants operate at Malvern, Hope, Fort Smith, and other towns, and a large tile plant at Texarkana.

In 1846 a Tennessean named William Crawley settled in Washington County, set up a potter's wheel, and for 25 years molded earthenware jugs, crocks, and jars, which he sold throughout northwest Arkansas. The excellent clays of the southwestern part of the State, although they were of great importance to Indian craftsmen, seem not to have been utilized by whites until 1866, when a pottery plant opened at Benton. By 1889 there were 7 plants in the vicinity and "large shipments [were] constantly being made to the outside world." With the development of the Niloak plant at Benton after 1909, and the Camark factory in Camden since 1927, pottery making became an industry rather than a handicraft.

Arkansas industries with an annual production valued at more than $5,000 numbered 1,048 in 1937. They employed about 37,000 wage earners to manufacture goods worth $164,676,277. There is a feeling that these totals will steadily rise, as additional hydroelectric energy is made available in the northern half of the State, and as the vast underground reservoirs of natural gas in southern Arkansas are converted into kilowatts.

Labor. The oldest labor organization in Arkansas is the Little Rock Typographical Union, chartered in 1865. This successful attempt at unionization was followed in the 1870's and 1880's by the organizing of railroad workers into brotherhood locals. As the unions grew in number and size, they began to engage in political activities. The Union Labor party, which adopted the national platform of the Agricultural Wheel, the Farmers' Alliance, and the Knights of Labor, polled 85,181 votes for its gubernatorial candidate in 1890. No farmer-labor organization has since attained a similar strength.

The coal beds of the upper Arkansas Valley, first mined in 1840, began to be worked extensively after the railroads reached them in the 1870's. For a time coal was dug by convicts hired from the State by private operators, but an early sit-down strike at Coal Hill in 1886 and later evidence of abuses aroused public opinion against the convict-leasing system. Thereafter miners were hired from farms in the neighborhood of the shafts, setting the pattern for an agricultural-industrial way of life that became common in the lumber industry as well as in the coal fields.

Unionization of miners started about 1900 and progressed rapidly, spreading to other trades. By 1904 the miners, formed into District 21 of the United Mine Workers, were ready to take the lead in setting up a State-wide labor organization. At that time central trades councils had been formed in Fort Smith, Hartford (a mining town in Sebastian County), and Little Rock.

The Arkansas State Federation of Labor, chartered in 1904, included 53 locals, the central trades councils, and the miners' district organization. Immediately after the formation of the Federation, labor laws began to appear among the Arkansas statutes. In 1905 the legislature prohibited blacklisting, ordered that shelters be provided for railroad workers engaged in constructing equipment, and established a 10-hour day for sawmill workers. Two years later it forbade payment of wages in scrip, made railroads liable for injuries suffered by employees because of the negligence of other employees, and passed a "full crew" law, specifying the minimum number of workers permitted to operate a train.

The rising tide of labor organization before the World War brought about enactment of a series of laws that were considered highly progressive. In 1913 the legislature established a bureau of labor and statistics as a permanent part of the State administration. An act passed in 1914 forbade the employment of children under 14 except by their parents or guardians, and then only during summer vacations. It also prohibited hiring children under 16 for "any occupation dangerous to the life and limb, or injurious to the health and morals of such child." In 1924 Arkansas became the first State to ratify the child labor amendment to the Federal Constitution.

The women's wage and hour law, enacted in 1915, prescribed a maximum of 9 hours work a day, 6 days a week, for women in manufacturing, mechanical, mercantile, and transportation industries. Cotton mill and farm workers alone were exempted. Along with other protective legislation, the act established a minimum wage of $1 a day for apprentices and $1.25 for experienced workers. The minimum wage provision was declared unconstitutional by the U. S. Supreme Court in 1925, but a 1937 decision of the same tribunal was interpreted by the State's attorney general as a reinstatement of the law.

Labor organization in Arkansas declined after the World War. The high wages that had been paid during a period of industrial stimulation were considered excessive by employers, and some unions that defended their scales lost members or went out of existence.

The walkout of workers employed by the Missouri and North Arkansas Railroad in 1921 was part of the unsuccessful Nation-wide railroad strike of that year. After the bitter struggle ended, the unions were unable to obtain contracts until passage of the National Railway Labor Act in 1924. Since that time the brotherhoods have strengthened their ranks and now include all the railroad employees in the State.

In 1925 the mining industry shifted to an open-shop basis when operators withdrew from an association that had signed a contract with the United Mine Workers. Scattered difficulties occurred for several years, as the miners strove to reorganize, mine owners occasionally requesting county authorities to provide protection. By 1933 the union was again firmly established, and coal mines now operate under a closed-shop, check-off agreement.

Until recent years few efforts were made to organize the lumber industry. Workers in some of the larger sawmills were drawn from the countryside, paid more money than they could earn by farming, provided low-rent homes, and treated by a company physician. These conditions were apparently satisfactory. Although organizers for the Industrial Workers of the World were active in the Louisiana forests, no record exists of their penetration into Arkansas. A series of strikes and shut-downs during 1911-12, arising from the organizing of Louisiana workers, closed several Arkansas mills belonging to the Sawmill Operators' Association, but no violence occurred in the State.

The National Recovery Act of 1933 brought sawmill workers higher wages than they had previously known. When the law was held invalid by the U.S. Supreme Court in 1935, several groups of workers organized in an effort to maintain their wage scales. At West Helena a brief strike, unsponsored by any union, ended with a compromise settlement. At Warren some 500 men were idle for more than a month as the result of an unsuccessful demand for union recognition. At Crossett, where 600 men were involved, a short strike was broken and the leaders dismissed. The men continued to meet, however, organizing into the Sawmill and Timber Workers division of the United

Brotherhood of Carpenters and Joiners. In 1938 the National Labor Relations Board ordered the reemployment of 44 workers discharged after the strike. The company followed this decision with recognition of the union.

Upholding of the National Labor Relations Act by the U.S. Supreme Court in 1937 cleared the way for organization of employees in several of the larger mills. The Sawmill and Timber Workers Union now has about 2,500 members in units at Crossett, Camden, Fordyce, Huttig, Sheridan, Warren, Malvern, and Little Rock. The two pulp-paper mills in the State, at Crossett and Camden, have been organized by the Pulp, Sulphide, and Paper Mill Workers and by the Paper Makers; in 1940 these unions set up a Southern Pulp Workers Council.

Other industrial workers who have begun to organize since 1937 include quarrymen and brick and clay plant employees. Bauxite miners, textile workers, and cottonseed-oil mill employees are largely unorganized.

Among craft unions are the various branches of the building trades, the typographers, bakers, barbers, teamsters and chauffeurs, and miscellaneous trades. Street railway employees in Little Rock have worked under union contracts since 1916. In Pine Bluff and Fort Smith, retail clerks are organized. The American Federation of Government Employees has a local at Little Rock and other members over the State. The State, County and Municipal Employees Union has members in Little Rock, North Little Rock, Pine Bluff, and Fort Smith.

Activities of the Congress of Industrial Organizations center around Fort Smith and the coal fields of western Arkansas. An organization drive in 1937 greatly increased the number of unions in Fort Smith. One of the industrial unions expelled from the American Federation of Labor in that year, the Federation of Flat Glass Workers, had the largest local in the city. Rather than lose the glass workers, most of the other Fort Smith unions joined the insurgents. A branch of Labor's Non-Partisan League established by Sebastian County union members in 1937 has been active in local politics.

In 1938 the Fort Smith unions and the United Mine Workers established a State organization called the Arkansas Industrial Council. Most important of the member unions, aside from the miners, is the United Furniture Workers, which has obtained contracts at several of the Fort Smith furniture factories. Oil field workers from southern Arkansas are also represented in the Industrial Council, as are the United Federal Workers of Little Rock and the United Cannery, Agricultural, Packing, and Allied Workers. The Fort Smith *Labor Journal* in 1939 became the official newspaper of the Arkansas Industrial Council. The State Federation of Labor sponsors the *Union Labor Bulletin,* a Little Rock union organ since 1898.

Negroes constitute a considerable percentage of the State's union membership, particularly in the lumber and clay products industries, where more than half the workers are Negro. White and Negro workers in a plant ordinarily belong to the same local. Few skilled Negro laborers are members of craft unions, aside from those employed by railroads.

Comparison of wage scales in Arkansas with those of other States, compiled by the U.S. Bureau of Labor Statistics in 1938, indicates that rates are somewhat lower than in most sections of the country. Common labor in Arkansas received, on the average, 28¢ an hour; the average for the South and Southwest was 34.8¢. The Arkansas average is probably brought down by the large number of Negro workers in the State, since analysis of the figures reveals that most workers receiving less than 35¢ an hour are Negro.

Rates for skilled labor in Little Rock are below those for cities of comparable population in the North and West, but sometimes above those in such Southern cities as Memphis and New Orleans. Comparisons, however, are too often affected by complex local factors to furnish any accurate guide to the student of labor conditions. Arkansas sawmill workers, for example, frequently reside on farms a few miles from their place of employment, raise crops during slack periods, and live better than men in similar occupations who draw higher wages in Northern lumber towns.

Recreation

I REMEMBER one spring," said the old man, "I'd been seeing some signs of turkeys on the old Bud Shanks place, and I slipped over there one morning before daylight. It was misting rain and I crawled up under a thorn bush with its limbs all growed down to the ground. I commenced giving a turkey hen's call, and directly I heard a tom answer, away over on a hill. I'd call, and he'd come a little piece and gobble, and then I'd make him wait a while. You don't want to git too anxious. A turkey hen is like a girl: if she acts too anxious, she'll lose her man for shore!" He waited for the chuckles. "The old field was all growed up in sumac and sassafras sprouts, and the tom stopped jest out of sight 'n' wouldn't come an inch further. Sometimes if your calling is jest the least bit off an old 'un won't come up to you. Mebbe he's been tolled up and shot at before. So I gave two long rakes on the ground with my fingers, like a turkey hen ascratchin'—they don't scuffle the dirt up like a chicken, you know—and jest then a real turkey hen walked out of the sumac thicket and headed straight for me."

The old man paused to let his predicament sink in upon his audience. If he frightened the hen she would fly, and with her would go the shrewd old tom. If she came in under the thorn canopy she was sure to take alarm.

"I thought a minute, and then I fell over on the ground and grunted like a hog." He demonstrated the action with a good imitation of a wallowing sow. "That fooled the hen and she walked right on past me. I laid real still and when Mr. Gobbler stepped in sight, I gave that gentleman a load of Number 4's."

Tales like this are told in Arkansas in the flickering firelight of deerhunters' camps, on the porches of crossroads stores, and at expensive desks in chromium-appointed offices. The stories may concern a matching of wits with a wary 'coon, the bringing down of an elusive deer, the trailing ability of a foxhound, or a struggle with a fabulous bass. There are few Arkansans who cannot spin some such yarn, for hunting and fishing have always been the favorite recreations of the State. Perhaps the emphasis on outdoor sports is not quite as strong today as is was in 1834, when a geologist complained that he could not hire a

guide to take him west of Hot Springs because the men preferred to
hunt bears, which were unusually fat that year.

Off the beaten track, where the rural men have behind them a tradition of more than 100 years of hunting, a fortunate visitor may coax
out a demonstration of turkey calling, the caller using devices such as
leaves, pipestems, quills, instruments whittled from chunks of cedar, or
pieces from a rubber balloon.   In a hunting camp there is always a
wit who can honk like a Canada goose, or double the listeners over
with his ludicrous mockery of the guinea's "Pot-rack! Pot-rack!"   To
demonstrate more artistic inflections the hunters urge the best of their
group to "owl for the stranger," and looking as solemn as the bird
itself, the expert, with hoots that echo eerily down the valleys, will
proceed to raise one of the great gray ghosts.   "Owling" is helpful in
hunting crows.   The gunner conceals himself near a dead tree and
turns out a medley of excited, corvine caws.   When he then gives an
irritated hoot or two, listening crows apparently think one of their
flock has cornered an owl, half-blinded by the daylight, and they swoop
down to worry their dreaded enemy.   Deer hunters also use hoots and
caws, Indian fashion, to signal each other without alarming the prey.
When a buck passes in sight but does not present a shot, the soft "who-
hoo" of an owl behind him seems natural, even in daylight, but it snaps
the hunter ahead to attention.

Though bear are now found only in a few remote districts and the
deer are not as plentiful as they once were, Arkansas still has its share
of large game and a great deal of small game—quail, opossum, squirrel,
rabbit, wildfowl.   It is likely that modern farming methods are increasing the quantities of small animals and wildfowl.   Strip-cropping, for
example, creates an ideal quail habitat.   In this type of cultivation the
clean-till crops such as corn and cotton are laced with bands of clover,
lespedeza, or small grain.   This food supply is often close to a patch
of woodland or a sheltering weed-grown fence.   Many farmers scat-
ter wheat or cracked grain in fence corners during the winter, sometimes setting a loosely bound shock of corn over the feed.   Such a
wigwam screens the coveys from hawks, and if a weasel should push
his snout through an opening the bobwhites can rocket through the
fodder into the sky.

Some of the low-lying, frequently flooded river valleys in eastern
and southern Arkansas still are dotted with canebrakes and stands of
thick timber; here large game is plentiful.   State and Federal legislation has set aside a number of these swampy areas, as well as many
mountainous tracts, for wildlife preserves.   Eighteen such refuges, covering nearly 300,000 acres, are controlled by the State Game and Fish
Commission through co-operative agreements with private owners.   In
addition, the Ozark National Forest contains five game sanctuaries and

Ouachita National Forest four.   The U.S. Fish and Wildlife Service maintains a 90,000-acre migratory waterfowl refuge on the lower White River and a smaller bird refuge at Big Lake on an arm of the St. Francis.

The climax of the sportsman's year is the deer hunting season, at present five days in November and five in December.   In the thick timber of the flatlands dogs are sometimes used to run deer, though there is a growing sentiment against the practice.   Most upland hunters do not use dogs.   The typical deer hunter leaves camp just before daylight and takes his stand at a "crossing," which may be a ford in a river, a gap in a ridge, or a fork in an old logging road.   While he waits the sun touches the hilltops, and the hollows begin to steam with early morning mists.   The birds awaken first, then the squirrels, and the hunter is kept on edge by a multitude of rustling sounds—the scrape of a leaf, the brushing of a bough, the sudden thump of a falling hickory nut.   A chipmunk pops his head from a hole and views the man with bright-eyed suspicion, then scurries after acorns.   The hunter glances casually at the crossing and is suddenly electrified: a buck is stealing by, antlers laid back on his neck, making, it seems, less noise in the dead leaves than the chipmunk.   After a split second of suffocation the hunter swings the gun to his shoulder.   At the motion the chipmunk whisks back into the hole, the buck leaps away in great bounds, now clattering like a mule in loose gravel.   There is time for just one shot as the deer clears the open space—and the hunter has downed or missed his buck of the season.

When dogs are used, shooting at anything except a deer while the hounds are in hearing becomes a high social offense; the unlucky gunner is branded a "potlicker" and finds invitations to deer hunts scarce the next year.   If a man on a stand shoots and fails to bring down his buck, campmates usually cut off his shirt tail and hang it in the breeze to flaunt his misfortune.

Fox hunting, still fairly common in the State, is a sport for dogs rather than for their masters.   The practice is the same as that in Southern mountain States; there is no riding to hounds or taking of the brush as in the English and Virginia chase.   Instead, the men lounge in the glow of a campfire on a hilltop and listen to the blended, echoing chorus of running dogs.   An Arkansan, Colonel Marcellus M. Davis, caught the excitement of the swiftly running pack in his story, *The Stranger* (J. B. Lippincott Co., 1938): "A low, dim buzz of sound from the distant foothills . . . came faintly sobbing on the night wind. Then it rose and freshened and died down and swelled forth as the pack topped the ridges and sank into the intervening valleys.   Then, stronger and stronger it grew, and louder and louder it rose, into a well-sustained stream of sound, melodious, magnificent, and mighty, without a halt or a hitch."

The "start dog" is released in fox territory to pick up a trail, and the pack rallies at his long-drawn notes. The listeners know from experience which points the quarry will probably include in his circle, so that by leaving the campfire they sometimes see the fox flash by, the pack boiling in his wake. "Trailing" means that the scent is cold, the music erratic. "Running" means that the fox is up, with the hounds in full cry.

Old foxhounds know that to chase rabbits at night is to fall from grace, but during the day they are sometimes used to bring up cottontails for a shot. The hunter posts himself near the spot where the rabbit is jumped. Since the latter's course is limited to the rather small territory with which he is familiar, it is only a matter of time until he circles back almost to the point from which he started. Then the hunter fires; if he misses, he waits until the scudding bundle of fur has made another, and probably longer, circle. Often the cottontail becomes exhausted and takes refuge under a thorny bush, where the yelping dogs cannot get at him.

Squirrels are sometimes still-hunted. The hunter stands near a hickory or pecan tree in the early morning or late evening and shoots the animals as they come to feed. Hunting quail, on the other hand, calls for long tramps across the clearings and through timber patches. Sportsmen from the cities generally use dogs to point the birds, but hundreds of farm-bred hunters kick up their coveys merely by walking through an outlying brushy pasture.

Eastern Arkansas is a part of the Mississippi flyway, the route taken southward by vast flights of ducks and geese each fall and winter. The scores of lakes and sloughs in the territory near the lower White and Arkansas Rivers, the broad fields of rice stubble, and the mountains of straw bring countless flocks of wildfowl to earth for food and rest. Though duck hunting is not confined to the rice-growing flatlands of the Grand Prairie, these are the counties that attract the nonresident hunters, some of whom come from as far away as New York and Chicago. In Stuttgart and other rice towns the duck season produces a mild business boom. Field hands take time off to act as guides to visitors in hip boots and canvas coats. The hunters stay in hotels, drive out to the blinds before daylight, and come back with ducks festooned on the fenders of their cars. While not as numerous as ducks, Canada geese are not rare. An unforgettable sight is a wary old gander leading his skein in several suspicious circles before setting his wings for the glide to earth.

Arkansas' half-million acres of water include streams ranging from tumbling mountain creeks to cypress-studded sloughs and broad lazy rivers. This variety of types of water makes nearly every sort of inland fishing possible. Upturned boats may be seen in city back yards as well as in barnyards, and on quiet summer evenings Little Rock businessmen whip their front lawns, practicing a delicate cast that will later be made through snags to the spot where a whopper rose last week. The huge Lonoke State Fish Hatchery encourages anglers by stocking the waters of every county with at least one truckload of fish annually.

In cold waters such as the upper White, Buffalo, and North Fork Rivers, smallmouthed bass furnish most of the sport. Although many flycasters wade these streams, as well as the smaller brooks of the Ozarks and Ouachitas, the most comfortable method of angling is by means of float trips. A guide, hired with the equipment, sits in the stern of a 16-foot skiff, paddling whenever necessary, while the passenger fishes from a low-backed chair in the middle. Ordinarily each fisherman has his own boat and guide. The boat drifts downstream with the current, nosing from one likely pool to another. Some of the popular starting points for float trips are Cotter, Henderson, Mountain Home, and Norfork. Crappie, the guide points out, lurk beneath the great submerged brush piles stacked up by spring floods. Bass and goggle-eye lie at the foot of riffles, in wait for tiny fish bewildered by the eddies.

At night the party camps ashore or on an island, renewing the downstream journey at daybreak. The trip ends at some specified bridge or landing where an automobile waits to portage the boats back to the starting point. Such vacations, which may last from a day to a week, are highly popular with Arkansas fishermen, and occasionally non-anglers take the outings purely for the relaxation and scenery.

Fishing the quiet lagoons of the plantation country has its special appeal. A Negro wise with years of angling experience smiles optimistically as he pulls the boat to some broad-skirted cypress "where dey *sho* to be bitin' dis mawnin'." Stiff-legged cranes rise and flap slowly away as the boat approaches, and turtles tumble into the dark water when the paddle splashes too near. The largemouthed black bass which inhabits the tepid water of the sloughs may lack the ferocity of his smallmouthed cousin, but he sometimes attains a weight of 12 pounds or more, and he strikes with zest. Other fish caught in the lowlands are striped bass, bream, goggle-eye, and the ever-present "pumpkin seed" sun perch. Campers pull out buffalo and catfish caught on trotlines. Even the spoonbill catfish, if his spine is drawn before cooking, yields white, flaky steaks, delicious with hot corn bread and cold buttermilk.

The long projectile-like gars that thrill novices by breaking water within reach of an oar are cordially hated as destroyers of game fish, and any attacks on them are welcomed both by fishermen and the State Game and Fish Commission. The gar, however, is a formidable antagonist. His bony mouth resists hooks (although he steals bait regularly), but even when hooked he is large and strong enough to wreck most tackle. The mesh of a legal seine is large enough for him to poke his nose through, and he can follow his nose anywhere—leaving a hole big enough for a horse. Various ingenious devices have been used to cope with gars. Along the larger lakes and rivers fishermen sometimes go after them with deep-sea tackle. Another method, employed by a few expert archers, is shooting from a bow an arrow fitted with a gig head. Gar parties sometimes go out in boats with floating snares made of watertight jugs and free-running wire loops baited with small fish. When the gar takes the bait the noose tightens and the fish dives, but the corked jug brings him up again. As soon as a jug begins bobbing the fishermen race for it. Since the jug often is pulled under just as a man leans over the boatside for it, the contest is spirited and hilarious.

For residents and visitors who wish to swim, hike, picnic, or go boating there are countless vacation spots in the State and national parks and the national forests. Most popular of the State parks are Petit Jean, atop the mountain of the same name, and Crowley's Ridge, near Paragould. Devil's Den State Park, in the high Ozarks, had more than 20,000 visitors in 1939, when its swimming and lodging facilities were completed. Mount Nebo, near Dardanelle, has been a resort for three generations. Buffalo River and Lake Catherine State Parks, named after the waters along which they lie, are not yet completely developed, but are sought out by fishermen as well as by hikers and picnickers. Motorists interested in historical spots drive through the rice country to Arkansas Post State Park, monument to a French settlement dating back to 1686. Negroes of Pine Bluff and the surrounding cotton country throng Watson State Park, which is being fitted with swimming and athletic facilities and dormitories.

The pines and oaks of the Ouachita and Ozark National Forests are broken regularly by camping places, some with swimming pools and cabins. In the Ouachita Forest is Mount Magazine, highest peak in Arkansas, where comfortable accommodations, excellent views, and two tree-banked lakes invite travelers up from the Arkansas and Petit Jean Valleys. Land utilization projects of the U.S. Soil Conservation Service, particularly at Lake Wedington near Fayetteville and along Crowley's Ridge between Marianna and Helena, include lakes and picnic areas. The U.S. Fish and Wildlife Service's Big Lake Bird Refuge near Manila has a picnic ground and beach used by an estimated 4,000 annual visitors.

Hot Springs National Park, which nearly encircles the Arkansas spa, offers a variety of recreation that has made it the most popular resort in the State. Trails, bridle paths, automobile drives, tennis, croquet, and horseshoe courts, a swimming pool, and a campground drew 178,755 visitors in 1939.

Privately owned areas also center around Hot Springs. The shores of Lakes Hamilton and Catherine, formed by hydroelectric dams in the Ouachita River, are dotted with fishing camps, clubhouses, and boat docks. Other concentration points for commercial and private outing-places are the northwestern Ozarks, from Sulphur Springs nearly to Fort Smith, the piney mountains encircling Mena, the icy trout-bearing waters of Spring River, and nearly the entire length of White River.

The larger cities of the State (Little Rock, Fort Smith, Pine Bluff, and Texarkana) have municipal parks and playgrounds, as do about 100 other towns. Seven of the counties maintain parks. Little Rock, Paragould, and Arkadelphia have municipal golf links, but the great majority of the 51 courses in the State are operated by clubs, ordinarily drawing their membership from near-by leading towns. Camps are owned by Boy Scouts and Girl Scouts, the Young Men's and Young Women's Christian Associations, and religious groups. Farm service organizations, such as Home Demonstration Clubs, 4-H Clubs, and Future Farmers of America, send hundreds of their members annually to camps, mostly temporary sites.

Since Arkansas is still uncrowded, there are thousands of outdoor havens where small groups gather to pick spring flowers, tramp among the trees, swim in cool water, or bask in the sun. In the hills such places are usually slopes and creek banks too steep or rocky for culti-vation. In the Delta there are hollows and sloughs where the back-water drains slowly and the trees and brush grow with the exuberance of a jungle. Although an increasing population may eventually cause these areas to be posted or fenced off, they are today open to any comer without payment. Tourists will not find them easily, but barefooted farm boys can walk to them blindfolded, and fathers and mothers remember them of a Sunday after church and dinner. Sunlight and air, relaxation and sport—these are the attractions of such random glades.

Religion

THE Quapaw, who called the French priests "black chiefs" because of their dark robes, had seen Roman Catholic missionaries at intervals for half a century before the Jesuit Paul du Poisson came to stay with them in the summer of 1727. In 1673 Father Marquette had visited the Indian villages on the west bank of the Mississippi and along the lower Arkansas. The priests of La Salle's party had conducted services in 1682. Father de Montigny had come from Quebec in 1698 but, after a few days, had decided that the Taensa, a larger tribe down the Mississippi, had greater need of him. The next priest to be stationed among the Quapaw was Father Foucault, who left the tribe in 1702, only to be murdered by his Koroa guides a few miles downstream.

Father du Poisson planned to become a permanent resident of Arkansas Post. He began to learn the Quapaw language and asked that religious pictures be sent to him from France, because the Indians "always get into ecstasies when they see a picture of St. Regis which I have in my chamber." The missionary also served as spiritual shepherd of the French garrison. In November 1729, while on a visit to Natchez, he was slain in an Indian massacre.

From 1737 until 1740 Father Avond was at the Post, living in a hut "the walls of which [were] made of splinters of wood; the roof of cypress bark; and the chimney of mud mixed with dry grass." Father Carette, who arrived about 1750, found that there was no longer a chapel, and Mass was held in the dining room of the fort. After a flood in 1758, Father Carette sold his belongings and closed the mission. The last resident missionary at Arkansas Post before the Louisiana Purchase was Father Janin, who served from 1796 to 1799.

Settlers who came from the Southern Appalachian States and Missouri brought Protestantism to Arkansas about the beginning of the nineteenth century. One of the earliest Methodists was William Patterson, a Kentuckian who moved to Little Prairie, north of Helena, in 1800, and is believed to have preached in the neighborhood shortly after his arrival. In 1804 he was appointed a circuit rider in Ohio. A Cumberland Presbyterian lay preacher, John P. Carnahan, delivered a sermon at Arkansas Post in 1811. Eight years later, Timothy Flint, Harvard graduate and Congregationalist from Massachusetts, conducted Sunday services at the Post in French, since that was still the language of most of his audience. "They are always . . . polite, and seem attentive," he wrote of his listeners. "But in regions like this . . . a few sermons, be they impressive or otherwise, cannot be expected to have much effect. . . . Hence it is, that the transient labours of itinerants . . . seem to operate on a region over which it passes like the flames of a stubble field. There is much appearance of flame and smoke; but the fire passes slightly over the surface, and in a few days the observer sees not a trace of the conflagration left. I did not flatter myself that my services were of much utility."

The great revival that swept over the United States early in the 1800's reached into Arkansas. A popular phrase of the day was, "If you hear something coming through the canebrake, you may know it is either a bear or a preacher."

Methodists organized their Spring River circuit in 1815, with the resourceful Eli Lindsay as pastor. The same denomination's Hot Springs circuit, including all the country south of the Arkansas River, was formed in 1816. John Henry, a Methodist on his way from Missouri to Hempstead County in 1818, is said to have preached the first sermon in Little Rock.

Another claimant for the honor of preaching the first sermon in the capital was a Congregational missionary, the Reverend Cephas Washburn. In his reminiscences Washburn wrote: "I was waited on by a committee of gentlemen . . . requesting me to preach a fourth of July sermon at Little Rock. I accepted the invitation and preached . . . to an audience of fourteen men and no women." This was in 1820, when Washburn was en route to the site of Dwight Mission, opened for the Cherokee on January 1, 1822. Washburn and his fellow missionaries in 1829 moved with the Indians into what is now Oklahoma.

Two sons of John P. Carnahan, the Cumberland Presbyterian exhorter, settled at Crystal Hill in 1811. The elder Carnahan, who followed them from Arkansas Post in 1812, was instructed to form a circuit along the Arkansas River. In 1816 he was ordained as a minister and held his first sacramental service. The Cumberland synod created an Arkansas presbytery in 1823. Five years later, the Reverend James Wilson Moore was sent by the Presbyterian Church (U.S.A.) to organize a congregation in Little Rock; there were seven charter members.

It is probable that the first Baptist church in the State was that of the Salem congregation, which met in 1818 near the present town of Pocahontas. A Little Rock group of the same faith built "a neat hewn log church house" in 1825; the structure was later used by the Territorial legislature as a meeting place. In 1828 a group of Baptist women living near Spring River invited the Reverend David Orr down from Missouri for a series of sermons and, shortly afterward, took the lead in forming the Spring River and Bayou Association. A Baptist church house, built at Hot Springs in 1842, was described years later by a man who said he had often sat on "one of the softest" of the split-log benches. The church had "three openings . . . the front door, a side opening or window about two and a half feet square, and an opening of about two feet square at the rear of the pulpit, so the darkies could hear, as they occupied seats outside of the building near the opening."

The first Episcopalians in the State looked for leadership to Leonidas Polk, installed as missionary bishop of Arkansas, Indian Territory, and the Southwest in 1838. A year after his appointment, Polk visited Little Rock, selected a site for a church, and donated $900 to buy the necessary lots. Renowned as a soldier as well as a churchman, Polk was killed at Pine Mountain, Georgia in 1864, while serving as Lieutenant General with the Confederate forces. The first Episcopalian minister sent to Arkansas was the Reverend William H. C. Yeager, who arrived in Little Rock in 1840 to become rector of Christ Church. In later years another rector of the same congregation "perfected a plan of supplying the Churchyard with shade, which was that the head of each family should plant an evergreen for each child in the family within the enclosure and an elm or maple on the outside as a border for the pavement." The trees were destroyed when the church burned in 1873.

Nearly all of the early Protestant congregations held camp meetings each summer, after the crops were "laid by." Families came in mule-drawn wagons from miles around, bringing food enough for three or four days. The summer religious session was such an important event that it often marked anniversaries and other dates. For example, a boy questioned about his age might say he would be "twelve years old come next camp meeting."

Until the last decade every Arkansan was familiar with the sight of the "brush arbors" that sheltered worshippers during summer revivals. The men in any neighborhood could build a brush arbor in a day or so by placing poles upright in the ground and making a roof of leafy boughs. These rustic structures had no walls, but around the four sides were scaffolds, where pine-knot torches burned at night to cast a fitful glow over the audience. Although summer religious sessions are still fairly common, they are now usually held in permanent camp buildings, in the open air, or in tents; brush arbors are seldom seen. The kerosene lanterns that eventually took the place of the pioneers' pine torches have now given way to electric lights dangling from a wire, or the headlamps of automobiles parked around the benches.

Before the War between the States there were a few Negro congregations, but after 1865 the number of such churches grew rapidly. Slaves usually accepted the faiths of their masters, and, since the largest religious groups of white people were Baptist and Methodist, these denominations have always led in Negro membership. The African Methodist Episcopal Church (which had its origin in the North) and the Colored Methodist Episcopal Church, encouraged in the South, were organized especially for Negroes.

When the railroads came, they often co-operated with the Roman Catholic Church in settling groups of European-born immigrants along their routes. Out of such a collaboration, begun in 1878, grew the Subiaco Abbey and Seminary. Around this Benedictine institution, a good many families of German and Austrian descent still reside. The church founded other German communities at Pocahontas, Jonesboro, and Altus. The Roman Catholic Polish colony at Marche was founded in 1878 by North Little Rock railroad-shop workers. In 1894 a number of Italians settled at Sunnyside, near Lake Chicot; some of these, led to Washington County by Father Pietro Bandini, established the flourishing settlement of Tontitown and introduced grape cultivation in the State. The 65 Germans who founded Stuttgart in 1878 were Evangelican Lutherans.

The first Jewish congregation in Arkansas erected a synagogue in Little Rock in 1870. Today (1941) there are temples in Pine Bluff, Hot Springs, Fort Smith, and other cities, and the membership totals about 5,000.

Jewish, Christian Science, and Episcopalian houses of worship are mostly in the cities and larger towns. Nearly half the Presbyterian congregations are urban, but the majority of buildings belonging to other denominations are in communities classed as rural.

In point of numbers the Baptists are the leading denomination, with Methodist, Church of Christ, Presbyterian, Roman Catholic, and Disciples of Christ memberships following in the order named. Members of the Methodist Episcopal Church, South, outnumbered communicants of the Methodist Episcopal Church before the two groups reunited in 1938. The American Baptist Association, sometimes called the "Landmarkers," has its national headquarters in Texarkana. The Southern Baptist Convention is the largest of the white Baptist branches.

Education

NEAR the crest of Mount Gaylor in the Boston Mountains stands an old log building in which Albert Pike taught country school a little more than a hundred years ago. Moved from its original location in the Arkansas River Valley and made into a memorial, the cabin now has electric lights and the appearance of having been restored, but a visitor here can still reconstruct the scene presented by an early-day schoolroom. Such a room had a puncheon floor, a stone fireplace, split logs for pupils' seats, a three-legged stool for the teacher, and perhaps a dried cowhide for a blackboard.

The pedagogue, often a wanderer of the Ichabod Crane type who came into the community and "boarded around," heard the recitations of from ten to thirty pupils. These students, who ranged from six-year-olds to grown men, were grouped according to their ability in reading or arithmetic, and the wayward were urged on with liberal doses of "peach limb tea." If an impudent pupil happened to be a six-footer the teacher might shed his coat and invite the gentleman out for a thrashing. In case the pedagogue won, the pupil could be expected to retaliate by placing several skunks in the schoolhouse during the night. If the teacher lost the fight, however, he was disgraced, and from then on found it almost impossible to keep order.

One-room log schoolhouses, which typified rural common-school education for most of the nineteenth century, were also the community centers. Here church services were sometimes held, and such favorite social gatherings as ciphering matches and spelling bees.

The audience that gathered at night for a ciphering match was divided into two teams, and each captain sent a contestant to the blackboard at the same time. Problems were usually in long division or multiplication of four-digit numbers. The old men hopped around spryly as they calculated, arrived at an answer, and whirled to the referee to see if the solution was correct. Children were given simple problems such as short division, or were asked to strike off with chalk as quickly as possible ten neat marks on the blackboard.

At spelling bees the "pronouncer," usually the school teacher, gave hard words to some grown-ups, easier ones to children and the less educated adults. Selecting the words a speller might be expected to know required tact, and the pronouncer would ask a child, "David, how far has your class got in the book?" If the pronouncer went out of bounds he would be rebuked in a shrill voice: "We ain't had that yet, Martin! Get back there where you belong!" The most approved spelling style was the syllabic, and thus the women who learned from Webster's blue-backed speller enunciated trimly: "Beautiful, B-e-a-u, byou; t-i, ty; f-u-l, full; byou-ty-full, beautiful."

Long before the American pioneers built their log schoolhouses, French Catholic missionaries had written the first paragraph in the history of education in Arkansas. Henri de Tonti, companion of the explorer La Salle, in 1689 deeded to the Jesuits several thousand acres of land near Arkansas Post, in return for the order's promise to "erect a cross fifteen feet high" and "instruct the Indians." Little is known about the extent and success of this seventeenth-century attempt at education, though it has been established that for a few years priests went from tribe to tribe teaching "Christian principles" and methods of agriculture.

Another, and better known, attempt to educate the Indians in Arkansas began with the founding of Dwight Mission, on Illinois Bayou in Pope County. Cephas Washburn and several other New England-trained Protestant missionaries arrived at the Bayou in 1820. For more than a year they cleared ground and erected buildings to house the Cherokee students, and on January 1, 1822 they opened school "with fifteen scholars; and such was the earnest entreaty of the people, that this number was soon increased to fifty." The "earnest entreaty" was not entirely due to the Indians' love of learning but was partly inspired by an Osage-Cherokee war then in progress: parents reasoned that their children would be safe at a boarding school conducted by white teachers. At first Washburn and his fellow workers could not speak nor understand Cherokee. Thus, undetected for some time, their Indian interpreter added his own irreligious comments when he translated the white missionaries' sermons to an audience.

After several years the student body at Dwight numbered more than 100 Cherokee boys and girls, as well as a few children of white settlers. In 1829, when the Cherokee were moved westward into Indian Territory the mission went with them. Washburn conducted classes at the Oklahoma site until 1840 and then returned to northwest Arkansas, where he taught in academies.

A public school system for Arkansas was first contemplated in 1819, when Congress, in creating the Territory, reserved the sixteenth section of land in each township as "an endowment for all public schools of the township." Ten years later the Territorial legislature empowered the appointment of trustees to lease the reserved land to individuals and use the revenue for schools. This act was followed in 1843 by legislation "to establish a system of common schools" and providing for a board of three trustees in each township.   In those days the school board had few duties besides interviewing prospective teachers and holding a meeting in the autumn to cut stovewood for the winter term.

While the system of public schools was slowly taking form, private seminaries and academies were flourishing throughout the State, and especially in the northwestern counties.   These institutions, of which about 90 were chartered between 1836 and 1860, reached their peak in influence and number just before the War between the States.   In the men's schools the emphasis was on logic, rhetoric, elocution, and the classics—studies proper for young men who looked to law, medicine, or the army for careers.   The sons of the wealthiest planters went to Eastern universities and following their graduation returned home to learn agriculture from a saddle on a blooded mare prancing down cotton headlands.   The curriculum in the young ladies' schools usually included instruction in languages, the piano and guitar, and sometimes the harp, needlework, the making of wax flowers, and painting.   Though the private seminaries went out of fashion as the public educational system matured, a few with strong denominational backing ripened into present-day colleges.

The War between the States closed virtually all schools in Arkansas. Efforts to re-establish them on a solid financial basis and to make them available to all classes were reflected in the constitution of 1868, a document which contained the basis of present-day popular education in the State.   Free schools were provided for every child between the ages of 5 and 21 years, the founding of a State university was authorized, income from a $1 tax levied on men over 21 years of age was allotted to the schools, and other taxes were set up to enable free schools to operate in each district for at least 3 months of the year.   The constitution of 1874 amended somewhat the previous arrangements for taxation but reaffirmed the principle of popular education.

Strengthened by the post-war legislation, education reached firmer ground in Arkansas.   By 1890 the number of public schools had passed 2,500, with an enrollment of some 240,000 children.   A long campaign waged by the Arkansas Teachers' Association culminated in 1903 with the passage of legislation outlining standard study courses and license requirements for teachers.

The University of Arkansas, at Fayetteville, was opened in 1872 as Arkansas Industrial University, the name it retained until 1899.   The University is a land grant school founded in accordance with the Federal Morrill Act of 1862, which donated public lands to States providing colleges "for the benefit of agriculture and mechanical arts." Since its establishment in 1879, the University School of Medicine has been located in Little Rock.   On the campus at Fayetteville a number of new buildings have been erected since 1934.

State support for higher education for Negroes was granted by an act of the legislature in 1873 creating an institution in Pine Bluff. This standard four-year school, now known as the Agricultural, Mechanical and Normal College, has steadily expanded its facilities since 1927, and today has an enrollment of about 450 students. Three denominational private colleges for Negroes operate in Little Rock and North Little Rock: Philander Smith College (Methodist), Shorter College (African Methodist Episcopal), Arkansas Baptist College. The total enrollment of the 3 private colleges is around 600. Dunbar Junior College, in Little Rock, is supported by the city and by tuition fees. Blind and deaf Negro students are placed in State schools maintained in Little Rock.

After 1900 the scope of education in the State grew broader. The legislature, in 1907, created the Arkansas State Normal School (now State Teachers' College) at Conway and, in 1909, provided for four district agricultural schools: State Agricultural and Mechanical College (Junior) at Magnolia; Arkansas Agricultural and Mechanical College, Monticello; Arkansas Polytechnic College (Junior), Russellville; and Arkansas State College, at Jonesboro. At these institutions in the last few years the emphasis has tended to shift away from strictly agricultural and vocational subjects. Henderson State Teachers' College was founded at Arkadelphia in 1929, and in the same year the legislature established the Junior Agricultural College, at Beebe. Municipal junior colleges are maintained by Little Rock, Fort Smith, and El Dorado.

Some of the denominational schools offering advanced work have developed from early-day academies. Thus, Arkansas College (Presbyterian) at Batesville grew from Batesville Academy, chartered in 1836. The College of the Ozarks, Clarksville, traces its history back to a seminary established by the Presbyterians at Cane Hill, Washington County, in the 1830's. Hendrix College (Methodist), at Conway, was begun as Central Collegiate Institute in 1876 at Altus. Other denominational colleges now operating in the State include Central College (for women), a Baptist Junior institution at Conway; Ouachita College (Baptist) at Arkadelphia; Harding College (Christian Church) at Searcy. St. John's Home Missions Seminary, a Roman Catholic theological institution in Little Rock, awards the Bachelor of Arts degree, as does Subiaco College (Roman Catholic), at Subiaco. John Brown University, an interdenominational institution at Siloam Springs, specializes in vocational education.

Commonwealth College, for about 17 years co-operatively maintained at Mena, has been closed, and its property sold (*see Tour 9b*). At one time it was one of the important schools in the country that trained for leadership in the labor movement.

The State's school for the blind was begun in 1859 at Arkadelphia, through the efforts of a blind Baptist minister, and moved to the capital in 1868. A deaf mute, Joseph Mount, in 1867 founded at Little Rock a school for deaf persons; this institution eventually became the Arkansas School for the Deaf. A similar school had been founded at Clarksville as early as 1851 by J. W. Woodward, but failed for lack of money.

Since the passage in 1911 of the first legislation authorizing consolidated schools, the public educational system of Arkansas has experienced greater changes than during the entire preceding century. The transition from old-fashioned to modern equipment is strikingly indicated by the fleets of school busses, which transport more than 100,000 pupils each year, and by the scores of consolidated school buildings that have been built in rural areas since 1930. During the last 20 years the number of school districts in the State has been reduced from more than 5,000 to about 3,000. Town after town offers as its most prominent building a neat, well-built schoolhouse of stone, often erected with Federal assistance. Since 1937 children in the first eight grades have been provided with free textbooks in basic subjects.

Other developments after 1911 kept pace with a growing interest in education. In 1917 Congress passed the Vocational Education (Smith-Hughes) Act, and the State matched Federal funds to finance a program of training in agriculture, home economics, and trades. A Free Library Service Bureau, its work later taken over by the Arkansas Library Commission, was created by the legislature in 1921. The Arkansas Congress of Parents and Teachers, a strong organization working in behalf of the schools and affiliated with the National Congress of Parents and Teachers, convened for the first time in 1925.

An active force for education is the Adult Education program of the Work Projects Administration. During a four-and-one-half-year period ending in 1939, the program's classes had greatly reduced illiteracy in the State by teaching 30,147 adults to read and write.

The budget for public school education in 1938 was $13,750,000. A survey made in 1937 under the direction of the State Department of Education in co-operation with the U. S. Office of Education estimated that an adequate program would require a yearly budget of $17,816,042, exclusive of debt service and capital outlay. The low salaries received by teachers, averaging $570 in 1938, illustrate graphically the need for additional school revenue.

Predominantly rural in population, Arkansas had but one public library in 1850, and the growth of such educational centers was slow for many years after the War between the States. In 1935 the State Library Commission was created by the legislature for the purpose of extending library service, especially in rural areas. The commission has aided in the establishment of 19 county libraries, and maintains a central book collection at Little Rock from which volumes are sent by mail to individuals, schools, clubs, and Work Projects Administration library projects, of which there are more than 100. Ten cities in Arkansas maintain free municipal libraries, and a few more than this number have public libraries requiring subscription fees. In the development of its rural libraries Arkansas ranks high among the Southern States.

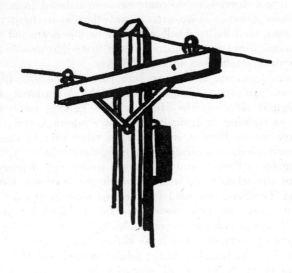

Newspapers and Radio

ON THE Territory's first election day, November 20, 1819, William E. Woodruff wrote in the initial issue of his *Arkansas Gazette:* "It has long been the wish of many citizens of this territory, that a press should be established here: their wish is now accomplished: we have established one . . . which we intend shall be permanent, and increase with the growth of the territory, and we look with confidence to a liberal public for a generous reward for our labors."

Woodruff had brought his small press from Franklin, Tennessee, overland to the Mississippi and then southward by water. The last stage of the trip, upriver to Arkansas Post, the place of publication, was made on a raft of two canoes lashed together. In 1940 the *Gazette* was in its 121st year and had an excellent claim to being the oldest newspaper west of the Mississippi.

The first issue of Arkansas' pioneer newspaper featured a story about American warships seizing the mouth of the Columbia River in the Pacific Northwest, and in it was printed a long letter denouncing the proposal of Tennessee's Governor McMinn to move Cherokee Indians from his State to Arkansas. There were also five marriage notices and a list of unclaimed letters, including three for Stephen F. Austin, of Texas fame.

When the legislature shifted the capital from Arkansas Post in 1821, the *Gazette* moved with the government to Little Rock, where it has since remained. During its first nine years in Little Rock, the Democratic *Gazette* had no competitors, but in 1830 Territorial Secretary Robert Crittenden persuaded Charles Bertrand, his brother-in-law, to start a Whig mouthpiece. The new publication, called the *Advocate,* after two years acquired Albert Pike as its editor. Pike, besides giving an air of literary distinction to the *Advocate's* columns, sometimes used them to defend his adopted home. In an 1835 issue, he wrote: "Our brethren of the East have some queer ideas about Arkansas and its people. . . . They talk about our exiling ourselves to this part of the world, as if we were exiled to St. Helena—and no doubt some of them take the little town of Helena to be that self-same Helena."

The "little town of Helena" itself had two newspapers by this time, the *State Democrat* and the *Herald.* Little Rock had obtained a third, the *Political Intelligencer.*

In the days when one man was able to gather the news, solicit advertisements, set type by hand, and operate his press, a weekly newspaper sooner or later was started wherever a few dozen people lived. In 1838 the *News* appeared at Batesville. The Washington *Telegraph* (which is still being published, as the *Journal Telegraph*), the Fayetteville *Witness,* and the Helena *Southern Shield* began publication in 1840. Of the *Arkansas Intelligencer,* established at Van Buren in 1842, the editor remarked that "it goes east from a point further west than was ever before paper published in these United States."

Advertisements in the early papers were often headed by a small engraving, used over and over. A picture of a Negro with a bundle of clothes dangling from a stick on his shoulder, and captioned "Stop the Runaway," was in nearly every print shop. About half the front page was ordinarily occupied by advertisements. Headlines were one column wide, printed in bold-face type slightly larger than the text. Since the flat-bed presses could, within limits, print a sheet of one size as well as another, there was little regularity as to the number of columns. A paper might have five columns one week, four the next, and seven the next, depending on the amount of news and the number of advertisements on hand.

The first Hoe cylinder press was brought to Arkansas for the Fort Smith *Times* in 1858 by John F. Wheeler, who had set type for Cherokee and Choctaw Bibles. In 1861 Wheeler and a partner launched a Fort Smith daily, the *Times and Herald.* In Little Rock the *True Democrat* had just previously become the first daily in the State. The Little Rock publishers obtained most of their outside news from the telegraph line that was completed from Memphis a few days after the paper was started. Although the capital at that time had only about 4,000 inhabitants, the excitement of the War between the States apparently justified a daily, and the *True Democrat* continued publication for nearly two years. Its demise was explained in its last issue, which was printed on brown wrapping paper: "Over two months since Mr. Yerkes [the publisher] started to Georgia for paper. He procured it and reached Natchez on his return, but the protracted sieges of Vicksburg and Port Hudson kept him on the wrong side of the river. It is possible that we may resume publication in a few weeks."

The war had drastic consequences for all Arkansas newspapers. After the Federals occupied Little Rock in September 1863, printing plants were taken over by Northern partisans, who issued sheets bearing such names as *The National Union* and *The Unconditional Union.* The weekly Washington *Telegraph* was one of the few papers in the South that came out all during the war; some of its issues were printed on wall paper.

During the Reconstruction period the State's most influential paper was the Little Rock *Republican*. Recapture of the government by the Democrats meant the end of official patronage for the *Republican,* which expired in 1875. Numerous other journals appeared and disappeared during the turbulent times, among them the State's first Negro paper, the *Arkansas Freeman*. The *Staats-Zeitung,* founded in 1877, was the most successful of several attempts to establish a German paper; it was published for nearly 40 years.

In the 1870's and '80's there were perhaps more "tramp" publishers than during other decades. When the principal financial backer of an owner-editor was a political candidate, and the election turned out wrong, the publisher was likely to move on to another town. One of the best known of the wandering journalists and typesetters was Opie Read (*see Literature*), who said of his fellow craftsmen that they "hopped like fleas from promise to promise." Read came to Carlisle in the 1870's and, with Harry C. Warner, began publishing *The Prairie Flower,* which (in the words of a newspaper historian) "soon withered and died." For several years afterward Read worked in various jobs on several Arkansas papers, including two in Little Rock and one in Conway. In 1882, he founded *The Arkansaw Traveler,* a weekly.

Read's ability to pick up a newspaper job whenever he needed one was largely due to his facility in concocting an amusing column or so out of trivial or imagined incidents. In the days before "boiler plate" fiction, household hints, and fashion notes were available, editors were often hard pressed for copy. Newspaper writing was rambling and informal, in sharp contrast to the compact style of modern journalism.

The number of newspapers in Arkansas reached its peak of 315 in 1909, the same year that lumber production was highest in the State. In 1940 there were 195 papers, of which 35 were dailies. Journals having a circulation of more than 10,000 were the *Arkansas Democrat* and the *Arkansas Gazette* of Little Rock, the Fort Smith *Southwest American,* and the Texarkana *Gazette and News*. During 1936, a number of Arkansas newspapers published large centennial editions commemorating 100 years of statehood.

The Arkansas Press Association, formed in 1873, is one of the oldest such organizations in the United States. The association now has 135 member papers, issues a weekly bulletin and a monthly magazine, and employs a secretary-manager at its office in Fayetteville.

Radio. WOK of Pine Bluff, opened in 1920, was the first Arkansas station to broadcast speech and music, although faculty members and students of the University of Arkansas College of Engineering had operated an experimental transmitter for several years before 1917, when military exigencies required its suspension. The Pine Bluff station was turned over to Henderson-Brown College at Arkadelphia in 1924. During the same year KTHS of Hot Springs, now the State's oldest continuously operated station, made its first broadcast.

Stations operating in 1940 were KLRA, KARK, and KGHI, Little Rock; KTHS and KWFC, Hot Springs; KFPW, Fort Smith; KOTN, Pine Bluff; KELD, El Dorado; KCMC, Texarkana; KLCN, Blytheville; KBTM, Jonesboro; and KUOA, Siloam Springs. The Arkansas State Police Department has its own shortwave system, as do several municipal police departments.

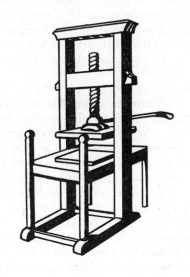

Country Folk and Country Ways

A BAPTIZING

Lange: F. S. A.

RAIL FENCE AND LOG BARN IN THE OZARKS

COUNTRY CHURCHYARD

Arkansas State Publicity Dept.

Lee: F. S. A.

TRAVELING GROCERY STORE

GOING TO TOWN

Arkansas State Publicity Dept.

WINSLOW, A MOUNTAIN TOWN

WAGON LOT, ARKADELPHIA

GENERAL MERCHANDISE STORE, BEAVER

OZARK FIDDLER

A SQUARE DANCE, NEAR HARDY

Shahn: F. S. A.   *Shahn: F. S. A.*

SHARECROPPERS

SUNDAY

Shahn: F. S. A.

Arkansas State Publicity Dept.

THE PELICAN, A MISSISSIPPI FREIGHT-CAR FERRY, AT HELENA

SHOWBOAT AT THE LEVEE

Shahn: F. S. A.

Folklore and Folkways

IT WAS nearly fifteen years ago, they say, that an unlucky woodcutter in the Ozarks had his first encounter with a hoopsnake—a reptile remarkable for its method of locomotion and for the poisonous stinger in its tail. The woodcutter promptly lit a shuck, that is, he started running. The snake tucked its tail in its mouth and rolled along in pursuit, like a wagonwheel bouncing downhill. While the panting woodsman was praying for his second wind, he came to a large white oak; here he took roundence. The snake, instead of swerving, rolled into the tree and accidentally buried its tail deep in the wood.

Talented as it is in some ways, the hoopsnake cannot pull out frontwise from anything it has stuck its tail into. The serpent began drilling backward through the tree, and the woodcutter ran for an ax. When he returned he saw that the poison from the stinger-tail had already got into the wood: dead leaves were sifting down like falling snow. The snake finally worked half its length from the bole, and the woodcutter chopped the writhing body in two.

Last spring when the woodsman was again cutting sawlogs in the same patch of timber he came upon the white oak. Though it had been dead for nearly fifteen years, the wood appeared to be sound enough for lumber. The woodsman cut it down, then rested on the fallen trunk while he ate his lunch. Without thinking, he yanked a splinter from the stump and picked his teeth. The hoopsnake's poison, which had long since penetrated every fiber of the tree, had never lost its strength. The woodcutter died before sundown.

When that yarn is told on the porch of a country store or around a campfire at night, it may be followed by the one about the exceptionally clever joint snake.

A farmer who found a joint snake in his barnyard whacked it with a stick. True to tradition, the serpent flew into several dozen pieces. After remaining scattered long enough to convince any ordinary observer of the snake's annihilation, the segments warily began to reassemble. The farmer, however, knowing the habits of joint snakes, had hidden one of the middle pieces in his pocket. For several minutes the completed front and rear ends of the snake searched for the missing link. At last, apparently deciding that the joint was forever lost, the snake coupled in a corncob instead, and glided away, darting out its tongue in high dudgeon.

That episode brings up the question of the whipsnake, which is accused of wrapping itself around a victim and fatally lashing the unfortunate person with its tail. The only way to escape, old-timers insist, is to keep cool and back up to a tree, against which the snake will flail itself to death.

And speaking of escapes, nearly every farm boy knows how a fox rids himself of fleas. With a piece of wood in his mouth, the fox wades slowly into a creek. As the water comes up to his body, the vermin climb to avoid getting wet, first to the neck of the fox, then to his head, then out onto the piece of wood. When only the tip of his nose remains above water, the fox darts down and swims away under the surface. The chunk of wood floats away laden with out-smarted fleas.

If mosquitoes become a subject of conversation, some member of the crowd may tell of the swarms that once attacked him on a frog-gigging trip. The hunter at first defended himself with a paddle, then with a shotgun. Later he went back to the swamp and caught one of the insects in a bear trap, intending to train it to bore wells. He shackled the mosquito in a mule's harness, but it broke away. Seizing a cow in its mouth, the mosquito flapped heavily away through the treetops. That, of course, is an exaggeration. Generally it takes two swampland mosquitoes to fly off with a cow.

The Arkansan has no monopoly on tall stories that deal with hoopsnakes and other fabulous fauna. Similar yarns are to be heard all through the Southern mountains and, for that matter, throughout the United States. Countless Arkansans, however, seem to have been blessed with an ability to concoct variations of the standard stories. These solemn fantasies (called "so-tales") occupy a prominent place in the State's folklore. More of the stories seem to have ripened in the hills than in the Delta, and nearly every upland county boasts of a citizen with a reputation for telling whoppers. Perhaps it was the isolation of the Ozarks and Ouachitas during the nineteenth century that nourished the imagination of mountaineers.

Almost as interesting as some of the tales is the etiquette that is observed in a story-telling session. For example, a veteran member of the circle once in a great while will voice a mild doubt as to the truth of a yarn, but an outsider who is fortunate enough to be listening in must never indicate skepticism. More than that, even the presence of an outsider may shut off the flow of so-tales. This kind of story is best told to a trusted audience, and it isn't told lightly—the mood and setting must be just right for the narrator.

When gristmills were found at regular intervals along the streams, they were ideal spots for storytellers, and many a myth was created by men who loafed while waiting for their corn to be ground. It might have been to the accompaniment of a turning mill wheel and the sound of running water that the legend of the Arkansas razorback was born. Like all true folk-myths, the razorback stories have an unknown origin. Assume that someone commented on a temporary scarcity of acorns and the consequent thinness of his hogs. A second man would agree, saying that his sows were able for the first time to squeeze through the garden gate. A third would testify that he could now hang his hat on the hips of his hogs. The next would aver that his swine had to stand up twice in order to cast a shadow. One man was almost bound to swear that *his* hogs were so desperately starved he could clasp one like a straight razor and shave with the bony ridge of its back.

Outside the imagination, a true razorback probably does not exist. There is no flesh-and-blood counterpart of the little bristle-backed emblem of the University of Arkansas football team, and a State official once vainly offered a reward for a genuine razorback, dead or alive. It has been said by some historians that De Soto's men brought hogs with them when they crossed the Mississippi into Arkansas. Some of these animals strayed into the woods and became gaunt, savage beasts living on mast. That was a long time ago, however, and the truly wild breed, if there ever was one, has forever disappeared. Though many farmers let their hogs forage in the forest for a good part of the year, the swine resemble those to be found in all parts of the United States.

The popular beliefs about, but not *of,* the mountain people in Arkansas and other Southern States contain many misconceptions. According to fiction, the hillman is a seven-foot combination of malnutrition and hookworm, asleep on his front porch with the dogs. His great bare feet, dangling off the porch, flap from time to time when the flies get too pesky, but nothing awakens him except a hound's salute to a stranger. Then he shoots up his astounding neck to its full length, ogles the visitor, and on his hunting horn blows a series of long and short blasts that means, "Hide yore stills and oil yore guns; they air a stranger h'yar." This feat of mountain Morse is all the more remarkable because he can neither read nor write, and, indeed, cannot count well enough to enumerate his hogs, but must identify them by name. Should one be missing for a day or two, he musters all his kin down to second cousins and step-uncles and goes across the "mounting" for a feud. While the menfolks shoot out one another's eyeballs at artillery distances, the "chillern" go down in the valley and throw rocks, it being considered unmanly to kill women and children except in a fit of anger.

At the height of the fighting, the hog in question reels in, red of eye, and the feudists deduce that he was not killed at all, but merely knocked over somebody's barrel of mash and subsequently went off down the valley, hunting wolves. The patriarchs and their relatives regretfully suspend the fighting and repair to a clan stronghold for a square dance. Between sets they hold spitting contests in the moonlight or mournfully intone Elizabethan ballads in purest Shakespearean idiom. When every keg of white lightning has been emptied, each man gathers up a rifle that saw service at Kings Mountain, and, followed by his twelve-year-old bride carrying a tub of clothes and two buckets of water, walks nine miles up the holler to his cabin.

Downing such an exaggeration is difficult, because there really is a rugged, homespun quality about the hill people. They appreciate a good pocketknife, a true rifle, and a cold-nosed coonhound. They look upon exceptional skill with an ax or a gun as an art. They take for granted an ability to "read sign" along creek banks, or to find a mule that has strayed in the woods.

If a traveler gets far enough back from the highway he will, of course, encounter a few old-timers who know ancient English and Scottish ballads, hear a few Elizabethan phrases, and learn that a good many old superstitions are still alive—although few adults put much faith in them. The folk beliefs that survive do so largely because many rural folk don't believe there's anything to be gained by taking chances. For example, it is just as *easy* to lay shingles at the proper time of the moon to keep them from warping. On the ground of either season *or* tradition, Good Friday is about the right time to plant a garden. Shaking a tablecloth after sundown is a sign of slack housekeeping as well as of bad luck. The girl who lets her dishwater boil *deserves* the seven more years of singleness she will have before getting a husband. If the "devil's darning needle" (praying mantis) is not poisonous, "who in tarnation's going to let himself get bit just to make sure?"

Many of the folk beliefs are handed down in the mock-serious manner that people often use in talking to children. A man who sends his son to look for the "pied muley cow that's been using yon side" may say, with every show of earnestness except for a faint flickering of the eyes: "Son, before you start, catch a daddy-long-legs and say you'll let it loose if it'll point to the direction the cow went. And when you're looking, if you see a toad, don't step on it, because that will make the cow go dry. If you see a red bird that means you'll have good luck. Now, you'd better hurry, because I heard a raincrow croaking a while ago, and so we're going to have a shower."

Negro folkways in the Arkansas Delta resemble those across the river in Mississippi. Cotton is the most important element in their lives and is associated with many beliefs. Picking the first boll that appears in a field and burying it under the back doorstep guarantees a successful year. Cotton in the sugar bowl is good luck, but in the pocket it keeps money away. If a Negro starts before dawn for the gin with a load of cotton that comes out exactly one standard bale (500 pounds) he knows that something unusually good will happen to him.

That the plantation Negro should believe in many superstitions is only reasonable. He was born in a cabin at the edge of a cottonfield, possibly while a granny-woman mumbled her incantations. In his home there was little distinction between the natural and dubious uses for various objects. Red flannel was the material for his baby petticoats, but it also made a bag for "asfeddity" (asafetida) worn around the neck to ward off contagious diseases. A piece of red flannel next to the skin kept the rheumatism from his mother's bones, and a bit in the kerosene lamp kept the oil from exploding.

Not far from the cabin door, behind a great man-made swell of earth, the mighty pulse of a river throbbed. Every few years the Negro saw that river sweep out a section of the levee and roar in to drown the cotton and livestock. He knew that the levee was something more than an ordinary wall of dirt—that engineers had laid out its every slope and curve, that huge machines had gnawed tons of earth and spat them out again to make that grass-covered fortification. If the levee could not stop the river, nothing could. And the levee sometimes did not stop the river. When he became older he learned about the cotton market, mysterious and destructive as the river, just as unpredictable in its movements. Like a cork in an eddy it bobbed up and down and occasionally plunged completely out of sight.

If the river or the market did not ruin the crop, a drought might sear the fields, or a blight of insects might leave the cotton stalks brown and spindling. So, at the mercy of vast inscrutable forces, the Negro sought whatever assurance he could get for the more personal elements of his life—women, health, enemies, luck. Love potions might help him win his wife, a persimmon sprout buried under the stoop would keep her faithful. Something silver under the pillow would prevent nightmares. Good luck flowed from conjure-doctors' charms, which might range from "lucky bones" out of crayfish to elaborate mixtures including May Water, John the Conqueror Root, the powdered lining of a chicken's gizzard, and hairs from the tail of a black cat. Dice might be influenced with Lucky Lucky Powder, or Fast Luck Drops, or Dice Special.

A great many Negro beliefs were learned by slaves from their masters and passed on from generation to generation, so that customs formerly thought to be of African origin have often turned out to be Anglo-Saxon. To the white boss and his family nowadays, witches are legendary hags who stir only on Hallowe'en. But many Negroes know persons who aver they have been forced from bed and ridden up and down the countryside by witches. People who sleep in the "big house" smile indulgently at ghost tales, but a man who pads down dim footpaths among the eerie swamp cypresses at night needs little imagination to *see* ghosts.

Wanting company and the excitement of even a village street, Negroes go to town every Saturday they can. Even without money it is possible to stroll up and down the sidewalks, looking in shop windows, and enjoying the higher tempo of life, much as the average small-city American expands when he walks through Times Square in New York. Loose change finds its way to the barber shops, pool halls, hamburger stands, and liquor stores. When he eats, the Negro is careful to remember that whisky and bananas do not mix, and that the combination of fried catfish and sweet milk is poisonous.

The difference between the city Negro and his rural relatives is probably wider than that between town and country white people. The urban Negro, frequently himself the son of a farmer, feels that he leaped a high hurdle in escaping from the cycle of cotton planting, chopping, and picking. He has money in his pocket the year around instead of during the few halcyon weeks after the fall crop settlement. He reads a newspaper devoted to happenings among members of his own race. Schools, parks, and playgrounds for his children are close at hand. These and other advantages of city life loom so large that he sometimes strives to build up additional distinctions. Remembering the callouses that walking barefoot gave him in childhood, he buys the biggest second-hand car he can find. He affects a contempt for country music and dancing, never misses a visit by a Memphis or New Orleans swing band if he has the money, and looks to Harlem for many of his dance steps.

Most white city-dwellers glance back toward the farm with nostalgia rather than resentment, and hardly ever make a self-conscious effort to shake off the patterns of rural life. The average businessman goes hunting or fishing whenever he can, and often owns a piece of land in the country. He is proud of his ability to keep a constant stream of milk running from the cow's udder to the pail, and to hold a plow steady.

Architecture

THE influence of the handful of Frenchmen who lived and traveled in Arkansas between 1686 and 1803 has been felt in the State's geographical and family names, but not in its architecture. Nor is there a heritage of Spanish architecture from the rule of Spain between 1769 and 1803. It remained for the Tennesseans and other Americans who came across the Mississippi after the Louisiana Purchase to bring the designs typical of the nineteenth century, and familiar in some parts of Arkansas today.

The first dwellings erected by homesteaders in the new Territory were one-room cabins of horizontal logs notched at the ends, to interlock, and chinked with mud. Cypress logs were favored in the Delta, oak and hickory in the mountains, and pine in the southern flatlands. The wide-throated fireplace that was placed at the end of a mountaineer's cabin was built of stone, but a clay-and-stick chimney was the rule in the lowlands, where rocks were scarce. If wild animals were especially numerous in the neighborhood, the settler might cut his door rather high in the wall and use a ladder for climbing in and out.

When the settler became firmly established, he replaced his cabin with a larger house, probably using squared logs. Usually the new dwelling was in the style most commonly known as dogtrot, but sometimes called saddlebag, breezeway, or "three P's" (two pens and a passage). Such a structure consisted of two separate one-room buildings set side by side and connected by a wide, covered hall open at both ends. In a day when walls were built of logs instead of boards, the dogtrot design was highly practical, because two men could easily handle logs long enough to build one-room buildings. The dogtrot style has other virtues, however, and long after sawmills had made boards available to nearly everyone this type of dwelling survived. In the western and southern parts of the State, examples are particularly numerous. A few of the squared-log dogtrots have been inhabited for a century. The cane-bottomed chairs in the breezeway are slick from long use, and begonias, geraniums, and ferns overflow from pots hanging from the eaves. Cool in summer, the breezeway is the place where the water bucket and washpan are kept, where the family rests in the evening, where during hot summer days the housewife does her sewing or piecing of quilts.

Although additions to dogtrot houses were usually made by adding rooms at the rear, sometimes a second story was built entirely across the top, leaving the first-floor hallway open. The Jacob Wolf house at Norfork, said to have been erected in 1809, is an excellent specimen.

In pioneer days, all shingles were made by hand. Whenever the fields were too muddy to work, or the crops were laid by, the farmer would set his shingle block, take his frow, and split "boards," as the hand-rived shingles are called. Though milled shingles now cover most roofs, the irregular pattern of shadows cast by handmade shingles has increasingly interested contemporary architects. In 1939 the architect of two recreation halls and a large gambrel-roof stable in Jonesboro's Craighead Forest made unusually effective use of cypress "boards" for roofing. A tentative step toward an indigenous architecture is to be seen in the occasional use of hand-rived shingles for siding. This type of building somewhat resembles the shingle-sided Cape Cod cottage.

Most of the ante bellum mansions now standing are in the cities, rather than on plantations. Little Rock, Van Buren, Fort Smith, Helena, Fayetteville, Washington, and other of the older towns have a few good examples of homes built before 1860. Though the one-story dwellings were usually frame, brick made and baked by slave labor from clay dug near by was used in some of the two-story houses. Among the most pleasing mansions built in the capital before the War between the States are the Albert Pike house and the Gracie house (now St. Andrew's School). Fayetteville has the Tibbetts house, the George Reed house, the Quesenbury residence, and Waxhaws, the latter built by Archibald Yell in the 1830's. Estevan Hall is Helena's most attractive example of an ante bellum house. In Van Buren and Washington are several white one-story cottages whose lines are essentially Georgian. An interesting experiment, successful though not copied, is the Belknap "adobe" house, built at St. Charles in the 1840's. The walls are of white clay mixed with straw and packed into a cypress framework. Dried by sun and air, the clay became hard as brick, and shows almost no signs of deterioration after a century.

In Little Rock are preserved a number of examples of the Victorian architectural vogues. On the south side, particularly, are immense houses of the 1880's and 1890's, with turrets, bay-windowed towers, and intricate wooden grillwork. Large sums of money were lavished on inlaid floors, stained-glass windows, chandeliers with hundreds of prisms, and curved staircases. Architects piled ornamentation on ornamentation, cupola on cupola.

Contemporary trends in small and medium-size dwellings are best presented in such a town as Magnolia, where recent oil prosperity has brought a wave of building. The narrow clapboards that were popular from about 1910 until a decade ago have given way to siding boards, eight to ten inches wide, overlapped or shiplapped. Exteriors are generally coated with sun-reflecting, clean-looking white paint. The preferred style is commonly called "Southern Colonial," a rather inexact term that usually implies Greek Revival (with slender square columns replacing the old-style massive round columns) or Georgian, and sometimes a pleasing blend of both.

The expensive residences such as are found on Pulaski Heights in Little Rock and on North Madison at the outskirts of El Dorado are similar to those in the more fashionable areas of the average American city. An Elizabethan half-timbered house may have, on its right, an example of modified Georgian and, on its left, a Norman adaptation. Down the street a few doors one may find an example of the so-called International style, with flat roof, horizontal lines, and at least one wall of glass brick.

The preference for wide clapboards instead of narrow is but one of three noticeable changes in material. Bricks, once uniformly soft red in color, are now made in a wide variety of tints; buffs and tans seem to be preferred. The Farm Security Administration popularized, in its small houses, the use of natural-color, knotty yellow pine for interior walls. This material is now found in a number of city residences, generally in playrooms and dens.

Planning dwellings that will be cool in summer and warm in winter is a problem that has engaged the attention of Arkansas architects. A cooling device increasingly used in four- to six-room houses is a ceiling vent at the center of the house leading into the attic air chamber, which has rather large openings at each end; the warm air ascends into the attic and escapes through the openings. The floor plan is such that all rooms open into a squarish central hall. Some householders install large electric fans above the attic vent to force the air out by way of the gable vents. Many homes in Little Rock, Fort Smith, and other cities are warmed in winter by floor heaters that burn natural gas. Since the need for furnaces is removed, the majority of the newer small dwellings have no basements—a fact that usually surprises Northerners. Outside the cities, most Arkansans burn wood for cooking and heating, and coal is seldom used except near the mining district of western Arkansas.

Although two- and three-story buildings take care of most business needs, several Arkansas cities had a touch of skyscraper fever during the 1920's. Shadowing smaller structures in Pine Bluff is the 11-story Simmons National Bank Building. Hot Springs has its 16-story Medical Arts Building. In Fort Smith a tall hotel looks down over Garrison Avenue's bulky three- and four-story commercial houses. The 8-story Exchange Building dominates El Dorado's skyline. Heading the list of near-skyscrapers in Little Rock are the Ben McGehee Hotel and the Donaghey Building.

As common in Arkansas as grain elevators in Kansas are the cotton gins alongside railroad tracks. The typical gin consists of two low, corrugated-iron buildings (the gin proper and a seedhouse) connected by a blower pipe for handling the seed. Mississippi County alone has more than 100 of these structures, and in the State there are nearly 1,200. In the larger cotton towns, a familiar sight is the warehouse of a cotton compress, usually painted a barn red and covered with a saw-toothed roof designed to admit a maximum of light. Large mills for extracting cottonseed oil are identifiable by their open-air batteries of huge storage tanks. Groups of industrial buildings processing materials other than cotton include the Lion Oil Refinery at El Dorado; brick plants at Malvern, Hope, and Texarkana; a kraft paper mill near Camden; a paper mill and large sawmill at Crossett; and furniture factories in Fort Smith.

In 1833, when Arkansas consisted of a few villages scattered in a wilderness, Territorial Governor John Pope took the lead in the construction of a Statehouse in Little Rock. Impressed by the appearance of the recently completed Kentucky Capitol at Frankfort, Pope engaged its architect, Gideon Shryock (sometimes spelled Shyrock) to draw the plans. Shryock, a Kentuckian, had been a pupil of William Strickland, who in turn had studied under Latrobe. Without visiting Little Rock, Shryock prepared a design, which was modified somewhat by Pope and by George Weigart, who supervised the construction. Renamed the War Memorial Building in 1921, the old Capitol remains the most distinguished structure in the State and an almost unexcelled example of Greek Revival architecture.

The present State Capitol was begun in 1899, occupied in 1911, and finished in 1916. The impressive use of mass and repetition of detail are in the best vein of its principal architects, Cass Gilbert and George R. Mann. Like the old Capitol, it was considered over-ambitious at the time of its construction, and was the subject of many a political argument.

County courthouses in the State range all the way from the heavy-arched masonry of Richardson Romanesque, in the old river towns of Arkansas City and Augusta, to the severe contemporary stone and brick structures of Monticello, Russellville, and numerous other communities. Variations of Romanesque and baroque were preferred in the early twentieth century, and the tall central or corner clock tower, surmounted by a minaret, was a favorite theme. The Columbia County building at Magnolia is an interesting experiment in adapting a stylized Classic exterior to an oblong first floor and a circular second-floor courtroom. A few Ozark towns have put up massive structures of heavy gray-limestone blocks, as at Evening Shade; others have used to advantage lighter, irregularly shaped stones. The Pulaski County Courthouse at Little Rock is one of the few examples of Renaissance architecture in Arkansas.

Building programs undertaken since 1930 have completely altered the appearance of a number of colleges in the State, though no dominant note characterizes campus architecture. The new buff-brick dormitories and classroom units at Arkansas State College, Jonesboro, have some resemblance to modern apartment houses in the outlying districts of large cities. The Tennessee-sandstone buildings at Monticello's Arkansas Agricultural and Mechanical College were designed by architect A. N. McAninch in the style termed "Collegiate Gothic." At the University of Arkansas, Fayetteville, recently completed academic halls of gray limestone harmonize with the red-brick walls and mansard roof of Old Main, erected more than 60 years ago.

Churches, particularly in the cities, also run a gamut of styles, although various versions of Gothic are naturally favored. St. Andrew's Cathedral, erected in 1882 in Little Rock, pioneered in the use of local stone by employing granite-like syenite quarried near the capital. Other ecclesiastical buildings, both Roman Catholic and Protestant, have utilized Arkansas limestones and sandstones. Rough sandstone blocks from the Ouachitas, erected into a towering mass around three sides of a court, give Subiaco Abbey and College an appearance of ruggedness. Set among green hills, this Benedictine institution looks not unlike European seats of the same order. In small towns and at rural crossings the usual church is a frame structure with front gable and square bell tower.

Among the more interesting recent developments in Arkansas architecture are the "forest houses," so far appearing almost exclusively in State parks and national forests. Varying from small cabins to elaborate lodges, such buildings ordinarily are of round logs, peeled and treated with a preservative. Every brace and joint is open to view, and the impression given is one of complete solidity and honesty. These cabins, at Petit Jean State Park and elsewhere, feature an adaptation of the breezeway, which vacationists find as cool as did the pioneers a century ago.

Literature

IN 1557, fifteen years after De Soto's men had broken winter camp and straggled southward along the banks of the Ouachita, there was published in Portugal a book that might be called the first literature of Arkansas. This volume, written by a "Gentleman of Elvas," was entitled the *True Relation of the Hardships Suffered by Governor Fernando de Soto . . . During the Discovery of the Province of Florida*. Like the other "De Soto narratives" (by Garcilaso de la Vega, Luys de Biedma, and Rodrigo Ranjel), the Elvas account contained descriptions of the swamplands west of the Mississippi, the hills that rose still farther to the west, and the Indians that had to be cajoled or conquered.

While translators were still bringing out French, English, and German editions of Garcilaso and Elvas in the seventeenth century, French explorers were beginning to produce a new body of literature descriptive of Arkansas. One of the first documents of this kind was the report prepared after Marquette and Joliet came down from Quebec to the vicinity of Arkansas Post in 1673. In another narrative Father Zénobe Membré wrote of La Salle's exploration of the Mississippi in 1682. Joutel and De Tonti left memoirs that throw a little light on a period of Mississippi Valley history that is still thickly shadowed.

Some of the documents and books written about Arkansas by the French are concise and reliable. Others, however, are leisurely blends of fact and fancy. Bénard de la Harpe's report on his journey up the Arkansas River in 1722 is perhaps a typical example of mild embroidering of the facts.

As a rule, the priests who visited or worked among the Quapaw during the eighteenth century were excellent observers of life in the wilderness. Such men as Father du Poisson and Father Gravier wrote to their superiors in France "Relations," still little known, that are characterized by insight and a wealth of detail.

One of the first descriptions of the Arkansas country to be written in English was the report of William Dunbar and George Hunter covering their Ouachita Valley explorations; this document was given to Congress in 1805. The earliest lengthy observations, however, were those of Henry Rowe Schoolcraft and Thomas Nuttall. Schoolcraft, a geologist who later became well known for his studies of American Indians, traveled through the Ozarks in 1818-19 and two years afterward published in London his *Journal of a Tour into the Interior of Missouri and Arkansaw*. Though the *Journal* is useful for its portrayal of some early-nineteenth-century aspects of Arkansas, it lacks the literary qualities found in Schoolcraft's later books.

Nuttall's *Journal of Travels into the Arkansa Territory, 1819* gives the author's impressions of the Arkansas Valley from the river's mouth to a point in present-day Oklahoma. Very little missed Nuttall's eye, and his book is replete with observations on plants, birds, minerals, and geography, as well as comments on the Indian and white inhabitants. About the time Nuttall was completing his trip, the Reverend Cephas Washburn and other missionaries were founding Dwight Mission, near Russellville. Washburn's *Reminiscences of the Indians* was published in 1869.

George William Featherstonhaugh, British-born, as was Nuttall, was the author of *Excursion through the Slave States . . . with Sketches of Popular Manners and Geological Notices,* published in 1844. In 1834, when Featherstonhaugh was in Arkansas gathering material, he found that the frontier bore little resemblance to his gentle English countryside; as a result, he often dipped his pen in vinegar to describe unfamiliar folkways. Despite the *Excursion's* amused and hypercritical point of view, it goes far in describing the appearance of Arkansas on the eve of statehood.

Frederick Gerstaecker, a popular and prolific German writer of the nineteenth century, spent several years in Arkansas between 1837 and 1843. His *Streif- und Jagdzüge durch die Vereinigten Staaten Nord-Amerikas* created an audience that grew with the publication of several fairly lurid novels; these included *The Regulators in Arkansas* (a story of horse thieves in Perry County) and *The River Pirates of the Mississippi*.

Contemporary with Featherstonhaugh and Gerstaecker was Albert Pike, a Bostonian who came to Van Buren in 1832. Newspaper editor, lawyer, and poet, Pike was one of the most versatile men in ante bellum Arkansas. While he was still in his twenties he wrote the first of his "Hymns to the Gods," several of which were later published in *Blackwood's Magazine* in Scotland. His "Isadore" has been credited with suggesting to Edgar Allan Poe the rhythms used in "The Raven." At the same time Pike was composing facile couplets for Arkansas newspapers, he was writing more serious verse in the manner of Keats and Shelley. A thoroughly romantic figure, Pike, before he died in 1891, had commanded a brigade of Cherokee fighting for the Confederacy, had fought at least one duel, and had made himself a world-renowned authority on Masonry.

In the two decades that preceded the War between the States, a trickle of backwoods humor grew into a stream of books printed throughout the United States. Arkansas was often the inspiration for these gusty writings, which make a vivid, if minor, contribution to American literature. Arkansans, including Charles Fenton Mercer Noland ("Pete Whetstone"), wrote a number of the popular items, but one of the most widely circulated stories, *The Big Bear of Arkansas,* was written by T. B. Thorpe, a Louisianan. In this tale, a settler from "the Forks of Cypress" tells how the bear "loomed up like a black mist" and "walked through the fence like a falling tree would through a cobweb. . . . It was in fact a creation bear, and if it had lived in Samson's time, and had met him, in a fair fight, it would have licked him in the twinkling of a dice-box."

Many of the best tales of the day were passed on from man to man until origins were hopelessly obscured. One of the most striking examples is the roaring bit of Americana known as *Change the Name of Arkansas,* believed by many readers to have been delivered as a speech before the general assembly in 1881 by a legislator named Cassius M. Johnson. (The general assembly's records show no legislator of this name.) There are countless versions of the address, some intended strictly for barroom audiences, and others more printable. Part of a rendition that has frequently been printed reads:

> The man who would change the name of Arkansas is the original, iron-jawed, brass-mouthed, copper-bellied corpse-maker from the wilds of the Ozarks! He is the man they call Sudden Death and General Desolation! Sired by a hurricane, dam'd by an earthquake, half-brother to the cholera, nearly related to the smallpox on his mother's side! Look at him! . . . He would use the meridians of longitude and the parallels of latitude for a seine, and drag the Atlantic Ocean for whales! He would scratch himself awake with the lightning and purr himself to sleep with the thunder. . . . When he's thirsty, he would reach up and suck a cloud dry like a sponge! When he's hungry, famine follows in his wake! . . . The man who would change the name of Arkansas would massacre isolated communities as a pastime. . . . He would attempt to extract sunshine from cucumbers, hide the stars in a nail-keg, put the sky to soak in a gourd, hang the Arkansas River on a clothes line, unbuckle the belly-band of time, and turn the sun and moon out to pasture. . . . The world will again pause and wonder at the audacity of the lop-eared, lantern-jawed . . . whiskey-soaked hyena who has proposed to change the name of Arkansas!

Except for a transposition to the third person, the speech is almost word for word the battle cry of a bragging raftsman in Mark Twain's *Life on the Mississippi.* Some unknown plagiarist may have rewritten Twain's classic and made a gift of it to Arkansas, or Twain may have picked the speech up in Helena or some other town while collecting material for the book, or he himself have copied it from Crockett's *Autobiography.* In those days stories fell like apples in the autumn, and the man prudent enough to gather them deserved any profit he might make.

Opie Read (1852-1939), though born in Tennessee, found material for the background of many of his novels while working as a newspaperman in Little Rock and Conway during the 1870's. *Emmett Bonlore* (1891) is a cross-section of life in the towns of the State during the 1880's, while *An Arkansas Planter* (1896) has as its scene a plantation not far from Pine Bluff. In 1882 Read and a partner founded *The Arkansaw Traveler,* a humorous and literary weekly that was published in Little Rock for five years before being moved to Chicago. Arkansans were never entranced with Read's treatment of the State, and their resentment nearly boiled over the levee with the publication of *On A Slow Train Through Arkansaw.* The humorist denied writing the book, and, in truth, he was not its author. In his autobiographical *I Remember* (1930), Read mourned gently about his long feud with the people of Arkansas: "It was of no use to print sketches descriptive of the beauty of the upper regions of the state, rivers nowhere equalled for bending graces, hills that seemed the breeding heights of gods and goddesses: it was of no effect to affirm that some of the noblest men and women of America were born and reared in this a favored land."

Among the popular authors who were associated with Arkansas from about 1880 until after the turn of the century were Ruth McEnery Stuart (1849-1917) and Alice French (1850-1934), whose pseudonym was "Octave Thanet." Mrs. Stuart, who lived for a few years at Washington, belonged to the school of local colorists who made extensive use of regional dialects and manners in late-nineteenth-century fiction. Her novel *Sonny* (1908) was a best seller, and her collections of character sketches were widely read; one of her best-known works in the latter group is *In Simpkinsville* (1904). Octave Thanet, for about 30 years before the World War, spent her winters at Clover Bend, where she acquired the background for her novels *Otto the Knight* (1893) and *By Inheritance* (1910), a study of Negro life after the War between the States.

The first State histories to be written by natives of Arkansas, or by men who had long lived there, were published in the late 1890's and early 1900's. Books such as William F. Pope's *Early Days in Arkansas* (1895), Josiah Shinn's *Pioneers and Makers of Arkansas* (1908), and Fay Hempstead's *Pictorial History of Arkansas* (1890) have only a local interest, but are valuable because their authors had witnessed many of the events of which they wrote. The two recent histories most widely used for reference purposes are Dallas Herndon's *Centennial History of Arkansas* (1922) and D. Y. Thomas' *Arkansas and Its People* (1930).

Although some of the well-known writers born in Arkansas have ranged far afield, about as many authors from elsewhere have made the State their adopted home or have used it as the setting for their books. A Tennessean, T. S. Stribling, wrote of the 1927 flood in Arkansas in *Backwater* (1930). James Street, a Mississippian, who worked for a time on a Little Rock newspaper, accumulated material he used later in *Look Away: a Dixie Notebook* (1936). Two public figures of an earlier day who spent their last years in Arkansas were William Hope ("Coin") Harvey and Carry Nation. At Monte Ne, near Rogers, Harvey wrote some of the tracts that advanced his "free silver" beliefs, and at Eureka Springs, Carry Nation wrote the story of her career as a prohibitionist, *The Use and Need of the Life of Carry A. Nation* (1904).

Fort Smith is the birthplace of Thyra Samter Winslow, who went East to study art and to write. She is the author of *Picture Frames* (1923), *Show Business* (1926), and other popular books. Katherine Susan Anthony, who lived in Fort Smith as a girl, always had a strong interest in feminism; this was the theme for her first book, *Mothers Who Must Earn* (1914), and is reflected in her biographies: *Catherine the Great* (1925), *Queen Elizabeth* (1929), and *Marie Antoinette* (1935).

Arkansans and outsiders alike have interpreted the Ozarks and Delta in a wide variety of books. A Missourian, Vance Randolph, made a careful study of the ways of mountain folk before writing *The Ozarks* (1931) and similar descriptive volumes. Eleanor de la Vergne Risley, who came to the Ouachitas to make her home, set down her experiences in *The Road to Wildcat* (1930).

Charlie May Simon, although best known for her juvenile books—*Robin on the Mountain* (1934) and *Lost Corner* (1935)—is also the author of *The Share-cropper* (1937). Before David Thibault died in 1933 he had completed most of the manuscript of *Salt for Mule,* chapters of which were published in *Harper's Magazine* and in the O. Henry Memorial Award collection of short stories. Thibault, who spent his early years on an Arkansas plantation, had an unusual understanding of the details and moods of Negro life. *The Unwilling Journey* (1940), a novel by C. P. Lee, has for its setting the author's home town—Pine Bluff.

A lifelong interest in Arkansiana is reflected in some of the works of Fred W. Allsopp, manager of a Little Rock newspaper; his published volumes include *Albert Pike, Folklore of Romantic Arkansas,* and *History of the Arkansas Press for a Hundred Years and More.* C. T. Davis, an editorial writer in the capital, was made poet laureate of the State in 1923, soon after the publication of his *Poems.* Another volume of his verse, *Riders in the Sun,* appeared in 1927.

During the last few years four writers have occupied especially prominent places on the literary horizon of Arkansas:

John Gould Fletcher, an outstanding poet, was born in Little Rock in 1886. After his college years at Harvard he spent long periods in England, and it was here that his first volumes appeared. Influenced by Amy Lowell and the growing army of free-verse writers, Fletcher soon identified himself with the group known as Imagists, publishing in rapid succession *Irradiations—Sand and Spray* (1915), *Goblins and Pagodas* (1916), *Japanese Prints* (1918), *Breakers and Granite* (1921), *Preludes and Symphonies* (1922). In other collections of poetry and in a long poem entitled "The Epic of Arkansas," Fletcher has employed a variety of verse forms. Best known among his prose works are *Paul Gauguin: His Life and Art* (1921) and *Life Is My Song,* an autobiography published in 1937. *Selected Poems* won for its author the 1938 Pulitzer Prize for poetry. Conrad Aiken has said of Fletcher that he achieves his finest effects "when allowed to develop rapidly successive musical variations on a theme capable of prolonged treatment."

The literary reputation of Bernie Babcock is based largely on her several novels dealing with the life of Abraham Lincoln. Born in Ohio, Mrs. Babcock as a young woman came to Arkansas, where she wrote *The Soul of Ann Rutledge* (1919), *The Soul of Abe Lincoln* (1923), and *Little Abe Lincoln* (1926). Not all of Mrs. Babcock's 20 books are fiction, though this is the medium she prefers for sponsoring movements such as prohibition, liberalism in religion, and feminism.

Charles J. Finger (1871-1941), born in England, led an adventurous life in South America, the Klondike, Mexico, and other corners of the world for many years before he became, in turn, an Ohio businessman, an associate of William Marion Reedy on *Reedy's Mirror,* and finally a prolific author of romantic books. One of his earliest volumes, *Tales from Silver Lands,* won the Newbery Medal for juvenile literature in 1925, five years after the author had come to Fayetteville as a permanent resident. In 1929 he won another prize for juvenile fiction with *Courageous Companions.* A bold, romantic flavor is found in *Highwaymen* (1923), *Bushrangers* (1924), *David Livingstone* (1927), *Adventures Under Sapphire Skies* (1931), and similar books dealing with (as one critic said) "historical vagabonds." *Ozark Fantasia* (1927) deals with the mountain people of Arkansas.

One of the younger generation of Arkansas writers who has found a sizable audience is Charles Morrow Wilson (1905-   ). Reared in Fayetteville, he chose the Ozarks as the setting for his first novel, *Acres of Sky* (1930). *Rabble Rouser* (1936) is the fictionized version of a politician's meteoric career, while *Backwoods America* (1934) is a collection of articles describing the lives of people who are far off the beaten track. Wilson (like Fletcher, Finger, and Mrs. Babcock) has not bounded himself by the Arkansas scene, his work having carried him far enough from the State to write *Aroostook* (1937), an account of Maine's potato-growing district, and *Corn Bread and Creek Water* (1940), a discussion of farm life in various parts of the United States.

The Theater

THE first theater in Little Rock was opened on January 16, 1839. A troupe headed by Sam Waters presented a double bill: a farce called *The Young Widow,* and John Howard Payne's *Charles the Second.* A few weeks previously the company had staged several plays in a warehouse that proved too small for the crowds. Waters, a veteran showman from Kentucky, thereupon converted the Arcade Saloon into an auditorium seating 500 people. There were boxes "for the accommodation of the ladies," elaborate gilt and mahogany decorations, and a drop curtain designed by a local house painter. These couplets from the facile pen of Albert Pike (who was then practicing law) celebrated the opening:

> Here late the Indian held undoubted sway—
> (Those not yet old, can recollect the day;)
> Here where we stand, a dense, dark forest stood,
> And the Arkansas rolled its troubled flood,
> Through pathless wilderness, to the ocean.
> All now is changed. Life, with its constant motion,
> Is eddying here, and wit, and grace, and beauty,
> Approve our humble efforts, and make duty
> A pleasure exquisite, while we engage,
> The first time here, to introduce THE STAGE.

Though the capital had a population of less than 2,000, it supported the productions until the end of the spring season.

Amateur theatricals had been staged several years before the first professionals appeared in the State. As early as November 1834 a group of young men calling themselves the Thalian Society presented *The Soldier's Daughter,* by Andrew Cherry. The Thalians followed this effort with the more ambitious *She Stoops to Conquer* and then, apparently, disbanded.

In the summer of 1839 a company under a Mr. and Mrs. Chapman gave the town of Pine Bluff its first professional performance, in a private house. In December, Waters reopened at Little Rock, presenting C. B. Parsons in *Julius Caesar* and *Virginius.* Parsons, who later became a noted preacher, had appeared in Philadelphia and Pittsburgh, playing in *Rip Van Winkle* as early as 1829.

The Little Rock Theater burned in 1840 and there were no more dramatic presentations in the capital for nearly 20 years. In 1858 a businessman who thought the time ripe for a new theatrical venture put up a three-story building designed to house a store, the town hall, and a playhouse. Nick Moroney and his wife Bettie, who played female leads, brought a company of 15 to the theater in October. The troupe presented two fairly complete seasons of melodrama and farce, with now and then a more ambitious effort such as *Macbeth* or *Richard III.*

After the Confederacy lost Little Rock in 1863, the capital was filled with General Frederick Steele's Federal soldiers, comparatively secure from attack and eager for amusement. A showman named Gus Mortimer, who had been captured by the Northern forces at Arkansas Post and then paroled, came to town. He found Mrs. Moroney keeping a boarding house, picked up a half-dozen barnstormers, rented an old carriage factory, and opened a theater. It was a turbulent affair.

"I remember," Mortimer told a reporter years afterward, "one night, the accidental discharge of a pistol in the audience killed someone. . . . All was excitement and I went to the footlights and suggested that probably the audience didn't under the circumstances want to proceed. 'Carry out the corpse and go on with yer show,' shouted some Federal soldier. . . . So the corpse went out and the show went on."

In March of 1868, T. L. Conner brought in a company which occupied the old Moroney theater building, and gave such notable plays as *Camille, The Bride of Lammermoor, Ten Nights in a Barroom,* and Schiller's *The Robbers.* A child actress known as La Petite Mattie scored a particular success by her recitations in *The Drunkard.* The audience gasped as a prop locomotive rolled on the stage toward the shrieking heroine of *Under the Gas Lights.* The season reached its climax with Alice Kingsbury playing *Fanchon, the Cricket.*

Grand opera was heard in Little Rock for the first time in 1870, when the McCullock-Brignoli Italian Opera troupe appeared. A $2.50 admission charge kept the customers away, and *Faust, Lucrezia Borgia, Martha,* and *Il Trovatore* were sung to disappointing houses.

In 1871 the Memphis and Little Rock Railroad was finally completed, giving the capital its first good rail connections. A year later J. H. Wood remodeled the old Moroney place into the Grand Opera House, elaborately decorated with crimson velvet hangings, prism-glass chandeliers, and new scenery. With the opening of this auditorium in 1873 Little Rock took its place on "the road." The town became a convenient one-night jump from either St. Louis or Memphis. During the next two seasons the opera house presented such attractions as Katie Putnam, Louie Lord, and Palmer's production of *The Black Crook.* Fay Templeton, a native of Little Rock, made her first professional home town appearance in 1875, playing *East Lynne* and

Jenny Lind among other billings. She was followed by Lotta Crabtree in Marsden's *Musette*. Light opera arrived in 1878 with *La Perichole* and other productions by Adah Richmond's Opera Bouffé Troupe. Operas, farces, "mellers," and tragedies alike had played against the backdrops (street scene, drawing room, classic portico, farm kitchen) which the Grand owned. Harry Weber's *Nip and Tuck* troupe (1880) was the first to bring its own sets. Musical companies grew popular in the 1880's, and the great Emma Abbott drew capacity houses in 1884 with *Faust, Rigoletto, Il Trovatore,* and *Mignon*. John McCullough and others brought Shakespeare. Light opera troupes gave Gilbert and Sullivan. Minnie Maddern appeared in Devereaux and Sardou pieces.

"Spectacle" plays created a vast impression among Arkansas audiences. Among the earliest of these was Herne's *Hearts of Oak* in 1882, with a grist-mill scene of splashing water, creaking machinery, and flying dust.

With the performance of *Private Secretary,* starring W. H. Gillette, the Grand closed its doors in 1885, to be replaced by the Capital. Adelaide Moore opened the new house with a revival of *The School for Scandal*. During the heyday of road shows, audiences at the Capital saw Kate Forsythe, Marie Wainwright, Joseph Jefferson, Sarah Bernhardt, and most of the other stars of the gaslight era.

Fort Smith opened an opera house in 1887, and many of the west-bound traveling companies made it their next stop after leaving Little Rock. Smaller cities along the railroads were visited by minstrel shows, barnstorming melodramas, and occasionally by big-time actors. To the river towns came the showboat, announced by a calliope, advertised by a parade, and patronized by almost the entire citizenry. Eagerly awaited from season to season, the showboat had perhaps a more loyal patronage than the road companies, and held out longer when the flickering films came; now, however, it too has disappeared.

During the 1930's Helen Hayes, Eva Le Gallienne, the Lunts, and the few other troupers still playing the road performed on the stage of the Little Rock High School auditorium. The Joseph Taylor Robinson Municipal Auditorium, completed in 1940, offers the best stage yet provided in the State, but the legitimate theater is today of small importance in Arkansas.

Towns of even a few hundred inhabitants, however, have their own motion picture theaters, often handsomely fitted. To many back-country dwellers touring tent shows bring pulse-stirring films of the Western plains. These wandering exhibitors, their outfits mounted complete on one or two trucks, usually follow the crop harvests, gleaning dimes from strawberry pickers and cotton choppers, detouring for Sunday School picnics or Fourth of July celebrations. When the operator finds a likely spot he pitches his tent, sets up folding chairs or planks, on cross trees, and gets out his projector and sound amplifier. Grown-ups and children watch tensely as the blurry heroes ride and fight, and the mountaineer's Adam's apple is likely to bob as the mortgage is foreclosed.

"Toby shows" also tour the crossroads villages and county seats, playing in tents, schoolhouses, or rented halls. The small cast is headed by "Toby," usually an aging professional who spiels at the gate, sells the tickets, and peddles the candy boxes containing prize tickets that may call for a brightly colored shawl or a plaster elephant, before he takes his place on the stage to play the comedy lead. Penetrating even farther into the rural sections are the medicine shows, complete with a ventriloquist, an Indian, or a girl dance-act to draw the crowd for the sales talk.

Carnivals with ferris wheels and acrobats come to the larger towns and the cities, where they can make a three- or five-day stand. Rodeos became popular in the late 1930's, drawing large crowds in Fort Smith, Jonesboro, North Little Rock, Pine Bluff, and other cities.

The Little Theater movement has thrived from time to time in Arkansas. In Little Rock such a group was organized in 1928, and despite periodic financial troubles has staged several seasons of contemporary plays. In 1938 the theater acquired its own building on West Seventh Street.

Several colleges have amateur theaters, the University of Arkansas taking the lead in 1932 with the founding of the University Theater at Fayetteville. The Hendrix College theater, at Conway, since its beginning in 1935 has given four full-length plays each year. Dramatic groups from high schools and colleges compete in an annual festival sponsored by the Arkansas Association of Teachers of Speech.

During the Centennial that celebrated 100 years of statehood two elaborate pageants were given, one in Rockport, another in Little Rock. The Little Rock pageant, *America Sings,* utilized more than 1,500 amateur actors, musicians, and singers.

The recreation division of the Work Projects Administration directed amateurs in the staging of 180 plays in Arkansas in 1939. The activities of this division, together with those of the Extension Service of the University of Arkansas, have given thousands of people their first glimpse of the stage.

Music

T HE Traveler was exasperated. Lost in the woods with night coming on, needing food and shelter for himself and his horse, he had learned exactly nothing in a half-hour's conversation with a sassy Squatter who seemed interested only in endlessly fiddling a single tune.

"What are you playing that tune over so often for?" demanded the Traveler. "Only heard it yisterday. 'Fraid I'll forget it." "Why don't you play the second part of it?" "It ain't got no second part." "Give me the fiddle," the Traveler ordered. He tuned it for a moment, then swung into the second part. The Squatter leaped up and began to dance, the sleeping hound awoke and thumped his tail, the children hopped up and down, and even the "old woman" came through the door with a smile twisting unaccustomed muscles on her face.

"Come in, stranger," roared the delighted Squatter. "Take a half a dozen cheers and sot down. Sall, stir yourself round like a six-horse team in a mud hole. Go round in the holler, whar I killed that buck this mornin', cut off some of the best pieces and fotch it and cook it for me and this gentleman directly. Raise up the board under the head of the bed and git the old black jug I hid and give us some whiskey; I know thar's some left yit. Dick, carry the gentleman's hoss around under the shed, give him some fodder and corn, as much as he kin eat. D—n me, stranger, ef you can't stay as long as you please, and I'll give you plenty to eat and drink. Play away, stranger, you kin sleep on the dry spot tonight!"

So goes part of the dialogue that accompanies one of the Nation's best known fiddle tunes, "The Arkansaw Traveler." The State's historians are generally agreed that both the story (which is narrated, not sung) and the melody were composed by Colonel Sandford C. Faulkner (1803-74). Faulkner, a prominent planter, is supposed to have been inspired by a conversation with a backwoodsman in 1840. A few folklore students have credited the authorship to an Ohio Valley fiddler named Jose Tasso, but Faulkner's claim was so fully recognized during his lifetime that the manager of the old St. Charles Hotel in New Orleans is said to have lettered "The Arkansaw Traveler" in gilt above the door of a room reserved for him.

The vogue of the tune and dialogue spread even more widely when they were used in a play, called *Kit, The Arkansas Traveler,* that delighted New York audiences of the 1880's. At the time, Arkansas people felt that the play was too full of pistol shots and bowie knives to be realistic. Even today many persons slightly resent the notion that the Squatter and his cabin were ever considered typical of the State. There was no gainsaying the appeal of the tune itself, however, and fiddles still quicken to its familiar rhythm after a hundred years. A Texas composer, David Guion, has used it as the theme of a symphonic score.

In the rural parts of Arkansas, as elsewhere, feet still occasionally jig to "The Arkansaw Traveler," "Turkey in the Straw," and other square-dance lilts beat out by a local-talent orchestra—or broadcast on the radio. Couples in jeans and ginghams shuffle gracefully through the figures, shouted by a hoarse-voiced caller. Youngsters too bashful to join in the dance peer through the windows or gather around the doorway. Now and then a really "country" program is varied by a "round dance," usually a waltz in rather fast tempo.

Square dances, held most often in schoolhouses and community centers, but sometimes in public dance halls, have taken the place of the old parlor hoe-downs and play parties. Though play parties are now very rare, up until two decades ago they were a favorite diversion of families who considered dancing to music irreligious. To an outsider, a play-party game would have seemed little different from a Virginia Reel or similar dance, except that there were no instruments and the tunes were sung by the participants.

Play-party songs and ballads (also seldom heard nowadays) were often of an old origin, particularly in isolated mountain communities. Some verses, as in the energetic game-song "Paw-paw Patch" and the rollicking "Let's Go Down to the Crawdad Hole," were improvisations crowded with local allusions. Others have been traced by authorities, such as Charles Morrow Wilson and Vance Randolph, to Elizabethan England, whence they were brought to Virginia and carried through Kentucky and Tennessee to Arkansas. To preserve some of the best ballads for future generations, Laurence Powell, onetime director of the Little Rock Symphony Orchestra, and John A. Lomax recorded more than 120 songs remembered by Mrs. Emma Dusenbury, the "Singing Lady of Mena."

Hymns have always been the most popular songs in Arkansas and make up most of the programs presented by scores of "singing conventions." Weekly, or at longer intervals, family and neighborhood groups gather informally for songfests. Having gained experience and confidence by practice, individual singers and choruses enter the contests held in each county during spring and summer months. The attendance at county contests has increased year after year, and the problem for the host town is now one of accommodating visitors rather than attracting them. For example, Viola, in Fulton County, has a singing convention attendance ten times the size of its population. The winners of county contests meet in district competitions, and district victors assemble in October at the Arkansas State Singing Convention.

Hymnals used by many of the singers are printed in shaped notes, far simpler for sight reading than the conventional "round" notes. The diatonic scale and the conventional staff and clef are used. For ease in identification, however, the tonic note, *do,* is drawn as a triangle, *re* as a semicircle, *mi* as a diamond, and so on. In the nineteenth century, shaped-note songbooks were widely used in the South and Southwest. During the last generation shaped-note music has survived only in the rural counties. One of the few publishing houses still specializing in shaped-note music is at Hartford, in Sebastian County. Singing schools conducted by the Hartford publishers in Arkansas, Oklahoma, and Texas offer three-week courses covering every phase of hymn writing and singing. Graduates of these schools write original lyrics and scores that are printed at Hartford and make up an important, although neglected, fund of contemporary folk music.

Negroes in the cotton country seldom use shaped-note or other songbooks. Many favorite Negro hymns follow a refrain so familiar that the preacher needs to announce only the first line of each stanza. Sometimes, when a song reaches so high a pitch of excitement that nobody wants to stop singing, the pastor or one of the congregation makes up new verses and recites them impromptu; the singers pick them up and repeat them, then swing into the chorus. Such a song may roll on for half an hour. When sharecropper organizations sprang up in the 1930's, some of the best-known hymns were converted into union songs. Tenants met and sang:

> It's a wonderful Union
> It's a wonderful Union
> It's a wonderful Union
> It's good enough for me.

Negroes sing lullabies, blues, and work songs as well as hymns and spirituals. Some of the songs come from Harlem, while others have a purely local origin. The scourge of the cottonfields is addressed half-humorously, half-resignedly, in the "Boll Weevil Song." Track layers on the railroads coordinate their work by a chant. When a strong-voiced husky booms "Little Rock!" as a signal, the crew grunts: "Memphis . . . Memphis . . . Memphis . . ." as they edge the rail into place. This work chant is said to date back to the construction of the Memphis and Little Rock Railroad, completed in 1871.

The radio and phonograph have, of course, leveled off sectional differences in music. Arkansas radio stations alternate New York swing bands with "mountain music" and sentimental ballads written in Tin Pan Alley. "Cowboy" orchestras, filtering in from Oklahoma and Texas, whang their guitars and banjos in Ozark county seats and Delta villages. Square-dance orchestras vary their programs with tunes familiar in metropolitan night clubs. The records in a nickel-in-the-slot phonograph at a crossroads lunchroom may include half a dozen hits from Hollywood movies, a couple of Negro blues numbers, two or three guitar renditions of unauthentic hill ballads, and a Louis Armstrong hot-trumpet version of the spiritual "When the Saints Go Marching By." A piece called "Little Rock Getaway" turns out to be a composition by Joe Sullivan of Chicago. Under the circumstances, it is impossible to point out any sort of music that is characteristic of Arkansas alone.

Classical music was first encouraged in the State by the young women's seminaries that appeared during the 1840's and 1850's. Directors advertised that harp and piano were taught. Private piano and voice schools helped the work along. The Little Rock Musical Coterie, organized nearly a half-century ago, presented Nordica, Schumann-Heink, Gadski, and other well-known artists in recitals at the capital. A similar organization was formed in Pine Bluff. After the World War a group successively known as the Little Rock Song Leaders' Club, the Community Music Association, and the Civic Music Association promoted weekly community musicales at the Majestic Theater for eight years, then built a band shell at City Park where it still offers free outdoor concerts in summer. Under the same sponsorship is an annual presentation by combined choral groups of Handel's *Messiah* during the Christmas season. A Little Rock Symphony Orchestra, organized in 1933 by Laurence Powell, dissolved when Powell, also its conductor, moved from the city in 1939. Its place was taken the following year by the Arkansas State Symphony Orchestra, which plays under the baton of David R. Robertson. Fort Smith has a symphony orchestra led by Mrs. Katherine Price Bailey. Degrees in music are conferred by the University of Arkansas, by Hendrix College, and Ouachita College. Public schools in the larger towns offer musical instruction; many high schools have bands, and a State high school singing festival is held in Little Rock each spring.

The Arkansas Federation of Music Clubs, formed in 1908, has about 40 senior and 30 junior clubs. The organization carries on a State-wide program to encourage musical appreciation and interest. Similar in intent are the programs of the Recreation and Music Projects of the Work Projects Administration. Endeavoring to correlate musical activities, the projects assist shaped-note singing conventions, give instrumental and vocal training, and create orchestras. Home

Demonstration and 4-H Clubs feature singing at their meetings and hold contests among their members.

Among well-known Arkansas musicians are: Mary McCormic, Belleville-born soprano who attained the Metropolitan stage; Mary Lewis, of Hot Springs, who went from the Ziegfield Follies to grand opera; Josef Rosenberg, pianist and founder of the Little Rock Choral Society; Frances Greer, of Piggott and Helena, a young coloratura with the Philadelphia Opera Company; William Grant Still, Negro composer of the *Afro-American Symphony* and other orchestral and ballet music.

Handicrafts and Painting

THE soft whir of spinning wheels and the rhythmic clack of looms could be heard throughout Arkansas during the first three quarters of the nineteenth century. Then the railroads came, first through the lowland forests, and later into the Ozarks and Ouachitas. When the wail of a train whistle rose above remote ridges the sounds of home industry faded, and handicrafts began to vanish from their last stronghold, the hill country. People started to wear factory-woven jeans and "store-boughten" Sunday suits instead of frontier homespun dyed in gray, red, and brown colors. Hosiery from Eastern mills replaced socks tediously knitted by firelight. In 1910 nearly every spinning wheel (whether for flax, cotton, or wool) had fallen apart or was gathering cobwebs and dust in the attic.

Home demonstration agents, who began their work in Arkansas about 1912, slowly revived old weaving skills and, in 1940, were able to report that more than 200 hand-operated looms were being used, including a few heavy-timbered machines constructed nearly a century ago. Most of the fabrics woven were for rugs, mats, and bags, although blankets, towels, and dress materials were run off the looms by the more expert operators. Nearly all of the weavers carded and wove wool that had been clipped on their own farms.

Quilting, less intricate than weaving and more of a communal affair, has had an uninterrupted popularity. Rural mothers still obey the custom of giving quilts to their marriageable daughters, and quilting parties are favorite "sociables" in the country, especially in the rainy winter reason. Around the frame as many as a dozen women can work and gossip. Perhaps they bring their own lunches, ready-cooked, and set them on the stove to keep warm until noon, when all the food is put on the table.

The underside of the quilt is often made of flour or sugar sacks sewed together and dyed turkey red or lemon yellow. This muslin-like foundation is stretched on the frame so that cotton "bats" can be spread over it evenly, and the entire coverlet is sewed through and through to prevent wadding. The top of the quilt is likely to be a pattern that was common on "cord-beds" in Kentucky or Tennessee six generations ago—the Wagon Wheel, the Flower Garden, the Wedding Ring, the Seven Star, or the Tulip. Sometimes quilting parties sew plain stitches, but an elaborate patchwork spread may have several dozen kinds of needlework, such as the featherstitch, the brier, lazy daisy, ocean wave, snail trail, dot-and-dash, French knot, and tepee. The scraps that are sewed in the patterns today are colored with inexpensive commercial dyes, but the housewife who quilted a few decades ago knew how to brew a deep-orange coloring liquid from madder root, a yellow from hickory bark, a rich green from oak galls, and a solid black from walnut hulls. For grays she had a wide choice of woody materials, such as maple, elm bark, and sweet gum.

The country craftsman, although he may not use his lore, still knows the art of making many household furnishings. He knows that the time to slice hickory sapwood for chair-bottom splints is "when the leaves are the size of squirrels' ears," and he remembers that if you want to make a basket of honeysuckle and buckbush runners you should rip up the materials from roadside ditches and rail-fence corners between September and March. Such a farmer is pretty sure that the ax handle he carved from hickory during an idle afternoon is better than the ones he hefted at the town hardware store last week, and he is convinced that water is at its best when sipped from a gourd dipper. The cornhusk doormat that his wife wove in an over-and-under pattern is familiar to him, and when he is resting after supper he silently admires the sewing basket that his wife fashioned from pine needles. Perhaps he has seen a chair bottomed with strips of inner tube and is deciding to make a seat like it.

Handicrafts have never been commercialized very much in Arkansas. Around Fayetteville, in the northwest corner of the State, a half-dozen families make baskets and sell them at highway stands to tourists in summer. A few of the women who treadle home-looms barter their fabrics or sell them for pin money. Most of the weavers, however, are interested in decorating their houses and clothing their families with the homespun that has again become fashionable. Straight-back, splint-bottom chairs can be bought at almost any furniture store on Seventh Street ("Furniture Row") in Little Rock or in the smaller cities. The most interesting chair designs, such as those made by the Civilian Conservation Corps' veterans' camp on Petit Jean Mountain, cannot be obtained in stores, although they invariably attract the attention of tourists in Arkansas State parks.

Rug making has a nationally known exponent in Mrs. Harry King, of Beebe, who has a collection of more than 2,500 hooked-rug patterns. The vogue for floor coverings of this type may foreshadow a revival of handicrafts in all parts of Arkansas.

Art in a formal sense probably was first represented in the State by George Catlin (1796-1872), whose 470 full-length paintings of Indians and tribal scenes now hang in the Catlin Gallery of the

National Museum in Washington, D.C. When Fort Smith was a frontier outpost, Catlin spent several summers in the adjoining Indian Territory. Portraits of a number of Arkansans who lived at the fort or at Van Buren are attributed to him.

The first resident professional artist in Arkansas, however, was John Henry Byrd, who had established a reputation in the lower Mississippi Valley before he settled in Little Rock in 1840. From the capital he traveled to the homes of planters who commissioned him to paint members of their families. During the War between the States, Byrd was with the Confederate armies and had as his subjects Lee, Jefferson Davis, Stonewall Jackson, and other leaders. A number of his oils now hang in the State Capitol, while others are prized by old families in Pine Bluff and Little Rock.

Massachusetts-born Chester Harding (1792-1866), a portraitist with a distinguished reputation in Eastern cities and in London, visited and worked at Pine Bluff in 1850. Besides painting the only known likeness of Daniel Boone, Harding is known for his portraits of Henry Clay, Daniel Webster, and other noted Americans.

Edward Payson Washburn, whose *Arkansas Traveler* is the best known of the State's paintings, was the son of Cephas Washburn, a missionary sent to the Arkansas Cherokee in 1820. After studying under Byrd and under Charles Loring Elliot in New York, the younger Washburn returned to Arkansas to paint landscapes and portraits. The enthusiastic reception given the *Traveler* in 1858 impelled him to begin a companion piece called *Turn of the Tune;* this was unfinished when he died in 1860, at the age of 28. The original of the *Traveler* now hangs in a private house at Russellville.

A contemporary of Washburn who also grew up in Arkansas was William Quesenbury (1822-88), who usually signed his work "Bill Cush." Best known as a caricaturist, newspaperman, and excellent soldier, Quesenbury (pronounced Cushenberry) nevertheless often worked in oils. Some of his paintings are still treasured in northwest Arkansas.

One of the first Arkansas women to gain a national reputation as a painter was Jennie Deloney Rice-Meyrowitz, born in 1866 at Washington, Hempstead County. After three years of teaching at the University of Arkansas, she went to New York in 1900 and won recognition almost overnight by painting the first portrait of Hetty Green, then widely known as "the richest woman in America." Her portraits of several Arkansas governors hang in the State Capitol. During the last few years the studio of Mrs. Rice-Meyrowitz in Little Rock has been a focal point for artists. The list of other Arkansas women who have been successful as painters includes Fern Edie Knecht, Fanny D. Hogan, Maude S. Holt, and Kathryne Hail Travis.

A State in the Making

STATE CAPITOL, LITTLE ROCK

ARRIVAL OF THE PIONEERS
Mural by Orville Carroll in Osceola Post Office

WOLF CABIN, NORFOLK

CLEARING THE LAND
Mural by H. Louis Freund in Heber Springs Post Office

ALBERT PIKE MUSEUM, MOUNT GAYLOR

L. E. Granger

THE HENDERLITER HOUSE IN LITTLE ROCK, THE
MEETING PLACE OF THE TERRITORIAL LEGISLATURE

HEMPSTEAD COUNTY COURTHOUSE AT WASHINGTON,
USED AS CONFEDERATE STATE CAPITOL (1863-65)

Arkansas State Publicity Dept.

ORIGINAL CANVAS OF *THE ARKANSAS TRAVELER*
Painted in 1858 by Edward Payson Washburn

OZARK STAGECOACH (*c.* 1905)

"MEN WHO RODE FOR PARKER"—U. S. DEPUTY MARSHALS
ATTACHED TO THE COURT OF JUDGE ISAAC PARKER
BETWEEN 1875 AND 1896

MOUNTAINEER IN COONSKIN CAP AND HOMESPUN JACKET
(*c.* 1900)

WASHING FOR DIAMONDS IN PIKE COUNTY (*c.* 1910)

NEWSPAPER MEN AND THEIR WIVES
VISIT THE DIAMOND MINE (*c.* 1910)

Louis Betts, portrait painter born in Little Rock, has been a member of the National Academy of Design since 1915 and has won notable awards. His work is represented in the Art Institute of Chicago and other metropolitan galleries. Benjamin C. Brantly in his Little Rock studio has painted both portraits and landscapes, examples of which may be seen in Arkansas museums and public buildings. Perhaps the capital's most active artist is Adrian Brewer, who came to Arkansas from Minnesota in 1926. Brewer, winner of a number of national awards and prizes, conducted an art school during the early 1930's. His most recent project is a series of woodcuts depicting historic public buildings.

Younger painters who are natives or long-time residents of Arkansas include J. Powell Scott, Thomas Arthur Robertson, and Everett Spruce. Scott, born in Kentucky, was for some years a leader in Little Rock art circles and is now an instructor at the University of Arizona. In 1940, after spending two years in a studio at New Orleans, Robertson returned to Little Rock to teach art at the capital's junior college. Spruce, of Conway, is registrar of the Dallas Museum of Fine Arts and has had exhibitions in Kansas City and New York; one of his oils, *The Hawk,* hangs in the New York Museum of Modern Art.

For many years the rich colors and striking perspectives of the Ozarks have attracted painters. Summer colonies of artists have grown up at Eureka Springs, at Winslow, and other points. A contemporary painter who has shown special interest in the highland region is H. Louis Freund, who came from Missouri to Hendrix College, Conway, as resident artist on a Carnegie grant. While he was in the State (1938-40), Freund painted United States Treasury murals for the post offices at Pocahontas and Heber Springs, delivered numerous lectures, and held classes in Conway and Little Rock.

Twentieth-century Arkansas has produced several cartoonists of note, including Jim R. Shaver of Evening Shade; J. P. Alley, creator of *Hambones;* Dan Glass of Harrison, originator of *Betty Boop;* and George Clark of Bentonville, who sketches the syndicated features *Side Glances* and *The Neighbors.*

Vinnie Ream Hoxie (1847-1914), who lived in Fort Smith during her girlhood, was the first woman sculptor to receive a commission from the United States Government. When she was only eighteen years old, she was asked by Congress to make a bust of President Lincoln; this work is now in the rotunda of the national Capitol.

In 1932 Howard Simon, a New Yorker well known for his illustrations, homesteaded in Perry County "thirty miles from the nearest railroad or telephone." Here, for about a year and a half, he depicted hill-country scenes in woodcuts and etchings. Simon's stay was especially valuable in stimulating the interest of other artists in Arkansas material.

A younger illustrator who is gaining a reputation because of her drawings for books is Helen Finger, of Fayetteville.

At the University of Arkansas and at Hendrix College are the State's leading art schools. A co-operative organization of unusual interest is the Little Rock Art League, which held its first classes in 1934 and soon attained high standards. Financial difficulties forced suspension of the league for a time, but it was revived in 1939.

The Arkansas Water Color Society, an active State-wide group of creative artists, was started in 1937 by Ralph M. Hudson, head of the University of Arkansas art department. Two years later the Arkansas Oil Painters and Sculptors Society was organized, partly under the sponsorship of Hendrix College.

The largest collection of paintings in the State is in the Little Rock Museum of Fine Arts, erected in 1937. The acquisitions include Italian primitive and Renaissance canvases; works by such painters as Inness, Peale, and Remington; and representative oils, water colors, and statuettes by Arkansans. Among the portraits exhibited is Samuel F. B. Morse's study of James I. Miller, the first Territorial Governor.

PART II

Cities and Towns

Blytheville

Railroad Stations: St. Louis-San Francisco Station, S. 3rd St. at Ash St., for St. Louis-San Francisco Ry.; St. Louis Southwestern Station, S. Elm St., for St. Louis Southwestern Ry.

Bus Stations: Greyhound Bus Terminal, 109 N. 5th St., for Dixie Greyhound and Mathis Bus Lines.

Airport: Municipal Airport, 1 m. S. on US 61; no scheduled service.

Taxis: Fare within city limits, 25¢ for 1 to 4 passengers.

Busses: Fare 5¢.

Traffic Regulations: No U-turns on Main St. between Franklin and 6th Sts.; speed limit 20 m.p.h. in downtown section.

Information Service: Chamber of Commerce, City Hall, 2nd and Walnut Sts.; Arkansas Automobile Club, Noble Hotel, Broadway and Walnut St.

Accommodations: Six hotels; tourist homes and camps.

Radio Station: KLCN (1320 kc.).

Theaters and Motion Picture Houses: High School Auditorium, 700 W. Chickasawba Ave., and City Hall Auditorium, for theatricals, concerts, and musicals; 2 motion picture houses.

Baseball: Mississippi County Fairgrounds, E. end Missouri Ave., independent teams.

Golf: Blytheville Country Club, 1.7 m. N. on US 61, 9 holes, greens fee 50¢.

Hunting and Fishing: Duck, quail, geese, and other game in season; freshwater angling in near-by lakes and streams for bream, crappie, bass, and catfish.

Tennis: Walker Park (2 courts), E. end Kentucky and Davis Sts., free.

Swimming: Walker Park, E. end Kentucky and Davis Sts., 10¢ and 25¢, suits and towels rented.

Annual Events: Mississippi County Fair in September; Cotton Picking Contest in October.

BLYTHEVILLE (257 alt., 10,652 pop.), in northeast Arkansas, lies almost within sight of the Missouri Line, and eight miles west of the twisting Mississippi River. Although the black Delta soil that stretches in all directions will grow many kinds of crops, cotton is the reason for Blytheville's existence, and the chief topic of conversation almost the entire year. Many of the town's thoroughfares run into cottonfields; Main Street has a cotton gin at the east end and a cotton garment factory at the west end.

In downtown Blytheville Main Street is a wide sunny avenue lined with one- and two-story brick stores and offices. Shoppers are most numerous on Saturdays. On this day the stores put on extra clerks, barbecue and hamburger stands prepare for a rush, and the motion picture theaters bill Western thrillers. Farm people, white and black, pack the sidewalks to sell produce, buy groceries and drygoods, and meet their friends. Sacks of feed and coops of squawking chickens are piled high outside the stores at the eastern end of Main Street. Perhaps a huge catfish, fresh-hooked from a Mississippi slough, dangles before a lunchroom. Farm wives throng the open-air markets while their husbands inspect bright red-painted plows and seeders in the implement houses. Farther west in the shopping district store windows are more sedate and the clerks less hurried. The press of people does not thin, however, until the business district comes to an abrupt end at Sixth Street, where Main narrows to become a tree-lined residential avenue.

Many of the Negroes do their trading a block south of Main, on Ash Street, which between Broadway and Fifth is almost a miniature Beale Street. Here, among the grocery stores and produce houses, are taverns, pool parlors, barbershops and other gathering-places. Most of Blytheville's 2,500 to 3,000 Negroes live along Ash, and south and southwest near the railroad tracks. Many of the men work in the compresses, where their adroitness in handling 500-pound bales amazes sightseers. Others are employed in the gins and seed oil mill; both men and women go into the surrounding fields to pick cotton in late summer and autumn.

Running southward into a maze of rails are the streets on which are concentrated Blytheville's chief shipping and industrial plants: Broadway, a block west of Third, is bordered by several gins, wholesale gasoline depots, and a large cannery; Elm, which heads southward from Ash just west of Fifth, passes a bottling plant, a gin, the jagged red roof of a compress, and a cottonseed oil mill. Wholesale houses are grouped along Ash, which parallels the railroad tracks.

At the beginning of the twentieth century Blytheville was a village centered around the corner of Main and Franklin Streets. The courthouse was a block north of Main, at Walnut and Second. Walnut Street is still the thoroughfare of public buildings, such as the present courthouse (on the site of the old), the city hall, and the Federal building. The city has grown almost entirely toward the west and northwest, although there is a new residential section to the northeast, near the Mississippi County Fairgrounds. Houses throughout Blytheville are fronted with deep porches shaded with bright awnings. Grounds are carefully tended, with flower-fringed walks, concrete birdbaths, and clumps of arbor vitae and other clipped hedges. Maples, catalpas, black locusts, Lombardy poplars, and a variety of oaks are set at regular intervals along the residential streets.

Blytheville was named for the Reverend Henry T. Blythe, a Virginia-born Methodist minister who came to Mississippi County in 1853. At that time the northeastern tip of Arkansas was covered with frequently flooded forests and almost impenetrable underbrush. Cotton growers would have laughed at the notion that the region would some day grow better crops than the soil of the Arkansas Valley, to the southwest. On a spot of fairly high land well back from the Mississippi, Blythe built his home and a small church. From this center he traveled throughout the region to conduct services and hold camp meetings. The community that grew up around the church became known as Blythe Chapel.

Among the most fondly remembered and colorful figures who settled in the neighborhood was Dr. Benjamin A. Bugg, a physician and planter famed for his extraordinary beard. Bugg thought that his six-and-a-half-foot adornment was the longest in the world, but in 1893 at Chicago's Columbian Exposition he saw a man with whiskers that were an inch longer. Chagrined, the doctor returned home and cut off his fabulous beard.

In 1880 Blythe divided some of his land into town lots, but the isolated village grew slowly for the next ten years because there was no way of reaching it except over boggy roads. After L. W. Gosnell installed a gin in 1888, however, a few cotton buyers from Jonesboro and Memphis began to come in each fall. In 1891, about the time its growth began, Blytheville was incorporated. A newspaper, the *Plain Dealer,* began publication in 1898, and shortly afterward a driller brought in an artesian well that gave the townspeople good water. In 1907, Blytheville ended a long rivalry with the Chickasawba community to the west by annexing it.

For a decade before the end of the nineteenth century the thick stands of timber near Blytheville had been a lure to lumber companies and railroads. The first effort to extend rails to the town began in 1893 with the formation of the Paragould Southeastern Railway Company, a line that now connects Blytheville with the St. Louis Southwestern at Paragould. The rails of the Jonesboro, Lake City and Eastern reached Blytheville in 1901, and the following year the St. Louis and Memphis (now St. Louis-San Francisco) came southward across the Missouri Line. For the first few years after the railroads came Blytheville depended largely on lumbering for its income, and muddy Main Street was filled with strings of mule-drawn wagons, often carrying one huge log apiece. As the timber was taken out inhabitants of the area began to see that the rich alluvial soil, if drained, was excellent crop land. In 1902 the first drainage district was organized, and despite the bitter opposition of some residents to "drainage districts, drainage commissioners, drainage engineers, and drainage lawyers" the land emerged from the stagnant water and became almost incredibly productive.

The establishment in 1911 of Blytheville's first compress, with storage space for 25,000 bales, symbolized the town's rise to importance as a cotton shipping point. Stimulated by high prices, production jumped sharply during the World War and continued to increase afterwards. In 1922 the Mississippi County crop totaled 93,953 bales, a figure that grew to 257,090 bales in 1937. Other crops that swell the incomes of local farmers and merchants include soybeans, alfalfa, and corn. The opening of a garment factory in 1937 indicates that Blytheville may become a manufacturing community as well as an agricultural center.

POINTS OF INTEREST

MISSISSIPPI COUNTY FAIRGROUNDS AND WALKER PARK (*open*), E. end of Missouri Ave., Kentucky St., and Davis St., together cover 67 acres. A half-mile race track, show buildings for white and Negro exhibitors, and a livestock building are on the grounds, where a fair is held each September. In the wooded park, used throughout the year by picnickers, is a six-acre lake and an open-air swimming pool. A grandstand overlooks the baseball field.

The AMERICAN LEGION HUT (*open*), 300 N. 2nd St., is built of cypress logs notched at the ends. Hand-rived cypress shingles form the roof, pegs in the oak flooring further simulate pioneer construction, and the large fireplaces are of Ozark stone. At the rear of the hut is a 700-seat athletic arena.

The MISSISSIPPI COUNTY COURTHOUSE, Walnut St. between 2nd and 3rd Sts., was erected in 1919. Buff brick walls rise to a cornice at the top of the third story, and the fourth story is set back from the lower walls. Exterior decoration consists of a small balcony above the main entrance and vertical concrete facings between the windows of the central section.

In the CITY HALL, SW. corner of Walnut and 2nd Sts., besides the usual municipal offices, are the offices of the Chamber of Commerce and the State police. An auditorium is on the second floor of the dark-red-brick building, which was completed in 1928.

The FEDERAL BUILDING, Walnut St. and Broadway, occupied since 1934 by the post office and other Federal agencies, is fronted by eight tall Ionic columns of white limestone. Doors and casements of the buff brick structure are framed in aluminum.

The BLYTHEVILLE CANNING COMPANY PLANT (*open 7-6 workdays*), S. end of Broadway, packs turnip and mustard greens, spinach, peas, and several varieties of beans grown on Mississippi County farms. Soybeans prepared for table use are a recent innovation here. The company, founded in 1929, employs as many as 300 workers at peak seasons (May and September).

The FEDERAL COMPRESS AND WAREHOUSE COMPANY PLANT (*open 8-12 and 1-5 workdays*), 400 S. Elm St., is one of Blytheville's three establishments for compressing, baling, and shipping cotton. Since cotton is highly inflammable, the storage sheds are divided by fireproof walls and protected by automatic sprinklers. Cotton sold to domestic mills is bound into standard size 500-pound bales, but that intended for export is compressed into less bulky bales.

The BLYTHEVILLE COTTON OIL MILL (*open 9-5 workdays*), S. end of Elm St. (L), annually buys about $1,000,000 worth of cottonseed from farmers and ginners within a radius of 50 miles. Products of the crushed seed include cooking oil and feed for livestock. The company, established in 1923, has its own railway spurs, artesian water system, and electric power plant. Warehouses at the mill have a capacity of 16,000 tons of seed.

In the BLYTHEVILLE PUBLIC LIBRARY (*open 2-6 week-days*), 523 W. Main St., are 6,000 volumes. The library, in a remodeled white frame house, is maintained by an association organized in 1921.

POINTS OF INTEREST IN ENVIRONS

Chickasawba Indian Mound, 1.3 *m.;* Fairfield Historical Museum, 3.2 *m.;* Big Lake Migratory Bird Refuge, 14.4 *m.* (*see Tour 10*).

El Dorado

Railroad Stations: Rock Island Station, 200 E. Hillsboro St., for Chicago, Rock Island & Pacific Ry.; Missouri Pacific Station, 425 E. Cedar St., for Missouri Pacific R.R.; El Dorado and Wesson Station, foot of S. West Ave., for El Dorado and Wesson Ry.
Bus Stations: Union Bus Station, 206 W. Elm St., for Tri-State Trailways and Gray Transportation Co.; 218 S. Washington Ave., for Missouri Pacific Trailways.
Airport: Municipal Airport, 1 m. S. on Washington Ave.; no scheduled service.
Taxis: Rates 15¢ within city limits; each additional passenger 10¢.
Traffic Regulations: Traffic lights in business district; one-hour parking limit in downtown section from 7 a.m. to 6 p.m., except Sundays and holidays. L-turns and U-turns prohibited on courthouse square.

Information Service: El Dorado Chamber of Commerce, S. Jefferson Ave. and Cedar St.

Accommodations: Five hotels; tourist homes, tourist camps.

Radio Station: KELD (1400 kc.).
Theaters and Motion Picture Houses: High School auditorium, Summit Ave., between Block and Wesson Sts., and Rialto Theater, 115 Cedar St., for theatricals, musicals, and concerts; four motion picture houses.
Baseball: Rowland Field, Cotton States League (Class C).
Golf: El Dorado Country Club, 2 m. N. on State 7, 18 holes, greens fee $1.
Hunting and Fishing: Duck, quail, squirrel, and geese in season; fresh-water angling in near-by lakes and streams.
Swimming: Norris Park Pool, 521 N. West Ave., adm. 15¢ and 25¢; YWCA pool, 118 Peach St., 10¢ and 25¢, suits and towels rented.
Tennis: Mellor Park (4 courts), E. 7th St. and Madison Ave., 20¢ an hour a person; El Dorado Junior College (2 courts), 320 S. West Ave., 5¢ a set a person; El Dorado City Park (3 courts), free.

Annual Events: Union County Fair in October; Christmas Street Festival.

EL DORADO (281 alt., 15,858 pop.), encircled by far-reaching forests of pine and hardwoods, lies halfway between the Mississippi River and Texas, within sight of the Louisiana border. The line of demarcation separating the city from the wooded countryside is almost as sharp as if drawn with a ruler. A quiet county seat for three-quarters of a century, El Dorado saw the prophecy of its name realized in 1921 when oil gushed from a well drilled a mile to the west. Since then the town has become a city and the "oil capital" of Arkansas.

In the center of a public square is the imposing four-story Union County Courthouse, faced by four thoroughfares lined with commercial buildings. Those erected since the discovery of petroleum are modern in design, with steel frames and stone or marble exteriors. Mingled with the new architecture, but more frequently found on side streets, are two- and three-story brick buildings of an earlier period. The wealth of El Dorado is reflected in the imposing churches and public buildings along Main Street, which faces the courthouse from the south.

Radiating from the square are the residential streets. Many of the homes are comfortable frame or brick houses of modern style and are occupied by the families of workers in the refinery and near-by oil fields. Shading scores of the dwellings are umbrella-shaped chinaberry trees. In the northeastern part of the city, off Champagnolle Road, are mansions that were built for cotton planters and businessmen long before the discovery of oil.

On the streets of El Dorado the oil field worker is recognizable by his khaki trousers and shirt, his clean-shaven face, and a bearing (such as railroad men have) that denotes steady work and good pay. Out among the derricks the men are a little less restrained than in town, and the atmosphere still has a trace of the robustness of boom days. Drilling for oil, however, has become almost prosaic, and the present orderly routine contrasts sharply with the noisy excitement that was a part of prospecting 20 years ago. Huge double-jointed trucks now rumble over suburban pavements where long lines of mules once slipped and struggled to pull heavy oil field equipment through the mud.

Approximately 4,000 Negroes live in El Dorado, the majority in an area called Fairview, in the southeast corner of the city, and in the St. Louis district, at the northwest edge. Negroes find little work in the oil fields, but are employed principally as domestic servants and laborers.

Though petroleum production and refining give El Dorado its present importance, the city has a wide tributary trade area. Almost exactly in the center of the southern Arkansas-northern Louisiana timber belt, it is a distribution center for a number of lumber towns and agricultural communities. The lines of two major railroads intersect here, and considerable quantities of gasoline and other petroleum products are shipped to Mississippi Valley and Gulf Coast ports on Ouachita River barges that tie up at Champagnolle Landing 12 miles to the northeast.

According to tradition, the first resident of El Dorado was an adventurer named Matthew F. Rainey whose wagon broke down at this point one day in 1843. Unable to go farther, the traveler held a sale of his possessions, and was so impressed with the neighboring farmers' eagerness to buy that he obtained more goods and put up a store. Whether Rainey called the place "El Dorado" in recognition of his good fortune is uncertain. The name was in use, however, the following year when Union County officials, seeking to move their county seat from the Ouachita River bluff now called Champagnolle, accepted Rainey's donation of 160 acres for the new site.

A courthouse and hotel, both of logs, were erected before the end of 1844. Shortly thereafter the Reverend William S. Lacey opened a private school in his home, teaching boys in one room while his wife taught girls in another. In 1851 the town, then one square mile in area, was incorporated. Cotton growers came up the Ouachita by steamboat and cleared plantations in the neighborhood. An early-day newspaper, the *Union,* began publication but, with the approach of the War between the States, changed its name to the *True Southern.*

In 1890 there were 455 people in El Dorado. The following year, however, the Camden & Alexander Railway (now Missouri Pacific) linked the village with the Iron Mountain branch at Camden. In 1903 the Little Rock Southern (now Chicago, Rock Island & Pacific) built a line through the forest from Haskell, giving El Dorado an almost direct north-south route to the Arkansas capital. Now less isolated, and sharing the prosperity of a timber-cutting boom, the town saw its population grow to 4,202 in 1910. Then there was a slump; much of the choice timber had been cut, and no important new industries had appeared. For a time it seemed that El Dorado was to sink again to the status of a rural trading center.

Development of adjacent Louisiana oil fields had for several years brought about prospecting and leasing of lands on the Arkansas side of the border. In the spring of 1920 a "wild gasser" blew in near El Dorado, but there was little excitement until January 10, 1921, when the Busey well began to flow.

The first film of oil had hardly covered the underbrush surrounding the derrick before El Dorado was swamped by an army of drillers, mechanics, speculators, contractors, engineers, merchants, mule skinners, and hangers-on. In a few weeks the population passed 20,000. People slept in hotel lobbies, in tents, in jerry-built shacks on empty lots. Feeding the newcomers became a critical problem, though hamburger stands sprang up everywhere. The sidewalk, said a newspaper, "became one great dining room, crowded and jammed, beautifully scented from the 'Hamburger With,' burned waffles, fried fish and boiling doughnut grease, looking like a great midway. . . . Resorts beyond the city limits, known as 'Pistol Hill,' 'Shotgun Valley,' 'The Chicken Farm,' flourished and prospered . . . roads loaded with a terrific burden of traffic got muddy, then boggy and in some cases disappeared entirely and it was a case of every man finding his own route through the woods and creek bottoms."

By the end of October 1921 some 460 producing wells had been drilled and 10,000,000 barrels of oil had been taken from an area of about 5,000 acres. Rigs were everywhere, and only prompt action by the city council checked enterprising drillers who were setting up derricks in the city itself. Overdrilling, inefficient methods, spectacular and costly fires, and seepage from the hurriedly constructed earth reservoirs wasted millions of barrels of petroleum. Until three pipelines were built during the first summer, crude oil was hauled by truck to El Dorado and from there shipped in railroad tank cars to refineries in other States. Regular discovery of new oil pools in the vicinity, conservation practices in both old and new fields under the Arkansas control statute of 1939, and huge estimated reserves give promise that El Dorado will long continue to be an oil center.

Recovering from the first impact of the boom, El Dorado steadied and soon transformed itself from an oil camp into a city. New buildings were erected to house supply firms, machine shops, foundries, and operations offices. The forests soon retreated before hundreds of new homes. The community climaxed its swift growth with an elaborate program of churches, streets and sewers, schools, and civic buildings.

POINTS OF INTEREST

1. The CITY HALL (*open 8-5 Mon.-Fri., 8-12 Sat.*), 210 N. West Ave., seat of El Dorado's aldermanic government, was built in 1927. Rising 45 feet above the two-story stone building is a central tower, whose windows and panels are ornamented with grillwork.

2. The UNION COUNTY COURTHOUSE (*open 9-5 weekdays*), Washington Ave. between Main and Elm Sts., designed by Mann and Stern, Little Rock architects, was completed in 1928. Extending around the four-story rectangular structure of white stone is an Ionic colonnade two stories high. On the fourth floor is the county jail. The courthouse square, a comparatively small landscaped plot, was a spring-fed lake until it was drained and cleared as the site of El Dorado's first courthouse in 1844.

3. The FIRST BAPTIST CHURCH, 210 W. Main St., houses a congregation which was organized in 1845 and worshipped in the courthouse until the original church was erected in 1848. The present structure, built in 1922 after the oil boom had greatly enlarged the membership, is a classic adaptation combined with a Moorish dome. Yellow brick walls roofed with dark red tile enclose the octagonal-shaped auditorium.

4. EL DORADO JUNIOR COLLEGE (*open 9-4 weekdays Sept.-June*), 320 S. West Ave., opened in 1925 as the first municipal junior college in Arkansas, occupies a three-story red-brick building with limestone trim, a Georgian entrance, and a steeply pitched roof with dormer windows. Erected in 1905 on land donated for school purposes by Albert Rust, an El Dorado pioneer, the building originally was the town high school. The present institution, which is coeducational and accredited, gives liberal arts courses and preprofessional training to about 100 students.

5. The LION OIL REFINERY (*open 9-5 weekdays; guides*), S. end of Marsh Ave., is one of the largest industrial plants in the State. Here each day about 15,000 barrels of crude oil are turned into gasoline, lubricating oil, kerosene, and other petroleum products. At first sight the $4,000,000 refinery looks like a jungle of gigantic tanks and curiously shaped pipes. Each still is an uncovered unit of black and silver-colored tanks shadowed by a brick smokestack. To the rear are steel reservoirs. Standing at the right of the entrance are laboratories for analyzing drill cores and crude and refined products. At the

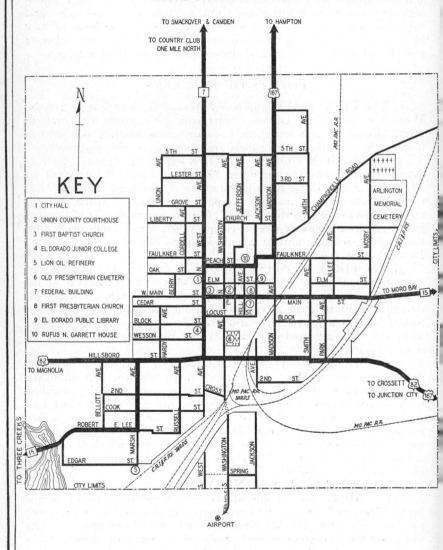

EL DORADO

1940

ARKANSAS WRITERS' PROJECT

TO SMACKOVER & CAMDEN   TO HAMPTON

TO COUNTRY CLUB
ONE MILE NORTH

KEY

1 CITY HALL
2 UNION COUNTY COURTHOUSE
3 FIRST BAPTIST CHURCH
4 EL DORADO JUNIOR COLLEGE
5 LION OIL REFINERY
6 OLD PRESBYTERIAN CEMETERY
7 FEDERAL BUILDING
8 FIRST PRESBYTERIAN CHURCH
9 EL DORADO PUBLIC LIBRARY
10 RUFUS N. GARRETT HOUSE

ARLINGTON MEMORIAL CEMETERY

TO MAGNOLIA
TO THREE CREEKS
TO MORO BAY
TO CROSSETT
TO JUNCTION CITY

AIRPORT

CITY LIMITS

north edge of the 160-acre plot are railroad spurs where tank cars are loaded for shipment to about 30 States. A part of the refinery's output is piped to Champagnolle Landing on the Ouachita River and shipped southward by barge. To avoid frictional sparks which might cause fires, some of the most inflammable liquids are not touched by pumps, but are pushed through the pipes by air pressure.

6. The OLD PRESBYTERIAN CEMETERY, 418 S. Washington Ave., was a country burial ground long before El Dorado existed. Among the pioneers buried here are Matthew Rainey, founder of the town, and the Reverend William S. Lacey, who opened the first school. The cemetery, now about a block square, was at one time much larger. Land was needed for a railroad right-of-way, however, and many of the bodies on the east side were moved. Most of the markers are old-fashioned narrow stone slabs and some of the inscriptions have been almost obliterated by time. Several old cedars and some young magnolia trees shade the spot, and along the fence of iron spikes Cherokee roses bloom.

7. The FEDERAL BUILDING (open 8-5 weekdays), SW. corner Main St. and Jackson Ave., follows the modified classical style typical of more recent Federal Government constructions. The three-story white building of Texas (Austin) stone is ornamented with marble trimmings and quoins from Vermont, Florida, and Georgia quarries. Since its completion in 1931 the structure has housed the El Dorado Post Office, the U. S. District Court, and the offices of various other Federal agencies.

8. The FIRST PRESBYTERIAN CHURCH, Main St. and Jackson Ave., with its flower garden and wide lawn occupies an entire block. The building, Gothic in style, is of red brick trimmed with white terra cotta. A green tile roof slopes down sharply on two sides to five double windows bordered with ivy. The congregation was organized in 1848.

9. The EL DORADO PUBLIC LIBRARY (open 12:30-6 p.m. weekdays), 402 E. Elm St., occupying a one-story remodeled frame building, has among its volumes a number of textbooks and reference works pertaining to the petroleum industry.

10. The RUFUS N. GARRETT HOUSE (private), Peach St. and Jefferson Ave., is set in landscaped grounds that include the site of the log cabin built by Matthew Rainey in 1844. The large gray-brick residence, roofed with red tile and faced with four stone columns, is screened by a giant oak. Leading up to the house is a long walk bordered with clumps of boxwood. In the east grounds is a snow garden in which all the flowers are white. The house, built in 1910, is typical of the splendid homes occasionally built in south-central Arkansas even before the discovery of oil.

POINTS OF INTEREST IN ENVIRONS

Smackover oil field, 12 m. (see Tour 8b). Shuler oil field, 14 m. (see Tour 14). Calion (river port), 12.1 m.; Calion Lake, 13.1 m. (see Tour 15).

Fort Smith

Railroad Stations: Union Station, 706 Rogers Ave., for St. Louis-San Francisco Ry. and Kansas City Southern Ry.; Missouri Pacific Station, 1st St. and Garrison Ave., for Missouri Pacific R.R.
Bus Stations: Union Bus Station, N. 11th St. and Garrison Ave., for Crown Coach Lines, Tri-State Trailways, and Oklahoma Transportation Lines; Trailways Union Bus Depot, 1000 Garrison Ave., for Missouri Pacific Trailways and Santa Fe Trailways.
Airport: Municipal Airport, 4.5 m. south on Greenwood Rd.; no scheduled service.
Taxis: Fare 10¢ and upward according to distance and number of passengers.
Busses: Fare 8¢; to Van Buren 10¢.
Traffic Regulations: Traffic lights in business district. One-hour parking limit in downtown section from 7 a.m. to 6 p.m. except Sundays and holidays. No all-night parking; no U-turns on Garrison Ave. except at 2nd, 3rd, 4th, 12th, and 13th Sts. Right turns permitted on red light after full stop.

Information Service: Chamber of Commerce, 613 Garrison Ave.; Arkansas Automobile Club, Goldman Hotel, 1215 Garrison Ave.

Accommodations: 8 hotels; numerous tourist homes and tourist camps.

Radio Station: KFPW (1400 kc.).
Theaters and Motion Picture Houses: Masonic Temple Auditorium, 200 N. 11th St., for theatricals, musicals, and concerts; 4 motion picture houses.
Baseball: Andrews Field, S. B and 7th Sts., Western Association (Class C).
Golf: Rolling Knolls Golf Course, 3215 N. O St., 9 holes, greens fee 25¢; United Commercial Travelers Country Club, 4 m. NE. on US 64, 9 holes, greens fee 25¢; Hardscrabble Country Club, 3.5 m. SE. on State 22, 18 holes, greens fee $1, $1.50 Sat., Sun., holidays.
Hunting and Fishing: Duck, quail, geese, deer, and other game in season; fresh-water angling in near-by lakes and streams.
Swimming: Whittaker Pool, 2312 N. 16th St., 15¢ and 25¢, suits and towels rented.
Tennis: Tilles Park (5 courts), free, 37th St. and Grand Ave.; Senior High School (2 courts), free, N. 23rd and B Sts.

Annual Events: Arkansas-Oklahoma Rodeo, Andrews Field, last week in May; Fort Smith-Van Buren Football Game, High School Stadium, Thanksgiving Day.

FORT SMITH (450 alt., 36,584 pop.), the second largest, and most industrialized city in Arkansas, spreads eastward from the Oklahoma Line at the point where the Arkansas River enters the State. At the approximate northern limit of cotton cultivation, Fort Smith has for its economic horizon factories that make furniture and brick, scissors and glass; farms that raise corn, livestock, and truck; and the coal mines in Sebastian County.

Running southeast from the river to the Church of the Immaculate Conception is Garrison Avenue, center of the business district and principal traffic artery. The exceptional width of the avenue, laid out as a parade ground for soldiers, gives downtown Fort Smith an air of Western spaciousness and makes even the larger buildings that line the sidewalks seem small. The bulky faded brick structures nearest the river show lines favored early in the twentieth century. Farther southeast, large steel-and-brick hotels, department stores, and gleaming restaurant fronts press together in an urban concentration surprising in view of the city's comparatively small population.

At a right angle to Garrison Avenue is Tenth Street, which after a few blocks becomes Midland Boulevard and several miles farther out crosses a loop of the Arkansas River into Van Buren. The older streets of Fort Smith, narrow and often heavily shaded, lie parallel with Tenth, north of Garrison. The entire district is laid out at a 45-degree angle to the cardinal points of the compass.

Later additions to the city were built along true north-south and east-west lines, but some of the first streets were carried through, and some of the newer ones (such as Grand Avenue) have been extended into the old district. The result is a pattern somewhat confusing to the visitor. At some intersections streets finger out in five directions; at others there are odd trapezoids and triangles of blocks that—away from the downtown district—are usually planted in shrubs and flowers. In July nearly the entire length of Midland Boulevard is a lavender blur of crape myrtle. Magnolias are fewer than in Little Rock or Pine Bluff, and venerable oaks are also less common, but their places are taken by round-topped elms, maples, and poplars. Several major streets are divided by grassy parkways, and vegetable gardens grow behind many of the houses.

South of the downtown section, in the angle formed by Garrison Avenue and the Poteau River, stood the fort (later replaced) that gave the city its name. On this site is one of the old buildings, and here also is the National Cemetery. At the apex of the angle, where the Poteau flows into the Arkansas, is a small tract of land claimed by neither Arkansas nor Oklahoma. For a quarter of a century after the last soldiers left Fort Smith in 1871, outlaws used this no-man's-land as a refuge. In 1898 the United States Government gave the city of Fort Smith police power over the strip, but the question of ownership has never been cleared up. Meanwhile the area, known as Coke (cocaine) Hill, has acquired a shantytown population which lives in shacks of scrap lumber and raises corn and vegetables within a stone's throw of Garrison Avenue's traffic.

Approximately 3,500 Negroes live in Fort Smith, not in one separate district, but grouped in various parts of the city. Work in the factories enables them to enjoy a living standard somewhat higher than that of members of their race in towns depending on cotton. Substantial brick residences owned by Negroes occasionally appear among the more common two- and three-room frame houses. There are a number of Negro churches, several amusement and recreational centers, and a swimming pool. In 1923 the Roman Catholic Church added a parochial school for Negroes to the already existing accredited public schools.

Fort Smith was founded in order to keep peace between the Osage farther up the Arkansas River and the Cherokee who lived downstream, as well as to protect the occasional trappers, hunters, and explorers from outlaws, both white and Indian. In the autumn of 1817 Major William C. Bradford, with Major Stephen H. Long, topographical engineer, and 82 riflemen, set out from St. Louis to establish the fort. Sickness among the men detained Bradford at Arkansas Post, so Long proceeded up the Arkansas River by skiff and set up a cantonment just before Christmas. He chose a site at the junction of the Arkansas and Poteau Rivers, called "Belle Point" by the French because of the unusual beauty of the oak-shaded bluff. The log fort, thrown up in a square fronting the river, was named for General Thomas A. Smith, the departmental commander who had given orders for its construction.

Thomas Nuttall, the English explorer-naturalist who visited the fort in 1819, reported that "the garrison, consisting of two block-houses, and lines of cabins or barracks for the accommodation of 70 men whom it contains, is agreeably situated at the junction of the Pottoe, on a rising ground of about 50 feet elevation, and surrounded by alluvial and uplands of unusual fertility. The view is more commanding and picturesque, than any other spot of equal elevation on the banks of the Arkansa."

Most of the garrison was moved west to Fort Gibson in 1824, and for several years Fort Smith was left in charge of only a small detachment. Meanwhile a few pioneer families had moved within shelter of the soldiers' rifles, and a village slowly took form. Apparently the first white settler was Captain John Rogers, who arrived in 1822 from New Orleans to become a sutler for the garrison. When a post office was established in 1829 Rogers became postmaster, and in 1834 he bought almost the entire town site for $450. Four years later the Federal Government decided to establish a new fort, and purchased 296 acres of Rogers' land for $15,000.

The fort begun in 1838 was much more substantial than the log stockade that had been the garrison's first protection. A quadrangle 450 feet by 600 feet was laid out. The 25-foot perpendicular rock wall that had been Belle Point was quarried down to the water's edge for building stone. Oak and walnut logs, floated down the Arkansas, went into a solid fortification that followed a design attributed to Vauban, famous French military engineer. Stonemasons, carpenters, and mechanics brought in to work on the fort mingled with soldiers and adventurers. A description of the town as it appeared during the time the fort was under construction was written years later by W. J. Weaver, a quarryman and logger. "On the bank fronting the river were about 15 buildings, reaching over two blocks from the avenue [Garrison Avenue] to Captain DuVal's store below. There was no wharf at the landing in front of the town, nothing but a side cut road down to the edge of the water. Upon the bank in front of Commercial Row . . . [one could see] ox wagons, a stir of trade . . . mounted officers charging about on spirited horses, many Indians with baskets and jugs, a few soldiers from the camp and laborers and mechanics going to and from their work on the new stone fort."

Into this scene rode General Zachary Taylor, then at the beginning of a career that brought him the nickname "Rough and Ready" and made him President of the United States. General Taylor took command of the unfinished fort in 1841 and with his family set up residence in a "plain one-story concern [building] with stone chimneys outside and ample porches in front and rear." This house was at the end of Garrison Avenue, where St. Anne's Academy now stands.

Late in 1842 the State general assembly incorporated Fort Smith, then a town of nearly 500 persons. Meanwhile work on the fort had lagged. Taylor shared the common feeling that there was no need for a strong fortification against the Indians, and at his suggestion orders to abandon work on the nearly completed structure came from Washington in 1843.

During the 1840's there was an epidemic of duels in the neighborhood, and keen interest in horse racing. Fort Smith's first church was financed in 1844 by sporting men who ran their horses on Race Track Prairie at the edge of town. The duels were usually fought on an Arkansas River sand bar in Indian Territory, beyond reach of antidueling laws. In 1844 Solon Borland and Benjamin J. Borden, editors of rival newspapers in Little Rock, made a steamboat trip up the river to Indian Territory to settle a dispute. Even more notable was the quarrel in 1848 between Albert Pike, prominent attorney and author, and John Selden Roane, later Governor of Arkansas. A large crowd followed the duelists to the sand bar in the early morning. Rigid etiquette was observed, with formal introductions, stiff bows, and handshakings. Pike wore an immaculate white shirt and puffed on a cigar. Each combatant cocked a pistol. At the word they fired— again and again. None of the shots took effect. A Cherokee spectator named Bill Fields grunted disgustedly that with such fine weapons he could kill a squirrel at 75 paces.

The year 1848 brought stirring news from the West: gold had been found in California. Fort Smith almost overnight became a noisy supply depot and point of departure for hundreds of emigrants who took the southern route across the plains. "Ho! for California!" pennants streamed from every river packet. Long lines of wagons, drawn by mules or oxen, creaked through the dusty streets or rumbled toward the camping grounds on the riverbank between Fort Smith and Van Buren. An Arkansas newspaper insisted that the supply of ore "is known to be inexhaustible," and asked, "who will sit quietly at home in the State pining in penury when fortunes are to be had merely for the labor of picking them up in California?"

These California-bound caravans lured so many emigrants by January 1849, only a few months after the steamboat *Pennywit* had tied up at the Choctaw wharf with news of gold, that families six miles from town were taking in boarders. Blacksmiths, hunters, and plainsmen were particularly welcome in the "Golden Army," but doctors, lawyers, farmers, geologists, shoemakers, and merchants also swelled its ranks. Despite contemporary newspapers' praise of the "sobriety and exemplary conduct" of the emigrants, gambling dens thrived, and Fort Smith passed ordinances to curb the flourishing iniquity. The council reserved the right to "license, regulate, tax or suppress . . . pawnbrokers, money changers . . . public masquerade balls, sparring exhibitions, dance houses, fortune tellers, pistol galleries, corn doctors . . . museums and menageries . . . horoscopic views, lung testers, muscle developers . . . billiard tables and other instruments used for gaming."

The prosperity that the gold rush brought Fort Smith and Van Buren was not felt all over the State. Senator Borland estimated that 1,000 people left Arkansas in 1849, and that twice that number would leave in 1850, a serious drain on the State's population. The military protection provided emigrants at Fort Smith was important in making the Fort Smith-Santa Fe route popular, along with the early grass of the southern region. Seeking to stop the westward flow of Arkansas people, Borland successfully urged that the Fort Smith garrison be removed to Fort Gibson. Western Arkansas seethed with indignation, and the Fort Smith *Herald* fumed: "The withdrawal of the last company of Infantry from this post has left about half a million dollars worth of public property exposed. . . . The public buildings for Military purposes at this place are the finest, largest, and best buildings on the Western frontier." Such pressure proved effective, and General Matthew Arbuckle was ordered to reoccupy the fort in 1851.

As the wagons continued to roll through the town, Fort Smith's population increased to 964 in 1850, or about twice the 1840 population. The general assembly in 1851 rechartered the community and pushed construction work on the Little Rock-Fort Smith highway. A contest between rival political factions kept the county seat of newly created Sebastian County shuttling back and forth between Fort Smith and the near-by settlement of Greenwood, until a compromise set up two judicial districts in the county. In 1858 the arrival of the first Butterfield stagecoach inaugurated rapid transportation to California and to St. Louis.

At the beginning of the War between the States, Fort Smith was taken by Confederate troops, and changed flags several times thereafter, but no major battles took place in or near the town. The fort's commissary building was used sometimes as a prison, sometimes as a refuge for women and children. More exciting were the years that came immediately after the war.

To the west of Fort Smith stretched Indian Territory, 74,000 square miles of scantily populated plains over which the Federal Government exercised only a shadowy jurisdiction. The Indian peoples made their own law, but their tribal courts had no authority over white offenders. Remote, with no communications except by horsemen, the Indian country was a haven for train robbers, murderers, and bank bandits. Men who lived and died by the gun thronged into it and made it their headquarters for forays into neighboring States.

The Federal District Court at Fort Smith was charged with enforcing the law in Indian Territory, in addition to handling Federal cases from western Arkansas. The size of the Territory, however, and the lack of peace officers, had long since resulted in a state of chaos. Such was the situation that confronted Judge Isaac C. Parker (1838-96), a Republican from Missouri, when he was appointed to the Fort Smith bench in 1875.

During 21 stern years in the courtroom, Parker sentenced 151 men to the gallows. Of those condemned, 83 were hanged. This amazing record was that of a man who did not favor capital punishment, who was described as "white of hair and beard, with pink cheeks, and slightly rotund," with "a twinkle in his eye and a little contagious chuckle which always made [the children] think of Santa Claus."

For the first 14 years of Parker's reign his court was unique in the history of Federal jurisprudence because, even in capital cases, his sentences could not be appealed to higher courts. In this period the only hope of a condemned man was executive clemency granted by the President. In 1889 and 1891 Congress enacted laws that, for the first time, permitted the Supreme Court of the United States to review capital cases decided in the Fort Smith courtroom.

Criminals were brought in from the Indian country by a force of 200 grim, hard-riding deputy marshals who always called themselves the "men who rode for Parker." So dangerous was their task that 65 of the officers were slain during Parker's years on the bench. News that the "hanging judge" had died in 1896 sent the Federal jail into a bedlam of celebration.

The desperadoes, white, Indian, Negro, or half-breed, with whom Fort Smith had to deal after the War between the States, ranged in small bands. Danger of organized attack on the city had ended long before. In 1871 the few troops still garrisoning the fort were withdrawn, and control of the military reservation passed to the Department of the Interior. The date marks the approximate beginning of Fort Smith's transformation from a frontier post into a city.

In 1879 the Little Rock & Fort Smith Railroad (now Missouri Pacific) reached its western destination. Down from Fayetteville three years later came the St. Louis, Arkansas & Texas (now St. Louis-San Francisco), whose trains crossed the Arkansas River from Van Buren by ferry for four years. The railroads stimulated coal mining in the area, and the mines increased the city's importance. Beginning in 1901 several natural gas wells were drilled just south of the city, and factories were attracted by the cheap fuel.

Although Fort Smith is the trading center of a large agricultural area, its principal income is from factories that normally employ about

5,000 workers and manufacture furniture, glass products, overalls, tents, scissors, brick, bedsprings, and other articles. Two smelters out Midland Boulevard refine zinc mined in southwest Missouri. Nearer downtown on the same thoroughfare are two glass factories, one producing flat glass and the other specializing in lamp chimneys, bottles, and similar small blown articles. Seven furniture factories, the largest group in Arkansas, line Factory Drive, reached from downtown by turning west on North I Street from North Second Street. Here workmen turn out furniture for every room in the average house.

A unionization drive that began in 1937 organized workers at most of the industrial plants and made Fort Smith the most labor-conscious city in the State. Signs in Garrison Avenue store windows advertise the union affiliation of employees, and the local labor council publishes a weekly newspaper, the *Labor Journal*.

Since 1913 municipal affairs have been managed by three salaried commissioners. A $409,000 bond issue for civic improvements voted in 1927 paid for new streets, sewers, parks, and playgrounds. Since 1936 clear mountain water from Lake Fort Smith, 28 miles to the northeast, has flowed through the city mains, instead of the salt- and gypsum-laden "Poteau punch" which housewives had complained about for many years. Recreational facilities, including a large swimming pool below the lake, are used by thousands of Fort Smith residents during the summer months.

For three decades the onetime frontier fort has had no challenge for its position as the second largest city in the State. The past, however, is still too near and too large a part of Fort Smith to be forgotten. Each year in May the city dons wide-brimmed sombreros, decorates Garrison Avenue with a Wild West motif, stages a rodeo, and exuberantly plays frontier town once more.

POINTS OF INTEREST

1. ST. ANNE'S ACADEMY (*open on application*), Garrison Ave. and N. 13th St., was established on its present site in 1853 by a band of Sisters of Mercy, in the residence abandoned by General Zachary Taylor. Only a vine-covered chimney, now converted into a grotto, remains of the old structure. The present group includes a three-story administration building, a red-brick convent, and the Church of the Immaculate Conception.

2. The NATIONAL CEMETERY (*open sunrise to sunset*), S. end of 6th St., overlooking the Poteau River, was set aside in 1832 as a burial ground for the soldiers at the fort and, in 1867, was given national status. Both Federal and Confederate dead were buried here during the War between the States, and some of the white markers carry such legends as "8 Confederate Soldiers," otherwise unidentified. The cemetery was retained by the War Department when the rest of the military reservation was turned over to the Department of the Interior.

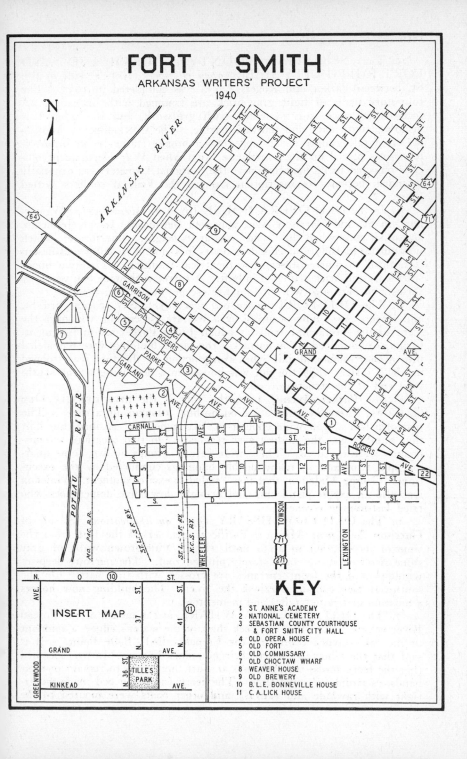

FORT SMITH

ARKANSAS WRITERS' PROJECT

1940

KEY

1. ST. ANNE'S ACADEMY
2. NATIONAL CEMETERY
3. SEBASTIAN COUNTY COURTHOUSE
   & FORT SMITH CITY HALL
4. OLD OPERA HOUSE
5. OLD FORT
6. OLD COMMISSARY
7. OLD CHOCTAW WHARF
8. WEAVER HOUSE
9. OLD BREWERY
10. B. L. E. BONNEVILLE HOUSE
11. C. A. LICK HOUSE

INSERT MAP

3. The SEBASTIAN COUNTY COURTHOUSE AND FORT SMITH CITY HALL (*open 9-5 weekdays*), E. side of 6th St. between Parker and Rogers Aves., was completed in 1937. The four-story walls of light gray brick are trimmed with limestone. A recessed entrance is ornamented with grillwork, and the interior is decorated with dark and mottled marble. The CONFEDERATE MONUMENT, a tall granite shaft topped by a bronze statue of an infantryman, was placed on the courthouse lawn when War Department officials objected to its installation at the National Cemetery, as originally intended, because its inscription ignored the Federal soldiers buried there.

4. In the OLD OPERA HOUSE (*open 8-6 weekdays*), SW. corner 5th St. and Garrison Ave., appeared Bernhardt, Joseph Jefferson, and other stars when the "road" was at its height. The theater, which was put up in 1887 and closed its doors in 1911, in its color and design is faithful to nineteenth-century theatrical tradition. The two upper stories are red brick trimmed in buff. A turret with wide bay windows forms a corner, and twin circular fire escapes descend on the side.

5. The OLD FORT (*open 8-6 weekdays*), SW. corner 3rd St. and Rogers Ave., now occupied by a welfare association, was once the scene of the spectacular trials at which Judge Parker sat in judgment. Originally intended as a barracks, the stone building was remodeled into a courtroom and jail when construction of the fort was stopped in 1843. After 1887 the jail was housed in a new wing at the southwest end of the structure.

Across Parker Avenue from the fort is the SITE OF THE OLD GALLOWS, where 83 men "stood on nothin', a-lookin' up a rope." The platform had a trap wide enough to "accommodate" 12 men, but half that number was the highest ever reached. On two occasions six miscreants were executed. There were several groups of five, some quartets and trios and so many double hangings conducted by the executioner, George Maledon, that they "failed to excite comment." Maledon was also an expert pistol shot and brought down five desperadoes who tried last-minute escapes.

6. The OLD COMMISSARY (*open on application*), S. side of Garrison Ave. near Missouri Pacific tracks, served the fort from the time of its erection in 1839 until 1871. Vine-grown walls of gray stone rise two stories to a steeply pitched roof. The narrow, deep-set windows and the front entrance are crossed with iron bars. On the southwest two cannon overlook the river. The building now houses a museum of frontier relics and mementoes.

7. The OLD CHOCTAW WHARF, at the mouth of the Poteau River behind Coke Hill, is a rock shelf at the water's edge—a remnant of the oak-crowned bluff that the French called "Belle Point." It is said that the Choctaw, when their boundary line was drawn, specified that the ferry across the Arkansas at Fort Smith was to remain in their hands, as it did for some time. The ferry (a wagon bed made watertight with rawhide and canvas) and other boats were moored to the

wharf by iron hooks driven into the rock. Several of these hooks still remain, bent in the direction of the current by the drag of the boats. About 100 yards north, almost under the Missouri Pacific bridge, is the SITE OF THE COMMERCIAL WHARVES, where a stone marker commemorates the arrival of Fort Smith's first steamboat.

8. The WEAVER HOUSE (*private*), NW. corner N. 4th and A Sts., a building of red brick and brown frame, was built in 1848 by William J. Weaver, and enlarged twice before 1867. Gables and chimneys vary the line of the gambrel roof. Weaver, who came to the town as a quarryman, later operated a ferry, became a merchant, edited a newspaper, and achieved some political prominence. His chronicles of early days are important source material for local historians.

9. The OLD BREWERY (*open on application*), SE. corner N. 3rd and E Sts., was built by Joseph Knobel, a native of Wittenberg, Germany, shortly after he arrived at Fort Smith in 1857. Thick stone walls rise three stories to encompass a cool and mellow interior. The first floor, now occupied by a grocery store, was once a beer hall popular with German settlers. Behind the building is a cave, dug into the hillside, that was used as a storeroom.

10. The B. L. E. BONNEVILLE HOUSE (*private*), 3215 N. O St., was the home of a soldier-adventurer who was thrice commander of Fort Smith and whose exploits were presented by Washington Irving in *The Adventures of Captain Bonneville*. Bonneville (1795-1878) was born in France, came to America as a boy, and graduated from West Point in 1819. In 1832 he set out from Fort Osage (near Kansas City, Missouri) with 110 men to explore the Far West, returning to Washington in 1835. Chosen one of the commissioners to select the site of the second army post at Fort Smith, he received his first appointment as commander of the fort in 1838. He became a Federal brigadier general during the War between the States, and returned to Fort Smith after retiring from the army in 1871.

During Bonneville's residence there, the house was the center of Fort Smith's social and intellectual life. The remodeled building is now owned by the Rolling Knolls Country Club, whose golf course sweeps toward the Arkansas River.

11. The C. A. LICK HOUSE (*private*), N. 41st St., one of Fort Smith's showplaces, stands behind a low red-brick wall that drops down a slope in long steps. In the yard towers a tall pine, a landmark in the city. Green venetian blinds and high green shutters contrast with the red roof. In the downtown shop (*private*) of the owner, Chauncey A. Lick, are printed millions of tickets, cafe checks, and other forms. Customers include major league baseball teams, railroads, theaters, and circuses.

The Lick residence is on the site of the Elias Rector house, scene of many frontier social affairs that attracted the notables of the day. Elias Rector (1802-78) was born in Virginia and came to Fort Smith in 1836, serving for 16 years as U. S. Marshal of Arkansas and Indian Territory. For removing Billy Bowlegs, Seminole chief, and his followers from Florida to Indian Territory, Rector was voted $10,000 and a resolution of thanks by Congress. When the War between the States broke out he was opposed both to dissolution of the Union and to bearing arms against the South. He retired to Texas and returned to Fort Smith after hostilities had ceased. The Rector home was destroyed by a tornado 20 years after the death of its owner.

POINTS OF INTEREST IN ENVIRONS

Bob Burns House (Van Buren), 5.6 *m.* (*see Tour 3b*). Arkansas Tuberculosis Sanatorium (branch), 5.4 *m.* (*see Tour 6*). Lake Fort Smith, 28 *m.*; Albert Pike Museum (*adm. 25¢*), 33.6 *m.*; Devil's Den State Park, 51.7 *m.* (*see Tour 9a*).

Hot Springs

Railroad Stations: Missouri Pacific Station, Broadway and Market St., for Missouri Pacific R.R.; Rock Island Station, Benton and Cottage Sts., for Chicago, Rock Island & Pacific Ry.

Bus Stations: Trailways Bus Depot, Citizens Bldg., Bridge St., between Central Ave. and Broadway, for Missouri Pacific Trailways, Dixie Motor Coaches, and Santa Fe Trailways; Union Bus Depot, Spencer Bldg., Bridge St. and Broadway, for Arkansas Motor Coaches and Tri-State Trailways.

Airport: Chamber of Commerce Airport, 2 m. SW. on US 70; no scheduled service; sightseeing trips over city, $1 a person.

Taxis: Zone rates 25¢ and up, according to number of persons and distance; 2-hr. 50 m. sightseeing tours, $1.50 a person, service in morning.

Busses: Fare 7¢, 4 tokens for 25¢; 3-hr. 50 m. sightseeing tours, $1.50 a person, service in afternoon.

Traffic Regulations: Traffic lights in business district; no U-turn where traffic lights are installed; area of limited parking time plainly marked; parking meters on Central Ave., rate 5¢ an hour; no all-night parking.

Information Service: Hot Springs National Park Administration Bldg., Central and Reserve Aves.; Chamber of Commerce, 115 Central Ave.

Accommodations: 72 hotels; numerous rooming houses, apartments, furnished cottages, trailer and tourist camps; lake cottages for rent by day or month; rates higher Jan.-Mar.; Government Free Tourist Camp, 2 m. N. on US 70, turn R. one-half mile.

Radio Stations: KTHS (1090 kc.); KWFC (1340 kc.).

Theaters and Motion Picture Houses: Municipal Auditorium in City Hall, Benton and Cottage Sts., for theatricals, musicals, and concerts; seven motion picture houses.

Baseball: Ban Johnson Field, W. end Whittington Ave., Cotton States League (Class C); Dean Field (2 diamonds), E. end Morrison Ave. off Central Ave., independent teams.

Boating: Lake Hamilton, 5 m. S. on State 7; Lake Catherine, 6 m. SE. on US 270; motor- and rowboats for rent by hour or day; boat landings maintained throughout lake areas.

Golf: Hot Springs Country Club, 2.5 m. SE. on US 270, three 18-hole courses, greens fee $1.75 winter, $1.25 summer; Oaklawn Golf Club, Central Ave. and Oaklawn Blvd., 9 holes, greens fee 50¢ (closed during racing season).

Hunting and Fishing: Duck, quail, geese, turkey, and deer in season; fresh-water angling in near-by lakes and streams.

Riding: Horses available at hotels and numerous riding stables with or without guides; bridle paths on Hot Springs Mountain, West Mountain, North Mountain, and Sugar Loaf Mountain.

Swimming: Fountain Lake, 5 m. N. on US 70, 15¢ and 25¢; Ozark Lithia Swimming Pool, 7 m. N. on US 70, 15¢ and 25¢, suits and towels rented.

Tennis: Courts at Whittington Park and Majestic Hotel; both courts free.

Annual Events: Horse Racing, 30-day season beginning last week in February; Easter Sunrise Service, Easter Sunday (Hot Springs Mountain); Outboard Speedboat Regatta, July 4 (Lake Hamilton); Christmas Carol Pageant, Dec. 24 (Arlington Park).

HOT SPRINGS (599 alt., 21,370 pop.), Arkansas' most cosmopolitan city, looks like a bit of a metropolis dropped among the green-clad Ouachita Mountains. To the west rise rocky slopes which form part of the Ouachita National Forest, a region of great natural beauty. The clear waters of Lake Hamilton and Lake Catherine, impounded from the Ouachita River as it descends in meandering S-loops toward the lowlands, curl among wide valleys toward the south and east.

Wedged between three forested hills, Hot Springs is compressed at its center into a curved, almost gorge-like valley wide enough only for Central Avenue. Along this single thoroughfare is famous Bathhouse Row and the downtown section. Sudden hills and valleys give the whole city a pleasantly unconventional layout. Business houses spread south and west from Central Avenue along streets that dart out at odd angles to take advantage of every level space. Some of the three- and four-story brick commercial buildings that typify the central shopping area back squarely into a steep shale bluff. The man-made structures in the valley are dwarfed by the hills that rise above them. Even the towering Medical Arts Building is almost overshadowed by the green slope of West Mountain.

The plan of Hot Springs' residential sections, like that of its business district, is dictated largely by the city's topography. Houses look upon little winding streets; often they are set high on a hillside and reached by long stairways of stone or wood. Architectural types include brick bungalows, white frame gingerbread, English manor houses, French provincial styles, and rambling old Southern mansions that seem to have grown up with the magnolias.

A hundred years of resort life have given the city an informal atmosphere. Outdoor photograph studios, where visitors have their pictures taken astride a slumbering burro or behind a prop saloon bar, spring up in vacant lots alongside sumptuous hotels. Small shops serve fresh sea food, fruit juices, or goats' milk, and stands display crystals, curios, souvenirs, and trinkets. In the narrow canyons patrons of shooting galleries blaze away into the mountainside without disturbing the chipmunks who scuttle unconcernedly after chinquapins through the bushes above. Among other tourist attractions are an alligator farm, an ostrich farm, and a cave containing unusual crystalline formations.

Bathhouse Row, a series of eight elaborate stone, brick, and terra cotta buildings, is the parade ground of Hot Springs' cosmopolitanism. The bathing establishments in their central setting of magnolias, young elms, and hedges furnish a back drop for an unceasing procession of vacationing businessmen with expensive clothes and graying temples, fox-furred and lorgnetted dowagers, and sightseers. An Easterner's derby bobbing briskly along the avenue is as common as a shapeless felt hat rocking gently over the loose-jointed gait of a native Arkansas woodcutter. Canes and monocles pass without a second glance from farmers in jumpers and overalls. The sight of a prominent motion picture star, prize fighter, or major league baseball player "down for the baths" starts only a ripple of comment along a hotel veranda as guests watch sunset shadows climb the wooded slope. During the racing season hundreds of afternoon visitors from Little Rock and other Arkansas cities join the crowds on the thronged sidewalks.

Behind Bathhouse Row rises Hot Springs Mountain, from the depths of which well the thermal waters responsible for the growth of Hot Springs as a spa and health resort. The 47 springs, sealed to prevent contamination, yield a daily flow of about 1,000,000 gallons with a constant temperature of about 143 degrees. Pipes collect the water from the springs and carry it to central reservoirs skillfully concealed under the west slope of the mountain. From here it is delivered to the bathhouses through conduits so carefully insulated that virtually none of the heat is lost. The houses are under the supervision of the National Park Service, whose local officers police the Hot Springs Park area adjoining the city. The Park Service also maintains a museum, a free bathhouse for indigent persons, and a free tourist camp.

A number of geological explanations have been advanced to account for the presence of the springs. Probably the most favored is the so-called meteoric theory, which holds that rain water sinking into the earth between West and Sugar Loaf Mountains descends until it comes in contact with either a mass of hot rock or gases escaping from such rock. After passing eastward beneath North Mountain the heated water finally emerges through a fault near the base of Hot Springs Mountain. Another theory is that the Hot Springs water has never before been at the earth's surface but is released from molten rock at the earth's interior. Supporting this idea of magmatic or juvenile water is the fact that neither the temperature of the air nor the amount of rainfall have any appreciable effect on the temperature or flow of the springs. Geologists have also suggested that the heat of the waters may be caused by radioactive materials, by chemical reactions taking place near the underground watercourse, or by friction between rock masses during periods of folding and faulting.

The standard bath as given in most bathhouses consists of about 15 minutes immersion, during which period the bather drinks hot water freely to assist perspiration. Then comes a vigorous massage, followed by a rubdown administered by an attendant. The bather rests in several rooms of successively cooler temperatures before going outdoors. Partial-immersion baths are given, and facilities are available in most of the bathing houses for sitz, leg, hand-and-arm, and vapor baths and various forms of hydrotherapy.

Although the social and economic life of Hot Springs is built around its medicinal waters and its vacation attractions, the city, third largest in Arkansas, also serves as the commercial center of a wide area. Women from the mountain towns look forward to shopping expeditions in the department stores while their husbands search for automobile parts in the used-car lots or bargain with dealers over the eggs and poultry they have brought in. Manufacturing is chiefly concerned with the needs of a spa and recreation center; industries include the production of bathrobes, slippers, and souvenirs.

Along Malvern Avenue and Pleasant Street in the southeast section of the city live the majority of Hot Springs' more than 4,000 Negroes. Their activities, like those of the city itself, revolve largely around the bathhouses, restaurants, and hotels, where they are employed as bath attendants, maids, cooks, waiters, and porters. They have their own business and recreation centers, hotels, schools, hospitals, and a Government-supervised bathhouse. Negro homes in Hot Springs, many of them substantial brick residences owned by their occupants, reflect a stable and fairly high income level.

Probably the first white men to visit the hot springs were De Soto and his followers, who are generally believed to have explored the region in 1541. According to tradition, the Indians thought the Great Spirit was present in the waters, and warring tribes made the valley a neutral ground where all might use the springs unmolested. Legends present the strange picture of braves from hostile tribes lying side by side in the hot mud to ease rheumatic pains resulting from exposure on the war trail.

Shortly after the Louisiana Purchase, President Thomas Jefferson commissioned William Dunbar and Dr. George Hunter to ascend the Ouachita River and make an official report on the hot springs. These explorers reached the springs in December 1804 and "found an open log cabin and a few huts of split boards, all calculated for summer encampment, and which had been erected by persons resorting to the springs for the recovery of their health." The huts were not of Indian construction, indicating that early white settlers and trappers in the region had erected them to use as temporary quarters while soaking a winter's kinks out of their knees and backs.

The first permanent house in the valley is credited to Jean Emanuel Prudhomme, a Louisiana planter who was guided to the spot in 1807 by Natchitoches Indians. The same year Isaac Cates and John Perciful (sometimes spelled Percival or Purcifull) were drawn from Alabama by reports of the springs' healing powers. Cates built a wooden trough in which to lie while the water flowed over his body. Perciful added to his income from hunting and trapping by renting to visitors cabins built or acquired from Prudhomme and other residents. Thomas Nuttall, English naturalist-explorer, described the hot springs in 1819:

The principal fountain, issuing from amidst huge masses of black rocks . . . has a stream of near a foot in diameter at its orifice, and hot enough to boil eggs or fish; a steam arises from it as from water in a state of ebullition, attended with a considerable discharge of bubbles. It is only after mixing with the cool water of a brook, at some distance from this spring, that it becomes of a temperature in which it is possible to bathe. . . . [The water] charged with an excess of carbonic acid, holding lime in solution, deposits a calcareous tufa, which incrusts leaves, moss, or any other substance which it meets in its course, to the great surprise of the ignorant, who commonly pronounce them petrefactions.

Except for a few cabins scattered irregularly in the valley or perched upon surrounding slopes, there was no accommodation for visitors at

Industry

COTTON AT THE GIN, LAKE DICK

REMOVING BALED COTTON FROM THE PRESS, LEHI

OIL DRILLING DERRICK, SOUTH ARKANSAS

Lion Oil Refining Co.

SPHERICAL TANK, EL DORADO

OIL REFINERY, EL DORADO

SAWMILL AT GLENWOOD

LOADING LOGS ON TRAIN, OUACHITA NATIONAL FOREST

PAPER MILL IN THE PINE BELT

BAUXITE PLANT, BAUXITE

SURFACE WORKINGS, BAUXITE

DRILLERS IN
BAUXITE MINE, BAUXITE
Republic Mining and Mfg. Co.

MAKING CORNCOB PIPES, EVERTON

QUICKSILVER REDUCTION FURNACE, PIKE COUNTY

WHITE RIVER BRIDGE AND DAM, BATESVILLE

CARPENTER DAM, OUACHITA RIVER

the spa until 1820, when Joseph Millard opened a hotel in a dogtrot log cabin. Millard's hostelry passed from existence in a few years, and when Ludovicus Belding, a native of Massachusetts, came with his wife and three children to live at the springs in 1828, he found the place almost unoccupied. Belding, too, built a hotel, drawing praise from a Little Rock newspaper which had remarked on the lack of "comfortable entertainment" for spa visitors.

The first bathhouses were built in 1830 by Asa Thompson. Small log cabins with plank tubs, they were a great advance over the jutting rocks and thickets previously utilized. At about the same time a vapor bath was constructed by building a rock-and-board shelter over a water-filled niche. These improvements made the baths so popular that in 1832 the United States Government, to prevent commercial exploitation of the waters, set aside four sections of land around the springs as a reservation.

This move retarded the construction of permanent buildings, because no one was willing to invest any large amount of work in property of which he might be dispossessed. The lack of adequate accommodations drew acid comment from the geologist George W. Featherstonhaugh, who came to the springs in 1834. His cabin was without furniture, complained the Englishman; "the floor was formed of boards roughly and unevenly hewn, and, unfortunately, some of them were wanting. . . . How invalids contrive to be comfortable, who come to this ragged place, I cannot imagine, yet I understand that ten or a dozen people are often crammed into this room, which my son and myself found much too small for two." However, he realized that he had penetrated to the farthest frontier: "All roads of every kind terminate at the Hot Springs; beyond them there is nothing but the unbroken wilderness, the trails and fords of which are only known to a few hunters."

While at the springs Featherstonhaugh met Hiram Abiff Whittington, a storekeeper who, like Ludovicus Belding, came from Massachusetts. With books sent from Boston, Whittington had established a library in his store, although it is doubtful that many of the hunters who wandered in to swap a catch of furs for supplies could read or sign their names. Whittington did about $6,000 worth of trading each year, entirely by barter. "We have no money here and never had," he wrote a brother in the East. "Our business is all done in cotton and skins."

When Arkansas was admitted to the Union in 1836 the spa was perhaps better known to outsiders than was the capital, Little Rock. At the time of its incorporation as a town in 1851, however, Hot Springs was still only a straggling village consisting of two rows of hotels, bathhouses, saloons, doctors' offices, and stores.

The War between the States doubly desolated the town: it shut off the flow of visitors from the North and East and caused a sudden migration of most of the 200 inhabitants to Texas.

Despite its decline, Hot Springs was unofficially the capital of

Arkansas for three months in 1862, when Governor Henry M. Rector, fearing capture of Little Rock by Federals, gathered up important State papers and records and fled to the spa. Many persons felt that Governor Rector's action, unauthorized by the legislature, was unduly precipitate, and the Little Rock *True Democrat* complained: "We would be glad if some patriotic gentleman would relieve the anxiety of the public by informing it of the locality of the State government. The last that was heard of it here, it was aboard of the steamer *Little Rock* . . . stemming the current of the Arkansas River. . . . If part of the State government is rusticating, we suppose there is some reason for it, but it is decidedly inconvenient to those who have business to transact with the State."

When Hot Springs was gradually rebuilt and repopulated after the war the question of title to the land about the springs claimed increasing attention. The town was named the seat of Garland County in 1874, but a site for the courthouse could not be obtained within a mile of the springs. Visitors and residents alike were inconvenienced by the absence of well-constructed buildings, although flimsy boardinghouses, hotels, and business establishments were put up despite title deficiencies of the land on which they stood. A United States Supreme Court decision in 1876 ended long litigation by voiding the titles of three principal claimants to property near the springs. The following year Hot Springs Reservation was separated from the town by an act of Congress, and part of the originally reserved territory was opened to private ownership. A commission appointed by President Hayes laid out Central Avenue and other streets, and surveyed the reservation for beautification purposes. It also decided which among the "squatters" should be entitled to purchase the newly available parcels of land.

General B. F. Kelly was appointed superintendent of the reservation, and one of his first acts was razing of "Ral City," an encampment of invalids too poor to pay for hotel accommodations. General Kelly moved the indigent bathers to a higher and more sanitary spot and built for them the first free bathhouse, a small shelter of rough boards.

Even before Hot Springs had fully begun its transformation from a crude village to a modern pleasure resort, it had attracted many notables. One of these was "Diamond Jo" Reynolds, Chicago capitalist who built the "Diamond Jo" narrow-gauge railroad between Hot Springs and Malvern (*see Tour 11*) in order to avoid the teeth-loosening stagecoach ride over the rocky mountain roads. The passengers who rode in the luxurious little coaches of the "Diamond Jo" included some of the most famous men of the time: Jay Gould, Phil Armour, Jake Kilraine, "Gentleman Jim" Corbett, John L. Sullivan, and Billy Sunday.

Completed in 1875, the railroad set Hot Springs' belated development in motion, and the sale of land adjoining the hot springs gave it added impetus. In 1882 ten bathhouses, some of them large and costly, were already in operation. During the same year Congress established the Army and Navy General Hospital to make the therapeutic benefits of the waters available to soldiers and sailors. As more hotels and stores sprang up, the city assumed its present form of two principal sections joined by a single street. One of the major improvements brought by the rapid expansion of the 1880's was the covering of Hot Springs Creek, whose course lies along Central Avenue underneath the Bathhouse Row promenade.

Shortly after 1900 a Federal board was created to examine and register physicians before they were permitted to prescribe baths in the hot waters. The "doctor-drumming" that had existed in the spa and its environs was thereby curbed. Further regulations forbade use of the waters to persons staying at hotels or boarding houses where "drumming" was permitted.

The latest of several devastating fires during the city's irregular growth, a blaze that swept Hot Springs in 1913, leveled 50 blocks of stores and residences. Water mains were destroyed by the flames, and gas jets flickered for days on the sites of burned homes. The electric power plant was one of the first buildings burned, and trolley transportation was crippled. A happy result of the calamity is the freshness of the city's present-day architecture.

In 1921 Hot Springs Reservation became Hot Springs National Park. Since that time, roads and trails on the overhanging mountains have been improved, picnic grounds have been laid out, and the entire park area has been made more attractive to tourists.

POINTS OF INTEREST

1. The ARMY AND NAVY GENERAL HOSPITAL (*open 2-4 daily*), in the U. S. Reservation, towers magnificently above the city from the southwest tip of Hot Springs Mountain. Two 5-story wings form a V to follow the natural sweep of the mountain and converge upon a 7-story central portion, from which mounts a 10-story tower strongly Spanish in conception. The walls are of light-toned brick with terra cotta trim and rise from a limestone base. At the front a one-story projection built of white stone contains the principal entrance and administrative offices. Private rooms and wards open upon sunporches extending the length of the wings on each floor. The colonnades bordering the roof enclose sundecks and an open-air theater for patients and personnel.

The hospital was established in 1882 and the first buildings were completed within the next three years. The present (1941) structure, finished in 1933 at a cost of $2,500,000, has a capacity of about 500 patients. It is supplied with water from the hot springs, and is equipped to provide hydrotherapy, heliotherapy, and physiotherapy treatments.

2. The HOT SPRINGS NATIONAL PARK ADMINISTRA-TION BUILDING (*open 9-4:30*), NE. corner Reserve and Central Aves., is the headquarters of the Park's administrative services. The structure, a two-story, cream stucco building with a red-tile roof, also contains a bureau of information for the public. Occupying the east

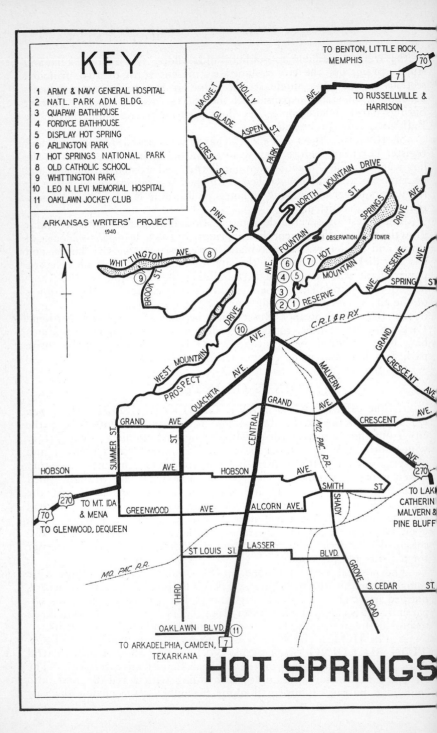

wing is a MUSEUM, with exhibits illustrating the natural and ethnological history of the Hot Springs region. Displays depict the formation of the neighboring mountains, the mechanism of the hot springs, Indian history and culture, early explorations, the coming of the pioneers, development of bathing shelters and bathhouses, plant and animal life in the vicinity, and the peculiar organisms found in the hot waters.

3. The QUAPAW BATHHOUSE (*open 7-5 weekdays; guides*), Central Ave. near the center of Bathhouse Row, is known for its GROTTO, where a hot spring flows at the rate of 180,000 gallons daily, with a constant temperature of 140.7 degrees. A stairway leads downward from the lobby into a narrow, warm cave winding to the spring, which some students believe was used by the Indians for vapor baths. Workmen discovered the grotto while excavating for the building's foundation. A long two-story plaster building with a red-tile roof and a mosaic dome, the Quapaw stands, like the other bathhouses on the street, within the limits of Hot Springs National Park and leases its site from the U. S. Government.

4. The FORDYCE BATHHOUSE (*open 7-5 weekdays; guides*), Central Ave., has on its top floor a MUSEUM containing a collection of Indian artifacts, many of which were found within a few miles of Hot Springs. The building is of brick in a crisscross, two-tone pattern, with the first story of limestone. A deep bath and therapeutic pool are available for treatment of arthritis and paralysis; bathers unable to walk are placed on a rubber mattress and lifted in and out of the pool by an electric hoist.

5. The DISPLAY HOT SPRING, at the rear of Maurice Bathhouse, gives an impression of the flow of the waters as they probably appeared to early explorers and pioneers, before they were enclosed and sealed. Approached by a promenade between the Fordyce and Maurice Bathhouses (the principal foot entrance to Hot Springs National Park), the spring filters through a rough rock sustaining wall and drops downward into a clear pool.

6. ARLINGTON PARK, fronting Central Ave. and Fountain St., is a grassy, landscaped crescent of ground north of Bathhouse Row at the base of Hot Springs Mountain. Among the cluster of weeping willows and shrubs is a large boulder of tufa, a porous rock resulting from the deposits of salts, especially silica and calcite, by the hot waters. Some of the local tufa encrustations, now covered by vegetation, are said to be 10 to 15 feet thick.

7. HOT SPRINGS NATIONAL PARK, covering 1,016 acres, ranges over the hills around the city and includes Hot Springs Mountain, North Mountain, West Mountain, Sugar Loaf Mountain, Indian Mountain, and Government Park. West Mountain, with a maximum elevation of 1,320 feet, rises more than 700 feet above the city proper. Throughout the park, hiking trails, bridle paths, and winding automobile roads lead to clearings overlooking the streets and houses below, and benches, tables, fireplaces, and shelters are available for use by picnickers. The region has a wide variety of plant life, including such

wild flowers as violets, wild hyacinth, blue larkspur, coreopsis, partridge pea, purple cone, goldenrod, foxglove, and great blue sage. Unusual plants are identified by signs. The American chameleon, a small lizard capable of changing its color to either brown or green, scuttles among the lichen-mantled rocks.

At the summit of Hot Springs Mountain is a 165-foot steel OBSERVATION TOWER (*open 7:30 to sundown; adm. 25¢*), whose lookout platform, reached by an elevator, commands a view for miles around. Far below, the roof gardens of Hot Springs' large hotels appear as small, bright rectangles of color, while in the distance the Ouachita glides through the forest, and Lake Catherine and Lake Hamilton are faintly visible in the sunlight.

8. The OLD CATHOLIC SCHOOL (*private*), 312 Whittington Ave., once housed the St. Mary's Academy and Convent, founded in 1881 by the Sisters of Mercy. A rambling white frame structure with a chapel attached, the building is given the appearance of an old log house by its grooved walls. Father P. McGowan, a Roman Catholic priest who figured in early Hot Springs history, donated the ground for its construction. Classes were conducted in the building until 1922, after which it became a rooming house.

9. WHITTINGTON PARK, Whittington Ave., is a privately owned area that includes a dance pavilion, a skating rink, and the Ban Johnson Baseball Field. The ball ground has been used for spring training by major league clubs, as well as for Cotton States League games. A hundred yards to the east is GOVERNMENT PARK, a division of Hot Springs National Park. Here are a public tennis court, a croquet court, and playgrounds.

10. The LEO N. LEVI MEMORIAL HOSPITAL (*open 2-4 daily*), Prospect Ave., accepts only charity patients, mostly arthritis sufferers to whom the hot waters of the springs are beneficial. Non-sectarian in character, it is supported by Jewish organizations and individuals. The red-brick building, its entrance almost hidden behind two spreading magnolias, is four stories high. A one-story addition on a high terraced fill to the east houses the Charles Steinberg Clinic, staffed by 32 Hot Springs physicians who donate part-time services. The hospital was completed in 1914; the clinic opened in 1928.

11. The OAKLAWN JOCKEY CLUB (*open 8-6 daily*), Central Ave. and Oaklawn Blvd., is the goal of every horse-loving Arkansan who can get to Hot Springs during the racing season, as well as of many outstaters. Secure from the February chill in the glass-enclosed, steam-heated grandstand, turf enthusiasts watch the horses tear around the mile track. Beyond the white rails of the track (which enclose a nine-hole golf course used after the season's end) green-cloaked foot-hills of the Ouachitas bear off against the horizon.

The Oaklawn plant was built in 1904 and the first racing meet held the following spring. In 1907 an act of the general assembly made gambling on horse races illegal, and racing was suspended until nine years later, the clubhouse, paddock, and track being used during some of the intervening years by the Arkansas State Fair. An attempt to legalize betting in 1915 failed, but racing was resumed nevertheless from 1916 through 1919. In 1934 another meet was held, and the next year the legislature sanctioned pari-mutuel betting and set up the Arkansas Racing Commission. Since that time 30-day spring seasons have been annual attractions. Operating approximately during the period between the closing of race tracks in Florida and Louisiana and the opening of Northern meets, Oaklawn is a stopover for many stables en route from South to North. Climaxing each meet is the Arkansas Derby, a mile-and-an-eighth event for three-year-olds.

POINTS OF INTEREST IN ENVIRONS

Lake Hamilton, 4.9 *m.*; Camp Quapaw, 31 *m.* (*see Tour 2b*). Mountain Valley Springs, 13.8 *m.* (*see Tour 8a*). Carpenter Hydroelectric Dam, 6.1 *m.;* Magnet Cove, 13.9 *m.;* Remmel Hydroelectric Dam and Lake Catherine State Park, 15.6 *m.;* Crystal Springs, 17.6 *m.;* Charlton Recreational Camp, 20.2 *m.* (*see Tour 11*).

Jonesboro

Railroad Stations: Union Station, Main St. and railroad tracks, for St. Louis-San Francisco Ry. and St. Louis Southwestern Ry.; Missouri Pacific Station, Nettleton, 3.5 m. E., for Missouri Pacific R.R. (passengers transferred by bus, fare 10¢).

Bus Stations: Union Bus Terminal, 328 S. Church St., for Arkansas Motor Coaches, Mo-Ark Trailways, and Mathis Bus Lines; Greyhound Bus Terminal, 593 S. Madison St., for Dixie Greyhound Lines and Missouri Pacific Trailways; Arroway Station, 103 W. Jackson St., for Arroway Coaches.

Airport: Municipal Airport, 2.5 m. E. on State 1; no scheduled service.

Taxis: Fare in city 15¢ for one or two passengers.

Busses: Fare 5¢ in city or to Arkansas State College; 10¢ to Nettleton.

Traffic Regulations: One-hour parking limit in business district except Sundays and holidays; U-turns prohibited on Main St.; speed limit 25 m.p.h.

Information Service: Noble Hotel, Jackson and Union Sts.; Jonesboro Chamber of Commerce, 320½ S. Main St.

Accommodations: Four hotels; tourist homes, tourist camps.

Radio Station: KBTM (1230 kc.).

Theaters and Motion Picture Houses: Community Center, S. Church St. at Elm St., and R.E. Lee Wilson Hall, Arkansas State College, 1.7 m. E. on State 1, for theatricals, musicals, and concerts; three motion picture houses.

Baseball: American Legion Park, 509 E. Washington St., Northeast Arkansas League; Kays' Athletic Field, Arkansas State College.

Golf: Jonesboro Country Club, 1 m. E. on US 63, 18 holes, greens fee 75¢.

Hunting and Fishing: Deer, quail, squirrel, turkey, duck, and geese in season; fishing in St. Francis River "Sunk Lands," 15 m. E. on State 18 (boats and guides at Lake City), and other near-by lakes and streams.

Tennis: Community Center (4 courts), S. Church St. at Elm St., 10¢ an hour a person, 9 a.m.-2 p.m., 25¢ an hour a person after 2 p.m.

Swimming: Keller's Bathing Pool and Beach, 1 m. S. on State 39, 15¢ and 25¢; Community Center, S. Church St. at Elm St., 15¢ and 25¢, suits rented.

Annual Events: Fall Festival in October.

JONESBORO (344 alt., 11,729 pop.), spread on a level expanse of Crowley's Ridge, is the largest town in the northeast corner of the State. A comfortable, conservative community in a diversified-farming area, Jonesboro bears more resemblance to a Midwestern corn-belt city than to the cotton towns only a few miles away in the Delta.

Nine miles wide and gently rolling, the Ridge at this point is subject to little erosion, except at the eastern and western edges. The land is divided into farms that produce beef and dairy cattle, poultry, corn, fruit, and vegetables. Most of the cotton that comes into Jonesboro is grown on alluvial soil east of the Ridge, where acres of stumps show how recently many tracts have been cleared and drained. West of the Ridge are new ricefields bounded by second-growth forests in the lowlands of Bayou de View and the Cache River.

Jonesboro's business district extends north from the courthouse square (laid out when the town was founded in 1859) to the railroad station. The main current of the city's life flows along four blocks of Main Street. Facing the sidewalks in unbroken rows are one- and two-story business buildings similar to each other in architecture but with a variety of colors in brick and tile. Establishments that require extensive floor space, such as automobile showrooms and print shops, are found on Union Street, west of Main, and Church Street, to the east. Unlike the leading thoroughfares of some cities, Jonesboro's Main Street has no contrasting stretches of old and new buildings.

North of the railroad tracks the tall concrete stack of the municipal water and light plant rises above a cluster of wholesale houses, bottling plants, coal and lumberyards, and truck depots. Beyond this industrial district are rows of frame houses where most of the city's 1,300 or more Negroes live. A smaller Negro area lies east of the American Legion baseball park.

South of the courthouse, lower Main Street broadens into an avenue that passes several large churches; of these imposing structures the city is justifiably proud. Still farther south, Main enters some of the older and more fashionable residential sections. Here fine houses are set far back from the sidewalk on parklike lawns that are shaded by oaks, maples, and elms. The newer residential areas spread to the south and west.

Ranging east and west along the parallel tracks of the St. Louis-San Francisco and the St. Louis Southwestern are two rice mills, three cotton gins, a cotton compress, half a dozen wholesale oil companies, a handle mill, a basket factory, and a feed and flour mill. Co-operative enterprises, rare in the State, have achieved some success in Jonesboro. A grocery, a feed and seed store, and a funeral home are maintained by members of the Arkansas Farmers' Union, which is affiliated nationally with the Farmers' Educational and Co-operative Union.

The first white settler in the neighborhood of Jonesboro was Daniel Martin, who in 1829 homesteaded with his family six miles southwest of the present city. Thirty years later the legislature created Craighead County despite the heated opposition of the man for whom it was named—State Senator Thomas B. Craighead. Craighead had objected to including in the new county some rich agricultural land then lying in his home county, Mississippi. The town selected as the seat of the new government unit was named for State Senator William Jones, who had advocated the formation of the county. Fergus Snoddy donated 15 acres on the crest of Crowley's Ridge as a town site.

"The spot was chosen," according to Harry Lee Williams (*The History of Craighead County*, 1930), "because there were not so many trees to cut down, the place being a large opening, a deer crossing, with great forest aisles under the large oak trees." Men in coonskin caps cleared away the underbrush and built a two-story frame court-house. Until the structure was completed county meetings were held at the log store of William Puryear, two miles north on the Greensboro road. Shortly afterward, Puryear moved his business into town, where he carried on a profitable trade with hunters. During one year, 1864, Puryear bought $3,700 worth of furs.

In 1863 a skirmish took place in the new town when Confederates drove out Federal troops quartered at the courthouse. After the war carpetbaggers and Klansmen had several encounters in the neighbor-hood, and a few partisans were killed. The Jonesboro *Register,* which began publication in 1867, spoke out so forthrightly against the carpet-bag militia that the editors were forced to flee for their lives, and the newspaper plant was burned.

About 1867 Jonesboro's community life began to take on its first polish. A Thespian Society staged amateur dramatics. A local minister set up an "ambrotype gallery" at the courthouse, where he made photo-graphs every Saturday. A Masonic lodge met "on Friday before the full moon in each month at early candle light." Professional men included two physicians, a dentist, and four attorneys.

In the early 1880's railroads reached the town in their race for the timber of northeast Arkansas. The main line of the Texas & St. Louis (now St. Louis Southwestern) came down Crowley's Ridge in 1882, and within a few months tracks now belonging to the St. Louis-San Francisco were laid. When the Iron Mountain & Helena (now Missouri Pacific) in 1881 had requested a bonus of $5,000 to bring its rails into Jonesboro, citizens had refused the demand. This line there-upon placed its tracks three miles to the east, and around the station grew the small town of Nettleton.

About the time of its incorporation in 1883 Jonesboro appeared to a railroad surveyor as "a remarkable village of some 300 or 400, all log buildings, with a 90-foot well in the middle of the square." By 1890 the population had passed the 2,000 mark, despite a fire the previous year that destroyed three blocks of buildings on Main Street.

The whine of sawmills and the sound of machinery in more than 30 woodworking plants filled the air at the turn of the century. As the forests were denuded of their first stands most of the mills moved away, but by that time Jonesboro's position as an agricultural trading center was secure. In 1909 a State board of trustees chose the town as the site for a district agricultural college. The institution, now called Arkansas State College, opened at Jonesboro in 1910 and moved to its present campus, a little more than a mile to the east, in 1911. Storekeepers began to design some of their window displays to catch the eyes of students rather than lumberjacks.

Notable among Jonesboro's citizens is Hattie W. Caraway (1878—), the first woman to be elected to the United States Senate. After the death of her husband, Senator Thaddeus H. Caraway (1871-1931), she was chosen at a special election, and was reelected to full terms in 1932 and 1938.

POINTS OF INTEREST

The CRAIGHEAD COUNTY COURTHOUSE, S. Main St. between Washington and Jackson Sts., is on the site chosen for Jonesboro's first courthouse in 1859. Unconventional in design, and almost resembling a pueblo, the building has a three-story central portion rising above four low corner wings. The structure was completed in 1934 at a cost of $125,000.

In the FEDERAL BUILDING (*open 9-4:30 weekdays*), Church St. facing Jackson St., are the Jonesboro Post Office and U. S. District Court. The building, remodeled in 1934, has a lower story of brick and an upper one faced with buff-colored cement.

The FIRST METHODIST CHURCH, S. Main and Matthews Sts., one of the city's largest, is constructed entirely of white Arkansas marble. Wide stone steps lead to the six massive columns and classic portico of the main entrance. At the rear a three-story Bible school building has been integrated into the design.

The JONESBORO COMMUNITY CENTER (*open*), S. Church and E. Elm Sts., is the scene of a wide variety of athletic and social events. The main building, set in a shallow valley, is of a design similar to that of the courthouse, with four one-story wings at the corners. Horizontal lines are emphasized in the decoration, and the central part of the building rises to a pointed roof. Inside is a gymnasium for boxing, basketball, and other athletic contests. A stage is available for theatrical and musical performances. To the right of the structure is a row of tennis courts, and in the rear is a large concrete swimming pool. The center was built in 1936.

The OLD COBB HOUSE (*private*), 812 Cobb St., was built in 1878 by the Reverend J. D. C. Cobb, who established the Jonesboro *Times*, an early-day newspaper. The simple one-story house is almost lost in a grove of towering oaks.

The JONESBORO RICE MILL (*open 9-5 workdays in milling season, Sept.-June*), Burke and Union Sts., is one of the two local plants that polish the rice grown west of Crowley's Ridge. Bran and other by-products are made into livestock feed.

POINTS OF INTEREST IN ENVIRONS

Arkansas State College, 1.7 *m.;* Crowley's Ridge State Park, 16 *m.;* St. Francis River "Sunk Lands," 14.3 *m.;* Craighead Forest and Camp Frierson (Boy Scouts), 5.1 *m.* (*see Tour 7*).

Little Rock and North Little Rock

Railroad Stations: Little Rock—Union Station, Markham and Victory Sts., for Missouri Pacific R.R.; Rock Island Station, 1007 E. 2nd St., for Chicago, Rock Island & Pacific Ry. *North Little Rock*—Served by Little Rock stations.
Bus Stations: Little Rock—Trailways Bus Depot, 203 W. Markham St., for Missouri Pacific Trailways and Santa Fe Trailways; Arkansas Motor Coach Depot, 100 E. Markham, for Arkansas Motor Coaches and Arroway Coaches; Greyhound Bus Depot, 123 W. 6th St., for Southwestern Greyhound Lines, Crown Coach Lines, and Interurban Transportation Co. *North Little Rock*—Busses of all major lines stop when flagged at the Hall Drug Store, 3rd and Main Sts.
Airport: Little Rock—Adams Field (Municipal), 14th St. and Harrington Ave., for American Airlines, Inc. and charter planes; taxi rate from downtown, 50¢ for passengers of American Airlines, Inc.
Taxis: Same rate both cities. Fare 25¢ first mile, one to five persons; 10¢ for each additional one-half mile.
Streetcars and Busses: Fare 6¢ in each city; intercity transfers 2¢ additional.
Traffic Regulations: Little Rock—Traffic lights in business district and at some intersections in residential districts. *Caution:* Stops at some through-streets are indicated by red iron buttons on pavement. Half-hour parking limit on Main St. and Capitol Ave., one-hour limit elsewhere in downtown section, from 8 a.m. to 6 p.m. except Sundays and holidays. No all-night parking; no U-turns where traffic lights are installed; left turns prohibited where warning posted; right turns permitted on red light after full stop. *North Little Rock*—No traffic lights; left and right turns on any street; no U-turns on Main St.

Information Service: Little Rock—Chamber of Commerce, 231 Lousiana St.; Arkansas Automobile Club, 115 Louisiana St. *North Little Rock*—Mayor's office, City Hall, 3rd and Main Sts.; North Little Rock *Times,* 217 Main St.

Accommodations: Little Rock—22 hotels (2 for Negroes); tourist homes, tourist camps. *North Little Rock*—3 hotels; tourist homes, tourist camps; auto camps numerous on major highways approaching both cities.

Radio Stations: Little Rock—KLRA (1420 kc.); KGHI (1230 kc.); KARK (920 kc.).
Theaters and Motion Picture Houses: Little Rock—Joseph Taylor Robinson Memorial Auditorium, Markham at Broadway; Senior High School Auditorium, 14th St. and Park Ave.; Parnell Hall, 2400 W. Markham St.; Community Little Theater, 711 W. 7th St., for theatricals, musicals, and concerts; 10 motion picture houses (1 for Negroes). *North Little Rock*—Senior High School Auditorium, 22nd and Main Sts., Community Building (North Little Rock Boys' Club), 13th and Main Sts., for theatricals, musicals, and concerts; 5 motion picture houses.
Baseball: Little Rock—Travelers' Field, Fair Park, Southern League (Class A-1); Lamar Porter Field, Little Rock Amateur Association, Boys' Club, and other amateur games. *North Little Rock*—Missouri Pacific Booster Park, Greater Little Rock Associated Amateurs.

Golf: *Little Rock*—Municipal Golf Links, Fair Park, 18 holes, greens fee 50¢; Riverside Country Club, 3 m. NW. of Little Rock on State 10, 18 holes, greens fee 50¢, 75¢ Sat. and Sunday; Little Rock Country Club, 4.5 m. W. of Little Rock on State 10, 18 holes, fee $1, $2 Sat. and Sun.; Concordia Country Club, 5 m. W. of Little Rock on US 70, 9 holes, fee 25¢.

Hunting and Fishing: Duck, geese, quail, turkey, deer, and other game in season; fresh-water angling in many near-by lakes and streams.

Swimming: *Little Rock*—YMCA, 6th St. and Broadway, adm. 25¢; open 10 a.m. to 9 p.m. weekdays, 1-6 p.m. Sundays; consult desk clerk for men's and women's hours. *North Little Rock*—North Little Rock Boys' Club, 13th and Main Sts., children 10¢, adults 20¢; open 1-9 p.m., June 1 to Sept. 15.

Tennis: *Little Rock*—Lamar Porter Field (4 courts), 7th and Johnson Sts., adm. 25¢ an hour in day, 65¢ an hour at night; Senior High School (5 courts), 14th St. and Park Ave., Sat. and Sun. only, 25¢ an hour.

Annual Events: *North Little Rock*—Arkansas Livestock Show and Rodeo, 5th and Beech Sts., variable date in October.

LITTLE ROCK (291 alt., 88,039 pop.), capital and leading city of Arkansas, and NORTH LITTLE ROCK (256 alt., 21,137 pop.), lie on opposite banks of the Arkansas River, very near the center of the State. Mounting abruptly to the west and northwest are the Ouachita foothills, and sweeping eastward are far-flung alluvial lands. The Arkansas, once a busy steamboat route, swings through a gap in the northwest bluffs, rounds the snub-nosed sandstone prominence that is Big Rock, and passes under five bridges that connect the two cities.

From the highest floors of office buildings on Little Rock's Main Street the residential districts appear as a dense screen of treetops interrupted by bright patches of red, gray, and green roofs. North of the river, and breaking the horizon, are sharply outlined factories, batteries of great cottonseed oil tanks, and tall industrial water towers shining in the sunlight. Main Street runs north and south. White-, brown-, and buff-brick buildings with modern store fronts stand among structures of the 1880's and 1890's. The brick walls of the older buildings have been mellowed to a deep red by the weather.

On the faded upper stories of East Markham Street, which parallels the river, half-obliterated signs such as *Choctaw Restaurant* and *Fine Wines and Whiskies* revive memories of a day when Markham Street rivaled Main in affluence. Markham's nearness to the river caused it to grow into a wholesale district when steamboats carried the commerce of the region, and it continued as a distributing section when railroad tracks were laid alongside the water.

Between East Markham and the Rock Island railroad shops, occupying level land once cultivated in cotton, is Little Rock's largest industrial district. Woodworking plants, a flour and feed mill, a furniture factory, two cottonseed oil plants, a chemical factory, and numerous other establishments spread along the railroad spurs. In the open spaces between the plants stand blocks of small frame houses where the workmen live, close to their jobs, but with room enough for gardens and perhaps a few chickens.

Residences south of the retail district illustrate strikingly the phases through which Little Rock architecture has passed. Venerable, pillared mansions sit grandly and time-stained behind magnolias. On the same streets, however, are late Victorian frame structures with gingerbread scrollwork; brick apartment buildings with balconies and Venetian blinds; and trim, new bungalows with white walls and blue roofs. The mixture of architecture in the city is represented most graphically at the intersection of Eighth and Scott Streets. Standing here on opposite corners are a Gothic Presbyterian church, a Baptist church of the Greek Revival order, a Classic Masonic Temple, and a Boys' Club building in the Georgian style.

Capitol Avenue, once called Fifth Street, links Main Street to Broadway, another north-south artery, and continues ten blocks westward to the Capitol. The slight elevation on which the Capitol stands is an outpost of the hills of Pulaski Heights, where terraced lawns, hedges, evergreens, and curved drives typify one of the community's newer residential sections. Higher and cooler than the rest of the city, Pulaski Heights attracts home owners and visitors who like the suburban atmosphere of pine-studded hillsides and ravines. South Broadway, after nearly a dozen blocks of showrooms and garages that give it the name "Automobile Row," becomes a shady boulevard lined by wide lawns and large homes similar to those on the Heights, but older.

Visitors in Little Rock often express delight at the clear, smokeless air (attributable to the use of natural gas instead of coal in factories and homes), and the profusion of hedges, trees, and flowers. Lawn mowing is a year-round activity for those householders who plant their yards in both Bermuda and Italian Rye (winter) grass. In the spring, sidewalks are bordered by violets and yellow jonquils that give way to an incredible variety of plants in summer, when almost any untended fence becomes a honeysuckle jungle. During a few summer weeks, the perfume from flowering magnolias hangs in the air. Fall brings chrysanthemums and colorful blends of leaves on hickory, oak, maple, pecan, persimmon and other species. On many Little Rock lawns are waxy-leafed holly trees covered with clusters of bright red berries in the winter.

Chromium-trimmed store fronts, air-conditioned buildings, and sleek busses give Little Rock its modern metropolitan aspects, but the city still stays fairly close to the earth. Mockingbirds sing in downtown districts on early summer mornings, and nighthawks wheel low over the streets at dusk. The thick foliage serves as a natural calendar to remind residents of the changing seasons, and at least once a year the newspapers tell of some small boy chasing a bewildered country 'possum up a tree on an urban lawn.

The rhythmically flowing arches of the Broadway and Main Street bridges carry pedestrian and vehicular traffic across the Arkansas River to North Little Rock, where large repair shops of the Missouri Pacific serve as a financial backlog for the smaller city. Any layoff of workers in the shops is a matter of community concern, and the "ship-by-rail" movement is enthusiastically supported. Of the three principal streets,

Main is the most solidly commercial. East Third becomes the Memphis Highway, where brilliant streaks of neon light wind away into the night advertising liquor stores, restaurants, tourist cabins, and beer parlors.

Washington Avenue, protected from the river by a recently constructed seawall, is North Little Rock's "Saturday" street. On that day farmers crowd the thoroughfare in such numbers that walking is difficult. After selling their produce in the curb market at Second and Poplar Streets they eat in little "Hot Fish" cafés or inspect the goods in the numerous second-hand stores, where a man can buy anything from a pair of used army shoes to an accordion. Farther to the east on Washington are the Negro honky-tonks whose "beedle-organ" records resound late into the night with the measured thump of blues rhythms and the frenzied trumpets of swing.

Overlooking the city from the north is Park Hill, an eminence developed into a residential district and reached by a winding road. Modern brick or frame houses, some of them commanding a view of the two cities and the river plains to the east, are the homes of workers and businessmen of both Little Rock and North Little Rock.

For the 20,000 Negroes in Little Rock and the more than 6,000 Negroes across the river, the chief sources of employment are the railroad shops, cotton oil mills, cooperage plants, wholesale houses, and the large processing plant for railroad ties east of North Little Rock. Women find work in domestic services and in laundries. Some small businesses are owned by Negroes, and there is a limited professional class of teachers, doctors, lawyers, and dentists. Little Rock has two denominational Negro colleges, Philander Smith College (Methodist) and Arkansas Baptist College, in addition to a Junior College housed in the imposing Paul Laurence Dunbar High School for Negroes. In North Little Rock is Shorter College, supported by the African Methodist Church.

West Ninth Street is Little Rock's Harlem. Negro restaurants, stores, beauty shops, pool and shoeshining parlors, and a motion picture theater give an impression of brisk metropolitanism, borne out by customers with brilliantly polished shoes, wide-bottomed, high-waisted trousers, and slicked hair. As darkness falls and neon lights glare above the sidewalk, West Ninth Street becomes filled with laughter, drawling conversation, and dance music. Gay groups in noisy automobiles "drag town," leaving clouds of exhaust smoke floating in their wake.

Beyond Ninth Street's gaiety lie rows of Negro houses, many of of them bleak shacks of the familiar "shotgun" design. There are more than one hundred Negro churches in the two cities, and Negroes operate two hospitals for members of their race.

Early explorers ascending the Arkansas River found that a moss-grown rock jutting out from the south bank about 150 miles above Arkansas Post marked the transition from a vast, alluvial plain to rough highlands. Bénard de la Harpe on an expedition from New Orleans in 1722 called this first stone outcrop the "Little Rock" in contradistinction to the huge bluff up the river on the north bank. The latter he apparently christened the "French Rock," but it has always been commonly known as the "Big Rock." Long before any permanent settlement grew up around the two rocks they had been landmarks for the Indians. White settlers, when they began moving from the upper Mississippi to the Southwest, found that the Little Rock marked a practicable ford.

A hunter, William Lewis, was perhaps the first white resident near the Little Rock. In July 1812 he built a rough clapboard hut, too low to permit standing erect inside, and scattered a few pumpkin seeds to meet pre-emption claim requirements. Lewis' tract, strategically situated at the crossing of two main avenues of travel, the Arkansas River and the Great Southwest Trail, was potentially valuable; obviously it would be a more logical site for the Arkansas Territorial capital than Arkansas Post. A land speculator from St. Louis, William Russell, bought the claim for $40 in 1819 and by May 1820 had staked out a town site.

Other claimants for the site appeared, among them Stephen F. Austin, of Texas fame, and his brother-in-law, James Bryan. In 1820 Bryan (who had purchased Austin's interest) and William O'Hara of St. Louis laid out a town over the one that had been surveyed shortly before by Russell and his co-claimants; the latter town site was named Arkopolis. Little Rock became the second capital of Arkansas Territory on June 1, 1821, and the same month the Territory's superior court recognized the claim of the Russell faction. The opposing group, determined to prevent its cabins and other improvements from falling into Russell's hands, blew up and burned some of the houses and dragged others off the site. Fearing that the dispute would result in removal of the seat of government to near-by Cadron, the rival land speculators sought a compromise. The disagreement was then amicably settled, and the town authoritatively named Little Rock.

Among the first men who came to the new capital was William E. Woodruff (1795-1885), who in 1819 had carried his printing press by Indian dugout to found the Territory's first newspaper, the *Arkansas Gazette,* at Arkansas Post. Dr. Matthew Cunningham, a graduate of the University of Pennsylvania School of Medicine, was the community's first physician. In 1820 Cunningham "built the second house in Little Rock, a log cabin, a short distance away from the 'little rock,' and in . . . a dense forest with deep shadows."

The dense forest gave way to streets, cultivated fields, and market places, but for some years Little Rock was a boisterous frontier village, slow to yield to tempering forces. An inclination, however, on the part of the citizens to tone down the early roughness is reflected in an ordinance passed February 4, 1826, by the committee of trustees. The regulation prohibited gambling between whites and Negroes, gaming in public taverns, and shooting in the streets on Sunday. The act of the Territorial legislature authorizing election of the trustees did not incorporate the town, but a supplementary measure passed in 1827 twice refers to the town as a "corporation." In 1831 formal chartering occurred, and an act of 1835, broadening the trustees' powers, re-incorporated Little Rock.

Early-day travelers arriving in the remote capital after journeys of hundreds of miles through thinly settled forests apparently could not resist expressing opinions about Little Rock. The comments, either given to interviewers on the spot or later published in diaries or travel books, reflected delight, amusement, or indignation—depending largely on the traveler. Thomas Nuttall, British-born botanist, who visited Edmund Hogan's cabin in 1819, about the time speculators were staking out their conflicting sites, wrote of the neighborhood: "After emerging as it were from so vast a tract of alluvial lands, as that through which I had now been travelling for more than three months, it is almost impossible to describe the pleasure which these romantic prospects again afforded me. Who can be insensible to the beauty of the verdant hill and valley, to the sublimity of the clouded mountain?"

In 1834, however, George Featherstonhaugh, a fellow-countryman of Nuttall's, visited Little Rock, and later wrote dourly in his *Excursion through the Slave States* (1844): "This territory of Arkansas was on the confines of the United States and of Mexico, and, as I had long known, was the occasional residence of many timid and nervous persons, against whom the laws of these respective countries had a grudge. *Gentlemen,* who had taken the liberty to imitate the signatures of other persons; *bankrupts,* who were not disposed to be plundered by their creditors . . . all admired Arkansas on account of the very gentle and tolerant state of public opinion which prevailed there." Not content with disapproving, Featherstonhaugh fell into the error of prophecy: "The town of Little Rock is surrounded by extremely poor land, and from a variety of concurring causes can never be very populous." But he conceded that "in virtue of it being the seat of government, it may in time become a respectable small town, have good seminaries of education for the youth of the territory and afford agreeable society."

The same year that Featherstonhaugh visited Little Rock the *Gazette* reported: "Among the distinguished characters who have honored our City with their presence, within the last week, was no less a personage than Colonel David Crockett—better known as Davy Crockett—the raal critter himself—who arrived on Thursday evening last, with some 6 or 8 followers, from the Western District of Tennessee, on their way to Texas, to join the patriots of that country in freeing it from the shackles of the Mexican Government."

Citizens staged a shooting match to celebrate the visit of the famous scout, gave him a banquet of fat bear-cub meat, venison, and wild turkey. Urged to stay and hunt bear, Crockett declined, but said: "If I could rest anywhere it would be in Arkansaw, where the men are of the real half-horse, half-alligator breed such as grow nowhere else on the face of the universal earth but just around the backbone of North America." In frontier fashion, his hosts insisted on lending him a horse, and a party accompanied him for the next 50 miles of his journey.

In the 1830's and 1840's great tracts of bottomland up and down the river from Little Rock began to bloom in cotton. There was little emphasis on industrial development, since cotton culture absorbed most of the available capital and labor. The town grew slowly, the census of 1850 listing a population of only 2,167. The scene of greatest activity was the wharf at the foot of Commerce Street, where southbound steamboats piled high with cotton bales cast loose to make room for boats from New Orleans loaded with clothing, tools, and great hogsheads of molasses.

The visit of the steamboat *Eagle* on March 16, 1822, had signaled the beginning of steamboat traffic on the upper Arkansas. The ensuing years saw a parade of shallow-draft paddle-wheelers bearing such names as *Reindeer, Cinderella, Trident, Industry, Revenue, Spy,* and *Siam.*

The first steam ferry between Little Rock and the opposite shore went into service in June 1838. A passenger wrote admiringly of its "comfortable cabin for passengers, officers' room, kitchen, etc. with ample gangways (forward and on each side of the boilers) sufficient for two of the largest wagons and teams, 3 or 4 smaller carriages, 20 or 30 head of horses or cattle, with sufficient other room for more than 200 foot passengers."

Arkansas seceded from the Union in 1861, despite some opposition from mountainous northern counties. Two years later General Frederick Steele and a Federal army advanced upon Little Rock from the east. General Sterling Price, commanding outnumbered Confederate troops, set fire to eight steamboats to prevent them from falling into the enemy's hands and retreated to Arkadelphia. The capital had already been moved to Washington, in Hempstead County. Little Rock became headquarters for the Northern invaders.

An eyewitness named Dickison Brugman, describing the entry of the city's captors, said, "The Federal troops were well received in Little Rock after the first contacts were made, and the occupation throughout was marked by orderliness and courtesy on both sides. Many of the Federal soldiers remained in Arkansas after the war."

The post-war reconstruction that crippled Little Rock along with the rest of the South culminated in 1874 in violent disorders called the Brooks-Baxter War (*see Government; History; Tour 13*).

War and upheavals past, Little Rock began the development of its commerce and industry. A population which had numbered 3,727 in 1860 grew to more than 12,000 in 1870. By 1876 there were mule-drawn cars, supplemented 12 years later by electric trolleys. Telephones made their appearance in the city in 1879, a waterworks system was installed in 1884, and four years later electric street lights began to replace the hand-lighted gas lamps.

The 1880's saw a great expansion of railroads in the State, and with the railroads came another upsurge in the city's population—from 13,138 inhabitants in 1880 to 25,874 ten years later. Little Rock's first locomotive had nosed up to the north bank of the Arkansas River in 1862, but construction was nearly at a standstill during the war and Reconstruction periods.

By 1890 there were more than 2,000 miles of steel tracks in the State, compared to about 800 miles in 1880, and 38½ miles in 1859. With the railroads came sawmills; and Arkansas' annual lumber production rose from 173,000,000 board feet to 526,000,000 board feet in a decade.

Extensive development of Pulaski Heights began in the 1890's. People rode out on open "summer" trolleys to Forest Park on the western edge of the new development, the motorman clanging his bell steadily on the long hills and treating the passengers to daring bursts of speed. Forest Park Theater offered concerts and plays in the summer; on one occasion Sarah Bernhardt appeared in *Camille.* The park's popularity began to decline after the World War, when automobiles placed other recreation areas and distant mountains and lakes within reach. The tract is now (1941) being transformed into a residential section.

Automobiles had appeared in Little Rock at about the same time that the gleam of Forest Park's colored lights first filtered through the trees of Pulaski Heights. There were 3 of the noisy vehicles in town in 1902, and a year later the number had jumped to 15. In 1914 there were nearly 5,000 automobiles in Arkansas. The capital's Motor Club begged defiant pedestrians, for their own safety, to drop their "hit-me-if-you-dare" attitude.

The World War ushered in days of unprecedented activity for Little Rock and North Little Rock. Businessmen of both cities organized the Army Post Development Company, bought or leased 13,000 acres of land north of the river, and offered the tract to the Government for an army cantonment. The War Department accepted the site June 11, 1917, allotting $3,500,000 for buildings, roads, and waterworks. During the summer of 1917 carpenters and masons put up barracks, kitchens, and storehouses for Camp Pike almost overnight. The soldiers came, thousands of them, and at times the camp's population exceeded that of Little Rock and North Little Rock combined. Both cities were filled to capacity by relatives of soldiers and by workers in the new jobs. Abandonment of the reservation was ordered in 1921 but it continued to serve as a Citizens' Military Training Camp, training grounds for the Arkansas National Guard, and annual encampment site for farm organizations. Camp Pike, renamed Camp Robinson, took on a semblance of its wartime look in 1940, as workmen erected quarters for 25,000 young men training under the national defense program.

In the 1920's Little Rock experienced a building boom of considerable proportions. The branch Federal Reserve Bank Building and the Albert Pike Memorial Temple, both built in 1924, were followed by the Donaghey Building (1926), highest structure in the city; three tall hotels—the Ben McGehee, Albert Pike, and LaFayette; the Worthen Bank and Union Trust Buildings; the Insurance, Wallace, and other office structures; the new Little Rock High School, the Paul Laurence Dunbar High School for Negroes, and the North Little Rock High School.

The tide began to recede in 1929, leaving Little Rock with an almost entirely new profile. Major construction projects during the 1930's included the Federal Building in Little Rock, the North Little Rock Post Office, and the Joseph Taylor Robinson Memorial Auditorium, all built wholly or partly with Federal funds.

Today, Little Rock divides its interests among industry, commerce, and government. With North Little Rock it has about 125 manufacturing plants, including railroad repair shops, cottonseed-oil, cooperage, furniture, garment, and printing plants, feed mills, foundries, mattress, and paper-box factories. Manufactured products reach an average annual value of more than $20,000,000. As the governmental seat of Arkansas, Little Rock is the headquarters for State departments and various Federal agencies working in Arkansas, including the U. S. Army Corps of Engineers.

North Little Rock prides itself on its balanced municipal budgets and shrewd financing, and makes easy-going comments on the larger city's spottier financial history. Indicative of the rivalry that has long existed between the two cities facing each other across the Arkansas was the platform plank adopted by a North Little Rock candidate for alderman. Cheerily he proposed that, as a flood-control measure, the river be widened seven miles on the south side. Aside from banter, however, and an occasional near-fracas at the annual football game between the cities' high schools, the rivalry has few manifestations.

In 1839, one year after the steam ferry began crossing the river at Little Rock, a United States Army officer laid out a town on the north side and named it De Cantillon after himself. His venture was unsuccessful, probably because a cypress bog covered a large part of the town site. Game continued to roam the tangled forests on the north bank, but the patch came to be known as Huntersville, and was slowly settled. Stagecoach lines operating from Fort Smith on the west and DeValls Bluff on the east met at Huntersville, whence passengers were ferried to and from Little Rock.

A Frenchman built a hotel at the ferry landing, and, apparently inspired by the sinking of a shaft intended to yield silver northeast of the town, called it the "Hotel Argenta." The name passed on to the settlement that took form around the inn. During the Reconstruction regime steamboat roustabouts and freed slaves gained for the village an unenviable notoriety.

Argenta was incorporated as a town in 1871, and the next year the Cairo & Fulton Railroad established its north-shore terminal. For a short time trains were ferried across the river. An English banker, Alexander Baring, then invested $300,000 in a railroad and vehicular bridge. Baring Cross Bridge, built in 1873, stood until 1927, when it was destroyed by a flood; it was replaced by a new structure in 1929.

Railroad shops were built near the bridgehead on the north side, and around them grew the village of Baring Cross, later joined to Argenta. In 1890 Little Rock annexed that part of Argenta between Clendenin Hill, the slight rise at Thirteenth and Main Streets, and the river, designating this section as the Eighth Ward. The move aroused resentment among Argenta citizens, who had been pushing plans for a high school and found that they would now have to reincorporate what was left of the town in order to raise funds for the new building. Reincorporation accomplished, the taxpayers built the school and began devising means of regaining their lost ward. This they did by causing to be introduced into the legislature a bill relating to districts lying between incorporated cities, and apparently affecting only the twin towns of Walnut Ridge and Hoxie in northern Arkansas. In 1903 North Little Rock, as south side realtors called the Eighth Ward, was voted back into Argenta. The name of the city was officially changed to North Little Rock in 1917 by the town council, and "Argenta" is seldom heard except when the capital city is jokingly called "South Argenta."

Recently the prime event of the year in North Little Rock has been the fall stock show and rodeo conducted by the Arkansas Livestock Show Association. The 1941 Arkansas general assembly appropriated $25,000 to be awarded as prizes for Arkansas-produced stock exhibited in the 1941 and 1942 shows.

LITTLE ROCK POINTS OF INTEREST

1. The PUBLIC LIBRARY (*open 9-9 weekdays, 2-6 Sun.; closed Sun. in summer*), 700 Louisiana St., built with Carnegie funds in 1910, has the restrained classic façade favored by Carnegie architects. The library is maintained by the city, though individuals assist in keeping its shelves well stocked with current fiction and non-fiction. In the north wing is the U. M. Rose Room containing 7,000 volumes, mostly French works, donated by a noted Little Rock jurist. Arkansiana is in the Charles H. Brough Room, named for a former Arkansas Governor whose gifts were the basis of the present collection. At the rear of the original building is a three-story annex completed in 1939.

2. ST. ANDREW'S CATHEDRAL (Roman Catholic), 7th and Louisiana Sts., was probably the first large building in Arkansas to be constructed of the granite-like syenite that is quarried near Little Rock. The structure is of English Gothic style, its vertical aspect emphasized by an octagonal steeple and buttresses that terminate in pinnacles. Completed in 1882, the cathedral succeeded a frame building at 2nd and Center which since 1845 had been the seat of the Arkansas diocese. The history of the Roman Catholic church in Little Rock, however, dates back to 1830, when Father Donnelly said the first Mass in a temporary chapel over a store at 2nd and Main Sts.

3. The WAR MEMORIAL BUILDING (*open 8-5 weekdays*), Markham St. facing Center St., for three-quarters of a century the

State Capitol, is generally considered the most beautiful building in Arkansas and one of the best examples of Greek Revival architecture in the South. Across a wide green lawn a walk, which divides at a chalice-like fountain, leads up to the façade—four massive Doric columns supporting a pediment. Two wings are linked to the central part of the building by galleries faced with railings of wrought iron. With its walls of thick handmade brick, plastered over and painted a creamy white, the edifice achieves an effect of rare serenity and charm. Framing the building against the blue sky and the Arkansas River, at its back, are magnolias with dark-hued trunks, evergreens, and tall elms.

Plans for the Capitol were drawn in Kentucky by Gideon Shryock (sometimes spelled Shyrock), who had previously designed the Kentucky Statehouse. Construction began in 1833 and was pushed forward by Territorial Governor John Pope. Though the building was still uncompleted in 1836, the general assembly of the newly created State met within its walls during that year. In 1885 the central portion was remodeled and the wings completed. After 1910 the legislature occupied chambers in the new Capitol, a mile to the southwest, and in the next 5 years most of the State offices were transferred from the old building, a part of which was then used for about 20 years by the University of Arkansas' School of Medicine. Renamed the War Memorial Building by an act of the 1921 legislature, the structure was repaired in 1935 and has since served as headquarters for several war veterans' organizations and for agencies of the Federal and State Governments.

On the lawn stands LADY BAXTER, a bulky iron cannon brought by the Confederates from New Orleans in 1861 for the defense of Little Rock, but still unused when Federals took the city two years later. During the Brooks-Baxter "war" of 1874, partisans of Governor Elisha Baxter repaired the gun and mounted it on the riverbank. The piece was never fired, however, until a blank charge was set off at the close of the "war" to celebrate Baxter's victory.

4. The OLD POST OFFICE BUILDING (*open 9-5 weekdays*), 2nd St. between Center and Spring Sts., was built in 1881 in the heavy style popular at the time. The rough-hewn blocks of the first story rise from a base of red mottled granite, and square chimneys thrusting upward add to the impression of weight. Postal offices were moved in 1932-33 to a new Federal building, and the structure now (1941) is the State headquarters of the Work Projects Administration.

5. In the PULASKI COUNTY COURTHOUSE (*open 9-5 weekdays*), SW. corner Markham and Spring Sts., are the offices and courts of the county named for Count Casimir Pulaski, Polish soldier who fought for the United States during the Revolution. The building, four stories of Bedford stone in an Italian Renaissance design of balustrades and arches, has an elaborate rotunda ornamented with marble pillars and gilded entablatures. A small park, running west to Broadway, is planted with shrubs and flowers.

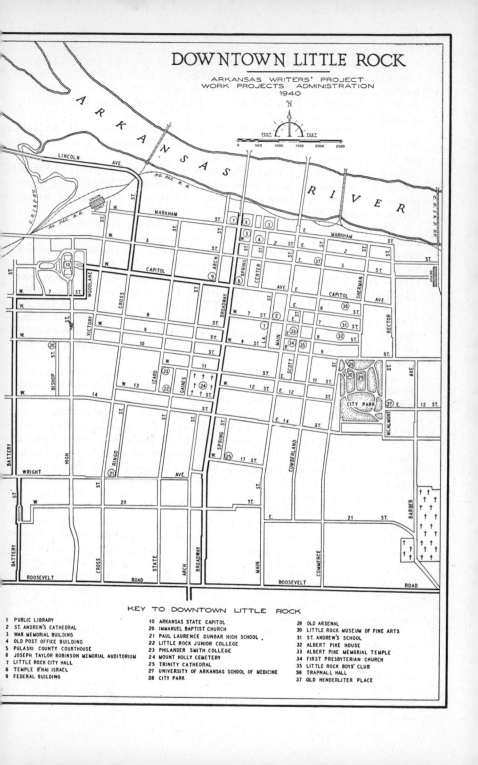

DOWNTOWN LITTLE ROCK

ARKANSAS WRITERS' PROJECT
WORK PROJECTS ADMINISTRATION
1940

KEY TO DOWNTOWN LITTLE ROCK

1 PUBLIC LIBRARY
2 ST. ANDREW'S CATHEDRAL
3 WAR MEMORIAL BUILDING
4 OLD POST OFFICE BUILDING
5 PULASKI COUNTY COURTHOUSE
6 JOSEPH TAYLOR ROBINSON MEMORIAL AUDITORIUM
7 LITTLE ROCK CITY HALL
8 TEMPLE B'NAI ISRAEL
9 FEDERAL BUILDING

10 ARKANSAS STATE CAPITOL
20 IMMANUEL BAPTIST CHURCH
21 PAUL LAURENCE DUNBAR HIGH SCHOOL
22 LITTLE ROCK JUNIOR COLLEGE
23 PHILANDER SMITH COLLEGE
24 MOUNT HOLLY CEMETERY
25 TRINITY CATHEDRAL
27 UNIVERSITY OF ARKANSAS SCHOOL OF MEDICINE
28 CITY PARK

29 OLD ARSENAL
30 LITTLE ROCK MUSEUM OF FINE ARTS
31 ST. ANDREW'S SCHOOL
32 ALBERT PIKE HOUSE
33 ALBERT PIKE MEMORIAL TEMPLE
34 FIRST PRESBYTERIAN CHURCH
35 LITTLE ROCK BOYS' CLUB
36 TRAPNALL HALL
37 OLD HENDERLITER PLACE

Adjoining the structure to the south is the OLD PULASKI COUNTY COURTHOUSE (*open 9-5 weekdays*), built in 1887 and looking like a medieval castle, with red-trimmed stone watchtowers and a moat-like walkway opening into the basement. The old courthouse, like the new, is used for county offices.

6. The JOSEPH TAYLOR ROBINSON MEMORIAL AUDITORIUM, NE. corner Markham St. and Broadway, was designed for the community's largest public gatherings. Its high walls of buff-colored brick enclose a convention hall, a lecture hall, and committee rooms, as well as the main 3,000-seat music hall. The building, completed in 1940, is named for former Governor and United States Senator Joseph Taylor ("Joe T.") Robinson (1872-1937).

Three of the walls rise sheer and windowless, their blankness relieved only by patterned brickwork and recesses decorated with Greek masks. Fronting on Markham Street is the main entrance, approached by a flight of stone steps and guarded by six heavy columns. The interior of the music hall is characterized by long curving lines, the elliptical sweep of a balcony, and molded vertical lines on the walls.

7. The LITTLE ROCK CITY HALL (*open 8-5 weekdays*), NW. corner Markham St. and Broadway, carries a red-tile dome above three stories of buff-colored brick. At the southeast corner of the City Hall lawn is a fragment of the "little rock" for which the city was named.

8. TEMPLE B'NAI ISRAEL, NE. corner Capitol Ave. and Broadway, is the meeting place of Little Rock's Reformed Jewish congregation. The yellow-brick building, put up in 1896, is topped by a cupola over the auditorium dome; a minaret rises at the corner.

9. The FEDERAL BUILDING (*open 8-5 weekdays*), W. Capitol Ave. and Arch St., is occupied by the Little Rock Post Office, Federal courtrooms, and various United States Government agencies. The block-long structure, five stories high, is built of Arkansas gray limestone on a granite base. Vertical facings between banks of windows extend from the second story to the cornices, adding an impression of height.

10. The ARKANSAS STATE CAPITOL (*open 8-5 weekdays; guides*), Wood Lane facing Capitol Ave., set on a knoll and framed by wide landscaped grounds, was designed by Cass Gilbert in a mode characteristic of this architect of capitols. Long wings extend north and south from a Classic portico which is repeated as a design across the entire façade. The tall dome which rises from the center of the building is encircled by Ionic columns and capped by a minaret with similar columns. At night floodlights throw the gray limestone walls into striking relief against the dark valley to the west.

The main doorway opens almost directly into the rotunda, finished in marble from the floor to the lower edge of the dome. At the end of the north wing is the Governor's reception room, a large wood-paneled chamber lined with portraits of former chief executives. The south wing contains the supreme court and its library of 40,000 volumes. Two marble stairways lead from the rotunda to the chambers of the senate and the house of representatives. On the third floor is the ARKANSAS STATE HISTORY MUSEUM, displaying aboriginal pottery, relics of pioneer times, portraits, and battle flags. The archives of the Arkansas History Commission are in the basement. Excavation for the foundations of the building began in 1899, but construction lagged for a decade. In 1909 George W. Donaghey became Governor partly because of his promise to complete the Capitol, and Cass Gilbert was engaged as architect. By 1911 the general assembly was able to hold its sessions in the new structure, and five years later the work was completed.

11. SQUATTERS' ISLAND, along railroad tracks between the Lincoln Ave. viaduct and the Arkansas River, is not actually an island, but a stretch of river-edge land which has been taken over by about a dozen homeless families. The inhabitants have thrown together shacks of scrap lumber and tar paper. Tomatoes, okra, and peppers thrive in the alluvial soil. Pumpkin vines dangle over the bank and jackbeans cover the sides of the cabins. When the river climbs toward the cabins, about once every three years, the squatters anchor their shacks to the giant cottonwoods, load their household goods into rowboats, and row to higher ground. When the flood recedes they shovel the mud off their floors and replant their drowned gardens.

12. The ARKANSAS SCHOOL FOR THE DEAF (*open 8:30-4:30 schooldays Sept.-June*), Markham St. and Park Ave., commands a broad view of the Arkansas River and Big Rock on the north side. The brush-covered bluff on which the school stands was noted for its turkey shooting in 1868, when the State received the site as a donation and began to educate deaf-mutes. The plant now consists of a number of red-brick buildings, among them Parnell Hall, an auditorium occasionally used by Little Rock groups for meetings and lectures. Negro children are housed and educated in Jenkins Hall, erected in 1931.

13. The ARKANSAS SCHOOL FOR THE BLIND (*open 8-4 schooldays Sept.-June*), 2600 W. Markham St., adjoining the School for the Deaf, occupies three red-brick buildings connected by passageways. In a fourth building is the hospital. The school includes an auditorium, a music hall, and a Braille library of more than 5,000 books. Vocational instructors give training in sewing, weaving, woodwork, and other crafts.

State education for the blind began in 1859 at Arkadelphia, and in 1868 the school was transferred to a building at 18th and Center Streets in Little Rock. The institution moved to its present buildings in 1939.

14. The LITTLE ROCK WATER FILTRATION PLANT (*open 24 hours daily*), E. end of Ozark St., built of reinforced concrete, might be mistaken for a modern apartment house on a high terrace, were it not for long stretches of windowless walls. Behind the plant are mixing pools where nine-foot paddle wheels slowly churn chemicals into the water. Inside the building the water passes through

gravity filters and enters the mains. Short-wave radio communication is maintained between the crew at the filtration plant and the reservoir superintendent at Lake Winona (*see Tour 13*) in the deep woods 45 miles west.

15. ST. MARY'S ACADEMY (*open 8-4 schooldays Sept.-June*), 3224 Kavanaugh Blvd., a Roman Catholic school for girls of kindergarten through high school age, is conducted by the Sisters of Mercy. The five-story main building, designed in a Gothic pattern of red brick, was erected in 1908 and enlarged by an annex in 1924.

16. ST. JOHN'S SEMINARY (*open 8-4 schooldays Sept.-June*), foot of N. Tyler St., a training school for the Roman Catholic priesthood, comprises three principal buildings grouped around a maple-fringed oval. The plant was built in 1916 for Little Rock College, no longer in existence, and has been occupied by the seminary since 1930. Students live under a modified monastic rule, being forbidden, among other things, to read secular newspapers or attend motion picture shows except during summer vacations.

17. FAIR PARK, W. Markham and Van Buren Sts., the largest park within the city limits of Little Rock, covers 200 acres. Here the State Fair was usually held until its discontinuance in 1930. The MUNICIPAL ZOO (*open 7-6:30 summer months, 7-5 winter months*), at the south end of the tract, has a notable new "monkey house" with bold pylons at the entrance. The "cat house" is also a favorite of visitors. Zoo officials have had unusual success in breeding tigers, and regularly trade young Bengals to other zoological gardens. At the southeast corner of the park is TRAVELERS' FIELD, where Little Rock baseball fans watch their Southern League team, the Travelers, play under floodlights at night, and in the sunshine on weekend afternoons.

18. The STATE HOSPITAL FOR NERVOUS DISEASES (*open 8-11 a.m., 1-5 p.m.*), W. Markham and Elm Sts., is a group of 18 white buildings set on a hilltop. The institution spreads over 160 acres and cares for 2,500 patients. Holly trees flank the entrance to the four-story administration building, built in 1882. Convalescent and mild chronic cases are sent to the hospital's Benton unit (*see Tour 1b*).

19. LITTLE ROCK SENIOR HIGH SCHOOL (*open 9-4 schooldays Sept.-June*), 14th St. and Park Ave., is attended by 2,500 students from all over the city. The school, completed in 1927, attracts the admiration of visitors because of the graceful crescent of its façade and the rich landscaping of its grounds. The wings mount story by story until they culminate in a five-floor central tower. West of the school is a 15,000-seat stadium with a floodlighted athletic field.

20. IMMANUEL BAPTIST CHURCH, 1000 Bishop St., completed in 1929, is a massive T-shaped buff-brick building. Six large stained glass windows designed by European craftsmen ornament the main auditorium.

21. When the PAUL LAURENCE DUNBAR HIGH SCHOOL (*open 9-4 schooldays Sept.-June*), Wright Ave. and Ringo St., was

dedicated in 1930, it was called "the dream of the colored people of Little Rock come true . . . far beyond in beauty, and modernity, and size what the boldest had ever hoped for." This three-story red-brick institution for Negro students includes a junior high school and Dunbar Junior College, as well as the senior high school.

22. LITTLE ROCK JUNIOR COLLEGE (*open 9-4 schooldays*), 13th and State Sts., supported in part by tuition fees, receives grants from the Donaghey Foundation. The income of the foundation is derived from several downtown office buildings. Founded in 1927, the junior college moved into its present quarters, a remodeled grammar school, in 1930. The 400 students receive two years of training in arts and sciences and in pre-professional subjects.

23. PHILANDER SMITH COLLEGE (*open 9-4 schooldays*), 11th and Izard Sts., with about 350 students, is the largest Negro college in Little Rock. A Methodist institution, it was founded in 1877 as Walden Seminary. The present name dates to 1883, when the widow of Philander Smith, of Oak Park, Illinois, gave a large donation to the school.

24. MOUNT HOLLY CEMETERY, entrance Broadway and 12th St., is crowded with ponderous headstones and tall marble shafts on which are chiseled many of the best-known names in Arkansas history. Here are the graves of the missionary Cephas Washburn and his son Edward Payson, painter of *The Arkansas Traveler;* William Woodruff; Fay Hempstead; Augustus Garland, and a host of other notables.

One of the most frequently visited graves is that of David Owen Dodd (1846-64), a youth hanged as a spy by Federal forces in Little Rock on January 8, 1864. Dodd was captured in the woods near the McHenry House (*see Tour 2b*) by General Frederick Steele's soldiers.

25. TRINITY CATHEDRAL, NE. corner 17th and Spring Sts., is the diocesan seat of the Episcopal Church in Arkansas. The faded brick building, erected 1884-88, is Gothic in style, with a steep shingle roof.

26. ADAMS FIELD, 14th St. and Harrington Ave., is Little Rock's municipal airport. Here transcontinental planes of American Airlines make daily scheduled landings. Private planes and those of the National Guard also use the port's hangars. The original field of 40.5 acres, made a supply depot for the Army Air Corps in 1917, was enlarged and turned into a National Guard airport in 1926. Subsequently, the field was taken over by the city, further increased in size, and equipped with hangars and runways. In 1940, it covered 231 acres, and plans had been made for the acquisition of additional land.

27. The UNIVERSITY OF ARKANSAS SCHOOL OF MEDICINE (*open 8-4 schooldays*), 12th and McAlmont Sts., was established in 1879 at Little Rock, rather than at Fayetteville, because of the capital's facilities, doctors, and clinical opportunities. In 1935, the School of Medicine moved into the present new six-story brick

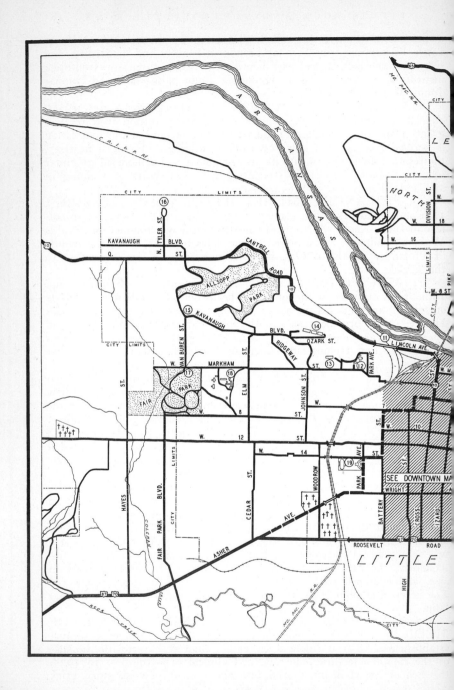

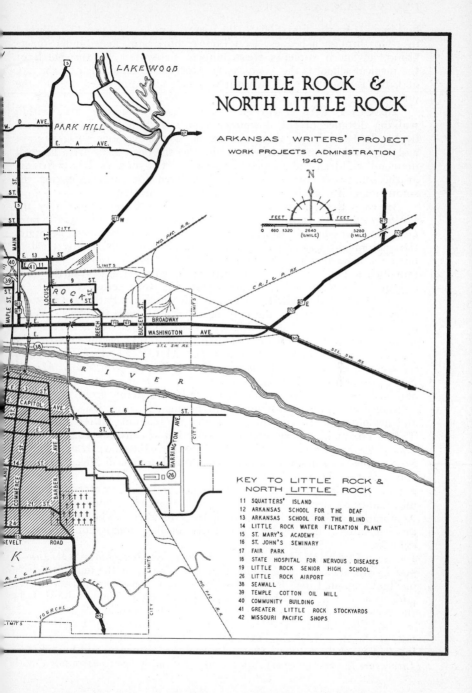

LITTLE ROCK &
NORTH LITTLE ROCK

ARKANSAS WRITERS' PROJECT
WORK PROJECTS ADMINISTRATION
1940

N

FEET   FEET
0   660   1320   2640   5280
(½ MILE)   (1 MILE)

LAKEWOOD

PARK HILL

KEY TO LITTLE ROCK &
NORTH LITTLE ROCK

11   SQUATTERS' ISLAND
12   ARKANSAS SCHOOL FOR THE DEAF
13   ARKANSAS SCHOOL FOR THE BLIND
14   LITTLE ROCK WATER FILTRATION PLANT
15   ST. MARY'S ACADEMY
16   ST. JOHN'S SEMINARY
17   FAIR PARK
18   STATE HOSPITAL FOR NERVOUS DISEASES
19   LITTLE ROCK SENIOR HIGH SCHOOL
26   LITTLE ROCK AIRPORT
38   SEAWALL
39   TEMPLE COTTON OIL MILL
40   COMMUNITY BUILDING
41   GREATER LITTLE ROCK STOCKYARDS
42   MISSOURI PACIFIC SHOPS

building. On the first floor is the ISAAC FOLSOM CLINIC, established in 1892 through a bequest by a Lonoke physician; here, under supervision, advanced students treat indigent patients. To the north of the medical school is the UNIVERSITY HOSPITAL, maintained by the city of Little Rock until 1939, when it was expanded and taken over by the university.

28. CITY PARK, entrance E. 9th and Commerce Sts., within walking distance of the downtown and East Side districts, is visited by hundreds of Little Rock citizens on warm evenings. Oaks, elms, and maples shade most of the 36 acres. In the open areas are a baseball diamond, children's playgrounds, tennis courts. FOSTER BAND SHELL, at the southwest corner of the park, is used for concerts during the summer and for political speeches preceding elections.

In 1836 the land now occupied by City Park was acquired by the United States Government for a military post, and two years later an arsenal was built. At the outbreak of the War between the States the cantonment was seized by Confederate forces, who vainly tried to burn the arsenal when they evacuated the capital in 1863. The tract remained a Federal army post until 1893, when it was traded to the city of Little Rock for 1,000 acres atop Big Rock across the river.

29. The OLD ARSENAL, N. side of City Park, a two-story white-brick structure, is the only post building now standing. Work of restoring the arsenal, which will shelter the city-owned Arkansas Museum of Natural History and Antiquities, was begun in 1940.

30. The LITTLE ROCK MUSEUM OF FINE ARTS (open winter 10-4 daily, 2-4 Sun.; summer 10-5 daily, 2-5 Sun.; closed Mon.), NW. corner of City Park, was built in 1937 at a cost of $70,000, obtained through private donations and a Federal grant. Here is assembled the State's most important permanent collection of paintings and art objects. In the foyer is a bust of Joaquin Miller by Lorado Taft. The main gallery displays a collection of canvases which includes The Adoration of the Shepherds by Francesco Bassano; Martyrdom of St. Stephen, an Italian primitive tempera by Lorenzo di Niccolo Gerini; and a portrait by Samuel F. B. Morse of James I. Miller, first Governor of Arkansas Territory. In the wings are prints, water colors, and miscellaneous pieces; in the print collection are signed etchings by Rembrandt, Whistler, Pennell, and Howard Pyle. The upper floor is divided into a lecture hall and three display rooms for temporary exhibits.

31. ST. ANDREW'S SCHOOL (open 8-4 schooldays Sept.-June), 502 E. 7th St., built as a residence in 1840, is one of the most attractive old buildings in Little Rock. The brick walls have been plastered over and painted white, without loss of the Georgian lines. Since 1924 the house has been used as a Roman Catholic parochial school.

32. The ALBERT PIKE HOUSE (private), 411 E. 7th St., is one of the most imposing ante bellum residences in the city. Erected in 1840 for Albert Pike (1809-91), explorer, attorney, and author (see Literature), the two-story brick house has long been surrounded with

Agriculture

WAGONLOADS OF COTTON WAITING AT THE GIN, LEHI

PLANTATION HANDS

Rothstein: F. S. A.

PLANTATION STORE, PLUM BAYOU

OZARK COUPLE

SHEEP GRAZING

HERD OF MULES

HAYSTACK

CORN IN SHOCKS

Extension Service, University of Arkansas

SPRAYING APPLE TREES IN NORTHWEST ARKANSAS

GRINDING CANE FOR SORGHUM MOLASSES

Arkansas State Publicity Dept.

THRESHING RICE, STUTTGART

RAKING SOYBEAN HAY

JUDGING AT A CATTLE SHOW, NORTH LITTLE ROCK

AT THE STOCKYARDS

trees and shrubs that give the grounds the appearance of a park. A brick walk leads from the street to the portico, where six great pillars are topped with a pediment broken by dormers. In this dwelling, now occupied by Congressman D. D. Terry, was reared John Gould Fletcher, imagist poet; his reminiscent poem, "The Ghosts of an Old House," concerns his memories of the place.

33. The ALBERT PIKE MEMORIAL TEMPLE (*private*), Scott St. between 7th and 8th Sts., is the headquarters of the Masonic Grand Lodge of Arkansas. The façade, a block-long row of 19 Ionic columns, is the building's most impressive feature. Pike's studies and writings made him an authority on Masonic law and symbolism. The temple named for him was completed in 1924.

34. The FIRST PRESBYTERIAN CHURCH, SW. corner 8th and Scott Sts., is the meeting place of a congregation organized in 1828. The present edifice, put up in 1920, is a brick Gothic structure with truncated spires flanking a deeply recessed window over the entrance.

35. In the LITTLE ROCK BOYS' CLUB (*open 9-9 weekdays*), SE. corner 8th and Scott Sts., young people have for their own use a swimming pool, an auditorium, and a gymnasium. The enrollment of nearly 5,000 includes more than 1,000 girls. Membership fees are graduated according to age, the highest being $1.80 a year. The building, completed in 1931, has a Georgian entrance and fanlight, with square white dormers and green shutters.

36. TRAPNALL HALL (*open 9-5 Thurs.*), 423 E. Capitol Ave., is another of Little Rock's well-preserved ante bellum houses. The walls are of red brick and the roof is green, matching the vine-hung shutters. Four slender columns give entrance to the main portico, the design of which is repeated twice in small porticoes at extensions on the east. The interior is built around a wide central hall with a marble-faced fireplace. Erected by Frederick W. Trapnall in 1843, the house is now the property of the Little Rock Junior League.

37. The OLD HENDERLITER PLACE, 3rd and Cumberland Sts., was built, says Judge William F. Pope in *Early Days in Arkansas* (1895) "by one Jesse Henderliter, a German, who kept a small grocery store in the west end of the building, occupying the balance as a family residence. The property afterwards . . . gained notoriety as having been the place of meeting of the last Territorial Legislature, in October, 1835." The original logs were boarded over in later years, and the place, once a quasi-State Capitol, in 1939 had become a rooming house. In that year State and Federal Governments collaborated to restore the structure and several adjacent small buildings in a half-block area.

NORTH LITTLE ROCK POINTS OF INTEREST

38. The SEAWALL, along the Arkansas River, was built in 1936 under supervision of the U. S. Engineers to protect North Little Rock from high water that had on several occasions flooded parts of the

town.   Nearly two thirds of the three-mile wall consists of earth levees, wide at the bottom and narrowing upwards; the remainder is of concrete.   The wall may be advantageously observed from the Main Street bridge.

39. The TEMPLE COTTON OIL MILL (*open 8-4 workdays*), 9th and Maple Sts., which opened in 1880, marked the beginning of an industry of importance to North Little Rock.   The city now (1941) has several other such establishments.   During the milling season (September to May or June) the plant crushes cottonseed and manufactures a variety of products, of which the most important are cottonseed oil, cake, and meal.

40. The COMMUNITY BUILDING (*open 9-9 weekdays*), 13th and Main Sts., is the home of the North Little Rock Boys' Club. Established by a newspaper publisher in 1920 to give his route carriers a place for leisure-time activities, the club by 1940 had grown into a municipally sponsored organization with a membership of 1,500 boys and 500 girls.   The building contains a gymnasium, game and athletic rooms, and a library.   Special departments give instruction in woodworking, art, photography, printing, and dramatics.   West of the building is an OPEN-AIR SWIMMING POOL (*open 1-9 weekdays in summer; 10¢ and 20¢*).

41. The GREATER LITTLE ROCK STOCKYARDS (*open 9-3 weekdays*), 200 E. 11th St., opened in 1938, handle feeder cattle for sale to farmers, and fattened stock for shipment to packing plants.

42. The MISSOURI PACIFIC SHOPS (*open on application to superintendent*), 8th St. and Pike Ave., form North Little Rock's most important industry, employing about 1,140 men with an average monthly pay roll of $153,350.   The present (1941) establishment, which includes 36 major shops on 160 acres of land, has grown from a roundhouse built by the Cairo & Fulton Railroad in 1874.

POINTS OF INTEREST IN ENVIRONS

Lakewood, 5.6 *m.;* State Forest Nursery, 15.6 *m.;* State Fish Hatchery, 22.9 *m.;* Toltec Mounds, 27 *m.* (*see Tour 2a*).   Boyle Park, 5.7 *m.;* McHenry House (*adm. 25¢*), 8.7 *m.;* Bauxite, 22.9 *m.* (*see Tour 2b*).   U. S. Veterans Administration Facility (Fort Roots), 5.1 *m.;* Camp Joe T. Robinson, 6.5 *m.* (*see Tour 5a*).   Negro Boys' Industrial School, 13.4 *m.* (*see Tour 5b*).   Pinnacle Mountain, 17 *m.;* Lake Winona, 44.5 *m.* (*see Tour 13*).

Pine Bluff

Railroad Stations: Union Station, 4th Ave. between State and Alabama Sts., for Missouri Pacific R.R. and St. Louis Southwestern (Cotton Belt) Ry.
Bus Stations: Union Bus Terminal, 4th Ave. and Chestnut St., for Missouri Pacific Trailways, Interurban Transportation Co., Tri-State Trailways, Dean's Bus Lines, and Southwestern Greyhound Lines.
Airport: Toney Field, 3.1 m. N. on US 79; no scheduled service.
Taxis: Rates 15¢ for one person, additional persons 10¢, within city limits.
Busses: Fare 5¢, 15-min. service.
Traffic Regulations: One-hour parking limit in downtown section from 7 a.m. to 6 p.m. except Sundays and holidays. No all-night parking; no U-turns on Main St. between courthouse and 6th Ave.

Information Service: Chamber of Commerce, 122 Main St.; Arkansas Automobile Club, Hotel Pines.

Accommodations: Two hotels; tourist homes, tourist camps.

Radio Station: KOTN (1490 kc.).
Theaters and Motion Picture Houses: High School Auditorium, 10th Ave. and Laurel St., Library Auditorium, 5th Ave. and Chestnut St., Oakland Tavern in Oakland Park, 1.5 m. W. on Pullen St., for theatricals, musicals, and concerts; 5 motion picture houses.
Baseball: Taylor Field, W. 17th Ave. just W. of Ohio Ave., independent teams.
Golf: Oakland Park, 9 holes, greens fee 25¢, second round 15¢; Memorial Park, 42nd Ave. and Poplar St., 9 holes, greens fee, 50¢ a day.
Hunting and Fishing: Duck, quail, and geese in season; fresh-water angling in near-by lakes and streams; Oakland Park bass lake, limit 15 all types, 50¢ a day.
Swimming: Atkins Lake, 7.5 m. SE. on Tamo Pike, then NE. 1.5 m., suits and towels rented; Memorial Park Natatorium, 36th Ave. and Poplar St., 15¢ and 25¢; Oakland Municipal Pool, Oakland Park, 10¢ and 15¢.
Tennis: Oakland Park (4 courts), 10¢ an hour a person; YWCA (1 court), 205 W. 6th Ave., 10¢ an hour a person; Merrill Civic Center (1 indoor court), 427 Main St., $1 an hour; Taylor Field (2 courts), free.

Annual Events: Livestock Shows in April and October.

PINE BLUFF (221 alt., 21,290 pop.), seat of Jefferson County, lies a little more than 50 miles southeast of the center of the State, alongside a deep bend of the Arkansas River. Spreading to the west are the pine and oak forests of southern Arkansas, and opening out to the east and southeast are wide cottonfields that begin almost at the ends of urban streets. Through the heart of the city two railroads parallel each other, and along these are strung the leading industries— lumber mills, cotton compresses and seed-oil mills, stockyards, and railroad repair shops.

Blocking the north end of Main Street is the Jefferson County courthouse, an ante bellum structure whose gilded clock is visible from most of the business section. The buildings on near-by Barraque Street, an early-day river front, have an age and dignity akin to that of the courthouse. Here is the old Jefferson Hotel, for decades a favorite of political notables, river pilots, and gamblers, now refurnished and air conditioned. Planters from far down the Arkansas Valley signed their notes and paid them off in the old bank, now occupied by a cleaning and dyeing establishment. Today (1941) the offices of cotton buyers share most of Barraque Street with garages, printing plants, and farm machinery salesrooms.

The shopping district extends southward along Main Street from the courthouse to an 11-story office building at Fifth Avenue. Between these two prominent structures are several large department stores with a metropolitan sparkle, as well as old-fashioned general stores that stock everything from plowshares to lamp chimneys for the farmers who throng the streets on Saturday afternoons. Each cross street in the business section has its own character. Second Avenue, with several motion picture theaters, is an amusement center. Third and Fourth are lined with businesses patronized largely by Negroes. Fifth is the route of US 65, which carries most of the tourist traffic.

Most residents of Pine Bluff live west and south of the downtown section—though a residential district marked by old homes runs a few blocks east of Main Street, and the Riverside community of railroad workers is at the far eastern end of the city. Many residential streets are shaded by towering elms and oaks. In the southwestern corner of the city, where large new homes push into the woods, landscape architects have created striking effects with shrubs and gardens.

Of the 6,000 or more Negroes in Pine Bluff, the majority live to the northwest, between the old river bed and the railroad tracks. They have their own stores, churches, cemetery, amusement houses, and schools, including the State Agricultural, Mechanical and Normal College. Negroes are employed as domestic servants, and in sawmills, warehouses, railroad shops, and cottonseed mills.

In 1819 the June rise of the Arkansas River flooded New Gascony, a settlement of French farmers a few miles below the site of Pine Bluff. Joseph Bonne, son of a Frenchman and a Quapaw woman, took his rifle and a few possessions and paddled his canoe up the Arkansas toward higher ground. He pitched camp in a forest of giant pines, and, after the water receded, found that he was perched on a bluff above a southward bending curve of the river. Before winter set in he put up a log cabin and brought to it his wife and his several small children. Bonne, who had signed the Quapaw Treaty of 1818 as interpreter, got along well with the Quapaw who lived in the region. On the high, dry ground he started a trading post, and the settlement that grew up around it was called Mount Marie. For the first few years after the trader came to the bluff most of the white men who visited him were roving hunters and trappers, but these gave way to home-seekers who cleared land and planted cotton.

A meeting held in Bonne's cabin led to the establishment of Jefferson County by the Territorial legislature in 1829. Three years later Mount Marie was renamed Pine Bluff, and in 1846 the State legislature passed an act that incorporated the town. The population grew slowly until 1850, numbering only 460 in that year. In the following decade, however, the population more than tripled, as increasing numbers of steamboats stopped at the landing to take out larger and larger cargoes of cotton. Planters built stately town houses, ornate with hand-carved woodwork, sparkling chandeliers, elaborate fireplaces, and imported rugs.

In April 1861 at Pine Bluff the Jefferson Guards halted several Federal boats steaming up the Arkansas with supplies for garrisons at Fort Smith and Fort Gibson. Because the act was carried out by regular troops under official orders, and because Governor Rector seized the cargoes for the Confederate Army, Pine Bluff citizens have long held that the warning musket discharged from the riverbank was the first shot fired in the War between the States.

Pine Bluff had its only real taste of battle, however, on October 25, 1863, when Confederate General John S. Marmaduke attempted to take the city from Colonel Powell Clayton. Early in the morning Marmaduke, heading about 2,000 Confederate troops, approached the town and demanded its surrender. Clayton set 300 Negroes to work erecting barricades of cotton bales. Cannons were rolled into position, sharpshooters were posted at strategic upper-story windows, and barrels were filled with water from the river to withstand a siege. In the fighting, several buildings, including the courthouse, were shelled, and fire swept along the cotton barricades. Deciding he could not dislodge Clayton without storming the breastworks at a high cost in men, Marmaduke withdrew.

Pine Bluff in 1874 was the scene of a violent episode in the Brooks-Baxter "war," an incident of Reconstruction days involving two claimants for the State governorship. At the end of April 1874, Colonel J. M. Murphy was reported on his way up the Arkansas River with reinforcements for Brooks. Colonel King White went down the river to intercept him on the steamboat *Hallie,* with about 200 Baxter volunteers. White stopped at Pine Bluff, then went on to surprise Murphy at New Gascony, killing 7 and wounding 30 of the latter's men.

In general, however, Reconstruction was a time of prosperity for Pine Bluff. Ginning, baling, and loading cotton on river boats gave work to returned soldiers and freed slaves, and the town became the State's leading cotton port. By 1870 the tracks of the Little Rock, Pine Bluff and New Orleans Railroad were laid from Pine Bluff to Chicot on the Mississippi River. During the next decade additions to this line (now part of the Missouri Pacific system) gave rail connections with Little Rock and various points in southeast Arkansas.

In 1882 the Texas and St. Louis Railway (now St. Louis Southwestern) was completed from Gatesville, Texas, to Pine Bluff, and a year later the route was extended to St. Louis. As the railroads penetrated the forests of eastern and southern Arkansas timber cutters invaded the woods, and large lumber mills began to belch smoke in Pine Bluff. The St. Louis Southwestern Railway repair shops, established in 1884 and gradually enlarged until they are now equipped to build entire locomotives, brought the city its largest single pay roll. Boom times in cotton and the establishment of new industries raised the population of Pine Bluff from 3,203 in 1880 to 9,952 in 1890.

During a major flood in 1908, the Arkansas River swept across a point of land north of the courthouse into a new channel and left muddy bottom lands where side-wheelers had once maneuvered toward the wharves. A few years earlier the shift would have been costly, but railroads had now taken the place of packets, so Pine Bluff people made the best of the situation by planting the new valley land in cotton and corn. The steep embankment of the old channel still marks the north edge of the city, although the river's current now touches only the eastern extremity of the bluff.

In 1936 Pine Bluff added large-scale trading in livestock to its other economic activities. The new stockyards, on a 16-acre tract at the eastern end of the city, have recently averaged sales of $2,000,000 a year. Most of the cattle go to East St. Louis, Chicago, and Birmingham.

POINTS OF INTEREST

1. The JEFFERSON COUNTY COURTHOUSE (*open 9-5 weekdays*), Barraque St., facing Main St., erected in 1858, has been remodeled and enlarged three times without loss of the original modified-Georgian lines. Stone steps rise directly from the sidewalk to the gray-brick walls. Terraced roofs slope from a central clock tower capped by a green dome. In the building are stored records dating back to court sessions held at Joseph Bonne's log cabin.

2. The PORTIS HOUSE (*private*), 216 E. 2nd Ave., was occupied in ante bellum days by the Taylor and Portis families, both prominent among Pine Bluff's plantation aristocracy. The one-and-one-half-story structure was built of hand-hewn lumber in 1844 by slave labor. Cypress columns and half-columns support the porch roof, and tall brick chimneys rise on each side of the end gables. Two magnolias in the yard are flanked by crape myrtles said to be a half century old.

3. The PINE BLUFF COTTON OIL MILL (*open on application*), Michigan St. at Missouri Pacific tracks, manufactures cottonseed oil, meal, and cake in several two-story buildings.

4. The PUBLIC LIBRARY (*open 9-7 weekdays, 9-9 Sat.*), NE. corner 5th Ave. and Chestnut St., is a cream-colored brick structure completed in 1931. Included in its 55,000 volumes is a collection of historical documents in French and Spanish.

5. The THOMPSON HOUSE (*private*), 519 W. Barraque St., erected about 1860, is a survivor of the mansions built in Pine Bluff during the slave and steamboat days. The design is of the late Greek Revival period, with four columns in the portico and two recessed columns. A heavy oak door, framed by fanlights and side lights, swings on hand-wrought brass hinges. Windows are set in groups of

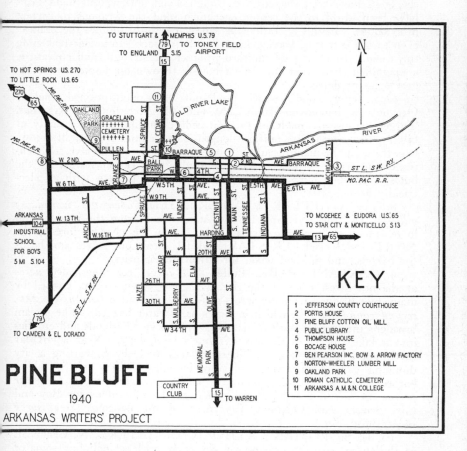

TO STUTTGART & MEMPHIS U.S.79
TO TONEY FIELD
TO ENGLAND S.15 AIRPORT

TO HOT SPRINGS U.S. 270
TO LITTLE ROCK U.S. 65

OLD RIVER LAKE

N

MO. PAC. R.R.

OAKLAND PARK

GRACELAND CEMETERY

PULLEN

ARKANSAS RIVER

W. 2ND.

BARRAQUE

BALL PARK

W. 6TH. AVE.

ST. L. SW. RY.

MO. PAC. R.R.

W.5TH.

W 9TH.

ARKANSAS
INDUSTRIAL
SCHOOL
FOR BOYS
5 MI S.104

W. 13TH.

W.16TH.

HARDING

TO MCGEHEE & EUDORA U.S.65
TO STAR CITY & MONTICELLO S13

20TH.

26TH.

30TH.

W. S.34TH.

TO CAMDEN & EL DORADO

MEMORIAL PARK

KEY

1 JEFFERSON COUNTY COURTHOUSE
2 PORTIS HOUSE
3 PINE BLUFF COTTON OIL MILL
4 PUBLIC LIBRARY
5 THOMPSON HOUSE
6 BOCAGE HOUSE
7 BEN PEARSON INC. BOW & ARROW FACTORY
8 NORTON-WHEELER LUMBER MILL
9 OAKLAND PARK
10 ROMAN CATHOLIC CEMETERY
11 ARKANSAS A. M. & N. COLLEGE

PINE BLUFF

1940

ARKANSAS WRITERS' PROJECT

COUNTRY CLUB

TO WARREN

three: two narrow openings on each side of a wide middle sash. A red trumpet vine mantles the southwest corner of the house, and three oak trees shade the landscaped grounds.

6. The BOCAGE HOUSE (*private*), 1115 W. 4th Ave., is set back from the street in a grove of oaks, one of which, a pin oak, is said to be the largest tree in Pine Bluff. The two-story white-frame structure, built in 1866, has steep gables and exceptionally wide eaves. A double porch is faced on the lower floor by a series of French

windows with old-fashioned green shutters. Inside the small central hall is a 21-step circular hanging stairway.

7. The BEN PEARSON INC. BOW AND ARROW FACTORY (*open to archers; guides*), 4th Ave. and Orange St., in a two-story brick building once occupied by a sorghum mill, has been furnished with machinery for manufacturing archery equipment. After the bows have been shaped from rough wood and walnut hand grips have been glued to the center, workmen sand the weapons to correct proportions. In this operation the sander carefully follows the grain— even to the extent of leaving knots on the surface—to avoid weakening the wood. In testing the finished product for strength and curvature, a magnified shadow of the drawn bow is thrown on a screen to exaggerate latent defects.

Good bow woods, which need not be straight-grained, include Oregon yew, lemonwood from Cuba, and *bois d'arc,* found in Arkansas. Target arrows are made of Oregon cedar, hunting arrows usually of birch or fir. To insure uniform length, balance, and weight, all arrows pass through the manufacturing processes in sheaves of twelve. Fletching of the arrows is done by girls, who glue split turkey feathers to the butts; men then burn the feathers to a desired pattern with an electrically heated wire.

8. The WHEELER LUMBER MILL (*open 9-4 workdays; guides*), W. 2nd Ave. and US 65, stands back from the road behind huge stacks of lumber. Using timber from the near-by forests, the NORTON-WHEELER STAVE MILL turns out staves and heads for barrels, and finished wood for furniture factories.

9. OAKLAND PARK, Pullen St., covers 64 tree-shaded acres at the northwest edge of the city. A cress-grown stream, crossed by many foot bridges, wanders across a 9-hole golf course (*greens fee 25¢, second round 15¢*) in which it serves as a water hazard. The stream broadens into a pool with miniature willow-covered islands and empties into a lake stocked with bass (*fishing 50¢ a day*). Near a circular turtle pond is a small zoo. The park was made by converting a city dumping ground in 1931, and now includes shelters, picnic tables, barbecue pits, a swimming pool (*10¢ and 15¢*), tennis courts (*10¢ per person an hour*), a baseball field and grandstand, cabins for Boy and Girl Scouts, and Oakland Tavern, used for dancing (*free, week nights; 40¢, Sat.*).

10. In the ROMAN CATHOLIC CEMETERY, N. Cedar St. at Pullen St., are the graves of many early settlers, including some of French blood. Here is the GRAVE OF SARASEN, a highly respected Quapaw chief who died in 1832 at the age of 97. An inscription on his tombstone recounts an incident of pioneer days—the kidnapping of two white children by an unfriendly tribe, and their rescue by Sarasen.

11. The ARKANSAS AGRICULTURAL, MECHANICAL AND NORMAL COLLEGE (*open 8-4 schooldays, Sept.-June*), at the north edge of Pine Bluff on US 79 (L), is a State-supported institution for higher education of Negroes. About 450 students attend

classes in the $500,000 plant, most of which has been erected since 1929. On the north side of the quadrangle is the LIBRARY, noteworthy for its functional architecture and its decoration. Horizontal lines dominate the buff-brick exterior; doors are of glass and chromium; floors and interior walls are painted pale blue and gray.

In 1873 the Arkansas general assembly authorized the establishment of a Negro Branch Normal College in Pine Bluff, mainly because the town was near the center of the State's Negro population. Two years later Professor J. C. Corbin taught the first class (seven students) in a rented frame building. The school had a slow growth, and from 1882 through 1894 awarded only ten A.B. degrees. Agriculture was first taught here in 1902, though in 1891 a woodworking shop, a foundry, forge, and machine shop had been in operation. Periodic financial difficulties were largely responsible for limiting the curriculum almost entirely to college preparatory work until 1929. In that year, under the direction of a new president, John Brown Watson, the program was expanded to include four-year, degree-granting courses.

POINTS OF INTEREST IN ENVIRONS

Cummins Prison Farm, 31.3 *m.;* South Bend Farm, 43.2 *m.* (*see Tour 5b*). Watson State Park, 8.9 *m.* (*see Tour 11*). St. Mary's Church (Catholic), 10.6 *m.;* Plum Bayou Resettlement Project, 27.6 *m.* (*see Tour 12*).

Texarkana

Railroad Stations: Union Station, State Line Ave. and Front St., for Missouri Pacific R.R., Texas & Pacific Ry., Kansas City Southern Ry., and St. Louis Southwestern Ry.

Bus Stations: Union Bus Terminal, 102 N. State Line Ave., for Missouri Pacific Trailways and Dixie Motor Coaches; McCartney Hotel Terminal, Front and Main Sts., for Southwestern Greyhound Lines, Tri-State Trailways, Nance Motor Coaches, and Arkansas Motor Coaches.

Airport: Municipal Airport, 3 m. NE. on US 67; no scheduled service.

Taxis: 10¢ for each passenger.

Busses: Fare 5¢.

Traffic Regulations: Traffic lights in business district; U-turns prohibited where traffic lights are installed; left turns on green light; one-hour parking limit in downtown section from 7 a.m. to 6 p.m., except Sundays and holidays.

Information Service: Texarkana Chamber of Commerce, 204 Foreman Bldg.; Arkansas Automobile Club, 7th and Laurel Sts.

Accommodations: Five hotels; tourist homes, tourist camps.

Radio Station: KCMC (1450 kc.).

Theaters and Motion Picture Houses: Five motion picture houses (two equipped for stage productions) in downtown area.

Baseball: Legion Park, 16th St. and Jefferson Ave., East Texas League and City League of Amateurs.

Golf: Texarkana Country Club, 2 m. SE. from business district near US 71, 18 holes, greens fee $1, $1.50 Sat. and Sun.; South Haven Course, 1.5 m. S. on Line Ferry Rd., 9 holes, greens fee 25¢; State Line Golf Course, 3 m. N. on State Line Ave., 9 holes, greens fee 25¢.

Hunting and Fishing: Duck, quail, and geese in season; fresh-water angling in near-by lakes and streams.

Swimming: Braumiller's Crystal Pool, 2 m. N. on Ghio Blvd., adm. 15¢ and 25¢, suits and towels rented.

Tennis: Spring Lake Park, 2 m. N. on Ghio Blvd., 2 courts; free.

Annual Events: Bowie County Fair, last week in September; Founders' Day, December 8 (street parade, banquet, and other festivities).

TEXARKANA (377 alt., 11,821 Ark. pop., 17,019 Tex. pop.), astride the boundary between Arkansas and Texas, is, formally, two cities in two States. The twin municipalities are separated, however, only by an imaginary line down the middle of State Line Avenue, which bisects the combined business section. The post office, placed on the boundary, is officially named "Texarkana, Ark.-Tex."

State Line Avenue follows the north-south direction of the border, but some of the most important downtown streets are laid out along the angle of the Missouri Pacific tracks. Consequently, many of the

business blocks are sliced into irregular patterns. Some office buildings are wedge-shaped, and others have walls staggered or even slightly
zigzagged to fit available ground space. Partly through necessity and
partly because more conventional designs would be inharmonious, the
roofs have also been chopped into odd angles, with curious gables and
diminutive towers springing up here and there. Bright bits of tile and
triangles of slate flash through the downtown skyline.

Texarkana streets are wide and the buildings low except in the
cluster at the intersection of Broad Street and State Line Avenue,
where banks and offices are in six- and eight-story structures. Broad
Street, most important of the business thoroughfares, parallels a maze
of railroad tracks, south of which lies the factory section. State Line
Avenue is divided into two segments by the Federal Building, erected
squarely across it: the section running south through the business district and ending at the Union Station is known as "Short State Line";
while "Long State Line," the route of US 71, extends north past service
stations, grocery stores, and residences toward a group of night clubs
at the city limits.

The older residential districts are on the west (Texas) side. Houses
here are set on ample lawns planted with shrubs and flowers and shaded
by trees. Private tennis courts, used during most of the year, are
numerous. On summer evenings Texarkana people gather in the dusk
on their lawns to rest and talk, the men cool in white linen suits, the
women fresh in starched cottons. Occasionally, a wide-brimmed hat
or, more rarely, a pair of high-heeled boots, reminds the visitor that
half the city is in Texas.

Although legally Texarkana is two towns, each with its own municipal government, school system, and police and fire departments, it is
socially and economically a unit. This situation gives rise to various
complications. For example, differences in the kinds and rates of taxes
put some Arkansas merchants at a disadvantage in meeting the prices
of Texas competitors across State Line Avenue. Therefore, the
Arkansas legislature makes special exemptions from such taxes for
Texarkana businessmen. Again, the Arkansas side has a monopoly
on the sale of legal liquor, since the Texas side is dry under Bowie
County's local option.

Police of the two towns have worked out an efficient arrangement
for dealing with lawbreakers who cross the boundary. In minor cases,
if the offender is in an automobile, the policeman simply notes the
license number and phones across the line to request the violator's
detention. In the event of a serious crime the pursuing officer makes
the arrest on either side of the border. Transfer of an offender back
to the proper jurisdiction is a formality requiring only a few minutes
at either police station.

The chamber of commerce, businessmen's clubs, and other civic
organizations draw on the entire city for their membership, and encourage industries on both sides of the line. These industries now
include a large clay-products plant, a variety of woodworking factories,

and several cottonseed oil mills. Most of Texarkana's business, however, is concerned with marketing and distribution. Carloads of cotton, dairystuffs, livestock, and other products that flow in from the surrounding agricultural region are made up for shipment over the four major railroads that enter the city. Other carloads of manufactured goods are received by wholesalers for shipment to small-town dealers and farmers in the four States—Arkansas, Texas, Louisiana, and Oklahoma—that contribute to Texarkana's trade territory.

Factories and warehouses employ many of Texarkana's more than 3,000 Negroes, although probably the greater proportion is in domestic service. Negro residential sections are in the outskirts of the city, the concentration being heaviest at the southwest corner. They have their own schools and churches, and one hospital, the Jamison.

Texarkana grew from construction camps set up at the western end of the Cairo & Fulton railroad tracks and at the eastern terminus of the Texas & Pacific rails. Railroad officials recognized the meeting-place of the two lines as a natural town site. The tracks at first were of different gauges, and for several years cars going through had to be shifted from one set of tracks to another. On December 8, 1873, usually given as the date of Texarkana's founding, the Texas & Pacific held a sale of building lots on the Texas side of the State Line. A few months later the Cairo & Fulton (now Missouri Pacific) laid off lots on the Arkansas side. Late in 1874 the Arkansas legislature established Miller County and made Texarkana its seat.

Of the several stories concerning the origin of the settlement's name, that most generally heard describes how Colonel Gus Knobel, upon completing his survey for the Cairo & Fulton's right-of-way to the Texas Line, wrote Tex-Ark-Ana on a board and nailed it to a tree, saying, "This is the name of the town that is to be built here." Colonel Knobel may have known that a packet plying the Red River in the early 1870's was called the *Texarkana*, and that a medicine was sold under the name of "Texarkana Bitters." Regardless of who first hit upon the combination of syllables, there is no doubt that they were taken from the names Texas, Arkansas, and Louisiana.

The city now smiles indulgently at tall tales of its first years. By all accounts it was an untamed locality. To its bars and hotels came adventurers and gamblers, Southern gentlemen impoverished by the War between the States, land-hungry settlers, and cattle rustlers. Guns blazed on the streets and set off feuds that lasted for years. Bowie knives were flashed with little warning. The State boundary line effectively curbed a sheriff's pursuit in either direction, and a frequent notation on Arkansas warrants for the arrest of some desperado was "G.T." (Gone to Texas). In private quarrels, however, such legal technicalities were ignored. An outraged citizen chasing a deck-switching card sharp did not stop when he came to the middle of State Line Avenue.

Gradually Texarkana settled down. The Texas & St. Louis Railway (now St. Louis Southwestern) swung through in 1882, opening the timberlands of southern Arkansas. Pioneer lumbermen built magnificent homes with forest-gained fortunes. In 1897 the Kansas City Southern linked Texarkana to Kansas City and the Gulf Coast. Cotton from Red River Valley plantations required the construction of warehouses, compresses, cottonseed mills. Hardwoods from the bottoms made possible factories that turned out tool handles, caskets, and baskets. Vegetables crowding the market gave rise to canneries.

Meanwhile the city's excellent transportation facilities enabled it to grow with the country. In 1890 the Arkansas population exceeded that of the Texas side, but since that time the proportion of Texas citizens has been consistently larger.

POINTS OF INTEREST

The FIRST CONGREGATIONAL CHURCH, NE. corner 6th St. and State Line Ave., on the site of Texarkana's first cemetery, is a low, wide building of red brick, with an eight-sided auditorium covered by a domed roof. Brick ells at the rear add still more facets to the unconventional design.

The TEXARKANA PUBLIC LIBRARY (*open 9-6 weekdays*), SE. corner 7th St. and State Line Ave., a remodeled frame building, stands behind a giant water oak and in a circle of small oaks. Among the volumes are many reference works on Arkansas and Texas history. Curiosities in the library's museum include a ladle used in serving Texarkana's first ice cream, shipped from Jefferson, Texas, in 1874, and sold at 50¢ a dish.

The plan of the FEDERAL BUILDING (*open 8-5 weekdays*), middle of State Line Ave. between 5th and 6th Sts., took into account its unusual function of housing two Federal courts. The east door is in Arkansas, the west in Texas, and the center entrance is immediately on the boundary line. On the third floor are the two courtrooms, separated by an unbroken wall extending the length of the building. The base of the five-story building is Texas granite and the walls are Arkansas limestone.

The SITE OF THE PARAGON SALOON, 119 W. Broad St., now occupied by a business house, is associated with one of Texarkana's most vividly remembered tragedies. During the city's youthful days the Paragon was a popular saloon and gambling house which also, on occasion, was used as a courtroom or a church. On July 12, 1882, a sudden downpour of rain drove pedestrians from the streets, and many of them took refuge in the Paragon. The violence of the storm caused the walls of an adjoining building to collapse, crushing the saloon. Coal oil lamps set the wreckage ablaze and 52 persons died in the fire.

Through the UNION STATION AND MAIL TERMINAL (*terminal open only by permit*), State Line Ave. at Front St., pass travelers and mail carried by four railroads. Visitors are invariably impressed by the speed with which mountains of mail are handled in the terminal, one of the largest in the Southwest. The State boundary cuts through a corner of the station's waiting room for white passengers, and divides the ticket office and the Negro waiting room. By this device the architects complied with Arkansas and Texas laws requiring separate waiting rooms for whites and Negroes in each State.

The TEXARKANA COTTON OIL PLANT (*open 9-5 workdays; guides*), Laurel and Broad Sts., processes cottonseed to produce oil, cake, meal, and other materials during the milling season (September to June). Machinery is so designed that with a few adjustments it can crush peanuts or oil-yielding beans. The building is two stories high, with one-story ells; from the ells run corrugated-iron sheds used for storing seed.

The DICKEY CLAY MANUFACTURING PLANT (*open 8-4 workdays; guides*), southwest corner of the city, bristles with more than 20 beehive-shaped kilns. For every two kilns there is a smokestack; and other chimneys rise from the plant's long main building. In the storage yards are huge honeycombs of tile pipe. Some varieties are only a few inches in diameter and others are large enough for a man to walk through.

Clay for the plant is mined west of Texarkana. At the factory it passes through grinders that mix the various types of earth and add water according to formulae. The tiles are stamped out, sometimes under 90 tons of pressure, by bell forms, then shunted into ovens and baked at a temperature of 2,200 degrees F. Salt, shoveled into the furnaces, turns into vapor and passes into the kilns, where it glazes the clay.

SPRING LAKE PARK (*tennis, picnicking, camping*), 2 miles N. on Ghio Blvd., covers 200 acres. Water from a large spring flows into fish ponds and a lake. Near the spring is a swimming pool for children.

POINTS OF INTEREST IN ENVIRONS

Washington (State capital 1863-65), 42.3 *m.* (*see Tour 1b*). Old Rondo Cemetery, 4.7 *m.* (*see Tour 14*).

PART III
Tours

Population figures in the Tours, marked with an asterisk (*), are for towns not covered by the 1940 census, and are taken from the 1937 edition of the Rand McNally Pocket Map of Arkansas. All other population figures are from the 1940 Census.

Tour 1

(Poplar Bluff, Mo.)—Newport—Searcy—Little Rock—Benton—Arkadelphia—Texarkana—(Texarkana, Tex.); US 67.
Missouri Line to Texas Line, 332.2 m.

Asphalt-paved for two short sections; elsewhere concrete-paved.
Missouri Pacific R.R. parallels route throughout.
Accommodations chiefly in cities.

US 67, cutting diagonally across Arkansas from northeast to southwest, divides the State into two triangles of sharply contrasting topography, geology, and economic and cultural patterns. To the southeast is the level, fertile Mississippi Delta, rising into the West Gulf Coastal Plain. To the northwest is the rocky, forested, upland region that includes the Ozark and Ouachita Mountains.

Along the line dividing these two regions the route follows a path picked out by the Indians centuries ago. This trail skirted hills, avoided swamps, and crossed the many rivers at their most practicable fords. Early in the nineteenth century the wagons of white settlers began following this great Southwest Trail through Arkansas. Pioneers drove herds of cattle ahead of their wagon trains, and sometimes brought families of slaves with them. At many points homeseekers turned off, selected tracts of bottomland, and made clearings in the wilderness. In 1831 Congress ordered the construction of a military road here, a road whose utility was proved a few years later in the War with Mexico.

When the railroads penetrated the Southwest in the 1870's, they followed the same natural pathway; and when, after another 50 years, the automobile made paved highways necessary, the concrete was laid almost on the path made by the Indians.

Section a. MISSOURI LINE to JUNCTION WITH US 70; 174.8 m., US 67

US 67 follows the Black and White Rivers through country that is alternately rich in cotton and corn or covered with swamp grass and pin oak, depending largely on whether the backwater has been drained off. A great part of this section of the road is built on fills, the construction of which took so much time and money that, despite its arterial importance, US 67 was not entirely paved until 1939.

South of Newport the route ascends from the White River Valley to higher land, where the soil is lighter and sandier. Here is the principal strawberry country of Arkansas. Near Little Rock the highway drops into the valley of the Arkansas, and cotton again becomes the leading crop.

Throughout the route small farms are the rule, owner-operated or rented on "thirds and fourths," an arrangement that gives the landowner as rental a third of the corn and a fourth of the cotton yield.

US 67 crosses the Missouri Line at MOARK, 0 m. (299 alt., 119 pop.*), 23.6 miles south of Poplar Bluff, Missouri.

In 1870 Moark was a bustling railroad roundhouse town, and for a few years basked in the prosperity brought by the railroad pay roll; but when the Cairo & Fulton (later the Missouri Pacific) tracks were completed to Little Rock the shops were moved there, and the border town was abandoned. It is now a scattering of filling stations.

CORNING, 7 m. (291 alt., 1,619 pop.), seat of the western district of Clay County, has a definite nineteenth-century flavor, with its rows of trees along the streets and tin marquees extending out over the sidewalks. In striking contrast is a brashly modernistic theater building, characterized by angles and broken lines.

At the CORNING NOVELTY COMPANY SHOP (*visitors admitted*), on the southeast edge of town, billiard tables are made from the black walnut and oak that still grow in small patches around Corning.

In Corning is the eastern junction with US 62 (*see Tour 4a*), with which the route unites for 27.5 miles.

The highway proceeds westward across level cultivated acres bearing little resemblance to the thick forest and tangled brush that once covered the land.

George Featherstonhaugh, an English geologist, was an early traveler along this route, and gave a colorful and detailed account of his journey in *Excursion through the Slave States* (1844). Featherstonhaugh made his trip in 1834, and complained that "one or more settlers here having quarreled about the direction of the Military Road, have taken the liberty to cut roads resembling it, and blazed the trees, to their own cabins; in consequence of this we got out of our way."

Other impulses of the pioneers Featherstonhaugh found more amusing. He noted, for example, that Yankee clock peddlers were everywhere, "and have contrived . . . to stick up a clock . . . in every dell of Arkansas, and in cabins where there was not a chair to sit on, there was sure to be a Connecticut clock. The clock pedlar is an irresistible person." If the backwoodsman at first refused to buy a clock, as was usually the case, the peddler persuaded the housewife to let him leave a clock without cost, until his next trip. "It is nailed up; he instructs her how to keep it in order, and takes leave. But what can equal their delight, when, with a bright, clear sound, it strikes the hours! 'Well,' they exclaim, 'if that don't beat all! Sartin, it is most delightful, curious company!'" When the shrewd peddler comes to reclaim his clock, the family cannot bring themselves to part with it, and so, "the clock becomes theirs for the mere formality of . . . giving a note, payable in six months, for some eighteen or twenty dollars. . . . He comes sure enough to dun the poor creatures, bringing one clock along with him; and as all the clocks have stopped . . . either because they were good for nothing, or because they have wound them up too often, he changes the clock at every place he stops, cobbling them up in succession as they come into his hands, and favouring every one of his customers with the bad clock of his neighbour."

The Mississippi Valley Fuel Company's glass-brick Booster Station (L), 25.2 *m.*, a rectilinear flare of electric light by night and of reflected sunlight by day, looks as though it had been dropped into the cottonfields from some Martian metropolis. Here natural gas flowing from the Louisiana fields to St. Louis and points farther north is pumped or "boosted" along its way.

US 67 crosses CURRENT RIVER, 26.6 *m.,* and immediately passes (L) CURRENT RIVER BEACH (*fishing, camping, houseboats*). The river here is clear, cold, and well stocked with crappie and bass; a sand beach slopes gradually into the stream.

POCAHONTAS, 34.5 *m.* (310 alt., 3,028 pop.), proud of the side-wheel packets that made it a booming Black River port in the 1870's, scorned the solicitations of two major railroads seeking right-of-way grants; later the town obtained the present branch line. Brick buildings of the river-trade period hem in the narrow streets that climb up the irregular valley wall.

The OLD RANDOLPH COUNTY COURTHOUSE, in the center of town, is a two-story brick structure with narrow arched windows, Christopher Wren spire, and elaborate lightning rod. In 1939 a new courthouse was built to the southwest, and the old building, erected in 1872, was bought by the city to be used for municipal and other governmental offices. On the lawn is a METEORITE about four feet high that fell into a near-by field in 1859.

A lobby wall of the POCAHONTAS POST OFFICE, in the downtown business district, is decorated with a mural painted in 1939 by H. Louis Freund under commission of the Section of Fine Arts, U. S. Treasury Department. Depicted as high points of local history are the old mill at near-by Birdell, river traffic of a half-century ago, a prairie schooner being ferried across the Black River, a Pocahontas street scene of 1900.

Stacks of short-length hardwood seasoning in the sun mark the SALLEE BROTHERS HANDLE FACTORY (*visitors admitted*) on the bank of the river. Handle factories, scattered throughout Arkansas, make most of their products from the tough wood of hickory and oak trees.

In Pocahontas is the western junction with US 62 (*see Tour 4a*).

US 67 crosses BLACK RIVER, 35 *m.,* and swings south through the bottoms. Though there are occasional two-story brick farmhouses, most of the homes in this area are of wood and follow the French story-and-a-half pattern, with the roof sloping steeply to the rear over the kitchen, less steeply to the front over the porch.

Unused streetcar tracks run down the main street of WALNUT RIDGE, 48 *m.* (270 alt., 2,013 pop.). In 1903 the Iron Mountain

Railway (now Missouri Pacific) built a roundhouse at Hoxie, a mile and a half distant. Walnut Ridge workers employed in the shops rode to their jobs in a mule-drawn car, later replaced by an electric line. The car line was abandoned in 1923, when the roundhouse was closed.

In the center of town is the LAWRENCE COUNTY COURTHOUSE, which serves the eastern district of the county. The yellow-brick building is in the Romanesque style, with a pointed tower at one end containing four clocks. On the lawn of the courthouse is the old town pump, still used by idlers on the square.

In Walnut Ridge are the junctions with State 25 and State 117 (*see Tour 7*).

Between Walnut Ridge and HOXIE, 49.7 *m*. (271 alt., 1,466 pop.), the line of houses along the road (R) is unbroken, and it is difficult to tell where one town stops and the other begins.

Founded as a railroad town, Hoxie was named for the Missouri Pacific's vice president, M. L. Hoxie. Negro section-hands chanted as they laid rails and drove spikes:

> Jay Gould he say to Hoxie,
> 'Hoxie, whar' yo gwine?'
> 'Down on de Iron Mountain,
> Ter pay dem niggers dey time.'

In Hoxie is the junction with US 63 (*see Tour 7*).

Depressed cotton prices have been partly responsible for diversification of crops in the country around Hoxie and Walnut Ridge. The flatness of the land along this section of US 67 has encouraged mechanized farming. Light tractors are used, instead of the heavy machines required to turn over the Delta's gumbo soil. Similarly, the mules that pull the plows of farmers here are smaller than the work stock bred in the Mississippi River counties.

As US 67 approaches White River the stands of water elm become more frequent, an indication that backwater lies here for long periods. Water-soaked land in time becomes "sour" and compact, and can be reclaimed for cultivation only by draining, plowing deeply, and allowing it to dry for several years.

NEWPORT, 86.7 *m*. (227 alt., 4,321 pop.), seat of Jackson County, derives its commercial importance from its position on the White River and as a railroad intersection. The town, in the bottom of the river valley, is protected from floods by a circle of levees.

Gathering and shipping pecans has become one of Newport's chief sources of income. Most of the harvest is from trees that grow wild in the river bottoms. Owners of groves divide the pecans equally with the pickers, who are usually families from the town or countryside. Sometimes great blankets, made of feed sacks sewed together, are spread on the ground, and the trees are thrashed with sticks; but many owners forbid this practice because of a belief that thrashing a tree reduces its subsequent yields. Nuts are sold for 8¢ to 10¢ a pound to Newport dealers, who frequently turn them back to gatherers for shelling.

North on Front St. near White River is BUTTONCUTTERS' ROW, a community of the economically lost. In 1937 local reformers and Works Progress Administration authorities attempted to improve the area. Some of the flimsiest shacks were pulled down; a café credited with at least one murder was refurnished and turned into a recreational center, where children are taught games and their mothers instructed in reading, writing, and sewing. The row now presents as respectable an appearance as do the poor sections of most towns.

The NEWPORT PEARL BUTTON FACTORY (*visitors admitted*), at the end of Buttoncutters' Row, manufactures button blanks from mussel shells. The cutting of the circular blanks is the only operation performed. Sorting, hole punching, and finishing take place in the East, where the garment industry provides markets. The Newport factory, one of a number of such establishments in towns along the White and Black Rivers, has recently felt severe competition from composition buttons and zippers.

Dredging the White River and its tributaries for fresh-water mussels used for button making affords farmers a part-time occupation spiced by the constant, though dim, anticipation of chancing across a valuable pearl. Mussels are gathered by waders or boatmen using long-handled rakes, or by "tonguing" (dragging along the river bed a bar set with hooks). Ordinarily, mussel-diggers are satisfied if their returns average $1 a day. The less expert prospectors trail old river hands who are familiar with probable locations of the shifting beds deposited by currents. The inedible meat is removed from the bivalves by boiling, and the shells are dried in the sun. Payment, made by the ton, varies according to the type of shell, "grandmaws," "pocketbooks," and "cucumbers" bringing less than "elephant ears" and "niggerheads." Most prized is the rare sand shell, sold to European markets for use on knife handles and for other decorative purposes.

Stories of finding valuable pearls in the shells are much more common than the pearls themselves, though a few have been found that eventually sold for several thousand dollars.

The HEINEMANN PEARL COLLECTION, 111 Walnut St., in the shop of a dealer, contains pearls and slugs in curious shapes, and a collection of Indian relics.

Among Newport's landmarks is the tall brick WATER TOWER at Second and Vine Sts. The octagon-shaped reservoir is filled from White River.

In REMMEL PARK (*golf, nominal fee*), at the southeast edge of Newport is long LAKE NEWPORT, artificially made in a section of the old river bed and stocked with crappie and bass.

Right from Newport on Front Street, which becomes a graveled road following the White River levee, to JACKSONPORT, 3.7 m. (226 alt., 215 pop.). A tall brick courthouse building, with cornice, full mansard roof, dormer windows, and bell-shaped tower stands in a cottonfield, surrounded by a few tumble-down houses. Nothing else remains of a town once noted throughout the lower Mississippi Valley for its social and commercial life; its belles attended balls in New Orleans, and its dowagers were invited to weddings at Louisville.

Jacksonport, strategically placed just below the confluence of the White and Black Rivers, was a port of call for side-wheelers from New Orleans, Memphis, and St. Louis. Cargoes were transferred to smaller boats for the voyage farther up the two rivers, or to oxcarts bound for inland villages. Settled in 1822, the town in 1854 became the seat of Jackson County.

Proud of their steamboat trade, Jacksonport citizens in the 1870's refused the Cairo & Fulton Railroad's requests for right-of-way grants. In reprisal the tracks were laid a few miles down the river, and the new town of Newport grew up there. In 1874 the county government was moved to Newport, and gradually the old town followed. The Jacksonport courthouse is now used as a poor farm, and the chief importance of the village today is as a mark of caste: the best insurance of social standing in Newport is a grandfather who moved down from Jacksonport.

US 67 crosses White River and continues westward to a junction at 88.8 *m.* with State 14 (*see Tour 17*).

In 1939 road workers jubilantly pitched their hats into the concrete mixer to celebrate the completion of the stretch of highway between Newport and Bradford. The swampy gumbo bottomland of the White River affords little foundation for a roadbed. Gravel was hauled in by rail, and the highway laid on a fill for miles to the point where US 67 ascends the valley wall and emerges into rolling lands.

BRADFORD, 105.4 *m.* (243 alt., 681 pop.), ships pecans from the bottomlands, strawberries from the higher country to the south, and cotton from almost every farm.

In Bradford is the junction with State 11 (*see Tour 17*).

In the neighborhood of RUSSELL, 110.7 *m.* (236 alt., 206 pop.), the road veers away from the ridge (R) that is one of the first outposts of the Ozarks.

BALD KNOB, 115.3 *m.* (223 alt., 1,445 pop.), a trading center, takes its name from a low ridge (R) that was a landmark for early-day travelers. From Bald Knob the Memphis line of the Missouri Pacific branches east.

In Bald Knob is the eastern junction with US 64 (*see Tour 3a*), with which the route unites for 32.5 miles.

From JUDSONIA, 120.3 *m.* (221 alt., 1,011 pop.), great quantities of strawberries are shipped in April and May of each year. The light sandy soil of the region has long yielded berries for out-of-State markets, and since the first co-operative marketing association was established in 1910 a dozen more have grown up in Judsonia and nearby towns. The ENTERPRISE BOX COMPANY PLANT (*open seasonally*) makes strawberry containers and crates of thin wood from gum trees.

White County leads Arkansas in strawberry production; 538 cars were shipped in 1940. The typical farmer along US 67 from Bradford to Beebe has perhaps ten acres in berries, about seven of which are in peak or near-peak production, while the rest have passed their prime and will soon be plowed under, to lie fallow or be planted in another crop. Expert cultivation and wise use of fertilizer greatly prolong the productivity of the fields. Some patches continue to bear well after

20 years, though most growers rotate their crops every 3 years. Five thousand plants (the usual number to an acre) set out in the early spring will produce 150,000 plants by the next spring. Farmers pluck off the blossoms so that vines will not bear the first year, since initial-crop berries are of low quality. The Klondike has been the preferred variety in the past, but the Blakemore, characterized by a waxy green cap, is increasing in popularity.

Several dozen carnivals and shows descend on the strawberry area during the picking season, melodramatic movies being the most popular attractions in the brown tents. Admission prices are 10¢ and 15¢, in keeping with the wage scales of the pickers, who generally receive 2¢ a quart and average perhaps $1.25 a day. In a heavy-bearing field, however, a skilled picker may garner 100 quarts between sunup and sundown. In the prosperous 1920's most of the workers were itinerants, but in the last few years these have been increasingly displaced by local townspeople and farmers. In order to release children for the harvest, schools close late in April, and reopen early in August. The dwindling regiments of itinerant workers begin picking berries in the Louisiana fields early in March. The southernmost crop gathered, they ride northward to central Arkansas in dilapidated automobiles. Here they divide into two streams, one group pushing on to Tennessee, Kentucky, and Virginia berry fields, the other going to northwest Arkansas and southwest Missouri. Many workers from both groups eventually meet again in Michigan fruit districts late in the summer.

Protected from the sun by straw hats and old-fashioned sunbonnets, berry pickers bend from the hips as they pinch the reddening fruit directly into quart boxes that later appear on grocers' counters. During the picking season rain is dreaded, because it splashes dirt on the berries and also softens them. After harvest the vines are untended, and weeds flourish in the fields. Killed by the frost, the weeds form a protective matting for the strawberry plants during the winter.

US 67 crosses LITTLE RED RIVER (*boats, fishing*) at 125.1 *m.*

SEARCY, 127.1 *m.* (264 alt., 3,670 pop.), was first called Sulphur Springs, for the medicinal waters that made the town a mid-nineteenth-century health resort. The springs that once attracted crowds to City Park, on Spring Street, disappeared when wells were drilled to supply the town's water system.

The present WHITE COUNTY COURTHOUSE, at the east end of the business district, exhibits the effects of an architectural imagination above the average. The first story is faced with white limestone, the second with red brick. The portico emphasizes the division, the upper part having a balcony and pediment in contrast to the general Romanesque style of the whole.

HARDING COLLEGE, Grand Ave. and East Center St., comprises a number of large brick buildings arranged in a semicircle. Galloway College for girls was established on this site in 1889 under the auspices of the Methodist Church, and in 1932 was merged into the Trinity System of Hendrix College at Conway. The Searcy plant was then purchased by the Christian Church, renamed and made coeducational. The present enrollment of the college is about 550.

Long storage and shipping sheds near the railroad station at BEEBE, 144.1 *m.* (246 alt., 1,189 pop.), stand unused except during the strawberry season. Among its other activities the JUNIOR AGRICULTURAL COLLEGE OF CENTRAL ARKANSAS (R), 144.7 *m.,* housed in three large brick buildings, encourages soil conservation and crop-diversification methods among neighborhood farmers.

At 147.8 *m.* is the western junction with US 64 (*see Tour 3a*).

AUSTIN, 153.5 *m.* (250 alt., 145 pop.), consists of a few scattered houses and filling stations marking the memory of vanished Old Austin, founded a mile to the east in 1821. Each August descendants of the early families hold a "homecoming" in a grove at the site of Old Austin.

Roark Bradford (1896—) came to CABOT, 156.1 *m.* (289 alt., 741 pop.), from a Tennessee plantation when he was 14. Here he spent his afternoons and Saturdays loafing around the cotton gin, absorbing patterns of Negro thought and details of Negro phraseology. When he grew up he moved to Georgia and began writing, later becoming a resident of New Orleans. In 1928 appeared his *Ol' Man Adam an' His Chillun,* which Marc Connelly used as the basis for his Pulitzer Prize play, *Green Pastures.* Bradford's parents live on a farm at the edge of Cabot.

Near JACKSONVILLE, 165.9 *m.* (279 alt., 323 pop.), are orchards whose fruit is sold mainly to the Little Rock market. In 1934 a hailstorm battered most of the peaches and pears from the trees. Resourceful public officials borrowed canning equipment from Little Rock relief authorities, took over an abandoned building, and set up an emergency canning plant, with merchants furnishing sugar and cans in exchange for a share of the products. So successful was the co-operative arrangement that it has since become a permanent institution.

At 174.8 *m.,* at a point 5.3 miles northeast of Little Rock, is the eastern junction with US 70 (*see Tour 2a*), with which the route unites for 28.8 miles (*see Tour 2b*).

Section b. BENTON to TEXAS LINE; 128.6 m., US 67

Gradually losing elevation as it slants southwestward from the center of Arkansas, US 67 passes through that quarter of the State drained by the Ouachita and Red Rivers. In the river valleys are level cotton lands, while the upcountry is covered with timber or planted with fruit trees or vegetables. Near Texarkana the route reaches pasture lands.

Long before white settlers came, southwestern Arkansas was occupied by the Caddo, a confederation of agricultural tribes who reached a higher stage of culture than most North American Indians. Remains of their beehive-shaped, mud-thatched houses, pottery and other artifacts, indicate that the Caddo approached the Pueblo of New Mexico in artistic ability.

French trappers and fur traders made their way up the Ouachita and the Red Rivers in the eighteenth century, leaving few traces besides an occasional Gallic name taken over by the Americans who followed them with ax and plow. The first towns grew up where these rivers were crossed by the old Southwest Trail, now followed by US 67.

The wide streets and low brick buildings of BENTON, 0 *m.* (291 alt., 3,502 pop.), are grouped around a courthouse and its square. About halfway between Little Rock and Hot Springs, the town is on a site that was subdivided in 1836 and sold on the installment plan. In 1838 Benton had a race track, long before the spa to the southwest had one. The first industry of record was a salt works, opened in 1827, and later abandoned. Pottery-making had become important before 1900, and about the turn of the century large numbers of lumberjacks went into the surrounding forests of pine, oak, and gum. In the last few years the manufacture of inexpensive furniture has employed several hundred of the town's workers.

The SALINE COUNTY COURTHOUSE, at North Market and Sevier Sts., is a two-story buff-brick structure completed in 1902. A pair of one-story wings were added during 1938-39. A Roman arch terminates both ends of the open hallway that divides the original building. The roof line, broken by many gables and chimneys, is dominated by a tall pointed clock tower rising at one corner.

The McCOY-COUCH FURNITURE PLANT (*guides furnished*), at Southeast St. and Sheridan Highway, specializes in living-room furniture. Because of heavy use and frequent style changes, living-room furniture becomes obsolescent rapidly, and the demand is therefore fairly constant.

Bedroom furniture is the principal product of the Owosso MANU-FACTURING PLANT (*open on application*), at the east edge of Benton. Adjoining the plant on the north is the VENEER MILL, where huge booms drop logs cut from the Saline River bottoms into vats of boiling water; here they are soaked until ready to be cut into thin plywood.

At the southern end of Market St. is the NILOAK POTTERY PLANT (*visitors admitted*), named from a reversed spelling of kaolin. Near-by deposits furnish the raw material for vases, jugs, churns, and other vessels. Pottery-making is essentially a hand industry, although the wheels are motorized. The Niloak plant maintains an exhibition shop east of Benton on US 70 (*see Tour 2b*).

In Benton is the western junction with US 70 (*see Tour 2b*).

US 67 crosses SALINE RIVER (*boating; bass, crappie, and bream fishing*) at 2 *m.*

The BENTON COLONY OF THE ARKANSAS STATE HOSPITAL (*guides furnished*), 5.7 *m.*, comprises 3,200 farmed and wooded acres on which some 40 buildings have been erected since 1931. Except for the dairy barns and a few cottages, all construction is of red brick, with white stone trim. Sixteen buildings have 2 stories each and house approximately 1,700 patients with nervous diseases, men and women transferred from the State Hospital in Little Rock because they are convalescent or have a chronic ailment not requiring constant care. As part of their treatment some patients perform tasks at the colony. The unit operates a 200-cow dairy and a large poultry and hog ranch and does general farming and land clearing. Women patients work in the four cafeterias, in sewing rooms, and in the dormitories.

Between Benton and Malvern US 67 passes old hill farms, their small cultivated patches set off from the surrounding pasture or timber by rail fences. Many of these farms have been in the same family for generations.

In the late fall the tall, waving sage grass turns yellowish brown, so that patches of red haw stand out. Grazing cows, some of them weighted down by cumbersome wooden yokes to discourage fence jumping, look wistfully across the pastures at fields of drying cornstalks. Autumn and winter rains lash the red-clay hills and expose the roots of scrub cedars that cling to eroding embankments.

At 20.5 *m.* is the eastern junction with US 270 (*see Tour 11*), with which the route unites for 2.4 miles.

The continuous-process PERLA PLANT (*open on application*), 21.2 *m.*, of the Acme Brick Company (R) consists of a series of corrugated-iron buildings and turret-roofed kilns, each on a different level, and all connected by a winding narrow-gauge track. From deposits a mile away, small cars carry clay to the plant; here they are hoisted up to the top of the first building and dumped. Wire cutters mold the raw clay into brick-shapes as it moves by on a belt; conveyors carry it continuously by gravity through kilns, and it emerges as finished brick. Enough bricks are turned out in 24 hours to build a six-room house.

Houses in MALVERN, 22.9 *m.* (311 alt., 5,290 pop.), seat of Hot Spring County, are fashioned of lumber taken from the virgin forests that once lay on all sides of town. The business structures, however, and the many gasoline service stations are, almost invariably, built of brick. This contrast between frame residences and brick or stone commercial sections is common in Arkansas cities.

Second-growth timber furnishes a steady supply of raw material for several lumber mills and a tool-handle factory. The well-watered soil in this region grows marketable timber in a surprisingly short time. Not far from town, for example, is land used as a wheatfield in 1918, but from which timber of sawmill size was cut 20 years later.

The INTERNATIONAL COTTON MILL (*visitors admitted*), at the north edge of Malvern on US 270, produces shoe linings for its parent firm, the International Shoe Company of St. Louis.

During the early 1870's, Malvern was a lively transfer point for passengers who got off the trains here and boarded the Concord Stage for Hot Springs. Many of the travelers wore diamonds and carried well-filled pocketbooks. Robberies were fairly frequent, of course, but probably not as colorful as presented by tradition. According to the newspaper yarns of the day, the bandits invariably behaved like perfect gentlemen, and a composite of the best-known legends would run something like this:

> As the stage was proceeding through a particularly desolate section the bandits suddenly leaped out into the road. The passengers recognized behind the masks Jesse and Frank James, Jim and Cole Younger, Arthur McCoy, and Belle Starr, each waving two pistols and a rifle.
> "Make no resistance, and none of you will be harmed," said the bandit leader courteously. "We want only your money and jewels. The ladies may keep their rings."
> The passengers stepped down, except for one gentleman who was badly afflicted with rheumatism—the desperadoes graciously permitted him to remain in the coach. The men were lined up along the road and searched, while the ladies seated themselves on handkerchiefs the robbers gallantly spread on the grass. One passenger, in a decided Southern drawl, said he had been a colonel in the Tennessee campaign under Stonewall Jackson. The bandits quickly insisted that he retain his purse, saying that they, too, had fought for the Confederacy.
> "We are sorry to have detained you," apologized the leader of the highwaymen, as the travelers climbed back into the Concord. "And now you may speed on your way to the beautiful city of Hot Springs and its healing waters. We wish you a pleasant good day."

In Malvern is the western junction with US 270 (see Tour 11).

At 44.3 m. is the northern junction with State 7 (see Tour 8b), with which the route unites for 4.5 miles.

A swift mountain stream, the Caddo River, runs under a bridge at 44.8 m., just before its entrance into the Ouachita River, east of the highway. Herds of sleek cattle graze in meadows near the river. The tall trees are thickly clustered with mistletoe, lost among the summer leaves but pleasantly green against bare branches in winter.

ARKADELPHIA, 48.8 m. (247 alt., 5,078 pop.), essentially a college community, is built along the bluffs of the Ouachita Valley wall. The first settlement in the neighborhood was at a salt works south of the present town (see Tour 8b). Founded in 1839, Arkadelphia became the seat of Clark County four years later, and was an important river port during steamboat days. By reason of its position on the Cairo & Fulton Railroad, the town maintained its commercial standing when locomotives replaced river steamers.

OUACHITA COLLEGE, Ouachita Ave. at Fifth St., overlooks the river for which it is named. The principal building, a turreted Gothic structure overgrown with ivy, was erected in 1886. Ten other buildings complete the plant of the coeducational Baptist institution, which has a regular enrollment of about 500. One of the school's music students, Mary McCormic, born in Belleville, gained national fame as an operatic soprano.

Giant water oaks and wild roses grow among the dozen red-brick buildings of HENDERSON STATE TEACHERS' COLLEGE, 11th St. at Henderson Ave. In 1929 the State took over the school from Henderson-Brown College, a Methodist institution established here in 1890, which merged with Hendrix College in Conway (see Tour 3a).

An expansion program begun in 1936 has enlarged the campus and added a science hall and three dormitories.

In Arkadelphia is the southern junction with State 7 (*see Tour 8b*).

Leaving the southern edge of Arkadelphia, US 67 stretches straight ahead for a long distance, and is paralleled by the tracks of the Missouri Pacific.

GURDON, 64.3 *m.* (210 alt., 2,045 pop.), is a railroad junction point where Missouri Pacific lines branch from the main route north to the lumber town of Norman and south through El Dorado into Louisiana.

One rainy day in 1892, when Arkansas was in the midst of its timber boom, six bored lumbermen, beleaguered in Gurdon by high water and bad roads, amused themselves by originating the Concatenated Order of Hoo Hoo. The order, conceived in a spirit of horseplay, and bestowing upon its officers such titles as "Grand Snark of the Universe" and "House of Ancients," amazed its originators by spreading throughout the lumber country. As lumber production in the Southern forests declined, the largest timber operators moved into the Northwest and into Canada; and with them went the ever-growing Hoo Hoo.

Between Gurdon and Prescott the pine and oak forests are broken by a few farms. Peach orchards appear here and there, indicating that the highway is approaching the fruit-growing region of southwestern Arkansas.

PRESCOTT, 80.7 *m.* (319 alt., 3,177 pop.), a lumber town in 1873, became a trading center and cotton-shipping point as the land was cleared. Fruit-marketing is now a leading activity.

Seat of Nevada County, Prescott was one of the first towns in Arkansas to operate its own public utilities, installing municipal light and water systems in 1899 with a bond issue of $16,500. No bonds have been issued since, and the plant is now valued at $250,000.

The grandfathers of Prescott's old families lived in Moscow, a mile south of the present town. Here, in 1864, occurred a battle of some strategic significance in the War between the States. General Frederick Steele, who was occupying Little Rock with Federal troops, attempted to effect a junction with General N. P. Banks, who was advancing up the Red River, so that together they might attack Shreveport. Confronted by Generals T. P. Dockery and Joe Shelby at Moscow, Steele was checked after a skirmish and turned south to Camden. Banks met reverses at the same time in Louisiana, and, after Steele encountered further difficulties, the attack on Shreveport was abandoned.

Left from Prescott on State 19, graveled after the first asphalt-paved mile, through the bottoms of sluggish Terre Rouge Creek. Stretches of shaggy water oak and swamp weed are brightened by the green blades of wild yucca, crowned in summer by white, bell-like blossoms. At 20.5 *m.* is the junction with a graveled road; L. here, passing decaying wooden derricks of an almost abandoned oil field, then through an operating field with steel derricks and storage tanks, 2.4 *m.*, to WATERLOO (300 alt., 500 pop.*), once an important oil center. Exhaustion of the high-grade petroleum in the district did not, however, result in Waterloo turning into a ghost town: the sludge pumped from declining wells assayed about 70 per cent asphalt, and became the basis of a new local industry. The BERRY ASPHALT PLANT (*visitors admitted*) consists of great, red oil tanks, smaller asphalt reservoirs, and a few office buildings and tool houses. Most of the work is done at the control valves. The company's output is used principally by road builders and shingle manufacturers. The greenish slate is shipped from quarries in the Ouachita Mountains.

State 19 continues south to WALDO, 35 *m.* (350 alt., 1,240 pop.) (*see Tour 14*), which is at the junction with US 82 (*see Tour 14*).

Between Prescott and Hope, US 67 traverses the eastern edge of southwest Arkansas' fruit-raising area. Peaches, pears, plums, and watermelons, as well as subsurface vegetables—sweet and Irish potatoes, and peanuts—thrive in the light soil.

At 93.6 *m.* is the junction with a graveled road.

Right on this road to the FRUIT AND TRUCK BRANCH EXPERIMENT STATION, 1.3 *m.*, of the University of Arkansas College of Agriculture. Broad test-fields and vineyards spread beyond a shrub-dotted quadrangle of brick buildings. Since its establishment in 1927, the station, by example, has induced many farmers to give up the unprofitable cultivation of cotton. Hundreds of varieties of fruit trees are grown, and experiments are conducted with vegetables, grapes, melons, and berries. Model farm cottages are demonstrated, along with barns, rural sewage disposal, and water and lighting systems.

HOPE, 96.5 *m.* (353 alt., 7,475 pop.), is a leading fruit-shipping point and the "watermelon capital" of the State. Melons as big as hogsheads are grown hereabouts, the champion (1939) being a 195-pound whopper.

Interest in producing oversized watermelons began some years ago when a new stock-feed variety grew to a previously unheard-of size in Hempstead County. A seed salesman stimulated informal competition among farmers by offering prizes. When specimens of 100 pounds and over began to appear, the businessmen of Hope realized the publicity value of the gargantuan fruit, and from 1926 until 1930 the town held August watermelon festivals to which visitors came from all over the State. A drouth in 1930 blighted the harvest and ended the festivals, which have not since been resumed.

Raising a giant watermelon requires as much art as growing a rare orchid. The farmer selects an exceptionally sturdy vine and clears the field around it. When the melons first appear he chooses the most promising and culls all the others. At this point solicitude begins in earnest. Castor beans or other plants are set around the pampered melon for shade; the soil is enriched with nitrogen-charged water from the manure trough or with commercial fertilizers; the melon is force-fed from shallow pans of water through lengths of wool yarn driven into the stem.

While the supermelons thus produced look well in the newspapers, they do not make particularly good eating. For the regular markets, therefore, Hempstead County grows watermelons of the more conventional 25- to 40-pound size.

At the junction of several railroad lines, including a branch to the Nashville peach district (*see Tour 2b*), Hope is an important commercial center. For 60 years its residents battled to make it the governmental center of Hempstead County as well. Washington (*see below*), the county seat since 1824, rich in history and tradition but with little business activity, resisted stoutly. Until 1938 repeated elections failed to give Hope the county seat. Meanwhile, the courthouse that Hope citizens had confidently erected some years before had been turned into a city hall, so that it was necessary to build a new courthouse.

While it depends largely upon fruit shipments, Hope also has a cotton compress and gins, a furniture factory, a basket and crate factory, a handle plant, and a brick kiln. The downtown streets are more lively with traffic and shoppers than most Southern towns; and new homes lining the residential avenues indicate the prosperity brought about by diversified farming.

The products of the BRUNER IVORY HANDLE FACTORY (*visitors admitted*), 301 North Laurel St., are made of hickory and white oak. In 1888 the plant's founder did his first work with hatchet and drawknife. Machine-turned handles are now shipped to tool manufacturing concerns in the North and East, where they are fitted to canthooks for Alaskan lumberjacks, hammers for South American carpenters, and axes for New Zealand woodsmen.

The HARRY J. LEMLEY ARCHEOLOGICAL COLLECTION (*open on application*), at 320 East Edgewood St., consists of pottery, Indian pipes, and thousands of stone artifacts. Authorities consider the display one of the most valuable privately owned collections in the United States. Though specimens from all parts of Arkansas have been gathered, perhaps the most outstanding relics are those of the Caddo tribes who once lived along the Ouachita and Red Rivers and made hard black pottery of high quality.

1. Right from Hope on a graveled road to the HOPE BRICK PLANT (*open on application*), 1.5 *m.*, which employs about 75 men in manufacturing brick from the clays of the district. The dozen beehive-shaped kilns are connected by tunnels so that excess heat from one oven can be diverted into another; time thus saved in preliminary heating of the kilns speeds the baking process.

2. Right from Hope on State 4, graveled, to WASHINGTON, 10.2 *m.* (374 alt., 432 pop.), one of the most highly civilized communities in early Arkansas, State capital in 1863-65, and now a living museum of old houses, old trees, and old memories.

Soon after the Louisiana Purchase, the first settlers came down the Southwest Trail, known also in this neighborhood as the Chihuahua Trail. In 1824 Elijah Stuart built a tavern that became Hempstead County's seat of government and the first building in Washington. The trail, widened and improved, brought a population of more than 2,000 to Washington before the War between the States. David Crockett stopped here on his way to Texas, and Sam Houston lived in the town for a time. When the Mexican

War broke out in 1846, Washington became military field headquarters for the American forces.

In 1840 a newspaper, the *Washington Telegraph,* was established. This weekly appeared regularly under the same name for more than 100 years, before it became the *Journal-Telegraph* through a merger made by its publisher, a great-grandson of the founder. In 1840, also, a young New Yorker named Nathan Douglas Smith began keeping weather records in the pioneer village. Long afterward, in presenting his *Meteorological Tables* (1840-60) to the Smithsonian Institution, he wrote: "My thermometer has hung all the time in the same place, in the open air . . . outside of the sash, on the north side of the house . . . and protected from any injurious reflection. My rain-gauge is a deep tin cup, set on the ground, in an exposed spot in the garden, and the rain measured after every fall."

Many distinguished attorneys of the Territory made their headquarters in Washington, among them Augustus H. Garland, who later became United States Attorney General (*see Tour 14*). Albert Pike was particularly amused by Major Thomas Hubbard's legal practice. This lawyer, Pike wrote, "contracted a great affection for his cases and became actually unwilling to see the most aged ones come to an end, as one dislikes to see that of an old friend. He had them of ten, fifteen and even more years of age, resented any attempt to bring them to what he considered untimely trial, and sincerely mourned for them and celebrated their obsequies, when, gray with age, they were gathered unto their fathers. To win one was almost as unwelcome to him as to lose it, when it had become hallowed and sanctified by time."

The War between the States brought Washington its greatest prominence. Imminent capture of Little Rock in 1863 by Federal forces under General Frederick Steele caused Governor Flanagin and his staff to move to Washington. Protected by Sterling Price's Confederate troops, the town became a gathering point for Southern refugees. The *Telegraph* was one of the few newspapers left west of the Mississippi to publish war news from a Confederate standpoint, and copies (sometimes printed on wallpaper) were eagerly sought.

An early-day smith in Washington, James Black, has often been called the inventor of the bowie knife, a weapon cherished by frontiersmen and renowned in dime novels. The story of this accomplishment usually accepted in Arkansas is that Black, who had once been a silversmith in Philadelphia, came to Washington and set up a blacksmith shop on the Chihuahua Trail; to this shop came James Bowie (or his brother Resin, sometimes spelled Rezin) with a hunting-knife pattern carved from the wood of a cigar box. Black altered Bowie's design, and of this collaboration the famous blade was born. In the following years Black hammered out many bowies, testing each one by whittling on a tough hickory ax handle for half an hour, then using the blade to shave hair from his arm. Black grew old and blind, jealously guarding the formula of his steel. In 1872, when he was dying, he tried to tell the secret to a friend, but to his consternation found that he had forgotten the dozen or more processes that gave the knife its unrivaled temper.

The legend has never been disproved, but strikingly similar versions—also never disproved—have grown for a hundred years in the South and Southwest. Some writers hold that the first bowie was shaped in New Orleans by a Spanish cutler named Pedro. In Texas the knife is attributed to one Noah Smithwick. Two descendants of the Bowie clan maintained that a plantation craftsman, Jesse Cliffe, wrought the original implement. Antiquarians in Philadelphia have claimed that James Bowie himself hammered out the first model when he visited that city. In Natchez it is said that a blacksmith's rasp furnished the crude steel, and that the cutler was a Natchez artificer. At any rate, bowies went into mass production, for at least one British cutlery firm began turning them out wholesale.

The blacksmiths who created the "first" bowie knife in the vast wilderness apparently all possessed something akin to the Damascus secret. Some scorned such prosaic tests as whittling hickory ax handles, and instead drove their bowies through silver dollars. Others rejected blades that did not quiver at the touch of a finger, or give off a vibrating bell-like tone when flipped with a thumbnail.

A Texas historian, J. Frank Dobie, attempted to unravel the stories connected with the nonpareil blade. He concluded, however, that "Bowie's knife has become nothing less than the American counterpart of King Arthur's 'Excalibur' or of Sigmund's great sword 'Gram,' . . . and its origin is wrapped in multiplied legends as conflicting and fantastic as those that glorify the master weapons of the Old World."

Authentic bowies are as rare as the legendary Arkansas razorback hog, but a deciphering of several descriptions indicates that the blade was about ten inches long, curved concavely on the back, convexly on the edge. At its broadest part the steel was about two inches across. The knife was equipped with a guard and hilt, and was well balanced for accurate throwing. The hilt, of horn or ivory, was often used as a pestle to grind coffee beans. An indispensable quality was a cutting edge that would remain razor sharp despite the roughest usage, and this edge was almost always termed "as keen as a lightning flash."

The pioneer used his bowie for carving willow whistles, for skinning game, cutting firewood on the trail, and hacking underbrush. It was the unexcelled weapon for infighting until Colt perfected the revolver, a few years after "Big Jim" Bowie fell in defense of the Alamo, wielding one of the knives that immortalized his name.

The old Chihuahua Trail ran down Franklin Avenue, still the main street of Washington. At the junction of Franklin and State 4 is WASHINGTON TAVERN or Travelers' Inn, built in 1830. The inn is a two-story building, constructed mostly of hand-hewn timber that was later weatherboarded. Eventually it was bought and remodeled into a residence by Colonel W. H. Etter, founder of the *Telegraph*.

The OLD HEMPSTEAD COUNTY COURTHOUSE AND STATE CAPITOL (*open*), on a low hill in the center of Washington, is a simple two-story building with a small classic portico, restored to an approximation of its original appearance by the United Daughters of the Confederacy in 1930. Completed in 1833, it served as legal headquarters of the county until 1875, and of the State from 1863 to 1865. State records were kept here until the close of the War between the States, except for a short period during which the approach of Federal troops caused them to be moved to Rondo (*see Tour 14*). The building was used as a schoolhouse from 1875 until 1914.

The OLD BAPTIST CHURCH, built about 1830 and still in use, is a small frame building with a pediment supported by four columns. Three of these are the original hewn cypress trunks; the fourth is a box column replacing one that was cut up for firewood during the War between the States when the church was used as a hospital.

The one-story frame A. O. STUART HOUSE (*open*), built of hand-finished lumber in 1852-57, is still in a fair state of repair. A. O. Stuart's fourth wife, Ruth McEnery Stuart (1849-1917), was the author of *Sonny* (1896), a dialect novel of Arkansas "poor whites" (*see Literature*).

US 67 continues southwest from Hope through orchards and watermelon patches, with fields of cotton becoming more frequent as the route nears the Red River.

FULTON, 109.6 *m.* (268 alt., 485 pop.), during the first half of the nineteenth century was a jumping-off place for expeditions into the turbulent Southwest. At Fulton the American section of the Southwest Trail ended; here and at Dooley's Ferry, a few miles up the Red River, were the crossings into Mexican territory. Founded in 1813, Fulton was a frontier trading post until, nurtured by land and water traffic, it grew into a commercial center.

Side-wheelers made their way among the shoals and snags of the Red River, bringing supplies from New Orleans. Townspeople came down to the wharf to sample bananas and other exotic fruits; small boys poked out knotholes in the hogsheads of sugar and dug the sugar out with spoons. Goods from the steamboats were transferred at Fulton to freighters, pulled by six mules apiece to Washington and other settlements. On each wagon, dangling in a bucket at the rear, was a supply of tar for greasing the wheels. From this practice arose the colloquialism "Hang me on for a tar-bucket" when a traveler wanted to board an already crowded vehicle. Drinking and gambling were conducted with pioneer lustiness in Fulton's early days. It is creditably reported that in one session of stud poker an entrepreneur lost $2,200, a cotton plantation, and the steamboat *Waukesha*.

Frequent floods and the building of a railroad terminal at Texarkana led to Fulton's decline. The rampaging Red River is now confined by levees, and in high-water seasons the residents go calmly about their business with the river booming past 20 feet higher than their heads.

US 67 crosses Red River at Fulton.

Near Texarkana the highway emerges from the cotton bottoms into livestock country. Here are fields of oats and lespedeza, herds of mules and cattle, high concrete silos, and great barns.

TEXARKANA, 128.6 *m.* (337 alt., 11,821 Ark. pop., 17,019 Tex. pop.), (*see Texarkana*).

Texarkana is at the junction with US 71 (*see Tour 9b*) and US 82 (*see Tour 14*).

In Texarkana, US 67 crosses the Texas Line into Texarkana, Texas.

〰〰〰〰〰〰〰〰〰〰〰〰〰〰〰〰〰〰〰〰〰〰〰〰〰〰〰〰〰〰〰

Tour 2

(Memphis, Tenn.)—Forrest City—Little Rock—Benton—Hot Springs —De Queen—(Durant, Okla.); US 70.
Tennessee Line to Oklahoma Line, 283.1 *m.*

Concrete-paved roadbed between Tennessee Line and Hot Springs, asphalt-paved between Hot Springs and Kirby; elsewhere graveled.

Chicago, Rock Island & Pacific Ry. roughly parallels route between Tennessee Line and Benton; Missouri Pacific R.R. between Little Rock and Hot Springs. Accommodations in larger towns; tourist camps numerous.

US 70 between Memphis and Hot Springs is part of a transcontinental highway sometimes called the Broadway of America. After leaving the Mississippi River the route in its swing through Arkansas crosses most of the rivers in the State. Sluggishly rolling under bridges east of the capital are the St. Francis, L'Anguille, Cache, and White. After crossing the Arkansas at Little Rock the road dips southwest through rugged country drained by streams that are clearer and faster —the Saline, Ouachita, Caddo, Little Missouri, and Cossatot.

Cotton, corn, and rice grow abundantly on the flat lands of eastern Arkansas. The soil of the hills to the west bears timber, fruit, and pasture. The hills themselves contain a variety of minerals that are mined today, or have been mined in the past: bauxite for aluminum and compounds, novaculite for whetstones, cinnabar for mercury, and precious stones from the only diamond mine yet discovered in North America.

*Section a.   TENNESSEE LINE to LITTLE ROCK; 135.9 m.,
US 70*

Once a stump-studded path wandering through the wilderness from the Mississippi River, the Memphis-Little Rock highway is now among the most heavily traveled routes in Arkansas, carrying a constant procession of tourist cars and interstate bus and truck lines. In St. Francis County the road climbs through the curious geologic formation of Crowley's Ridge (*see Natural Setting*), noted for its peaches. Descending at Forrest City, the highway passes through level farmlands and skirts the northern edge of the Grand Prairie rice belt between Wheatley and Lonoke. Cotton plantations reappear in the Arkansas River Valley.

US 70 crosses the TENNESSEE LINE, 0 *m.,* in the center of the muddy Mississippi, on the Harahan Bridge, which carries the trains of three major railroads as well as automobile traffic. Arkansas baseball fans point out the bridge as the spot from which the manager of the Memphis team of the Southern Association promised to dive into the river if his team did not finish ahead of the Little Rock Travelers in the 1936 pennant race. Memphis trailed the Travelers, but the manager resigned in midseason, and was spared the leap.

At 0.7 *m.* is the junction with a graveled road.

Right (*straight ahead*) from the bridgehead to the Greyhound Race Track, 0.2 *m.,* where for two 40-night seasons each year streamlined hounds chase a fleeing mechanical rabbit. The stadium holds 2,500 spectators, whose money is scientifically tithed by pari-mutuel machines. The track is under the jurisdiction of the Arkansas Racing Commission.

Right from the race track on a dirt road to a fork at 0.5 *m.*; R. here through cottonfields to the Site of Hopefield, 1.5 *m.,* marked by a frame cabin set high on pilings. One of the first towns in Arkansas, Hopefield was founded by Benjamin Foy, a Hollander, who moved across the Mississippi from the Chickasaw Bluffs (now Memphis) about 1797. Foy had been sent to the Bluffs in 1794 as an agent to the Chickasaw by Gayoso, Spanish governor of Louisiana. Gayoso built Fort San Fernando de las Barrancas on the site of Memphis in May 1795, but after pressure by the United States the Spaniards abandoned their Tennessee outpost and withdrew to the west bank of the river, where they built Fort Esperanza in 1797. Foy moved with the soldiers and settled on a point above the fort.

The Spaniards soon departed, but the former agent to the Chickasaw remained and prospered. A dozen years later, in *Sketches of a Tour to the Western Country* (1810), Fortescue Cuming mentioned "a fine stock of horses, cows and oxen" at "Mr. Foy's handsome settlement and good frame house." Foy also kept a store and owned "a small barge which he sends occasionally for goods to New Orleans, from whence she returns, generally in forty days, and did so once in thirty."

Under the American regime Foy became a magistrate, and accounts agree that he was a man of attainments. He "appears to have possessed a far more extensive and correct knowledge of the country than any other man in it," reported James B. Davis in his *History of the City of Memphis* (1873), "and his statements were held by the government as the most reliable, which caused the point to be visited, not only by many of our most able statesmen of that day, but also by distinguished tourists from foreign countries. Among the latter I might name the great philosopher, historian, poet, deist, etc., Volney, who spent the winter of 1805 with the Judge in quest of knowledge." Reuben Gold Thwaites, in his notable collection of *Early Western Travels* (1905), comments that Foy's settlement was "said to have been the most healthful, moral, and intelligent community between the Ohio and Natchez."

The Americans who settled around Foy's store translated the name of Fort Esperanza to Hope Encampment, then to Hopefield. The town flourished as a river port, and in 1857 became the eastern starting point of Arkansas' first railroad, the Memphis & Little Rock. Hopefield burned during the War between the States, and the ruins were swept away by the Mississippi.

An optimistic farmer raises cotton on the adjoining acres when they are above water. Since the land, lying outside the levee system, has been flooded nearly every winter since 1923, cultivation is apparently planned on the assumption that a flood is certain. When there is "late water" (March-April) no crop is made. In 1937 the field was under 16 feet of water. The farmer once more moved back to higher land, and, as he expressed it, "rested and tried to figure out how to cross cotton with water lilies."

At the PERMIT STATION (L), 0.8 *m.*, of the Arkansas Department of Revenues, interstate trucks must stop to be weighed and to obtain permits for travel within the State. Since most trucks can carry loads heavier than the law allows, there is a temptation to overload, and drivers carry on a constant battle of wits with permit stations and weight officers.

At 1.4 *m.* on US 70 is the junction with a private road.

Left on this asphalt-paved road to the U. S. ENGINEER OFFICE, 0.5 *m.*, under the jurisdiction of the United States War Department. Buildings are of modern, industrial design; the principal one is a four-story, concrete, fireproof structure. Activities of the office began in 1890 and have increased until they now include channel and harbor maintenance, flood control, levee building, and bank protection. Here are the shops at which the various boats of the Revetment Fleet (*see Tour 10*) are maintained.

In the golden days of river steamboats (1840-80), packets lined the shores of Mississippi ports so thickly that one could sometimes walk across decks for nearly a mile without stepping ashore. It was not uncommon for a dozen boats to dock or depart each day, and in very active seasons a single steamer would be loaded to the smokestacks with 3,000 bales of cotton. Though the fabulous days of the packet are gone, vast tonnages of freight are transported up and down the Mississippi in less ornamental but more efficient steel barges. A single barge tow has been known to carry enough steel to fill more than 100 railway freight cars. Eight oil barges in a string, a fairly common sight, carry the same amount of gasoline or crude oil as 9 freight trains of 40 tank cars each. Grain, pipe, and machinery for the petroleum fields of Oklahoma and Texas, cotton for New Orleans warehouses, and other bulky freight not requiring rapid transportation, are piled by cranes on barges pushed by little stern-wheelers that look like seagoing lawnmowers as they thrash up and down the river.

In WEST MEMPHIS, 5.8 *m.* (221 alt., 3,369 pop.), the well-built stores, service stations, cafés, and tourist camps that stretch for more than a mile along US 70 have an air of being new and busy. At first glance the town appears to be a thriving suburban district of Memphis, but it has had an independent growth. Founded about 1910 as a logging camp, it was known as Bragg's Spur until its incorporation in 1927, when the name was changed to take advantage of the premium price that lumber identified with the Memphis basin commanded in foreign markets. Behind the façade of neon signs, elaborate gasoline stations, and fruit stands are the industries of the town—a sawmill, two gins, a large compress, and a cottonseed oil mill. West Memphis has grown so rapidly in the last decade that its population almost quadrupled between 1930 and 1940.

In West Memphis is the junction with US 61 (*see Tour 10*).

LEHI, 12.6 *m.,* marks the junction with US 79 (*see Tour 12*),

West of Lehi, where sizable stretches of land have not been cleared, cottonfields break between forests of willow, oak, and cypress. The plantation centers usually have a store, a bright corrugated-iron gin, and a loading platform. Farmers in overalls and wide-brimmed straw hats lounge about the store on hot summer days, when the most common sound is the thump-thump-thump of a hound's leg on the floor as he scratches contentedly. Oldtime hunters say that fleas are a hound's salvation: his constant twisting and clawing in pursuit of the tormentors keep his joints supple.

Not so fast as his highly bred brothers at the race track, the farm hound is a master in the art of unraveling the twisted trail of that swamp phantom, the wildcat. Lazy during the day, the dog frisks like an excited puppy at night when lanterns are refilled or carbide head-lights brought out for a hunt. Padding down a dim trail, he suddenly jerks his nose to the ground and snuffles anxiously, his soft nose making little noises over each stick and leaf; then his quavering, exultant baying floats across the swamp. To an experienced ear the baying tells a story. If the trail is cold, the cry at first is hesitant and indecisive. As the hounds become more certain, their voices are more enthusiastic, and if they finally jump the wildcat their sudden full sound fills the bottom with a steady, rhythmic music. They lose the trail at the slough, then find it again, and drive closer and closer, until finally the panting cat, his breath and tricks both exhausted, ascends a tall cypress and spits down at the clamoring dogs. Ordinarily the quarry is shot down by hunters, or jumps from his perch at their approach. Once on the ground he lays about him, sometimes fighting from his back so that he can use all four sets of claws as well as his teeth. Again, he may back up against a tree, and with ears and lips laid back, dare the dogs to close in. His breath recovered, he may break through the circle of hounds and make a dash for the thickest tangle of canebrake and brier, where as often as not he eludes his pursuers and skulks off through the swamp, more lean, ragged, and ill-tempered than ever.

The shore of BLACK FISH LAKE (*cottages, boats, bait*), 21.9 *m.*, has been developed as a recreational area, and the lake enjoys a reputation for catfish, crappie, bream, and bass. In 1839 Frederick Gerstaecker, the German adventurer-romancer, wrapped himself in a buffalo skin and slept on the shore while mosquitoes hummed around him. In his *Wild Sports in the Far West* (trans. 1870) he describes the lake as a "coffee-coloured piece of water, several miles long, and some hundreds of yards wide . . . its gloom . . . increased by overhanging cypresses."

US 70 crosses the ST. FRANCIS RIVER at 38.3 *m.,* and the wooded hills of Crowley's Ridge rise up immediately to the west.

At 39.9 *m.* the route crosses a boundary of a Soil Conservation Service demonstration project, with headquarters at Forrest City. Here many gullies on the Ridge have been sodded with grass and partly filled with brush. Some land has been withdrawn from cultivation and turned into pasture. On the remaining acres crops have been planted in strips, and according to the contour of the land.

FORREST CITY, 43.5 *m.* (276 alt., 5,699 pop.), on the western slope of Crowley's Ridge, is the commercial center of St. Francis County. The town grew from a construction camp of the Memphis & Little Rock Railroad in 1867, and was named for Confederate General Nathan Bedford Forrest, who had contracted to put the railroad through the Ridge. The business houses, often on terraces above the street level, are of brick and stucco. Residences are typical of those in a Southern county seat: a few are brick, two-storied structures, but the majority are white frame cottages with wide cool porches.

Beginning about 1920, Elberta and Early Wheeler peach trees were planted in large numbers on the Ridge, and peach growing has now become an important enterprise. The picking season usually reaches its height late in July.

COMMUNITY PARK (*adm. 15¢-25¢*), north end of Washington St., a landscaped community center, has a one-story white frame auditorium and a concrete swimming pool.

The ST. FRANCIS COUNTY COURTHOUSE, Izard and South Front Sts., is a massive two-story yellow-brick structure with a raised field-stone foundation. Deep bays break the lines of the exterior walls, and a clock tower rises from the northwest corner.

The FORREST CITY OIL MILL (*open on application*), South Division St. at the railroad tracks, centers around a two-story red-brick structure where cottonseed is crushed and the oil extracted. Connected with the mill by suction pipe conveyors are four corrugated-iron seed storage houses.

The FEDERAL COMPRESS (*open on application*), at the western edge of the town, south of the railroad tracks, is housed in an immense, rectangular, red-brick-and-frame building, divided into sections by brick fire walls that extend a few feet above the roof line. Here cotton bales delivered by the gins are compressed into smaller sizes and stored for shipment.

West of Crowley's Ridge the highway crosses a gently rolling area where cotton and corn fields have a backdrop of white oak, red oak, hickory, gum, beech, and elm trees.

US 70 crosses L'ANGUILLE RIVER (*fishing*) at 50 m. Flooding of the bottomlands, once common here, has now been eliminated to a considerable extent by drainage projects.

A RICE ELEVATOR (R) 59.4 m., a low red frame building with a square corrugated-iron tower, marks the fact that the route passes through the northern edge of the Grand Prairie rice-growing region of Arkansas (*see Tour 12*).

WHEATLEY, 63.3 m. (202 alt., 362 pop.), with its low brick stores lining the highway, divides its interest between rice and cotton. The town, first known as Dennis Station, was named for Wheatley Dennis; about 1876 it was given its present name.

BRINKLEY, 68.2 m. (204 alt., 3,409 pop.), a cotton and lumbering center, is built around a triangular park of which the railroad tracks form the northern edge. The business district is L-shaped. The man on the street wearing overalls and brogans is a small cotton farmer; if he wears gum boots he is from the Cache River bottoms. The man in work shirt and pants is probably from the lumber mill, and if he is slightly stooped, with glasses and a studious look, he is probably a foreman, or perhaps the sawyer who glances at the bark and waves for the carriage man to "turn her over" before the carriage runs the log back to the whirling saw.

When construction of the Memphis & Little Rock Railroad was proceeding again after the War between the States, a railroad camp was established here on a site that had been cleared by two small sawmills working the hardwood forest. Merchants with an eye for the construction camp's pay roll soon erected three or four stores, and the town that grew up was named for R. C. Brinkley, president of the railroad. In 1871 the first train in Brinkley arrived from Memphis. The laying of this initial track in the State was beset with serious engineering and financial problems. A bridge builder employed by the road wrote in his reminiscences:

There was a dense canebrake a large part of the way from Cache River to the high land west of Brinkley, which made the work tedious and expensive. . . . The [bridge construction] force numbered about twice as many men as needed, owing to sickness from chills and fever. . . . The men were nearly all Irish. . . . I wrote the assistant chief engineer explaining the condition of the force and asked him to send me one barrel of good whiskey, and two dozen ounces of quinine. . . . I had the barrel mounted in my private office. . . . I put an ounce of quinine in a jug of whiskey and sent it up to camp with orders . . . to "jigger" the men three to four times a day. By the time I had used up the quinine there was not a sick man on the job.

Brinkley, taking advantage of its position on the railroad, rapidly developed as a shipping point for lumber. As the densely wooded land was cleared, cotton cultivation began, and cotton gins and compresses were established.

The DOOLEY LUMBER COMPANY PLANT (*open on application*), at the northern edge of town, occupies frame and brick structures surrounded by platforms and lumber stacks. The high overtone of the saw penetrates every corner of the mill, singing when it runs free, sharpening into a scream when it bites the log. Everyone squints just a little from the fine sawdust that is always in the air, and noses smart from the smell of fresh, raw lumber.

Right from Brinkley on State 17, graveled, to the FARGO AGRICULTURAL SCHOOL, 7 *m.,* a vocational self-help school for Negro boys and girls, established in 1920 by a young Tuskegee alumnus, Floyd Brown. On the landscaped campus are two dormitories, a two-story white frame academic building, and several cottages and barns. Some 200 acres adjoining the campus are cultivated in corn, cotton, potatoes, and truck crops by the students, who raise practically everything served in the dining room. Tuition in the school, which receives no government aid and depends on contributions, is about $5 a month; enrollment averages 175.

State 17 continues north to COTTON PLANT, 11.4 *m.* (192 alt., 1,778 pop.), its main street lined with long rows of red-brick stores. William D. Lynch, owner of a near-by cotton plantation, laid out the town in 1840 and named it for his lint-covered acres. On the Hill Plantation west of Cotton Plant occurred, on July 7, 1862, the Battle of the Cache, sometimes called the Battle of Hill's Plantation, or the Battle of Cotton Plant. Following the Battle of Pea Ridge in northwest Arkansas General Samuel R. Curtis took his invading army southeastward through the hills to Batesville, where he planned a campaign against the Arkansas capital. Proceeding down the east side of White River, Curtis encountered Confederates under General Albert Rust at Cotton Plant. After the battle Rust retreated across the Cache. Curtis, however, surprised at the organized resistance and uncertain as to the whereabouts of reinforcing gunboats he had expected to come up the White River, turned eastward and moved down to Helena, postponing the attack on Little Rock until the following summer.

The LYNCH HOUSE (*open*), a dogtrot log cabin, was the first house built in Cotton Plant. Part of the original structure still stands. A flagstone walk leads through the chinaberry-shaded grounds to the front gate.

The SOUTHWESTERN VENEER COMPANY PLANT (*open on application*), at the southern edge of town, is housed in a group of long, low, corrugated-iron buildings. Here tupelo, gum, and other hardwoods taken from the Cache and White River bottoms are cut into workable lengths, soaked in vats for several hours, and then cut into thin sheets. The finished plywood is shipped to furniture manufacturers in Northern states.

West of Brinkley US 70 lies atop a high earthen fill built across several miles of bottomland. Trestles span the occasional drainage ditches. When it was new, this stretch of excellent highway tempted motorists to such high speeds that wrecks were frequent. Guard rails, warning signs, and improved contours have since reduced the number of accidents.

CACHE RIVER, 80.3 *m.*, is almost hidden in canebrakes and willow thickets. In the curves of the river, secluded from civilization, the rare otter still exists. Looping his way along like an aquatic dachshund, swimming under water for long distances with incredible speed, the otter catches both the slow moving carp and the darting bass. Among the merriest of animals, otters will establish themselves in whole families on a clay bank and spend hours sliding down on their bellies, like boys with sleds on a snow-covered hill. Having been hunted to near-extinction for their glossy brown coats, otter are protected by law in Arkansas until 1943.

BISCOE, 83.3 *m.* (189 alt., 395 pop.), also known as Fredonia, is the headquarters of a Farm Security Administration resettlement project, one of several in the State.

DE VALLS BLUFF, 86.8 *m.* (192 alt., 686 pop.), on the western bank of White River, is a shipping point for rice, fish, cotton, and hay. The highway forms the main street, bordered by weather-worn commercial houses. Overlooking the river are the bluffs that made the settlement an active steamboat port long before 1860. During the War between the States a large Federal army camped here and erected an arsenal and a large frame barracks (later used as a hotel, a courthouse, and an opera house). Federal General Frederick Steele reported to the War Department: "This is a healthy locality, no swamps in the vicinity, and the current in the river rapid. The health of the command has improved perceptibly since our arrival here."

The western section of the trouble-beset Memphis & Little Rock Railroad was completed from Little Rock to De Valls Bluff in 1862, but the war suspended further construction. For several years eastbound rail passengers transferred to steamboats that took them down White River to Clarendon. Here they boarded the stage for Madison, and later Brinkley, in order to reach the eastern section of the tracks. In 1871 White River was finally bridged, the mayor of De Valls Bluff drove a last spike, and the first interstate railroad in Arkansas was complete.

In 1873 De Valls Bluff was made one of the seats of Prairie County, the other being at Des Arc.

HAZEN, 93.9 *m.* (235 alt., 819 pop.), a central point for storing and shipping rice and cotton, was named for Dr. W. C. Hazen, who, in 1854, brought his family and slaves here from Covington, Kentucky. The prairie was covered then with high grass that sheltered abundant game. Settlers found it difficult to keep herds of deer away from the first vegetable gardens.

Right from Hazen on State 11, graveled, to DES ARC, 18.4 *m.* (203 alt., 1,410 pop.), one of the oldest river ports in the State. The town is active as a railroad shipping point for farm products and lumber. Along the water front are several docks, where White River catfish and buffalo fish, caught by commercial fishermen with trotlines and seines, are kept until shipped to Little Rock or Midwestern cities. Des Arc was settled in the 1820's and incorporated in 1854. In 1860 river steamers took out 13,000 bales of cotton.

CARLISLE, 103.1 *m.* (222 alt., 1,080 pop.), is a trading center for farmers who sell rice, cotton, and dairy products. Founded in 1871, Carlisle had among its earliest citizens Albert Emonson, a Norwegian, who brought to the community excellent draft horses and Holstein cattle. Emonson later acquired the town's first general store, and ran a newspaper, a lumber mill, and a large plantation on the Grand Prairie.

In the 1870's there also came to Carlisle a young printer, Opie Read (1852-1939), who later became a best-selling novelist (*Emmett Bonlore, An Arkansas Planter, A Yankee from the West,* and others). Read and a partner, H. C. Warner, founded the first of a series of Arkansas papers, *The Prairie Flower.* Of Read's first venture into Arkansas journalism Fred W. Allsopp, in his *History of the Arkansas Press* (1922) says, "The Prairie Flower was pretty, but frail and lonely, and soon withered and died."

The ARKANSAS STATE RICE MILLING COMPANY PLANT (*open on application*), at the western edge of the business district, is a four-story, corrugated-iron building. Rice is brought to the plant by truck and is carried through conveyors into storage bins. Milling includes extraction, grading, and polishing the kernels. The mill has a processing capacity of 1,800 "pockets" of rice a day, a pocket being a trade term for 100 pounds. The busy season of the mill is from September through January.

The KRAFT-PHOENIX CHEESE PLANT (*open on application*), west of the rice plant, was established in 1927 and later enlarged to handle the 50,000 pounds of raw milk brought in daily by dairymen. Approximately ten pounds of whole milk are required to produce one pound of cheese. A by-product of cheese-making is whey, which is returned to farmers and used by them as feed for chickens and hogs.

LONOKE, 111.9 *m.* (239 alt., 1,715 pop.), at the junction of roads from the ricefields to the east, the strawberry patches to the north, and the cotton plantations to the west and south, is a shipping point for all three crops. The town was named for a landmark of pioneer days, a solitary red oak that stood near the present railroad station.

The LONOKE COUNTY COURTHOUSE, erected in 1928, is a three-story brick building to which a classic note has been added by the four pillars of the façade. On the top floor, concealed by an ornamental wall, is the county jail.

The JOSEPH T. ROBINSON HOUSE (*private*), facing the railroad track at the east end of town, is a rambling two-story white frame house in which Lonoke's best-known citizen lived. Joseph T. Robinson (1872-1937) was elected Governor of Arkansas in 1912 while serving his fourth term in Congress; he resigned from Congress, was inaugurated as Governor, and within a few weeks was elected by the general assembly to the United States Senate, where he remained until his death, acting as leader of Senate Democrats after 1922. In 1928 he was running-mate to Al Smith in the latter's unsuccessful campaign for the presidency. "Joe T.," as all Arkansas called him, was a bulky man with a powerful voice, and a master of American politics. He won wide approval by such activities as sponsoring relief for poverty-stricken farmers and his attacks on religious prejudice.

A cottonfield (R) at 112.8 m. was an Army aviation school during the World War. The tract, donated to the Federal Government in 1917, was named for Captain Melchior M. Eberts, an Arkansas flyer who crashed and was killed at Columbus, New Mexico. The field was in use until the end of the war, when hangars and equipment were removed.

At 113.6 m. is the junction with an asphalt-paved road.

Left on this road to the STATE FISH HATCHERY (*open daylight to dark; guides*), 0.6 m. The hatchery, one of the largest in the United States, covers 267 acres and includes 58 artificial ponds, surrounded by bright green weeping willow trees, shrubs, and flowers. Brood stock is placed at spawning time in special ponds, outfitted with "nests" made by screening off corners. When the fish are newly hatched they are transferred to rearing ponds where they are kept and fed until they reach fingerling size. They are then shipped by tank truck and placed in streams and lakes throughout the State. More than 1,500,000 bream, crappie, and catfish are hatched here each year. The artificial ponds afford a refuge to thousands of wild ducks which feed in the near-by ricefields.

HILL LAKE (*fishing prohibited*), at 124.2 m., winds alongside the highway (L) for several miles. Filling an abandoned curve of the Arkansas River, the water is shadowed by dense foliage and dotted with huge-kneed cypress trees. Near the lake the road passes between long rows of pecan trees into rich cotton land, cultivated in large plantations.

At 130.6 m. is the northern junction with US 67 (*see Tour 1a*), with which the route unites for 28.8 miles.

Between the junction with US 67 and the city limits of North Little Rock is a series of cafés and small roadhouses patronized by visitors from Little Rock and neighboring towns.

At 132.1 m. on US 70 is the junction with State 30.

Left on this concrete-paved road, which follows the levee of the Arkansas River as it cuts through the valley, to SCOTT, 9.4 m. (248 alt., 225 pop.*), the headquarters of the 6,000-acre George Alexander Plantation, with cotton gin, loading sheds, and commissary.

Right from Scott on a paved road 2.4 m. to the STATE FOREST NURSERY (*open 8-4*), comprising 40 acres and operated by the State for the purpose of propagating seedling oak, pine, and walnut trees. The physical plant, including machinery for threshing pine seed, is housed in two white frame buildings that overlook the river. Cover crops of peas and velvet beans are grown to condition the soil for the seedlings. The first year's growth of pine reaches a height of 8 to 12 inches. Oaks, which later grow slowly, produce a first year's seedling of 12 to 18 inches. At "lifting" and shipping times 30 men are employed.

State 30 continues from Scott to a junction with a graveled road, 13 *m.;* R. here 0.8 *m.* to the tree-covered TOLTEC INDIAN MOUNDS. Two large and several smaller mounds overlooking a crescent-shaped lake are all that remain of the group, reputed to have once numbered 40. A report by a United States Bureau of Ethnology representative in 1891 called the group "one of the most important in the United States." Fragments of pottery, stone implements, and some human and animal bones have been taken from the smaller mounds. The name "Toltec" is a conjectural title, since no scientific warrant yet exists for associating the mounds with the Toltec, who preceded the Aztec as rulers of Mexico (*see Archeology and Indians*). Several times the elevations have been useful to bottoms farmers as places of refuge during floods.

NORTH LITTLE ROCK, 134.7 *m.* (256 alt., 21,137 pop.) (*see Little Rock and North Little Rock*).

North Little Rock is at the northern junction with US 65 (*see Tour 5a*), with which the route unites for 1.2 miles.

Right from North Little Rock on Main Street, which becomes State 5, to a junction with an asphalt-paved road, 3.6 *m.;* R. here to another junction, 3.8 *m.;* R. again to the center of LAKEWOOD (*open; fishing, swimming in lowest lake*), 4.4 *m.* Developed by real estate promoters, the park, surrounding a chain of artificial lakes in a timbered valley, is a favorite picnic spot. The OLD MILL, on the central lake, is an ingeniously built concrete reproduction of an ancient moss-grown gristmill, complete with water wheel and grinding stones. Rustic bridges, stiles, and other structures surround the mill.

From North Little Rock US 70 crosses the Arkansas River on the Broadway Bridge.

LITTLE ROCK, 135.9 *m.* (291 alt., 88,039 pop.) (*see Little Rock and North Little Rock*).

Little Rock is at the junction with US 167 (*see Tour 15*), State 10 (*see Tour 13*), and the southern junction with US 65 (*see Tour 5b*).

Section b. LITTLE ROCK *to* OKLAHOMA LINE; 147.2 *m.,* US 70

At Little Rock US 70 turns southwest and, in its course between the capital and the Oklahoma Line, passes through a region of strikingly varied natural resources. A short distance from the center of the State are mines that yield most of the bauxite dug in the United States. The ore is used to make aluminum, abrasives, and aluminum chemicals. Near Benton are clay deposits long used for making pottery. For about 50 miles the highway skirts the Ouachita National Forest, a splendid wooded playground for sportsmen and vacationers. Farther along are deposits of cinnabar, the source of mercury. Vast peach orchards border the route as it nears Oklahoma.

Leaving LITTLE ROCK, 0 *m.,* on Roosevelt Road, US 70 passes a line of tourist camps, service stations, restaurants, general stores, and small farms. Gradually, the buildings spread farther apart, giving way to fields and, increasingly, to woods.

BOYLE PARK (R), 5.7 *m.,* is a 231-acre tract of pine- and oak-covered slopes owned by the city of Little Rock. Good roads lead through the park to picnic areas containing pavilions, tables, and fireplaces. Horses can be rented at the stables west of the pavilion for rides along the cypress-grown creek, through dogwood, service berry, and redbud.

The old brick STAGECOACH HOUSE (*adm. 25¢*), 8.7 *m.,* in a yard fringed with cedars, is rich in Arkansas history. Designed in 1836 by Gideon Shryock, Kentucky architect of the Old Capitol (War Memorial Building) in Little Rock, the brick house is built between broad chimneys. A paneled door, with the original lock and brass key, opens into a central hall, from which a walnut stairway leads to the second floor. Early-day chandeliers and furniture ornament the place.

Intended as an overnight stopping point on the old Southwest Trail, the inn was originally known as the Ten-Mile House. When General Frederick Steele's Federal Army occupied Little Rock the house became a military headquarters, and a few Confederate prisoners were kept here; one name and the autographer's profane opinion of "damn Yankees" is still a legible scrawl on the wall. The woods near by witnessed the capture of David O. Dodd, 17-year-old Confederate dispatch bearer, who was hanged in Little Rock. The onetime inn is now a tearoom and antique shop.

At 13.5 *m.* is the junction with a graveled road.

Left on this road to the THOMAS C. MCRAE MEMORIAL SANATORIUM (Negro), 2.2 *m.* The institution, named for a former Governor who was also president of the Arkansas Tuberculosis Association, was authorized in 1923 and opened in 1931. The original building, a white-brick, T-shaped structure surmounted by cupolas, served about 35 patients. A large new addition completed in 1940 increased the capacity to nearly 200 beds.

COLLEGEVILLE, 15.5 *m.* (440 alt., 80 pop.*), was named in 1823 by Ezra M. Owen, who set aside 40 acres of land and laid out a town site, hoping to have a State college located here. The school was never built, however, and the town is now a crossroads trading post.

Alongside US 70 in Collegeville is a concrete marker (R) erected in 1936 by the Arkansas Society of American Colonists. A bronze plate on the marker reads: "The geographical center of Arkansas is a few steps north of this highway." Though this spot is traditionally the geographical center of the State, Bulletin 817 of the U. S. Geological Survey (1930) gives the exact center as "twelve miles North of West of Little Rock," which would be in the neighborhood of Palarm Creek where it is crossed by US 65.

Right from Collegeville on State 111, graveled, to the STATE TRAINING SCHOOL FOR GIRLS and the STATE REFORMATORY FOR WOMEN (*open 2 Sundays each month*), 1 *m.* The institutions, under the same management, have an average of 100 inmates. Women and girls make their own clothes, cultivate gardens, and can food. A school is conducted during 9 months of the year.

At 16.8 *m.* on US 70 is the junction with a graveled road.

Left on this road to BAUXITE, 6.1 *m.* (358 alt., 2,063 twp. pop.), owned by the Republic Mining and Manufacturing Company. Workers in the town are nearly all engaged in mining and refining bauxite. Houses are not arranged in regimented rows, as in many company towns, but string out along the curves of three intersecting roads, and are surrounded by trees and gardens.

The community centers around a small circular park opposite the Republic mill. Near the park are the company offices, a post office, school, church, a community building with a wide veranda, and the general store. Farther off is the railroad depot and the motion picture theater.

The REPUBLIC MINING AND MANUFACTURING COMPANY PLANT (*visited by permission 8-4 workdays; guides*), a property of the Aluminum Company of America, crushes ore dug from the near-by mines, and removes the moisture. That part of the bauxite intended for the manufacture of aluminum is shipped to a reducing plant in East St. Louis, Illinois, where it is converted into alumina. The alumina is sent on to mills in the East for manufacture into metal and metal products. A portion of the ore is calcined in Bauxite and sold for use in chemicals and aluminum abrasives. About 450 workers are employed in the milling processes. A semicircular MUSEUM in the Republic office contains exhibits of aluminum products and a photographic frieze illustrating the manufacture and uses of the metal. An illuminated map indicates the flow of the ore from mine to manufacturer.

Two smaller refining mills operate in the outskirts of Bauxite: the NORTON COMPANY PLANT, at the northern end of town, with about 50 employees, and the independently owned ARKANSAS BAUXITE CORPORATION PLANT in West Bauxite, employing some 60 workers. Each of these mills has its own group of employees' homes.

A few minutes' drive in any direction from the town will bring one to a bauxite mine. There are some slope and shaft mines running a few hundred yards underground, but most of the deposits lie so near the surface that they are worked by stripping. Steam shovels peel off the topsoil and bite into the rust-colored friable rock.

The Arkansas deposits of bauxite were discovered in 1887. Shortly before this time an Ohio college student, Charles M. Hall, had devised the electrolytic refining process that was to change aluminum from a scientific curiosity to a widely used material. The first shipment from Arkansas (20 tons) was made in 1896, and production increased steadily. In 1918 the peak was reached, with an output of 563,000 tons. Today (1941) Arkansas diggings produce 95 per cent of the bauxite mined in the United States, but vast deposits in Guiana have supplemented domestic production. About half of Arkansas bauxite is now used for aluminum products, the remainder going into abrasives and chemicals.

Farm houses along US 70 are fairly substantial, protected from the road by groves of pine and cedar. In the back yards three-legged black iron washpots are standard equipment.

A hill (L), 21.4 *m.,* contains a deposit of kaolin, showing deep red with green and yellow streaks; from this clay Niloak pottery is made at Benton (*see Tour 1b*). The shallow excavations have made no appreciable impression on the vein, although for more than 20 years clay has been dug in this vicinity.

BENTON, 23.5 *m.* (291 alt., 3,502 pop.) (*see Tour 1b*), is at the southern junction with US 67 (*see Tour 1b*).

West of Benton oak, hickory, and elm forests reappear, and the ground pitches more steeply. US 70 twists through cut-banks that show red clay and gravel, and small white rocks dot the fields.

At 28.2 *m.* is the junction with a graveled road.

Left on this road to CAMP QUAPAW, 1.2 *m.,* a Boy Scout summer camp, high on a wooded bluff overlooking Saline River. The 22 buildings accommodate about 100 boys, and a pump and concrete tank supplies water for the pine-log shower house.

Near ALUM FORK, 34.5 *m.,* cuts made to lessen the grade of the road over the hilltops show shale as well as gravel, and highland pines give way to black and sweet gum in the creek bottoms. Alum Fork is the stream that is dammed to obtain a water supply for Little Rock (*see Tour 13*).

Close to Hot Springs the hills grow more humpbacked, and the road twists and doubles across narrow mountain streams. Roadside stands sell woodwork, pottery, and baskets to tourists visiting the spa. The rounded bulk of Hot Springs Mountain looms near the town.

At 50.8 *m.* is the northern junction with State 7 (*see Tour 8a*), with which the route unites for 7.2 miles.

On a hill back of a service station at 53 *m.* a NOVACULITE QUARRY is worked intermittently. Light charges of blasting powder loosen the stone, which is then pried out with crowbars. Novaculite (Lat., *novacula,* razor) for whetstones has been taken from the hills near Hot Springs for more than 100 years, and several quarries still operate from time to time. Germany remained the principal market for whetstones after synthetic carborundum largely replaced them in the United States. Before white men began mining novaculite, Indians used the material for fashioning arrowheads and tools. Henry Schoolcraft, a geologist who visited Arkansas in 1818, was favorably impressed with the deposits: "A quarry of this mineral three miles above the Hot Springs of the Washitaw [Ouachita] has often been noticed by travelers, for its extent and the excellency of its quality. A specimen now before me is of a grayish white color, partaking a little of green, translucent in an uncommon degree. . . . Oilstones . . . are procured from this place, and considerable quantities have been taken lately to New Orleans" (*A View of the Lead Mines of Missouri,* 1819).

HOT SPRINGS, 58 *m.* (599 alt., 21,370 pop.) (*see Hot Springs*).

Hot Springs is at the southern junction with State 7 (*see Tour 8b*) and at the eastern junction with US 270 (*see Tour 11*), with which US 70 unites for 2.2 miles.

West of Hot Springs the highway curves past tourist camps and roadside restaurants. At 60.1 *m.* is the western junction with US 270 (*see Tour 11*).

US 70 crosses LAKE HAMILTON at 62.9 *m.* The 9,000-acre lake, created by Carpenter Dam on the Ouachita River in 1931, is a hydroelectric development which has become equally important for recreation. Thousands gather each summer for the swimming, motor-boat regattas, and fishing. The lake is restocked regularly, and black bass up to 10 pounds have been taken there. Cabins and lodges dot the shores; their occupants may turn from water sports on the lake to hunting squirrel and rabbit in the Ouachita National Forest. Deer and turkey are also hunted in season. Near the lake roads lead from the highway to boatlandings and vacation camps.

A few miles south of Lake Hamilton conifers close in, pines whose timber adds to the income derived from rocky wayside farms. Farmhouses are set well back from the road, with pine trees in the front yards topped to make the branches widespreading. Flocks of hens scratch busily in clumps of scrub oak and around the sheds. Here and there is a deserted house, where peach trees bloom around a crumbling stone chimney. Roses from cuttings planted by a pioneer wife ramble among weeds in the overgrown front yard. Old rail fences surround fields taken over by pine shoots and sassafras sprouts.

Little country cemeteries under gnarled cedars along the road are filled with modest white markers. Yellow jonquils nod in the wind, and around the mounds are scattered mussel shells and bits of broken glass, once arranged in simple decorative patterns, but now dispersed by the rains among the leaves of honeysuckle and English ivy that have covered the almost forgotten graves.

GLENWOOD, 81.5 m. (547 alt., 854 pop.), is bordered with peach orchards laid out in precise alignment, in contrast to the usual informal planting of the hill farmer. The town grew up around a sawmill. The mill burned, and the shipment of pulp pine then became the chief activity. The central building is the log AMERICAN LEGION HUT, which serves as town hall and municipal dance floor.

Right from Glenwood on State 27, graveled, through rugged country, with a great blue hogback looming on the right. CADDO GAP, 5 m., is a break in the hogback through which pass the Caddo River, the highway, and a lumber-carrying spur of the Missouri Pacific Railroad. The road, cut high in the side of the bluff, affords a magnificent view of the green pines and the blue stream rushing past gravel banks.

The town of CADDO GAP, 8.2 m. (619 alt., 311 pop.), is enriched each summer by tourists who come for the bass and crappie fishing and for the mountain scenery. A bronze statue of a Tula Indian stands at the Caddo Gap crossroads; according to an inscription, confirmed by the United States De Soto Expedition Commission, it marks the farthest westward point reached by De Soto in his journey from Florida.

KIRBY, 90.7 m. (666 alt., 80 pop.), is a cluster of dwellings, filling stations, and stores.

Left from Kirby on State 27, paved to the junction with a dirt road, 5.8 m., at the brow of a hill; R. on this road, winding through rough back country underbrush, 5 m. to a CINNABAR MINE (open on application), owned by the Southwestern Quicksilver Company and operated at intervals. From the shaft on the side of a hill (R) the ruby-red crystals are brought up by cable and buckets. The ore is heated until the metallic mercury passes off as vapor, which is condensed and purified of the accompanying sulphur. A ton of good ore yields about ten pounds of mercury, the only metal that is liquid at ordinary temperatures. The product is shipped in steel flasks holding 76 pounds, and is used in the manufacture of chemicals, explosives, and electrical apparatus. Only recently (1930) were rich deposits of cinnabar discovered in Pike and Clark Counties; in the past world trade has depended largely on the mines in Spain. Uncertainty about the market price and troubled international conditions have made capital reluctant to invest heavily in the equipment necessary for large-scale mercury production in Arkansas. Nevertheless, in 1939 more than 1,200 flasks were shipped from the several Arkansas cinnabar mines.

State 27 continues south to MURFREESBORO, 15.2 *m.* (367 alt., 835 pop.), centering around Pike County's three-storied red-brick courthouse. The town leads a quiet, agricultural existence. Peach cultivation is slowly extending up from the south, and local businessmen await development of the cinnabar deposits discovered to the north.

Left from Murfreesboro on a dirt road 3.3 *m.* to a closed DIAMOND MINE, covering nearly 80 acres surrounded by a wire fence and patrolled by a guard. Though small quantities of diamonds have been found in the western gold fields and other parts of the country, the claim that the deposit here is the only diamond mine ever to be discovered and exploited in the United States is not questioned.

John M. Huddleston, who owned and farmed the site after 1900, was puzzled because a part of his land would grow no crops. Tramping over his sterile acres one day in 1906 he picked up two crystals that aroused his curiosity. He sent them to a Little Rock jeweler for identification. To the astonishment of the jeweler, the farmer, and his neighbors, the stones were diamonds. Huddleston, according to old residents, sold his holdings to a hastily organized mining corporation for $38,000. Geologists sent to the site discovered that the barren acres covered the "pipe" of an ancient volcano. Though the existence of peridotite in the region had been noted by a geologist as early as 1842, and the volcanic area had been mapped in 1890 by John C. Branner, then State geologist, Huddleston was the first man to discover the diamonds.

From 1908 until 1925 a small plant operated fairly steadily at the mine. The ore was washed, crushed, and sluiced over a grease table that retained the white, yellow, and brown stones. Diamonds found here have been brilliant and of an excellent luster. A high proportion of the crystals, however, were very small (the mine's average was 50 stones to a carat), and many had a structural distortion that made them unsuitable as jewels, though not lessening their worth for industrial uses. A few of the stones taken out have been very valuable—one specimen weighed more than 40 carats and was valued at $8,000. Increasing use of diamonds in hard-edged cutting tools and instruments may result in the reopening of the mine.

The HIGHLAND PEACH ORCHARD (R), 19.2 *m.,* on State 27, with nearly a million Elberta peach trees, reaches as far as the eye can follow, over gently rolling ridges. The trees are set out with mathematical precision to permit passage of cultivators and wagons down the rows, and a network of pipes sprays insecticides. The first seedlings were planted in 1902, and some of the original trees are still bearing—low, knotty, fruit producers that are carefully and constantly tended. The county's crop ranges up to 2,000,000 bushels a year, and the price averages 90¢ a bushel. About March 1 the Nashville Chamber of Commerce makes an accurate forecast of the date the orchards will be in full bloom. The sight of limitless acres of bright blossoms attracts thousands of visitors to the neighborhood each year.

NASHVILLE, 29.5 *m.* (373 alt., 2,782 pop.), has been called by sociologist Edmund de S. Brunner, of Columbia University, "a typical village of the New South." Farmers in this territory have practiced with more than average success the diversification of crops long advocated by agricultural economists as a cure for the ills of the cotton belt. Peaches now outrank cotton as the chief crop. Corn and alfalfa are grown for feed; and the raising of such vegetables as cabbage, onions, tomatoes, and cucumbers, and the breeding of livestock, have created a steady prosperity. The seat of Howard County is a clean little city with wide streets and neat brick buildings. More than the usual number of motion-picture theaters and brisk department stores indicate that the farmers and townspeople spend, as well as earn, their income in a modern manner. Artist John Tazewell Robertson chose peach growing as the subject of his mural on the wall of the United States Post Office lobby.

Southwest of Kirby US 70 passes through country even more sparsely populated than the Ouachita Forest border. Pines line the road for miles, their green needles a bit dusty in the late summer, bright after the winter rains. The scattered farmers live almost completely self-sufficient lives. Perhaps their philosophy was expressed by the old Confederate soldier who, returning home from the war to find his credit gone, penned the following letter to his grocer:

Go to hell, Mr. Merchant, with your supplies. The woods is full of 'simmons, the vines is full of grapes, the 'possum is fat and slick, the coon is as good as ever; and we can live on these till springtime comes; then we can live on blackberries till roasting ears come; then on them till the corn gets hard, and the old woman and boys can grind it on our old steel mill the Yankees left in the yard, while I hunt and fish. (From *Folklore of Romantic Arkansas*, Fred Allsopp, by permission of the publisher, The Grolier Society, Inc., New York, 1931).

At 111.2 *m.* on US 70 is the junction with a graveled road.

Right on this road to a STATE GAME REFUGE, 5.2 *m.*, where a number of beaver colonies have built dams and are increasing rapidly. An interesting and highly successful experiment in wild turkey restocking has been carried on here by the Arkansas Game and Fish Commission. Instead of using tame turkey hens to breed with wild toms, which produces a chunkier, less agile fowl than the purebred wild turkey, the Commission procures undomesticated hens and keeps them with their wings clipped in open-top pens into which wild gobblers fly. The eggs are hatched in incubators, and the young fowls, when three or four months old, are released in specially prepared coverts, as untamed as their forest cousins who have never seen a hunter.

DIERKS, 113.8 *m.* (422 alt., 1,459 pop.), has a red-brick, two-storied school (R), a row of stores, and a central strip of paving in its main street. South of the hip-roofed company houses is the community's economic base—the giant DIERKS LUMBER AND COAL COMPANY MILL (*open on application*). Long tin-roofed loading sheds lead out like fingers from the bulk of the main plant, and the high-pitched hum of swift power belts is punctuated from time to time by the piercing sound of the saws, explosive puffs, and the roar of machinery. The specialty of the mill is pine vegetable crates, sold to Texas firms and distributors in the North and East.

The vast and complicated operations of this huge plant are in marked contrast to those of the small mills worked as part-time projects by farmers here and there throughout Arkansas. A typical small sawmill involves the use of a light gasoline engine, or an old steam roller which has been countersunk and bolstered by heavy oak pilings. When the slab-roofed framework to shelter the workers has been erected and the carriage and track laid, the mill is ready for operation. A belt is run from a high wheel to transmit power. In slack times farmers snake out logs and haul them to the slope above the mill, and then roll them with cant hooks to the bed of the carriage, where they are held in place by adjustable blocks. About four men operate one of these small mills, including the off-bearer and the sawyer, who directs the movements of the log so as to get the most lumber out of a tree trunk. Where a steam outfit is used a fireman chops waste lumber and feeds it to the roaring fire under the boiler.

West of Dierks the hills fade into the bottoms of the Saline and Cossatot Rivers. The woods thicken and become gloomy; pines grow taller among great, straight hickories and bulky white oaks, and such near-river vegetation as vines and creepers appears in abundance.

At 137 *m.* is the eastern junction with US 71 (*see Tour 9b*), with which the route unites for 1.2 miles.

Service stations are scattered along the highway, and houses are spaced so that there is room for chickens and a garden and sometimes a cow. Buildings accumulate into a settlement just before the road turns right into De Queen.

DE QUEEN, 138.2 *m.* (432 alt., 3,055 pop.), was originally named Calamity. At a later date, in return for financial assistance, the Kansas City Southern Railway offered a Dutch capitalist, DeGeoijen, the privilege of christening several towns along the right-of-way. He gave his surname to the settlement built where the old Fort Towson trail crossed the railroad, and in a short time DeGeoijen was anglicized to De Queen. A weekly newspaper in the community is named, perhaps inevitably, *De Queen Bee.* Incorporated in 1897, and made the seat of Sevier County in 1905, De Queen has grown steadily. Two railroads (the De Queen & Eastern, and the Texas, Oklahoma & Eastern) built by the Dierks Lumber and Coal Company connect here. The town is also a division point on the Kansas City Southern.

The SEVIER COUNTY COURTHOUSE is a three-story brick structure, surrounded by arborvitae and elms. Proceeds of the bond issue that financed the building were tied up in a closed bank at Little Rock for more than two years (1930-33), and the courthouse stood uncompleted while De Queen attorneys united in a complicated legal battle that finally freed the funds.

In De Queen is the western junction with US 71 (*see Tour 9b*).

US 70 crosses SALT LAKE, 145.3 *m.*, a brackish pond that before and during the War between the States furnished a supply of salt, then a scarce commodity. Sometimes a day's wages consisted of a peck of salt, valued at about $10 a bushel in Confederate money. Fragments of large Indian vessels, the size of wash boilers, found in a mound

near the lake have been taken as evidence that the Indians, too, used
the water for salt making.

At 147.2 *m.* US 70 crosses the Oklahoma Line, 130 miles east of
Durant, Oklahoma.

<<<<<<<<<<<<<<<<<<<<<<<<<<<<<<<<<<<<<<<<<<<<<<<<<>>>

Tour 3

Marion—Searcy—Conway—Russellville—Fort Smith—(Muskogee,
Okla.) ; 287.6 *m.,* US 64.

Concrete- or asphalt-paved roadbed except for several short graveled stretches.
Missouri Pacific R.R. parallels route between Marion and Beebe, Conway and
the Oklahoma Line.
Accommodations in larger towns only.

US 64 is the most direct route across the middle of Arkansas. From
the Delta it runs directly west to intersect US 67, which it follows
southwest for some 30 miles. It then turns west again, reaches the
Arkansas River near Conway, and follows the northern valley wall to
Fort Smith.

Cotton and corn are the dominant crops along the whole length of
the route, but the patterns of cultivation vary considerably. In the
"black wax" soil of the Delta are great plantations, farmed principally
by Negro sharecroppers or day laborers. Beyond Crowley's Ridge
most farmers either rent or own their moderate-sized farms, and a
few ricefields appear. On the higher land west of the White River
cotton alternates with strawberries and livestock feed. The rolling
land along the Arkansas River is cut into small farms; here cotton
grows only in bottom patches.

Section a. MARION to CONWAY; 152.7 m., US 64

Before the Louisiana Purchase eastern Arkansas was a wilderness
of marshes and lowlands, crossed by many rivers and covered with
luxuriant hardwood, vines, and brush. Early travelers mentioned
difficult fords, mosquito-infested swamps, and trackless forests. Perhaps the least difficult of the few trails that penetrated the wilderness
was the Indian trace that ran from Chickasaw Bluffs (Memphis, Tennessee) to join the Southwest Trail in the neighborhood of Little Rock.

Most of the early white settlers and explorers who traveled by land followed this path, whether they intended to clear a homestead in the lowlands, or push on to the Arkansas River and thence westward. Many of the 2,000 Cherokee who were living in Arkansas by 1816 had moved westward over this route to their new homes. Improvements made the trail a military highway used during the Mexican War and the War between the States.

The old road, which US 64 approximates as far as L'Anguille River, was the most easily traveled route between Memphis and Little Rock until the construction of US 70 through the bottoms farther south (*see Tour 2*). The latter highway, many miles shorter, now carries nearly all of the through traffic, and US 64 is used chiefly by farmers, salesmen, and produce trucks.

US 64 branches west from US 61 (*see Tour 10*) in MARION, 0 *m.* (227 alt., 758 pop.). Paralleling the latter highway, which serves as the main street, are the tracks of the St. Louis-San Francisco Railway. To the east are old brick buildings used as general stores, barber shops, and the like. To the west are filling stations and business places for the highway trade, along with the more recently erected homes. Cotton ginning is an important source of income in the town.

The CRITTENDEN COUNTY COURTHOUSE, in the center of Marion, is a two-story brick building with a low green dome. A parkway planted with weeping willows leads to the six-columned entrance.

The county was named for Robert Crittenden (1797-1834), a brilliant young Kentuckian who fought in the War of 1812, and at 22 was appointed Secretary of the newly created Arkansas Territory. Arriving at Arkansas Post in 1819, Crittenden undertook the organization of the Territorial government while Governor James I. Miller made a tour down the Ohio and Mississippi Rivers (*see Tour 5a*). Despite his administrative and forensic abilities, Crittenden made many enemies by his political maneuvers, his disrespect for the Governors, and his habit of quarreling with his closest associates. In 1827 a dispute with Henry Conway, whose election as a delegate to Congress Crittenden had brought about four years earlier, resulted in a duel. Crittenden was a notoriously bad shot. Urged by friends to brush up his marksmanship, he took three shots at a tree, missed each time, and gave up in disgust. In the duel, however, he mortally wounded Conway with his first bullet. The death of the popular Congressman cast a deeper shadow over Crittenden's career, but he continued in law and politics until 1834. In that year, after arguing a case before the Mississippi supreme court at Vicksburg, he collapsed, and died shortly afterward.

In Marion is the junction with US 61 (*see Tour 10*).

Cottonfields border US 64 west of Marion. Occasionally a solitary sycamore or oak stands in the middle of a cultivated flat, or a streak of deep green brush marks the course of a creek. The irregular outlines of timber patches break the distant horizon. Houses of sharecroppers are sometimes bordered by a few hills of corn, almost always by a row of bright flowers.

Census figures for 1930 indicated that 86.6 per cent of the families engaged in agriculture in Crittenden County were tenants; 80.9 per cent of the entire population was Negro. These figures, both the highest of any county in the State, are probably connected with the difficult relations in the district between planters and sharecroppers.

As the cotton tenancy system changed after the World War, increasing economic pressure on the planters intensified old dissatisfactions and created new ones. The "furnish" arrangement, whereby planters maintained commissaries and extended credit to tenants to carry them over the nongrowing season, made the accumulation of savings difficult and offered little basis for future security. Generally illiterate, suffering from a poor diet, from malaria and pellagra, the sharecroppers were among the least favored economic groups in the United States.

In 1934 the Southern Tenant Farmers' Union was formed in eastern Arkansas. Locals met secretly, and under cover of darkness, in schoolhouses, churches, and swamps. The movement had the fervor of a crusade, and preachers were the most popular organizers. Strikes were called, and as union members marched past the fields, sharecroppers dropped their hoes to join them. The upheaval was given widespread publicity in newspapers.

Leadership of the union by white Socialists, several of them Easterners, increased the bitterness of the planters' fight for their own existence, and violent attempts were made to repress the newly organized labor movement. Vigilante groups broke up union meetings, attacked leaders, and burned strikers' homes. The union gained some concessions as a result of the struggle, and maintained its organization. Both the State and Federal Governments investigated the mass of charges and countercharges. Recommendations of the Federal Committee on Farm Tenancy had some influence on the present semiexperimental program for the reduction of tenancy under the Farm Security Administration.

CRAWFORDSVILLE, 8.9 m. (227 alt., 656 pop.), once a plantation headquarters, has grown into a cotton town. The more elaborate houses in the east end are shaded by luxuriant willows and surrounded by hedges.

The main street of EARLE, 19.3 m. (224 alt., 1,872 pop.), runs at right angles to the highway. A little more than a quarter century ago, when the country was covered with timber, Earle was a busy lumber center, and two small sawmills still remain. Today (1941) the town owes its leading position in Crittenden County to gins and compress and cotton-marketing facilities.

US 64 crosses the St. Francis River at PARKIN, 24.4 m. (223 alt., 1,412 pop.), and for a mile or so gives a view of the stream's lazy curves. The high Missouri Pacific roadbed then cuts off the scene to the south. On the opposite side of the road small farms press back the timber. Houses here are few, but rather large, and are occupied by farmers who own their stock and equipment and rent or own land.

LEVESQUE, 34.5 *m.* (229 alt., 15 pop.*), on the east side of Crowley's Ridge, is a railroad stop and crossroads trading center.

Left from Levesque on a narrow, graveled road that winds along the steep brush-covered side of the Ridge to WITTSBURG, 2.1 *m.* (230 alt.). At this point, where the St. Francis loops against Crowley's Ridge, was one of the few permanent crossings of the unruly river. In 1739 Bienville, who governed Louisiana for France, had a fort built here for use in a war against the Chickasaw. American settlers, in their turn, found the site a fortunate one, since not many places on the Ridge were accessible by water. After steamboats began to come up the river, Wittsburg, then known as Strong's Point, became an active port. Isolated pioneers traveled as far as 100 miles to buy salt, sugar, coffee, and bullets, bringing oxcarts loaded with cotton in exchange.

The port became the seat of Cross County in 1862, but began to feel the decrease of steamboat trade in less than a decade. In 1886 the county seat was moved to more centrally placed Vanndale, where it remained for a few years. Today nothing remains of Wittsburg but a store, a school, and a few houses. The level spot once occupied by the leading hotel, left of the road, is marked by two magnolias and a cistern.

Immediately west of Levesque US 64 enters a gap in Crowley's Ridge and passes between the rolling slopes.

WYNNE, 39.6 *m.* (266 alt., 3,633 pop.), on the western slope of the Ridge, is the seat and largest town of Cross County. At the junction of the Memphis-Little Rock and Knobel-Helena lines of the Missouri Pacific, the town is a division point for the railroad.

For about a month each summer Wynne almost forgets cotton in the rush of harvesting and shipping the Crowley's Ridge peach crop. Truckers from as far away as Michigan bring their transports to town. Filling stations set up "Peach Information Bureaus" to direct the drivers to orchards. Pickers and packers crowd the streets, and restaurants feature peaches.

The SUMMERSWEET ORCHARDS PACKING SHED, on the railroad track in the middle of town, is a center of peach-shipping activity. Lines of trucks piled high with bulging baskets pull up to the west side of the shed and unload. The fruit is dumped into a hopper, and on a series of rollers passes the alert eyes of women who pick out the damaged peaches. The sound fruit rolls on to a conveyor belt along which other women are posted at 10-foot intervals. These workers select the most handsome peaches for use as "facers," which are placed in baskets atop orchard-run fruit. Ornamental curls of green serpentine are dropped on the top layer just before the lids are wired to the baskets. The containers are then stacked for loading into refrigerator cars.

Unchilled peaches are highly perishable, so packers work each night until the entire day's harvest is ready for shipment. Girls and their grandmothers, high school boys and elderly men, find work at the shed during the season, and such of the townspeople as are not employed gather to watch the packing.

Left from Wynne on State 1, a concrete-paved road that runs along the west side of Crowley's Ridge, to the junction with a graveled road, 5.6 *m.*; L. here (straight ahead) to another junction, 6.7 *m.*; L. again to the SUMMER-SWEET ORCHARDS, 10.8 *m.*, source of most of Wynne's peaches. The orchards, stretching for miles over the rolling lands of the Ridge, were planted in 1930 by Herbert South, a Nebraskan. An experiment was made at the same time with raspberries, but this venture was later abandoned. Two hundred acres of apples are also under cultivation.

West of Wynne, the timber closes in on the L'Anguille bottoms. There is an occasional patch of late corn, planted perhaps in May or even in June when the soil has dried sufficiently to take the plow. In the water-filled roadside ditches, from which earth was taken for the highway, float the broad green leaves and yellow, cornucopia-shaped blossoms of yoncopins and other lilies.

L'ANGUILLE RIVER (Fr., the eel), 48.4 *m.*, was apparently named for its serpentine shape rather than for the eels rarely seen in its waters. Early-day engineers found the stream hard to bridge.

Between L'Anguille and Bayou de View, 60.2 *m.*, the road occasionally breaks from the heavy woods into a cleared area of ricefields, with drainage ditches, pumphouses, and an occasional windmill. As late as 1933 these lush fields were part of the forest. Successful rice growing in the Stuttgart area (*see Tour 12*) inspired farmers to buy up the second-growth timberland for a dollar or so an acre. They cleared off the trees, installed equipment, and began planting rice, with highly successful results. The cost of land clearing was paid in part by cutting the larger hardwoods into railroad ties, and selling the less valuable timber to a chemical factory.

Mainstays of McCRORY, 65.3 *m.* (211 alt., 1,010 pop.), are cotton gins, trade with rice growers, and some shipping of peaches. Named for Cyrus Wade McCrory, whose plantation provided its site, the town is built around a long main street lined with stores. McCrory was one of Woodruff County's three seats until 1931, when the legislature unified the county government, making Augusta the headquarters.

JELKS, 67.8 *m.* (200 alt., 284 pop.), is a village with two names, the Missouri Pacific Railroad and the United States Post Office Department calling the place Patterson. A factory here manufactures implement handles from the hardwoods of the near-by Cache River bottoms.

At 75.9 *m.* is the junction with the asphalt-paved Augusta Road.

Left here to AUGUSTA, 1.2 *m.* (224 alt., 2,235 pop.), built along the high east bank of the White River, on the site of an Indian village which white settlers called Chickasaw Crossing. In 1848 Thomas Hough, a wealthy Quaker from Maryland, established a trading camp for lumbermen who floated their rafts of 60-foot logs down the White and Mississippi Rivers to New Orleans, where the timbers were sold for masts on sailing vessels. In 1852 Hough obtained a charter for Augusta, which he named for his niece.

The town was beginning to flourish as a cotton port when the War between the States interrupted shipping. In 1862 General Frederick Steele's Federal Army, on its way down the White River, occupied Augusta, and troops camped for a time on the courthouse lawn.

Post-war years were troubled by the disorders of Reconstruction prevalent all over the State. The Ku Klux Klan, organized to combat carpetbagger oppression, was active in Augusta. In 1868, ten citizens were killed by militia-men searching the town for Klansmen, and martial law was declared in the county.

To connect Augusta with the Iron Mountain Railway (now the Missouri Pacific), which passed a mile to the south in the 1880's, the town built its own one-mile railroad. Formally named the Augusta Railway, the line was affec-tionately called the "Little Dummy." A mule-drawn St. Louis streetcar with bright yellow paint and red-plush seats was the road's initial equipment. In 1903 a locomotive and passenger coach were purchased. Automobile and highway development ruined passenger traffic on the "Little Dummy," but the line is still (1941) used for hauling freight.

The link with a railroad, in addition to a sawmill, cotton gins, and com-mercial fishing and mussel gathering, saved Augusta from the fate of many old river towns that all but vanished when steamboats left the waters. The river front is lined with houseboats whose occupants sell "Catfish 12½¢" or, for bait, "Minnows 50¢ for 100." Now and then a mussel scow, stacked with shells, is pushed slowly upstream by a chugging motor dory toward a button factory at Newport (*see Tour 1a*), or a barge docks at the sawmill with a load of logs brought from the river bottoms.

The WOODRUFF COUNTY COURTHOUSE, on Third St., is a Romanesque brick structure whose most prominent detail is a square corner tower topped by a Roman-type arched cupola and a pyramidal spire. The OLD JAIL in the rear was once the dining room and kitchen for slaves of Thomas Hough, Augusta's founder. The county was named for William E. Woodruff (1795-1885), pioneer Arkansas journalist.

Woodrow Wilson as a youth worshiped in the PRESBYTERIAN CHURCH, on Third St., when he resided for a time with his sister, wife of Reverend A. R. Kennedy, then the church's pastor.

At the end of Third Street is the carefully tended, century-old AUGUSTA CEMETERY. This spot may be the resting place of the notorious Missouri guerilla, Francis Quantrell. Quantrell is generally supposed to have died in prison. However, a Captain L. J. Crocker, who moved to Augusta shortly after the War between the States, asserted just before his death in 1917 that he was Quantrell, and that he had escaped clad in a dress brought him by his wife.

West of Augusta US 64 crosses the WHITE RIVER, 77.9 *m.*, and runs for ten miles on a series of high fills. This section of the road resembles a park: poplars line the highway, which looks down upon grass-covered meadows and timber, bright green even in the driest summer weather because of the backwater from the river.

In a newspaper article Dr. John A. Wyeth described the White River bottoms as they appeared about 1870:

> It is difficult to imagine anything more suggestive of helplessness and loneliness than one of these vast and seemingly endless stretches of cane, with now and then an open slash full of tall and stately cypress. . . . Deer were so plentiful that any excursion into the brush of the uplands or second bottoms would start up a herd of from six to a dozen. . . . They seemed to avoid the lowlands or canebrakes, and for good reason; the cane grew so thick they could not jump or run through it.

BALD KNOB, 88.6 *m.* (223 alt., 1,445 pop.) (*see Tour 1a*), is at the northern junction with US 67 (*see Tour 1a*), with which the route unites for 32.9 miles (*see Tour 1a*).

At 121.5 *m.* is the southern junction with US 67 (*see Tour 1a*). Between this junction and Conway the first ridge of the Ozarks is noticeable to the north. Far to the south, across the Arkansas, the foothills of the Ouachitas are barely visible. Occasional orchards and truck plots indicate the nearness of the Little Rock market. The land in this region has been worked for a long time. Fields are bounded by weathered rail fences. A number of the houses are decorated with the jigsaw scrollwork of the 1880's. Sometimes a gaunt brick or stone chimney rears out of a cottonfield, the solitary remnant of a burned homestead.

CONWAY, 152.7 *m.* (321 alt., 5,782 pop.), founded in 1871, is the home of three colleges, whose students make up a large part of the town's population. Some of the big, tree-shaded houses were built by farmers who moved to town in order to send their children to school.

The Conways for whom the community was named moved down from Missouri to a Red River plantation in the pioneer days of Arkansas settlement. Ann Conway was an early leader of the Methodist Church in the State. Of her seven sons, Henry, the oldest, was a Territorial Delegate to Congress, and two others became Governor of the State.

Opie Read (1852-1939), one of the greatest in the long line of Arkansas humorists, edited a Conway newspaper in the late 1870's. Typical of the farcical exaggeration which characterized Read's writing is the story he tells of going to the Conway town well for a bucket of water. An acquaintance stopped him for a drink; others joined them, and the bucket was passed around, while stories were told and gossip was exchanged. Finally Read said: "Well, gentlemen, I don't want to hurry you, but the printing office is on fire, and I just came down for a bucket of water to put the fire out."

The FAULKNER COUNTY COURTHOUSE, Faulkner St. and Robinson Ave., across the Missouri Pacific tracks from the business section, is a square cream-colored brick structure with pleasingly simple lines. Indicative of the taste of an earlier generation is the pyramidal roof and pointed corner tower of the OLD FAULKNER COUNTY JAIL, in the corner of the courthouse square. This building contains the public library.

ARKANSAS STATE TEACHERS' COLLEGE, at the southwest corner of Bruce St. and Donaghey Ave., is a co-educational training school maintained by the State. It provides a four-year course, and has an average enrollment of 800. An apartment building with housekeeping quarters for students is located among the lecture halls, laboratories, and dormitories scattered over the 40-acre campus of the college.

Baptist CENTRAL COLLEGE (for women), Conway Blvd. and College Ave., offers junior college work, including training in music, fine arts, and home economics. The principal building is a large two-and-a-half-story brick structure topped by a row of dormer windows, with tall columns along the front and a tower at each end. The school's other building, Bruce Hall, is a dormitory.

HENDRIX COLLEGE, 1400 Front St., began in 1876 at Altus as Central Collegiate Institute. During the next 15 years it was taken over by the State Methodist Conference, had its name changed to Hendrix, and was moved to Conway. In 1929-33 Henderson-Brown College of Arkadelphia and Galloway College of Searcy were merged with Hendrix. The whole is known as the Trinity System.

Buildings of the college occupy 38 acres along the city route of US 64 (R). The school, with an enrollment of about 440 men and women in 1939, offers pre-professional training in medicine and dentistry, as well as general college work; in its 38,000-volume library are many old newspapers, magazines, court records, and similar material of historical importance. One of the few Southern colleges to be given assistance by the Rockefeller General Education Board, Hendrix had by 1939 received about $600,000 from this source.

Of interest to students and historians is the PAUL CLAYTON LIBRARY (*open on application*), on Caldwell St., a private collection of old and rare books and Arkansiana. The library includes the journals of Bossu, La Harpe, and other early explorers.

The Jo E. FRAUENTHAL HOUSE (*private*), at the west end of Louvena Ave., a large three-story red-brick building with sun porches and a conservatory, is one of the town's show places.

In Conway is the southern junction with US 65 (*see Tour 5a*), with which the route unites for 1.7 miles (*see Tour 5a*).

Section b. NORTHERN JUNCTION WITH US 65 to OKLAHOMA LINE; 133.2 m., US 64

Between Conway and Fort Smith US 64 runs along the north valley wall of the Arkansas River, a natural westward path that was used for centuries by Indians and white hunters and trappers before the first trading towns sprang up along it and steamboats began to ascend the river.

Throughout most of the Arkansas Valley are prosperous cotton plantations, cornfields, and livestock farms. In the region between Clarksville and Mulberry, however, the Ozark ridges, blue shapes to the north along the entire route, roll down to the river's edge; and here field crops tend to give way to peaches, grapes, and other fruits and vegetables. Deposits of coal and natural gas have been developed in the Clarksville area.

West of the northern junction with US 65 (*see Tour 5a*), 0 m., US 64 curves around the high hill which rises from Conway. The quarter-mile MISSOURI PACIFIC TUNNEL, 1.8 m., where the tracks cross under the highway and plunge into the hillside (L) was considered a remarkable feat of engineering by the residents of Conway in 1903, when it was constructed. Previously, the railroad had rounded the hill, following the route that US 64 now takes.

At 4.1 *m.* is the junction with an unimproved road.

Left on this road, impassable in wet weather, to a fork, 1.2 *m.*; L. again to CEDAR PARK (*tables, benches*), 1.6 *m.*, a grove of cedar trees on the bank of the Arkansas which marks the SITE OF CADRON.

In 1778 a trapper named John Standlee, wandering up the Arkansas, decided that the bluff at the mouth of Cadron Creek would make an excellent site for a settlement. In 1814 he returned and built a house on the spot he had selected 36 years previously.

For a few years Cadron showed promise of becoming important. John Englebright established a tannery and boot shop. A general store stocked merchandise brought in by keelboat and dugout. Three gristmills were built on the north fork of the creek. A mail route ran from St. Louis to Cadron and thence to Arkansas Post, at the mouth of the Arkansas, without stopping at Little Rock.

Rivalry between Cadron and Little Rock reached a climax in 1820 when they contested for the seat of Pulaski County, which at that time embraced most of central Arkansas. The real prize was the Territorial capital, which everyone knew would soon be moved from Arkansas Post (*see Tour 12B*). The Territorial legislature voted Little Rock the county seat and the capital of Arkansas Territory. The defeated town survived for some years, but the bell of the first locomotive to pass through Conway, seven miles away, sounded the death knell of Cadron. Purely a river town, it died when men turned their backs on the river.

Samuel Plummer acquired a cabin at PLUMMERVILLE, 12.7 *m.* (287 alt., 541 pop.), in 1825; he enlarged it, installed machinery, and made saddles for sale to the Cherokee. When the Little Rock-Fort Smith stage line was established the house became known as Plummerville Station, and the town that grew up took the same name.

Jolting over the wilderness road in coaches whose bodies were suspended on leather straps must have been something of an ordeal. Nevertheless, owners of the stage line advertised complacently:

U. S. MAIL LINE
From Little Rock to Fort Smith
Leaves every Monday, Wednesday and Friday at 8 o'clock, A.M.
Passengers will go through by this line in comfortable post-coaches, with excellent stock and careful drivers, in about fifty-four hours.

In one of the last flare-ups of Reconstruction hatreds, John M. Clayton, defeated Republican candidate for Congress and brother of former Governor Powell Clayton, was murdered in 1889 as he sat at the window of a hotel in Plummerville, where he had come to investigate an election fraud. The killing aroused strong feelings, since Clayton was highly respected, but the assassin was never found.

Plummerville is the birthplace of Rupert B. Vance (1899-   ), sociologist and author of several books dealing with Southern conditions and problems. Among his works are *Human Factors in Cotton Culture* and *Human Geography of the South.*

MORRILTON, 18.5 *m.* (389 alt., 4,608 pop.), built on the Little Rock & Fort Smith Railroad in the 1870's, soon became the seat of Conway County and absorbed the old river port of Lewisburg, a short distance to the south.   An early highway bridge across the Arkansas River enlarged the town's trade territory.   In addition to the stores that line its several business streets, Morrilton today has a cotton-oil mill, a lumber mill, a meat-packing plant, and a large textile factory on its outskirts.

The MORRILTON PUBLIC LIBRARY (*open 2-8 weekdays, 10-6 Sat.*), on Division St. a block south of US 64, contains the William Porter collection of rare books, which includes catalogues of *Le Musée français* and of *Le Musée royale,* printed by order of Napoleon Bonaparte and supposed to have been the former property of the Spanish royal family.

Left from Morrilton on State 9, an asphalt-paved road that crosses the ARKANSAS RIVER at 2.6 *m.*   At 3.9 *m.* is the junction with State 154.   R. on State 154, asphalt-paved, which strikes across the level cotton-growing river valley directly toward the looming bulk of PETIT JEAN MOUNTAIN (1,100 alt.), 9 *m.*   The mountain, actually a part of the Arkansas River's southern valley wall, is reputed to have been named for Jean la Caze, a French aristocrat who fled the Revolution with his wife and eight-year-old son, outfitted a boat at New Orleans, and made his way up the Mississippi and Arkansas.   The wife and son, unable to stand the rigors of the wild country, soon died, but La Caze lived on, subsisting on berries.   The first American settlers who came up the valley found him, driven mad by his misfortunes, playing a flute he had brought with him.   Old-timers say that when the wind whistles around the south side of the mountain, where La Caze lived, the sound of his flute can be plainly heard.

PETIT JEAN STATE PARK, 14.7 *m.,* is reached after a steep ascent that permits impressive views of the winding river and the hills on its farther side.   The park, established in 1923, comprises 2,999 acres of pine-covered plateau on the edge of the Arkansas Valley wall.   Improvements include foot trails, bridle paths, picnic grounds, swimming and fishing lakes, and campsites.

LAKE BAILEY (*fishing, boating*), which covers 100 acres near the park entrance (R), is stocked with crappie and bream for the angler.

A PIONEER CABIN (R), 15.6 *m.,* built of square-hewn logs and chinked with mud, shows in its construction and furnishings the type of houses, even to the zigzag rail fence and log stile, in which the first settlers in the valley lived; many such cabins are still in use in the hill country.   Here also is the trail to CARPET ROCK, one of the many queerly shaped outcrops of greenish stone.

The path to CEDAR FALLS (R), 15.9 *m.,* ends abruptly on the edge of a deep gorge that widens out into a tremendous natural amphitheater, almost circular, whose steep walls are broken by the recess from which the waters of Cedar Creek drop 75 feet into the pool at the bottom.

MATHER LODGE (R), 16.2 *m.,* constructed of logs and stone, is a well-equipped tourist hotel built by the State.   On the edge of Cedar Canyon, its veranda affords sweeping views of the gorge and glimpses of the Arkansas Valley beyond.   Cabins are also available here.

BEAR CAVE (R), 16.9 *m.,* is not an underground cavern but a great heap of rock with curiously twisted and shaped crevasses.   Rock deposits of some types have been washed out, leaving passageways that are as much as 15 feet wide at the bottom and very narrow at the top.

The PALISADES (R), 17.4 *m.,* are at the point where Cedar Canyon opens into the wide Arkansas Valley.   From the top of the canyon one can see across the meandering blue Petit Jean Creek to the Arkansas River and the foothills beyond; the canyon wall drops straight down 500 feet.

At 19 *m.* on US 64 is the junction (L) with a hard-surfaced road.

Left on this road, which passes under the Missouri Pacific tracks, turning (R) at 0.2 *m.*, to the MORRILTON COTTON MILL (*open on application*), 0.8 *m.*, one of the largest in the State. The mill occupies a one-story building whose walls and roof are almost entirely of glass. Here between 80 and 150 men and women are employed in manufacturing wide duck cloth, sold to cutters in the East and North, who turn it into tents, tarpaulins, filters, and similar commodities. Twine and yarn are also manufactured.

ATKINS, 32.2 *m.* (357 alt., 1,322 pop.), incorporated in 1876, is another of the railroad towns which attracted business away from older river settlements like Galla Rock (*see below*). To the north of Atkins a long ridge called CROW MOUNTAIN parallels US 64 for several miles; on this higher land the crops are principally fruit and potatoes.

Near the mouth of GALLA CREEK, 38.2 *m.*, was the Indian village of Galla Rock, one of several established by the Western Cherokee on the upper Arkansas early in the nineteenth century. A few Cherokee had crossed the Mississippi in 1794 to escape reprisals after a so-called massacre at Muscle Shoals, Tennessee. After the Osage had vacated northern Arkansas by treaty in 1808, Chief Tahlonteskee led 300 Cherokee into the new land, and large numbers of the tribe followed, settling in the fertile valley of the Arkansas River.

In 1813 the United States Government sent a veteran of the American Revolution, Major William L. Lovely, to the Western Cherokee as agent. For four years Major Lovely lived alone with his wife among the Indians, "upwards of three hundred miles from a post office." Among his accomplishments was the gigantic deal, known as Lovely's Purchase, by which he obtained from the Osage what is now northwestern Arkansas and northeastern Oklahoma. After Lovely's death in 1817 his wife, Persis, continued to live among the Cherokee, and when a treaty signed in the same year required all whites to vacate the Cherokee territory, Mrs. Lovely alone was excepted.

The treaty of 1817, by which the Cherokee in Tennessee agreed to exchange their land for homes in northern Arkansas, was unacceptable to many members of the Eastern nation. Despite this, a considerable number migrated, including a group of 331 led by John Jolly, brother of Tahlonteskee. On the death of Tahlonteskee, Jolly became head of the Western Cherokee, and under his chieftainship Galla Rock was a model village. "You must not think that by removing we shall return to the savage life," he had written Secretary of War Calhoun. "You have learned us to be herdsmen & cultivators, and to spin and weave. Our women will raise the cotton & the Indigo & spin & weave cloth to cloath our children."

When Thomas Nuttall journeyed up the Arkansas in 1819 he found both banks "lined with the houses and farms of the Cherokees, and though their dress was a mixture of indigenous and European taste, yet in their houses, which are decently furnished, and in their farms, which were well fenced and stocked with cattle, we perceive a happy approach towards civilization. . . . some of them are possessed of property to the amount of many thousands of dollars, have houses handsomely and conveniently furnished, and their tables spread with our dainties and luxuries."

In 1829 the Cherokee were shifted still farther west, into what is now Oklahoma. When Sam Houston suddenly abandoned his bride and the governorship of Tennessee in 1829, he went westward to the new home of Jolly and the Cherokee, his childhood friends. Here he set up a trading post, entered into an informal marriage with an Indian girl, and ignored white civilization except for occasional letters to the Arkansas newspapers, which he signed "Tallentusky," a variation of the name of his foster father, Chief Tahlonteskee. Houston lived among the Indians four years before going on to Washington, Arkansas, and then into the limelight of the Texas revolution.

Galla Rock prospered as a steamboat landing and trading center until the railroad was built, away from the river, in the 1870's.

At 38.7 m. is the junction with a narrow hard-surfaced road.

Left on this road to POTTSVILLE, 0.2 m. (370 alt., 308 pop.), named for Kirkbride Potts, who came from Pennsylvania to Galla Creek in 1828 and who erected a house at this spot in 1854.

The POTTS HOUSE (*private*), on the old route of US 64 (L) in the center of the town, took six years to build. Doors and windows were shipped up the Arkansas; bricks for the chimneys were baked in a kiln on the place. The house served as home, trading post, post office, tavern, and overnight stop on the Little Rock-Fort Smith stagecoach route.

RUSSELLVILLE, 44.8 m. (351 alt., 5,927 pop.), seat of Pope County, is the largest town between Little Rock and Fort Smith and the center of a trading territory that extends northward into the Ozarks and southward across the Arkansas through the Ouachitas. Coal mines in the vicinity, a lumber mill, a woodworking plant, gins, and a cotton compress support the population.

Although Dr. T. J. Russell, British-born and British-educated physician, for whom the town was named, lived here as early as 1835, Russellville was not incorporated until 1870, and its real growth began a few years later with the construction of the Little Rock & Fort Smith Railroad (now the Missouri Pacific).

Russellville was long the residence of Jeff Davis (1862-1913), United States Senator and three times Governor, and still remembered for the homespun wit that flavored his campaign speeches. To one political opponent Davis shouted: "You threatened to kill me. I am not afraid of you. I can take a corncob with a lightning bug on the end of it and can run you into the river." His fearless orations were studded with such gems as: "a farmer with a patch on the seat of his pants as big as the map of South America"; and, "When I licked that gang in Little Rock during the last campaign they went around on the streets with faces as long as a saddle blanket." His credo read: "I am a Hard Shell Baptist in religion; I believe in foot-washing, saving your seed potatoes, and paying your honest debts."

In the Cities

WAR MEMORIAL BUILDING (STATE
CAPITOL, 1836-1911) LITTLE ROCK

AIRVIEW, LITTLE ROCK

Jungkind Photo Supply Co.

GARRISON AVENUE LOOKING TOWARD
THE ARKANSAS RIVER, FORT SMITH

STATE LINE AVENUE, TEXARKANA

HOT SPRINGS

SKYLINE, LITTLE ROCK

BATH HOUSE ROW

EUREKA SPRINGS

TIBBETTS HOUSE, FAYETTEVILLE

SIMMONS HOUSE, PINE BLUFF

ZOO BUILDING, LITTLE ROCK

Wilson: W P A

MUSEUM OF FINE ARTS, LITTLE ROCK

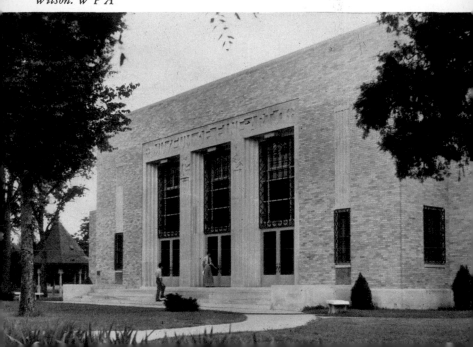

In the GEORGE BLACK HOUSE (*open*), 313 W. Eighth St. (end of Denver St.), is the most famed Arkansas picture—*The Arkansas Traveler,* done in oils in 1858 by Edward Payson Washburn (1831-60), son of a pioneer missionary to the Cherokee, Cephas Washburn. Dulled by time, damaged by water and folding, the painting depicts in somber blue and gray the meeting between the well-dressed, mounted Traveler, and the fiddle-playing Squatter seated on a keg. Washburn painted a number of mediocre landscapes and a few portraits, some of which hang in the Black home, but his fame depends on the *Traveler,* which was lithographed, copied, distorted beyond recognition, and hung in drawing rooms all over America during the Victorian era. He gave the original to his sister, who turned it over to her daughter, Mrs. Black.

The POPE COUNTY COURTHOUSE, on Main St., shows the straight lines and vertical emphasis characteristic of many public buildings constructed in the 1930's.

The OZARK NATIONAL FOREST SERVICE HEADQUARTERS (*open*), on US 64 (L) at the west end of town, are in a handsome two-story building completed in 1939. The lower half of this Georgian adaptation is of field stone, and the upper portion of wide, vertical planking. Here are housed the administrative offices of the national forest which covers more than 800,000 acres north and west of Russellville.

ARKANSAS POLYTECHNIC COLLEGE, at the north edge of town on State 7, is a State-supported, co-educational institution which offers a two-year course in agriculture, engineering, home economics, music, and the liberal arts. The school comprises several large brick buildings with hipped roofs and dormer windows. Enrollment averages 600.

In Russellville is the junction with State 7 (*see Tour 8a*).

On the west bank of Illinois Bayou is the SITE OF DWIGHT MISSION (L), 49.3 *m.,* opened by Reverend Cephas Washburn (1792-1860) for the Cherokee in 1822 (*see Education*). The settlement was named for Timothy Dwight, president of Yale College. Most distinguished of the Indians who gathered around the mission was Sequoyah (1770-1843), also known as George Gist or Guess, the lame silversmith and blacksmith who invented the Cherokee alphabet.

Born in Tennessee, son of a Dutch trader and an Indian mother who may also have had some white blood, Sequoyah came to Arkansas after the Cherokee Treaty of 1817. Fascinated by the ability of white men to communicate by written characters, he had begun to work out an alphabetical system for the Cherokee language. Using berry juice for ink and writing upon bark with a quill, he experimented with word-pictures and syllable-sounds, ignoring the ridicule of his friends and the petulance of his wife, who is said to have cast all his work into the fire on one occasion.

By 1825 Sequoyah had produced an alphabet so simple and complete that literacy spread rapidly throughout the Cherokee Nation. By 1828 type had been cast for his 86 characters, and a newspaper called the *Cherokee Phoenix* was being printed in Georgia, where the main body of the tribe still lived. About the same time a Bible was printed in Cherokee and used with great success by missionaries. Sequoyah traveled widely, teaching his tribesmen to read and write. He died in Mexico, while searching for material concerning the history of the Cherokee Nation, and his name has been given to the giant redwood trees (*Sequoia gigantea* and *Sequoia sempervirens*) of the Pacific coast.

Dwight, which had acquired a post office in 1823, remained as a trading post and river port after the departure of the missionaries in 1829, and later became a stagecoach stop. The inhabitants drifted to Russellville after 1870.

Each July the streets of CLARKSVILLE, 71 *m.* (370 alt., 3,118 pop.), are crowded with trucks that have come to carry away the peach crop. Drivers sleep even on the courthouse lawn, ready to leave at daybreak for the near-by orchards, where they bargain with the farmers, obtain cargoes, and drive off to distant cities. Clarksville celebrates the harvest with a festival and tour through the orchards.

For many decades coal mining has been an important activity in the district, and Johnson County ranked third in the State in 1937-38, with an output of 224,565 tons. Natural gas northwest of Clarksville was first tapped in 1929, and is piped to cities in Arkansas and adjoining States.

In the center of town, where US 64 becomes the main street, is the JOHNSON COUNTY COURTHOUSE (L). The three-story-and-basement building, completed in 1936, has clean lines, with an emphasis on the vertical, and is of concrete and steel construction, faced with white stone in front.

The COLLEGE OF THE OZARKS, at the north end of College Ave., a co-educational institution maintained by the Presbyterian Church, offers a four-year course. Until 1920 the school was known as Arkansas Cumberland College. MARIE MACLEAN HALL, the principal building, is a tall brick structure with projecting wings framing the four-pillared portico. Limestone MUNGER MEMORIAL CHAPEL, built in 1933, is modernized Gothic.

On the land now occupied by the campus once stood the home of Augustus M. Ward, where John W. Woodward (1820-65), as a private venture, taught Arkansas' first school for deaf children in 1851. Woodward, a newspaper editor, acquired a local reputation as a poet, particularly for his "Legend of the Broken Sword."

Left from Clarksville on a graveled road passing the FAIR GROUNDS (R), 1.9 *m.,* where horse races are held annually on a half-mile track, to SPADRA, 5.5 *m.* (372 alt.), a group of miners' houses, marking the center of a century-old coal field.

Spadra may be derived from a play on the Spanish noun *espada,* meaning sword, and the verb *espadar,* meaning to break. The legend goes that a member of De Soto's ubiquitous band, a young man named Pedro, wandered off into the forest and fell in love with an Indian girl. Their plans for elopement were discovered, and the girl's father and his warriors trapped the couple. Pedro fought valiantly, but fell. According to Woodward's poem, referred to above, Pedro's broken sword was later discovered by De Soto, who picked it up and exclaimed " 'Spadra!"

Mining operations began at Spadra in 1840, and in March of the following year Little Rock greeted the arrival of its first boatload of coal with tremendous enthusiasm. "This marks a new era in the history of Little Rock," said the *Arkansas Gazette*. "The coal is of excellent quality, and is much cheaper fuel than wood. In a year's time everybody will be burning coal. Hooraw for Arkansas!"

The abundance of timber in the State, however, and the inadequacy of transportation, retarded development of the coal mines for a good many years. Mining in Johnson County did not become as important as in Sebastian, to the west, but it has been a part of the economic pattern since about 1880.

In Territorial days Spadra was the last home of Matthew Lyon (1746-1822), a stormy Irishman who ran for Congress wherever he lived. Settling first in Vermont, Lyon was sent by his neighbors to Washington, and cast the vote that made Thomas Jefferson President, instead of Aaron Burr. Kentucky next attracted Lyon, and here he was again made a Congressman. He followed the frontier to Missouri, but this time he was defeated in the Congressional election. Appointed agent to the Western Cherokee, Lyon came to Spadra Bluff in 1821, and promptly entered the race for Territorial Delegate to Congress. Though he lost the election, he went to Washington to claim the seat. Rejected, he came back to Spadra, took a boatload of furs to New Orleans, and returned with the machinery for one of the first cotton gins in Arkansas.

The SUNSHINE MINE (R), 6 *m.*, provides an example of the latest mechanized techniques used in working coal veins. A slope mine, its shaft enters the ground at an angle of 45 degrees. The coal, after being blasted out, is cut with electrically driven saws, tossed on a conveyor belt, and carried out of the mine and up a long tramway to be dumped directly into railroad cars.

West of Clarksville, as US 64 enters the southern fringe of the Ozarks, the level fields give place to hillsides covered with feed crops or pasture. Small patches of corn or cotton grow in the valley bottoms or on the flat tops of ridges, but much of the land is too steep for cultivation.

COAL HILL, 83.7 *m.* (471 alt., 1,040 pop.), was the scene of one of the earliest sit-down strikes in American labor history. Here, in 1886, convicts were engaged in mining coal for a private operator. At that time the State leased prisoners to contractors in agriculture and industry, and provided no regulation of working conditions. The convict miners' discontent with harsh treatment and long hours without pay flamed into open protest, and at a signal they sat down in the tunnels and refused to leave the mine. They erected barricades, killed the car mules for food, and fashioned crude cannon from iron pipe, loaded with scrap metal and blasting powder. After 18 days the sit-downers' terms were met. They emerged triumphantly from their underground fortress, and, after an investigation of the treatment of convict workers, the system of leasing State prisoners was eventually modified, then abolished.

ALTUS, 88.7 *m.* (538 alt., 541 pop.), received this name, from the Latin, because it was at the highest elevation between Little Rock and Fort Smith on the railroad built between the two points in the 1870's.

On top of Pond Creek Mountain (R) is the towering white bulk of St. Mary's Catholic Church, looming like a castle over the hills above the Arkansas River.   Finished in 1902, the church was built mostly by the labor of the parishioners.   Paintings of scenes from the life of Christ were done by local priests, using residents of Altus as models.

OZARK, 94.5 m. (400 alt., 1,402 pop.), has been one of the seats of Franklin County since 1838, the other being Charleston (see Tour 6), across the Arkansas.   The difficulty of crossing the river (now spanned by a highway bridge at this point) necessitated the establishment of two seats of government.

The Franklin County Courthouse is built of brown brick in two tones; above the four clocks of its tower is a small minaret, with a classic pediment and pillars.

At 94.9 m. is the junction with State 23.

Right on this graveled road to the junction with another graveled road, 15.6 m.; L. here to the BLACK MOUNTAIN GAME REFUGE, 16.5 m., a part of the Ozark National Forest.   The refuge, maintained by the Federal Government, is a 19,700-acre tract reserved for the propagation of deer and turkey.

The eastern bank of BIG MULBERRY CREEK, 106.8 m., is a solid rock wall some 20 feet high at the point where it is crossed by US 64.   The stream affords fishing for smallmouthed bass, buffalo, cat, bream, and perch.

MULBERRY, 108 m. (394 alt., 973 pop.), a trading center, was a Methodist campground early in the nineteenth century.   Near here US 64 emerges from the Ozark foothills into the Arkansas Valley. The market furnished by Fort Smith has brought about the cultivation of vegetables and fruits, and the raising of dairy cattle.

ALMA, 118.8 m. (430 alt., 774 pop.), besides filling stations and restaurants typical of a main-highway junction, has platforms for shipping strawberries and other truck crops grown in the neighborhood.

In Alma is the northern junction with US 71 (see Tour 9a), with which the route unites for 13.6 miles.

VAN BUREN, 126.8 m. (411 alt., 5,422 pop.), seat of Crawford County, would be known primarily as a once-important frontier post and stagecoach stop which eventually became subordinated to the adjoining city of Fort Smith, had it not been given national publicity by the radio programs of a popular humorist: large signs now inform the visitor that Van Buren is the home of Bob Burns.

The inventor of the "bazooka" stems directly from the line of frontier humorists that includes Bret Harte, Mark Twain, and Opie Read.   His mosquitoes that can be identified by the two-inch white spot between their eyes come from the same zoological dream book that produced the jumping frog of Calaveras.   Burns' exaggerations concerning his mythical kinfolk have made Van Buren seem to radio audiences an isolated village in the remotest Arkansas backwoods, and some Arkansans feel that Burns does the State a disservice in helping to perpetuate the fable of the hill-billy in connection with it. Yet Van Buren loves him and celebrates his periodic return to the town.

There were settlers at Van Buren as early as 1818, but the place was known as Phillip's Landing until 20 years later, when two promoters named David Thompson and John Drennen purchased the site, renamed it for President Martin Van Buren, and made it the seat of Crawford County. The site of the village on the Arkansas River, at the edge of American territory and across from the military post of Fort Smith, made it an outfitting place for expeditions into the Indian country and Texas, and a distributing point for goods shipped up the river.

The steamer *Robert Thompson* reached Fort Smith as early as 1822, but the upper Arkansas offered steamboats little business to compensate for its shoals and snags, and only occasional supply boats for Fort Smith and transports loaded with Indian emigrants to the upper river risked the trip during the next decade. By 1840, however, regular schedules had been established to Fort Smith and Van Buren. Freight rates were surprisingly low; whisky could be shipped from Cincinnati in 1846 for $1.50 a barrel, and the general rate from Little Rock was 40¢ for 100 pounds.

The necessity of putting large stern-wheelers through shoals where the Indians had sometimes portaged canoes led to the building of craft with amazingly light drafts. It was a common jest that Arkansas steamboats would run anywhere that the ground was a little damp. The *Fort Gibson,* built especially for the upper Arkansas, actually drew only 12 inches, but was one of the most luxurious steamers on the river, with staterooms painted peachblow and furniture upholstered in brocatelle.

Wagons traveling the State Road from Missouri to Van Buren, paralleling Arkansas' western boundary (approximately the route of present US 71), brought immigrants and increased the town's commercial standing. Freight shipped up the Arkansas on steamboats was hauled north over this road as far as Springfield, Missouri. In 1849 Van Buren became an outfitting point for gold hunters on their way to California; and the Butterfield stage route to the coast, established a decade later, came down from St. Louis by way of the State Road and turned west here. The town's narrow Main Street, with its old brick buildings, was once a major highway to the West, and something of the frontier spirit still clings to it.

The BOB BURNS HOUSE, a two-story frame house atop a high terrace at 9th and Jefferson, is marked with a sign. The humorist lived here from his childhood until he left high school.

US 64 crosses the ARKANSAS RIVER at 127.6 *m.,* on a drawbridge now seldom called upon to lift for passing boats.

FORT SMITH, 132.4 *m.* (450 alt., 36,584 pop.) (*see Fort Smith*).

Fort Smith is at the junction with State 22 (*see Tour 6*) and the southern junction with US 71 (*see Tour 9b*).

At 133.2 *m.* US 64 crosses the OKLAHOMA LINE, 77 miles east of Muskogee, Oklahoma.

⟨⟨⟨⟩⟩⟩

Tour 4

(Malden, Mo.) — Corning — Hardy — Harrison — Eureka Springs — Rogers — Fayetteville — (Muskogee, Okla.) ; US 62.
Missouri Line to Oklahoma Line, 344.2 *m.*

Concrete-paved between Corning and Pocahontas, asphalt-paved between Harrison and Oklahoma Line; elsewhere graveled.
St. Louis-San Francisco Ry. roughly parallels route between Corning and Pocahontas, Imboden and Hardy, and between Gateway and Oklahoma Line; Missouri Pacific R.R. between Cotter and Pyatt; Missouri & Arkansas Ry. between Olvey and Eureka Springs.
Accommodations in all larger towns.

Though its eastern and western extremities pass through comparatively level country, US 62 zigzags for most of its length through the Ozark hills of northern Arkansas. The slopes, gradual as they rise from the Black River, become increasingly steep as the route moves westward, until they reach a dramatic height in the breath-taking gorge of the upper White River near Eureka Springs.

Visitors expecting to find bearded hill farmers blasting away with squirrel rifles at blood-enemies will be disappointed. The romanticized isolation of the Arkansas mountaineers has been broken down by railroads and automobiles, movies and radios. Log cabins are giving way to houses of field stone, and there are few stretches of more than ten miles without a filling station. The highway generally follows the river valleys, the most fertile and prosperous land in the Ozarks; back in the rocky hills, life is harder and more meager.

While improved transportation and communication facilities have brought about important social changes in two or three decades, economic advance has lagged. Most Ozark families are still virtually self-sustaining. Cash to buy overalls and shoes, schoolbooks and store whisky is raised by the occasional sale of a calf, a few bushels of apples or peaches, or a load of cedar fence posts. The comparatively recent introduction of Hereford beef cattle, which graze in the forests, is gradually providing a larger and more stable money income for the hill farmers.

Section a. **MISSOURI LINE to JUNCTION WITH US 65;**
212.3 m., US 62

From the St. Francis River Valley, US 62 crosses narrow, isolated Crowley's Ridge, then sweeps through the low land of the Black and Current River bottoms to the hills at Pocahontas. Seldom following a straight line for a quarter of a mile, the route curves through the Ozarks, where the succession of hills and ravines is broken by the deep-cut valleys of swift-flowing streams, well stocked with bass, catfish, and bream.

US 62 crosses the ST. FRANCIS RIVER, 0 *m.*, the boundary between Missouri and Arkansas, 13 miles southeast of Malden, Missouri.

ST. FRANCIS, 0.3 *m.* (297 alt., 266 pop.), a sleepy market town, grew around the St. Louis Southwestern Railway built through this point in 1882. Residents of an older settlement, Chalk Bluff (*see below*), moved here. Rapid development of timbering boomed St. Francis. Besides sawmills there were shingle, box, stave, and barrel mills. Five two-story hotels were filled to capacity. Lumbermen sweated all week fighting mosquitoes and mud, then riotously celebrated Saturday nights in a saloon at the Missouri end of the bridge.

The timber began to run out just before the World War, and St. Francis declined more rapidly than it had grown.

Right from St. Francis on a graveled road, impassable during high water, that follows the St. Francis River to CHALK BLUFF, 1.2 *m.*, site of a vanished town. At this point the river breaks through Crowley's Ridge, which extends from the Missouri Ozarks down through the level plains of eastern Arkansas. The first trail into northeastern Arkansas followed the Ridge from Missouri, since it was the only high land in a wilderness of swamps and backwater. Here a settlement grew up in the early 1840's as a trail ferry crossing. Troops passed up and down the trail during the War between the States and, in May 1863, General John S. Marmaduke, after a raid into Missouri, erected rude fortifications on the bluff, from which he exchanged artillery fire with the Federal forces across the river.

PIGGOTT, 7.8 *m.* (303 alt., 2,034 pop.), is the eastern seat of Clay County; Corning (*see Tour 1a*) is the western. Like many other Arkansas counties, Clay was forced to establish two governmental headquarters because the legislature, in determining county boundaries, failed to consider such natural barriers as the almost impassable Black River bottoms. Good roads and high-water bridges in recent years have largely eliminated the need for duplicate county governments, but in most units where there were two seats both are still retained.

Situated on the eastern slope of Crowley's Ridge, Piggott is a typical Arkansas farm town. The business district centers around the courthouse square, and tree-lined streets lead off into the residential districts. On the lawn of the courthouse is a 12-foot PETRIFIED HICKORY, dug out of the Ridge, which yields numerous such specimens.

The HARLAN GEOLOGICAL COLLECTION (*open on application*), in a private home on Third St. just east of the business section, includes petrified wood, fossils, and drill cores from the Ridge. Part of the collection is out of doors.

1. Left from Piggott on a graveled road to the PIGGOTT NURSERY (*open*), 0.5 *m.*, where rows of young fruit trees, mostly peach, are grown to stock the orchards of Ridge farmers, whose soil is well adapted to fruit growing.

2. Right from Piggott on a graveled road to the PIGGOTT CEMETERY, 0.5 *m.*, an old tree-shaded burial ground. Several of the graves are marked by chunks of petrified wood instead of the more ordinary limestone or granite slabs.

From Piggott US 62 winds westward among steep ravines and rolling hills. The loess topsoil, deposited by wind, is light in texture and offers little resistance to erosion. Hillsides are deeply scarred by water-channels wherever the timber has been cleared off.

As the road descends from Crowley's Ridge into the Black River bottoms, the character of the country changes completely. The road is built on a fill, usually lined with oaks standing in backwater. Where the land has been cleared and drained, cotton and corn grow luxuriantly. To early settlers the bottoms were simply a wilderness. A woodsman could follow obscure trails along the tops of ridges, ford the sloughs, and circle around impassable growths of brush and timber. No one made the trip eagerly, and no farmer would have dreamed of homesteading in the morass. The lumber companies that came with the railroads turned the region into one of feverish activity, but only big trees were milled, and sometimes a score of saplings were felled and left lying crisscross in order to remove one giant oak.

Little attempt was made to utilize the wilderness until about 1910, when a few enterprising men started burning cut-over jungles and digging drainage ditches. Here and there along the highway, between well-cultivated farms, there are still occasional fields of slowly rotting stumps.

US 62 crosses the BLACK RIVER (*boating; bream, crappie, and bass fishing*), at 31.5 *m.*

CORNING, 34 *m.* (291 alt., 1,619 pop.) (*see Tour 1a*), is at the northern junction with US 67 (*see Tour 1a*), with which the route unites for 27.5 miles.

POCAHONTAS, 61.5 *m.* (310 alt., 3,028 pop.) (*see Tour 1a*), is at the southern junction with US 67 (*see Tour 1a*).

Climbing the Black River Valley wall at Pocahontas, US 62 leaves the flat country and enters the hills. The contrast between the rocky, tree-covered slopes and the fertile crop land only a few miles away is startling. No less remarkable is the difference in the lives of the inhabitants. The valley farmer is often menaced by floods, insect plagues, and market prices. The hill farmer, however, always seems to make out somehow with his corn patch, his few vegetables, his rifle, and fishing rod. This self-contained economy creates in the hillman a comparative disinterest in the world's affairs, along with a disdain of lowland ways. "I don't go to question the good Lord in his wisdom," runs the phrasing attributed to a typical mountaineer, "but I jest cain't see why He put valleys in between the hills."

IMBODEN, 74.9 *m.* (276 alt., 525 pop.) (*see Tour 7*), is at the southern junction with US 63 (*see Tour 7*), with which the route unites for 24.9 miles (*see Tour 7*).

Seat of the northern district of Sharp County, HARDY, 99.8 *m.* (362 alt., 721 pop.), is a resort town on the bank of cold, clear Spring River. The business buildings, of local stone, are strung along the highway.

In Hardy is the northern junction with US 63 (*see Tour 7*).

US 62 crosses Spring River (*fishing*) at Hardy and turns south. At 100.1 *m.* is the junction with a graveled road.

Right on this road to the ruins of WAHPETON INN, 0.4 *m.*, which was destroyed by fire in 1939. The large stone lodge on the edge of the bluff overlooking the river had been the scene of many State-wide gatherings. Near-by octagonal cabins with pointed roofs somewhat resemble the tepees of an Indian village that once occupied the site.

The road, difficult in wet weather, continues over steep, rocky hills to REO VISTA, 0.9 *m.*, a cluster of cabins. R. here a foot trail slopes down 0.3 *m.* to WHITE WATER BEACH, where Spring River tumbles over a waterfall into a natural swimming pool.

A GIRL SCOUT CAMP (*private*), is on the main side road at 1.9 *m.*, and a YWCA CAMP (*private*), at 2.2 *m.*, by the river.

The rounded Ozark hills west of Spring River are covered with oak, cedar, and gum. Cedar, growing in the shallow soil of ledges too rocky to support larger species, was sought by the Indians because its tattered bark made good tinder. White settlers found it a strong, light, straight-grained wood, easily split and handled. Cedar fence posts have been known to stand 30 years without rotting. Storm-cellar beams, porch supports, furniture, and poles are made of the abundant red trunks.

The storm cellars, resistant to heat and cold, serve also as storehouses for canned fruit. With thick stone walls, and a roof strengthened by cedar supports imbedded in cement, these shelters are almost indestructible, and seem hardly necessary in a region where twisters are extremely rare.

At 110.3 *m.* is the junction with State 11, a graveled road.

Left on State 11 to EVENING SHADE, 13 *m.* (458 alt., 347 pop.), as placid as its name. When Arkansans say "evening" they mean the period between noon and sundown. The "evening shade" originally referred to the refuge from the afternoon sun afforded by tall trees in the neighborhood of an old gristmill (*see below*) around which the town grew. The alternative name of Hookrum was given Evening Shade, according to an apocryphal story, by a visiting farmer who was plied with rum and "hooked" of his money. "Hookrum" struck some peculiar chord in Arkansas folk humorists, who used the word until it had become identified all over the State with backwoods rusticity. The name has been disavowed by the citizens of Evening Shade.

The SHARP COUNTY COURTHOUSE for the southern district is a square limestone building whose formidable appearance is accentuated by iron bars on its lower windows.

At 13.4 *m.* on State 11 is the junction with a dirt road; L. here 0.1 *m.* to MILL CREEK DAM, the power from which is used both to operate a turbine that furnishes electricity for Evening Shade and to turn a gristmill. This mill, at which corn is still ground, is the third to occupy the site since 1817.

State 11 continues south to CAVE CITY, 23.6 *m.* (659 alt., 427 pop.), a resort village whose field-stone buildings straggle along the road. The CAVE (*adm. 10¢*) consists of three chambers, the largest of which is about 80 feet wide and 10 feet high.

BATESVILLE, 38.3 *m.* (266 alt., 5,267 pop.) (*see Tour 17*), is at the junction with State 69 (*see Tour 17*).

Not far from the junction with State 11, US 62 swings back to the north. Here most of the slopes are too steep for cultivation, but the valley bottoms and ridge tops are planted in corn, vegetables, and soil-restoring lespedeza. Numerous hogs forage the woods; the acorns and chinquapins on which they feed give their meat a flavor that Ozark people maintain is far superior to that of corn-fed swine.

Outstaters who have heard tales of Ozark shiftlessness may be surprised by the industry evidenced in the frequent use of stone for ornamental and technical purposes on hill farms. Rock walls encircling duckponds, flower gardens, and houses are common, and often show a genuine feeling for landscape effects.

SALEM, 127.8 *m.* (664 alt., 574 pop.), derives its income from marketing cattle, hogs, and feed crops, and from the business of county government.

The FULTON COUNTY COURTHOUSE, in its square at the middle of the town, is a two-story brick structure erected in 1892, with high mansard roof and dormer windows. Farmers in town on Saturday afternoons gather around the local creamery to receive their weekly checks for milk.

In Salem is the junction with State 9 (*see Tour 17*).

Money was seldom seen when this remote Ozark country was being settled during the middle nineteenth century, and the pioneers used products of the land as mediums of exchange. "When my father first located," wrote William Monks (*History of Southern Missouri and Northern Arkansas,* 1907), "beeswax, peltry and fur skins almost constituted the currency of the country. . . . A man thought nothing of buying a horse or a yoke of oxen, or to make any other common debt on the promise of discharging the same in beeswax and peltry, in one month's time."

Bee trees rich in honey were considered veritable pots of gold by the settlers. "After they had found a sufficient number of bee trees and marked them," related Monks, "the morning following they would go out and kill nothing but large deer; caseskin them until they had a sufficient number of hides to contain the honey that they expected to take from the trees, take the hides to the camp, tie a knot in the fore legs of the hide . . . run two rows of stitches, draw it tight . . . knot the hind legs of the skins . . . take their tub, a knife and spoon, proceed to the trees . . . take out the honey, place it in the tub, and when the tub was filled carry it to the wagon where the hides were prepared, empty their tubs into the deerskins . . . then they would return home. . . .

"The labor of the women then commenced. They would proceed to separate the honey from the beeswax, pouring the honey into hogsheads, kegs or barrels prepared for it, and running the beeswax into cakes ready for the market, while the men were stretching and drying the deerskins."

VIOLA, 137.9 m. (692 alt., 280 pop.*), for several years has been the scene of a singing festival, usually held on the fourth Saturday and Sunday in April. Chairs and benches are packed into the school gymnasium, and more than 3,500 people come from the Ozark region of north-central Arkansas for the two-day sing. Sheet-music companies send quartets, and occasionally a featured soloist is imported, but most of the singers are amateurs whose church hymns, the true folk music of Arkansas, make up the greater part of the program. No prizes are offered and no admission is charged; people come to the festival because they like to sing and to hear singing.

At the NORTH FORK OF WHITE RIVER (fishing, float trips), 155.4 m., flowing through a deep cleft in the hills, are arresting views of green and blue mountains through the hazy atmosphere, and one realizes suddenly that US 62 has almost imperceptibly climbed to an elevation of some 800 feet. The stream, clear and cold from the many Ozark springs that feed it, offers excellent fishing for smallmouthed bass.

MOUNTAIN HOME, 164.3 m. (799 alt., 927 pop.), is the seat and largest town of Baxter County. On a high plateau between the North Fork and White Rivers, it is an outfitting point for four- or five-day vacation float trips as far as Clarendon.

Left from Mountain Home on State 5, graveled, to the old town of NORFORK, 13.6 m. (455 alt., 304 pop.), at the joining of North Fork and White River. Above this point shoals and rapids make the two streams normally impassable for any craft heavier than a flatboat; hence at the beginning of the nineteenth century Norfolk was the usual head of navigation. Here homeseekers disembarked from keelboats, piled their belongings into ox-drawn wagons, and creaked into the wilderness. Many of the early settlers in southwest Missouri followed this route. With the advent of the steamboat in the 1840's Norfolk's importance increased. Loads of salt and other necessities were freighted from this river port through the hills as far as Springfield, Missouri, over a road that roughly followed the White River to Branson and was known as the Old Salt Trail. "A mile and a half to two miles an hour," says a local chronicler, "was good time for the old oxcart caravans loaded with salt that made their way slowly through the narrow defiles of the Three Brothers Mountains in north Baxter County, and clung tightly to the old trail as it wound dangerously around the side of Bald Jess in Ozark County, Mo." The building of a railroad to Rolla, Missouri, just before the War between the States, reversed the direction of traffic. The wagons now brought supplies southward through the Ozarks, and Norfolk became the end of the trail instead of the beginning. Work on a Federal flood-control dam across the North Fork River here in 1940 brought the town renewed activity.

The WOLF HOUSE (*open on application*), on State 5 (R) overlooking White River, remains to remind Norfolk of its history. This "saddlebag" cabin is said to have been erected in 1809 by Jacob Wolf, Indian agent, blacksmith and trader; its accessibility soon made it an unofficial governmental center for northern Arkansas. Eventually, the dwelling served as the first Izard County Courthouse. In 1938 the house was purchased by the town of Norfolk and turned into a museum. Exhibits include corded bedsteads, spinning wheels, and ox yokes.

South of Norfolk, State 5 follows the course of White River, which here bounds a section of the Ozark National Forest. At intervals skeleton-like towers on high knobs overlook the forest in constant vigilance against fire. The mountains run blue in the distance, sharpening at close range to irregular hogbacks with jagged ends and sides that slant into tilted pine- and cedar-grown glades.

CALICO ROCK, 26.5 *m.* (364 alt., 738 pop.), spreads over the high north bank of White River. Because of the steep grade, Main Street has been built in three decks. Business houses on the east side stand even with the traffic level; the west half of the street, held in place by a rock sustaining wall, is about six feet higher. The third deck is a stone and cement walkway whose buildings overlook the roofs across the way.

Like many other points along the river, Calico Rock was named by boatmen before any settlement had begun. The bluff "is one of those rare and fanciful works of nature which are seldom met with, and is approached under circumstances well calculated to heighten the effect of a scene in itself very striking and picturesque," wrote Henry Schoolcraft (*Journal of a Tour into the Interior of Missouri and Arkansaw,* 1821). "On turning a bend in the river, suddenly the rock appears before you. . . . It is a lofty smooth wall of stratified lime-stone rock, presenting a diversity of colour in squares, stripes, spots, or angles, all confusedly mixed and arranged according to the inimitable pencil of nature." When the Missouri Pacific's White River line reached the town in 1903, the vividly patterned face of the bluff was blasted away to make room for a roadbed. The newly exposed stone, being unweathered, lacked the color of the destroyed surface. With the passage of years, however, the colors have begun to reappear.

The best view of the "calico" rock is from the south bank of the river. The ferry (*cars 25¢, pedestrians 5¢*) is held at an angle by tackle fastened to a wheel that moves on a cable stretched across the stream. The force of the current is used to move the boat. During the deer hunting season cars and trucks loaded with sportsmen jam the natural ramp that runs down to the ferry. Forest rangers check hunting licenses here, and the khaki-clad hunters stock up on supplies and ammunition.

Despite its position on the bluff, Calico Rock has three times been flooded by White River. The 1916 flood reached a stage of 51 feet, 3 inches. Such torrents seem incredible to visitors who view this quiet mountain stream, wide, shallow, and so clear that the bedrock in its center can be seen from the bank.

In Calico Rock, the route turns (L) on State 56 and continues to a junction with State 9 at 41.1 *m.* (*see Tour 17*).

West of Mountain Home US 62 winds around the higher hills and rides the tops of the lower ridges. Patches of cotton, hay, and potatoes alternate with corn and another tall, headed stalk that resembles corn but bears no ears. This is sorghum cane, grown to make "long sweetnin' " for the syrup pitcher on the hill-family table.

In the fall, the sorghum-maker brings his portable mill to grind the harvested cane. His pay is usually a fourth of the syrup, and his mill is a simple crushing device with a log boom hauled around and around by a patient mule. A trench is dug for fires, and a series of shallow pans astride it serves as the refining apparatus. Impurities that accumulate in a froth above the boiling juice are skimmed off, and the liquid becomes purer as it passes from pan to pan, until it pours from the last one clear, sweet, and sparkling.

COTTER, 175.8 m. (441 alt., 903 pop.), was built in 1903 with the arrival of the White River line of the Missouri Pacific Railroad, a major factor in ending the traditional isolation of the Ozarks. The railroad shops have given Cotter an industrial aspect unfamiliar in this section of the State. Situated on the banks of White River, the town is a popular starting point for fishermen's float trips (see Recreation).

The low price of shells has diminished mussel-digging in the White River in recent years, but shipments are still made by barge from Cotter to the button factories at Newport (see Tour 1a) and Clarendon (see Tour 12).

At Cotter US 62 crosses the White River on a graceful rainbow-arch bridge.

YELLVILLE, 186.8 m. (860 alt., 546 pop.), once known as Shawneetown, was named for Colonel Archibald Yell (1797-1847), a romantic figure in early Arkansas politics. A North Carolinian by birth, Yell went to Tennessee as a youth. At the Battle of New Orleans in 1815, and again during the Seminole War in 1818, he served under Andrew Jackson. When Jackson became President, he appointed his young subordinate Territorial judge for western Arkansas, and Yell settled at Fayetteville. He was elected Arkansas' first Congressman in 1837, and three years later became Governor. In 1844 Democratic leaders, believing Yell the only man in the State who could defeat the Whig nominee for Congress, induced him to resign the governorship and enter the race. During the heated campaign Yell is said to have visited Shawneetown, named for an Indian village that had occupied the site, and paid the residents $50 to rechristen the settlement with his name. In 1846 Yell resigned from Congress to lead an Arkansas cavalry detachment in the Mexican War, and the following year he was killed at Buena Vista.

Imposing for this thinly settled country, the MARION COUNTY COURTHOUSE is a two-story limestone building with a Romanesque four-clock tower.

The JAMES BERRY HOUSE (private), on Berry St. overlooking Crooked Creek, is a story-and-a-half, white frame house built in 1853. The front of the structure has been remodeled, but the projecting rear wing shows the original lines. One of the few big houses in the region during the War between the States, it was used as a barracks by Federal troops during their occupancy of Yellville in 1862.

Left from Yellville on State 14, graveled, to BUFFALO RIVER STATE PARK, 16.9 *m.* The 1,735-acre tract of woodland, acquired by the State in 1938, overlooks Buffalo River from sheer rock cliffs. Fishing in the clear spring-fed stream is now the park's major attraction, but contemplated improvements will add a bathing beach, a lodge and cabins, and trails leading through the rugged hills to curious rock formations.

West of Yellville, US 62 skirts the rim of Crooked Creek Valley as it ascends toward Harrison. In this higher altitude the forests of oak and gum become considerably thinner and in places disappear altogether. On the steep sides of the hills occasional curving rows of corn and vegetables indicate farmers' experiments in contour-farming, intended to conserve water and soil.

At 212.3 *m.*, at a point 5.4 miles southwest of Harrison, is the southern junction with US 65 (*see Tour 5a*), with which this route unites for 11.9 miles (*see Tour 5a*).

Section b. FRANCIS to OKLAHOMA LINE; 120 m., US 62

Although the western part of US 62 traverses the highest country of the route, the elevation is strikingly perceptible only where the highway makes its way through the deep gorges of the White River or one of its tributaries. Between Harrison and Gateway, these dips are frequent enough to give the country a genuinely mountainous appearance; thereafter the land is a plateau. Farmers of the level land in this northwestern corner of the State have perhaps the highest living standard of any rural people in Arkansas. Houses and barns are well-kept and painted; carefully tended orchards and vineyards yield important cash crops.

West of FRANCIS, 0 *m.* (*see Tour 5a*), at the northern junction with US 65 (*see Tour 5a*), the route nears the high Ozarks.

In the neighborhood of ALPENA, 6.6 *m.* (1,135 alt., 313 pop.), shadowy blue bulks of mountains punctuate the horizon and deep ravines drop abruptly from the ridge tops that carry the highway. As a visitor once said, "It's not that the mountains are so high, but that the valleys are so deep."

Unlike most Arkansas towns, BERRYVILLE, 23.6 *m.* (1,256 alt., 1,482 pop.), is built around a circle rather than a square. Here, on Saturday evenings during the summer, fruit and dairy farmers and their families from the near-by hills and valleys join the town workers from the sawmill and woodworking plant to go shopping in the crowded stores.

Imposing GRAND VIEW HOTEL, built on the circle in 1902, when the coming of the Missouri & North Arkansas (now Missouri & Arkansas) Railway promised a lively future for Berryville, is a brick building with prominent wooden galleries girdling each of its three floors, and a high peaked roof with a pointed tower.

In the SAUNDERS GUN COLLECTION (*open on application*), at 186 Forsythe St., are more than 1,000 firearms, including a Chinese pistol more than 500 years old, and sidearms that reputedly belonged to Wild Bill Hickok and Jesse James.

1. Right from Berryville on State 21, a graveled road, to the BRASHEAR HARDWOOD PLANT (*visitors admitted*), 0.5 *m.* At the plant a wide variety of products are manufactured: wagon tongues, axles, cedar novelties, flooring, and bows and arrows. The office is a cedar-panelled log cabin.

2. Right from Berryville on graveled State 21 to the junction with a graveled road, 4.9 *m.*; L. here to the BRASHEAR FROG FARM (*open; frogs hibernate Nov.-April*), 6.1 *m.*, a well-fenced half-acre pen surrounding a lake, where breeding frogs, fed on crayfish, grasshoppers, and other insects, are raised for sale to other frog farmers. Moist sacks in ventilated boxes are used for shipment. Watercress and moss, used to provide oxygen for the pond, are sold as a side line.

West of Berryville US 62 takes on the characteristics of a typical mountain road, as it twists across valleys, looping around hairpin turns and cutting through crags.

At 35.9 *m.* on US 62 is the junction with State 23.

Left on State 23, asphalt-paved, to the junction with the Lake Lucerne Road, 0.2 *m.*; L. here to LAKE LUCERNE (*swimming, fishing, riding, golf*), 1.1 *m.*, a cottage resort on the shore of a deep-green pool.

EUREKA SPRINGS, 36.8 *m.* (1,463 alt., 1,770 pop.), a spa, clings to valley slopes so steep that townspeople say there is no level spot here large enough for a circus to pitch its tents.

Although Eureka Springs is the western seat of Carroll County, its principal business is catering to the health-seekers who have visited it for half a century. Most of the older homes are large frame buildings, now turned into boarding houses. Springs emerge every few yards along the single through street that winds between the valley walls; 63 springs have been counted inside the city limits. Caves, usually found in the neighborhood of limestone springs, also abound, some of them opening directly from the main street.

Each of the seven floors of the BASIN PARK HOTEL, on Spring St., may be reached without riding an elevator or climbing stairs, since the position of the building against the side of the mountain makes every floor a ground floor. Similarly, the parishioners of ST. ELIZABETH'S CHURCH (Catholic), on Crescent Drive, walk directly into the second-floor auditorium—although the frequent claim that the church is entered through the steeple is a literary exaggeration.

Carry Nation (1846-1911) lived for a time in the Arkansas Ozarks, and made her last temperance speech in Eureka Springs a few months before her death. In the reformer's declining years her followers built HATCHET HALL, a barn-like frame building on Steel St. (R), to house an academy for the training of young prohibitionists. The project was abandoned when the stormy hatchet-wielder died, before any classes had met. The building has recently been used by artists as a museum and studio.

West of Eureka Springs US 62 passes through the most rugged country of its entire route, skirting canyons 500 or 600 feet deep and rearing over summits that reveal similar canyons winding away to the horizon. The road reaches White River's most impressive gorge at INSPIRATION POINT, 43.9 m. In winter the bare brown hills, fading into the characteristic smoky blue of the Ozark horizon, give the vista a resemblance to Arizona mesas. Spring covers them with tones of green and blue found nowhere but in the Southern mountains. On the far side of the valley range after range of hills, rolling northward into Missouri, repeat the pattern.

The highway descends steeply and crosses WHITE RIVER, 46.4 m. Once the valley has been passed, the country becomes surprisingly flat.

The name of GATEWAY, 55.9 m., refers to its position at the portal of the Ozarks—at least a dozen towns call themselves the "gateway to the Ozarks." This community, with perhaps the clearest claim to the title, is hardly a town, but a group of filling stations and tourist camps.

At 60.9 m. is the junction with State 72, graveled.

Right on State 72 to ELKHORN TAVERN, 1.8 m., site of the Battle of Pea Ridge, Arkansas' most important engagement in the War between the States. Federal General Samuel R. Curtis' maneuvers in Missouri in 1861 led Southern leaders to fear an invasion of Arkansas, and troops that had been concentrated near the State Line retreated below Fayetteville in the hope of drawing him into the Boston Mountains. Northwestern Arkansas became a no man's land, harried by detachments from both sides. When Curtis had proceeded from Springfield as far south as Pea Ridge, just across the Arkansas Line, General Earl Van Dorn, who was in charge of the Southern forces, determined to wipe out the Federal army. Accordingly, Sterling Price's Missourians and Ben McCulloch's Texans advanced northward to meet Curtis, burning the rail fences along the road at night to light their march. From Oklahoma General Albert Pike brought a brigade of Cherokee to join the Southern armies.

Near Bentonville on March 6, 1862, Van Dorn found Federal General Franz Sigel with a small artillery detachment. Sigel retreated until he reached the main body of Curtis' troops. Meanwhile Curtis had time to fell trees across the roads and erect camouflaged shelters for his batteries. March 8, 1862, on a snow-covered field, thousands of ill-trained Confederates hurled themselves gallantly against withering Federal grapeshot. Two Confederate generals, McCulloch and James I. McIntosh, were killed and General W. Y. Slack was mortally wounded, thus leaving the Confederate troops confused. Though the battle is considered by Southern historians as a victory, it failed to destroy Curtis' force.

The Confederate soldiers went southward; Van Dorn and Price rallied them, but were shortly thereafter ordered to Mississippi, leaving Arkansas virtually undefended. Curtis proceeded southeastward and occupied Bates-

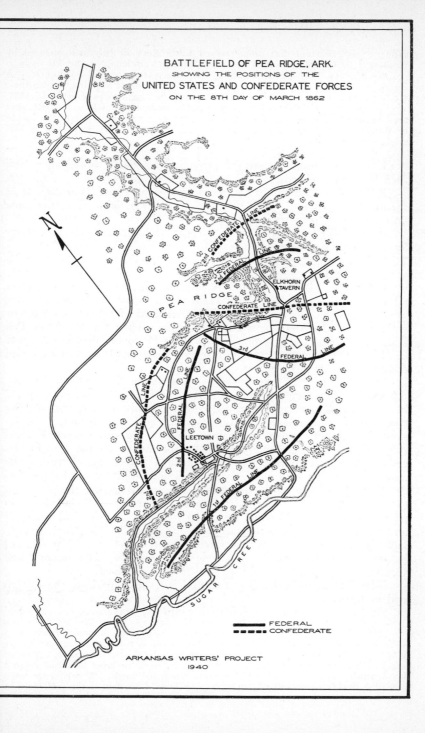

BATTLEFIELD OF PEA RIDGE, ARK.
SHOWING THE POSITIONS OF THE
UNITED STATES AND CONFEDERATE FORCES
ON THE 8TH DAY OF MARCH 1862

ARKANSAS WRITERS' PROJECT
1940

ville; a gesture from that point toward Little Rock in July was opposed by Hindman, so Curtis continued southeast and took Helena, on the Mississippi.

The Tavern itself, built in 1833, and once a stop on the Springfield-Van Buren stage route, was burned by guerillas. The present building, a two-story, white-painted structure with an overhanging pediment, was erected in 1886, against the original chimney. In the yard a walnut tree whose top was shot away in the battle has spread out to a width of more than 100 feet; 16 inches in diameter when the first tavern was built, the tree trunk is now 4 feet thick.

US 62 continues southward through level fields, broken now and then by apple orchards.

ROGERS, 72.8 m. (1,371 alt., 3,550 pop.) (see Tour 9a), is at the northern junction with US 71 (see Tour 9a), with which the route unites for 19.5 miles (see Tour 9a).

FAYETTEVILLE, 92.3 m. (1,427 alt., 8,212 pop.) (see Tour 9a), is at the southern junction with US 71 (see Tour 9a).

US 62 swings west from Fayetteville through the rolling foothills of the mountainous country to the south.

PRAIRIE GROVE, 104.5 m. (1,180 alt., 887 pop.), a country village with the usual store-lined Main Street, is the site of an encounter that marked the renewal in northwest Arkansas of fighting on a major scale during the War between the States. After the Battle of Pea Ridge (see above) the section was overrun by roving detachments that lived off the country, raiding farmers' barns and smokehouses and dodging the patrols of both regular armies.

On November 28, 1862, while on the march from Missouri to the Arkansas River, General James F. Blount's Federal army was attacked by General Thomas Hindman's newly organized Arkansas defense troops in a preliminary skirmish at Cane Hill (see below). In response to Blount's request for reinforcements, General Francis J. Herron marched down from Springfield, to be met at Prairie Grove, December 7, by Hindman, who had made a forced march across the mountains hoping to annihilate the Federal reinforcements before they could reach Blount. Blount's unexpected arrival during the afternoon extended the fighting until dark, when, according to Hindman's report, the enemy "fled beyond the prairie, leaving his dead and wounded and the colors of several regiments in our hands." The Confederates' lack of food and ammunition forced them to retire to Van Buren, however, and thus Herron was able to report four days later: "The victory is more complete and decisive than I imagined."

The PRAIRIE GROVE BATTLEFIELD is a small park at the eastern end of town.

At 108.9 m. is the junction with State 45, graveled.

Left on State 45 to CANE HILL, 3.3 m. (1,691 alt., 70 pop.), founded in 1827 by settlers who led pack horses over buffalo trails too narrow for ox wagons. The town, however, claims white habitation far earlier. According to local tradition, walls of an old fort believed to have been constructed by Spanish explorers once stood in the center of town. A writer in 1859 recorded that a four-foot oak was growing from a section of the wall at that time, and that the stone bore the marks of steel tools. All traces of the supposed fort have long since vanished.

Here in 1835 Presbyterians opened an academy in a two-room log house. Chartered in 1852 as Cane Hill College, the school was burned during the War between the States along with most of the other buildings in town. It was rebuilt, and operated until about 1892; from it grew the College of the Ozarks at Clarksville (*see Tour 3b*).

At 120 *m.* US 62 crosses the Oklahoma Line, 63 miles east of Muskogee, Oklahoma.

Tour 5

(Springfield, Mo.)—Harrison—Conway—Little Rock—Pine Bluff—McGehee—Lake Village—(Tallulah, La.); US 65.
Missouri Line to Louisiana Line, 326.7 *m.*

Asphalt- and concrete-paved roadbed.
Missouri & Arkansas Ry. roughly parallels route between Harrison and Leslie; Missouri Pacific R.R. between Conway and Louisiana Line.
Accommodations in larger towns only.

US 65 curves southeastward through the Ozarks, crosses the Arkansas River at Little Rock near the geographical center of the State, then follows the stream southeast almost to its confluence with the Mississippi and continues down the valley of the larger river to the Louisiana border.

The northern section of the route is the more varied and attractive. In spring the rolling hills gleam with dogwood, redbud, the misty foam of wild plum thickets, and occasionally a silver sycamore. In fall the ridges blaze with turning leaves that grow dimmer near the horizon until they become smoke blue with distance. Farms are small and worked by their owners, who live much as their grandparents did, growing their own food and adding to their incomes by work in the forests.

South of Pine Bluff the Arkansas River dominates the scene, and its man-made levees are the only elevations. The countless cottonfields are often bordered by cypress and pin oak. The ever-present tenant shacks are no shabbier than many cabins in the mountains, but they look less attractive, partly because the fields, coming to the door, afford no cover for their plainness.

Section a. **MISSOURI LINE to LITTLE ROCK; 166.2 m., US 65**

The Ozarks, through which US 65 twists, are so ancient that they have been weathered down to rounded hills. Busses now carry mountain children to consolidated schools that have replaced the one-room schoolhouses with high-backed recitation seats, but back-country dwellings today are similar to those of the pupils' grandparents. A squirrel rifle and hunting horn hang over the front door of the typical mountain home. A wide-throated fireplace still keeps the family warm, though the cooking is likely to be done on a wood-burning stove. Coal oil lamps light most of the rural houses, and the refrigerator is frequently a log springhouse. Hogs and cattle run the range. Chickens and turkeys often roost in a tree in the farmyard, and occasionally the domestic gobbler meets his wild cousin in the farm's pea patch. With the hens are a few guineas, scolding fowl valued mostly for the chatter they set up at the approach of a red fox or destroying hawk.

US 65 crosses the MISSOURI LINE, 0 *m.,* 74 miles south of Springfield, Missouri, in a mountainous, thinly populated region.

OMAHA, 5.2 *m.* (1,354 alt., 146 pop.), which presumably commemorates the Indian tribe of that name, is on the site of Sha-wa-nah, once an important village on a heavily traveled trail. Pieces of armor and Spanish coins found near Omaha have been ascribed to De Soto, but were probably left by later Spanish explorers. A tunnel of the Missouri Pacific's White River branch runs directly under the ridge on which the town is situated.

The fields of corn and hay in roadside clearings south of Omaha are occasionally varied by small patches of tomatoes, growing low and bushy on the rocky ground. Raising tomatoes for small canneries in the region is a rather recent venture for farmers in half a dozen Ozark counties. As a rule, canneries supply young plants to growers, and buy the entire crop at a fixed price.

FRANCIS, 18.1 *m.* (1,140 alt.), is a mountain village named for Major Henry Francis (1757-1840), who fought in the Battle of King's Mountain in South Carolina and settled in northern Arkansas after the Revolutionary War.

In Francis is the western junction with US 62 (*see Tour 4b*), with which the route unites for 11.9 miles.

To the HARRISON SALES AND COMMISSION COMPANY'S BARN (L), 22.5 *m.,* farmers and traders bring mules, hogs, sheep, and cattle for the Tuesday auctions. On that day the entire family comes to town, and while wives exchange neighborhood gossip and children play games, the farmers pull reflectively on pipes as they listen to the auctioneer's pleading, or go from pen to pen inspecting the stock. Farm implements, grain, and furniture are sometimes auctioned here. Sales at an average session run from $6,000 to $8,000.

The metropolis of the northern Ozarks, HARRISON, 24.6 *m.* (1,049 alt., 4,238 pop.), lies in the valley of Crooked Creek. The BOONE COUNTY COURTHOUSE, in the town square, is a two-story red-brick structure trimmed with white flagging. At the northeast corner of the square is the three-story limestone-trimmed FEDERAL BUILDING, set off by a small park. Here a division of the Western Arkansas United States District Court holds sessions for seven northwest Arkansas counties.

The return of legalized liquor in 1933 brought about a boom in stave milling at Harrison and for a time 5 such plants were running, some of them 24 hours a day. A branch of the Lansing Motor Wheel Corporation, erected to manufacture wooden wheels for automobiles, installed stave cutting equipment, and for several years millions of beer barrel staves were stacked in its drying yards. The town is a shipping point for red cedar and hardwood taken from Ozark forests. Other industries include a cheese factory owned by the Cudahy Packing Company, a flour mill and grain elevator, and produce houses that handle poultry and eggs brought in from near-by counties.

Deposits of marble in the hills west and south of Harrison have been worked from time to time. Some historians say that, in 1849, a 2,000-pound block from these quarries was hauled by ox team through the mountains to Van Buren, whence it went by river to New Orleans and by sea to Washington, D. C. The block was intended for the Washington Monument, then being planned by a memorial society.

In 1873 Bellefonte (*see below*) hotly opposed Harrison in an election held to designate a county seat. Harrisonites distributed watermelons to the voters, and won the election by 18 votes. The victory bonfire that night could be seen for miles, and the jubilant winners fired anvils until dawn. In this old-fashioned type of noisemaking a blacksmith's anvil was placed upside down atop another, with a charge of black powder between the two. Touching off the powder created a clear, exultant boom that went ringing across the hills.

Harrison was incorporated in 1876 and grew slowly until the beginning of the century, when the Missouri & North Arkansas Railway (now the Missouri & Arkansas) was built through from Eureka Springs. As headquarters for the railroad's offices and shops the town progressed rapidly, more than doubling its population in 20 years. In 1922-23 a strike by the railroad's workers aroused unprecedented bitterness in the quiet community.

Like other railroads in the country, the Missouri & North Arkansas had been operated by the Federal Government during the war, and workers had been paid union wages. Returned to private operation, the road, unprofitable and burdened by debt, was unable to meet expenses. After various expedients had been tried a wage reduction was announced, and the workers walked out. The national railroad brotherhoods, fearing wage cuts all over the country if the reduction stood, gave the strike full support.

Farmers who had donated the right-of-way and townspeople who lived by railroad commerce feared that a successful strike would mean abandonment of the road. The people of Harrison, knit together by blood-ties and generations of friendship, were split on the issue. Bridges were burned and rails torn up; vigilantes combatted the strike, and dozens of strikers and sympathizers were flogged. A striker was taken from his home by a mob and hanged from the railroad bridge that spans Crooked Creek. A Methodist minister who defended the strikers eventually lost his pastorate. He then wrote a book condemning the townspeople. Another minister answered with a book denouncing the strikers, many of whom were driven from the country. The railroad operated on an open-shop basis for a time, but the unions reorganized after passage of the National Railway Labor Act in 1924.

In Harrison is the junction with State 7 (*see Tour 8a*).

A spring in BELLEFONTE, 29 m. (1,062 alt., 226 pop.), gave the town its name. For many years it was a trading center and campground for drivers who hauled freight to or from Springfield, Missouri, in ox-drawn wagons. Oxen, while slower than mules, were steadier and not so likely to bog down in mudholes. Yokes of straining oxen, belly-deep in mud, the driver's tongue and whip cracking with equal acerbity, are now used only in timbered bottoms where good roads have not penetrated.

Bellefonte slumped when Harrison was made the county seat in 1873. Today (1941) the industrial mainstay of the neighborhood is the cutting of cedar fence posts. Considerable cedar is used by mountain artificers in making souvenir desk sets, paper knives, and silhouettes of Ozark scenes.

At 30 m. is the eastern junction with US 62 (*see Tour 4a*).

Sweet-smelling azaleas, known in this region as "mountain honeysuckle," grow in profusion on the rocky soil. The salmon-pink flowers are at their best in May.

At 33.5 m. is the junction with a graveled road.

Left on this road to EVERTON, 5 m. (845 alt., 190 pop.), whose surrounding hills are dotted with red oak that is in demand for railroad ties. Farmers chop out the ties with broadax and adze. Near Everton is a large deposit of fine silica, mined from time to time for sale to glass factories.

Left from Everton on a dirt road 1.6 m. to the UNCLE SAM COB PIPE FACTORY (*visitors admitted*), on the bank of Clear Creek. The St. Charles White variety of corn grown near by yields the desirable large cobs, which are cut, bored, and varnished by mechanical processes. The dozen or so workers turn out 10 to 12 gross of pipes daily.

In the hills around WESTERN GROVE, 38.4 m. (1,102 alt., 206 pop.), small farms are the rule. The mountaineers who till the clearings grow up lean and tall, and not infrequently grim-visaged. The hill mother, instead of carrying her child in her arms, usually seats the baby astride her hip, taking most of the weight off her arm, and leaving her other hand free to carry a pail of water, a bucket of blackberries, or a gunny sack of provisions. In the more remote valleys a man, wife, and children walk single file. The woman and children often bear the burdens, following a custom going back to the days when a man's hands had to be free to hold a gun. Even now the farmer using back-country footpaths often carries a rifle on errands; at the slightest flash of gray in the treetops the gun leaps to his shoulder and a squirrel tumbles to the ground.

At 42.5 *m.* on US 65 is the junction with a graveled road.

Right on this road to the BIG HURRICANE CAVERN (*adm. adults 40¢, children 20¢; guides furnished*), 1.2 *m.*, so named many years ago because a violent storm hurled uprooted trees into the mouth of the cave. The cavern was once noted for the bear and wildcats killed within its shelter. The passageways are lighted by electricity, and board walks lead through chambers adorned with fantastic formations, including an onyx parrot, a stone airplane, and rocks that ring like steel chimes.

ST. JOE, 50.7 *m.* (794 alt., 213 pop.), once attracted the attention of O. O. McIntyre, who wrote in his syndicated column that Will Rice, a resident, was a man "who lives at a crossroads place in the deep Ozarks, where nothing happens, and yet turns out readable columns for a group of country newspapers. . . . Trains run through twice a week and night life consists of an owl's hoot or so, or perhaps the mournful strains of a mouth organ from across a far-away ridge. Yet Rice manages to winnow full-blooded observations about life and its meaning amid such desolation" (reprinted by permission of McNaught Syndicate, Inc.).

Rice is better known among Arkansans for his full-blooded exaggerations, such as the following: "John Byrd, whose migrating pumpkins caused some neighborhood disputes a few years ago when the vines wandered into neighboring fields, breaking down rail fences by growing big pumpkins on top of them and even blocking water courses . . . states that the pumpkins will be used this year to move some heavy log granaries and barns, and the seed is being planted around these buildings. As the pumpkins grow they will lift the buildings off the foundations and then the buildings can be rolled along as on ball bearings."

At the south end of a bridge is BUFFALO RIVER CAMP (*fishing, boating, float trips; guides*), 55.4 *m.* The waters of this stream, cold and blue-green, shelter an abundance of bass and bream, which are gamier than those taken in lowland rivers and lakes. The accessibility of this point on the river makes it a popular starting point for fishing-float trips (*see Recreation*).

When physicians and drugstores were few and far between in the Ozarks many housewives doctored common ailments with herbs and home remedies. Each year the use of these homespun medicines declines, but some of the more popular are still used. Hives are treated with sweet milk in which wild raspberry root has been boiled. Oil from the Jimson weed leaf is supposed to soothe boils. Slippery elm bark is prescribed for stomach disorders. Nightshade is applied to poison ivy rash. Catnip is used as a mild sedative for children. Tea made from the root of the sassafras is widely used as a spring tonic "to thin the blood"; the Cherokee regarded sassafras so highly that they forbade the cutting or burning of the tree.

The store buildings facing the town square of MARSHALL, 66.7 m. (1,050 alt., 822 pop.), have the tin marquees, small windows, and narrow double doors that indicate an old Ozark settlement. The solid two-story SEARCY COUNTY COURTHOUSE, standing in the small square, was built of stone taken from the hills in 1856, and still serves as the seat of government.

One hot Saturday afternoon in 1932 the roar of a shotgun from a second-story window on the square announced that a simmering political feud had progressed from words to actions. The target of the blast ducked behind a wagon and returned the fire. During the ensuing week both feudists rallied their friends, and on the following Saturday afternoon several participants were wounded by gunfire. After a trial that attracted spectators from all parts of the Ozarks one of the instigators was freed and the other imprisoned. Political ramifications of this feud attracted State-wide attention. Such affrays are rare nowadays, but were more common in the Ozark back country when every man owned a gun, corn liquor was potent, and blood-ties strong.

Left from Marshall on State 27, graveled, which follows a tree-lined creek between long, narrow fields. The hills that wall in the valley are a green bank in summer, but winter turns them startlingly bare. Twisting from one valley to another over a high ridge, the road overhangs itself, so that far below, and almost directly beneath, it appears as a tiny strand weaving through miniature trees.

In HARRIET, 11.2 m. (1,000 alt., 20 pop.*), is the junction with State 14. Right on State 14 is a swinging bridge across Big Creek, 14.4 m., strung in 1911, when a hay-laden wagon was about the heaviest traffic. It still accommodates passenger automobiles, undulating as they cross.

State 14 crosses, at 23.9 m., the western boundary of the OZARK NATIONAL FOREST, an almost uninhabited area of rolling hills and deep-hewn valleys. SYLAMORE CAMP, 40.6 m., is a gathering point for hunters who stalk deer and turkey along the forest borders and for fishermen who wade in Sylamore Creek and the near-by White River.

A common method of clearing land in the Ozarks is by girdling (locally called "deadening"). A ring is hacked around the tree, establishing a gap in the cambium, so that the sap cannot reach the leaves. The tree dies and in a few months it is thoroughly dry and can be burned. The stump resists the flames and stands for days on the hillside, the fire glowing through its knotholes like a monster Halloween head.

The hills surrounding LESLIE, 74.2 m. (975 alt., 779 pop.), were once covered with stands of white oak, and mills were built in the town to turn out barrel staves and heads. Operation now is usually on a part-time basis.

Twittie Baker, youngest survivor of the Mountain Meadow Massacre, spent the last years of his life in Leslie as a drayman. In 1857, when Baker was seven months old, his parents joined a wagon train bound for California from northwest Arkansas. At Mountain Meadow, Utah, south of Salt Lake City, the caravan was attacked by several hundred men. The emigrants surrendered upon the word of John D. Lee, Mormon farmer and Indian agent, that they would be protected. All over seven years old—more than 100 Arkansans—were slain. A few months before the massacre a Mormon missionary had been shot in Van Buren while attempting to add an Arkansan's wife to his collection, and most Arkansans believed the slaughter was an act of reprisal by Mormons. Though Mormon historians insist that Indians were the perpetrators, Lee later confessed his part in the affair and was executed.

In the massacre Baker and his two sisters were spared, and were cared for by Mormon families. A year later an army detachment took charge of the children and returned them to their relatives.

At 93.3 *m.* is the junction with State 16, a graveled road.

Left on this road alongside the Little Red River, then over piney hills where knotty cedars carry two telephone wires along the right-of-way. The road crosses modest valleys hemmed in by a hogback on one side, a sheer rock face and hills on the other. A little creek feints uncertainly at the road, hurries under a wooden bridge, and darts back and forth several times before finally dashing away.

The Little Red River at SHIRLEY, 10.7 *m.* (542 alt., 365 pop.), at one time was used by local residents to raft hardwood logs down to Heber Springs. The town now serves mainly as a mart for neighboring farmers.

At 14.3 *m.* is the junction with a graveled road; R. here 0.7 *m.* to the INDIAN ROCK HOUSE (*adm. 10¢*), a series of high, short caverns in the face of a cliff. Indian markings on the walls have not been deciphered satisfactorily, but archeologists say they probably antedate the tribal civilizations existing at the time of European exploration. Several Indian skeletons and pottery and arrowheads have been dug up in the main chamber.

State 16 crosses LITTLE RED RIVER at 28.1 *m.*, on a one-way suspension bridge.

HEBER SPRINGS, 35.3 *m.* (354 alt., 1,656 pop.), the seat of Cleburne County, is at the foot of Round Mountain. The town takes its name from the mineral springs in a ten-acre municipal park; each of the several varieties—sulphur, alum, magnesia, iron, and arsenic—is said to have its special curative powers. A creosoting plant treats timber taken from the surrounding countryside. The loops of Little Red River to the north furnish about 60 miles of good fishing waters. In the HEBER SPRINGS POST OFFICE is a mural by Louis Freund, once an artist at Hendrix College, in Conway. The central portion of the painting depicts a young pioneer couple clearing an Ozark farm.

Left from Heber Springs on a graveled road 2.5 *m.* to SUGAR LOAF MOUNTAIN, which rises almost perpendicularly for 500 feet. Its flat top is capped by a massive layer of limestone and studded with pine trees. Heber Springs boys act as guides for tourists who climb the mountain, the summit of which is accessible by only a few routes. A legend holds that Sugar Loaf was shaped by Indians who sought to make the plateau impregnable in time of war.

CLINTON, 94.3 *m.* (505 alt., 915 pop.), founded in 1842, has uneventfully grown up around the courthouse square. Each Friday a small stock auction is held on the north edge of town. Several buildings in Clinton, including the courthouse, are made of native stone.

The VOCATIONAL SCHOOL (R), with an average enrollment of about 250, is supported by the State. The institution comprises three buildings and 92 acres of land.

Between Clinton and Conway the highway glides down from the Ozarks and passes among farms where decades of cotton growing have depleted the red, sandy loam. Federal farm agencies are here encouraging diversified farming and terracing the eroded hillsides.

US 65 crosses North Fork of Cadron Creek at 120.1 *m.* and East Fork at 129.6 *m.* The bottom land of these streams is known as buckshot; if plowed when wet, it forms blocks of sticky earth that become hard and untillable.

At 133.1 *m.* is the western junction with US 64 (*see Tour 3b*), with which the route unites for 1.7 miles.

South of the junction fields give way to a row of filling stations that marks the approach to Conway.

CONWAY, 134.8 *m.* (321 alt., 5,782 pop.) (*see Tour 3a*), is at the eastern junction with US 64 (*see Tour 3a*).

At the north end of the bridge over Palarm Creek, 147.8 *m.,* a granite memorial stone (R) marks the SITE OF THE JAMES I. MILLER HOUSE. Miller, later to become first Territorial Governor of Arkansas, was an officer in the Battle of Lundy's Lane (War of 1812) when his superior asked him whether he could capture a certain British battery. "I'll try, sir," he answered, and took the battery, whereupon he became a national hero and gave the country a new catchword.

Appointed Governor of Arkansas Territory in 1819, Miller, by this time a general, proceeded from Pittsburgh down the Ohio and Mississippi, his journey a tour of triumph. His private keelboat, the *Arkansas,* fitted up at government expense, carried a banner at her masthead bearing the words "I'll try, Sir." At every river port men used the phrase to accept invitations for drinks. Such was the enthusiasm that the trip from Pittsburgh to Arkansas Post took 75 days, an average, as some Arkansans caustically pointed out, of 10 miles a day, downstream.

Governor Miller, disliking the topography of Little Rock, built his home 15 miles up the Arkansas, and made unsuccessful efforts to have the Territorial capital removed to near-by Crystal Hill. He is remembered less for his executive accomplishments than for his motto, which was taught to schoolboys all through the nineteenth century.

At 153.8 *m.* is the junction with a graveled road.

Right on this road to MARCHÉ (Fr., the market), 1.6 *m.* (268 alt., 72 pop.*), a Polish community founded by Count Timothy von Choinski and his wife in 1878. The titled pair, who had emigrated to America, determined to establish a community for their countrymen where they might struggle together with the strange language and strange occupations. About 300 families settled, cleared land, and built cabins, though all did not remain. Today (1941) Marché is one of the few settlements in Arkansas retaining European customs and language. All social life centers around the church built on *Jasna Gora* (Sky-blue Mountain), but weddings, followed by enormous feasts, are the most important occasions.

LEVY, 162.6 *m.* (282 alt., 1,306 pop.), was a rough and roaring rendezvous for off-duty soldiers in 1917 and 1918. With the abandonment of the near-by military cantonment after the World War, the community resumed its quiet status as a suburb, but came to life again in 1940 when the camp was reopened.

Left from Levy on an asphalt-paved road to CAMP JOE T. ROBINSON (*open 8-6*), 2.9 *m.,* a military reservation that, during the World War, was known as Camp Pike. In 1918 as many as 100,000 men were stationed here at one time, housed in hundreds of barracks. After the Armistice most of the buildings were torn down, although some 5,000 acres of land were retained. Under the national defense program of 1940, new buildings were erected to shelter some 25,000 men, and an artillery range of 39,500 acres was added by lease to the original camp.

At 162.9 *m.* is the junction with the Fort Roots Road.

Right on this road to the U. S. VETERANS ADMINISTRATION FACILITY (*private*), 1.8 *m.,* occupying buildings once a part of Fort Roots. The hospital has a commanding view of the Arkansas River from its site on Big Rock, so named by the early explorers to distinguish it from the Little Rock just across the river.

On the 1,100-acre reservation are 9 dormitories, a clinical building, a tuberculosis ward, a power and boiler house, the hospital building, and dozens of smaller structures. The hospital was opened in 1921 by the Federal Government for mental and nervous patients who are veterans of American wars; it now has nearly 1,200 beds.

A few traces of military occupancy remain of Fort Logan H. Roots. Beginning in 1893, the grounds were laid out and several buildings of the post erected, but operations were stopped by the Spanish-American War in 1898, when the troops occupying the fort were ordered to Puerto Rico. A small garrison was maintained until the World War, when Camp Pike was built a few miles away.

NORTH LITTLE ROCK, 165 *m.* (256 alt., 21,137 pop.) (*see Little Rock and North Little Rock*).

North Little Rock is at the northern junction with US 70 (*see Tour 2a*), with which the route unites for 1.2 miles (*see Tour 2a*).

LITTLE ROCK, 166.2 *m.* (291 alt., 88,039 pop.) (*see Little Rock and North Little Rock*).

Little Rock is at the junction with US 167 (*see Tour 15*), State 10 (*see Tour 13*), and the southern junction with US 70 (*see Tour 2b*).

Section b.   LITTLE ROCK to LOUISIANA LINE; 160.5 m.,
US 65

South of Little Rock US 65 slips down from the low Ouachita foothills into the broad valley of the Arkansas at Pine Bluff and passes through plantation country to the Louisiana Line. Along the bayous and creek bottoms the dense forests that once covered this region still maintain strategic footholds, and seem ready to overrun cultivated fields at the first faltering of the farmers' vigilance. Beyond the levees, in the swampy regions which men have conceded to the rivers, saplings and brush grow luxuriantly, affording shelter to a few bear and wild-cats as well as to rabbit, raccoon, turkey, and deer.

Leaving LITTLE ROCK, 0 *m.,* on Roosevelt Road, US 65 crosses Fourche Creek at the city limits and follows the irregular valley wall of the Arkansas River.

The main building of the ARKANSAS CONFEDERATE HOME (R), 5.2 *m.,* is a red-brick two-story structure that faces the highway from the top of a wooded hill. The white frame gallery across the front is much in use, attesting that the inhabitants are of rocking-chair age. The L-shaped structure south of the main building is the dormitory.

Former Confederate soldiers, who in 1889 formed an association to care for needy veterans and their widows, obtained these 54 forested acres in 1891. Two years later the State took over the institution, erected a new building, and assumed maintenance. Approximately 140 veterans, widows, and daughters were inmates of the home in 1939.

WRIGHTSVILLE, 11.8 *m.* (257 alt., 317 pop.*), is a small trading town which grew up to serve the timber workers to the west and the plantations which lie between the highway and the Arkansas at this point.

Left from Wrightsville on a graveled road to the NEGRO BOYS' INDUSTRIAL SCHOOL, 1.6 *m.,* a State institution for the correction of delinquent juvenile Negroes, established in 1921 and rebuilt with Federal assistance in 1936-38. The youthful inmates are given instruction in farming, blacksmithing, and carpentry. The principal buildings are arranged in a rough oval, and include a commissary, dormitories, dining room, hospital, and offices.

WOODSON, 17.5 *m.* (250 alt., 314 pop.*), populated mostly by Negroes, is a sun-baked town that hunches over a sawmill and a cor-rugated-iron gin. The settlement was named for a family who once owned large plantations in the vicinity.

Fragments of the old "Dollarway," the first hard-surfaced road in Arkansas (built 1912-13), are seen alongside the present highway from the Pulaski-Jefferson County line to Pine Bluff. The road, slightly more than 23 miles long, was let out on the then customary "one dollar per square yard" contract rate—hence its name. Farmers have dug out chunks of the abandoned roadbed for retaining walls, house foun-dations, and walks.

To the neighborhood of REDFIELD, 23.4 *m.* (301 alt., 339 pop.), came M. Le Noir de Serville, after serving with the French marines in the Revolutionary War and being wounded at Yorktown. Killed by a falling tree in 1828, he was buried with military honors, and his funeral was attended by Arkansas political and military notables. The location of De Serville's grave is unknown.

South of Redfield dense woods of scrub oak close in upon the high-way, which tunnels through them as far as Pine Bluff.

At 39.3 *m.* is the junction (R) with US 270 (*see Tour 11*).

PINE BLUFF, 44.1 *m.* (221 alt., 21,290 pop.) (*see Pine Bluff*). Pine Bluff is at the junction with US 79 (*see Tour 12*).

South of Pine Bluff US 65 passes through the cotton land of the Arkansas Delta. The great plantations are sharply differentiated by the color of the sharecroppers' houses set in rows at regular intervals in the level fields; one group of cabins may be red, the next white, the next (probably belonging to a planter who held his cotton for a higher price) unpainted. Some of the 'cropper homes are surrounded by fences, gardens, and a few sheds, but most of them have neither fences nor outbuildings. The mules are usually kept in great stables at the "big house." These plantation houses are frequently set among groves of trees and bordered by green lawns. A common architectural feature is a railing around the flat sections of the roof, perhaps a survival of the days when the planter mounted his housetop to observe the work of his slaves.

The endless fields, bleak brown in winter, green in spring, snowy white in fall when the bolls burst, are broken here and there by patches of brush and timber along the creeks and bayous. Here the 'croppers hunt rabbit, 'possum, and 'coon, and fish for perch, bream, crappie, and catfish. While the catfish is not a flashy warrior like bass or trout, he fights with a stubborn tenacity. When the hook is set this sullen sluggard dives for deep water like a miniature whale and has to be tugged inch by inch from the bottom. Even after being dragged to the surface he lives up to his alternate name "bullhead," and sometimes stands on his head and pulls doggedly for a submerged drift, where he will snare the line and tear himself loose, then wriggle tiredly down under a cypress stump.

Although the country is well-populated, such towns as MOSCOW, 59.1 *m.* (195 alt., 225 pop.*), and GRADY, 66.5 *m.* (185 alt., 472 pop.), consist of little besides a railroad station, a long row of cotton-loading platforms, a couple of gins, a few stores, a church, a school, and a handful of small houses.

At VARNER, 72.1 *m.* (181 alt., 5 pop.), is a crossroads filling station and store.

Left from Varner on a graded road to the CUMMINS PRISON FARM (*open 1-4 first Sunday in month*), 3.3 *m.*, which, with Tucker Farm (*see Tour 12*), constitutes the basis of the present Arkansas penal system, the old penitentiary at Little Rock having been closed in 1933. Negro felons, men and women, have been confined here since 1901, and the more difficult white male prisoners since 1936. Most of the convicts work on the farm, growing cotton, livestock, and vegetables. The institution also manufactures clothing and lumber.

From 1849 to 1893 all Arkansas convicts were leased to private individuals. Widespread protest over abuses growing from irresponsible supervision and competition with free labor finally forced the establishment of State control. Some penitentiary labor, however, was hired out to planters, contractors, and manufacturers until 1913.

At a country store on Cypress Bend of the Arkansas, east of US 65 at this point, Henry Morton Stanley (1841-1904), African explorer, once passed a quiet interlude in his adventurous life, selling groceries, calico, and whisky to planters.

Born John Rowlands, of a poor Welsh family, Stanley spent his early years in a British workhouse, whence he escaped after thrashing the schoolmaster, and eventually made his way as a cabin boy to New Orleans, where he was adopted by Henry Morton Stanley and took his foster father's name. Invited in 1860 by a Saline River planter to visit his Arkansas estate, Stanley became weary of the table fare and indignant at the brutality of the overseer. He walked 40 miles overland to the Arkansas River and obtained a clerk's job at Louis Altshul's store. Caught by the war fever the following spring, he enlisted in the 6th Arkansas Volunteers, survived a cholera epidemic that swept the camp at Searcy, and was sent to the Tennessee front, where he was captured in April 1862 during the battle of Shiloh. He secured his release by joining a Federal artillery company, but was in such poor health that he was discharged in a few weeks and left for England.

Unable to earn a living in his native country, Stanley soon went to sea again, was wrecked off Barcelona, and returned to America, where he joined the Federal navy in 1864. At the close of the war he attached himself to an overland expedition that took him to Colorado and Utah, and acquired a reputation with New York editors for vivid correspondence; he was thus enabled to wander all over the world as an explorer-reporter. James Gordon Bennett of the New York *Herald* sent him to Africa, and around 1870 Gordon Bennett, Jr., commissioned him to go in search of the long-lost Livingstone. The jungle meeting brought forth his "Dr. Livingstone, I presume," a phrase whose casualness made it a symbol everywhere of British aplomb. After spectacular experiences in Africa during the next two decades as explorer, soldier, and political manipulator, he returned to England, where he was elected to Parliament, and knighted.

Stanley found Arkansas malaria worse than the African fevers. "It was a strange disease," he wrote in his autobiography, "preceded by a violent shaking, and a congealed feeling as though the blood was suddenly iced, during which I had to be half-smothered in blankets, and surrounded by hot-water bottles. After a couple of hours' shivering, a hot fit followed, accompanied by delirium, which, about the twelfth hour, was relieved by exhausting perspiration. When, about six hours later, I became cool and sane, my appetite was almost ravenous from quinine and emptiness. . . . During the few months I remained at Cypress Bend, I suffered . . . three times a month."

The planters Stanley found "stiff and constrained. . . . They lived like princelings, were owners of hundreds of slaves over whom they were absolute except as to life or limb, and all their environments catered to their egotism. Though genially sociable to each other, to landless people like myself they conducted themselves as though they were under no obligations." And to make matters worse, "every new immigrant soon became infected with the proud and sensitive spirit prevailing in Arkansas. The poor American settler, the Irish employee, the German-Jew storekeeper, in a brief time grew as liable to bursts of deadly passion, or fits of cold-blooded malignity, as the Virginian aristocrat. In New Orleans, and other great cities, the social rule was to give and take, to assert an opinion, and hear it contradicted without resort to lethal weapons, but, in Arkansas, to refute a statement was tantamount to giving the lie direct, and was likely to be followed by an instant appeal to the revolver or bowie." (*Autobiography of Sir Henry Morton Stanley,* Houghton Mifflin Co., 1909.)

GOULD, 77.3 *m.* (167 alt., 908 pop.), larger than most of the cotton towns, but much like them otherwise, was named for Jay Gould, Wall Street financier and railroad magnate. Gould began operations in the Southwest by buying the St. Louis, Iron Mountain & Southern in 1881. To this line, which had absorbed the old Cairo & Fulton from Moark to Texarkana, he added in the following year the Little Rock & Fort Smith. During the ensuing decade he bought up a network of roads in eastern and southern Arkansas. Gould frequently visited the State while he was acquiring his railroad empire. On these occasions the lamp chimneys in the Little Rock station were polished and crowds turned out to see the famous man. Resented by monopoly-hating farmers, Gould strove to win the loyalty of his employees by fraternizing with trainmen and section-hands.

Left from Gould on State 114, graveled, to the junction with a dirt road, 5.4 *m.;* R. here to the SOUTH BEND FARMS (*private*), 10 *m.* The plantation house, built in the 1850's for Dr. John A. Jordan, a Kentuckian, utilized handmade brick produced by slave labor, and some woodwork brought from Kentucky. The structure is an interesting adaptation of the style of the dogtrot cabin, with wings extending backward to form a court. It once fronted on the Arkansas, but the river has long since shifted its course, and the view is now terminated abruptly by a high, grass-covered levee.

DUMAS, 85.1 *m.* (166 alt., 2,323 pop.), was named not for the French novelist but for a county surveyor. It has facetiously appropriated as the town anthem the ragtime tune *Ding Dong Daddy from Dumas,* which local musicians play whenever possible. Though Dumas is primarily a cotton town, part of the population is employed by a sawmill. Missouri Pacific Valley Line tracks run down the middle of the wide main street, which is lined with brick stores, shaded by wooden marquees.

South of WINCHESTER, 93.9 *m.* (155 alt., 171 pop.), the highway winds along the course of a sluggish bayou, the banks of which are covered with canes and vines that tangle with the overhanging branches of cypress, willow, and water oak. Here, a white crane may pose rigidly in the shallow water until an unwary fish comes near; then the head whizzes out and spears its prey and the crane stalks awkwardly to a cypress knob, where he bangs the victim a couple of times to quiet him, and gulps him headfirst. The bird preens a feather or two and assumes his statuesque immobility.

In TILLAR, 100.3 *m.* (154 alt., 229 pop.), shade trees and well-kept lawns distinguish the residential district.

Right from Tillar on State 138, graveled, across the level Bartholomew Bayou Valley, to the junction with graveled State 4, 6.7 *m.;* R. here to MONTICELLO, 21.9 *m.* (273 alt., 3,650 pop.). Lying among timber-covered hills that roll up from Bartholomew Bayou, Monticello has little resemblance to the cotton towns of the Arkansas Valley a few miles away. A small park containing a fountain and flower beds occupies the center of the town. Radiating from the park are tree-shaded streets lined with substantial brick residences. The DREW COUNTY COURTHOUSE, south of the square, was built in 1932. This four-story, flat-topped building has six Corinthian columns set into the façade. A college (*see below*) joins with a wide variety of industrial and agricultural enterprises to support the town.

In June or July Monticello stages a festival to honor the ripening products of the neighboring ridges. A Tomato Queen is chosen, visitors are shown crated displays and packing sheds, and a parade and dance are held.

On the hilltop at the east end of Shelton Avenue (R) is the WILLIAMSON OBSERVATORY (*visitors admitted*), a small square building with a low round-pointed tower, set behind the home of its owner, an amateur astronomer.

At the MONTICELLO COTTON MILL (*open on application*), on East Shelton Ave. (R), about 250 workers weave duck, drill, and other coarse cloths which are marketed to wholesalers.

The DREW COTTON OIL MILL (*open on application*), on State 4 at the Missouri Pacific tracks (L), produces cottonseed oil and cake. The same company also operates a sawmill, stave mill, and ice plant, and cans tomatoes in the summer and early fall.

Left from Monticello on State 13, asphalt-paved, 0.7 *m.* to a graveled road; L. here along the town's edge 0.5 *m.* to the SITE OF ROUGH AND READY, an early trading point which became the first seat of Drew County in 1847. The settlement, presumably named after Zachary Taylor's sobriquet, was noted for a number of fatal fights that took place here. From the eminence which it occupied there is a view of timbered hills which drop into the Saline Valley and of the smoke from the lumber mills of Warren (*see Tour 12*).

At 3.4 *m.* on State 13 (R) is MONTICELLO AGRICULTURAL AND MECHANICAL COLLEGE (State). The campus is covered with flowers, shrubbery, and ancient trees. Nearly all the buildings are of recent construction. Some are of red brick with hipped roofs, others are of buff brick with pointed gables and dormer windows, some of stone in Gothic design. Accredited as a four-year college, the school offers bachelor's degrees in the arts and sciences. The curriculum emphasizes courses in agriculture, engineering, education, and home economics. Enrollment is about 500. Near the north end of the campus is a magnificent SPANISH OAK, said to be 125 years old, its lower branches nearly touching the ground. The tree once shaded the home of William Harrison Wells, who became the first judge of Drew County in 1847, and was host to many Arkansas notables.

McGEHEE, 107.1 *m.* (149 alt., 3,663 pop.), was familiar to passengers on the Valley Line of the old Iron Mountain Railway as a stop where they ate dinner at the plantation home (no longer standing) of Colonel Abner McGehee, while the train refueled for its trip to Arkansas City. Establishment of railroad shops in 1905 catapulted the village into industrial prominence, and accounted for its rapid growth. The sun-baked, treeless business streets are lined with brick buildings clustering along the railroad tracks that have brought them into existence. The Missouri Pacific shops still provide the leading pay roll of the town, and its position as a junction helps to make it the principal commercial center of southeast Arkansas. The C. A. LINAKER WHOLESALE PROVISION COMPANY (*open on application*), on the railroad tracks near the center of town, buys beef and pork raised by farmers who have turned part of their cotton acreage into pasture and feed crops.

At 108.8 *m.* is the junction (R) with US 165 (*see Tour 16*).

At 111.8 *m.* is the junction with State 4, asphalt-paved.

Left on State 4 to ARKANSAS CITY, 7.7 *m.* (140 alt., 1,446 pop.), a Mississippi River port whose fortunes have gone up and down. The town was established about 1873 when the river engulfed Napoleon, at the mouth of the Arkansas, and the inhabitants of that famous old shipping point were forced to seek other homes.

Napoleon had been founded in the 1820's by Frederick Notrebe, a French general and subordinate of Bonaparte. It had soon become one of Arkansas' chief outlets on the Mississippi. Some of the stern-wheelers that ascended the Arkansas and White Rivers were not adapted to Mississippi navigation, and Napoleon was the transfer point for cargoes from one type of boat to the other. Accounts agree that it was a roaring, wide-open town, full of suave cardsharps and rough rivermen. A combination steamboat-stagecoach line, from Napoleon to Pine Bluff by water and thence to Little Rock by road, was opened in 1853. The United States Government in 1855 completed a three-story marine hospital accommodating 100 patients. Napoleon was nearly destroyed by fire at the time of its capture by Federal forces during the War between the States. Year after year its buildings were undermined by the ever-encroaching Arkansas and Mississippi Rivers. After an especially devastating assault by the waters in 1874 the remaining citizens gave up the fight and moved southward. A decade later Mark Twain wrote its requiem in *Life on the Mississippi* (Harper & Brothers, 1927):

"It was an astonishing thing to see the Mississippi rolling between un-peopled shores and straight over the spot where I used to see a good big self-complacent town twenty years ago. Town that was county-seat of a great and important county; town with a big United States marine hospital; town of innumerable fights—an inquest every day; town where I had used to know the prettiest girl, and the most accomplished, in the whole Mississippi valley . . . a town no more—swallowed up, vanished, gone to feed the fishes; nothing left but a fragment of a shanty and a crumbling brick chimney!"

Today an occasional excursion boat docks at the Arkansas City landing, and strings of barges pass up and down the river. The single row of business houses, overshadowed by the high Mississippi levee, have been under water so often that they look mildewed. The two most impressive buildings, the three-story DESHA BANK on Main St. and the DESHA COUNTY COURTHOUSE to the north, were built in 1896 and 1900 respectively. The functions of county government keep Arkansas City alive, and the enterprising town of McGehee is already clamoring for these.

US 65 continues south through plantation country, here more frequently broken by bottom timber patches, into Chicot County, so celebrated among Arkansans for its deer, turkey, and waterfowl that it has special game laws, enforced by a large crew of wardens (*see General Information*).

In the fall of 1935 Chicot and Desha Counties witnessed a land rush that reenacted on a minor scale scenes associated with the opening of the Cherokee Strip of Indian Territory in 1889. Some 75,000 acres of fertile land, cut over by lumber companies and forfeited to the State for taxes, became available for homesteading in October. Jobless factory workers, bankrupt storekeepers, and other city-bred victims of the economic depression joined dispossessed sharecroppers and

hill farmers from the Ozarks in the scramble for land made rich by
countless overflows of the Mississippi. They crowded Lake Village
and Arkansas City, picked their home sites from section maps, paid
a $10 filing fee, and set to work "proving up" their claims. After
they had cleared a minimum of 5 of their 160 acres, lived on the land
at least 2 years, and improved its value by at least $200, the State
granted title in the form of "donation" certificates; thus the settlers
became known, somewhat paradoxically, as "donators."

Some of these twentieth-century pioneers have surrendered to the
tremendous difficulties confronting them—the tangled wilderness of
fallen trees and undergrowth that had to be cut and burned, the
swamps that had to be drained, the water-soaked soil that had to be
plowed up and cultivated. These have given up their land and returned
to the cities. But many of the "donators" are making steady if toil-
some progress toward establishing homes and livelihoods for themselves
and their families.

LAKE VILLAGE, 132.5 *m.* (127 alt., 2,045 pop.), built on the
curving shore of Lake Chicot, has long been a resort where south-
Arkansans have gathered for fishing, swimming, motorboating, and
sailing on the lake and for hunting in the near-by river bottoms. Cotton
gins, barrel-stave mills, and commercial catching of buffalo and other
"rough fish" provide the town's income. The CHICOT COUNTY
COURTHOUSE, a buff-brick structure with Classic portico and four
pillars of pieced stone, overlooks the lake. The homes of wealthier
citizens spread along the shore, and the business district centers on
the three streets that bound the courthouse square.

Established in the 1850's, Lake Village was occupied on June 7,
1864, by about 10,000 Federal troops recuperating from the Battle of
Ditch Bayou below the town. Confederate General J. S. Marmaduke
had harassed Northern transportation on the river so successfully that
Federal troops under General A. J. Smith were landed at Sunnyside,
at the lower end of the lake, to destroy his force. Marmaduke's troops
met Smith's at Ditch Bayou, and an all-day battle ensued. The Confederates, out of ammunition and vastly outnumbered, withdrew, and
the Federals entered Lake Village, to remain only one day before
marching again to Sunnyside. Here they re-embarked under scattered
fire.

Horseshoe-shaped LAKE CHICOT (L), an abandoned channel
of the Mississippi, is now separated from the river by high levees.
Arkansas' largest natural lake, Chicot is about 15 miles long and a
half-mile wide. Its 32 miles of shore line afford countless vantage
points for fishermen and duck hunters. Near its upper end is
STUART'S ISLAND, once a stronghold of the outlaw band headed
by John Murrell (1803-44). Murrell, who claimed that his mother
"learnt me and all her children to steal so soon as we could walk,"
was one of the most deadly brigands of the early nineteenth century.
His operations, which extended over a number of States, included
robbery of mails, banks, stores, piracy of river boats, counterfeiting, and

slave-kidnapping. Murrell's boldness, ruthlessness, and lavish distribution of spoils attracted scores of followers among frontier adventurers, and his band was reputed to number 1,000 members. His spectacular career was cut short by capture in Tennessee in 1834. Miraculously, he escaped the gallows, spent ten years in prison, and died shortly after his release. The stronghold on Stuart's Island was attacked and burned by indignant citizens of Chicot County, who so thoroughly obliterated it that no trace remains.

In Lake Village is the junction with US 82 (*see Tour 14*).

For several miles below Lake Village US 65 skirts the shore of Lake Chicot. Cypresses, distinguished by their curious conical trunks, stand in the water. Here and there a large turtle suns himself on a stump. Beyond the lake, past the levee that separates it from the Mississippi, are the swamp lands of the great Mississippi flyway, used by thousands of wild duck and geese each year in their passage southward. In season hunters come here from all parts of the South.

CHICOT, 141.7 *m.* (127 alt., 160 pop.*), a small collection of stores and houses, is the headquarters of the 8,700-acre HAMMOND RANCH which stretches along the highway toward Eudora. The place was purchased in 1935 by a Memphis newspaperman interested in the possibility of turning cotton land into a stock ranch. About 120 families occupy the tract, each with cows, hogs, and chickens. A sawmill in Chicot cuts lumber used on the ranch, and a gin processes the cotton.

EUDORA, 148.6 *m.* (129 alt., 1,808 pop.), is a cotton-ginning and sawmill town with the usual red-brick stores and offices. The name is associated by Arkansans with the controversial floodway, or "fuse-plug" levee, proposals. Concerned about the disastrous floods of 1927, the United States Congress in 1928 enacted legislation to rebuild and strengthen the levees of the lower Mississippi. The Flood Control Act provided, however, that levees from Yancopin, near the mouth of the Arkansas, to Luna Landing, above Lake Village, should remain low so that extra high water could be diverted through a great floodway west of Eudora, down the Bœuf River and thence through Louisiana.

Mississippians endorsed the floodway heartily, since it would relieve pressure on the Mississippi levees. Louisianans, however, objected to having the flood waters pouring over their State. Arkansans proposed alternative floodways that would go through Louisiana but miss Arkansas. Around Eudora sentiment was also divided. Landowners in the path of the proposed floodway disliked the prospect of having their cotton washed away in high-water periods in order to save someone else's crop, but persons on higher ground welcomed a plan that offered protection against a general flood. In 1936 the projected spillway was shifted from the Bœuf Basin to another route east of Eudora. Fresh protests arose. Finally, after a decade of debate, army engineers reported that dredging of the Mississippi's channel and building of reservoirs in the river's watershed had brought about an unexpected lowering of flood crests and made the need for the floodway less imperative. Consequently, orders were given in 1939 to build up the "fuse-plug" section to the same height as the rest of the 1928 levees. While the floodway may still be constructed, likelihood that it will ever be used has greatly diminished.

At 152.4 *m.*, US 65 reaches GRAND LAKE (L), another old Mississippi bend now completely cut off from the parent river, and follows its edge about four miles. South of the lake the plantations give way to smaller farms, mostly operated by Negro renters. A renter's house can usually be distinguished from a sharecropper's, because the renter keeps his own mules. Oaks line the road, and beyond the cottonfields are heavier patches of timber, many of which were once cleared but allowed to go back to forest because of the decline of cotton growing.

At 160.5 *m.* US 65 crosses the Louisiana Line, 44.6 miles north of Tallulah, Louisiana.

Tour 6

Dardanelle — Subiaco — Paris — Charleston — Fort Smith; 75.3 *m.*, State 22.

Missouri Pacific R.R. roughly parallels route between Paris and Fort Smith. Concrete-paved roadbed.
Accommodations in larger towns only.

In 1834 young Jefferson Davis served in western Arkansas as lieutenant of a company of dragoons. When State 22 was built about a hundred years later to make a short route from Dardanelle to Fort Smith and to lessen the flow of traffic on US 64, north of the Arkansas River, the new highway was named for the lieutenant who later became President of the Confederate States.

The Jefferson Davis Highway winds over the low hills that rise between the Arkansas River bottom and the chain of higher peaks farther south. Pastures, interrupted by fields of cotton and corn, border most of the route. Near Paris towering piles of slag indicate the proximity of an important coal field. Large barns and silos near Fort Smith denote a flourishing cattle and dairy industry.

A rocky peak jutting into the Arkansas River made DARDA-NELLE, 0 *m.* (325 alt., 1,807 pop.), a landmark for explorers and homeseekers who struggled upriver with keelboats; and the settlement that grew in the shadow of the cliff was among the first in the valley. Thomas Nuttall, one of the earliest travelers to write of the territory, found a Mr. Raphael managing a Cherokee trading post here in 1819. Other families moved in steadily, although the town was not platted until 1843. The origin of the name has often been debated. An earlier version seems to have been Derdonnai, which may be either of Indian-French origin or derived from the family name of Jean Baptiste Dardenne, who owned a land grant across the river while Arkansas was still under Spanish rule. The transition to Dardanelle may have come about because of a fancied resemblance of the rock to a peninsula on the straits below the Black Sea in Europe.

Dardanelle changed hands several times during the fighting between Federals and Confederates for control of the upper Arkansas River, but the settlement's value was strategic rather than economic, since its population was then very small. Building of railroads in the 1870's and the development of near-by Mount Nebo as a recreation center boomed the town.

Present-day Dardanelle's Front Street stretches for more than a mile along the tree-bordered Arkansas. The residential section spreads out to the southwest. The YELL COUNTY COURTHOUSE, which serves the north half of the county, is at the upper end of Front Street near the bridgehead. A creamery and a sawmill in the center of town provide the chief sources of income.

Two great COUNCIL OAKS, on the riverbank behind the waterworks on North Front Street, shaded an important meeting in 1820 between Robert Crittenden, Secretary of Arkansas Territory, and leaders of the Cherokee. The purpose of the conference was to arrange an agreement whereby the Indians would yield for white settlement part of their treaty-granted land in Arkansas. Under the direction of Colonel David Brearly, Indian agent, trees were felled to seat the assemblage of more than a hundred chiefs and tribesmen. As Brearly's son tells the story, Chief Black Fox placed himself next to Crittenden, and repeatedly asked the official to give him a little more room on the log. At last Crittenden angrily replied that he had reached the end of the log, and that there was no more room. "That is just the way with us," Black Fox replied blandly. "Our Great Father has moved us from place to place until we can get no farther." Despite the Indian's eloquent allegory, the white man's power prevailed, and the Cherokee finally agreed to withdraw into the hills north of the Arkansas. In a tiny, grassy park the trees that shaded the council still stand, one of them fenced and marked.

The north end of Front Street runs into a foot trail. A stiff 20 minute hike up the trail, among jagged boulders and through crevasses, will bring a sure-footed climber to the top of DARDANELLE ROCK. The peak, much higher than it appears from below, affords the same "sublime view of the surrounding country" that Nuttall found in 1819. The wide current of the Arkansas sweeps past in an almost straight channel. To the north are the houses of Russellville, looking no bigger than children's blocks, with the first ridges of the Ozarks rising behind them. To the south is Dardanelle, nearly hidden by trees, with fields and forests checkerboarded around it. To the east is the cloven peak of Petit Jean. Flat-topped Mount Nebo is to the west, and rising beyond Nebo is the huge blue bulk of Magazine.

In the 1890's Captain Joe Evans somehow managed to set a 41-ton iron tank atop Dardanelle Rock to hold the town's water supply. Thereafter, water gushed out of Dardanelle faucets under a pressure of 148 pounds to the square inch. In 1939 the big tank was skidded half-way down the mountain to reduce the strong pressure, and one of the best-known landmarks of the Arkansas Valley disappeared.

In Dardanelle is the junction with State 7 (*see Tour 8*).

Left from Dardanelle on State 155, which cuts across the valley and then zigzags steeply (*drive in low gear both climbing and descending the elevation*) up the side of MOUNT NEBO, 6.8 *m.* (1,750 alt.). Overlooking a fertile valley and offering a view of far horizons, the mountain was aptly named for the peak from which Moses saw the Promised Land.

The mountain became quite widely known in the 1870's when Colonel E. F. Babcock, a horticulturist from up-State New York, set out an apple orchard on its flat top. Kentucky Redstreaks, Ben Davises, and Shannons raised from stock grown in Colonel Babcock's lofty nursery won prizes in national expositions.

Pine-covered, rugged, and cool during the summer weeks when the Arkansas Valley sweltered, Nebo became an early-day resort. In 1928 it was made a State park. The 3,375-acre park area includes picnic grounds, a baseball diamond, a pavilion, cabins, and bridle paths. Scattered over the summit are summer homes, many of them 20 or 30 years old, and numerous water tanks, filled by means of gasoline pumps. Oddly enough, water is obtainable from shallow wells, despite the mountain's considerable elevation above the surrounding country. The striking view from SUNSET POINT, on the west flank, embraces Petit Jean Valley to the south and Chickalah Mountain on the west, as well as the Arkansas Valley to the north.

West of Dardanelle State 22 runs through low rolling hills. Out-croppings of rock dot the pastures that alternate with forests. To the south is a long chain of mountains, sometimes blue in the distance, sometimes so near the highway that individual green pines can be distinguished. Trading towns, such as NEW BLAINE, 16.1 *m.* (398 alt., 200 pop.*), and MIDWAY, 22.5 *m.*, occupy level spaces, and are bordered by corn and cotton fields and potato patches.

SUBIACO, 28.6 *m.* (465 alt., 202 pop.), is dominated by the twin medieval-style towers of SUBIACO COLLEGE AND ABBEY (*open, guides*), on a hill north of the highway. The principal building, containing a chapel, classrooms, dormitories, and a museum, is a massive four-story sandstone structure that extends around three sides of a courtyard. Sloping down from the building are wide cultivated fields and vineyards. A chicken farm, an apiary, a printshop, and a smithy make the institution nearly self-sustaining.

The first Benedictines came to Subiaco from St. Meinrad's Abbey in Indiana; St. Meinrad's had been established by members of the order from Switzerland. The Little Rock & Fort Smith Railroad was anxious to secure settlers along its line and offered the order part of its State-granted land and funds for buildings. The expectation was that German immigrants would follow the church. Three monks arrived at the site in 1878, and for their first service used an unhinged cabin door as an altar table. The mission became a priory the following year, and an abbey in 1892. A theological school was opened in 1887. Meanwhile, the anticipated colony had begun to flourish in the community, and many of the descendants of German settlers still live around Subiaco.

The institution now includes a general high school, as well as a seminary for training novices to the priesthood. Almost all students board at the school, many of them receiving limited scholarships. Enrollment averages around 175, and about 20 resident members of the order act as instructors and administrators. Summers are spent working the farm lands and canning fruits and vegetables. The SUBIACO MUSEUM contains rare books and manuscripts, sacred relics, and specimens of taxidermy and minerals.

PARIS, 34.1 m. (410 alt., 3,430 pop.), is built around the LOGAN COUNTY COURTHOUSE, a two-story red-brick building with Classic porticoes on two sides. Spreading in all directions from the town are the dozen or more coal mines from which came 400,000 tons in 1937-38.

Years of activity by the United Mine Workers have made Paris one of the few strong union towns in Arkansas. Here approximately 1,000 miners are enrolled in 7 locals. Social and political, as well as economic, life centers around the unions. Each month the locals take turns in holding an "Open-Door House" featured by entertainment and dancing. Wives and daughters of the miners belong to a ladies' auxiliary. Local office-seekers vie for the endorsement of the union. The presence of this organized support made possible in 1939 the launching of a new union, the Industrial Workers of America, with a membership consisting of farm day-laborers.

Logan County coal miners, working 6 shifts a week at a scale of $5.29 a shift, earn more than the average Arkansas worker. Seasonal layoffs, however, which begin in March, reduce the working year to 8 or 9 months. During the off season most miners must rely on their gardens, cows, and unemployment compensation.

The GILL HOUSE (*private*), three blocks west of the courthouse on Main St. (L), is a curiosity in stone. House, patio, and garage are built of yellow rocks in unusual shapes. Over the fireplace in the living room is a map of the United States with each State represented by a native rock—Arkansas having a piece of Pike County diamond-bearing peridotite.

In Paris is the junction with the Mount Magazine Road (*see Tour 13*).

Right from Paris on a graveled road to the junction with a dirt road at 1.5 m.; L. here to the JEWEL MINE (*open 7-4 workdays, guides*), 2 m. Largest coal producer in the vicinity of Paris, the Jewel is a slope mine; that is, the shaft bores into the earth at a 45-degree angle instead of entering vertically. After descending about 150 feet, the main shaft straightens out and runs horizontally for about a mile and a half. Coal is cut from the vein, loaded on mule-drawn cars, and hauled to the surface, where 60,000 tons a year are crushed, graded, and loaded.

Forest-covered buttes rise on each side of State 22 west of Paris. Visible through occasional breaks in the ridge to the south are hazy blue hills, undulating like waves in a seascape to the majestic peak of Mount Magazine. Along the road the land is fairly level, grass-grown, and dotted with small trees and clumps of brush. Cows graze the pastures, sometimes by twos and threes and sometimes in large herds.

CHARLESTON, 51.8 m. (511 alt., 958 pop.), ships an increasing number of beef and dairy cattle, as well as poultry and eggs, to Fort Smith and Kansas City. The community is largely agricultural, although there are a few small coal mines near by. The FRANKLIN COUNTY COURTHOUSE, which serves that part of the county south of the Arkansas, is a flat-topped two-story brick building, with no suggestion of courthouse architecture except for the arched windows opening from the second-floor courtroom.

The largest business in BLOOMER, 57.5 m., is a creamery, which buys dairy products from farmers as far distant as Booneville.

Between Bloomer and Fort Smith the route takes on the appearance of a prosperous cattle country. Haystacks dot the fields in which large herds pasture. Barns here are often larger than the farmhouses, and concrete silos tower above the trees. Some of the large houses passed occasionally are the country homes of residents of Fort Smith.

At 70.6 m. is the junction with an asphalt-paved road.

Right on this road to the ARKANSAS TUBERCULOSIS SANATORIUM'S WILDCAT MOUNTAIN BRANCH (R), 0.7 m., a circle of low white-painted buildings. Here are sent patients rated by the main sanatorium at Booneville (*see Tour 13*) as being in an advanced stage of tuberculosis. The central building contains the offices, clinic, and examination rooms.

FORT SMITH, 75.3 m. (450 alt., 36,584 pop.) (*see Fort Smith*).

Fort Smith is at the junction with US 64 (*see Tour 3*) and US 71 (*see Tour 9*).

Tour 7

(Rolla, Mo.)—Mammoth Spring—Hardy—Jonesboro—Turrell; **133.5** *m.,* US 63.

Asphalt-paved between Bono and Trumann, Marked Tree and Turrell; else-where graveled.
St. Louis-San Francisco Ry. roughly parallels entire route.
Accommodations in larger towns only.

As US 63 cuts across the northeast corner of Arkansas it traverses three different kinds of countryside. South of the Missouri Line are the tree-covered Ozark hills, attractive to vacationers. Between Black River and Crowley's Ridge the terrain becomes level, and is partly planted in corn and cotton and worked by individual renters or owners. The black, rich soil of the Delta stretches between Crowley's Ridge and the Mississippi. Virtually all of this land, almost incredibly fertile, is planted in cotton and cultivated by the plantation system. The inhabitants of the three contrasting areas encountered on this short route constitute a cross-section of the State's population groups—mountaineers, white farmers with small acreages, planters, and Negro sharecroppers.

US 63 crosses the MISSOURI LINE, 0 *m.,* 138 miles south of Rolla, Missouri.

MAMMOTH SPRING, 0.3 *m.* (549 alt., 666 pop.), is named for one of the largest springs in the world. At the north end of town a torrent of cold, blue water rushes from the earth at the rate of about 200,000,000 gallons a day to form a pool that is the source of Spring River. In his *Geological Reconnaissance of the Northern Counties of Arkansas* (1858), David Dale Owen, first geologist to make an official survey of the State, surmised that this "respectable lake" stemmed from Howel's Valley, in Missouri. His theory that Mammoth Spring is the outlet of a subterranean river beginning many miles to the north has been confirmed by later geologists.

"In the early settlement of the country," Owen reported, "herds of herbivorous wild animals traveled from great distances to this fountain, of both food and water, as well as flocks of wild fowl . . . it is, also, a general resort of ducks, geese, and other aquatic birds. . . . Small and rude as the present grist-mill is . . . with its two run of 40 inch stones, it attracts the custom of farmers living 30 or 40 miles distant, who throng to its door—even though they may have to wait days and nights for their turn to come around. . . . If it [the water] were all saved . . . there would be enough for many grist-mills as well as woolen factories, which would be well adapted to the resources of the country, since both the climate and herbage seem to be well suited to raising sheep."

Sheep raising never became important around the spring, and the woolen mills were never built, but the water is now stored behind two hydroelectric dams whose generators furnish power to communities in Arkansas and Missouri. The upper dam is inside the Mammoth Spring town limits.

A bright green moss (*Myriophyllum*), used for oxygenation of water in goldfish bowls and aquariums, is gathered from Spring River and shipped to cities throughout the country.

Operated by the United States Government, the MAMMOTH SPRING FISH HATCHERY (*visitors admitted*), at the south end of town, covers 7½ acres and includes 9 ponds fed by the spring. About 350,000 bass and other game fish are propagated here each year for stocking streams in several States.

Only 50 miles long, SPRING RIVER (*fishing, float trips*), which US 63 follows south from Mammoth Spring, is noted for its great natural beauty. Shoals and spray-edged rapids alternate with deep clear pools. Rainbow trout thrive in the upper part of the river, attracting fly-fishermen from afar. Several dirt roads branch (R) from US 63 to vantage points on the river.

HARDY, 18.3 *m*. (362 alt., 721 pop.) (*see Tour 4a*), is at the western junction with US 62 (*see Tour 4a*), with which the route unites for 24.9 miles.

East of Hardy US 63 winds and dips through the hills past small unpainted cabins, shaded by oaks and gums, and often banked by flowers.

Near WILLIFORD, 27.9 *m*. (322 alt., 272 pop.), quarrying of limestone in the hills is carried on occasionally. The stone is used for building and, more recently, in the manufacture of rock wool, an insulating material.

At 37.1 *m*. is the junction with a graveled road, impassable in wet weather.

Left on this road to RAVENDEN SPRINGS, 6.4 *m*. (500 alt., 200 pop.), one of the many health resorts that flourished toward the end of the nineteenth century and began to wane after 1910. The extent of the now-vanished spa trade is indicated by the abandoned SOUTHERN HOTEL (R), a 40-room frame structure with a double gallery across its wide façade. Wooden stairs lead from the hotel down a steep hill to the spring. Across the road is CITY PARK, where health seekers once paid high rentals to stake their tents. LONE ROCK, a well-known landmark, rears away from the base of the cliff just beyond the hotel.

The healing power of the spring, according to local tradition, was first revealed about 1880 to Reverend William Bailey, who was suffering from a stomach ailment. Three times in one night Bailey dreamed that he had drunk of the waters and been cured. The next day he accordingly went to the spring and began his treatment. Apparently, the waters were helpful, for the minister lived until 1909.

IMBODEN, 43.2 m. (276 alt., 525 pop.), on the bank of Spring River, was named for Benjamin Imboden, a pioneer of Swiss descent who settled amid canebrakes that flourished here in 1824.

In Imboden is the eastern junction with US 62 (*see Tour 4a*).

POWHATAN, 52.6 m. (265 alt., 137 pop.), was founded in 1820 as a ferry landing on the Black River, and with the rise of the steamboat trade became a thriving port. In 1883 the building of the Springfield & Memphis (now St. Louis-San Francisco) Railroad two miles away halted its development. Powhatan clung to its position as county seat though most of its citizens moved away to the railroad towns of Black Rock and Portia. Today (1941) it retains the LAWRENCE COUNTY COURTHOUSE, a red-brick structure standing among a cluster of small houses; most of the official business, however, is now transacted in the county's other seat, Walnut Ridge (*see Tour 1a*). The old building at Powhatan contains a set of records dating back to 1815, when Lawrence County included most of northern Arkansas and part of Missouri. Neatly written with quill pens, the records describe sales of land and slaves and appointments of officers throughout the Black and White River country. The many French names in these early documents indicate how large was the number of French hunters and trappers who wandered over northeast Arkansas.

Left from Powhatan on State 117, graveled, to BLACK ROCK, 2.4 m. (249 alt., 769 pop.), supported by sawmills and the oldest button factory in Arkansas. In 1897 nacreous mussels were first found in marketable quantities in the Black River. Many persons soon engaged in shell gathering, and a button factory was established in 1900. The plant, since rebuilt, now turns out blank buttons that are shipped to New York State for finishing.

Right from Black Rock 6.2 m. on a graveled road (*impassable in wet weather*), to the SITE OF DAVIDSONVILLE, overgrown with wild iris and marked only by a deserted dwelling and by a sunken spot under a giant oak where the town well once stood. Davidsonville, founded as the seat of Lawrence County in 1815, became Arkansas' first post office two years later. Mail was brought from St. Louis once a month by a carrier on horseback, who rode on to Arkansas Post (*see Tour 12B*) and Monroe, Louisiana. Besides its courthouse and post office the town had, in 1817, general stores, a blacksmith shop, a land office, a distillery, and a smelter. Just why Davidsonville was abandoned is not entirely clear. According to old settlers in the region, passengers landing from a New Orleans packet brought the germs of yellow fever, and the ensuing epidemic raged so fiercely that the few townspeople who escaped the pestilence gathered their belongings and fled.

State 117 crosses the Black River at Black Rock on a State-owned ferry (*free*) and continues to WALNUT RIDGE, 11.4 m. (270 alt., 2,013 pop.) (*see Tour 1a*), which is at the junction with US 67 (*see Tour 1a*).

US 63 crosses the Black River at Powhatan and runs through the bottomlands, timbered and swampy where they have not been drained, verdant with cotton and corn where ditches have been dug.

HOXIE, 63.3 m. (271 alt., 1,466 pop.) (*see Tour 1a*), is at the junction with US 67 (*see Tour 1a*).

Southeast of Hoxie US 63 runs close alongside the man-made bank which carries the roadbed of the St. Louis-San Francisco Railway.

JONESBORO, 87 m. (344 alt., 11,729 pop.) (*see Jonesboro*).

1. Right from Jonesboro on graveled State 1, 4.2 *m.;* R. here on a graveled road to CRAIGHEAD FOREST (*fishing, picnicking, hiking, bridle paths*), 5.1 *m.,* the only municipally owned recreational forest in the State. On 612 oak- and hickory-covered acres donated to the city of Jonesboro by the Young Men's Civic Club, facilities were erected in 1939 and 1940. Alongside a lake formed by an earth dam stands a two-story clubhouse and dance pavilion built of cypress logs and roofed with hand-drawn cypress shingles, called "boards." Near by is an administration building, an outdoor theater, and an observation tower, from which a climber may view the rolling countryside. Outdoor fireplaces, tables, and benches are well spaced in seven picnic areas.

Adjoining the forest is CAMP FRIERSON, belonging to the Boy Scouts of America. Several cottages and a swimming pool are on the 126 acres of wooded land.

2. Left from Jonesboro on State 1, graveled, to ARKANSAS STATE COLLEGE, 1.7 *m.,* a co-educational school supported by the State. The campus, on the top of Crowley's Ridge, includes a number of buff-brick buildings centering around WILSON HALL. Established in 1909 as a junior college, the institution added senior work in 1930 and first conferred degrees the next year. Emphasis is placed on training teachers and agricultural technicians, but liberal arts, engineering, music, and preprofessional courses are also offered to the 900 students.

PARAGOULD, 23.6 *m.* (295 alt., 7,079 pop.), seat of Greene County, is at the intersection of the St. Louis Southwestern Railway's main line with its Blytheville branch, and is served also by the Missouri Pacific. Originally a lumber town named for two railroad men, J. W. Paramore and Jay Gould, Paragould has become a community of varied industrial and agricultural activities. Besides railroad shops and woodworking plants, there are cotton gins, cold storage plants, canneries, and a shirt factory. HARMON FIELD, at the northern edge of town, is a 13-acre playground equipped with tennis courts, a field house, pavilion, wading pool, and other facilities, presented to Paragould in 1925 by the Harmon Foundation. Although a caretaker is employed, the town as a whole makes itself responsible for the upkeep of the park. Several times a year business and professional men don overalls and work on the field. As the result of such public spiritedness, Paragould won for three consecutive years the national Harmon award for the best-kept playground.

Left from Paragould on State 25 to the junction with a graveled road, 31.7 *m.;* L. here 3.6 *m.* to CROWLEY'S RIDGE STATE PARK (*swimming, boating, camping; cabins $1.50*), a 347-acre tract on the western slope of the Ridge. The park marks the home site and burial place of Benjamin Crowley (1758-1842), a soldier in the War of 1812. Like many other veterans, he was rewarded for his war services by an Arkansas land grant. On arriving in the State with his family and slaves, he found his grant to be swampy and jungle-covered, and about 1820 moved to the high ground which bears his name.

Crowley's Ridge served the Arkansas pioneers as a landmark, trail, and goal. Immigrants struggling through the morasses of the St. Francis Valley rejoiced at the sight of the high land, and many of them settled down among the rolling bluffs. Travelers from southeast Missouri were always certain of a dry trail as far as Helena. If they wanted to go west they could move down the Ridge until they reached a promising path through the river bottoms toward Little Rock. The St. Louis Southwestern Railway follows the strip from the Missouri Line to Jonesboro, the Missouri Pacific nearly its entire length.

Plowing up the grasslands and cutting the timber left the loose-packed soil at the mercy of heavy winter rains, which sluiced and gullied the Ridge until it presented bleak eroded landscapes in many places. Now thousands of acres are embraced in soil conservation projects, designed to save and improve the Ridge by turning it into a land of orchards, pastures, and recreation areas.

State 25 continues west to WALNUT RIDGE, 48.4 *m*. (270 alt., 2,013 pop.) (*see Tour 1a*), which is at the junction with US 67 (*see Tour 1a*).

NETTLETON, 91.2 *m*. (251 alt., 909 pop.), a shipping point for farm products, grew up alongside the Iron Mountain tracks in 1881 when the citizens of near-by Jonesboro, with two other railroads in prospect, refused to give the customary land grants and bonus, and the Iron Mountain located its line a few miles to the east.

Left from Nettleton on concrete-paved State 18 to the junction with State 135, 11.1 *m.*; L. on this graveled road through the SUNKEN LANDS of the St. Francis Valley. This region was turned into a wilderness of marshes, lakes, and sloughs by the New Madrid earthquake of 1811-12, the greatest recorded geological disturbance in the history of the Mississippi Valley. The first shock came on December 16, 1811, and minor quakes continued at intervals for more than a year. The destruction was most severe at New Madrid, Missouri, one of the few towns of any size in the thinly settled valley. Extending 300 miles up and down the river, the earthquake changed river courses and land contours.

An eyewitness quoted by Richard Edwards in his *Great West* (1860) recalled that, "The agitation which convulsed the earth, and the waters of the mighty Mississippi, filled every living creature with horror. . . . Directly a loud roaring and hissing was heard, like the escape of steam from a boiler, accompanied by the most violent agitation of the shores, and tremendous boiling up of the waters of the Mississippi in huge swells. . . . Sand bars and points of the islands gave way, swallowed up in the tumultuous bosom of the river, carrying down with them cottonwood trees, cracking and crashing, tossing their arms to and fro. . . . [The water] changed to a reddish hue and became thick with mud thrown up from the bottom. . . . The earth on the shores opened in wide fissures, and closing again, threw the water, sand, and mud, in huge jets, higher than the tops of the trees . . . the river rose in a few minutes five or six feet. . . . Numerous boats were wrecked on the snags and old trees thrown up from the bottom of the Mississippi, where they had quietly rested for ages. . . . The sulphureted gases that were discharged during the shocks, tainted the air with the noxious effluvia, and so strongly impregnated the waters of the river . . . that it could hardly be used for any purpose for several days."

A few islands in the "sunk land" have been cleared and are cultivated, but many of the inhabitants depend for a livelihood on fishing and serving as guides for hunters who come to the area for game and wild fowl. Some families live on cabin boats, moored to overhanging willows or tall cypresses.

TRUMANN, 104.2 *m*. (231 alt., 3,381 pop.), is built around the POINSETT LUMBER AND MANUFACTURING PLANT (*open on application*), the main woodworking establishment of the Singer Sewing Machine Company. The company owns thousands of acres of timberland in the vicinity, from which it cuts gum and hardwood for machine bases, and walnut for veneer. Although the sewing machine company's plant was not started until 1912, Trumann has been a lumber center since its founding in the early 1890's. In recent years farmers who have moved into the cutover timberlands have brought the town some agricultural trade.

MARKED TREE, 118.5 *m*. (217 alt., 2,685 pop.), at the confluence of the St. Francis and Little Rivers, takes its name from a blazed oak that once indicated the ford across the St. Francis. According to tradition, the tree was marked by the Murrell outlaw band that terrorized eastern Arkansas and Tennessee (*see Tour 5b*). The landmark was washed away by the river during a flood in 1890.

At the edge of the plantation country, Marked Tree is a cotton center, with a large Negro population. In 1934, the Southern Tenant Farmers' Union was organized near here (*see Tour 3a*).

After the flood of 1927 the town was the scene of an important experiment with powdered yeast as a treatment for pellagra. Paul de Kruif describes the episode in *The Fight for Life* (Harcourt, Brace and Co., 1938):

> With him [De Kleine] were Red Cross Nurse Annie Gabriel, and an old country doctor who had forgotten how many people he had seen die of pellagra but who knew mighty well when he was looking at one who had not long to live. Here lay an eighteen-year-old Negro girl. She was a bag of bones at the end of pellagra's final starvation. . . . Her mouth was half-open and her eyes were a blank. Asked questions, she answered with an unintelligible, high-pitched whining. . . .
> "You wouldn't mind our trying this yeast, Doctor?" asked De Kleine. Of course not. Why not try anything, so long as she hadn't more than a week or ten days to live. The old doctor was tolerant of any remedy, however new-fangled, in this extremity. And who blames him for his being skeptical, in view of this yeast's commonness, its simplicity? It had no jawcracker scientific label. It had been tied up too long with plain beer and bread. Now followed a teaching of new ultra-modern, homespun science. Now De Kleine made the dying girl's mammy, herself, measure out the two spoonfuls of the yeast powder, then stir it up in an old cup in a little water. . . .
> So all that day De Kleine, Nurse Gabriel, and the old country doctor went from cabin to yet more dilapidated hovel. Was this medical science? They didn't themselves quite believe in what they did, not even De Kleine. . . . Then De Kleine crossed the Mississippi to spread this new yeast science further. He left faithful Annie Gabriel to do the follow-ups in Arkansas, to go back and back to every cabin, to teach, to cajole the inmates. Then in less than two weeks De Kleine came back to Marked Tree. To that first cabin he came with Nurse Gabriel and now the ex-dying girl was sitting up in bed. Her sores had healed. Her eyes were bright. She was hungry. Now she could keep down all she ate. Now she was no longer starving. . . .
> This was the first field test, under practical conditions, under the worst possible scientific surroundings, of a cure as powerful and as sure as any in death-fighting's history.

But pellagra was not so easily conquered. The yeast had only served as a substitute for the dietary essentials the lack of which had caused the disease to appear. As soon as the yeast was stopped, pellagra returned. It was not until the collapse of cotton prices that the share-croppers began to grow green vegetables for themselves around their cabins. De Kruif continues the story: "Not to fight pellagra, but to stave off actual starvation of the rural southern masses, the men of the Red Cross chapters distributed hundreds of thousands of pounds of garden seeds. They were guided by the Federal and State Departments of Agriculture. . . . You see gardening had become a lost art with many of the sharecroppers and tenant farmers, because, to get the last penny out of the cash-crop, cotton, many planters, landowners—themselves near ruin—forbade their toilers space and time to raise their own garden truck on the soil round their own cabins." Treatment and increased use of green food reduced the pellagra deaths in Arkansas from 657 in 1927 to 184 in 1938.

South of Marked Tree US 63 passes through the plantation land of Poinsett and Crittenden Counties, where cottonfields run for miles from each side of the highway. The plantation houses, appearing at long intervals, are large, well built, and usually set on beautifully landscaped grounds.

TURRELL, 133.5 m. (230 alt., 515 pop.), is built around the cotton gin and loading sheds on the west side of the highway, which forms its main street. On the east side are red-brick mercantile establishments.

In Turrell is the junction with US 61 (see Tour 10).

Tour 8

Harrison—Russellville—Hot Springs—Arkadelphia—Camden—El Dorado; 289.4 m., State 7, State 128, State 9.

Graveled roadbed between Harrison and Dover, Dardanelle and Hot Springs, Arkadelphia and Eagle Mills; elsewhere asphalt-paved.
Dardanelle & Russellville Ry. parallels route between Russellville and Arkansas River; Chicago, Rock Island & Pacific Ry. between Sparkman and Camden; Missouri Pacific R.R. between Camden and El Dorado.
Accommodations in larger towns.

This route follows a zigzag course north and south through Arkansas, about halfway between the middle of the State and the Oklahoma border. Beginning high in the Ozark uplands, it rides the mountain ridges until it drops into the Arkansas Valley, a rich swath of farming country which separates the northern hills from the gentler dips and sways of the Ouachitas to the south. In the neighborhood of Hot Springs the Ouachitas fade away to the west, and the route then follows the Ouachita River through lowlands to El Dorado. Timber cutting, furniture making, and petroleum production have made south Arkansas fairly prosperous.

Section a. HARRISON *to* JUNCTION WITH US 70;
159.4 m., State 7

The northern part of State 7 passes through both the Ozark and Ouachita National Forests, which together make up nearly half its mileage. The tourist sees wooded crests extending to the horizon in all directions. Dogwood, rhododendron, wild plum, and wood violets set the tone in spring, while summer brings the sun-spotted shade of deep green forests. The yellow of hickory leaves and the blazing red of sumac and gum combine with brown oak foliage and evergreens to make fall the most colorful of the seasons.

State 7 branches south from US 65 (*see Tour 5a*) in HARRISON, 0 *m.* (1,049 alt., 4,238 pop.) (*see Tour 5a*), and runs southward in Crooked Creek Valley. Sturdy white-faced Herefords stand knee-deep in pastures surrounded by tight wire fences. Ponderous barns are near comfortable houses with trim lawns. However, as the road climbs into the mountains that at first loom far on the left, the farms change with the character of the soil. Houses become ramshackle and unpainted, and sprawling rail fences replace the neat barbed wire.

Two hydraulic rams at OZARKADIA PARK (L), 9.9 *m.*, pump water up to homes on the hill across the road. Guided by the muffled thumping of the rams, the visitor will find on the east side of the park the spring that operates them, a small stream issuing from a fissure in the mountain. Crayfish that wander out from under the ledge are snow-white, and occasionally blind fish are caught near the opening of the subterranean stream.

A small sign (L) at a roadside parking-place points out MARBLE FALLS, 10.5 *m.*, where Mill Creek leaps a ledge from a cedar glade. At 14.4 m. the road crosses blue-green BUFFALO RIVER (*bass, crappie, redhorse*), banked on the south by a rock cliff.

A grocery and dance hall perched on the side of a mountain has added to its more conventional offerings a ROADSIDE ZOO, 16.8 *m.* The monkeys and bear were bought from a circus, but the wildcats, 'coons, skunks, squirrels, and rattlesnakes were captured in the near-by woods.

At 20.3 *m.* is the junction with a graveled road.

Right on this road to DIAMOND CAVE (*guides furnished; 3 hr. tour; adm. $1.12*), 4 *m.*, discovered in 1832 by Sam and Andrew Hudson, who followed a bear more than half a mile into it. Explorers have since penetrated 21 miles without reaching the end. From its mouth, an inconspicuous opening 500 feet up Mill Creek Mountain, the throat of the cave descends abruptly into the main body. The cavern has been wired in a series of circuits, so that the guide throws a switch as he enters each division, and extinguishes the lights behind him. Smoke-blackened formations near the entrance remind one that earlier explorers used pine torches. The Red Room, a chamber in which ferrous oxide has given a vivid red color to the walls and roof, is the first notable widening of the passage. The "Icicle Ceiling" blends into the "Shredded Cocoanut Ceiling." At the next broadening are white stalagmites of such size and shape that they are referred to as the Ku Klux Konclave. Water in the cave here is so clear that it is almost impossible to see it, and despite the guide's repeated warnings, tourists sometimes step into shallow puddles. After the "Garden of Eden," where a miniature Adam embraces an even smaller Eve, is the "Japanese Tea Garden," containing pagoda-like formations. Beyond a low passage is the wilder portion of the cave. Here stalagmites and stalactites are in some instances as large as tree trunks, some slender, graceful columns running from the ceiling to the floor.

The formations are caused by calcareous water dripping so slowly that the lime is deposited instead of being carried away with the runoff water. If the rate is slow enough, a stalactite is formed, hanging from the ceiling, gradually growing into the shape of a giant icicle, unless air currents twist it or changes in the mineral content modify its structure. If the drip is somewhat faster a stalagmite is built up from the floor. An intermediate rate results in both a stalactite and stalagmite which eventually meet and grow together. A uniform number of drops each day, if maintained long enough, will form an almost perfect pillar; the best example of this process is in the chamber at the end of the tour—a slender shaft about 4 inches through and fully 30 feet high.

At the foot of Mill Creek Mountain are cabins, a café, and the old HUDSON LOG CABIN (*open*), erected in 1832. The building is now a museum containing such pioneer relics as a spinning wheel, a loom, wool cards, and old guns.

JASPER, 20.5 *m.* (857 alt., 412 pop.), lies in a hollow overlooked by cedar-clad mountains that contribute timber, poultry, dairy products, and fruit. Newton County, of which Jasper is the seat, is the only Arkansas county that has never had a mile of railroad. The business section surrounds the courthouse, built in 1940 from stone quarried in the near-by Little Buffalo River bed.

South of Jasper State 7 climbs steeply into some of the roughest mountains in the State. Though most of the Ozarks are low and gently rounded, these fall away in breath-taking descents and present wide views of tumbled forests that fade into a blue haze. Because of the sharp angles of the terrain the farmer usually cultivates only the top of a hill. Pawpaws, a rich, banana-like fruit of the mountain country, grow here. Mayapples, low plants that prefer the moist, shaded loam of a wooded hillside, bear their yellow, egg-shaped fruit among the dogwood, ash, and elm.

Such typical pioneer contrivances as rail fences, with their corners locked together by upright stakes, and horse troughs made from half a hollow log, bespeak the isolation that the mountains have forced upon inhabitants of this region. Elderly persons reproduce distinctly the pioneer's "bar" for bear, and "thar" for there. They use such Elizabethan expressions as "yon side" (the other side) and "Air you agoin' to camp meetin', come Tuesday?" (next Tuesday) as easily as did early American settlers. The women wear sunbonnets, and many of them use snuff, taking a small quantity on the end of a "rough elm toothbrush," and chewing it like plug tobacco. Hill people consider dipping snuff, or putting it in the lower lip, an unclean habit, fit only for white trash and lowlanders. The men are weatherbeaten and have the tiny wrinkles around their eyes that also characterize aviators and seamen—perhaps from customarily looking at distant objects. Their loose-kneed, shambling gait is ungraceful, but deceptively fast, whether they strike out for town, six or eight miles away, or are just making a circle to kill a few squirrels. The homes of these older residents are nearly always clean, although sometimes bare. An ancient clock on the mantle above the fireplace ("fire-board," they call it), several calendars with pictures, photographs of the old folks, and a spray of peach blossoms in season, round out the interior decoration. The women are fond of bright colors: vivid red geraniums and pink begonias are favorite potted plants, and the patchwork quilts they make are almost gaudy.

The cultivated plots in this rugged area are planted in corn, vegetables and feed crops, and farmers are nearly independent of the outside world for their food. Attics are packed with canned and dried peaches and apples, strings of dried peppers, beans, onions, and home-cured salt pork. Corn bread is cooked in a heavy skillet. "Johnnybread," also made of corn meal, is baked slowly on a grease-soaked johnnyboard. Hot biscuits and molasses are preferred for breakfast, while salt pork and thickened gravy are often on the table three times a day. A winter favorite is "crackling bread"—corn bread with bits of fried-out pork rind mixed in the batter.

State 7 crosses the northern boundary of the OZARK NATIONAL FOREST (*see Resources and Conservation*), at 31.9 *m.* At 46.9 *m.* is a planting of young pine shoots, one of many set out by forest officials; and (R), at 56.9 *m.,* is a LOOKOUT TOWER (*open*).

Most of the farmers living within the forest boundaries occupy land that their families have owned for generations. Old traditions were preserved here long after they had been abandoned elsewhere. Many novelists have found rich material in the Ozarks. An example of an imaginative use of mountain folklore is contained in Charles Morrow Wilson's *Acres of Sky* (G. P. Putnam's Sons, 1930):

> An old wife announced in a carrying whisper that he was dead. Nolen Dye pulled open the door to let out the departing spirit. . . . Squire Bass stepped over and stopped the clock. . . . Women folk busied themselves at hanging white cloths over the mirrors. . . . For if one sees his own reflection in a house of death, he will not live to see another year. . . . No one was surprised. All the signs had pointed on towards death. . . . Cattle had bawled the night before, and a window sash had fallen, and a rooster had crowed close by the sick room. For that matter the signs had long been bad. Neighbor people months before saw Snowbelle building a fire out of sassafras wood. Such doings as that only goes to lure on the death of such an old one.

The highway crosses the southern boundary of the OZARK NATIONAL FOREST at 72 *m.* and drops down between the hills.

DOVER, 84 *m.* (447 alt., 493 pop.), approached through deep honeysuckle banks on the north edge of town, was selected seat of Pope County in 1841, and for a time was one of the most flourishing towns between Little Rock and Fort Smith. Supplies were hauled to Dover from boat landings on the Arkansas River and distributed through the Ozark country. After the War between the States, railroad tracks were laid through Russellville, and the county seat was removed to the same place in 1887. Routing the railroad through Russellville ended Dover's importance. It was a logical move, however, since Illinois Bayou backs up over its banks whenever the Arkansas River rises sharply, and makes an island of the bluff on which Dover is built.

The OLD JAIL is a 20-foot cube on a foundation of solid rock with walls 12 inches thick. The unknown pioneer who built the jail made it two stories high, with no door in the lower room, so that the only way to get in or out was through an opening in the ceiling of the bottom chamber. However, the story goes that some of those incarcerated were as ingenious as the architect, and burned their way out. Not Lee Barnes. Convicted of the murder of a professional gambler, he was successfully imprisoned in the jail, and hanged near by in 1885, the last person legally executed in Pope County.

RUSSELLVILLE, 93.1 m. (351 alt., 5,927 pop.) (see Tour 3b), is at the junction with US 64 (see Tour 3b).

Running between Russellville and the north bank of the Arkansas River is the four-mile Dardanelle & Russellville Railway, built in 1883 and at once dubbed the "Dinky" because of its narrow-gauge track and diminutive equipment. About 1908 the road was changed to standard gauge, but the rolling stock is still tiny, compared to ordinary trains. The locomotive used in the motion picture Jesse James (1939) was a Dardanelle & Russellville engine with its fittings polished up and an old-fashioned smokestack affixed. The same engine is in regular use.

At 95.2 m. is the junction with a graveled road.

Right on this road, passing the slag heap of a coal mine, to a fork, 0.7 m.; L. here to the CEPHAS WASHBURN HOUSE, 1.2 m. The teacher-minister who founded Dwight Mission west of Russellville in 1822 (see Tour 3b), returned to Arkansas after spending nearly 20 years with his Cherokee charges in Indian Territory and taught for a time in Washington and Benton Counties. About 1855 he came back to the neighborhood of Russellville and built this dogtrot cabin. The Reverend Washburn and his family occupied the house for several years, and Edward Payson Washburn's noted picture, The Arkansas Traveler, was painted here (see Tour 3b). The breezeway has been closed at the ends and converted into a room, a kitchen lean-to has been added, and the ancient brick chimneys have been boarded over. The log building is still in excellent repair, and is occupied by a farm family.

State 7 crosses the ARKANSAS RIVER, 97.3 m., on a bridge which in 1929 replaced a pontoon bridge that had served for 38 years. The pontoon-supported structure, more than 2,000 feet long, had been useful to Dardanelle residents in more ways than one. Boys fished from the decks of the 72 pontoons; lovers watched the moon rise over the river; a wedding once took place on the central span. A month after the bridge was completed in 1891 a storm washed it downstream. Thereafter the bridge was "taken in" during high water and moored to the banks, while a ferry provided temporary service.

Richard Keilch, Irish-born construction boss who helped build the pontoon bridge, remained as tollkeeper throughout its existence. Tolls were 15¢ for a horseman, 35¢ for a wagon or prairie schooner. Foot-travelers paid 10¢, but many were allowed to cross for nothing when they had no money.

DARDANELLE, 97.7 *m.* (325 alt., 1,807 pop.) (*see Tour 6*), is at the junction with State 22 (*see Tour 6*).

CENTERVILLE, 105.8 *m.* (350 alt., 224 pop.), so named because it is halfway between Ola and Dardanelle, has a gin and a sawmill. South of town, low hills appear as the road nears the Ouachitas.

OLA, 112.7 *m.* (355 alt., 839 pop.) (*see Tour 13*), is at the junction with State 10 (*see Tour 13*).

State 7 crosses the northern boundary of the OUACHITA NATIONAL FOREST (*see Resources and Conservation*), at 121.3 *m.* At 126.8 *m.* is the junction with the Cove Mountain Road.

Right on this graveled road to the COVE MOUNTAIN LOOKOUT TOWER (*open*), 4.9 *m.*, a square cab that perches like a huge glass eye atop a derrick. Binoculars in hand, the watchman sits from sunrise to dark in dry seasons watching for signs of fire. The telephone at his knee connects him with other towers; by means of another observation, taken at an angle different from his own, the exact location of a fire can be calculated. When the fire is too small to be spotted from some other tower, the watcher determines its distance with a range finder.

IRON SPRINGS PARK (*open*), 142 *m.* (R), is protected from wandering stock by sturdy posts and hog wire. In open sheds are ponderous log tables and benches. Stacks of wood are ricked beside stone fireplaces, and at the back of the park is a pool for swimming. The name comes from a spring with a high iron content that trickles from under a hill into the creek.

The JESSIEVILLE FORESTRY HEADQUARTERS (L), 147.4 *m.*, a white building, marks the southern boundary of the OUACHITA NATIONAL FOREST.

At 153.3 *m.* is the junction with a graveled road.

Right on this road through a pine grove to MOUNTAIN VALLEY SPRINGS, 0.5 *m.*, whose water has been sold throughout the country since the War between the States. Two ancient hot-air pumps, the original apparatus for conveying water to the bottling house, have been whitewashed, and their wheels and air-bulbs remain as ornaments.

Selling water from the neighborhood of Hot Springs is a larger industry than might be expected. Five companies operating in the county in 1937 bottled more than 3,000,000 gallons.

At 159.4 *m.* is the eastern junction with US 70 (*see Tour 2b*), with which the route unites for 7.2 miles (*see Tour 2b*).

Section b. HOT SPRINGS to EL DORADO; 122.8 m., State 7, State 128, State 9

The floor-like Ouachita bottoms offer no views comparable to those of the hills, but their covering of pine sustains the countryside. Lumber for building, for making crates, furniture, and caskets, and for general purposes comes from the mills along the way. The lumber company that owns the giant pulp plant near Camden follows the "plant-two-where-you-cut-one" policy that assures future stands of marketable timber.

Cotton and corn predominate on many of the small farms, but stock and food raising are gradually increasing.

State 7 leads south from the western junction with US 70 (*see Tour 2b*) and a junction with US 270 (*see Tour 11*) in HOT SPRINGS, 0 *m.* (*see Hot Springs*). The road between the spa and Lake Hamilton is lined with filling stations and grocery stores that cater to the vacationers who throng the area, summer or winter, and live in cottages on the lake's many inlets.

LAKE HAMILTON (*see Tour 2b*), 5.6 *m.*, is in sight for several miles. The highway crosses an arm of the lake to an island, swings over the main body of water on a long concrete bridge, then follows the southern shore. South of the lake the mountains fall back from the road, leaving the scene part farm, part forest, with blue hills hovering in the background.

At 31.5 *m.* is the northern junction with US 67 (*see Tour 1b*), with which the route unites for 4.5 miles (*see Tour 1b*).

ARKADELPHIA, 36 *m.* (247 alt., 5,078 pop.) (*see Tour 1b*), is at the southern junction with US 67 (*see Tour 1b*).

State 7 crosses the Ouachita River at Arkadelphia and swings east through a forest of tupelos and oaks. The trees open out at the SITE OF THE HEMPHILL SALT WORKS, 36.6 *m.,* where a marker commemorates "one of the first manufactories in Arkansas." In 1811 John Hemphill came from South Carolina to the Ouachita and found Indians making salt from a spring near the river. Acquiring the spring by barter, Hemphill obtained great iron kettles for boiling the water and metal pans for drying the salt. The business was continued until competition from heavier deposits in Louisiana brought about its abandonment after 1850. The War between the States, however, interrupted commerce of every kind, and the need for salt became urgent. Confederate troops took over the old works, drilled new wells, made drying pans out of discarded steamboat boilers, and worked Negro slaves in day and night shifts. Even this feverish activity failed to furnish an adequate supply, and farmers fed their stock corn soaked in salt water. The capture of Arkadelphia by Federal forces under General Frederick Steele put an end to salt manufacturing once more, and attempts to revive the business after the war's end were not successful. A few of the great kettles are still owned by farmers.

The thick matting of vegetation that entangles the delicate twigs of elms and the rough limbs of water oaks makes the country through which this section of State 7 passes seem like a jungle. Back in the shade are clumps of rattan, whose long, snake-like withes are used as whips by country boys to play "burn-out." Two boys select five- or six-foot lengths of limber rattan, lock their left hands, and lay on until one or the other has had enough.

A less punishing sport of back-country children is riding the bag swing. A gunny sack is stuffed with cotton and rags and suspended from a tree by a rope long enough to allow the bag to describe a considerable arc. One of the larger boys, as "leader," mounts the bag from a platform on the top of a fence, and sails away. When the swing returns to its original position youngsters crowding the platform leap out, settling like horseshoes ringing a post. One object of the game seems to be to jolt the leader off the bag, if possible. In the more lonely districts stately cranes are sometimes startled out of their dignity by the whoop of a solitary youngster swinging back and forth over a creek from a high bank, by a grapevine tangled in the overhanging branches.

The shade in the small, cedar-enclosed CEMETERY (L), 46 m., is almost deep enough to create an effect of twilight. Honeysuckle trails over the stones marking quiet graves almost hidden by beds of white and purple iris.

DALARK, 49.7 m. (243 alt., 152 pop.), is a hamlet that hardly extends beyond the shade of a single huge oak (L). Dalark's name is composed of the first three letters of Dallas and the last three of Clark, names of the two counties on whose boundary Dalark is situated. Overflow of game from the refuge in Ouachita County makes the region good deer-hunting country.

SPARKMAN, 59.5 m. (170 alt., 840 pop.), is supported by two mills, one cutting pine and one hardwood. The Ouachita River (bass, bream, perch), is only a few miles west of Sparkman, and fishing camps are fairly common in this vicinity.

At 65 m. is the junction with State 128, graveled, on which the route turns left.

HOLLY SPRINGS, 71.9 m. (253 alt., 150 pop.*), is at the junction with State 9, graveled, where the route turns right again.

At 81.2 m. is the northern junction with US 79 (see Tour 12), with which the route unites for 10.6 miles (see Tour 12).

CAMDEN, 91.8 m. (198 alt., 8,975 pop.), seat of Ouachita County, is one of the leading towns of southern Arkansas. Three railroads (St. Louis Southwestern; Missouri Pacific; Chicago, Rock Island & Pacific) together with Ouachita River traffic make it an important shipping and distributing point. Woodworking establishments, the larger of the State's two pulp mills, and a pottery plant give the town industrial stability. The streets and buildings are new, fresh-looking, clean. Much of the city's expansion has occurred in the last two decades, and the population more than doubled between 1920 and 1930.

The Ouachita River bluff on which Camden is situated was a trail crossing for Indian tribes hundreds of years ago. De Soto and his 300 surviving men passed here on their way down the Ouachita, according to the United States De Soto Expedition Commission, and possibly spent the winter of 1541 on the bluff. The earliest permanent white settler, a Frenchman named Fabre, gave the place the name of Écore á Fabre (Fabre's Bluff), which it retained until Camden was incorporated in 1844.

American pioneers began to arrive before 1820, and a steamboat reached the bluff in 1824. Many more boats came in the ensuing decades, for Écore á Fabre was among the few good landings on the Ouachita. The obstacles to navigation in the Red River (*see Tour 9b*) led settlers to come up the Ouachita and travel from Camden overland.

The settlement became the seat of Ouachita County in 1843 and was renamed the following year by General Thomas Woodward for his home at Camden, Alabama. Schools and a newspaper appeared shortly thereafter, and in 1860 a woolen mill was turning out cloth which soon was made into uniforms for Confederate soldiers. Camden continued to flourish as a river port after the war, and when the steamboat traffic began to wane it retained its commerce as a railroad center. Deepening of the Ouachita by a series of locks and dams between 1915 and 1926 reawakened interest in river transportation, and the city is now the head of a barge-line service to New Orleans. The improvement of the Ouachita channel represents an investment of more than $4,500,000 by the Federal Government, and maintaining a 6½-foot depth costs an additional $205,000 annually.

Visible (R) as the highway enters the city are the long, low roofs of the CAMDEN FURNITURE COMPANY BUILDINGS (*visited by permission*). Camden was chosen for the factory site because of the dual advantage of transportation facilities and the nearness of great stands of tupelo. The company specializes in bedroom furniture and ships the finished product all over the United States.

The CAMARK POTTERY PLANT (*open on application*), at the south end of town on State 7, is probably the best known of Camden's industries. Some clay is received from a brickyard at Malvern. The raw material is poured into plaster of Paris molds and then poured out, leaving a layer clinging to the sides in the exact shape of the molds. The soft vessels are removed, trimmed, and placed on slowly moving racks that convey them through tunnel-like ovens. When they emerge from the ovens, baked hard, they are dipped into solutions of silica and mineral oxides; still colorless, they are again passed through the kilns, whence they reappear tinted according to the contents of the solution, and ready for sale.

South of the business section is the OUACHITA COUNTY COURTHOUSE, a brick structure overlooked by a four-faced clock. Double windows under arches flank the two columns that mark the door.

In Camden is the southern junction with US 79 (*see Tour 12*). Here the route turns south on State 7.

South of Camden is CULLENDALE, 94.8 *m.*, built around the vast SOUTHERN KRAFT CORPORATION PULP PLANT (*open on application*), a long, red-brick factory, with a tangle of electrical equipment on the north end and a 250-foot smokestack just behind it. Rows of glittering windows line the sides of the building, and the odor of pine wood, lime, and salt cake hangs over the countryside for miles around, day and night.

Camdenites donated the site in 1927 for the $4,000,000 mill, whose pay roll is $16,000 each week. Cutters in the woods earn another $10,-000, and the cost of the wood is something over $10,000 weekly. The pulp plant uses more electricity, more natural gas, and more water than the entire residential section of Little Rock.

The small pine logs ricked along the highway are pulp billets. Specifications call for pine, 4 to 14 inches in diameter and 5 feet long. Bark, which is used for fuel, is stripped from the billets by a huge drum. Then the naked logs are chipped and the fiber thoroughly washed and chemically treated. The pulp, by now a slush, flows through pipes to the paper mill, where it is beaten to a fine mixture and is passed through great drums, filled with steam, to be pressed into the familiar brown kraft paper. The plant produces 275 tons of paper a day. Two paper-bag plants adjoining the mill turn out 80 tons of bags daily.

Travelers reaching SMACKOVER, 111.1 *m.* (121 alt., 2,235 pop.), are informed by acres of stacked boards, advertised as "Field and Rig Lumber," and the smell of crude petroleum that they have reached one of Arkansas' principal oil towns.

Dense sumac thickets in the neighborhood led early French hunters to call the place *Sumac-couvert,* a name corrupted to Smackover by American settlers. In 1922 the town was a backwoods village of about 100 people, inaccessible even from near-by El Dorado in wet weather. Then oil was discovered, and while the amazed farmers looked on, the population jumped to about 10,000. The three stores, the blacksmith shop, and the post office were swamped by jerry-built frame and sheet-iron shacks, and by cabins and tents, as Smackover swept into the delirium of a wild oil boom. People slept on floors, in barns, on the ground, in wagon beds, anywhere. In the wake of speculators, investors, and oil field roughnecks came gamblers and confidence men. Smackover saw its first "barrel house," a combination saloon, gambling den, hotel, and brothel. The spewing of wild gas wells, some of them on fire, added to the general excitement. Revolvers were carried openly, and fights and killings were common. Eight- and ten-yoke teams of oxen, hauling heavy oil field equipment, churned the main street into mud. Property owners, attempting to keep the street open for traffic, piled thousands of feet of lumber on the street and watched it sink from sight.

Smackover is still one of the major oil fields of the United States. Of the 2,954 producing wells in Arkansas by the middle of 1940, Smackover had 1,705. A total of 381,406,000 barrels of oil had been taken from this field, 72,144,000 of them in 1925 alone.

The roughneck days are over, however, and with them the times when drillers earned $25 a day, and farmers whose lands bordered impassable roads made comfortable livings by charging toll fees for permission to pass over their property.

Right from Smackover on a dirt road to the UNION COUNTY TRAINING SCHOOL, 0.9 *m.*, a vocational school for Negroes, begun in 1928 and supported by Smith-Hughes grants. Girls are taught home economics, while boys learn agriculture and shop work. Regular school courses include the twelfth grade.

South of Smackover, State 7 passes through the heavy Union County forests, which lead the State in production of railroad ties. Although lumber mills turn out a few ties, they find it more profitable to slice logs into boards, beams, and laths. Tie-cutting is essentially a poor man's industry. Nearly every Arkansas farmer has his cross-cut saw and double-bit ax for cutting firewood, and the only additional equipment necessary to produce ties is a broadax to square and smooth the logs. An expert handler of a broadax can finish off a surface almost as neatly as if he used a plane, but such ability comes only with years of practice. Beginners may struggle for 3 or 4 days with one tie, whereas an old hand can cut as many as 10 in a day. The market price varies from about 20¢ to 60¢ each, delivered at the railroad siding. The farmer who uses his own timber, who has a couple of healthy sons to fell the trees, and hauls with his own truck clears the full price of the tie; otherwise, charges for timber, labor, and hauling may cut the return by half. Next to farming, tie-hacking is perhaps the most common occupation in rural Arkansas, and there are few parts of the State where a pile of squared logs is not to be seen crisscrossed near a siding. The ties are usually sent to a creosoting plant for preservation treatment before being delivered to a railroad maintenance crew.

EL DORADO, 122.8 *m.* (281 alt., 15,858 pop.) (*see El Dorado*).

El Dorado is at the junction with US 82 (*see Tour 14*) and US 167 (*see Tour 15*).

Tour 9

(Neosho, Mo.)—Fayetteville—Fort Smith—Mena—Texarkana—(Shreveport, La.); US 71.
Missouri Line to Louisiana Line, 331.8 *m.*

Asphalt-paved between Missouri Line and Bentonville; concrete-paved between Bentonville and Waldron, Wilton and Fouke; elsewhere graveled.
St. Louis-San Francisco Ry. roughly parallels route between Gravette and Greenwood; Kansas City Southern Ry. between Mena and Texarkana.
Accommodations in larger towns; numerous tourist camps in the Ozarks.

The principal north-south route running alongside the western border of Arkansas, US 71 first crosses the fertile plateau lying in the State's northwest corner, then plunges southward through the Ozarks. Straightening its course across the Arkansas Valley, the highway winds through the pine-covered Ouachitas and comes again to level land in the extreme southwest corner of Arkansas.

Along the way modes of life vary greatly, according to the character of the land. Farmers on the intensively cultivated northwestern plateau raise fruit, poultry, and dairystuffs in abundance. Agriculture in the Arkansas Valley near Fort Smith is typified by truck farms that supply vegetables to near-by canneries. Coal mining in the same region is a leading industry. In the rugged hill country to the south, however, the sparse mountain population maintains itself like its ancestors—with forest-bordered patches of corn, vegetables, and upland cotton. Most mountaineers keep a few cattle and pigs. Where the Ouachitas dwindle into sandy ridges, near De Queen, there is a notable production of peaches.

Section a. MISSOURI LINE to ALMA; 99.1 m., US 71

Set apart from the rest of the State by the Ozarks to the south and east, and climatically distinguished by a rather high altitude, Benton and Washington Counties offer a scene unlike other parts of Arkansas. Though their land is rich, the people here have never known a plantation economy. Culturally oriented toward the Midwest rather than the South, and owning few slaves, they nevertheless fought for the Confederacy. Diversified agriculture gives to this northwest corner a degree of prosperity comparable to that found in the average good farming area in the United States.

In 1816 Major William L. Lovely, acting for the Federal Government, obtained the entire section, along with a large part of northeast Oklahoma, from the Osage Indians. Later treaties made the tract Cherokee territory, but white settlers filtered into Lovely's Purchase despite official discouragement, and the Arkansas Territorial legislature in 1827 organized the district as Lovely County. The Cherokee treaty of 1828 gave the western part of the Purchase to the Indians, and the remainder was renamed Washington County. The area was divided in 1836, and the northern portion called Benton.

The highway, after crossing the level land of Benton and Washington Counties, cuts through the Boston Mountains to the Arkansas Valley, then swings westward to Fort Smith.

US 71 crosses the MISSOURI LINE, 0 m., 32.1 miles south of Neosho, Missouri.

SULPHUR SPRINGS, 2 m. (930 alt., 435 pop.), has tourist camps, souvenir shops, and small stores for visitors, who have sought its waters since the building of the "Splitlog" (now Kansas City Southern) Railway by Mathias Splitlog, a Wyandotte Indian, made them accessible from Joplin, Missouri, about 1890. LITHIA SPRING

(L), largest of the group, lies in the valley of Butler Creek just above the highway bridge; it has been dammed to make a swimming pool. Two blocks farther south are several other springs in a small park; the bathhouses near by offer sulphur baths. John Brown Academy, a private interdenominational institution, once occupied a large part of the town but was destroyed by fire in 1940.

GRAVETTE, 6.7 *m.* (1,227 alt., 865 pop.), at the intersection of the Kansas City Southern and the St. Louis-San Francisco railways, is a shipping point for apples, dairy products, and grain.

US 71 swings eastward to pass through the heart of Benton County. Pastures and fields of oats, hay, and wheat alternate with apple orchards. Benton County apples (Jonathan, Ben Davis, Winesap, Delicious, Yellow Transparent, Grimes Golden) have been widely known for half a century. Cold winters here destroy many insect pests. Cool summer nights and warm days ripen the apples quickly, and the early autumn freeze brings out the color that makes them attractive to the eye.

Each April the apple-shipping centers (Bentonville, Rogers, Siloam Springs, Springdale, and Fayetteville) sponsor an Apple Blossom Tour, in the course of which the visitors are shown acres of the white blooms. Because cross-pollination is vital to the productivity of the orchards, beehives are placed in some groups of trees.

BENTONVILLE, 24.2 *m.* (1,305 alt., 2,359 pop.), is the seat of Benton County and a commercial rival of Rogers, a few miles farther east. The town's shipments of broilers and dairy products now overshadow apples in cash importance. Two hatcheries and several feed mills serve poultry and stock raisers. A cheese factory utilizes milk from scores of farms. Much of the poultry and dairystuff goes directly to the Chicago market.

Bentonville, founded in 1837, and Benton County were both named for Thomas Hart Benton (1782-1858), Missouri's first Senator and a militant champion of frontiersmen. He was a leading figure in the discussions of 1819-20 that were to make Missouri a State and Arkansas a separate Territory, and he fought in Congress to extend Arkansas' boundary westward at the expense of the Indians.

During the War between the States, Bentonville was the scene of a skirmish preliminary to the Battle of Pea Ridge. Confederate General Earl Van Dorn found a Federal artillery unit under Franz Sigel here on March 6, 1862. Sigel retreated, firing as he went, to the main Federal force at Pea Ridge (*see Tour 4b*).

In 1881 the main line of the St. Louis, Arkansas and Texas (now St. Louis-San Francisco) Railway was built from Missouri, passing a few miles east of Bentonville and spawning a new town, Rogers. Bentonville constructed a branch line to the railroad in 1883 but, for a time, lost some trade to its young rival.

On the wooded grounds of the old PARK SPRINGS HOTEL, at the northeast corner of Bentonville, are the springs that attracted visitors during the early days of the town's settlement. The hotel, a huge, rambling two-story brick building with verandas on all sides, was purchased by the Ozark Christian College in 1940.

The TAYLOR HATCHERY (*visitors admitted*), 109 S. Main St., provides many Benton County farmers with the chicks that are later sold as broilers. Two incubators, with a combined capacity of 105,000 eggs, are heated electrically. The trays of eggs are turned twice a day for 18 days; they then produce their hatches. Chicks are sold within 24 hours after they emerge from the shell.

The ARMOUR CREAMERY (*visitors admitted*), 512 Fourth St., bought about 5,000,000 pounds of milk from local farmers in 1938 to manufacture approximately 500,000 pounds of cheese. The creamery was established in 1935 by the consolidation of several small plants.

In the McPHETRIDGE HOUSE, a wide, white story-and-a-half building at 616 W. Central St., was reared Mrs. Louise McPhetridge Thaden (1906-   ), aviatrix who in 1936 was awarded the Harmon Trophy as the outstanding woman flier in the United States.

Left from Bentonville on State 100, a concrete-paved road, to BELLA VISTA (*golf $1-day, tennis, horses, swimming, dancing*), 4.9 *m.* (1,250 alt.), a resort visited by some 200,000 people annually.

Right from Bella Vista on a graveled road 0.8 *m.* to WONDERLAND CAVERN (*adm. 55¢*), where nationally known orchestras play dance music throughout the summer at an underground night club. The large cool central cavern, reached by a long passageway, is used for many purposes: conventions frequently meet here, and church services are held regularly in summer. Wine from a small winery on the Bella Vista grounds is aged in the cave.

ROGERS, 31.4 *m.* (1,371 alt., 3,550 pop.), retains its marketing and industrial leadership in Benton County despite Bentonville's challenge. Here in January 1939 was held the first of the annual live-broiler shows, intended primarily to advertise the fact that Benton County produces several million young chickens each year. Varieties raised are chiefly White and Barred Rocks and White Wyandottes. Modern methods have elevated broiler-raising into an industry: the young chicks are confined in coops from the day of their hatching, stuffed with feed carried on conveyor belts, permitted no exercise, and shipped to market hardly able to stand on their feet but tender and succulent.

Besides shipping farm products, Rogers processes apples in a large vinegar factory, milk in a cannery, and rock in a silica plant. Hardwood, stave, and heading mills, together with various service industries, add variety to the town's occupations.

The GREGORY-ROBINSON-SPEAS VINEGAR PLANT (*open on application*), US 62 at West Cedar St., converts apples into cider vinegar by grinding, fermentation, and oxidation. The grinding season begins August 15 and lasts about three months. During the remainder of the year the plant, which works on a 24-hour, 365-day schedule, manufactures vinegar from the apple cider. About 3,000,000 gallons of vinegar are produced in a year, and shipped in wooden tank cars all over the South and Southwest. Grinders were formerly maintained at various points in the apple country, but truck transportation has now made grinding at the central factory more economical.

The CORONA PRODUCTS MILL (*open on application*), North A St., grinds silica which is quarried near Rogers and ships it for use as a concrete admixture and as an ingredient in filters, paints, and polishes. The rock is crushed wet in a ball mill and dried on a steam plate.

In Rogers is the northern junction with US 62 (*see Tour 4b*), with which the route unites for 19.7 miles.

Left from Rogers on State 94, graveled, to MONTE NE, 5.8 *m.* (1,102 alt., 116 pop.), a village surrounded by several resort hotels and lodges; R. here on a dirt road to the HARVEY TOMB AND AMPHITHEATER, 6.3 *m.* In 1894, when farmers all over the country were chafing under the yoke of "tight money," and Western mining interests were pressing for free coinage of silver as a remedy, a book called *Coin's Financial School* appeared in Chicago. In it an eight-year-old boy lecturer named Coin was represented as confounding the financial wizards and economic pundits of the Nation by the clarity and overwhelming force of his arguments for silver. The book swept the country and sold more than a million copies. The author, William Hope Harvey (1851-1936), emerged from his anonymity to become a trusted counsellor of young William Jennings Bryan, who two years later was to electrify America and capture the Democratic nomination for the Presidency by denouncing mankind's crucifixion on a cross of gold.

Harvey, a native of West Virginia trained as a lawyer, had gained wealth and a high regard for silver in Colorado. *Coin's Financial School* and succeeding books reputedly made him a millionaire. Throughout the hectic Free Silver campaign of 1896 he applied his genius as a pamphleteer to promoting Bryan's candidacy and denouncing the Eastern bankers, who, he claimed, sought to make the United States a financial vassal of England. Thousands of readers chuckled over such jingles from his pen as:

the prise uv wheet was fawling fast
as up wall street a banker past
hiz klose perfumed and smellin nise
while threw hiz hed ran this devise
sownd munney

from albion's shores heed just arrived
with plans mature & well kontrived
& softly in the kokney tung
he warbled owt with hiz wun lung
sownd munney

in church you mite have herd him sing
& thank the lord fer everything
& if perchanse he fell asleep
heed mix with amens lowd & deep
sownd munney

in happy homes he saw the lite
uv big log fires blaze up at nite
& az he thot uv morgege lones
he sang agen in lowder tones
sownd munney

Crushed by the defeat of Bryan and Free Silver, Harvey turned his back upon a gold-mad world and retired to the Arkansas hills, where he built a house in the upper White River Valley at Monte Ne. Here he lived quietly, writing an occasional book, until the economic collapse of 1929 bore out his jeremiads against usury and Wall Street: In the emergency he returned briefly to public life, organized the Liberty Party, and ran for President in 1932 as its candidate, receiving some 50,000 votes.

Convinced that the American people, who had twice rejected his message, could not long survive, Harvey, now past 80, spent the remainder of his life on a long-cherished plan to preserve a record of their cultural achievements in a great American pyramid at Monte Ne. His death in 1936 stopped the project before it was well begun. The amount of preliminary work which survives indicates the breadth of Harvey's conception. A pavilion with a stone bench has been built in the middle of a large spring. The encircling hillside has been turned into an amphitheater. Pavilion and amphitheater are constructed of heavy limestone and concrete, hand-tooled and of a solidity calculated to last through the ages which Harvey expected to intervene before a new civilization discovered his repository of culture. The amphitheater is now used for plays, stunts, and other performances by members of CAMP JOYZELLE (*private*), a girls' vacation development with cabins named for Greek goddesses.

South of Rogers US 71 again traverses farm and orchard country, passing the BENTON COUNTY NURSERY (L), 33.5 *m.,* which sells young trees to apple, plum, and peach growers of the region. Farther south occasional vineyards appear, reminders that grapes from some 4,000,000 vines rank next to apples as a commercial fruit in northwest Arkansas. Concords are the most important variety, although Moore's Early and Niagara are also cultivated.

SPRINGDALE, 41.7 *m.* (1,324 alt., 3,319 pop.), is a market town for grapes, apples, and vegetables. The settlement grew up around the spring that still flows from the hollow just north of present Main Street; at one time it was called Spring-in-the-Dale. The arrival of the St. Louis-San Francisco Railway in 1881 shortened the name and increased the town's commercial importance.

The WELCH GRAPE JUICE FACTORY (*open on application*), at the northeast corner of Springdale, along the railroad tracks, usually employs between 50 and 100 people. Building of this plant in the early 1920's encouraged grape-growing in the area. Previously there had been few vineyards except at Tontitown (*see below*).

The NELSON WINE & DISTILLERY COMPANY PLANT (*open on application*), on US 71 at the north end of Springdale (L), produces about 100,000 gallons of sherry, claret, and port each year.

The NELSON PACKING PLANT (*open on application*), adjoining the distillery, cans tomatoes, spinach, beans, and apples. Most of the vegetables are grown on northwest Arkansas farms, but the greater part of the spinach comes from Sebastian County, farther south. At its peak, during the height of the tomato season, employment reaches 300.

Right from Springdale on State 68, an asphalt-paved road, is the WELCH GRAPE JUICE COMPANY'S VINEYARD (L), 4.1 *m.,* maintained principally to give neighboring farmers instruction in practical methods of grape-growing.

TONTITOWN, 5.4 *m.* (1,311 alt., 189 pop.), named for Henri de Tonti (c. 1660-1704), Italian lieutenant of the explorer La Salle and founder of Arkansas Post (*see Tour 12B*), is the nucleus of an Italian settlement responsible for the introduction of grape-growing in northwest Arkansas. In 1897,

Education and Social Welfare

CHILDREN IN SCHOOL AT LAKEVIEW RESETTLEMENT COMMUNITY

RECITATION, LAKE DICK RESETTLEMENT COMMUNITY SCHOOL

SCHOOL LUNCH

TIME FOR COD LIVER OIL IN THE NURSERY
SCHOOL, LAKEVIEW RESETTLEMENT COMMUNITY

THE PUBLIC HEALTH NURSE VISITS A RURAL MOTHER

PARNELL HALL, STATE SCHOOL
FOR THE DEAF, LITTLE ROCK

LOG CABIN BUILT BY REHABILITATION CLIENT

Lee: F. S. A.

FARM BOYS

CAMPUS OF ARKANSAS COLLEGE, BATESVILLE
Extension Service, University of Arkansas

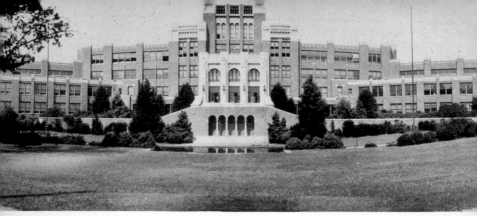

LITTLE ROCK HIGH SCHOOL

FINE ARTS BUILDINGS, STATE AGRICULTURAL
AND MECHANICAL COLLEGE, MONTICELLO

Lee: F. S. A.

HOUSES, LAKE DICK RESETTLEMENT COMMUNITY

DORMITORY, ARKANSAS STATE COLLEGE, JONESBORO

Arkansas State Publicity Dept.

Extension Service, University of Arkansas
DOORWAY OF THE AGRICULTURAL BUILDING,
UNIVERSITY OF ARKANSAS, FAYETTEVILLE

a priest named Pietro Bandini, sent from Italy to investigate the condition of Italian emigrants to America, found a half-starved, malaria-ridden colony of his people on Lake Chicot (*see Tour 5b*) in the cotton country of southeast Arkansas. He purchased 1,000 acres of rolling land in Washington County and moved 35 families there to live on wild rabbits while they cleared the land. Planting of grape slips on the congenial Washington County slopes began immediately, and the members of Father Bandini's group cultivated vineyards and made wine for a quarter of a century before neighboring farmers began to think seriously of grapes as a cash crop. A Grape Festival has been an August event at Tontitown for 40 years. At first a simple folk fiesta, it has lately taken on promotional aspects, such as the importation of carnivals and speech-making political notables and the staging of old-fiddlers' contests.

Now rather thoroughly Americanized, though the older folks still speak both Italian and English, the community guards its reputation for making good wine. Many roadside stands sell revenue-stamped port and claret pressed from grapes grown in the neighborhood.

Since its founding as a resort in 1880 SILOAM SPRINGS, 31.4 *m.* (1,154 alt., 2,764 pop.), strung along the bank of Sager Creek, has grown to rank with Rogers and Bentonville as a leading town of Benton County. Shipments of poultry and apples largely account for Siloam Springs' commercial importance. Students from near-by John Brown University and delegates to the religious gatherings frequently held here bring added activity to the town. The IRON and SULPHUR SPRINGS that attracted the first residents are in small parks along the main street, which follows the creek. Opposite is a steep bluff, atop which the town spreads westward. Paths have been cut into the side of the bluff for walkers.

1. Left from Siloam Springs on asphalt-paved State 59, 2.1 *m.*, to the BAPTIST CAMP GROUND (*private*), where cabins and dormitories cling to the hillsides around a central dining hall and meeting-place. About 1,000 delegates of the church from Arkansas and other Southern States gather at the camp for a two-week "retreat" each June, to hear lectures, take part in study courses, and relax.

2. Right from Siloam Springs on an asphalt-paved road 1.2 *m.* to JOHN BROWN UNIVERSITY, an accredited interdenominational institution specializing in vocational training, and headed by evangelist John E. Brown. The college grounds include about 800 acres of campus and farm lands. Buildings are long and low, covered with brown shingles and set off by green-painted window frames. The tall steel broadcasting mast of station KUOA, operated by the school, towers over the campus. Besides the four-year academic courses, the school trains its 350 students in printing, sheet-metal work, aeronautics, electrical engineering, lumber milling, office work, farming. Emphasis is laid on Bible study. Tuitions and contributions support the college.

South of Springdale US 71 passes through fairly flat country dotted with orchards and vineyards. Blue hills are visible to the east and south.

The U.S. VETERANS ADMINISTRATION FACILITY (*visitors admitted*), 48.9 *m.* (R) is a group of seven red-brick buildings, where war veterans receive general care. The hospital has 250 beds.

FAYETTEVILLE, 50.4 *m.* (1,427 alt., 8,212 pop.), seat of Washington County and of the State University, has been the leading town of northwest Arkansas since the first lots were sold in 1828. The settlement soon acquired a reputation for its interest in education, and was the home of several small colleges in the 1840's and 1850's. The Fayetteville Female Seminary, a pioneer girls' school, was founded as early as 1838.

Colleges, stores, and most of the houses in Fayetteville went up in smoke during the War between the States. The importance of the town, and its location halfway between the Federal base at Springfield, Missouri, and the Confederate positions on the Arkansas River made it a goal for both armies; it changed flags frequently, and when the harassed citizens were not having their homes requisitioned for barracks and their rail fences burned for campfires, they were trying to hide their horses and their winter supply of salt meat from guerilla bands.

Washington County's promise of $100,000 in 1871 brought about the establishment of the Arkansas Industrial University at Fayetteville. The school, later renamed the University of Arkansas, has since furnished the town's chief motif. The presence of the university, together with a healthful climate and nearness to the mountains, has attracted an unusual number of professional men, writers, artists, and retired farmers. Industries include fruit and vegetable canneries and a veneer mill using gum, walnut, cherry, and sycamore trees from the surrounding hills. Another specialized plant, not now operating, made textile shuttles from the exceptionally tough hardwoods—persimmon, dogwood, and *bois d'arc*.

The UNIVERSITY OF ARKANSAS, Arkansas Ave. and West Dickson St., centers around the ADMINISTRATION BUILDING, in use since 1875, a four-story brick building with mansard roof and dormer windows; the two mansard towers at the corners are visible for miles. Chicago architect John M. Van Osdel designed the building as an approximate copy of Illinois University's "Old Main." Stones used in the foundation were hauled 70 miles by ox-wagon over rough mountain roads. The legislative act that established the University failed to exclude women students, so despite considerable popular disapproval the school was co-educational from its inception, and the first graduating class in 1876 consisted of five men and four women.

A building program, aided by Federal funds, during the last decade has increased the number of structures on the campus to about 30. Among these is the VOL WALKER MEMORIAL LIBRARY (1935), an outdoor Greek theater, and an athletic stadium seating some 13,500 people.

The University comprises schools of liberal arts, education, engineering, agriculture, business administration, law, extension, and graduate work, and has a school of medicine at Little Rock (*see Little Rock and North Little Rock*). Average enrollment at Fayetteville is about 2,000.

WAXHAWS (*private*), on South College Ave., is a frame house built in the 1830's by Archibald Yell (*see Tour 4a*) and named for Yell's birthplace in North Carolina. The walnut casings of the fireplace remain as Yell saw them when he resided in Fayetteville; on the slope outside is a well dating back to the same period.

The GEORGE REED HOUSE (*private*), on West Dickson St., nearly as old as Waxhaws, was occupied between 1851 and 1866 by J.W. Washburn, son of missionary Cephas Washburn. J.W. Washburn's wife, Susan, was a Cherokee, as were several of Fayetteville's early-day prominent citizens. Elias Boudinot (1835-90), editor, and a leading attorney of western Arkansas, was one of the distinguished Cherokee-blood residents of Fayetteville.

The QUESENBURY HOUSE (*private*), on South Duncan St., was built in 1854 by William Quesenbury (1822-88), known throughout the State, and to a certain degree nationally, for his cartoons, which he signed "Bill Cush." Quesenbury was also an artist in oils, and several of his paintings of Washington County citizens and buildings are still cherished in northwest Arkansas. He served in the Mexican War as quartermaster under Archibald Yell and in the War between the States under Albert Pike. Returning to Fayetteville, Quesenbury became associate editor and cartoonist on Boudinot's newspaper, the *Arkansian*.

The TIBBETTS HOUSE (*private*), 118 E. Dickson St., half-hidden behind a century-old elm, is a low white building frequently admired by architects. Built in the late 1840's by William Baxter, it was used as headquarters by Federal troops in 1863, and holes torn by Confederate musket balls during a hot skirmish are still visible in the interior woodwork.

TIN CUP, a section on the east side of Fayetteville, just back of the Washington County Courthouse, is one of the few Negro settlements in northwest Arkansas. The inhabitants, nearly all descendants of slaves owned by wealthy Fayetteville people, live around Lincoln School and two churches. Most of them are employed as domestics in homes or at the university. Negroes in this community have little contact with the customs and habits of plantation Negroes, 200 miles or less to the southeast.

In Fayetteville is the southern junction with US 62 (*see Tour 4b*).

1. Right from Fayetteville on State 112, a graveled road, to the AGRICULTURAL EXPERIMENT STATION, 3.7 *m.*, of the University of Arkansas College of Agriculture. Established in 1888, the station has provided Arkansas farmers with scientific advice on agricultural and agronomic problems. Besides issuing reports on production, shipping, and marketing of crops, the station has turned out bulletins on such varied subjects as rural housing conditions, medical facilities, standards of living, and landlord-tenant relations.
The 646-acre tract at the main station is used principally for experimentation with field crops, horticulture, forestry, livestock feed and pasture, and plant diseases. A large part of the field work is now done at branch stations: cotton at Marianna (*see Tour 12A*), rice at Stuttgart (*see Tour 12B*), fruit and truck crops at Hope (*see Tour 1b*), and livestock and forestry at Batesville (*see Tour 17*).

2. Right from Fayetteville on State 16, graveled, to a junction with a graveled road, 15.6 *m.*; L. on this road to LAKE WEDINGTON (*swimming 10¢ and 5¢, suits and towels rented; boats 20¢ hour; fishing 25¢ day; cabins; picnic grounds*), 15.9 *m.* The 100-acre lake, bathhouse, lodge, and cabins were constructed by the Land Utilization Division of the United States Soil Conservation Service, which administers 16,963 acres of hill land near the Arkansas-Oklahoma border.

3. Left from Fayetteville on an asphalt-paved road up MOUNT SE-QUOYAH to the METHODIST CAMP, 1.5 *m.*, marked throughout the summer by a huge electric cross. The camp, property of the General Board of Christian Education of the Methodist Church, was opened in 1923 as a place for summer conferences and training schools. More than 1,500 church workers, young and old, enroll for courses each year, with about 300 remaining through the summer. A chapel, assembly hall, library, office, cafeteria, and several dormitories are the focal point for the camp; around them are summer homes and cottages.

The 400-acre site was donated by the city of Fayetteville. The hill, once known as East Mountain, was renamed Mount Sequoyah for Sequoyah, inventor of the Cherokee alphabet (*see Tour 3b*).

South of Fayetteville the hills close in upon US 71, until by the time WEST FORK, 60.4 *m.* (1,340 alt., 359 pop.), is reached, the road and the St. Louis-San Francisco tracks are pressed side by side within the narrow valley of White River's West Fork. Jagged shoulders of limestone project from the valley wall, ranging in color from slate to brown and yellow.

Small stacks of logs along the highway in this region may be firewood cut by farmers, or they may be piles of hard *bois d'arc,* going through a four-year period of seasoning. *Bois d'arc,* known variously as ironwood, Osage orange, mock orange, bowwood, yellowwood, hedge, applewood, or rabbit hedge, is highly prized by makers of archery equipment. It was used by the Osage for the bows with which they killed bear and buffalo. Early white settlers found that this wood made hedge fences "pig tight, bull strong, and horse high"; they used it for singletrees, felloes, and neck yokes, and sometimes built wagons of it; but they cursed it when they tried to clear their fields, because its roots extend for long distances, and every bruised or cut root produced new sprouts. Much of the best *bois d'arc* has long since been cut out, but now and then a farmer finds a few trees that he cuts for sale to bow-and-arrow factories. Only perfectly straight trees, eight or nine inches thick, are suitable; most of these are sold through a dealer in Little Rock. Crooked or small *bois d'arc* is ideal for fence posts, taking staples without a crack and lasting indefinitely.

WINSLOW, 72.8 *m.* (1,744 alt., 248 pop.), with the highest altitude of any incorporated town in Arkansas, is at the crest of the divide between the watersheds of the White and Arkansas Rivers. Its single row of business buildings, crowded between the limestone wall of the roadbed and the fast-flowing West Fork, dates back more than half a century. Before the coming of railroads and good highways the village was a taking-off point for the difficult journey through the mountains from northwest Arkansas to the Arkansas Valley.

Right from Winslow on State 74, a graveled road that climbs through ridges of constantly increasing height, to DEVIL'S DEN STATE PARK, 11.3 *m.* The park, established in 1933, is a 4,320-acre tract of heavily wooded mountain country, notable for numerous deep cracks and crevices in the sandstone, caused by folding of the earth's surface.

The road corkscrews down the steep valley wall to LEE'S CREEK (*fishing*), 12.8 *m.*, where the park headquarters are situated. Here are cabins, a lake (*swimming*) formed by damming the creek, a large stone lodge, and camping areas. Foot trails and bridle paths lead off into the woods.

South of Winslow US 71 passes through the most rugged country of its route. Unable to find a creek valley sufficiently wide to admit passage, it careens over a series of ridges, whipping from curve into curve as it climbs and descends. Passengers on the St. Louis to California Butterfield stage line, which followed this route between 1858 and 1861, were alternately thrilled by the views and terrified by the hazardous highway. One traveler wrote:

> I might say our road was steep, rugged, jagged, rough and mountainous . . . and then wish for some more expressive words in the language. The wiry, light, little animals tugged and pulled as if they would tear themselves to pieces, and our heavy wagon bounded along the crags as if it would be shaken to pieces every minute. . . . As the road winds along the ridges you are afforded most magnificent views of the surrounding hills and valleys . . . and I can only say that our mountain views in the highlands of the Hudson are but children's toys in comparison with these vast works of nature. The term 'Boston Mountain' is, I believe, derived from a prevailing Western fashion of applying that name to anything which is considered very difficult. But Connecticut hills and roads are mere pimples and sandpaper compared with the Ozark ranges. By hard tugging we got up, and with the aid of brakes and drags we got down; and I can assure you we were by no means sorry when that herculean feat was accomplished. . . . We reached Fort Smith . . . at five minutes after two o'clock A.M., having made the sixty-five miles from Fayetteville in fourteen hours and seven minutes.

Good automobile drivers now cover the distance in two hours.

From the top of MOUNT GAYLOR, 77.1 *m.,* spreads a vista (L) of Ozark peaks and valleys, the nearer slopes green in summer and brown in winter, the farther ones invariably dust-blue shadows against the clearer blue of the sky. Here are several lodges and cabins where travelers may stay overnight and rise early to see sunrises unexcelled this side of the Rockies.

The ALBERT PIKE MUSEUM (*adm. 25¢*), 79.1 *m.* (L), is the log schoolroom in which the explorer, soldier, and writer for whom it was named taught in 1832. The building has been moved from its original site near Van Buren, where it was in use as a cattle barn, and partly restored. Pike had just returned from an exploring trip to Santa Fe when he took the teaching job. His fortunes were at a low ebb. "I had on a pair of leather pantaloons, scorched and wrinkled by fire, and full of grease," he wrote, "an old grimy jacket and vest; a pair of huge moccasins, in the mending of which I had expended all my skill during the space of two months . . . a shirt made of what is commonly called counterpane which had not been washed since I left Santa Fe; and to crown it all, my beard and mustachios had never been trimmed during the entire trip." Under the circumstances, he was glad enough to undertake the instruction of 22 students for a stipend of $3 per month.

The museum contains a quill pen made by Pike, pieces of a slate, a slate pencil, and a teacher's pointer found in the old building; it has a saddle reputed to have belonged to the female desperado, Belle Starr, and other historical items.

Also housed in the building is the HENDERSON EARLY AMERICAN GLASSWARE COLLECTION. There are 5,000 pieces including such patterns as the Atlantic Cable, designed in 1860 to commemorate the laying of the first inter-continental telegraph line, the Jacob's Ladder, the Jacob's Coat, the Old Man of the Mountain, and many others. A mountaintop at 84.7 m. affords the first view of LAKE FORT SMITH (L), a long blue ribbon twisting through the valley. The 640-acre lake, formed by an earth dam across Clear Creek, furnishes Fort Smith's water supply. There is now a large, modern swimming pool and recreational park below the dam. As US 71 descends rapidly into Clear Creek Valley the lake is almost constantly in sight, and numerous side roads run down to it.

MOUNTAINBURG, 87.4 m. (716 alt., 185 pop.), is a resort village at the southern edge of the mountains, easily accessible to Fort Smith residents and popular for week ends. Summer homes appear frequently along the highway.

A post office called "The Narrows" existed at Mountainburg in the 1840's, but the town's growth did not begin until after the War between the States. An early-day missionary service resulted in a clash between hill-country factions that was described as a "terrible battle . . . the men using clubs, fists, stones and what weapons they could find, while the women used the knives and forks they had brought to serve the dinner that was supposed to follow the preaching." This "Bloody Sunday" left such bitter memories that Mountainburg had no religious services of any kind for 70 years thereafter. A Bible school was opened in 1927 and a community church was built in 1934.

ALMA, 99.1 m. (430 alt., 774 pop.) (see Tour 3b), is at the eastern junction with US 64 (see Tour 3b), with which the route unites for 13.6 miles (see Tour 3b) to Fort Smith.

Section b.   FORT SMITH to LOUISIANA LINE; 219.1 m., US 71

South of Fort Smith US 71 crosses the Arkansas Valley, which has coal and gas fields at its southern edge. Entering the Ouachita Mountains, the route winds over and alongside ridges covered with straight, slim pines and white oaks. Beyond the divide separating the Arkansas, Ouachita, and Red River valleys at Rich Mountain the slopes gradually diminish, but heavy woods, periodically decimated by snorting portable sawmills, continue as far as De Queen. At Red River the highway crosses briefly into Texas, returning to Arkansas at Texarkana and continuing through swampy wilds to the Louisiana border.

US 71 leaves FORT SMITH, 0 m., on Towson Avenue and levels off southeastward across the Arkansas Valley, bisecting small farms that raise fruit and truck for sale in the city. Spinach, canned in Fort

Smith and Van Buren, is an important crop in this area; eggs are also sold to canneries.

GREENWOOD, 17.5 *m.* (518 alt., 1,219 pop.), is the southern seat and chief coal-shipping point of Sebastian County, which ranks first in Arkansas coal production. Half a million tons were dug in the county in 1937-38 by some 1,600 miners. Most of the coal found hereabouts is in "low" veins, from 28 to 32 inches thick, lying at an angle of about 20 degrees. Miners work about seven hours a day in less room than a mechanic has under an automobile, digging the coal loose from the rock above it and slicing out a space below the vein to insert a dynamite charge. Nervous strain is added to physical by the possibility that the blast may open a gas fissure and lead to an accidental explosion.

Principal markets for coal, besides the railroad companies, are manufacturers and domestic consumers in St. Louis, Kansas City, and Omaha. All mines close down about April 1 and reopen in July, in time to supply the early winter demand. Miners spend their summers in their vegetable gardens, with perhaps a couple of weeks of cotton chopping on the plantations farther down the Arkansas Valley.

In Greenwood is the junction (L) with State 10 (*see Tour 13*).

Right from Greenwood on State 10, graveled, passing the tipples and stacks of several mines. Where coal operations have been abandoned the slag mounds soon become covered with weeds and saplings; the unconquerable Arkansas forest reaches for every inch of earth, whether it be silt or slag, when it is relinquished by man.

The main street of HACKETT, 10 *m.* (436 pop.), once boasted a dozen saloons and rang with the sound of quarrels, for Hackett was one of the string of border towns that sprang up along the edge of Indian Territory in the 1870's to sell supplies and liquor to the Indians. Today the saloons have given place to one-story brick store buildings, and the only memento of the town's youthful enterprise is the ponderous three-story limestone-block OLD SCHOOLHOUSE, now abandoned, a block north of the business district.

Near MANSFIELD, 29.4 *m.* (594 alt., 1,002 pop.), royalties from natural gas wells supplement some farmers' incomes from cotton, fruit, and truck. A brick plant here supplied the material for homes and stores in western Arkansas and eastern Oklahoma from 1901 until the collapse of markets and credit caused its closing in 1929. Farmers around Mansfield have recently experimented with a giant peach, producing specimens ranging up to 19 inches in circumference.

WALDRON, 49.3 *m.* (654 alt., 1,298 pop.), like many of the towns near the Oklahoma border, has a distinctly Western atmosphere. Broad-brimmed hats are common, and overalls are tucked into boot tops. Red, blue, and green flannel shirts stand out against the dull brick of Main Street business buildings. Waldron has a modest summer tourist trade, based on fishing in Poteau River and Buffalo Creek and on camping in the near-by woods.

The SCOTT COUNTY COURTHOUSE is a two-story red-brick building with an archway supported by stone columns over the front door. Shrubs set along the foundation soften the façade.

South of Waldron US 71 enters the Ouachita Mountains. When a ridge cannot be avoided by an easy sweep, the road makes a climb along the face of the hill, passing through a cut at the top. Sometimes the mountains press close, sometimes they drop back until they are only blue bulks in the distance. Occasionally a turbulent stream rushes down a hillside, crosses under the road through a culvert, and blusters on. A few of the farms along the way maintain service stations built of logs and lighted at night by gasoline flares; and a cabin or two may be maintained to accommodate deer hunters in season.

At 63.4 *m.* is the eastern junction with US 270 (*see Tour 11*), with which the route unites for 15.8 miles. A swift boulder-strewn stream plunges past the junction on its way into Fourche la Fave, and thence into the Arkansas. Local anglers prefer to tramp over the ridge to the south and fish for bass and crappie in the headwaters of the Ouachita. The highway swings to the west and winds its way over the divide between the two major river basins.

At 79.2 *m.* is the western junction with US 270 (*see Tour 11*). Here the highway emerges briefly from the hills into the valley of Big Creek.

MENA, 84.8 *m.* (1,143 alt., 3,510 pop.), the seat of Polk County, was founded in 1896 when the Kansas City Southern Railway came through. The name Mena, a contraction of Wilhelmina, was a tribute to the reigning queen of the Netherlands by the Dutch investors who aided in financing the road.

In the middle of the town site stood an old log cabin erected in 1851, reputedly a rendezvous for border bandits and guerillas in the hectic 1860's and 1870's. Surveyors and civil engineers for the railroad used the cabin as headquarters, then left it standing in the middle of a square which they called JANNSEN PARK after one of the Dutch capitalists. Eventually the cabin became the Mena city hall and a gathering point for public assemblies. Such notables as William Jennings Bryan, Carry Nation, and Huey Long made speeches here. The original structure is very little changed, except that a brick chimney built in 1872 replaces the original stick-and-mud fireplace. A new city hall was built in 1939.

During the last years of his life Will Dilg (1869-1927) lived in Mena. Founder of the Izaak Walton League of America, one of the first and most vigorous conservation clubs, Dilg attracted wide attention to the need of game, fish, and forest conservation. The work of the league has now been largely taken over by the National Wildlife Association, Ducks Unlimited, and similar organizations, bolstered by Federal and State legislation.

The most interesting expression of Mena's interest in recreation is the Polk County 'Possum Club, founded in 1913 when a west Arkansas attorney challenged the mayor of Mena to a 'possum-hunting contest. The match ended in a draw, and members of both parties joined forces to eat the night's bag and establish the club. The annual meeting of the club has since become a major occasion. One day each December persimmon trees are set up on the town's main street and festooned with live opossums, while hounds bay frantically in all directions. A verbal feud is always renewed by representatives of the Ozark country and the Ouachita Mountain residents, each claiming that 'possums from their district are blue-blooded, pedigreed, royal food for the gods, fattened on golden persimmons and choicest yams, and that animals from the opposing section are mangy creatures unfit even for hog feed. Festivities culminate in a banquet to which anyone who has a dollar bill and can jam himself into the Mena armory is welcome. Here senators and sharecroppers, bankers and backwoodsmen mingle to eat their fill of baked 'possum and steaming sweet potatoes, while political bigwigs and country-store humorists retail anecdotes and pay tribute to the succulent marsupial. Any departure from the spirit of levity is taboo: Oklahoma's onetime Governor Bill Murray was roared to his seat in 1938 for attempting to make a serious speech.

Aside from its attractions to sportsmen, Mena is the center of a wide trade area, since it is the only large town in the Ouachitas excepting Hot Springs at their eastern extremity. Industrial plants include flour and feed mills, gins, a heading and stave mill, a brick and tile works, several sawmills, and a handle factory.

The NORRIS GOFF HOUSE (*private*), 203 Reine St., is one of Mena's showplaces. Double columns set off the cream-colored porch which rises the full two stories of the house to the hipped roof with its dormer windows. The landscaped lawn, studded with magnolias and elms, is encircled by a cobblestone wall. Norris Goff and Chester Lauck, also a onetime Mena resident, formed the radio team of Lum and Abner.

1. Right from Mena on Mena Street, which becomes Rich Mountain Drive, over a "skyline highway" to the top of RICH MOUNTAIN, 11.6 *m*. (2,750 alt.). The slopes of the peak, one of the highest in Arkansas, are covered with a remarkable variety of flora. Though the temperature is consistently ten degrees below that of the surrounding valleys, farmers grow all sorts of vegetables in the mountain's rich black soil. A 700-pound black bear was shot here in 1936 by an enraged 'coon hunter, whose prized hounds were being savagely mauled. Occasional shooting of bears, forbidden by game laws, is sometimes excused on the grounds of necessity or on the basis of affidavits as to sheep-killing activities. Many of the depredations blamed on bears could be more justifiably ascribed to mountain lions. Atop the mountain is WILHELMINA INN, better known locally as "The Castle," a grand-scale yellow-sandstone edifice erected in 1896, in the somewhat far-fetched hope that the Dutch Queen would make it her summer residence. It was turned into a hotel and was partly burned after a few years' use; picnicking parties like to inspect the ruins of the great fireplaces and sweeping staircases. LOVER'S LEAP, a quarter-mile walk from the inn, gives an extensive view of winding, pine-covered ridges, cleared valleys, and other ridges blue with distance.

The road descends Rich Mountain steeply to a junction with US 270 (*see Tour 11*) at 12.9 *m*.

2. Right from Mena on a graveled road to the junction with a dirt road, 10.4 *m.;* R. here to the SITE OF COMMONWEALTH COLLEGE, 11.7 *m*. In 1923, dissidents from the Newllano co-operative colony in Louisiana established the school as a place where students might make their own living by farming, while they studied courses of a general nature. No degrees were offered, and

the social aspects of the usual American college were absent. Social and psychological differences between the faculty members and students, mostly Easterners, and the neighboring hill farmers were enlarged upon and widely publicized by sensational magazine articles, with the result that the school was twice investigated by the Arkansas legislature. In 1940 the college closed, and plans were made to turn it into a theater school; but, while the transfer was pending, the institution was charged with teaching anarchy in violation of Arkansas statutes, and its property was sold to satisfy a fine imposed by a Mena justice of the peace.

The school consisted of about 25 white-painted frame buildings, including a library with more than 10,000 items. In the dining hall was a large mural completed in 1934 by Joe Jones, St. Louis artist.

HATFIELD, 96.2 m. (971 alt., 437 pop.), is separated by the Kansas City Southern tracks from its chief source of income, a large sawmill half hidden behind stacks of drying lumber. When the railroad was being built Hatfield was as lusty as a mining town and was a favorite spot with gamblers and confidence men, who preyed upon the construction workers, tie-hackers, and mill hands. The drifters left with the boom, and Hatfield is now a trading village.

COVE, 100.2 m. (1,046 alt., 381 pop.), is another mill town whose quiet is disturbed only by the high hum of the planer back of the long red lumber shed (L).

For the cannery at WICKES, 111.6 m. (1,027 alt., 121 pop.), farmers 20 miles away grow vegetables, strawberries, and blackberries. Daniel LeBow in 1884 homesteaded what is now the town site, and it was bought a few years later by the Arkansas Townsite Company, apparently an organization having contacts with the surveying crew of the Kansas City Southern. Wickes now has two lumber mills, and watches with anxious eyes the supply of timber on the hills to the east and west.

Besides being depleted by the large established mills, the forests suffer serious inroads from small portable mills, which need little equipment besides their saw table and motor. Such outfits can be moved by truck and set down anywhere that a road penetrates. Most of their labor is supplied by neighboring farmers, glad of the opportunity to pick up a few dollars cash for a week's work, or to exchange their services for needed lumber. The few permanent employees needed to operate the gasoline engine and the carriage live at the millsite in tents or knockdown shacks, where their wives haul water and bake cornpone, while their children play in the sawdust piles or range the woods, paying little heed to maternal cautions against wolves and wildcats. Ordinarily the area immediately surrounding the mill is cut out within six weeks or two months; saw and household equipment is then loaded on trucks, and the trek to another cutting site begins.

Landmarks of GRANNIS, 116.2 m. (921 alt., 225 pop.), are a white frame church and a red log house with a green roof.

DE QUEEN, 132.2 m. (432 alt., 3,055 pop.) (see Tour 2b), is at the western junction with US 70 (see Tour 2b), with which the route unites for 8.1 miles (see Tour 2b).

At 140.3 *m.* is the eastern junction with US 70 (*see Tour 2b*).

The Cossatot and Bear Creek bottoms below De Queen mark the edge of the Ouachitas; south of these streams US 71 runs in long straight drives through flat country timbered with dense stands of pine, varied along creek banks by gaunt, naked sycamores. Caution should be used in crossing the smaller bridges in this vicinity, since many of them are built for one-way traffic.

LOCKESBURG, 146.1 *m.* (407 alt., 764 pop.), in the heart of the truck belt, is distinguished by neat white houses and a silvered water tank. Lockesburg girls find seasonal employment at wrapping tomatoes. Cucumbers, cantaloupes, radishes, and peas are also shipped. Some logs are concentrated here for trucking to the mill at Dierks (*see Tour 2b*). Fishermen idle on the shady banks of the Cossatot, waiting for a strike by the black bass in the stream.

Near the Little River bottoms the woods move back to the hills, leaving wide flat fields flanking the road, except for the thickets that now and then line a meandering brook. Cows seek out these sheltered spots in midsummer heat and stand knee deep in cool water, chewing their cuds and switching at flies. Farmhouses on stilts and the elevation of the highway on a long fill indicate the proximity of the river. Brackish backwater stretches away on each side into uncleared forests.

LITTLE RIVER flows under a highway bridge at 159.4 *m.* between high, washed-out banks that show its uncertain temper. The barge and crane usually visible from the bridge are used in gravel-digging operations.

WILTON, 162.3 *m.* (321 alt., 319 pop.), where a few houses, service stations, and stores straggle along the highway, supplies workers for the Little River gravel barge. Wilton ships some truck produce, ties, and logs.

The north end of ASHDOWN, 167.2 *m.* (329 alt., 2,332 pop.), is overshadowed by an L-shaped compress and warehouse. Besides cotton, cottonseed oil, and truck, Ashdown products include lumber cut by a large sawmill.

Founded in 1892, the town was named in honor of Judge Lawrence Ashdown Byrne. Its location at the junction of the Kansas City Southern, the St. Louis-San Francisco, and the Memphis, Dallas & Gulf railroads caused the removal of the county seat from Richmond to Ashdown. The LITTLE RIVER COUNTY COURTHOUSE is a two-story red-brick building with a large dome in the center of the roof.

US 71 approaches RED RIVER, 177.6 *m.*, through wide fields that produce phenomenal yields of cotton and corn in the years that the crops are not drowned out. Behind the fields is the comforting bulk of the levee, winding out of sight. The bridge has a center drawspan, and is sufficiently high to allow gravel barges and other present-day craft to chug underneath without tying up highway traffic by requiring the raising of the draw section.

During the early days of Arkansas settlement, the Great Raft in Red River near here caused valley planters and Government engineers endless grief. Composed of driftwood, brush, and debris, grown over with weeds and even saplings, the raft covered the stream from shore to shore for about 100 miles, and blocked navigation. William Dunbar described it in 1805 as supporting "a vegetation of everything abounding in the neighboring forest, not excepting trees of considerable size; and the river may be frequently passed, without any knowledge of its existence" (*American State Papers, Indian Affairs*). "There were many theories to account for the origin and growth of the Great Raft," says Grant Foreman (*Mississippi Valley Historical Review,* 1928). "The Red River is a very crooked stream and it readily lent itself to the collection of logs in the numerous sharp bends. The Raft was supposed to have been growing at the upper end at the rate of one mile per year and wearing away at the lower extremity at a similar rate, from which it was deduced that it was at least 300 years old. It not only obstructed navigation, but it effectually dammed the river, and caused great tracts of adjacent land to overflow, rendering worthless a strip of land twenty miles wide."

Steamboats had ascended the Red River as far as Nachitoches, Louisiana, in 1820, and Arkansans were anxious to have the Raft cleared away so as to open the upper river to navigation. As early as 1825 General Winfield Scott at Louisville, Kentucky, sent a detail to clear the channel, but the soldiers could do little except to report on the magnitude of the task. In 1833 a determined effort was made to destroy the Raft by Captain Henry Shreve with 4 snag boats and 150 men; the effort was completed 5 years later. However, the obstruction immediately began to rebuild itself, and the Federal Government made appropriation after appropriation, expending over $300,000 on the channel. Navigation remained hazardous for some years, until the Raft was finally cleared away permanently.

South of the Red River bridge, US 71 crosses briefly into Texas, then rides the State boundary line into Texarkana through acres of deep green alfalfa, punctuated by clumps of oats. The road passes golf courses, night clubs, and rows of trailer and tourist camps as it nears the city.

TEXARKANA, 186.3 *m.* (337 alt., 11,821 Ark. pop., 17,019 Tex. pop.) (*see Texarkana*).

Texarkana is at the junction with US 67 (*see Tour 1b*) and US 82 (*see Tour 14*).

South of the border city US 71 makes an easy eastward arch through pine forests, then follows Red River. The country seems almost uninhabited; trees are tall and blanketed with moss. Breezes bring the fresh smell of lush growth and the cool dampness of dark mud.

This region was long in dispute between Arkansas and the Mexican government, having been apparently given to Mexico when the Louisiana Purchase line was drawn but included within the boundaries of the Territory of Arkansas in 1819. The ambiguity of its status made it a resort for outlaws and renegades. Even after Texas became a republic the border was so indefinite that, it is said, a family residing here had one son in the Arkansas legislature and another in the Texas legislature. An Arkansas judge complained in 1838 that he had been unable to hold court in the region because Texas had usurped jurisdiction and divided it into two counties. The present line was not finally determined until 1874.

At 219.1 *m.* US 71 crosses the Louisiana Line, 38.8 miles north of Shreveport, Louisiana.

〈〈〈〉〉

Tour 10

(Sikeston, Mo.)—Blytheville—Osceola—West Memphis; 70.6 *m.,* US 61.

Concrete-paved roadbed between Missouri Line and Yarbro, Jericho and West Memphis; elsewhere asphalt-paved.
St. Louis-San Francisco Ry. parallels route.
Limited accommodations except in larger towns.
Caution: Cross bridges carefully in this section; flooring is placed lengthwise and after even slight rains cars will skid easily.

US 61, swinging southward from the northeast corner of Arkansas, cuts directly through the richest of the Mississippi cotton bottoms. The earth is as black as the cotton is white, and the foliage along the route shows the deep green characteristic of near-river vegetation.

The people in this section of the State talk about cotton, they dream about it, they wear it, and like millions of Americans they eat foods made from cottonseed oil. In the off-season they are, like other Southerners, slow of both movement and speech, but when cotton is in their devotion to the crop alters them completely. Hours before daybreak they are up fighting its enemies, and their days are spent coddling and pampering it. Even when "the river comes to see them" they do not measure the flood in terms of personal inconvenience so much as by the damage inflicted upon the cotton.

Of the river Mark Twain said (*Life on the Mississippi*, Harper & Brothers, 1927) that because of the constant shifting of the channel and deposits of silt, "nearly the whole of that one thousand three hundred miles of old Mississippi River which La Salle floated down in his canoes, two hundred years ago, is good solid dry ground now. The river lies to the right of it, in places, and to the left of it in other places."

So the traveler, on this route, may drive his automobile over farm lands where French explorers paddled canoes.

US 61 crosses the MISSOURI LINE, 0 *m.,* 71.5 miles south of Sikeston, Missouri.

YARBRO, 1.5 *m.* (238 alt., 88 pop.*), is astir from morning till night during the ginning season in August, September, October, and November. In the hot summer months life in the town is quieter. Sharecroppers, mules, and hounds alike move with an easy rhythm that invokes the notice and sometimes the amusement of Northern tourists. An open account at the plantation commissaries insures the "three M's": meat, meal, and molasses. Only in the autumn is there any heavy demand for such few clothes as are needed—overalls, shoes, hats for the men, and bright gingham dresses for the women.

The BLYTHEVILLE COUNTRY CLUB (*9 holes; open to public; fee 50¢*), 3.9 *m.,* has a white clubhouse with a green roof and a spacious porch that extends across the entire front. A circular drive leads in from the highway across grounds landscaped with willows, poplars, and cottonwood trees.

BLYTHEVILLE, 5.6 *m.* (257 alt., 10,652 pop.) (*see Blytheville*).

1. Right from Blytheville on State 18, an asphalt-paved road, to the BIG LAKE MIGRATORY BIRD REFUGE (*open*), 14.4 *m.,* 9,821 acres of swamps and shallow lakes maintained by the United States Fish and Wildlife Service as a sanctuary. Here, in addition to the usual varieties of waterfowl of this region, are the shy and beautiful wood duck and the snowy American egret—both approaching extinction. The snowy egret is a large, non-crested member of the heron family, blessed and cursed with a magnificent train of long, white plumes extending a foot or so beyond his tail in the breeding season.

The reservation centers about BIG LAKE (*fishing*), 14.8 *m.,* formed by a widening of Little River. During the flood of February 1937, the natives of this eastern section of the State watched the levees around the lake with the care an engineer gives his steam gauge, because a break here would have inundated about 400,000 acres of the finest cotton land. The National Guard patrolled the dikes day and night, and shortwave radio sets were installed in rowboats so that immediate warnings could be given as to the location of weak spots. Bags of sand were kept in readiness to be rushed to danger zones, and the inhabitants spoke glibly about flood stages. A $16,000,000 project is now under way (1941) to reconstruct and raise levees around Big Lake and the entire Little and St. Francis River area in order to insure flood control in the future.

West of Big Lake State 18 rides an earth fill and crosses a number of trestles.

MANILA, 18.3 *m.* (245 alt., 1,248 pop.), formerly known as Big Lake Island, was founded in 1852 by Ed Smith. The early stands of virgin red oak, cypress, gum, and walnut made profitable the laying of narrow-gauge tramways into the forest to haul out timber, and Manila became a lumber town. In 1901, when the Jonesboro, Lake City, and Eastern Railroad (now St. Louis-San Francisco) came through, the community was renamed in honor of Dewey's victory at Manila Bay. Principal streets, such as Baltimore and Olympia, bear the names of battleships that engaged in the contest.

The HERMAN DAVIS MONUMENT, on State 18 at the southern edge of Manila, honors a local World War hero, Private Herman Davis (1888-1923), of the 113th Infantry of the American Expeditionary Forces. Davis first achieved distinction by killing, single-handed, four German machine gunners, a feat described as "almost impossible," thereby saving an entire American company from annihilation. In another skirmish he killed 47 enemy gunners as fast as they peeped from behind parapets, picking them off as accurately as he had "barked" squirrels back home in Big Lake. He was cited by General John J. Pershing for bravery and extraordinary heroism in action. The General also called Davis Arkansas' greatest soldier, and listed him as fourth among 100 American heroes of the war. Davis was decorated with the Distinguished Service Cross, the French *Croix de Guerre* with Palm Leaf and Gilt Star, and the French *Médaille Militaire*. After the war he returned to his home, where he carried on his former pursuits of farming, hunting, and trapping until he died in 1923 of tuberculosis contracted during his service overseas.

2. Right from Blytheville on Chickasawba Avenue, which becomes Gosnell Road, to the CHICKASAWBA INDIAN MOUND (R), 1.3 *m.*, in a cottonfield. The mound is about 25 feet high and has a circumference at its base of approximately 130 feet. The most recent opinion among experts is that the mound was neither a refuge from high water nor a burial place; no weapons have been found among the many pieces of pottery unearthed. The peace-loving Chickasawba possibly built the mound as a temple upon which to chant their prayers to the sun, fire, and water.

3. Left from Blytheville on Main Street, which becomes Armorel Road, to the junction with the Clear Lake Road, 1.2 *m.;* R. here to the A. G. LITTLE MANOR HOUSE (*private*), 2 *m.*, a white frame building with a one-story ell on each side and a six-columned portico facing the lawn. East of the house is the FAIRFIELD HISTORICAL MUSEUM (*free*), furnished and maintained by A. G. Little as a memorial to the Mississippi County pioneers. The museum is the old Huffman log cabin, a familiar landmark on the bank of the Mississippi for 97 years, transplanted and equipped with typical pioneer furnishings: an early-day handmade bed with its "cord," a crane and pot for cooking over the open fireplace, a dough board, a handmade churn, an old sugar bucket.

Near LUXORA, 18.3 *m.* (237 alt., 1,258 pop.), part of the Mississippi River levee system comes into view (L), resembling a low, winding hill. The first settler of Luxora was D.T. Waller, who built a one-room store on the bank of the river in 1882 and named the settlement after his daughter. Until about 1900 the town bustled with river life. Anchor, Collar, and Lee Line steamers made regular stops.

The cabins and saloons on these floating palaces were hand carved in rosewood and walnut, magnificently carpeted and draped, and furnished with huge French mirrors, crystal chandeliers, oil paintings and frescoes, and grand pianos. The bridal suite, when occupied, was serenaded by Negroes with gourd fiddles. Even the gamblers were gracious and ornamental, with their elaborate courtesy, their lace cuffs, and tall hats. But the passengers on the steamboats remained frontiersmen, however luxurious their surroundings. Their daily contact with elemental dangers made them hot-blooded and high-headed; and even an imagined insult would often provoke a fight.

The arrival of a railroad in 1899 helped Luxora to survive its colorful past. Today (1941) it provides an agricultural community with the gins and warehouses characteristic of Arkansas cotton towns.

OSCEOLA, 23.3 *m.* (238 alt., 3,226 pop.), the southern seat of Mississippi County, is named for the Indian chief Osceola (1804-38), who led his people during the Seminole War in Florida. In 1830 when William B. Edrington bartered for the town site, it was occupied by an Indian village. Realizing that the settlement was too small to warrant calls by steamboats, the shrewd woodsmen persuaded captains to stop by keeping cheap firewood corded on the shore. The town was first incorporated in 1838 as Plum Point.

The faint-hearted were not particularly fond of this section of the State in the early days. One story recounts that a Tennessean, after a single day in the then almost impenetrable tangle of cypress, briars, and canebrakes, pestered by myriads of mosquitoes, and bogged in the heavy gumbo mud, declared: "Arkansas is not part of the world for which Jesus Christ died—I want none of it." He returned to Memphis on the next boat.

Hardier souls remained. J.W. DeWitt, the first postmaster, built his shanty from lumber retrieved from steamboat disasters. His post office was an old cracker box into which the mail was dumped without sorting. Trappers in coonskin caps would saunter in and rummage through the post office for their letters.

In competition with DeWitt's and other stores built along the banks were the merchandise boats that plied the navigable rivers of the South, carrying everything from thimbles to iron kettles. The mellow blast of a hunter's horn or a conch shell announced to the planters and their wives that the river storekeeper was drawing near. In payment for drygoods, groceries, and hardware the settlers gave grain, cotton, tobacco, dried venison, and furs. In some localities the boatmen were required by law to obtain permits for trade with Negroes. Lacking these, the traders would anchor their boats under cover of night and barter with the slaves for cotton, chickens, and equipment filched from the plantations.

Some of the boats were equipped with copper stills for making peach and apple brandy. This trade was a lively one among the poorer whites and Negroes. The more prosperous farmers quaffed the smoother liquors brought up from New Orleans, though the jug of homemade corn was never out of place at any backwoods festivity.

Reconstruction trouble broke out between the whites and Negroes in 1868 and culminated in 1872. Despite protests, a Negro regiment was sent to Osceola while Governor Powell Clayton was in office. The whites banded together and ranged the country, terrorizing rebellious Negroes. Clayton offered $5,000 reward for the capture of the white band's leader, Captain Billy Erwin, but Erwin escaped to New Orleans.

The visitor who sees the Mississippi smiling and twinkling in the sunshine is likely to take the river too lightly. The "Old Man" should also be seen when he swells himself into a hideous yellow monster who gnaws at the levees with an insatiable appetite, snapping up in a single gulp great strips of the bank, with houses and barns. Or when he insidiously undermines some moss-bearded cypress and tosses it head over heels into the turbulent water. Or when he leaps from his bed and in a single night tunnels himself a new channel, and lies there, miles from his accustomed haunts, gurgling at the amazement and fear of his new neighbors. Or when, having broken his man-made chains, he steals into the far back country and awakens the startled native by the quiet lap, lap, lap of muddy water on his floor. You should see him when you can row a boat through your parlor, when your marooned family peeps out from the attic upon surrounding forests that look like an immense, turbid lake studded with treetops, when catfish glide down cotton rows that were to have paid your mortgage, when alligator gars disport themselves above your smokehouse, and when ears, weary of listening to the eternal slap of the wavelets, long to hear the distant put-put of a rescuer's motorboat.

With the deforestation of large areas, the monster has grown more powerful each year. In 1859 the gauge at Arkansas City (*see Tour 5b*) registered 46 feet, but the flood of 1912-13 reached 55.4. In 1916 the gauge read 56.4 and in 1922 the high-water mark was 58.0. In 1927 the astounding depth of 60.4 caused levees to collapse. In some places the water stood 19 feet on level ground.

During times of high water in the Mississippi Valley, restrictions similar to martial law prevail and are accepted. Thousands of sandbags, tents, shovels, and lanterns, along with clothing, lumber, and manpower are pressed into service. The Red Cross sets up its organization to care for the horde of refugees. Food, money, and clothing pour into the stricken areas. Railroads set out strings of boxcars on sidings to house the homeless, four families to a car. Lawyers and laborers, clerks and convicts, all work side by side, regardless of class or color.

The Negroes, who are the worst sufferers, contribute the most toil to save the levees. When cold, lead-colored skies pour rain day after day to soften levees already strained to the breaking point, and one cut is patched only to have another spot give way, the steady, measured beat of the Negro songs can be heard all up and down the river. Sometimes the shout, "Sandboil!" goes up: a spot has been found where a long arm of water has reached under the levee and come up in a small spot that boils like oatmeal. The scurrying workers stack sandbags in a ring around the boil. When, within the circle of sandbags, the water reaches the height of the river, pressure is equalized and the flow stops.

The bitterest time of a flood is not when the water is high, and airplanes and motorboats are seeking out the stranded families. It is after the water has gone down and the farmer goes back to his home, and finds, perhaps, a sand bar where his alfalfa field had been, or discovers that the river now runs through his back yard. He takes his furniture out of the attic—if his house is still there—and starts quietly about the work of reconstruction.

Two stone pillars mark the entrance to GRIDER PARK (L), 27.9 *m.*, a memorial to Lieutenant John McGavock Grider of the Royal Flying Corps, killed at Armentières, France, June 18, 1918. The park is a ten-acre wooded grove, outlined sharply against the flat treeless fields that surround it.

At 28.3 *m.* is the junction with a graveled road.

Left on this road, crossing the Mississippi levee at 2.9 *m.*, to a REVETMENT FLEET (*operates approx. Aug.-Dec.; visitors admitted*), 3.3 *m.*, belonging to the Memphis District of the United States Engineer Office. The fleet, which comprises about 100 boats and barges of various types, has been stationed here since 1931. Its normal function is the manufacture of concrete revetment mats, which are placed at strategic points along the bank to curb the river's current. The concrete mats are cast in articulated sections, 4 feet by 25 feet, made up of 15-inch slabs. Sections are wired together and sunk where the underwater bank is to be protected. As far back as 1850 woven willow mats were weighted down with stones to serve the same purpose.

DRIVER, 31.4 *m.* (232 alt., 24 pop.*), is the center of the Driver Cotton Plantation, on which some of the tenant families have resided for several generations.

WILSON, 35 *m.* (237 alt., 1,500 pop.*), controlled by the cotton-growing R.E. Lee Wilson Company, is built around a small landscaped park faced by a general merchandise store, a pharmacy, bank, restaurant, and gasoline station. Across the railroad tracks, east of the park, are the Wilson-owned soybean mill, cotton gin, and seedhouse. The electric power plant was sold to outside interests in 1930. Beyond the industrial section are Negro houses, small and unassuming, but superior to similar dwellings in the average cotton town.

An excellent example of business paternalism, the town is the creation of Robert E. Lee Wilson (1863-1933), whose career amounts to one of the best success stories in Arkansas. Wilson, an orphan when he was 15 years old, was a farmer on a small scale a few years later. In the 1890's he invested his savings in a sawmill, and a short time afterwards traded part of his cleared quarter section of farm land for 2,100 acres of swampy timberland. He cut and sold the trees from his swamps, drained the rich black soil (incurring the wrath of taxpayers who resented the assessments levied for drainage ditches), and in the course of years planted enough cotton to make his plantation one of the largest in the world.

Right from Wilson on a graveled road to DYESS FARMS, 10.4 *m.*, consisting of some 16,000 acres of Mississippi County overflow land divided into about 500 farms. Named for W. R. Dyess (1884-1936), first administrator of the Works Progress Administration in Arkansas, the colony was founded in 1934 as an initial experiment toward relieving the farm tenancy problem by means of an agricultural co-operative assisted by the Federal Government. Tenants were selected from relief rolls throughout the State. Dwellings were centered around a community hospital, a bank, feed mill, cotton gin, canning shed, library, and other service buildings. Farms have been worked on an individual basis, the community tasks being performed by colonists co-operatively hired. Dyess Colony soon after its beginning received much notice in the national press because of the large scale of the enterprise and the attention it attracted from highly placed governmental officials. On the other hand, there was some criticism of the project by dissatisfied tenants and others, who claimed that too high a price had been paid for the buckshot soil (land that is rich but lumpy and hard to work in wet weather) and that the farm dwellings were too hastily built. Until 1939 the colony was directed by a board composed of Work Projects Administration and other governmental officials. Shortly before 1940 the Farm Security Administration assumed control of the project and renamed it Dyess Farms.

For eight miles south of Wilson stretch cotton plantations owned by the Wilson Company, marked by green-painted and red-roofed tenant houses. Cotton here, as elsewhere in the county, is usually planted during the latter part of March or the first part of April, in carefully prepared soil. A series of gears in the bottom of a mechanical planter causes the seed to drop at regular intervals. About four weeks after planting, side plows tuck the earth around the young plants, leaving them on ridges so that crews of Negro men, women, and children can thin the cotton and hoe out the grass and weeds. The successive warm days and nights and the endless weaving of cultivators and shovel plows to pulverize the soil promote a rapidity of growth which is almost tropical, and in early June the blossoms appear. The blossom is white in the first stage, pink in the second, and at the end of the third stage falls off, being replaced by a rudimentary boll, or square.

The dreaded boll weevil lays eggs in some of these squares; these drop off in two or three days. Mature bolls are menaced by the army worm that goes from field to field stripping the foliage and exposing the bolls to the intense sunlight. To combat these insect enemies the plants are sprayed with arsenate of lead or cyanide. A Negro rides a horse between the rows with a pole held crosswise and a dusting bag of the poison on each end, the jolting movement of the horse causing the poison dust to billow out of the bags and down on the cotton. As the dust will adhere only to moist surfaces, the work is done in the early mornings before the dew evaporates. A few large plantation owners spray by airplane, as a plane can cover 500 acres or more a day in contrast to 30 or 40 acres by horseback. Birds are also an important factor in insect control.

During the summer the cotton choppers clean grass and weeds from the rows, grunting with each stroke of their hoes. In mid-July cultivation ceases. There is then little or no work for the tenants to do, so entire families spend long, lazy days on the near-by bayous and sloughs fishing for catfish, a prized delicacy. The first bolls of cotton open early in August, and now every able-bodied worker in the entire countryside crawls with bent back from daylight till dark to pick his 200 or 300 pounds of cotton, dragging a long bag behind him as an ant drags a crumb of bread.

Though the Rust brothers have proven that their queer assortment of cogs and spindles is practicable for harvesting cotton, the bulk of the crop is still gathered by nimble black fingers. The deep, quiet voices of the men, the high-pitched giggles of the women, the scrape of the long pick sacks, and perhaps the chuckle of a solemn pickaninny riding in state behind his mother, all blend into a hum that rises from the foamy field. And then a clear tenor rings out, "A'comin' across Jor-dan, what did Ah see-e?" All join him, "A'comin' for to carry me home. . . ." The tenor again, "A band of an-gels, comin' after me-e," and the gentle response, " 'Comin' for to car-ree me home." And then they "swing low" together as they deftly gather the cotton in great, soft handfuls—one of the most typical, and beautiful, pictures of the rural Southland.

Nor is it merely a pretty picture. The hat on the visitor's head, the rayon socks on his feet, his shirt—even the upholstery he sits upon and the artificial leather bag from which he takes his camera to capture the scene—all owe something to some such field. Cottonseed gave him the salad oil he had for lunch. He slept under linters last night. Combs, cosmetics, dyestuffs, the lacquer on the traveler's car, the box his battery sits in, fertilizer, stock feed, soap, camera film, writing paper, and gunpowder are just a few of the articles that can claim cotton and cottonseed as ancestors.

BASSETT, 40.5 m. (288 alt., 39 pop.*), has grown from a general store and steam gin in 1900 to several brick buildings with a modern electric gin that handles thousands of bales of cotton each fall.

When Arkansas was admitted to the Union in 1836, the flat bottoms of Mississippi County supported a magnificent growth of cypress, red oak, gum, and walnut. The first steam sawmill had been set up at Helena ten years before, but operators only nibbled at the forests until railroads were built at the close of the nineteenth century. Since that time the great mills have run through the timber and moved on. Deforestation uncovered the rich black soil that produces from one to five bales of cotton to the acre, the average yield being twice the rate of the State as a whole and three times that of the entire cotton belt.

In 1915, 48,267 bales (500 pound equivalent) were ginned in Mississippi County. In 1920 the total was 62,615. The many gins in 1925 turned out 157,067 bales. The floods of 1927 and 1928 took their toll, and the drouth in 1930 cut production to 100,040. The yield jumped to 215,350 in 1931; the next growing season was less favorable and resulted in only 190,100 bales. Since 1932 the Federal cotton-acreage-reduction program has attempted to hold the totals down, but 1937 saw a new all-time high of 257,090 bales, with Mississippi County producing 1.7 per cent of the world's output of cotton and ranking among the 10 leading counties of the world in value of farm products.

TURRELL, 54.2 m. (230 alt., 515 pop.) (see Tour 7), is at the junction with US 63 (see Tour 7).

The southernmost 20 miles of the route pass through Crittenden County, second only to Mississippi in cotton production. Here the gumbo soil is heavier than in the region near the Missouri border; larger mules, or tractors with stepped-up horsepower, are required to drag the plows. Occasional bright splashes of flowers—princess feathers, Shasta daisies, chrysanthemums—border cabins set among the unending waves of cotton.

MARION, 65.7 m. (227 alt., 758 pop.) (see Tour 3a), is at the junction with US 64 (see Tour 3a).

WEST MEMPHIS, 70.6 m. (221 alt., 3,369 pop.) (see Tour 2a), is at the junction with US 70 (see Tour 2a).

Tour II

Junction with US 65—Malvern—Hot Springs—Mount Ida—(Mc-Alester, Okla.); 170 m., US 270.

Asphalt-paved for two short sections; elsewhere graveled.
Missouri Pacific R.R. roughly parallels route between junction with US 65 and Sheridan; Chicago, Rock Island & Pacific Ry. roughly parallels route between Malvern and Hot Springs.
Accommodations limited except in larger cities.

US 270 passes through corn and cotton land, grazing country for blooded cattle and race horses, and heavily timbered territory. West of Hot Springs the route traverses the Ouachita National Forest, emerges briefly into a strip of prairie near Mena, and plunges into the forest again, following the high ridges of the Ouachitas to the Oklahoma Line.

Except for the cosmopolitan population adjacent to the Hot Springs territory, the people of this section are of Kentucky, Tennessee, and Virginia stock. Difficulty of communication has brought about considerable isolation for some of these hill-dwellers, whose language, it is asserted, resembles Elizabethan English. Travelers usually find little difference, however, between these Arkansans and the hill people of neighboring States.

US 270 branches west from a junction with US 65 (see Tour 5b), 0 m., at a point 4.8 miles west of Pine Bluff. Along the sweeping curve of the highway at the "Y" of the junction is a row of service stations and lunch stands, catering largely to the truck drivers who transport pine logs from Grant County to the sawmills at Pine Bluff.

Between the junction and Sheridan, the route traverses a densely wooded area of second-growth yellow pine and scrub red oak. Small cleared plots are cultivated in cotton and truck. At intervals are roadside booths where, during the spring and summer garden seasons, farmers' wives sell fresh vegetables, eggs, and poultry. The dwellings are of pine slabs, and usually have two or three rooms, with a lean-to at the rear for a kitchen.

WATSON STATE PARK, 4.1 m., is a recreational area for Negroes that covers about 100 acres of pine woods. A dining hall, baseball grounds, and other facilities have been constructed, and a community hall is scheduled for completion in 1941.

SHERIDAN, 20.3 m. (237 alt., 1,338 pop.), is built around the GRANT COUNTY COURTHOUSE, the grounds of which become a social and bartering center on Saturdays. The two-story building is of red brick, and its flat-topped hipped roof is broken by four chimneys; a tall steeple on the north contains three clocks—the town timepieces.

The WILLIAMS LUMBER COMPANY PLANT (*visitors admitted*) covers 40 acres in the eastern part of town. The long shed used for sawing and planing is surrounded by stacks of green-cut shortleaf pine as well as hardwoods drying in the air. Many of the logs are cut by farmers from their own lands and hauled to the mill by truck and wagon. The lumber is generally used for building forms and inexpensive structures. At the southern edge of the yard is the commissary, where the mill workers purchase most of their supplies. Farmers, too, are sometimes paid for their logs with due bills drawn on the company store.

Each summer the Grant County Singing Convention is held in Sheridan. Hymns are almost the only songs, but the square and triangular "shaped notes" of former times are giving way to the conventional round notes of the city-printed hymnbooks. The singing starts about nine in the morning and continues until ten at night. Dinner at noon is a major social event. The people of the district bring their lunches of fried chicken, country ham, and cakes. Women greet old friends and catch up on gossip from the other end of the county. Men discuss crops as they range up and down picking out the choicest pieces of chicken.

The singing itself, held at the church or the school gymnasium, brings out talents developed by long evenings of home music. Small groups of farmers gathered around a fireplace on a winter night decide to have some "old-time singing"; someone turns the screw stool to the proper height and sits down at the bellows-organ or piano, and everybody joins in *Give Me the Old Time Religion* or *In the Sweet Bye and Bye*.

Children brought up on such music are sometimes sent to the singing classes held at the schoolhouses in July, when the cotton is laid by. The instructor is usually an itinerant preacher or a local song-leader. From these schools and from the farms and churches come the competitors in the county meets. Winners go on to the State conventions and have an opportunity to get on radio programs or city church quartets.

In Sheridan is the junction with US 167 (*see Tour 15*).

Left from Sheridan on State 46, a graveled road, to MASONIC PARK (*picnics, swimming, fishing*), 11.5 m., site of the Battle of Jenkins Ferry. The landscaped 40-acre tract commemorates the skirmish which occurred in April 1864 on the sloping bank of the Saline River.

General Frederick Steele, whose Federal army had been occupying Little Rock, moved southwestward in the spring of 1864 and occupied Camden. The capture of his supply train at Marks' Mill (*see Tour 12*) left his men without ammunition and food, and he determined to retreat to Little Rock. Confederate forces took advantage of his embarrassment to attack him as he was attempting to cross the Saline at Jenkins Ferry. The battle, which lasted half the day, was bloody but indecisive. After both sides had suffered considerable losses, Steele succeeded in crossing the river on pontoons and, unpursued, made his way back to Little Rock.

West of Sheridan the forest along the highway is broken by small farms and meadows. Hereford cattle fatten on the abundant wild grasses.

At 28.2 *m*. is the junction with a dirt road.

Right on this road to a FOREST LOOKOUT TOWER (*open*), 4.6 *m.,* a steel structure 100 feet high supporting a glassed-in square cab. The view is one of rolling woodland and farms.

PRATTSVILLE, 29.1 *m*. (250 alt., 114 pop.*), is the trade center of a district where the sandy loam is adapted to the growing of Irish potatoes and truck. A potato growers' association prospered here until a price collapse in 1931 made further operations unprofitable. Now the grower raises only enough potatoes to fill the igloo-shaped storage mound in his back yard. The mounds are used because they are less expensive than underground cellars.

West of Prattsville the highway winds through the swamps and sloughs of the Saline River. The bottomland is a wilderness of towering cypress, gum trees, and thick underbrush. In late evening are heard the weird calls of swamp animals, the hooting of owls, and the baying of hounds. Dancing will-o'-the-wisps and "fox-fire" add mystery to the night.

The SALINE RIVER, 31.1 *m.,* wanders back and forth across its valley to south Arkansas, flooding alluvial bottomlands after each heavy rainfall.

POYEN, 34.7 *m*. (230 alt., 400 pop.*), was developed in 1916 by the lumber and piling industries as a railroad shipping point. When the virgin timber supply was exhausted, some residents turned for a living to cutting second-growth pine and stripping it of its bark, making telephone poles and piling for bridges and other structures. The industry is at its height in the spring, when the bark is easily removed by a flattened-out hoe. The piling is eventually sent to creosoting plants in Missouri and North Little Rock.

At 43.1 *m*. is the northern junction with US 67 (*see Tour 1b*), with which the route unites for 2.4 miles (*see Tour 1b*).

MALVERN, 45.5 *m*. (311 alt., 5,290 pop.) (*see Tour 1b*), is at the southern junction with US 67 (*see Tour 1b*).

BUTTERFIELD, 50.2 *m*. (388 alt., 280 pop.*), was at one time an important stop-over on the stagecoach line to Hot Springs, but when the "Diamond Jo" railroad (*see below*) was carried to Hot Springs the glamorous coach route was doomed. The Stagecoach Inn, a sumptuous building furnished with full-grained leather lounge chairs and other luxuries, soon deteriorated and was eventually scrapped for building material.

The village was named for D.A. Butterfield, who supervised the building of the "Diamond Jo" line. Incidentally, dairy farmers near here produced much butter for the tourist trade. Wealthy visitors stopping at the Stagecoach Inn on their way to the spa learned to recognize the intricate designs of flowers and animals on the cakes of butter, hardened in homemade wooden molds. One of the favorite designs was that of a race horse, because of association with the horse races at Hot Springs. Buttermolds are handed down in families from generation to generation, not only here but in all parts of Arkansas. Small-town grocers well acquainted with their community can tell at a glance what kitchen produced a particular pound of butter.

MAGNET, 53.6 *m.* (525 alt., 252 pop.*), is strung along US 270 for approximately a mile. A new brick high school and a vocational agriculture building made of logs are at the eastern end of the village. The several stores along the way have changed their wares from gingham and calico, cheese and crackers, to modern packaged groceries, gasoline, oil, and quick-lunches for motorists.

1. Right from Magnet on an ungraded road to the KIMZEY MINERAL COLLECTION (*free*), 1.3 *m.* The collection was begun several years ago when the Kimzey family made a hobby of gathering odd-shaped and colored stones from the neighboring fields of Magnet Cove (*see below*). The exhibit is kept in glass cases on the front porch of the family log house, which has the conventional breezeway.

2. Right from Magnet on an ungraded road, turning left at each fork, to a TITANIUM MINE, 2.1 *m.* The weathered ore is dug from the surface by steam shovel, crushed, and washed with the water from a near-by creek. When the creek is dry the mine does not operate. Production in 1937 amounted to 948 tons, with a value of $37,904. The mine at Magnet is the only one in Arkansas, and the mineral is comparatively scarce in the United States. Chief sources of world supply are in Quebec, Norway, and India.

Titanium is used principally in the manufacture of pigment for paint, but of recent years it has been increasingly employed as an alloy for steel, brass, and other light metals. Further uses are as a coloring material for the production of ceramics, textiles, and leather goods, and for making artificial teeth.

MAGNET COVE (R), 54.1 *m.,* a valley surrounded by low hills, looks much like any other piece of pasture land in the Ouachita foothills, but its small area (5.1 square miles) comprises one of the most remarkable assortments of minerals in America. Geologists have counted 42 kinds of minerals here.

Early Ouachita Valley settlers, puzzled by the erratic behavior of their compass needles in this valley, discovered quantities of lodestone (magnetite ore) underlying the slope and appearing frequently in pebbles on the surface. The name "Magnet" was applied to the cove and to the settlement that grew up near by. George Featherstonhaugh, British geologist, who visited Colonel James Sevier Conway at the Cove in 1834, was so enthusiastic about the spot that he thought "the proprietor would certainly possess one of the most enviable estates in America" if it were not so isolated.

"Upon considering all the circumstances connected with this cove, the intrusive character of its rocks, their distinct origin and separation from the sandstone, its minerals, the quasi-crateri form of the cove, and the immense deposits of magnetic iron," wrote Featherstonhaugh (*Excursion through the Slave States,* 1844), "I could not but be impressed with the opinion that Magnet Cove owes its origin to an ancient volcanic action, and that it is one of those extinct craters that may have preceded that class where basalt and lava are the principal products. . . . I left this rare place full of admiration."

The volcano-crater theory of Magnet Cove's origin is probably the most common, but the supposition has also been advanced that it may be the relic of a prehistoric lake basin. Another suggestion is that the Cove was once a lone island rising above a great sea that extended to the Rocky Mountains, to the Ozarks, and to the Appalachians.

Apparently Magnet Cove had attracted the interest of Indians long before white settlers appeared. Archeologists have found artifacts in the Southwest made from rocks and minerals presumably of Cove origin, and Featherstonhaugh discovered in the Cove "a great many Indian arrow heads made of a beautiful semi-transparent kind of novaculite." The source of the novaculite puzzled the geologist but it probably came from deposits in the neighborhood of Hot Springs (*see Tour 2b*).

About 1878 St. Louis capitalists bought a ten-acre tract and planned to mine lodestone. After they had done considerable work they found the paying ore existed only in small quantities, and abandoned the project. Since that time the deposit has been worked in a small way at different times to supply collectors and museums. Some superstitious people believe that the lodestone, which has the power of attracting metallic substances, will also attract members of the opposite sex. In former years many tons of magnetite were dislodged and shipped from the Cove to "love charm" markets in Chicago and New York.

Lodestone still exists in the Cove, and a bed of it is said to underlie the pavement of US 270. It occurs in loose fragments, from the size of a grain of sand up to chunks several inches in diameter, distributed through a dark clay, and is generally black in color, with a metallic luster. Large specimens occasionally contain six to eight varieties of minerals, many of them in colored crystals. The only Cove ore now being commercially mined is titanium (*see above*). Barite (barium sulphate) deposits are also occasionally worked.

The highway gradually ascends COOK MOUNTAIN, 54.4 *m.,* following sharp curves blasted from rock. Fertile green valleys indicate the trend to diversified farming of wheat, rye, oats, and garden produce. The work of the soil-conservation agencies is evidenced by the terraced hillsides and rapidly filling gullies.

Between Magnet and Hot Springs the highway dips from one hill to another, occasionally riding the shore lines of Lakes Catherine and Hamilton. Highway signs reading "Live minnow bait for sale" dot the roadside. Near Cook Mountain sections of the circular fences of the once-famous Essex race track, until 1910 one of the leading courses in the South, are visible above the water line of Lake Catherine, which now covers the track.

At 55.2 *m.* is the junction with a dirt road.

Left on this road to the REMMEL HYDROELECTRIC DAM, 2.8 *m.,* built in 1923-24 across the Ouachita River. Turbines in the brick powerhouse at the eastern end of the dam produce 13,000 horsepower.

LAKE CATHERINE, formed by the dam, affords good fishing (*bream, crappie, largemouthed black bass*).

LAKE CATHERINE STATE PARK (*hiking, boating*), comprising 2,048 acres of rolling woodland, stretches from the dam up the western shore of the lake. Roads and trails run through the pine forest. Plans for development include the building of housekeeping cabins along the water front.

At 64.4 *m.* is the junction with a graveled road.

Left on this road to the CARPENTER HYDROELECTRIC DAM, 2.5 *m.,* the second of a series built on the Ouachita River. Turbines here have a capacity of 80,000 horsepower. The dam, named for a river captain of the old school, forms Lake Hamilton (*see Tours 2b and 8b*).

In 1874, "Diamond Jo" Reynolds, a Chicago industrialist and steamboat operator, jolted over 25 miles of rocky mountain road in a stagecoach on his way between Malvern and Hot Springs, where he was going to take baths for his rheumatism. After complaining of the rough ride, he told the hotel keeper, "I've got to come back here some day but I promise you I'll never ride that way again." And he didn't. Instead, he built a narrow-gauge railroad from Malvern to Hot Springs and returned in style.

The "Diamond Jo" Line, completed in 1875, was the wonder of the countryside, with its rosewood and mahogany furnishings, its genuine leather upholstery, and its velvet drapes. Reynolds kept the equipment in perfect condition, and reduced the fare to one-third the stage rate. Besieged by his friends for passes, he printed facsimile two-dollar bills to use for "Annie Oakleys," so that the paying passengers could not detect the free riders. The wood-burning locomotive consumed more fuel than the little tender could carry, and a stop had to be made at Magnet to load up; here such wealthy and notable figures as Jay Gould and Jim Corbett would hop off to help the fireman pitch cordwood into the tender.

Just west of Magnet lay "Coffee-pot Curve," so named by the train crew because the pot of coffee that they were in the habit of making during the wood-loading would usually overturn at this point. At the end of the curve was a trestle over a small stream. One day as the little train, with its precious cargo of wide cravats and diamond stickpins, rounded the curve, Engineer Johnny Ryan found the trestle in flames. There was no time to stop, so he jammed the throttle wide open and roared safely across.

Billy Sunday, then a ballplayer, was among the sobered passengers who walked back to inspect the red-hot rails. Later he cited the incident as one of the major determinants in his decision to become an evangelist.

Whereas hundreds had endured the jerking stage journey to enjoy the healing waters of the spa, the luxury of the "Diamond Jo" Line attracted thousands, and the popularity of Hot Springs with Easterners increased enormously. Eventually, the railroad was rebuilt into a standard-gauge line, and after the death of Reynolds in 1902 it became a part of the Choctaw, Oklahoma & Gulf (now Rock Island) Railroad.

HOT SPRINGS, 68 *m.* (599 alt., 21,370 pop.) (*see Hot Springs*).

Hot Springs is at a junction with State 7 (*see Tour 8b*) and the eastern junction with US 70 (*see Tour 2b*), with which the route unites for 2.2 miles (*see Tour 2b*).

At 70.2 *m.* is the western junction with US 70 (*see Tour 2b*).

The highway crosses the OUACHITA RIVER, 76 *m.*, curving in a great "S" from the western mountains through the flat lands of southern Arkansas into Louisiana. This river has played an important role in the development of the southwestern part of the State. Many of the large towns owe their growth to the river traffic of the early 1800's. Most scholars believe that Ouachita (or Washita, as anglicized by early geographers and writers) meant "people of the clear, sparkling waters," though the meaning may also be "good hunting grounds." Immediately west of the river US 270 enters the Ouachita Mountains.

The route crosses the eastern boundary of the OUACHITA NATIONAL FOREST (*see Resources and Conservation*) at 82.6 *m.*

CRYSTAL SPRINGS, 85.6 *m.*, is a recreational center with lodges and campsites. The springs come from the base of Crystal Mountain, to the west.

CHARLTON RECREATIONAL CAMP (*picnicking, boating*), 88.2 *m.*, (R) under supervision of the United States Forest Service, was constructed by the CCC.

Five acres comprising a SHORTLEAF PINE PLANTATION, 89.3 *m.*, are used as an experimental plot by the Forest Service. Similar plantations throughout the Ouachita National Forest are covered with seedlings used to restock sections that will not naturally continue their growth, and to reinforce areas now understocked. The effect on growth of various soil, moisture, altitude, and climatic conditions are observed. The information gained from these studies is available to lumber companies or individuals interested in the practical aspects of reforestation.

CRYSTAL MOUNTAIN (R), 90.1 *m.*, received its name from the quartz crystals veined abundantly through its sandstone. The translucent hexagons and octagons, pointed at one end, range up to two or three feet in length, and with weathering take on soft tones of rose and yellow. Roadside stands sell chunks of the crystals, which are used for rock gardens and occasionally for interior ornament. Many people like to watch the flicker of lamp or firelight in the quartz.

A footpath at this point leads to the MONTE CRISTO MINES (*visitors admitted*), where crystals are hacked out of the surface rock and washed.

At 90.7 *m.* is the junction with the Womble Silver Trail.

Left on this graveled road, which winds among high mountains and dips through rocky ravines, all covered with virgin pine. The country along here was completely inaccessible until the Forest Service road was constructed. Public camps have been constructed at intervals. Usually the camps have shelter houses, tables, and fireplaces, and frequently there are swimming facilities.

At 13.7 *m.* is the junction with another graveled road; L. 2.4 *m.* on this trail to the HIGH PEAK LOOKOUT TOWER (*open*), where Forest Service men maintain their watch for the smoke cloud that indicates the beginning of a fire.

On the Trail is the WOMBLE FOREST RANGER'S STATION (R), 17.4 *m.*, a two-story white frame cottage. This is a part of the network of ranger, guard, and lookout stations, all linked by telephone, which protects the forest.

At 18.3 *m.* is the junction with State 27; L. on State 27 to NORMAN, 19.2 *m.* (707 alt., 512 pop.), a lumber town on the Caddo River.

Right from Norman on a graveled road to the ALBERT PIKE RECREATIONAL AREA, 35 *m.*, lying on a flat bench along a sweeping curve of the Little Missouri River. At the apex of the curve is a natural swimming pool; the river cascades into the pool over huge boulders. The camping area, shaded by tall oaks and beeches, is the center of a magnificent vacation country. Below precipitous cliffs the Little Missouri leaps from one clear pool to another; it affords smallmouthed bass fishing.

After Albert Pike (1809-91), explorer, newspaperman, poet, general, and Indian Commissioner for the Confederacy, had led troops from the Five Nations in the Battle of Pea Ridge (*see Tour 4b*), he quarreled with his superiors, lashing the Arkansas military leaders in a letter to the Confederate Congress, and resigned his command. His movements thereafter until the close of the war are obscure, but considerable evidence indicates that toward the end of 1862 he retired to this wild and beautiful spot on the Little Missouri. One account describes him as arriving in magnificent style in a buggy drawn by white horses, followed by a wagon loaded with furniture and gold and a procession of two score slaves. Here he built a house, according to old settlers, and commenced the major work of his life, the writing of the philosophy of Freemasonry. His labors were interrupted after several months by a band of guerillas that drove him from his home, destroyed his belongings, and threw his excellent library into the river. At the conclusion of the war he reappeared in Little Rock for a time, moved to Memphis, and eventually completed his Masonic writings in Washington, D. C.

The history of MOUNT IDA, 104.7 *m.* (663 alt., 490 pop.), seat of Montgomery County, began in 1836 when Granville Whittington, who had come to Hot Springs from Massachusetts the previous year, opened a general store in the hills. His old ledgers carried the names of many prominent figures of the time. Whittington was secretary of a meeting in June 1835 that petitioned Congress to make Arkansas a State. His store was a mile and a half north of present-day Mount Ida. The town that grew up here was called Montgomery at first, then Salem until 1850.

The first settlers of Mount Ida traveled in dugouts up the Ouachita and its tributaries, or in carts drawn by horses, mules, or cattle. The early vehicles were lubricated with pine tar; oil greases were unavailable. In cold weather the tar became stiff, and fires had to be built under the spindles of the wagons before the wheels would turn.

The livestock yards in the northern part of the town, where beef cattle are shipped for the Kansas City market, represent the principal source of livelihood in the county. Cattle graze freely over the wooded areas unfit for agriculture. All but the southern edge of Montgomery County is in the Ouachita Forest.

US 270 crosses the OUACHITA RIVER, 111.4 *m.* At 114.3 *m.* is the junction with State 88, a graveled road.

Left on this road is ODEN, 2.8 *m.* (771 alt., 102 pop.), on a high bluff and fertile lands. Here are a number of general stores, a cotton gin, and a plant that cuts shortleaf pine. Many of the homes are constructed of stone quarried from the near-by hills.

The name of PINE RIDGE, 12.1 *m.* (840 alt., 45 pop.*), results from the fact that the town is an example of life imitating art. Some years ago two radio performers known as Lum and Abner devised a "hillbilly humor" program. For material they used the inhabitants and background of the village of Waters, Arkansas, where as vacationers from near-by Mena they had spent much of their boyhood. The program was successful, and the people of Waters were soon astounded and delighted to find their names, their jokes and incidents in their lives being broadcast to millions of radio listeners. As the genuinely Arkansan and the conventionally vaudevillian were blended on the Lum 'n Abner program, so the actual mountain town of Waters attempted to adapt itself to the traditional Broadway conception of the Arkansas hill country. Tourists were interested; the village's back-wardness became a commercial asset. Eventually, the process reached its climax when the people of Waters changed their town's name to Pine Ridge, the name Lum and Abner had given it on the radio program. Elaborate ceremonies attended the formal rechristening. The proceedings, broadcast over a national hookup, were held on the steps of the State Capitol in Little Rock, with Lum and Abner, the Governor of the State, and other prominent person-ages participating. The self-consciousness of Pine Ridge manifests itself at the village's edge in such signs as "Drive Keerful," "Don't Hit Our Young 'uns," and "You-all Hurry Back"—locutions which nearly all Arkansas hill people use daily but would never dream of putting in print. The weather-beaten crossroads store, otherwise like hundreds of others, sells souvenir photographs, knives, pipes, and pottery, along with the customary lamp wicks, soap kettles, work shoes, women's dresses, and harness. Dick Huddleston, the proprietor and a leading figure in the broadcasts, keeps a register of all visitors. A few dozen yards away on the Ouachita is a tourist camp and fishing lodge, with rowboats named for Lum and Abner and their characters.

West of Mount Ida US 270 continues through the sparsely settled Ouachita Forest—land of so little value agriculturally that most of the inhabitants were delighted with the Government's small purchase price. Since in many cases the amount received for the land was not enough to set the farmer up elsewhere, arrangements were made whereby he continued to live on his farm, paying a nominal rental, with his agricultural operations under strict supervision. Thus he is not per-mitted to plant soil-depleting crops, but is encouraged to develop pasture grasses and to change to a livestock economy. He is instructed in soil terracing and contour plowing and is permitted to cut firewood only in accordance with the conservation and reforestation program. A recent development is the introduction of timber farming. Shortleaf pine can be planted, cultivated, and harvested like any other crop except that the growing time is a period of years rather than months, and the stands must be set out so that they reach maturity in rotation.

At 138.2 *m.* is the northern junction with US 71 (*see Tour 9b*), with which the route unites for 15.8 miles (*see Tour 9b*); at 154 *m.* is the southern junction with US 71 (*see Tour 9b*).

US 270, swinging to the west, winds past the base of RICH MOUNTAIN (*see Tour 9b*). In the fall this long ridge is covered with a rich variety of color patterns. Then the red, gold, and brown of the dying oak and hickory leaves is interrupted by the deep-green patches of pines, and low-lying clouds add a haziness that obliterates the horizon and blends the polychromatic hills into the sky.

At 163 *m.* is the junction with the Rich Mountain Road from Mena (*see Tour 9b*).

US 270 continues between the high Ouachita ridges to cross the OKLAHOMA LINE, 170 *m.,* at a point 103 miles east of McAlester, Oklahoma.

Tour 12

Junction with US 70—Marianna—Stuttgart—Pine Bluff—Camden—Magnolia—(Shreveport, La.) ; 272.5 *m.,* US 79.

Asphalt-paved between Rison and Camden, and for three shorter stretches; elsewhere graveled.
Missouri Pacific R.R. roughly parallels route between Lehi and Marianna; St. Louis Southwestern Ry. between Clarendon and McNeil; Louisiana & Northwest R.R. between McNeil and Louisiana Line.
Accommodations in larger towns only.

One of a network of highways beginning near the Mississippi River opposite Memphis and spreading through the Southwest, US 79 slants diagonally across the southern half of Arkansas to Magnolia, then drops down to cross the Louisiana Line. The route, graveled for most of its distance, receives only a slight stream of interstate traffic, but connects several of the State's smaller cities, and provides farmers with a convenient road to markets.

The first miles of US 79 run across the cotton-blanketed Delta; the next section traverses the rice-growing territory between the White and Arkansas Rivers. Broad fields then disappear, and in the rolling, wooded country southwest of Pine Bluff small farms make up the agricultural scene. Though much of the best timber in this territory was cut by the time of the World War, lumbering is still an active

Sport and Recreation

Rothstein: F. S. A.

SWIMMING HOLE

FISHING IN HILL LAKE

Guy Amsler

WILD DUCKS, ARKANSAS COUNTY

HUNTING QUAIL

Owen Lyon

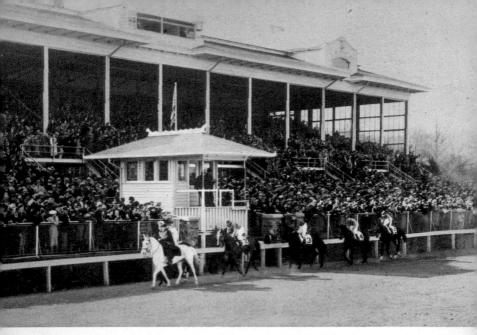

GOING TO THE POST AT OAKLAWN, HOT SPRINGS

PADDOCK AT OAKLAWN TRACK, HOT SPRINGS

Vitous Photo

EQUESTRIENNES UNDER A MAGNOLIA,
IN HOT SPRINGS NATIONAL PARK

AN OUTING ON WHITE ROCK, OZARK NATIONAL FOREST

OUTBOARD MOTOR RACE AT
LAKE HAMILTON, HOT SPRINGS

LAKE WINONA

FISHING FOR SUPPER

SEINING FISH FOR SHIPMENT
FROM STATE HATCHERY, LONOKE

industry, and has been stimulated the last few years by increased furniture manufacture in Arkansas.

The crowds on the streets of Delta towns and the workers in the plantation fields are Negro; the few whites are landowners, merchants, and professional men. On the other hand, rice culture does not lend itself to the plantation system, and in this grain section the population is white. White descendants of early emigrants from Tennessee and Kentucky live on the small farms in the rolling, timbered country. Near the Louisiana Line, where many old plantations have been broken up, the proportion of Negroes in the population again increases.

At LEHI, 0 *m.*, US 79 branches south from US 70 (*see Tour 2a*). Just south of the junction is the first of the cotton gins that rise alongside the railroad tracks every few miles in plantation country. From early September until Christmas or later, high-sided wagons and trucks carrying one or two trailers loaded with snowy cotton stand near the gins. Driven into the building, or under an adjoining marquee, the wagon box is emptied by a suction pipe that conveys the average 1,600-pound load in from 5 to 8 minutes. Inside the gin, rows of small circular saws on spindles tear up the cotton, loosening the seeds. The lint is then carried by another suction pipe to the baler, and the seeds are moved by a blower to the seedhouse.

Ginning a typical wagonload of cotton requires 15 to 20 minutes, depending on the moisture content of the lint. The 500-pound bales that emerge from the gin are hauled to compresses which reduce the bulk by about half, for more economical shipping. Electric motors and Diesel engines have largely replaced the steam boilers that supplied the power for early-day gins.

HUGHES, 20.1 *m.* (205 alt., 1,004 pop.), was started in 1913 when the Iron Mountain (now the Missouri Pacific) built its costly "mud line" across the Delta from West Memphis to Marianna through difficult swamps and brushland. After the railroad came, the land was cleared on such a large scale that cottonfields now reach to the horizon.

Left from Hughes on State 50, graveled, to HORSESHOE LAKE (*hunting, fishing, cabins, guides*), 7 *m.*, an old channel abandoned by the Mississippi. White-tailed deer, raccoon, and squirrels inhabit the woods surrounding the lake.

Some of the sharecropper houses a few miles west of Hughes are two-story buildings. Besides its use as dwelling space, the second story serves as a refuge when the adjacent St. Francis River overflows its low banks.

US 79 crosses the ST. FRANCIS RIVER at 32.4 *m.* and L'ANGUILLE at 41 *m.* The husky mosquitoes found in summer near such rivers were the subject of an early-day steamboat conversation described by T. B. Thorpe in *The Big Bear of Arkansas.* A Hoosier admitted the State was without a fault, except the annoying lowland insects. "Well, stranger," replied an Arkansan, "mosquitoes is natur, and I never find fault with her.   If they ar large, Arkansaw is large, her varmints ar large, her trees ar large, her rivers ar large, and a small mosquito would be of no more use in Arkansaw than preaching in a cane-brake."

MARIANNA, 42 m. (233 alt., 4,449 pop.), a cotton town atop Crowley's Ridge, has grown around a well-tended, tree-dotted park faced on three sides by business houses.   The seat of Lee County, Marianna was named for the wife of an early settler; the county itself takes its name from the Confederate military chief.   The new LEE COUNTY COURTHOUSE, at one edge of the square, has a lower story faced with limestone and an upper of brick; a railed balcony runs across the second-floor facade.

In Marianna is the junction with State 1 (*see Tour 12A*).

Left from Marianna on the Crowley's Ridge Road, graded, past small apple and peach orchards to the PATTERSON HOME SITE (R), 2.1 m., now occupied by a brown-painted farmhouse. A marker here indicates the grave of John Patterson (1790-1886), often called "the first white child born in Arkansas," though it is probable that white children were born at Arkansas Post during French and Spanish occupancy prior to 1790. Patterson used to say that he was "raised in the wilds of Arkansas, uncultivated as a poke stalk, unlettered as a savage; birthplace caved in when I was young; father was shot from ambush while asleep at home." In his old age he often recited a riddle now engraved on the marker:

> I was born in a Kingdom,
> Raised in an Empire,
> Attained manhood in a Territory,
> Am now a citizen of a State,
> And have never been 100 miles from where I now live.

The kingdom was Spain, the empire France, and Arkansas was first a Territory, then a State.

The MARIANNA-HELENA LAND PROJECT, 2.7 m., covers 22,000 acres of badly eroded Ridge land, running southward almost to Helena. Under the direction of the United States Soil Conservation Service, the section has been taken out of cultivation and is being developed for grazing and forestry, wildlife retreats, and recreational purposes. Two artificial lakes have been constructed on the project for fishing and swimming, and cabins and bathhouses are planned.

West of Marianna, the soil is brown rather than black, and small farms, usually operated by Negro renters, look out on the road.   As US 79 runs still farther west patches of swamp timber become larger, until the forest is dominant and farms become the intruders.   Occasionally a small sawmill with a sawdust heap beside it appears in a clearing.

CLARENDON, 75.8 m. (176 alt., 2,551 pop.), at the confluence of Cache and White Rivers, is an old river town which is still supported to a considerable extent by river products and traffic.   In 1819 a post office was established here and called "Mouth of the Cache." By 1838 the settlement, then known as Roe Rock or Rockroe (to give only two of many spellings), became the eastern terminus of a stagecoach line from Little Rock; here travelers transferred to White River steamboats.

Like other river ports, Clarendon has often seen floods. In 1927 the levee was under such terrific pressure that when it finally went out the water rose at the rate of a foot an hour, and the town was under 18 feet of water. Levees built in 1935-37 have greatly reduced the danger of future floods.

Cat, drum, buffalo, and carp, locally called "rough fish," are taken in great quantities from the White River by fishermen equipped with trotlines and seines. Gasoline-powered boats collect the fish from "shanty boatmen" and bring them to Clarendon and other river towns for packing and shipment to cities in the East and North. About $2,500,000 worth of rough fish are caught in eastern Arkansas rivers and lakes each year.

Mussels, some of them pearl-bearing, also grow on the White River bottom, and are scooped out by diggers and sold to Clarendon's pearl button factories. The PEARL ANN BUTTON PLANT (*visitors admitted*), on South Main St., is a typical industry of its type. About 30 workers are employed seasonally in cutting blanks from the shells. Most of the blanks are sent to Iowa for finishing, although some go to upstate New York.

Present-day river traffic centers around the CHOCTAW TRANSPORTA-TION COMPANY DOCK, just below the White River highway bridge. The company operates steel barges and light draft steamboats on the White, Mississippi, Yazoo, and Ohio Rivers. Two sawmills at Clarendon receive cargoes of logs regularly.

The MONROE COUNTY COURTHOUSE, a block from the levee, is a large two-story gray-brick structure whose red hipped roof is broken by dormer windows and drawn up into a peak at each corner. From the middle of the façade rises a tower twice as tall as the courthouse proper and visible for miles through the trees. The business district surrounds the courthouse and spreads down along the levee.

US 79 crosses White River from Clarendon and passes over the swampy bottomland beyond on a series of fills and trestles. The western valley wall marks the beginning of the ROC-ROE STATE GAME REFUGE, 80.3 *m.*, 13,000 brush-covered acres reserved for the propagation of deer, turkey, and quail.

To ROE, 83.6 *m.* (230 alt., 200 pop.*), hunters from Arkansas and other States bring their favorite bird dogs each November for competition under the auspices of the Arkansas Amateur Field Trials Association. The winning dogs, divided into age classes, are awarded prizes according to ability in locating and pointing quail, plentiful in this area.

Near ULM, 90.2 *m.* (210 alt., 146 pop.), rice farms come into view, distinguishable by large farmhouses and barns, stacks of straw, irrigation ditches, and pumphouses over wells that supply the great amounts of water needed for rice growing.

The Grand Prairie of Arkansas is a vast level tract between the lower White and Arkansas Rivers. It lay directly in the path of the settlers who spread out from Arkansas Post, and has been in cultivation for more than 100 years. In 1819 Thomas Nuttall, viewing the great savannah as he traveled up the Arkansas, remarked (*Journal of Travels into the Arkansa Territory, 1819*): "Amongst other kinds of grain, rice has been tried on a small scale, and found to answer every expectation. The price of this grain, brought from New Orleans, was no less than 25 to 37½ cents per lb. by retail. Under the influence of a climate mild as the south of Europe, and a soil equal to that of Kentucky, wealth will ere long flow, no doubt, to the banks of the Arkansa."

But the American settlers whose plows broke the prairie forgot the early-day experiment with rice, and pinned their hopes to cotton. Gradually they moved off to seek more fertile land. By 1900 farmers considered the prairie soil worn out, and used much of its acreage for pasture. A Nebraskan, William H. Fuller, had settled near Carlisle (*see Tour 2a*) in 1892, and had made a trial planting of rice near that town in 1897. His initial experiment was not highly successful, however, and he went to Louisiana to study rice cultivation. Returning to Arkansas, he produced in 1904 the first successful stand of rice in the State, raising 5,225 bushels on 70 acres near Carlisle. The new crop soon spread over the Grand Prairie, and in a little more than 25 years has revolutionized the agriculture of a large area southeast of Little Rock.

Grand Prairie land is adapted to rice culture because its level topsoil is underlaid by an impervious hardpan that holds water on the surface for days at a time. Rice must be flooded during the growing season for several reasons: to assist germination of the seed, to kill weeds and grass, and to produce good heads of grain.

Land that could be bought for $5 an acre before the coming of rice now sells for as much as $145 an acre. Equipment, too, is costly. Some of the hundreds of deep-well pumps are powered by electric motors, others by Diesel engines. The operations are highly mechanized, and the hired man, almost unknown elsewhere in Arkansas, appears here, usually living with the farmer's family, prepared to quit the chores at any time in order to tinker with a broken pump or a stalled engine. Many of the rice farmers are not native Arkansans, but are experienced grain growers who have come from Midwestern States. In recent years low prices for rice, together with the necessity for rotating the crop with legumes to restore soil fertility, have led to an increase in cattle raising.

In the middle of the Grand Prairie is STUTTGART, 98.7 *m.* (217 alt., 5,628 pop.), the "rice capital" of Arkansas, and a town of clean buildings, wide streets, and busy stores. While there is some lumbering and woodworking, most of the local industry centers around rice—mills, elevators, pump and storage-tank works, well-drilling companies, implement houses, and machine shops.

The ARKANSAS RICE GROWERS' CO-OPERATIVE MILL (*open on application*), on North Grand at the St. Louis Southwestern tracks, one of Stuttgart's four large mills, employs about 200 workers during the fall and winter. Admission to membership in the co-operative, which extends throughout the rice country, is determined by an elected board of directors. Each member possesses a vote, regardless of the volume of his business. Growers receive a cash advance of 75 per cent when their crop is brought to the co-operative mill, and are paid the remainder of the market price when the grain is sold.

The RICELAND HOTEL, on Main St., from the middle of November until the end of December is a gathering place for duck hunters who come to shoot on the Grand Prairie. Duck, quail, and other game birds feed in the ricefields. The entire section is a near-paradise for followers of hunting dogs.

In Stuttgart is the junction with State 30 (*see Tour 12B*).

HUMPHREY, 110.2 *m.* (191 alt., 595 pop.), a market town astride the line dividing Arkansas and Jefferson Counties, is, by an act of the State legislature, incorporated in both counties.

Near WABBASEKA, 117.6 *m.* (198 alt., 258 pop.), ricefields fade out and cotton plantations appear again.

ALTHEIMER, 121.9 *m.* (207 alt., 494 pop.), was founded as the headquarters of the Altheimer brothers' plantation in 1883. A typical cotton town, it contains gins, commissaries, stores, and homes strung along the parallel highway and railroad track.

Left from Altheimer on a graveled road to the junction with the Lake Dick Road, 2.7 *m.;* R. here to LAKE DICK, 7.3 *m.,* an experimental farm co-operative established in 1936 by the Farm Security Administration. Eighty modern frame houses of various designs form a rough circle around the lake. In a nuclear group are an L-shaped school, a retail store, a gin, feed and syrup mills, and implement sheds. Land, buildings, and equipment are leased by the co-operative association. The workers, all white, are paid semimonthly in cash according to the tasks performed, and profits at the end of the year are divided among the members. Of the 3,669 acres of land, about 2,300 are cultivated in common. Families comprising the co-operative were selected for farming ability and financial need.

At 128.8 *m.* on US 79 is the junction with a graveled road.

Right on this road to ST. MARY'S CHURCH (Roman Catholic), 0.3 *m.,* a yellow-brick building with a pedimented portico and a Christopher Wren spire. The original St. Mary's was built at Arkansas Post in 1782.

US 79 continues west through plantation country to a junction with State 15 at 130.7 *m.*

Right on this graveled road through SHERRILL, 6.8 *m.* (215 alt., 258 pop.), and TUCKER, 10.5 *m.* (221 alt., 74 pop.), to the junction with a graveled crossroad, 11.2 *m.*

1. Left at this junction 8 *m.* to the headquarters of PLUM BAYOU RESETTLEMENT PROJECT, one of the most ambitious of the Farm Security Administration's colonies. The land, once a plantation operated by convict labor, is now divided into 30- and 40-acre holdings, each with its house, garden, and barn. The four- to six-room houses are of simple but varied architectural types—some adaptations of the French end-gable house common throughout

Arkansas, others square-built around a central chimney, several L-shaped with extending kitchens. Each family works its own tract, instead of cultivating the entire farm together, as at Lake Dick. The general store and other community projects are owned co-operatively. For the first five years occupants rent the land, and repay government loans for livestock, implements, and seed; thereafter they may buy their place on payments spaced over a 40-year period.

2. Right at the junction 2.3 *m.* to TUCKER STATE PRISON FARM (*open 1-4 second Sunday in month*), where most of Arkansas' white prisoners work in the fields, and in shoe, clothing, and auto-license tag factories. Tucker Farm was established in 1916, shortly after the system of leasing State prisoners to private contractors was abolished. Negroes were sent to Cummins (*see Tour 5b*), but since 1936 some white male criminals have also been assigned to Cummins.

In the 1870's some plantations in Jefferson County tried a curious experiment with imported agricultural labor; more than 100 Chinese were brought into eastern Arkansas from California to work in the cottonfields. Among other inducements offered was an allowance of a half pound of opium monthly for each worker. The cost of the narcotic ($15 to $18 a pound) was said to be one of the reasons for planters abandoning the use of Chinese workers after a few years. Though most of the Chinese drifted back to California, a few remained to open stores and laundries in Arkansas towns.

US 79 crosses the ARKANSAS RIVER at 132.9 *m.* and passes TONEY FIELD (L), a Pine Bluff airport, at 136 *m.*

PINE BLUFF, 139.1 *m.* (221 alt., 21,290 pop.) (*see Pine Bluff*).

Pine Bluff is at the junction with US 65 (*see Tour 5b*).

Southwest of Pine Bluff the highway weaves through the low, rolling hills of the Arkansas Valley wall. Pines begin to outnumber oaks in the clumps of woods between small farms, pastures, and orchards.

RISON, 169.5 *m.* (236 alt., 1,005 pop.), seat and commercial center of wooded Cleveland County, covers a larger area than the average cotton-country town of similar population. Houses are spaced widely and surrounded by lawns and trees. The CLEVELAND COUNTY COURTHOUSE is a two-story, gray-brick building, whose red-tile roof slopes up to a clock tower encircled by a balcony and capped by a hexagonal dome.

Much of the topsoil along the highway west of Rison is red clay. In the slanting light of sunset the earth appears blood scarlet, laced with black shadows from the pines.

The Cleveland County farmer, like those in most parts of Arkansas, cocks his head toward the gray sky when the winter rains begin to fall and wonders if it is cold enough for hog killing. When the day comes he gets out the black wash kettle and sets it over a roaring fire, sharpens the butcher knives, and scours the smokehouse. The hog is beguiled with an ear of corn, and shot between the eyes with a small caliber rifle. As the animal slumps to the ground it is stabbed in the throat so that the meat will not be bloodshot. The carcass is sloshed about in a tank or barrel of hot water to loosen the hair, scraped until it is as white and slick as a peeled hickory pole, and hung up by the hind feet to be chilled and then carved into hams, bacon, and other cuts. Though some of the meat is smoked, the present-day farmer does not cure as much meat in this manner as did his father. Making hogshead cheese, however, cooking the fresh backbones and spareribs, and salting down the wide slabs in the meat box are events rural folk look forward to on thousands of Arkansas farms. And while the farmer's wife prepares a great pan of sausage with sage and other flavoring, one of the children is dispatched with "a bit of fresh meat" to each of the neighbors.

KINGSLAND, 179 m. (214 alt., 473 pop.), is a railroad shipping point.

Left from Kingsland on State 8, graveled, to the junction with a dirt road, 6 m. In the woods near here on April 25, 1864, occurred the Battle of Marks' Mill, an incident in General Frederick Steele's attempt to move his Federal troops southwestward from Little Rock toward Shreveport. Steele got as far as Camden, where he waited for General Powell Clayton to bring up a supply train from Pine Bluff. A Confederate force under General James F. Fagan surprised Clayton at Marks' Mill, capturing 240 wagonloads of supplies and a large number of prisoners. Steele gave up his expedition and returned to Little Rock (see Tour 11).

State 8 continues to WARREN, 23.1 m. (206 alt., 2,516 pop.), near the Saline River, one of Arkansas' leading lumber towns and a sizable cotton market. Warren existed as a county seat and trading center for half a century before the lumber industry became important to southeast Arkansas. The BRADLEY COUNTY COURTHOUSE, a two-story buff-brick building with a tall clock tower at one end and a smaller tower at the other, occupies the center of the square; around it the business district gives way to tree-shaded residential sections.

The BRADLEY LUMBER COMPANY MILL (open on application), at Wheeler Ave. and Martin St., is one of the largest buyers of hardwoods in the South; it employs some 1,100 workers. The mill comprises five units, including a hickory products department and a flooring plant. A leading product is unassembled furniture, which is crated compactly and shipped to Eastern assembly plants. Other specialties include ladder rungs and uprights, and blocks from which skis are cut. Adjoining the mill, but outside the Warren city limits, the company maintains a village of four- and five-room houses for its employees. Workers, however, are not required to live in the company houses or to trade at the company store, and all pay rolls are in cash.

The SOUTHERN LUMBER COMPANY MILL (open on application), at the west end of Pine St., employs about 400 workers and specializes in cutting pine and oak flooring. Just outside of Warren the Southern Company also owns a community for its workers, and follows a policy similar to the one used in directing the Bradley settlement. The well-built houses are surrounded by trees, shrubs, and gardens.

FORDYCE, 187 m. (290 alt., 3,429 pop.), has numerous gins, a large lumber mill and several smaller woodworking plants, a casket factory, and service industries. The DALLAS COUNTY COURTHOUSE is a two-story, brown-brick structure with a classic portico and domed clock tower. On the highway (R) at the east end of the town is the impressive A. B. BANKS HOUSE (private), built about 1910, decorated with classic porticos and balustraded roofs. The landscaped grounds contain rosebushes, magnolias, and shade trees, as well as arbors.

The FORDYCE LUMBER COMPANY MILL (*open on application*), distinguishable at the north end of town by its tall smokestacks, produces pine lumber and oak flooring. Fifty company-owned houses near the mill are rented to white and Negro employees.

In Fordyce is the northern junction with US 167 (*see Tour 15*), with which the route unites for 5.7 miles.

The country along US 79 southwest of Fordyce is almost entirely covered with stands of pine and oak, which shelter deer, turkey, and smaller game.

THORNTON, 192.7 *m.* (314 alt., 550 pop.*), once had its own railroad, the Thornton & Alexander, which ran southeast from the St. Louis Southwestern tracks to tap the Calhoun County woods and connect with the Rock Island at Tinsman. After sawmills thinned the forests the line was abandoned.

In Thornton is the southern junction with US 167 (*see Tour 15*).

BEARDEN, 200.7 *m.* (239 alt., 961 pop.), built with the Cotton Belt in 1882, was incorporated in 1892. Lumbering and agriculture have been the mainstays of the town.

At 206.5 *m.* is the northern junction with State 9 (*see Tour 8b*).

The forests give way to level land and a few cotton plantations appear as US 79 enters the Ouachita Valley. The fields then merge into swamp bottoms overgrown with pin oak until the Ouachita River is crossed at 216.2 *m.*

CAMDEN, 217.1 *m.* (198 alt., 8,975 pop.) (*see Tour 8b*), is at the southern junction with State 7 (*see Tour 8b*).

The valley of the Ouachita, like those of the Arkansas, the White, and the Black Rivers, was among the earliest-settled sections in the State. The few pioneers who lived here were much more familiar with New Orleans, easily accessible by water, than with Little Rock, which could be reached only by a long journey through uninhabited forests. Enforcement of laws made at the capital was therefore sometimes a haphazard matter. George Featherstonhaugh tells a humorous, if not too credible, story of a frontier court session at which three persons accused of murder and one of horse stealing were arraigned (*Excursion through the Slave States,* 1844):

The place where they were to be tried consisted of a single house in the wilderness, which represented the future county town; the witnesses were on the spot, and all the appliances to constitute a Court. Twelve men had been with some difficulty got to leave home, and come to this place to perform the part of a jury. At the critical moment, however, one of these men was not to be found; and as a panel could not be formed, the judge stated the fact, and asked what step the prosecuting attorney intended to take. The counsel of the accused, after many protestations of their innocence, and their strong desire to prove it without loss of time, now proposed to fill the panel *de circumstantibus.* It so happened that the only *circumstantes* were the three murderers and the horse-stealer, so they put one of the murderers into the jury, and first tried the horse-stealer and acquitted him, and then put the horse-stealer into the panel and acquitted the murderer; and by this sort of admirable contrivance the whole four were honourably acquitted, and returned perfectly whitewashed into the bosom of society. . . .

A steel derrick at the northern edge of STEPHENS, 237.4 *m.* (231 alt., 998 pop.), heralds the approach to the southwest Arkansas oil fields. The Hunter Discovery well, drilled near here in 1919, first revealed the presence of petroleum in the State. Most of the business buildings of Stephens are of brown brick, and were built in the 1920's when the early wells came in. Production in the local field has declined, though several wells are still pumping. North of Stephens are onetime oil producers that now yield asphalt.

McNEIL, 247.9 *m.* (323 alt., 694 pop.), established in the 1880's, inherited the population and trade of the old College Hill settlement, where William B. McNeil had conducted a school before 1860.

McNEIL PARK, a grove at the east end of the town, was purchased by the Southwest Confederate Veterans' Association in 1892. The site, now used as a town park, was given to the American Legion in 1933.

The State-supported MAGNOLIA AGRICULTURAL AND MECHANICAL COLLEGE (L), 252.5 *m.*, consists of a dozen red-brick structures arranged around the three-story Administration Building, which was erected in 1910. The institution, originally established as a vocational school and high school, added junior college work in 1925.

MAGNOLIA, 254.1 *m.* (207 alt., 4,326 pop.), once depended largely on cotton ginning and marketing and a textile mill just west of town on US 82 (*see Tour 14*). Opening of an oil field in 1938 brought a new source of income which, husbanded according to scientific conservation methods, may continue for decades.

The COLUMBIA COUNTY COURTHOUSE, in the center of town, appropriately surrounded by magnolias, is a successful attempt at functionalism in courthouse architecture. A box-shaped first floor is divided into county offices, with a circular courtroom rising from its center. The idea is faithfully carried out on the exterior, the courtroom rising into a flat dome; the circular center is brought into harmony with the rectangular outline of the building by a gallery of linked Corinthian pillars on each side.

The MAGNOLIA POST OFFICE, just east of the courthouse, is a severe, modern brick building with strips of limestone facing along the windows. On a wall of the lobby is a small mural, depicting a harvest scene, by the St. Louis artist, Joe Jones.

In Magnolia is the junction with US 82 (*see Tour 14*).

From Magnolia US 79 swings south and passes between small level farms that are generally tilled by Negro renters.

EMERSON, 266.5 *m.* (310 alt., 501 pop.), a cotton town, also has a small sawmill that specializes in timbers for the southwest Arkansas oil field riggings.

At 272.5 *m.* US 79 crosses the LOUISIANA LINE, 65.4 miles north of Shreveport, Louisiana.

Tour 12A

Marianna—West Helena—Helena—Elaine; 51.9 *m.*, State 1, State 20, State 44.

Asphalt-paved roadbed.
Missouri Pacific R. R. roughly parallels most of the route.
Accommodations in Helena.

The route to Helena, leading city on the Arkansas bank of the Mississippi, crowds into its few miles most of the Delta's characteristics. In the summer sunshine green fields of cotton stretch away to deeper green patches of timber. Negroes guide cultivators down the rows, or sprawl on the porches of cabins. Children walk along dangling a string of fish hooked at a slough or bayou. On the narrow highway are mule-drawn wagons loaded with feed, trucks hauling logs to the mills at West Helena, the shiny new cars of traveling salesmen.

Growing cotton and cutting timber are the occupations of the farmers. Processing the timber and cotton are the chief industries of Helena and West Helena. No clear line exists between farm and city dwellers, for many rural men come into town during the winter to work in the mills, and townspeople go out into the fields to earn money during cotton chopping and picking time.

State 1, branching south from US 79 (*see Tour 12*) in MARIANNA, 0 *m.* (233 alt., 4,449 pop.) (*see Tour 12*), runs to the west of Crowley's Ridge, which here swings toward the Mississippi.

The COTTON BRANCH EXPERIMENT STATION (*visitors admitted*), 3 *m.*, of the University of Arkansas College of Agriculture covers (L) 245 acres purchased in 1926. Experiments with cotton yields devised at the University in Fayetteville are worked out in practice here. Buildings as well as agricultural methods are intended as models. The director's home is a simply designed, modern plantation house. The Negro families who do the farming live in well-built tenant houses with running water and electricity. Groups of planters inspect the station on visiting days held about the middle of April and in August.

WALNUT CORNER, 15 *m.*, is at the junction with State 20; L. here.

Founded in 1909, WEST HELENA, 22.8 *m.* (255 alt., 4,717 pop.), is an industrial extension of Helena, and is built around the factories and mills for which the older town had no space. Workers followed the industries, and retail stores followed the workers; along

West Helena's busiest street, Plaza, there are no banks or hotels, and very few doctors and lawyers, because these services are obtained in the older city.

A number of sawmills in Arkansas and Louisiana supply nearly 3,500,000 board feet of lumber each month to the CHICAGO MILL (*open on application*), on West Plaza St. The plant, which makes boxes and crates, operates 24 hours a day during busy seasons, employing about 1,600 workers.

The PEKIN WOOD PRODUCTS MILL (*open on application*), also on West Plaza, is owned by the Chrysler Motors Corporation and manufactures wood parts and cratings for automobiles. Operations require approximately 250 workers seasonally.

State 20 winds through the rolling slopes of Crowley's Ridge between West Helena and Helena, cutting through banks covered in summer with Virginia creeper and blazing with patches of flowers. The stretch is suburban in character, but set back from the highway are small farms.

In ante bellum days HELENA, 26.3 *m.* (190 alt., 8,546 pop.), was a center of culture on the Delta, a town of old families and traditions, and lively with the coming and going of river packets. Mark Twain, who piloted steamboats past the town, wrote in his *Life on the Mississippi* (Harper & Brothers, 1927): "Helena occupies one of the prettiest situations on the Mississippi. Her perch is the last, the southernmost group of hills which one sees on that [the west] side of the river." Just before one of Twain's visits Helena had been flooded, and he commented that "a Mississippi inundation is the next most wasting and desolating infliction to a fire." Nevertheless he "had an enjoyable time here, on this sunny Sunday; two full hours' liberty ashore while the boat discharged freight. In the back streets but few white people were visible, but there were plenty of colored folk . . . and almost without exception upholstered in bright new clothes of swell and elaborate style and cut—a glaring and hilarious contrast to the mournful mud and the pensive puddles."

Helena, the one city in Arkansas to which the Mississippi is still important as a traffic artery, is called by local civic organizations "Arkansas' Only Seaport." Like most lower Mississippi ports the city is walled off from the river by the levee. Cherry Street, the chief thoroughfare, parallels the levee and ends near the ferry landing. Intersecting Cherry are secondary business streets that become residential avenues as they go up towards the hills of Crowley's Ridge. The entire city is hemmed in by the Ridge on the west and the levee on the east. In their design and in the patina of coal smoke that covers them, the brick commercial buildings show a respectable age.

Before white men came to the region an Indian village occupied the site of Helena. Local historians say this village was the "Pacaha" visited by De Soto in 1541. An early American settler was Sylvanus Phillips (1766-1830) for whom the county was named and for whose daughter, Helena, the town was named about 1820. In 1829 the

Territorial legislature authorized the building of a road from Helena to Mouth of the Cache (Clarendon), where it would connect with the Little Rock-Arkansas Post highway. As the black land was cleared and planted in cotton steamboats began to stop regularly.

Helena was of strategic value during the War between the States, and was occupied by Federal General Samuel Curtis in 1862. On July 4, 1863, Confederates under Generals T. H. Holmes, J. S. Marmaduke, and L. M. Walker vainly attacked Curtis in an effort to divert Federal forces from the siege of Vicksburg. Ill feeling arose between Marmaduke and Walker after the Battle of Helena, reaching a climax in a duel at Little Rock two months later in which Walker was killed.

Of the seven generals which Helena gave the Confederacy, the best known are Major Generals Thomas C. Hindman (1828-68) and Patrick R. Cleburne (1828-64). Hindman, Tennessee-born, lived in Mississippi for a time, served in the Mexican War, and came to Helena to practice law in 1854. "Almost fresh from the blood-stained fields of Mexico, where he had been promoted for valorous conduct from a private to a first lieutenant," says a biographer (C. E. Nash, *Biographical Sketches of Gen. Pat Cleburne and Gen. T. C. Hindman,* 1898), he "regarded Arkansas as an empire of which he should be emperor. At this time fire ran through all his veins and dynamite through his brains." In Helena Hindman met Cleburne, a young Irish immigrant who had recently come from Cincinnati to clerk in a drugstore. Working together as nurses in a yellow fever epidemic that swept the town in 1855, they became fast friends, Cleburne serving Hindman as best man at his wedding and defending him in a political shooting scrape in which both were wounded.

In 1862 Hindman was placed in charge of the State's defense, commanding the Confederate army at the Battle of Prairie Grove (*see Tour 4b*) and subsequent maneuvers. Smarting under what he considered unjust criticism, he was transferred to the East at his own request. He refused to surrender with the Confederate army at Bentonville, North Carolina, and fled instead to Mexico, returning to Helena about a year later. In 1868 an unknown assailant shot him as he bent over his mother's bed. Mortally wounded, he made his way to the front gallery, where some neighbors had gathered, and said, "I do not know who killed me; but I can say, whoever it was, I forgive him!"

Cleburne's military career was no less dramatic. He enlisted from Helena as a private in the Yell Rifles, but almost immediately was made a captain and then a colonel. He fought in Kentucky, Alabama, Georgia, and Tennessee, his most spectacular exploit being the covering of the retreat of General Braxton Bragg from Lookout Mountain at Ringgold Gap, in Georgia near Missionary Ridge. His death at Franklin, Tennessee, is described by Irvin S. Cobb (*Tennessee Historical Magazine,* January 1931):

> Pat Cleburne died on one of the bloodiest battlefields of Christendom in his stocking feet because, as he rode into battle that morning he saw one of his Irish boys from Little Rock tramping barefooted over the frozen

furrows of a wintry cornfield and leaving tracks of blood behind him. So
he drew off his boots and bade the soldier put them on, and fifteen minutes
later he went to his God in his stocking feet. Raleigh laid down his coat
before Good Queen Bess, and has been immortalized for his chivalry, but
I think a more courtly deed was that of the gallant Irishman, Pat Cleburne.

In the 1870's a railroad was built to Helena along the route of the
old road from Clarendon. The Iron Mountain a few years later ran a
branch south along Crowley's Ridge from Knobel on its main line.
Both of these roads now belong to the Missouri Pacific system. In
1909 a third line, the Missouri & North Arkansas (now Missouri &
Arkansas), reached its southern terminal at Helena. Freight cars are
ferried across the river by the Yazoo & Mississippi Valley, an Illinois
Central branch.

The HELENA PUBLIC LIBRARY (*open 12:30-6 weekdays*), on Pecan
St. at Perry, contains about 12,500 volumes and local historical records.
The adjoining PHILLIPS COUNTY MUSEUM (*open 12:30-6 weekdays*)
has collections of Indian and pre-Columbian relics, war mementoes,
pioneer exhibits, letters, valuable maps, and an art gallery.

At the foot of Missouri St. is the HELENA FERRY (*car $1, round
trip $1.50*), a steel-hulled steamer which runs to Glendale, Mississippi,
leaving on the hour. Service is maintained day and night.

The FEDERAL BARGE LINE TERMINAL (*visitors admitted*), a series
of large sheds atop the levee, is Helena's principal port facility. Railroads now honeycomb southeast Arkansas, so that cotton is no longer
the chief outgoing water cargo, although much of it is still shipped from
the terminal. Rice, trucked from the Grand Prairie country, has
become the leading export, with peanuts and hay filling many barges.
Incoming craft bring oil from Baton Rouge, coffee and sugar imported
by way of New Orleans, beer from St. Louis.

The NEW SOUTH MILL (*open on application*), at O'Connor and
Pontotoc Sts., rebuilt in 1938 after a fire, extracts oil from cottonseed.
Eight presses are used in this large plant, which runs 24 hours a day
for most of the year.

The LOOKOUT OIL AND REFINING COMPANY PLANT and the
ARMOUR MEAT PACKING PLANT (*open on application*), which share a
building against the levee on Elm St., are packaging divisions for
Armour and Company products.

The WALRIDGE KNITTING MILL (*open on application*), at 314
Perry St., began operations in 1938. The company, which manufactures anklets for women and children and half-hose for men, employs
about 65 workers.

From the west end of York Street, a few blocks from the downtown
section, a foot trail climbs steeply to the top of RESERVOIR HILL. The
eminence, used for storage of the city's water supply, gives an extensive
view of Helena's homes and factories, the apparently blue Mississippi
beyond the levee, and the woods on the farther shore. Along with the
high school hill to the south, this elevation was fortified by General
Curtis, and was the scene of heavy fighting during the Battle of Helena.

South of Helena the route continues on State 44.

LAKEVIEW (*open*), 44.5 *m.*, stretching for miles along Old Town Lake, is a Farm Security Administration project for Negroes. Until 1937 part of the 5,600-acre tract was comprised of plantations, some of them in cultivation 100 years ago when the lake was still an arm of the Mississippi and supplies were delivered to planters by boat. Purchased by the Federal Government, it has been divided into 95 farms of about 44 acres, each with its house and barns. Each family cultivates its own plot, but the Lakeview Co-operative, comprising the heads of all the families, operates the general store, the gin and feed mill, repair shops, and a livestock herd. The community also includes schools—elementary, high, vocational, and nursery. After a trial period colonists may arrange to purchase their land.

ELAINE, 51.9 *m.* (173 alt., 634 pop.), in the fall of 1919 was the scene of a bitter interracial struggle, in which several white men and probably more than 100 Negroes lost their lives.

Fundamentally the trouble grew out of those social and economic problems of the farm tenancy system which such experiments as Lakeview are intended to guide toward solution. In the upsurge of labor organization that followed the World War the Negro sharecroppers around Elaine, chafing under such grievances as poor housing, low income, and questionable bookkeeping in some commissaries, formed units of the Progressive Farmers and Household Union of America.

On the night of September 30, 1919, a deputy sheriff and another white man drove up to a schoolhouse near Elaine where one of these groups was meeting. The deputy claimed that he was repairing a tire and that the Negroes fired upon him without warning. Negroes contended that they were fired upon by the whites and returned the shots. At any rate a white man was killed, and almost instantly the whole region was inflamed; posses hurried to Elaine. A newspaper reported that "the bodies of at least fifteen Negroes were lying in the streets and outskirts of the town and more probably would be found in the woods."

Rumors flew about the countryside. It was reported that an armed Negro insurrection had been planned for months, and that more than 1,000 Negroes equipped with high-powered rifles were hidden in the woods near Elaine. Sporadic battles that raged in the bottoms for nearly a week were ended only when Governor Charles H. Brough sent 500 regular army troops from Camp Pike to restore order, and appointed a 7-man investigating commission. A large number of Negroes were arrested, 87 sentenced to the penitentiary, 12 to the electric chair. The death sentences were eventually reversed by the United States Supreme Court, and all the defendants finally freed.

Today (1941) Elaine seems much like any other Delta town, with its row of brick stores, its church, its schoolhouse, and its gin. Negroes laugh on the streets and in the pool halls. White planters and storekeepers grumble over cotton prices and agree that something has to be done. A new generation has grown up since 1919, and no outward evidence of the disturbance remains.

Tour 12B

Stuttgart—De Witt—Arkansas Post; 50.9 *m.*, State 30, State 1.

Asphalt-paved between Stuttgart and Gillett; elsewhere graveled
St. Louis Southwestern Ry. parallels route between Stuttgart and Gillett.
Accommodations in Stuttgart and De Witt.

The area lying between the lower reaches of the White and Arkansas Rivers was the first land in Arkansas to be touched by the pirogues of the early French explorers. For more than a century it remained the most populous and most important part of the State. Eventually the settlers moved westward and northward seeking better land, and much of the region was turned into pasture or went back to trees. Rice growing, which began early in the twentieth century, brought new settlers and a fresh prosperity.

A large part of this territory is included in Arkansas County, through which the route passes from Stuttgart, its leading town, to Arkansas Post, the first permanent white settlement in the Louisiana Purchase territory.

State 30, branching east from US 79 (*see Tour 12*) in STUTTGART, 0 *m.* (217 alt., 5,628 pop.) (*see Tour 12*), runs through level fields in which rice alternates with legumes. The cultivation of soybeans, which restore to the soil the fertility that grain removes, has recently become widespread in Arkansas County, now one of the leading soybean areas in the State.

Since 1927 the RICE BRANCH EXPERIMENT STATION (*visitors admitted*), 9.6 *m.* (R), of the University of Arkansas College of Agriculture, has been the scene of tests designed to improve rice yields. On the 160 acres of this model farm the staff of technicians also works with the legumes used for crop rotation, combats plant diseases, and experiments with irrigation methods. Results of the tests are made available to rice growers throughout the State. On special days in April and September throngs of visitors, mostly members of farm organizations, make excursions to the station.

DE WITT, 26.9 *m.* (189 alt., 2,498 pop.), second town of Arkansas County, has three rice mills and several cotton gins, and is a shipping point for timber and livestock. In the ARKANSAS COUNTY COURTHOUSE, a three-story, cream-colored brick structure erected in 1932, are the State's oldest records, inherited by De Witt when the county seat was moved from Arkansas Post in 1855. Here are registers of civil proceedings dating back to 1803 (earlier ones were moved by the Spaniards to Havana, Cuba) ; land titles in Spanish, French, and English; a county assessment list for 1817, when the total levy covering several thousand square miles was only $782.18.

On Halliburton St. at the north end of town is (R) the HALLIBURTON HOUSE (*private*), a white two-story building with a projecting rear wing, its lines preserved despite remodelings. The house was built in 1854 by Colonel W. H. Halliburton (1816-1912), whose *History of Arkansas County* is a valuable source book.

Left from De Witt on State 1, asphalt-paved, to ST. CHARLES, 16.2 *m.* (200 alt., 412 pop.), in early days a steamboat port, and now a center for White River commercial fishing.

Right from St. Charles on State 17 to the headquarters (L) of the U. S. MIGRATORY GAME BIRD REFUGE (*camping and fishing by permit; no hunting*), 16.6 *m.,* which extends 62 miles along White River and includes more than 90,000 acres of bottom country. Corn and other grains are planted to encourage wild duck and geese to winter at the refuge, rather than feeding in the near-by rice-fields, which have suffered considerable damage from this source in the past.

The White River bank at this point was the scene of a battle on June 7, 1862. On this day, say some historians, was fired "the most destructive single shot of the War between the States." To stop a fleet of Federal ironclads ascending the stream, Confederates under Captain Joseph Fry set up a shore battery at St. Charles and engaged the armored boats, at first futilely. The *Mound City,* however, unwisely opened a porthole. Captain Fry, a West Point graduate and ordnance expert, plumped a cannon ball through the opening, smashing a steam pipe and killing nearly 150 soldiers packed in the ironclad.

Right from the Game Refuge headquarters 0.2 *m.* to (L) the ADOBE HOUSE (*adm. 20¢*), which still bears bullet scars of the battle. Built on the river bank in the 1840's by Colonel Charles Belknap, founder of St. Charles, the house is of dogtrot style but the breezeway has been closed at both ends. The walls are of clay, covered with hard plaster.

South from De Witt, State 1 runs between ricefields which sometimes give way to forests, then open out again beyond the belt of trees.

GILLETT, 40.7 *m.* (183 alt., 781 pop.), at the end of the St. Louis Southwestern Railway's Arkansas County branch, has a rice and a lumber mill on its wide main street, and in season ships pecans from the river bottoms.

At 41.8 *m.* is the junction with the Arkansas Post Road; L. here.

ARKANSAS POST, 50.9 *m.* (178 alt., 64 pop.*), established in 1686, is the oldest white settlement in Arkansas, and was the Territory's first capital. Crude fortifications that once stood near here were manned by the only white garrison in the western valley of the Mississippi.

René Robert Cavelier de la Salle landed at the mouth of the Arkansas on March 14, 1682, on the first journey ever made by white men down the entire length of the Mississippi. For the King of France he claimed all the land drained by the tributary river. Four years later Henri de Tonti descended from the Illinois country to the mouth of the Mississippi to meet La Salle, but failed to find his chief, who had been stranded on the Texas coast, and left a garrison at Arkansas Post on his return trip. A halfway point between the Illinois settlements and the Gulf, the post was maintained by the French during the next three decades with a few soldiers and was visited by an occasional priest.

In 1717 Louisiana passed into control of the Edinburgh promotional genius John Law, whose elaborate plan was later called the "Mississippi Bubble." Law proposed securing control of the monetary system of France and issuing an unlimited quantity of notes. The notes were to be paid off with the wealth expected to flow from the Mississippi Valley.

The project involved populating Louisiana with white settlers, so Law began to recruit immigrants. Most Frenchmen were skeptical of his alluring descriptions of a new country filled with gold, precious stones, and languorous Indian maidens. But the Rhineland gave his pamphlets a warm reception, entire parishes of Germans enrolling as colonists. Many died during the hard voyages, but a number arrived at New Orleans.

Law had reserved for himself the country around Arkansas Post, which he intended to erect into a duchy. In the spring of 1719 he shipped 500 Negroes to the post. The following year about 800 white settlers arrived, mostly Alsatians. Unaccustomed to pioneer life and without food for the winter, they built houses and existed as best they could, mostly by the charity of friendly Indians.

In December 1720, the "Mississippi Bubble" burst, and Law left France. When news of the collapse reached the half-starved colonists at Arkansas Post the following June, they immediately set out for New Orleans, with the intention of returning to Europe. Governor Bienville, however, persuaded them to remain. He gave them land on the Mississippi above New Orleans, in a district still known as the German Coast.

In 1722 Bénard de la Harpe, sent from New Orleans to explore the Arkansas River, wrote that there were 47 persons living at the post in 20 cabins, "badly placed." When he returned a few weeks later, he noted that a shipment of flour, sent by Bienville to prevent abandonment of the colony, had come just in time, "since the settlers had nothing for subsistence and were not able to trade with the Savages." In 1727 Father du Poisson, a newly arrived priest, wrote that 30 Frenchmen had remained.

"Only the excellence of the soil and climate has kept them," Poisson noted, "for in other respects they have received no assistance . . . they now think that the Company of the Indies had no intention of abandoning this district . . . in as much as they had sent a missionary here."

For the remainder of the eighteenth century the post struggled along, its inhabitants living by hunting, fishing, and growing a little wheat. A census taken in 1744 by the Marquis de Vaudreuil, who succeeded Bienville as Governor of Louisiana, indicated that there were 20 white soldiers and 10 Negroes at the post, besides the settlers and traders. Much to the annoyance of the French authorities, outlaws and fugitives from justice sought refuge in the Arkansas country.

British Captain Philip Pittman in 1770 described the post as consisting chiefly of a stockade fort "situated three leagues up the river Arcansas . . . the sides of the interior polygon are about 180 feet, and one three-pounder is mounted in the flanks and faces of each bastion. . . . The fort stands about 200 yards from the waterside and is garrisoned by a captain, a lieutenant, and 30 French soldiers, including sergeants and corporals. There are eight houses without the fort, occupied by as many families. . . . These people subsist mostly by hunting, and every season send to New Orleans great quantities of bear's oil, tallow, salted buffalo meat and a few skins."

In 1763 France had ceded to Spain all of Louisiana west of the Mississippi. When the Spaniards took possession of Arkansas Post they rechristened it Fort Charles III and planned to strengthen and improve its fortifications. They knew that the Arkansas River, with its tributaries the Cimarron and the Canadian, was the road to the Southwest, as American explorers were laboriously to discover half a century later. While nothing came of these plans, the Spaniards continued the French policy of maintaining a close friendship with the Quapaw Indians, who lived up the Arkansas.

In 1783 Chickasaw attacked Arkansas Post so vigorously that its commandant, Jacobo Dubreuil, was compelled to buy "one cask of brandy to revive the troops" and "three rolls of tobacco to please the troops and volunteers who went in pursuit of the enemy." Possibly this battle was only another incident in the long series of difficulties that the French and their allied Quapaw had had with the Chickasaw, but Dubreuil suspected larger designs. An Englishman named James Colbert was living with the Chickasaw. Dubreuil believed that the attack was instigated by the British in an attempt to gain territory west of the Mississippi to replace that lost to the American revolutionaries on the eastern side.

Nevertheless the Spaniards failed to develop the possibilities of their outpost on the Arkansas. In 1800 Napoleon regained Louisiana for France. In 1803 he sold the territory to the United States, and the post was occupied by American troops in 1804.

The low country around the mouth of the Arkansas did not appear particularly inviting to travelers who came down the Mississippi to investigate the new territory. Nuttall observed:

> On this [north] side of the Arkansa the floods cover the whole inter-
> mediate space to White river, a distance of 30 miles. Within this tract,
> cultivation can never take place without recourse to the same industry,
> which has redeemed Holland from the ocean. The singular caprice of the
> river, as it accidentally seeks its way to the sea, meandering through its
> alluvial valley, is truly remarkable. The variation of its channel is almost
> incredible, and the action which it exercises over the destiny of the soil,
> can scarcely be conceived. After pursuing a given course for many ages,
> and slowly encroaching, it has, at length, in many instances cut through
> an isthmus, and thus abandoned perhaps a course of six or eight miles,
> in which the water stagnating, at length becomes totally insulated, and
> thus presents a lagoon or lake . . . nothing yet appears but one vast

trackless wilderness of trees, a dead solemnity. . . . All is rude nature
as it sprang into existence, still preserving its primeval type, its unreclaimed
exuberance.

The settlers from Tennessee and other States pushed on up the river
from the post, seeking higher land. When, after the War of 1812,
American homeseekers in greater numbers began to come down the
Southwest Trail from Missouri, the center of population in the Arkansas country rapidly shifted toward the point where the trail crossed the
Arkansas River, at Little Rock. Despite this the post maintained its
dominant position for a few years longer. A post office was established
here in 1817, and in 1819 William E. Woodruff brought a printing
press up the river and founded the *Arkansas Gazette*. In the latter
year the Arkansas Territory was split off from Missouri and the post
was made its capital. In 1821 the capital was removed to Little Rock
and the *Gazette* followed it shortly.

Arkansas Post still thrived, however, growing to a population of
3,500, because steamboats now churned the river. During the War
between the States both sides recognized the post's military value as
the key to the Arkansas. Assigned 3,000 men by the Confederacy to
defend it, General Thomas J. Churchill built fortifications here. On
January 10, 1863, General John A. McClernand, supported by gunboats, attacked the post with 30,000 Federal troops and, after a two-
day battle, captured the remains of Churchill's army. The post remained in Federal hands for the duration of the war.

After the war railroads penetrated the Southwest and drove the
packets from the rivers. Arkansas Post, birthplace of a region's history, was without a rail connection, and slowly faded. The few families
still in the neighborhood live by farming. The post office was discontinued in 1934, but sentiment brought about its re-establishment in
1939.

ARKANSAS POST STATE PARK (*swimming; unfurnished
cabins 50¢*), created in 1930, adjoins the town. A 62-acre grove
surrounds the lake which covers Confederate trenches. The log cabins
that housed the Arkansas Territorial legislature are long since gone,
but the handmade-brick cistern which lay between them remains. Also
on the grounds is an old well that was probably dug by the eighteenth
century Spanish garrison. A caretaker guides visitors through the park,
pointing out the sites of vanished buildings and of semilegendary
incidents.

Tour 13

Little Rock—Danville—Booneville—Greenwood; 136.2 *m.*, State 10.

Asphalt-paved roadbed between Danville and Havana, Booneville and Green-
wood; elsewhere graveled.
Chicago, Rock Island & Pacific Ry. roughly parallels route between Little
Rock and Booneville.
Accommodations in larger towns only.

High, isolated peaks and ridges rise immediately south of the Arkansas River as it flows through the western third of the State. Between
these isolated elevations and the Ouachita Mountains flows Petit Jean
Creek in a wide valley which parallels long stretches of the Arkansas
River.

After leaving the capital State 10 wedges through the Ouachitas
into Petit Jean Valley, which it follows for some 50 miles. At Booneville the road leaves the valley and passes into the State's most productive coal fields. Except for the mining district the country is thinly
settled, with buildings and folkways reminiscent of pioneer days. Cabins
made of squared logs are not uncommon, and gingham dresses and
overalls are the predominant costume. Subsistence farms are the rule,
the hills not being adapted to large-scale cotton and corn production.

The section is rich in recreational possibilities, and each year more
and more Arkansans fish the clear streams and hunt deer, turkey, 'possum, and 'coon. Development of the Ouachita National Forest and the
Mount Magazine area by the Federal Government is attracting increasing numbers of visitors from outside the State.

Leaving LITTLE ROCK, 0 *m.*, on Cross Street, State 10 finds
itself in the midst of heavily wooded slopes almost before it reaches the
city limits. The road rides a hogback out of the capital. To the south
are rolling ridges of the Ouachitas, to the north, across the Arkansas, is
the impressive bulk of Big Rock, crowned by Fort Roots (*see Tour
5a*). A 92-million-gallon RESERVOIR (L), flashes in the sunlight at
6.8 *m.* Intended as an auxiliary water supply for Little Rock in case
of damage to the pipe line from Lake Winona (*see below*), the reservoir
covers 25 acres and holds enough water to maintain the city for 10
days.

At 10.8 *m.* is the junction with a graveled road.

Right on this road to another junction, 1.5 *m.;* R. (straight ahead) here
to the PULASKI COUNTY PRISON FARM (*visitors admitted*), 3.5 *m.*, a group of

low, white-painted buildings on the sandy Arkansas River bank. Surrounding the buildings are fields of corn, cotton, and vegetables. Here county prisoners work out their misdemeanor sentences to such good advantage that the institution shows an annual profit.

The Joe T. Robinson Consolidated School (L), 14.6 *m.*, is a one-story field-stone building with windows extending almost the full height of the rooms. The school, built with Federal assistance, is typical of the modern centers of instruction which are replacing the traditional one-room schoolhouses where pupils of all grades learned the three R's. Children from as far away as 25 miles are brought each morning and taken home each evening by bus. A gymnasium, a primary unit, and a home-economics cottage adjoin the main building.

Right from the school on a graveled road to PINNACLE MOUNTAIN (R), 2.4 *m.*, an almost symmetrical, cone-shaped peak that rises abruptly from a level cornfield. The elevation, a landmark for early explorers, was called *Mamelle* by the French because of its resemblance to a woman's breast. The name, corrupted to Maumelle, has also been given to two streams in the neighborhood. The steep slopes of Pinnacle, unbroken by motor roads, are frequently climbed by Sunday picnickers from Little Rock.

The road continues, crossing BIG MAUMELLE at 3 *m.*, to the crossroads store at NATURAL STEPS, 3.9 *m.* (268 alt., 85 pop.*); R. here to an old cemetery, 4.2 *m.*, where huge oaks and stunted cedars shade lichen-covered tombstones hand-hewn from native rock; R. again to the end of the road in a farmyard, 4.8 *m.*, which contains the remains of the "natural steps" that gave the community its name. The steps, great chunks of rock projecting from the hillside, descended into the Arkansas River and formed a ready-made steamboat landing. Most of the stone has now been blasted away in the course of revetment work. The river traffic has been taken over by railroads and the stream itself abandoned the landing after the flood of 1927.

At the mouth of Palarm Creek, a short distance up the river from the natural steps, occurred one of the principal military encounters in the Brooks-Baxter "war" of 1874. The struggle, an outgrowth of Reconstruction difficulties, arose over the claims of Elisha Baxter and Joseph Brooks to the governorship. Little Rock was in a state of armed tension, with the Brooks forces holding the Statehouse, from which they had ejected Baxter. A flatboat loaded with munitions was coming to Brooks from Fort Smith. A group of Baxter men boarded the steamer *Hallie,* which had just returned from a successful skirmish near Pine Bluff (*see Pine Bluff*) and set off up the river to intercept the flatboat. The Brooks faction countered by sending a detachment up the Little Rock & Fort Smith Railroad to the Palarm, where they ambushed the *Hallie.* In the exchange of fire three Baxter men were killed. The boat, disabled, drifted ashore near the natural steps, where it was abandoned by its occupants. Several of the wounded were left with farmers to be cared for until they recovered, while the main body returned to Little Rock by land. The Brooks forces meanwhile occupied the *Hallie,* repaired her, and triumphantly docked her at the Statehouse.

State 10 continues westward through forests. A few large stone houses of Little Rock businessmen stand on the tree-covered hillsides, but the neighboring clearings are most often occupied by log homes roofed with hand-cut shingles.

At 24.9 *m.* is the junction with State 113.

Right on this dirt road to a junction at 5.4 *m.;* R. (straight ahead) here to LITTLE ITALY, 8.3 *m.*, an agricultural community of Italians who came from Chicago about 1912. A white church (R) with a pointed steeple on a hilltop marks the center of the settlement. Long rows of grapevines descend the slopes toward Fourche la Fave River and the Arkansas, and there are bonded wineries in the community. Well-cultivated cornfields and cottonfields among the vineyards give the colony a refreshing air of prosperity.

At 33.5 *m.* is the junction with State 9.

Left on this graveled road through rugged woodlands of the Ouachita National Forest to a junction with the Lake Winona road, 6 *m.;* R. here to LAKE WINONA (*fishing, swimming, camping, and picnicking prohibited above dam*), 11 *m.,* a 1,240-acre reservoir backed up into the wooded hills by a dam across Alum Fork. The lake, which holds 14 billion gallons, is the principal source of Little Rock's water supply. A 39-inch pipe line carries the water to the city, where it is filtered. From a field-stone cottage, set in landscaped grounds alongside the dam, the superintendent keeps in constant radio contact with the Little Rock plant.

Turning north at the junction, State 10 runs along the border of the OUACHITA NATIONAL FOREST (*see Resources and Conservation*), passing entrances (L) at 35.1 *m.* and at 37.7 *m.* The road crosses FOURCHE LA FAVE RIVER (Lefevre's Fork), 42.9 *m.,* named for an early French settler. Many Little Rock fishermen contend that this stream provides the finest fishing in the State for bass, crappie, and bream.

The business district of PERRYVILLE, 43.8 *m.* (325 alt., 577 pop.), is built on two sides of the steel-fenced PERRY COUNTY COURT-HOUSE, a two-story brick structure. Perryville, like the county which it serves as a seat of government, depends almost exclusively on agricultural products for its support.

In 1882 Perryville was the scene of a feud which "disturbed the catfish and impelled the bullfrog to lower the tone of his evening hymn," and which gave Opie Read (1852-1939), then with a Little Rock newspaper, an opportunity for one of his classics of humorous reporting. He wrote:

One man was killed, another wounded, and an old lady who had no blood relationship to the affair affirmed before a justice of the peace that her brindled cow had sustained such a fright as to sour her milk. . . . The sheriff came down to Little Rock, called on the governor and swore his inability to handle the trouble. . . . [The governor] took an instantaneous view of the situation and declared Perryville and its back yard under martial law.

The Army got on board a train at Argenta [North Little Rock] and got off at Morrilton, thence marched over to the scene of military activity. The *Gazette* appointed me as war correspondent. Once I had helped Wat Worthen pull a Negro crap game, and was now regarded as a veteran at arms. . . .

The town did not sit up to wait for us, and when we arrived Perryville was asleep. A dog barked and there was talk of immediate court martial, but this was set aside by sane judgment. . . .

Along about 5:16 a rooster crew, and at 7:10 he was served rather raw but hot. At 10 o'clock the court house bell summoned the citizens. They assembled on the public square, shook hands with us and asked us how long we expected to stay. They said that if we weren't in a hurry they might take us fishing.

North of Perryville State 10 cuts through a range of hills which divides Fourche la Fave River from Open Lake Creek.

The two-block-long main street of PERRY, 47.2 m. (295 alt., 377 pop.), at right angles to the highway, is lined with frame stores. On the railroad, Perry is the chief shipping point of the county and has a small lumber mill.

At Perry State 10 turns west and flanks a main line of the Chicago, Rock Island & Pacific Railway, which was pushed through the hills from Little Rock in 1898. The railroad, then the Choctaw & Memphis, spent thousands of dollars advertising in the East to bring settlers to its route. Most of the villages along the tracks were founded by these immigrants.

At OLA, 72.4 m. (355 alt., 839 pop.), the Dardanelle branch of the Chicago, Rock Island & Pacific Railway connects with the main line. General merchandise stores in this quiet little town sell everything from harness to perfume. Two sawmills are the principal sources of occupation for the townspeople.

In Ola is the junction with State 7 (see Tour 8a).

State 10 continues westward through hills that border Petit Jean Valley, crossing country almost uncultivated. Now and then a cornfield interrupts the stretches of brush-covered pasture and small timber. Peas are sometimes grown with corn, serving a double purpose by keeping the weeds down and furnishing food. The road passes another entrance (L) to the OUACHITA NATIONAL FOREST at 82.1 m.

DANVILLE, 83.4 m. (387 alt., 1,010 pop.), on the bank of Petit Jean Creek, is encircled by a rim of hazy blue mountains. The highway, as it passes through the town from east to west, encounters a sawmill and a double row of stores. The YELL COUNTY COURTHOUSE, a two-story stuccoed structure with an open arched hallway through the middle, is topped by a white, railed dome. The square is surrounded by concrete posts set with iron hitching rings.

Danville was founded in 1841 as the seat of Yell County, named for Governor Archibald Yell (see Tour 4b). In 1875 the governmental functions for the northern part of the unit were assigned to Dardanelle (see Tour 6), which has the county's other courthouse. A strictly individual approach to electoral machinery and the counting of ballots has caused the county to be known throughout Arkansas as the "Free State of Yell." Defeated political candidates have sometimes wryly claimed that tombstones and bird dogs voted. A legislative inquiry once revealed that the number of votes in a hill-country township rose on an especially urgent occasion from 16 to 312.

Petit Jean Creek, which State 10 crosses at Danville, is a pleasant, shaded stream that has good fishing. In 1872 Captain Howell put his steamboat, the *Danville,* into regular service carrying freight and passengers down this small river to the Arkansas.

BELLEVILLE, 87.6 *m.* (368 alt., 411 pop.), is the birthplace of Mamie Harris, who later took the name Mary McCormic, and gained international recognition as a singer. Reared in Dardanelle and Ola, the girl attended Ouachita College in Arkadelphia. By way of a Methodist choir in Chicago and a national singing contest sponsored by Mary Garden, she rose to fame, and sang leading soprano roles in American and European opera companies.

GATEWAY PARK (*open*), at the north end of Belleville on the Spring Creek Road, is a tree-shaded municipal grove, with picnic tables and a playground for children.

Right from Belleville on the graveled Spring Creek Road, which passes fertile fields of corn and cotton, to the boundary of the OUACHITA NATIONAL FOREST, 4.1 *m.;* thence through forested hills to SPRING LAKE (*swimming, boating, fishing*), 4.7 *m.*, an 86-acre body of water impounded for recreational purposes in 1937. Along the top of the arched masonry dam runs a walk to the north side of the lake, where the boathouse and bathing beach are situated. The road circles the upper end of the lake and reaches the BEACH at 7.5 *m.*

HAVANA, 92.4 *m.* (375 alt., 449 pop.), in order to accommodate the tourists attracted to Mount Magazine, has erected a string of stores along the highway at right angles to its older business section.

Right from Havana on the graveled Mount Magazine Road toward the huge bulk of MOUNT MAGAZINE, towering above every other peak in Arkansas (2,850 alt.). This "magnificent empurpled mountain," said Nuttall (*Journal of Travels into the Arkansa Territory, 1819*), ". . . from its peculiar form . . . has received the name of the Magazine or Barn by the French hunters." Though the origin of the name is disputed, some historians maintaining that the elevation was the site of Confederate ammunition stores, Nuttall's version seems the most plausible.

The road leaves the fields and enters the Mount Magazine section of the OUACHITA NATIONAL FOREST at 1.9 *m.* Some 90,000 acres of the mountain and its environs were added to the forest in 1938, after several years of development by the Resettlement Administration. The region is used for reforestation and grazing as well as for recreational purposes; experimental plantings of trees and pasture grasses appear in level spots. Curving rapidly upward, the road reaches a PETIT JEAN VALLEY OVERLOOK, 8.6 *m.*, which affords an impressive view of the wide valley and the undulating Ouachitas. At 10.5 *m.* is the junction with a graveled road; L. on this road 2 *m.* to an elaborate lodge and a group of cabins that cling to the edge of the precipice. From CAMERON'S BLUFF, 3 *m.*, a lofty serrated cliff studded with wind-blown cedars on the north side of the mountain, the vast Arkansas Valley comes into view. The blue line of the river itself, limned by its sandy shore, is clearly visible, although some 20 miles distant, and beyond it rise the rugged Boston Mountains, the first great escarpment of the Ozarks. Cut into the sheer edge of the mountain is an amphitheater for public meetings and entertainments. The seating capacity is 1,600. The main Mount Magazine Road descends the north side of the peak to COVE LAKE (*fishing, swimming*), 19.2 *m.*, a beautiful 170-acre body of water backed up among the pine-covered hills by an earth dam across Cove Creek. The road continues down the mountain to PARIS, 27.8 *m.* (410 alt., 3,430 pop.) (*see Tour 6*), which is at the junction with State 22 (*see Tour 6*).

West of Havana State 10 runs for some 20 miles along the ridges at the base of Mount Magazine. The great folds in the peak's façade throw shadows over the pines and oaks, creating innumerable nuances of green as the shade moves with the sun. Old houses on the hillside farms are surrounded with bright red laurel and pink myrtle, set off now and then by the yellow flare of sunflowers.

Between the village of MAGAZINE, 109.1 *m.* (456 alt., 385 pop.), at the western end of the mountain, and Booneville, State 10 descends again into the excellent farm land of Petit Jean Valley. The road is bordered with fields of corn, cotton, tomatoes, and other vegetables. Farmhouses here are large and freshly painted; well-built barns indicate a prospering dairy industry.

BOONEVILLE, 115.7 *m.* (511 alt., 2,324 pop.), southern seat of Logan County, centers around two-story red-brick business buildings at the widened intersection of State 10 and State 23. Three sawmills, railroad switching operations on the Rock Island, and two cotton gins contribute to the support of the town. Its principal income, however, is provided by the Arkansas Tuberculosis Sanatorium (*see below*), which has a monthly pay roll of $11,000 and an annual maintenance cost of some $400,000. Farmers in the neighborhood find the institution a steady market for eggs and poultry, and to a less extent (since the sanatorium has its own herds and gardens) for dairy produce and truck. Eggs, butter, and milk are also shipped west from Booneville on the Rock Island to Oklahoma cities, and northward to the creamery at Bloomer (*see Tour 6*). Within a short distance of Mount Magazine and of the Ouachita National Forest, Booneville has become in recent years a headquarters for quail and deer hunters and for fishermen.

Left from Booneville on asphalt-paved State 116 is the ARKANSAS TUBERCULOSIS SANATORIUM, 3.6 *m.,* high on a hill overlooking the round-topped Ouachitas. The five-story brick and concrete main hospital, completed in 1940, is surrounded by long, low two-story structures, some stuccoed and some frame. Total capacity is about 1,100 patients. The sanatorium has its own post office, school, power plant, and cannery. In the valley below are gardens, vineyards, orchards, and cattle barns. The institution was conceived in 1907 by three Arkansans, who became acquainted at Tucson, Arizona, and laid plans that culminated in the passage of an appropriation by the legislature two years later and the opening of the sanatorium in 1910.

Right from the sanatorium on a graveled road 4.1 *m.* to GOLDEN CITY (550 alt.), a quiet mountain village which was laid out and named in the flush of a gold boom in 1886-87. Little Rock and Fort Smith newspapers carried accounts of lode discoveries running $400 to the ton. Several companies were organized, shafts were sunk, and land speculation became feverish. An "expert" who visited the diggings announced that the discovery was "not a myth by any means." Gold and silver had been found in four distinct lodes, he reported. Many buildings had been erected and the town had grown rapidly when, "in the midst of development the only available sawmill broke down. . . . It is high time," the writer remarked reprovingly, "that the disparagement ignorantly or otherwise leveled at the Golden City discoveries be called off." The town was "bound to be the Leadville of Arkansas," according to one of the mine owners.

The excitement gradually died down, and there were ugly rumors that the mines had been salted with gold from Colorado. The *coup de grâce* was

administered to the boom by the assistant State geologist, Dr. Theo. B. Comstock, who examined the ores and found iron pyrites and copper percussion
caps, but no gold.

From Booneville State 10 swings westward through the Ouachitas.
At times the road rides the ridges and overlooks valleys on each side.
The lowlands are checkered with cornfields, pastures, and patches of
timber.

GREENWOOD, 136.2 *m.* (518 alt., 1,219 pop.) (*see Tour 9b*),
is at the junction with US 71 (*see Tour 9b*).

Tour 14

(Greenville, Miss.)—Lake Village—Crossett—El Dorado—Magnolia
—Texarkana—(Texarkana, Tex.) ; US 82.
Mississippi Line to Texas Line, 192 *m.*

Graveled roadbed between Lake Village and Crossett, Magnolia and Garland
City; elsewhere asphalt-paved.
Missouri Pacific R.R. roughly parallels route between Montrose and Crossett
and between Strong and El Dorado; St. Louis Southwestern Ry. between
Waldo and Texarkana.
Accommodations in larger towns.

In its progress from east to west US 82 recapitulates the economic
history of Arkansas. In the Mississippi Delta the route crosses the rich
cotton land which brought the State its first wealth; near Hamburg it
passes into the remnants of the forests that were cut with reckless
enterprise between 1880 and 1910; next come the second-growth timberlands that were revivified by the first oil boom of the 1920's. The road
then traverses more recently developed oil territory, which utilizes the
latest production methods. Along the westernmost section of the route
are the livestock-raising areas that are probably the eventual hope of
prosperity for the greatest part of the State.

The route crosses the Mississippi near the southeastern corner of
Arkansas and runs generally parallel to the Louisiana Line. The
countryside, part of the Coastal Plain, is flat or rolling; there are no
high peaks or steep valleys.

US 82 crosses the MISSISSIPPI LINE, 0 *m.,* in the middle of the Mississippi River, at a point six miles southwest of Greenville, Mississippi. The bridge, completed in 1940, was the first to span the river between Memphis and Vicksburg.

Following the shore line of horseshoe-shaped LAKE CHICOT (*fishing; crappie, black bass*), formed when the Mississippi cut through one of its own deep curves, US 82 winds among overhanging willows.

Thousands of deer, larger, darker in color, and somewhat slower of movement than upland deer, range the bottoms of Chicot County, particularly the Bœuf River and Macon Bayou regions north of Lake Village. During the hunting season parties come from all over eastern United States and establish camps. The unregistered kill, together with the drownings that occur during each flood, make any accurate count of the deer difficult; apparently, however, the animals continue to increase in number. Special hunting licenses are required in Chicot County.

The LINDBERGH MEMORIAL MONUMENT (R), 7.7 *m.,* commemorates the first night airplane flight made by Charles Lindbergh, in April 1923. The aviator was on his way from St. Louis to Houston and stopped en route at Lake Village. Capitalizing on the novelty of aviation at that time, Lindbergh remained several days to take passengers on short flights over the town. One exceptionally clear moon-lit night he ventured into the air for the first time after dark.

LAKE VILLAGE, 11.3 *m.* (127 alt., 2,045 pop.) (*see Tour 5b*), is at the junction with US 65 (*see Tour 5b*).

Continuing west, US 82 passes through rich black cotton lands representative of the Delta. White-painted manor houses, each with its barns and implement sheds, are set amid acres of cotton dotted with two-room tenant homes. The latter are rough clapboard dwellings sometimes insulated from the tide of cotton by a narrow border of flowers; the scarlets and blues are astonishingly vivid in the limitless snow-white fields. Characteristic of southeast Arkansas farms are small gardens, usually surrounded by a rough picket fence, alongside or behind the tenant's house. In these gardens the 'croppers grow vegetables and greens for their own use.

MONTROSE, 24 *m.* (126 alt., 343 pop.), sometimes called Mount Rose, is a cotton ginning and shipping center on the Missouri Pacific Railroad. Gaudy red shirts, gay ginghams, and shiny new washtubs hang from pegs on the front of general stores to tempt the sharecroppers who come to town on Saturday afternoons. There is little cash in circulation, and buying goes on by a credit system. Purchases are charged to the landlord and are paid for at the close of the season out of the tenant's share of the crop.

In Montrose is the junction with US 165 (*see Tour 16*).

BARTHOLOMEW BAYOU, 28 *m.,* was named for a French settler who lived on the rising end of the bayou near Pine Bluff about 1819. This otherwise sluggish creek clears in April and May, and bream or crappie spiritedly take live minnows, red worms, or crayfish tails.

Between Montrose and Hamburg the highway emerges from the low hills at the Delta's edge to the level reaches of the Coastal Plain. Here the soil has worn thin under a century of unbroken cultivation in cotton, and is now used largely as pasture for cattle and horses. Diversified farming is making some headway, as indicated by patches of corn and vegetables.

The series of low, grass-covered MOUNDS (R), 35.6 m., which dot the level pasture at regular intervals of 15 or 20 yards, are of geological rather than archeological interest. For years they were assumed to have been constructed by the primitive mound-building peoples who inhabited the Mississippi Valley prior to the historical Indians, partly because such burial mounds had actually been found near by along Bartholomew Bayou. Excavations, however, revealed no sign that they were of human origin. There is no agreement among geologists as to the significance of the mounds.

HAMBURG, 43.6 m. (177 alt., 1,939 pop.), seat of Ashley County, is built around a three-story buff-brick courthouse in the middle of the town square, fenced by low iron pickets. Small sawmills add to Hamburg's income, but most of the timber in the region is milled at Crossett, 13 miles west.

Left from Hamburg on State 13, graveled, to a STATE GAME REFUGE, 15 m., a 28,000-acre haven for deer, turkey, migratory birds, and small game. The tract, consisting of cutover timber and swamp land, was leased to the State by landowners and sportsmen of the district in 1931 with the expectation that the game raised here would restock this section of Arkansas.

Between Hamburg and Strong US 82 weaves through a region heavily grown with shortleaf and loblolly pine. The Crossett Lumber Company (see below) insures a perpetual timber supply here by planned cutting and replanting. Fire hazard is reduced by frequent corridors cut through the forest and kept clear of underbrush.

The entire town of CROSSETT, 56.6 m. (159 alt., 4,891 pop.), is owned by the Crossett Lumber Company. Most of the houses are alike, four- and five-room frame structures painted steel gray and surrounded by picket fences. All phases of life—commercial, educational, social, and religious—are controlled by the company; ministers and barbers as well as sawmill workers draw company salaries.

The huge CROSSETT LUMBER COMPANY MILL (open on application), in the center of town, turns out a hundred million board feet of pine a year, besides a quantity of hardwood. A portion of the lumber is processed for protection against dampness and termites. A chemical plant operated in conjunction with the mill manufactures such by-products as charcoal, alcohol, and various types of acid and oil. Logs are hauled by truck to central stations in the forests, from which they are taken by rail to the mill. A pioneer in the practice of scientific reforestation, the company has gained national distinction for its methods. Each summer the senior class of the Yale School of Forestry comes to Crossett for a six-week field-study course.

The KRAFT PAPER AND PULP MILL (*open on application*), owned by the Crossett Company, consumes young yellow pine logs, culled out of the newly planted forests in accordance with the reforestation program.

US 82 crosses the OUACHITA RIVER, 65.5 *m.*, and passes through its swampy bottoms on a long straight fill. Between this point and Strong, lumber activity diminishes. Instead, a few oil derricks appear like rangy skeletons on the horizon.

In STRONG, 80.4 *m.* (115 alt., 762 pop.), called Victoria until 1905, cotton processing and lumbering are the chief sources of revenue. The oil boom of the early 1920's affected this town but little, although some extra cash filtered in from workers in near-by fields. A tornado which caused more than 30 deaths in May 1927 destroyed most of the business district and a part of the residential section. Nearly all the structures were soon rebuilt.

Left from Strong on State 129, graveled, to HUTTIG, 12.6 *m.* (92 alt., 1,379 pop.), another company town, with streets of workers' houses all alike, and a long two-story commissary at its center.

The UNION SAWMILL (*open on application*) is technologically modern. The building is of steel and concrete. The carriages are operated by steam, and the kilns are under thermostatic control. The daily output is about 100,000 board feet.

Between Strong and El Dorado the pine-studded hills that rise from the Ouachita bottoms are spotted with clusters of old wooden derricks, erected during the oil boom of 1921. The oil was drained as wantonly as the timber which covered this country had been cut in the preceding decades. A strike of rich sand meant the sinking of a dozen new wells as close as possible to the first. Large vacant slush pits, their earthen walls blackened, attest the feverish haste of the boom. When a gusher came in there was no time to erect storage tanks or build pipe lines. Frantic owners wanted the oil at once, and the only way of storing it was to build earthen pits, some with a million-barrel capacity. Farmers look back wistfully to the days when oil men begged for the use of their teams at $1 an hour to haul earth.

To the astounded proprietors of the bonanza lands the boom brought a prosperity still more incredible. They moved to town and built pretentious houses. Dazzled by fashionable landscapers, they bought tropical shrubs that quickly died. Characteristic Arkansas wit has exaggerated or invented stories of the absurdities committed by these parvenus. Among the most delightful tales is that of the family suddenly possessed of six wells. The dazed mother, father, and children moved to Dallas and cruised the city in a taxi looking for a house to buy. At last they found one which was not for sale but suited their fancy. The owner, who had no thought of leaving his home, finally agreed to sell the house and its furnishings at an enormous profit. When the family portraits were being taken from the walls preparatory to vacating, the new oil princess objected strenuously: "No, you don't! Pitchers is furniture!"

Exaggeration aside, there is no question that the unexpected wealth produced grotesque results. As the quality and price of petroleum sank, the fortunes of its possessors fell. Checked suits and yellow shoes, tiaras and evening gowns, were put away. Families sold their magnificent homes and retired to less sumptuous residences.

By 1938 the pools of the 1921 boom were nearly dry. The reverberating crude-oil engines pounded at only 1 well in 10, and the oil they pumped was almost asphalt, selling for as little as 16¢ a barrel. The rotting black timbers of the abandoned derricks remain as evidence of Arkansas' first oil boom.

At 98.6 *m.* is the southern junction with US 167 (*see Tour 15*), with which the route unites for 2 miles (*see Tour 15*).

EL DORADO, 100.6 *m.* (281 alt., 15,858 pop.) (*see El Dorado*).

El Dorado is at the junction with State 7 (*see Tour 8b*) and the northern junction of US 167 (*see Tour 15*).

West of El Dorado lies the SHULER OIL FIELD (sometimes spelled Schuler), one of the richest in the State, opened in 1937. The riggings are not found in clusters, as in the old fields farther east, but are spaced at regular intervals, one to each 20-acre tract, in conformity with State regulations designed to maintain gas and water pressure in the pools. A maximum of the reserves can thus be obtained. The derricks are constructed of portable angle-iron sections instead of heavy timbers. When a well is brought in the derrick is dismantled and moved to another drilling site.

Nowhere in the southwest Arkansas fields do the oil wells dominate the scene. The road passes among oak and pine forests broken by small farms but apparently untouched by twentieth-century industry. The odor of gas signalizes the nearness of a producing well. Then the rigging comes into view, surrounded by a cluster of shacks. Beyond, the forest closes in again.

In sections where depletion of a field has reduced the natural gas and water pressure so that the wells no longer gush, pumps are often operated by one-inch steel cables running off into the underbrush, through eyelets bored in wooden posts. The cables lead to a central power station, where a Diesel engine drives a dozen pumps at once, some of them as far as a half-mile away. Where electric power is available, light motors at each pump lift the oil efficiently and economically.

MAGNOLIA, 136 *m.* (207 alt., 4,326 pop.) (*see Tour 12*), is at the junction with US 79 (*see Tour 12*).

Broadcloth produced at the MAGNOLIA COTTON TEXTILE MILL (*open on application*), 137 *m.* (L), is sent to New England to be bleached, dyed, and printed. The plant, opened in 1928 and operated seasonally since then, is one of the few in the Southwest producing high quality cotton cloth of this type.

The employees' houses surrounding the mill constitute an experiment in paternalism that was welcomed by the tenant farmers who furnish the labor. Equipped with electric lights and running water, the dwellings rent for 40¢ a room per week. A community pasture and a small truck patch are available for employees who want to keep milch cows or grow their own vegetables. In summer flowers surround the houses and the mill.

WALDO, 143.5 m. (350 alt., 1,240 pop.), midway between two oil fields, is far enough away from both to have gained little beyond rumors of excitement. Its surrounding cotton lands depleted by 100 years of one-crop cultivation, its best timber taken out by lumber companies at the turn of the century, Waldo exhibits a sleepiness which would typify most southern Arkansas towns but for the rejuvenating influence of oil.

The community, one of the oldest in the region, grew up in the late 1830's along the military road which connected Fort Towson on the upper Red River with the forts on the lower Red. It was known as Lamartine, after the French poet, until the building of the Texas and St. Louis (now St. Louis Southwestern) Railway in the 1880's caused a shift of the town site and of the name.

In Waldo is the junction with State 19 (see Tour 1b).

The worn-out cotton country between Bayou Dorcheat, 150.5 m., and Stamps witnessed an oil boom in 1937. Heavy trucks loaded with rigging labored over hastily built corduroy roads of pine and oak saplings. Men worked all night under the illumination of great floodlights, operated by current from a providentially completed Rural Electrification Administration power line, while the cattle and hogs looked on in amazement.

Said a filling station attendant in BUCKNER, 151.7 m. (274 alt., 450 pop.), in 1937: "We cain't grow cotton no more, and our timber's gone, and I don't see where in hell any cash is ever comin' from."

A few weeks later the oil rush brought hundreds of newcomers to the town, temporarily. Food prices went sky high and beds were at a premium. Wagons and rattletrap Fords gave way to shiny new cars. Repair shops were established for heavy drilling equipment. Buckner's first "skyscraper," a two-story red-brick bank building, appeared.

Conservation of oil resources, enforced by legislative action and use of improved methods, will, apparently, insure Buckner a stable affluence.

STAMPS, 155.8 m. (267 alt., 2,405 pop.), is another waning cotton and lumber town revivified by the oil industry. LAKE JUNE (fishing, motorboating), a 93-acre lake inside the city limits, affords excellent fishing for crappie and largemouthed black bass, as well as white perch, cat, and bream.

Between Stamps and Texarkana US 82 passes through the bottomlands of the Red River. Frequent floods, often severe enough to close the highway, demonstrate here the end-result of heedless cutting of forests and the perennial planting of soil-destroying crops. With all cover removed, there is nothing to restrain the water. Thousands of acres of rich alluvial land are too swampy for cultivation, and lakes and sloughs are common.

Where crops can be raised the deep silt topsoil makes first-rate cotton land, so that large plantations again appear along the highway. Instead of occupying country houses, as do the landlords of the Mississippi Delta, Red River planters usually live in the towns (Lewisville, Garland City, and Texarkana), where social life is not so restricted and where recreational opportunities are more varied.

LEWISVILLE, 160.9 m. (237 alt., 1,314 pop.), like many other Arkansas towns, was spawned by a railroad, and the Texas & St. Louis (now St. Louis Southwestern) station was the first building in the town. Residents moved from Old Lewisville, a few miles away. Lewisville is the seat of Lafayette County.

The steel bridge on which US 82 crosses the Red River, 169 m., cost nearly a half-million dollars. The bridge is approached on long, high fills, built above the high-water line; the earth of which they are constructed was dug out along the sides of the road, leaving deep pits that are usually filled with water.

Shooting alligators is a sport of the Red River bottom dwellers. Hunts are usually held at night, with the hunter cruising the sloughs and swamps in a flat-bottomed boat, playing a flashlight on the water to catch the gleam of a 'gator's eyes. The animals will not attack humans except during the mating season or to protect their young. Sometimes the sport is varied by lassoing—even children can rope 'gators on dry land. The hides dry and crack within a day or so unless special treatment is given them, so no attempt is made to market them commercially.

No great number of alligators inhabit the Red River bottoms. Occasional specimens reach a length of 12 or 14 feet. When the river is low the reptiles burrow into the bank and hibernate for as long as six months. They feed on turtles, fish, wild fowl, and small land animals which they sweep off the bank with their tails. During the mating time, between February and July, the bulls have terrific fights, and their bellowing can be heard a mile away through the swamps. The female deposits her eggs in an above-water nest about four feet high and six feet long, built of logs and grass, and leaves them to hatch in the heat of the decaying grass.

GARLAND CITY, 169.1 m. (227 alt., 325 pop.), is one of the most "washed away" towns in Arkansas. Mud marks on homes and public buildings indicate the height of the latest flood. Several times the river has isolated the town, so that food and medicines have had to be parachuted from airplanes.

Backwater and swamps breed mosquitoes, and mosquitoes bring malaria. As a result, towns in the neighborhood of Garland City are meccas for the itinerant medicine shows that peddle quinine and patented cures to the farm laborers during cotton-gathering time. Actors, stage equipment, and pharmaceutical supplies travel in a truck, the back of which drops down to form a stage. Although the performance sometimes includes monologues, banjo solos, or other forms of entertainment, the favorite attraction is the Indian show. A tired trouper in red paint, feathers, and blanket jigs up and down and utters warwhoops. The barker then gives his spiel about "this wonderful Indian herb medicine, made according to a secret formula handed down from generation to generation, brewed from rare plants and herbs known only to the Red Man, which sells regularly for one dollar a bottle, but tonight—and tonight only—we are making a special price for our friends of *two* bottles for one dollar. . . ."

Garland City was named for Rufus Garland, once owner of the town site. Augustus H. Garland (1832-99), son of Rufus, became a leader in the State's struggle for civil and political rights during the Reconstruction period. A member of the Provisional Congress of the Confederacy during the War between the States, Augustus Garland was refused readmission to practice in the Federal courts after the war. He fought the discrimination, and in the United States Supreme Court won the case known as *ex parte* Garland, in which the law excluding him was declared unconstitutional. In 1867 he was elected to the United States Senate, but was refused a seat by that body. The battle against the carpetbag regime was ended in 1874 with his election as Governor. He surveyed the State's finances and remarked that there was not enough money in the Arkansas treasury to buy kindling wood for his office. His administration made considerable progress toward setting the State on its feet, and in 1877 he was again elected Senator and this time seated. At the conclusion of his term he became Attorney General in President Grover Cleveland's cabinet.

As US 82 emerges from the bottom lands, the rows of cotton give way to alfalfa, clover, and peas, indicative of the switch to stock raising that has occurred under the double pressure of economic interest and governmental encouragement. Between 1930 and 1935 the number of cattle in Miller County doubled and the number of hogs increased 50 per cent. Many students of Arkansas economy believe that eventually cotton growing will yield to cattle raising all over the State except in the richest of the Delta sections. They consider beef production, along with timber farming and truck growing, a likely foundation for future rural prosperity.

At 189.8 *m.* is the junction with a graveled road.

Right on this road to RONDO, 2.1 *m.,* of which nothing now remains but a frame church built in 1861. The church bell is reputed by local tradition to be cast of Mexican dollars.

The first settlers who came to Rondo in the 1830's were not certain whether they were in the United States or Mexico. In 1820, the Territory of Arkansas had defined its boundaries so as to include large stretches of land west of Red River; but Mexico disputed the claim, and many of the settlers in Miller County found it more convenient to adhere to the non-existent authority of the Texas provincial government.

Rondo, despite its position on the Southwest Trail that ran from St. Louis and bisected Arkansas, grew slowly and did not receive a post office until 1858. The name was taken from the French game of chance, *rondeau.*

When Federal armies invaded Arkansas during the War between the States, refugees poured into this southwestern frontier town. Among the fleeing non-combatants was Mrs. Albert Pike, wife of the pioneer poet and general. It was she who advised back-country housewives on Eastern fashions in hats and gowns. Settlers from Texas tramped through Rondo on their way eastward to join Confederate armies.

The State Government of Arkansas had been moved in 1863 from Little Rock to Washington (see Tour 1b), the seat of Hempstead County, in order to escape capture by Federal forces. In 1864 Washington in turn was threatened by General Frederick Steele's army, and the State archives were removed to Rondo, where they were kept in a general store for three months. Thus arose Rondo's claim to have been a wartime capital of the State.

RONDO CEMETERY, 2.5 m., contains the graves of 85 unidentified Confederate soldiers belonging to a regiment swept by disease while stationed at Rondo. The burying ground is maintained by the United Daughters of the Confederacy.

TEXARKANA, 192 m. (337 alt., 11,821 Ark. pop., 17,019 Tex. pop.) (see Texarkana).

Texarkana is at the junction with US 67 (see Tour 1b) and US 71 (see Tour 9b).

At Texarkana, US 82 crosses the Texas Line into Texarkana, Texas.

Tour 15

Little Rock—Fordyce—Hampton—El Dorado—(Ruston, La.) ; 135.7 *m., US* 167.

Asphalt-paved roadbed.
St. Louis Southwestern Ry. roughly parallels route between Fordyce and Thornton; Chicago, Rock Island & Pacific Ry. between Ouachita River and Junction City.
Accommodations in larger towns.

US 167, which drops south from Little Rock to the Louisiana Line, is a point-to-point highway. For long stretches it disregards small settlements to the right and left, and shows neither the wide curves of a road following a water course nor the intricate doublings of a mountain lane that must accommodate itself to ridges and gaps.

Bottomlands through which the road passes are heavily timbered with pine, oak, gum, and hickory. Where sawmills have cut away the shade from the black loam, peanuts, sweet potatoes, corn, and cotton thrive. Deer, turkey, and other game that were part of this country's lure for the first settlers remain in sufficient numbers to attract sportsmen.

US 167 leads south from LITTLE ROCK, 0 *m.,* on Arch Street Pike, and runs through a thinly populated farming region, made to seem even less inhabited by the absence of towns on the route, and by reaches of pine forest. Here and there along the roadside are small sheds, built to shelter children on wet or windy days as they wait for the school bus.

A favorite sport of boys in neighborhoods such as this is "twisting cottontails." Armed only with an ax and pocketknife, the youngsters look for an old field, clover patch, or clearing where the brush piles have not been burned. They take with them the fastest dogs available (it is a good daytime workout for foxhounds), and rabbits are so plentiful here, the sniffing hounds ordinarily lose no time in picking up a warm trail. Pressed closely, the cottontail takes refuge in a hollow log or tree, which he climbs by squeezing his back against one side of the hollow, his feet against the other. The juvenile hunters cut and notch a pole, push the notched end up the hollow against the huddled rabbit, and turn. The twisting takes up the slack in the animal's loose skin, and when the pole is retracted by an experienced hand the rabbit is dragged out, squeaking and kicking.

SHERIDAN, 33.2 *m.* (237 alt., 1,338 pop.) (*see Tour 11*), is at the junction with US 270 (*See Tour 11*).

SALINE RIVER, 46.8 *m.,* winds its way through wild back country that is the habitat of deer, squirrel, and turkey. Farms are scattered, and the land is so flat that high water spreads itself over a considerable area of what might otherwise be good farming soil. Small lakes back from the road, as well as the Saline River, abound in bass and bream.

Much of this land has never been cultivated. The timber cutters were preceded by pioneer hunters, who moved in on what was Quapaw hunting territory. The first settlers who came up the valley of the Saline and settled along Hurricane Creek remembered that the Indians who passed along the trails were a friendly lot, and that they took deerskins, bear oil, venison, and pelts to Pine Bluff. Cotton-growing in the creek bottoms did not begin until the 1840's.

FORDYCE, 68.4 *m.* (290 alt., 3,429 pop.) (*see Tour 12*), is at the northern junction with US 79 (*see Tour 12*), with which the route unites for 5.7 miles (*see Tour 12*).

THORNTON, 74.1 *m.* (314 alt., 550 pop.*) (*see Tour 12*), is at the southern junction with US 79 (*see Tour 12*).

South of Thornton US 167 cuts through tall bottoms forests, pines with a few clumps of willow huddled near the roadside.

At and near HAMPTON, 90.9 *m.* (200 alt., 686 pop.), are several sawmills. Hampton was founded in 1851 as the seat of newly established Calhoun County and incorporated two years later. Business languished during the War between the States, and according to some historians not a merchant remained in the place at the close of the war. Reincorporated in 1871, the town prospered with the growth of the lumber industry and was at one time linked to the Cotton Belt and Rock Island railroads by the short Thornton & Alexander line. With the dwindling of the timber and the development of highways the route was abandoned.

CALION, 106.3 *m.* (93 alt., 712 pop.), at the south end of a bridge spanning the Ouachita River, is named for Calhoun and Union Counties. The bluff on which the town is built marked a crossing for the Indian traces, several of which joined here, and has a fairly creditable claim to being the site of Utiangue, the Indian village at which De Soto and his party built a stockade and passed the winter of 1541.

In the latter half of the nineteenth century the bluff, then known as El Dorado Landing, was a regular stopping point for the packets that went on to Camden and Arkadelphia. Building of the Iron Mountain and Cotton Belt railroads through southwest Arkansas in the 1870's and 1880's reduced the river traffic, and by the end of the century El Dorado Landing, no longer a steamboat port, had disappeared from the map. In 1903, however, the Little Rock Southern (now Chicago, Rock Island, & Pacific) Railway constructed a line from Haskell

Junction, near Benton, to the town of El Dorado. The abandoned landing was the best spot for the tracks to cross the Ouachita River, and the new town of Calion soon grew here. In 1908 a store and post office was established, and shortly afterwards sawmills began to appear. In 1920 the town was incorporated. Floods in 1927 and 1930 took lumber from Calion mill yards and scattered the boards all over Louisiana. Nevertheless, the settlement went on growing, and construction of a highway bridge across the Ouachita in 1930 increased its trade.

The final chapter in Calion's comeback was written with the building in 1931-32 of the long corrugated-iron SHIPPING TERMINAL and DOCKS by a newly organized barge line. Today, strings of barges ascend the Ouachita, made navigable by Government-constructed dams and locks, and Calion ships thousands of bales of cotton each year to the warehouses at New Orleans.

Left from Calion on a graveled road, which follows the Ouachita, to 1,800-acre CALION LAKE, 1 m., created in 1936 by damming a creek at the base of a high bluff. Besides being popular for crappie and bass fishing, the lake is used by an El Dorado motorboat club for races every August.

At CHAMPAGNOLLE LANDING, 2.6 m. (98 alt., 15 pop.*), a few tumble-down houses mark the site of one of the oldest settlements in southern Arkansas. Carvings on beech trees have led residents to believe that the first settlers came in 1818. There is also a local tradition that Daniel Boone was in the habit of camping on this hill in his wanderings. First called Scarborough Landing, the settlement was renamed Union Courthouse when it became the first headquarters of Union County in 1840. Four years later the seat of government was moved to El Dorado and the landing was given its present name. Champagnolle continued as a cotton and lumber port for another quarter-century, but declined after the railroads were built.

In 1934 Colonel T. H. Barton, head of the Lion Oil Refining Company of El Dorado (*see El Dorado*), decided to establish an oil-shipping station at Champagnolle. A 4-inch pipe line was laid from the refinery at El Dorado, 15 miles away. Petroleum products are now pumped directly from the refinery into tank barges at the terminal. Company equipment consists of a dock and a valve-control house, set in landscaped grounds. Although Champagnolle has again become a port, the bustling and sometimes rowdy atmosphere of the old river days has given way to quiet efficiency.

At 107.8 m. is a roadside campsite built by El Dorado businessmen. Farther south are great, red, petroleum storage tanks, 112.5 m., some with a network of lightning rods built around them, like the web of a giant spider.

A blackened scar (R) shows where a tank burned. Intense heat shriveled the near-by pines and melted the tank walls like solder. The roar of the conflagration was heard and the long flames shooting skyward were discernible all over the countryside. Billowy masses of black smoke, typical of petroleum fires, reflected the light of the reddish-orange flames, shedding a glow over the neighborhood. As the walls crumpled, the oil, bearing its peculiar fire (the flames, which are the combustion of gases released by the heated oil, seldom touch the face of the petroleum but play a little above it), spilled out and ran down the slope northward, where it completed the work of destroying the pine grove and searing the earth. Safety methods now employed reduce fire hazards to a minimum.

EL DORADO, 118.4 *m.* (281 alt., 15,858 pop.) (*see El Dorado*). El Dorado is at the junction with State 7 (*see Tour 8b*), and the western junction with US 82 (*see Tour 14*), with which the route unites for two miles.

Cotton appears between forest lands south of El Dorado, but woods still predominate in the low, flat bottoms. The moss becomes more luxuriant. Giant cypresses, with their peculiar knees and wide, spreading bases, become more numerous.

At 120.4 *m.* is the eastern junction with US 82 (*see Tour 14*).

JUNCTION CITY, 135.7 *m.* (176 alt., 797 pop.), is astride the Arkansas-Louisiana Line. Most of the business establishments facing the main street are on the Arkansas side of the boundary, as is the town's principal industrial plant, a lumber mill. The combined population of the Louisiana and Arkansas portions of the settlement is 1,152. US 167 crosses the LOUISIANA LINE here, 36.3 miles north of Ruston, Louisiana.

Tour 16

Junction with US 65—Dermott—Montrose—Wilmot—(Monroe, La.); 46.6 *m.,* US 165.

Asphalt-paved between Junction with US 65 and Jerome; elsewhere graveled.
Missouri Pacific R.R. parallels route throughout.
Accommodations in Dermott.

US 165 follows the valley of Bartholomew Bayou through the western edge of the lower Arkansas Delta. Plantations stretch alongside the road and continue east to the Mississippi levees. In the opposite direction, beyond the bayou, the land rises gradually in tree-covered slopes, then drops again into the valleys of the Saline and Ouachita Rivers.

The country along this highway, like most of the Delta region, was covered with virgin timber a half-century ago. Towns on the route usually began as lumber camps and gradually became cotton-marketing centers when the land was cleared and planted. Small sawmills and woodworking plants still operate, along with gins and cotton-loading sheds. Diversified farming and stock raising have gained momentum during the last decade and promise higher living standards than either lumber or cotton provided.

US 165 branches from US 65 (*see Tour 5b*), 0 *m.*, at a point 1.7 miles east of McGehee (*see Tour 5b*), passing rows of sharecropper houses as it progresses southward. Patches of timber occasionally break the expanse of fields. Some of the stands contain new clearings, with acres of stumps still surrounding the recently constructed cabins.

DERMOTT, 7.1 *m.* (148 alt., 3,083 pop.), a trading point for four adjacent counties, was named for members of the McDermott family who settled here in 1832. Charles McDermott's house was an overnight stopping point for westward travelers who crossed the Mississippi at Gaines' Landing. Slaves brought water in cedar tubs for the guests. McDermott's enthusiasm for building flying machines took him to Washington to secure patents, and brought him the nickname of "Flying Machine Charlie."

The building of the Iron Mountain Railway (now Missouri Pacific) in 1887 brought about Dermott's beginning as a town. The lumber industry boomed population and supported two large hotels. Exhaustion of the first-rate timber brought the inevitable slump, but agricultural marketing stabilized business and income.

Railroad tracks mark the center of Dermott; the business district spreads from a park beside them. Present-day industry includes sawmills, stave mills, a handle factory which ships much of its output to England, and a pecan-shelling plant employing about 100 people seasonally.

At 11.1 *m.* is the junction with a graveled road.

Right on this road to LAKE WALLACE (*bass, crappie, bream*), 0.5 *m.*, artificially created in an abandoned bend of Bartholomew Bayou. The lake, studded with cypress trees and stumps, is 8 miles long and is bordered by a 200-acre park belonging to the town of Dermott.

US 165 continues southward past two- and three-room Negro houses frequently bordered by vegetable patches and chicken yards. Sometimes the farmers go to Dermott on Saturday afternoons to exchange their poultry, eggs, and produce for shoes and store clothes. Some of the trade, however, is carried on by "rolling stores," necessary institutions in rural Arkansas. These trucks, outfitted with stocks of manufactured goods, groceries, and farm implements, chug up to the farmers' doors. The drivers take payment in kind, and make the return trip with hen coops lashed on top of their vehicles and egg crates piled inside. Broilers and eggs are picked up at Dermott and other towns by cross-country trucks and sold in the large-city markets.

JEROME, 17.3 *m.* (133 alt., 112 pop.), at the beginning of 1939 was well on its way toward becoming a ghost town. The timber that had once made the place a noisy lumber camp was gone. Farmers were unwilling or unable to rent the cleared land. The new cotton gin, erected about 1933, had never been used. Population had shrunk to about a quarter of the 1920 figure.

In March 1939 the Farm Security Administration purchased the town and made it the headquarters of a 3,535-acre rehabilitation project for low-income families. Old houses were repaired, mill sheds converted into barns, and other buildings utilized for community purposes. The land was divided into farm units averaging 54 acres, each with its residence, barn, and garden.

MONTROSE, 24.5 m. (126 alt., 343 pop.) (see Tour 14), is at the junction with US 82 (see Tour 14).

Horses, occasionally used for saddle purposes by the planters, graze along the highway with the cattle, and now and then a bewildered colt may get into the middle of the road in front of an automobile and race awkwardly along for several hundred feet, uncertain which way to turn off. Motorists attentive to the variety of fauna encountered on Arkansas roads may remember that wild birds invariably get out of the way, hens make two or three false starts but usually escape unharmed, a litter of pigs will parade soberly across with no monkeyshines, horses ordinarily stick to the shoulders and ditches, mules are unpredictable but know how to take care of themselves, dogs dart from under the wheel at the last moment, and only cows are completely oblivious; a herd of cattle on the road is the signal to slow down to five miles an hour or to come to a full stop.

PORTLAND, 28.9 m. (129 alt., 518 pop.), and PARKDALE, 37.1 m. (119 alt., 278 pop.), are rows of brick stores along the road opposite the railroad track, with blocks of frame houses behind them fading into small farms and distant cottonfields.

WILMOT, 41.5 m. (115 alt., 625 pop.), is similarly constructed; across the track (R) is ENTERPRISE LAKE (bass, crappie, bream), a cut-off horseshoe of Bartholomew Bayou owned and stocked by the State. Cypresses projecting over the lake's entire area give it a deceptive appearance of shallowness, but actually it is 10 to 15 feet deep in most places.

US 165 crosses the LOUISIANA LINE at 46.6 m., at a point 52.1 miles north of Monroe, Louisiana.

Tour 17

Mammoth Spring—Salem—Melbourne—Batesville—Bradford; 106 *m., State 9, State 69, State 11.*

Graveled roadbed, one short asphalt- and concrete-paved section. Accommodations in Mammoth Spring and Batesville.

This route loops southward through thinly settled Ozark Mountain country to reach the White River at Batesville, one of the oldest and most important of the upland towns. South of the river the slopes become gentler, softening the contrast between the mountain region and the level country east of Bradford, where the route joins US 67.

Timber and native stone are the building materials of the hills. Hand-split rails fence the fields from wandering stock. Older homes are built of logs, usually squared, and sometimes given a thick coating of whitewash. Or, to harmonize with the forest colors, the logs are painted green and the chinking white. Many of the newer houses are trim rock structures, occasionally in original designs, set off by low stone walls around which chipmunks scurry.

State 9 branches southwest from US 63 (*see Tour 7*) in MAMMOTH SPRING, 0 *m.* (549 alt., 666 pop.) (*see Tour 7*), and climbs immediately into hills covered by red and white oak. Only the valley bottoms and more gentle hillsides are in cultivation, and the rocks in creek beds show why this is so. Farmers pick the larger slabs from the sward and stack them to bolster a caving bank or block a gully, or, like New England plowmen, heap them into walls between the fields. When farms in this area have been stripped of their trees the earth is easily washed away, so that fields of considerable fertility may in a decade become useless even for pasture unless erosion is carefully controlled. An occasional deserted log cabin, with its back broken and windows gaping, bears evidence to the difficulty of grubbing a living from rocky soil by means of agriculture designed for the lowlands. A few vineyards and cattle indicate a trend toward a type of agriculture adapted to the rugged terrain. Terraces to check the runoff water run like welts across nearly every cultivated field. Contour plowing, strip farming, and cover cropping are increasingly practiced in the region.

CAMP, 13.4 *m.* (121 pop.*), was originally named Indian Camp, because the presence of mounds near by suggested to the settlement's founders that the spot had once been a tribal center. An old log cabin

(L), built about 1870, was the first building of the town. The second structure was a general store, erected in 1876; its walls seem to be preserved in the present store (R).

State 9 crosses SOUTH FORK, a branch of Spring River, at 18.2 m.

SALEM, 19.5 m. (665 alt., 574 pop.) (see Tour 4a), is at the junction with US 62 (see Tour 4a).

South of OXFORD, 32.1 m. (811 alt., 225 pop.*), is a cedar thicket typical of the growth that springs up on slopes where rocks and shallow soil starve out oaks and hickories. Watercourses, filled to the brim after a rain but dry between showers, thread through the clearings.

At 37.6 m. is the junction (R) with State 56 (see Tour 4a).

Whitewashed sentinel poles along the sides of the road mark concrete culvert heads, which are often hidden under the ballast piled by road graders.

MELBOURNE, 44.3 m. (604 alt., 567 pop.), affords a stretch of pavement and a glimpse of the American Legion white-mortared log hut (R). The town extends around the IZARD COUNTY COURTHOUSE, a two-story structure of rough-chipped Batesville limestone, which harmonizes well with the buildings surrounding it.

Apparently, the first white settler in what is now Izard County was John Lafferty, a Revolutionary War veteran who settled originally in North Carolina. After his marriage he went to the Cumberland district of Tennessee, then moved with his family to Arkansas in 1807. Lafferty put up a log cabin alongside a creek that was later named for him, and cleared a small farm in the "Barrens." His first crops were seriously damaged by "bears and buffaloes . . . in the fall." During the War of 1812 Lafferty went back to Tennessee to join the army. At the Battle of New Orleans he received a wound that caused his death shortly after he came back to his Arkansas cabin in 1815.

In Melbourne is the junction with State 69; L. here.

At 52.1 m. is the junction with a graveled road.

Right on this road to a timbered LOOKOUT TOWER (open), 0.3 m., manned by enrollees from the Negro CCC camp at its base. The tower commands a view of about 35 miles, and maintains communication with other lookout stations by telephone.

The early morning traveler who happens to see a short, bulky animal scuttle across the road to a den in the roots of an old stump has probably surprised a woodchuck. Very common in the region, the woodchuck, or groundhog, is about 20 inches long, heavy, thickly furred, and has long claws for digging. Though no mean antagonist when cornered, he usually prefers to run for a hollow tree or burrow, and to extract him from it is a perplexing task. Twisting a rabbit out of a log is not difficult, but the woodchuck, braced with his short, powerful forelegs, is almost impossible to budge. Only smoke, or a barbed-wire twist, can bring him out to face the dog. The woodchuck is quite capable of besting an ordinary mongrel in a rough and tumble, but fares badly with a trained hunting dog or an Airedale.

MOUNT PLEASANT, 57 m. (500 alt., 200 pop.*), was first called Barren Fork, because settlers erroneously supposed that the treeless tract between Poke (now Polk) Bayou and Lafferty Creek was not fertile. The post office established in 1876 was given the name Barren Fork, as was an academy which operated from 1878 until it burned in 1902. A few years later, according to the Melbourne *Times,* a girl from the village attending boarding school was plagued by her classmates with jokes about her home town's name. On her return she got her father to circulate a petition that resulted in an official change to "Mount Pleasant" in 1914. The township still appears on the map as Barren Fork.

CUSHMAN, 64.1 m. (712 alt., 427 pop.), owes its existence largely to intermittent booms in the manganese fields that surround the town. The earliest boom occurred in 1850-52, when the mineral was discovered. Ore then was ground in crude mills made of logs set with railroad spikes, and hauled to the White River by ox teams. The area became important in the 1880's, but the most extensive activity occurred during the World War, when more than 200 pits were worked. A new boom began in 1939.

The principal use of manganese is as an alloy for steel. In the Cushman area today, individual pit mining, on a hit-or-miss basis, is the rule. Prospectors select a likely looking spot and begin digging with pick and shovel. If they happen to strike a vein of ore they haul the rock to the surface with a hand- or mule-powered windlass. Proceeds are shared with the owner of the land. On rare occasions somebody hits a vein that nets a few hundred dollars, but until now most of the miners have scraped out a scant living.

Geologists believe that the Independence County fields could be developed to compete with manganese areas abroad if a certain process of extracting the metal were used. Such a process has been discovered, but requires furnaces that use cheap fuel or power, not yet available.

Right from Cushman on an unimproved road that follows the base of the first hill to the CLUBHOUSE MINE, 0.7 m., one of the few mechanized manganese workings in the district. Compressed air for drills is carried by pipes from an engine room a mile or more away. Ore is blasted from tunnels in the hillside and moved out of the mine on handcars running on tracks. The ventilation shafts on the mountain top are surmounted by sapling towers that carry a red flag, used by drill operators to signal engineers at the powerhouse.

A spring (L) at 68 m. was dammed many years ago, forming a pool large enough to be called a small lake. The water provides power for SPRING MILL (*open*). A later frame addition almost hides the original mill structure, made of hand-hewed logs fastened with wooden pegs, and partly covered with weather-boarding held in place by old-fashioned square nails. Almost all of the equipment stands just as it was fashioned—the wheel, out of sight under the floor, the shafts and gears that transmit the power, and the wooden crane used to lift the heavy stone burrs out for sharpening. About the time the mill was built considerable wheat was grown in this part of the State. Harvesting was done with scythes, and rack-like attachments called "cradles" caught the wheat as it was mowed. The sheaves were flailed on a blanket or wagon sheet to beat the grain from the heads. Then the grain was poured from an edge of the roof while men standing on the porch fanned the stream vigorously to blow out the chaff. When cheap flour from the Western wheat belt caused a shift to corn planting, new burrs designed for grinding corn were shipped in from France. The old cedar worm-drive and casing used in bolting the crushed wheat still hang across the rafters.

At 69.1 *m.* is the junction with a graveled road.

Right on this road is the BATESVILLE WHITE LIME COMPANY PLANT (*open 1-4 workdays; guides*), 1.9 *m.* The plant is housed in a series of corrugated-iron buildings set into the side of a hill. Limestone is quarried about three miles west and hauled in narrow-gauge railroad cars. In the yard long ricks of hardwood, cut by farmers, furnish fuel for furnaces that swallow nine cords apiece at a burning.

Limestone is dumped into the top of the kilns, kept glowing 24 hours a day. The heat releases carbon dioxide, leaving pure lime. Between 36 and 48 hours are required for the process, after which the burned lime is drawn off in trundles at the bottom. Most of the lime is sold to what the trade calls "chemical industries." Paper-making pulp mills are among the largest purchasers. At the back of the plant limestone rubble is crushed into railroad ballast and road gravel.

The LIVESTOCK AND FORESTRY BRANCH EXPERIMENT STATION (*visitors admitted*), 7.8 *m.,* is the largest of four branch stations maintained by the University of Arkansas College of Agriculture. Selection of the 3,000-acre tract, given to the University by Independence County in 1937, was based on the fact that its hills and valleys contain practically every kind of soil in northern Arkansas, from light sand to alluvium and heavy clay. Work of the staff includes field experimentation in pasture and feed crops, breeding and developing varieties of beef and dairy cattle, sheep, hogs, and goats, research and demonstration of soil conservation methods, and studies of timber-growing.

Rocky knolls, hillsides, and hollows on the station area afford an unusual opportunity for studying soil erosion under varying conditions. The U. S. Soil Conservation Service has set up devices to measure the quantities of soil washed away from test plots under various crops and systems of cultivation. Test acres are banked on three sides by ridges to prevent any escape of runoff water or dirt, while a concrete trough is sunk along the fourth side, at the foot of the field. The trough carries all drainage water through a flume to instruments which record its volume and take samples for analysis.

Striking examples of gully redemption are demonstrated on badly eroded slopes. Most impressive of the object-lessons is a mile-long sodded watercourse with its head near the administration buildings. When the land was taken over in 1937 a deep cut had ripped open the lower fields. Now the water that pours from the sodded, smoothed-in gully after a heavy rain is almost as clear as the flow from a spring.

BATESVILLE, 74.1 *m.* (266 alt., 5,267 pop.), at the point where the White River emerges from the Ozarks, is a processing center for both lowland and upland products. Here are gins and a compress, as well as stave-bolt mills. From the rolling farms of the valley edge come fruits, poultry, and milk. From the mountains come marble and manganese. The town is the seat of Independence County.

About 1812 John Reed, from Missouri, built a house at the mouth of Poke Bayou, where a fork of the Southwest Trail crossed the White River. Here he traded whisky and supplies for hides and furs. Wild game was amazingly abundant in the valley in Reed's day. Indeed, a half-century later a politician reputedly climaxed his appeals to voters by harking back to the times when he had heard resounding through the forests "the angry roar of the lion and the fierce scream of the panther and the heavy tread of the elephant."

A ferry was put into use at Poke Bayou as early as 1818, and the thriving village that grew up was renamed Batesville for Territorial Judge James Woodson Bates. In 1831 the *Waverly,* first steamboat to ascend the White River to this point, docked at Batesville, and after that stern-wheelers called at the town whenever the river was high enough. Among the early residents of Batesville was Colonel Charles Fenton Mercer Noland, who gained fame in the East for his humorous sketches published under the name "Pete Whetstone."

The pioneers found deposits of black marble in the Ozarks north and west of Batesville, and polished pieces of the jet stone to ornament their homes, but commercial quarrying awaited railroads and highways. Operations today depend upon orders, and shift from point to point as veins run out or become streaked. There are no well-established quarries where long-continued operations are carried on. Marble from Batesville has been used in the Arkansas State Capitol, in the Army and Navy Hospital at Hot Springs, and in public buildings throughout the United States. In recent years the product has begun to compete with Belgian jet stone. Small pieces are used for table tops and other decoration, and scraps for terrazzo.

ARKANSAS COLLEGE, near the center of town at Boswell and 8th Sts., was incorporated in 1836 as Batesville Academy. Townspeople erected a costly building that burned before the first class had met. The rebuilt academy passed into the hands of the Presbyterian Church, but classes were discontinued during the War between the States. In 1868 the school was re-established, and four years later became Arkansas College. In the poverty-stricken Reconstruction period classes met in kitchens, and the president sadly wrote that "it would have been from a human standpoint a more hopeful undertaking at the time and under all the existing circumstances to have started to build a railroad from the White River to the Pacific Ocean with a pick and shovel and $50 to start on." The school, still operated by the Presbyterian Church, is an accredited co-educational institution, which offers a 4-year course and has an average attendance of 200.

Batesville's WHITE RIVER WHARF-STADIUM, on the river front, is the scene of an annual water carnival that attracts spectators and contestants from the entire Ozark area. Diving and swimming meets, speedboat regattas, and a bathing beauty contest feature the program, usually held in August. The concrete stadium, completed in 1939, seats about 6,000 persons, and has a landing chute and dock.

In Batesville is the junction (L) with State 11 (*see Tour 4a*); here also is the junction (R) with State 11, on which the route continues south.

1. Left from Batesville on an unimproved road to the WHITE RIVER DAM AND LOCKS, 1.6 *m.*, built in 1900 for flood control and navigation purposes. This dam, with two others at ten-mile intervals up the river, enables boats of three-foot draft to ascend as far as Guion, above Batesville. River traffic is light; the principal utility of the dams is in restraining high water. A small park borders the dam, and near by are buildings of the U. S. Engineers, who maintain dredges to keep the channel clear and supervise revetment work.

2. Left from Batesville on State 14, a graveled road which winds among low hills covered with stands of second-growth oak and gum. In the neighborhood of SULPHUR ROCK, 8.7 *m.* (312 alt., 181 pop.), the road emerges into the White River bottoms and passes rich fields of cotton and corn.

The town of NEWARK, 14.8 *m.* (243 alt., 802 pop.), has erected a row of elaborate electric light standards down the middle of its broad main street, which is bounded on the south side by the tracks of the Missouri Pacific's White River line.

Left from Newark on a graveled road to the junction with an unimproved road, 2.3 *m.;* L. here 3.4 *m.* to KOLETA'S KURIO KABIN (*contributions voluntary*), filled with a collection of minerals, precious stones, Indian relics, pioneer furniture, fossils, and miscellanea. Koleta Walker, the owner, began the collection casually a few years ago by gathering curious rock specimens.

At 19.6 *m.* on State 14 is a FERRY (*passenger cars 25¢, trucks 50¢*) crossing the White River. The "Oil Trough Barge," as the ferry is called, is a flat-bottomed, engine-propelled scow, held on its course by trolleys riding a steel cable.

OIL TROUGH, 20.6 *m.* (237 alt., 200 pop.*), takes its name, according to residents, from the bear oil shipped from here during the earliest days of white settlement. Tree trunks were hollowed out with axes, the troughs were packed with bear grease, rafted together, and floated as far as New Orleans. The grease was used for cooking, grooming the hair, and dressing leather. Other uses were sometimes found for bear fat: an early-day Mississippi naturalist told of an Arkansas hunter "caught out many miles from home in the snow" who "only preserved himself (not being able to procure a fire) by opening the bear, removing the viscera & laying himself in the body, which in morning was frozen stiff."

At 30.2 *m.* on State 14 is the junction with US 67 (*see Tour 1a*).

South of Batesville State 11 crosses WHITE RIVER, 75 *m.*, on a $300,000 steel and concrete bridge. At Batesville the stream leaves the mountains, to wander through alluvial regions toward the Mississippi. Of White River's upper reaches, Henry Rowe Schoolcraft said in 1819: "Its waters, unlike most of the western rivers, are beautifully clear and transparent, being wholly made up of springs which gush from the flinty hills that are found for more than half its length, within a few miles of, often immediately upon its banks."

Ramsey Mountain, where State 11 tops the crest of the valley wall, gives an excellent view across the green river bottoms to Batesville, with Ozark hills in the background, and a sheet of water spilling over the White River dam in the right foreground.

At 76.6 *m.* is the junction with State 110.

Left on this graveled road, which follows the valley downstream, to the SALADO CREEK BRIDGE, 6.8 *m.,* an impressive example of stone-masonry. The graceful double arch was in use from 1870 until 1939.

Almost hidden among cedars between two hills is a SPRINGHOUSE (*open*), 85.3 *m.,* constructed in 1850, a structure of rough stone blocks tapering to a gable. The roof is of rafter and beam construction, covered by shingles. Many such shelters appear in the Ozarks, although most of them are neither so old nor so solidly built. Springhouses serve to protect the water in which milk, butter, and eggs are chilled. Mountain boys, after a hot day in the fields or an arduous squirrel hunt, sometimes steal into the nearest springhouse and refresh themselves with cold buttermilk taken from a crock set deep in the gravelly spring bottom.

A few steps up the hill from the springhouse is a cave, one of many in the limestone country. Exploring parties have wandered through the various passageways without finding any end.

PLEASANT PLAINS, 92 *m.* (552 alt., 156 pop.), is the last of the mountain towns on the route, Bradford being more than 300 feet lower, and just on the edge of the foothills.

BRADFORD, 106 *m.* (243 alt., 681 pop.) (*see Tour 1a*), is at the junction with US 67 (*see Tour 1a*).

PART IV

Appendices

Chronology

1541   Hernando de Soto and his followers, first white men to visit Arkansas, spend nearly a year in explorations.

1542   De Soto party leaves Arkansas, following the Ouachita River southeastward.

1673   Marquette and Joliet descend the Mississippi River to the mouth of the Arkansas.

1682   La Salle descends Mississippi to its mouth and claims the entire valley for France, naming it Louisiana.

1686   De Tonti establishes Arkansas Post, first white settlement in lower Mississippi Valley.

1687   Survivors of La Salle colonizing party, headed by Joutel, reach Arkansas Post after difficult journey from the Texas coast.

1719   John Law colony established at Arkansas Post.

1721   John Law colony abandoned, as "Mississippi Bubble" bursts.

1722   La Harpe expedition from New Orleans explores the Arkansas River.

1744   French census lists 20 white soldiers, 10 Negroes at Arkansas Post, besides settlers and traders.

1766   François d'Armand opens fur trading post at mouth of White River.

1769   Spaniards take over Louisiana, rename Arkansas Post Fort Charles III.

1794   Cherokee involved in Muscle Shoals (Tennessee) "massacre" migrate to Arkansas.

1797   Spanish garrison, retreating from site of Memphis, erects Fort Esperanza, later called Hopefield.

1799   Spanish census lists 368 people in Arkansas District.

1800   Spain returns Louisiana to France by secret treaty.

1803   United States purchases Louisiana for $15,000,000.

1804   United States troops occupy Arkansas Post.
William Dunbar and George Hunter explore the Ouachita River, visit Hot Springs.

1806   Lieutenant James B. Wilkinson, detached from Pike's party in Kansas, explores Arkansas River to the Mississippi.
District of Arkansas set up as part of Louisiana Territory.

1807   John Lafferty settles near upper White River.
Major John Pyeatt founds community at Crystal Hill.

1808   Osage vacate area within limits of present Arkansas.

1809   Jacob Wolf builds house at Norfork and opens trading post.

1810   Population 1,062 (first United States census).

1811   New Madrid earthquake shakes central Mississippi Valley, causing topographical changes in Arkansas.

John Hemphill sets up salt works at Blakeleytown, near Arkadelphia.

1812   Territory of Missouri (including Arkansas) created.

1813   Missouri Territorial Legislature establishes Arkansas County.

Major William Lovely sent as Indian agent to Cherokee.

1815   Lawrence County set up, Davidsonville becomes county seat.

1817   Davidsonville acquires first Arkansas post office, Arkansas Post the second.

Large group of Cherokee exchange eastern holdings for land in Arkansas.

Major William Bradford builds Fort Smith as Indian outpost.

1818   Quapaw treaty cedes to United States nearly all land between Arkansas and Red Rivers.

Ferry operates at Batesville (then called Poke Bayou).

Henry Schoolcraft explores upper White River.

Three new counties (Clark, Hempstead, Pulaski) created.

1819   Arkansas becomes a Territory, James I. Miller first Governor.

Arkansas Gazette founded at Arkansas Post.

Joseph Bonne settles at Pine Bluff (first called Mount Marie).

Thomas Nuttall, scientist and writer, explores the Arkansas.

1820   Population 14,273.

Post office opens at Little Rock.

1821   Capital moved from Arkansas Post to Little Rock.

1822   Dwight Mission, near present-day Russellville, opens school for Cherokee.

First steamboat, *Eagle,* reaches Little Rock.

1824   Congress grants $15,000 for military road from Memphis to Little Rock.

1826   First steam sawmill in Arkansas begins operations at Helena.

1827   Robert Crittenden, Secretary of Arkansas Territory, kills Henry Conway, Territorial Delegate to Congress, in duel.

1828   Cherokee by treaty agree to leave Arkansas; present western boundary line established.

1830   Population 30,388.

Congress passes Indian Removal Act, and great migration through Arkansas to Indian Territory begins.

1831   Steamboat *Waverly* reaches Batesville.

1832   Congress makes Hot Springs a Federal reservation.

1833   Sam Houston leaves Cherokee and, in Washington, plans Texas revolution.

1834   First theatrical performance given in Little Rock.

George Featherstonhaugh, English geologist, visits Arkansas.

Little Rock lionizes Davy Crockett, passing through on his way to Texas.

1836   Convention draws up first constitution.

1836   Arkansas admitted to the Union as the 25th State; James Sevier Conway is first Governor.

Statehouse (now War Memorial Building) virtually completed, used by first general assembly.

Bank of the State of Arkansas and Real Estate Bank chartered.

Batesville Academy incorporated.

1838   Sophia Sawyer founds Fayetteville Female Seminary.

First revised code of Arkansas laws published.

1840   Population 97,574.

Coal mining begins at Spadra.

1844   Real Estate Bank, insolvent, forfeits charter.

1846   Archibald Yell resigns from Congress to lead Arkansas cavalry regiment against Mexico.

Battalion organized to defend western frontier.

1847   Arkansas regiment fights at Buena Vista, Yell killed.

1849   Fort Smith and Van Buren become starting points for gold seekers taking overland trail to California.

1850   Population 209,897.

1852   Cane Hill College receives charter.

1853   Legislature grants first railroad charters.

1857   David Dale Owen begins first geological survey.

1858   Edward Payson Washburn paints *The Arkansas Traveler*.

Butterfield Stage Lines (St. Louis-California) operate through northwest Arkansas.

1860   Population 435,450.

Telegraph line opens between St. Louis and Fayetteville.

First State Fair held at Little Rock.

1861   State authorities seize Little Rock Arsenal.

Arkansas secedes from the Union and joins the Confederacy.

1862   Federal troops burn Napoleon.

Battle of Pea Ridge, first major Arkansas encounter of War between the States, ends indecisively.

Federal troops occupy Helena.

Battle of Prairie Grove fought.

1863   Federals capture Arkansas Post.

Confederates unsuccessfully attack Helena.

State Government moves to Washington.

Federals take Little Rock.

1864   Union State Government organized at Little Rock.

Federal movement toward southwest Arkansas defeated by capture of supply trains; Battle of Jenkins Ferry occurs.

Price makes spectacular raid into Missouri.

1865   Confederates cease military resistance.

Confederate State Government suspends.

1867   Military law established in Arkansas by Congress.

1868   "Reconstruction" constitution adopted.

Arkansas readmitted to the Union.

Free public school system established.

1868   General T. C. Hindman assassinated.
1870   Population 484,471.
1871   Railroad from Little Rock to Memphis completed.
1872   Arkansas Industrial University (now University of Arkansas) opens.
1873   First bridge across the Arkansas (Baring Cross) completed.
1874   Brooks-Baxter "war" brings armed encounters at Little Rock and other points.
         Constitution of 1874 marks end of Reconstruction era.
1876   Democratic Party regains control of Arkansas.
1879   United States Weather Bureau office set up in Little Rock.
1880   Population 802,525.
1881   General assembly determines proper pronunciation of "Arkansas."
1882   State Bar Association formed.
         Prairie County farmers organize Agricultural Wheel.
1883   Cleburne County, 75th and last in the State, created.
1884   Arkansas apples win first prizes at New Orleans Exposition.
1887   Bauxite discovered south of Little Rock.
1888   Agricultural Experiment Station opened at Arkansas Industrial University.
1890   Population 1,128,211.
1892   Poll tax made prerequisite for voting.
1893   Convict leasing system abolished.
1898   Tornado kills 50 people in Fort Smith.
         Arkansas sends two regiments to Spanish-American War.
1899   Construction of new Capitol begins.
1900   Population 1,311,564.
1901   Natural gas discovered at Fort Smith.
1904   Arkansas Supreme Court invalidates poll tax amendment.
         First successful rice crop made.
         Arkansas Federation of Labor chartered.
1906   John Huddleston discovers diamonds in Pike County.
         First railroad (St. Louis, Iron Mountain, and Southern) completed through Ozarks; resort business increases.
1907   Ouachita National Forest established.
1908   Ozark National Forest established.
         Poll tax amendment again adopted.
1909   Lumber production reaches all-time peak of 2,111,000,000 board feet.
         General assembly authorizes four district agricultural schools.
1910   Population 1,574,449.
         Arkansas Tuberculosis Sanatorium opens at Booneville.
1911   Legislature meets in new Capitol.
1913   State Highway Department established.
1915   State-wide prohibition law passed.
         Child labor law and women's minimum wage-and-hour act passed.
1917   Camp Pike built near Little Rock.
         Arkansas sends 63,632 men to World War.

1918   Women admitted to Democratic primaries.
1919   Elaine race riot occurs.
1920   Population 1,752,204.
1921   Oil production begins in southern Arkansas.
1922   Railroad strike culminates in violence at Harrison.
1923   General assembly names Arkansas the "Wonder State."
1924   Remmel Dam, first major hydroelectric development, completed.
1925   Arkansas becomes first State to ratify Federal child labor amendment.
        Petit Jean State Park, first in the State, dedicated.
1927   Greatest flood in State's history covers a fifth of Arkansas land.
1928   Senator Joe T. Robinson becomes Democratic nominee for Vice President.
        Teaching of evolution prohibited.
1930   Population 1,854,482.
1931   Air mail service begins at Little Rock.
1932   Arkansas elects first woman (Hattie W. Caraway) to United States Senate for full term.
1935   State prohibition act repealed.
        Legislature creates State Planning Board.
1936   Arkansas celebrates 100 years of statehood.
1938   All State-owned bridges made toll-free.
        First State livestock show held at North Little Rock.
1940   Population 1,949,387.

Bibliography

PHYSICAL SETTING

Adams, George I. *Zinc and Lead Deposits of Northern Arkansas.* Washington, Govt. Printing Office, 1904. 118 p. il., plates, maps. (U. S. Geological Survey. Professional Paper 24.)

Baerg, W. J. *Birds of Arkansas.* Fayetteville, University of Arkansas, 1931. 197 p. il. (University of Arkansas. Agricultural Experiment Station. Bulletin 258.)

Bramlette, M. N. *Geology of the Arkansas Bauxite Region.* Little Rock, 1936. 68 p. il., tables, maps. (Arkansas Geological Survey. Information Circular 8.)

Branner, George C. *Cinnabar in Southwestern Arkansas.* Little Rock, 1932. 51 p. il., plates, charts, maps. (Arkansas Geological Survey. Information Circular 2.)

Branner, John C. *The Zinc and Lead Region of North Arkansas.* Little Rock, Thompson Lithographing and Printing Co., 1900. 395 p. il., tables, maps. (Annual Report of the Geological Survey of Arkansas for 1892, Vol. V.) One of 14 geological studies prepared by Dr. Branner and his assistants during his incumbency as State Geologist (1887-93). Other volumes deal with Arkansas coal, manganese, novaculite, marble, iron deposits, and mineral waters; authors include Arthur Winslow, R. A. F. Penrose, L. S. Griswold, T. C. Hopkins, J. Francis Williams, and Theo. B. Comstock.

———. *The Clays of Arkansas.* Washington, Govt. Printing Office, 1908. 247 p. il., tables, charts, maps. (U. S. Geological Survey. Bulletin 351.)

Buchholz, John T., and Matton, Wilbur R. *Common Forest Trees of Arkansas.* Little Rock, Agricultural Extension Service, 1924. 84 p. il. (University of Arkansas. College of Agriculture. Extension Circular 180.)

Ferguson, Jim C. *Minerals in Arkansas.* Little Rock, Bureau of Mines, Manufactures, and Agriculture, 1922. 160 p. il., tables, charts, maps.

Fuller, Myron L. *The New Madrid Earthquake.* Washington, Govt. Printing Office, 1912. 119 p. plates. (U. S. Geological Survey. Bulletin 494.)

Giles, Albert W. *St. Peter and Older Ordovician Sandstones of Northern Arkansas.* Little Rock, 1930. 187 p. il., plates, charts, tables, diagrs., maps. (Arkansas Geological Survey. Bulletin 4.) With a section on the use of northern Arkansas sands for glass making and other purposes.

Owen, David Dale. *First Report of a Geological Reconnaissance of the Northern Counties of Arkansas, Made During the Years 1857 and 1858.* Little Rock, Johnson and Yerkes, 1858. 256 p. il., charts, tables, plates.

——. *Second Report of a Geological Reconnaissance of the Middle and Southern Counties of Arkansas, Made During the Years 1859 and 1860.* Philadelphia, C. Sherman and Son, 1860. 433 p. il., tables, plates.

Turner, Lewis M. *Trees of Arkansas.* Little Rock, Agricultural Extension Service, 1937. 112 p. il. (University of Arkansas. College of Agriculture. Extension Circular 180.)

Veatch, A. C. *Geology and Underground Water Resources of Northern Louisiana and Southern Arkansas.* Washington, Govt. Printing Office, 1906. 422 p. il., charts, tables, diagrs., maps. (U. S. Geological Survey. Professional Paper 46.)

ARCHEOLOGY AND INDIANS

Foreman, Grant, ed. *A Traveler in Indian Territory.* Cedar Rapids, Iowa, The Torch Press, 1930. 270 p. il. Ethan Allen Hitchcock's journal during his investigation of Indian mistreatment by contractors and Government agents.

——. *Indians and Pioneers.* New Haven, Yale University Press, 1930. 327 p. il. Authentic reference on early nineteenth-century history of Arkansas.

——. *The Five Civilized Tribes.* Norman, University of Oklahoma Press, 1934. 455 p. il. History of the emigration of the Choctaw, Chickasaw, Creek, Seminole, and Cherokee.

Harrington, M. R. *Certain Caddo Sites in Arkansas.* New York, Museum of the American Indian (Heye Foundation), 1920. 349 p. il.

Hodge, Frederick W., ed. *Handbook of American Indians North of Mexico.* Washington, Govt. Printing Office, 1910. 2 v. il., maps. (Smithsonian Institution. Bureau of American Ethnology. Bulletin 30.)

Lowrie, Walter, and Franklin, Walter S., eds. *American State Papers.* Vol. II, U. S. Congress Indian Affairs, Dec. 4, 1815-March 3, 1827. Washington, Gales and Seaton, 1834. 872 p.

Moore, Clarence B. *Antiquities of the St. Francis, White, and Black Rivers.* Philadelphia, P. C. Stockhausen, 1910. 362 p. plates. (Reprint from *Journal of the Academy of Natural Sciences of Philadelphia,* Vol. XIV.)

——. *Certain Mounds of Arkansas and of Mississippi.* Philadelphia, P. C. Stockhausen, 1908. 605 p. il., plates, maps. (Reprint from *Journal of the Academy of Natural Sciences of Philadelphia,* Vol. XIII.)

Moorehead, Warren King. *Archeology of the Arkansas River Valley.* New Haven, Yale University Press, 1931. 204 p. il., charts, tables, maps.

Shetrone, Henry Clyde. *The Mound Builders*. New York, D. Appleton and Co., 1930. 508 p. il., maps, biblio. Contains a section on Arkansas tumuli.

Swanton, John R. *Indians of the Lower Mississippi Valley and Adjacent Coast of the Gulf of Mexico*. Washington, Govt. Printing Office, 1911. 387 p. il., maps. (Smithsonian Institution. Bureau of American Ethnology. Bulletin 43.)

Washburn, Cephas. *Reminiscences of the Indians*. Richmond, Presbyterian Committee of Publication, 1869. 236 p. Life at Dwight Mission described by one of its best-known missionaries, with a biographical sketch of Washburn by the Rev. J. W. Moore.

TRAVEL AND EXPLORATION

Bossu, Jean Bernard. *Nouveaux Voyages dans l'Amérique Septentrionale* . . . Amsterdam, 1777. 392 p. Bossu explored the Mississippi and Arkansas Rivers in the eighteenth century.

Coues, Elliot, ed. *The Expeditions of Zebulon Montgomery Pike to the Head Waters of the Mississippi River, through Louisiana Territory, and in New Spain, during the years 1805-6-7*. New York, Francis P. Harper, 1895. 3 v. il., maps.

Cuming, Fortescue. *Sketches of a Tour to the Western Country (1807-1809)*. Cleveland, Arthur H. Clark Co., 1904. 377 p. facsim. (Vol. IV of Reuben Gold Thwaites' *Early Western Travels: 1748-1846*. Orig. pub. 1810.)

Featherstonhaugh, George William. *Excursion through the Slave States* . . . London, 1844. 2 v. il. Featherstonhaugh traversed Arkansas from the northeast to the southwest in 1834-35. His journal provides a realistic picture of pioneer conditions.

Foreman, Grant, ed. *Adventure on Red River*. Norman, University of Oklahoma Press, 1937. 199 p. il., facsim. Report of explorations along Red River by Capt. Randolph B. Marcy and Capt. C. B. McClelland, with route map.

French, B. F. *Historical Collections of Louisiana* . . . New York, Wiley and Putnam, 1846-53. (Parts I-V. New Ser. New York, J. Sabin and Sons, 1869. Second Ser. New York, Albert Mason, 1875.) An invaluable compilation of descriptive material written by early travelers and explorers.

Gerstaecker, Frederick. *Wild Sports in the Far West*. Translated from the German. Philadelphia, Lippincott, 1876. 396 p. il. Arkansas pioneer life as seen by a German adventurer between 1837 and 1843.

———. *Western Lands and Western Waters*. London, 1864. 388 p. il. Contains several references to Little Rock.

Jefferson, Thomas, and others. *The Debates and Proceedings in the Congress of the United States; with an Appendix Containing Important State Papers and Public Documents* . . . Ninth Congress. Second Session. Washington, Gales and Seaton, 1852. A report of the "Expedition of Lewis and Clarke" (cols. 1,036-1,146) contains "a statistical view" of the Indians in Arkansas and a description of the Red River country as seen by John Sibley, and an account of the Dunbar and Hunter exploration of the Ouachita River in 1804.

Lewis, Anna. *Along the Arkansas.* Dallas, The Southwest Press, 1932. 207 p. maps. Explorations of La Harpe, Joutel, and Du Tisne.

Nuttall, Thomas. *Journal of Travels into the Arkansa Territory, 1819.* Glendale, Calif., Arthur H. Clark Co., 1905. 366 p. il., facsim., maps. (Vol. XIII of Reuben Gold Thwaites' *Early Western Travels: 1748-1846.*) Arkansas life and natural setting in 1819, pictured by the English explorer-naturalist.

Schoolcraft, Henry Rowe. *Journal of a Tour into the Interior of Missouri and Arkansaw . . . in the Years 1818 and 1819.* London, 1821. 102 p. map.

————. *Scenes and Adventures in the Semi-Alpine Regions of the Ozark Mountains of Missouri and Arkansas . . .* Philadelphia, Lippincott, 1853. 256 p.

U. S. De Soto Expedition Commission. *Final Report of the United States De Soto Expedition Commission.* Washington, Govt. Printing Office, 1939. 400 p. il. facsim., maps, biblio. (76th Congress. 1st Session. House Document 71.) An exhaustive study of De Soto's exploration through the southern United States in 1539-42, with reproductions of numerous old maps.

HISTORY

A History of the Northwest Editorial Excursion to Arkansas. Little Rock, T. B. Mills and Co., 1876. 384 p. A compilation of descriptions of Arkansas written by newspaper editors from Illinois, Kansas, Michigan, Ohio, and other Northern States following a promotional excursion in the 1870's.

Arkansas Democrat. Arkansas Centennial Edition: 1836-1936. Little Rock, Arkansas Democrat Publishing Co., 1936. 98 p. il.

Arkansas Democrat. Little Rock, files for 1878 to 1940.

Arkansas Gazette. Little Rock, files for 1819 to 1940.

Arkansas Gazette. State Centennial Edition: 1836-1936. (*Arkansas Gazette,* Vol. 117, No. 209.) Little Rock, Gazette Publishing Co., 1936. 224 p. il. Contains a year-by-year chronology of significant events during Arkansas' first hundred years of statehood.

(During 1936 a number of Arkansas newspapers, in addition to the *Democrat* and the *Gazette,* published centennial editions commemorating Arkansas' one hundredth anniversary as a State. Newspapers whose editions serve as a valuable reference for the history of their respective towns and cities include the El Dorado *Sunday News,* Fayetteville *Daily Democrat,* Fort Smith *Southwest-Times Record,* Harrison *Daily Times,* Hope *Star,* Van Buren *Press-Argus,* Camden *News,* Blytheville *Courier News,* Texarkana *Gazette and Daily News,* Smackover *Journal,* Baxter *Bulletin,* Jonesboro *Daily Tribune,* Hot Springs *New Era,* and the Mena *Weekly Star.*)

Baxter, William. *Pea Ridge and Prairie Grove.* Cincinnati, Poe and Hitchcock, 1864. 262 p. An account of Arkansas' two most important battles of the War between the States.

Biographical and Historical Memoirs of Central Arkansas. Chicago, Goodspeed Publishing Co., 1889. 811 p. il.

Biographical and Historical Memoirs of Eastern Arkansas. Chicago, Goodspeed Publishing Co., 1890. 820 p. il.

Biographical and Historical Memoirs of Southern Arkansas. Chicago, Goodspeed Publishing Co., 1890. 1,080 p. il.

Bowers, Claude G. *The Tragic Era.* Cambridge, Mass., The Riverside Press (Houghton Mifflin Co.), 1929. 557 p. il. Includes a vivid description of Reconstruction in Arkansas.

Britton, Wiley. *The Civil War on the Border.* New York, G. P. Putnam's Sons, 1890. 2 v. front.

Clayton, Powell. *The Aftermath of the Civil War, in Arkansas.* New York, Neale Publishing Co., 1915. 378 p. front. Clayton was Governor of Arkansas 1868-71.

Crockett, David. *Life of David Crockett. The Original Humorist and Irrepressible Backwoodsman* . . . New York, The Perkins Book Co., n.d. 415 p. il. Includes a lively account of Crockett's visit to Little Rock.

Foreman, Grant. *Marcy & the Gold-Seekers. The Journal of Captain R. B. Marcy,* with an *Account of the Gold Rush over the Southern Route.* Norman, University of Oklahoma Press, 1939. 433 p. il., map.

Gibbs, Mifflin W. *Shadow and Light.* Washington, 1902. 372 p. The autobiography of a Negro lawyer who served as municipal judge in Little Rock and held other offices. With an introduction by Booker T. Washington.

Goodspeed, Weston Arthur. *Arkansas.* Madison, The Western Historical Association, 1904. 500 p. il. (Vol. VII of *The Province and the States.*)

Goodwin, Cardinal. *The Trans-Mississippi West (1803-1853).* New York, D. Appleton and Co., 1922. 528 p. maps.

Halliburton, W. H. *History of Arkansas County,* n.p., n.d. 190 p.

Hallum, John. *Biographical and Pictorial History of Arkansas.* Albany, Weed, Parsons and Co., 1887. 581 p. il.

———. *Reminiscences of the Civil War.* Little Rock, Tunnah and Pittard, 1903. 400 p.

Harmon, S. W. *Hell on the Border.* Fort Smith, Phoenix Publishing Co., 1898. 718 p. il. The reign of "Hanging Judge" Isaac C. Parker.

Harrell, John M. *The Brooks and Baxter War.* St. Louis, Slawson Printing Co., 1893. 276 p.

Hempstead, Fay. *A Pictorial History of Arkansas.* St. Louis, N. D. Thompson Publishing Co., 1890. 1,240 p. il.

———. *Historical Review of Arkansas.* Chicago, Lewis Publishing Co., 1911. 3 v. il.

Herndon, Dallas T. *Centennial History of Arkansas.* Chicago, The S. J. Clarke Publishing Co., 1922. 3 v. il. Vol. 1 is historical; 2 and 3 contain biographies. Mr. Herndon has been secretary of the Arkansas History Commission since 1911.

Herndon, Dallas T. *Highlights of Arkansas History.* Little Rock, Arkansas History Commission, 1922. 174 p.

———, ed. *The Arkansas Handbook: 1937–1938.* Little Rock, Arkansas History Commission, 1938. 235 p. il.

———. *Why Little Rock Was Born.* Little Rock, Central Printing Co., 1933. 181 p. The story of land "deals" and legislative manipulations behind the founding of Arkansas' capital.

History of Benton, Washington, Carroll, Madison, Crawford, Franklin and Sebastian Counties, Ark. Chicago, Goodspeed Publishing Co., 1889. 1,382 p. il.

McNutt, Walter Scott; McKnight, Olin Eli; and Hubbell, George Allen. *A History of Arkansas.* Little Rock, Democrat Printing and Lithographing Co., 1932. 622 p. il.

Monks, William. *A History of Southern Missouri and Northern Arkansas.* West Plains, Mo., West Plains Journal Co., 1907. 247 p.

Nash, Charles Edward. *Biographical Sketches of Gen. Pat Cleburne and Gen. T. C. Hindman.* Little Rock, Tunnah and Pittard, 1898. 800 p. il. Cleburne and Hindman were Confederate leaders from Arkansas.

North Little Rock Times. Industrial Recovery Number. North Little Rock, Times Printing and Publishing Co., 1936. 68 p. il. A valuable reference for North Little Rock history.

Pope, William F. *Early Days in Arkansas.* Little Rock, Fred W. Allsopp, 1895. 330 p. il. One of Arkansas' earliest histories.

Reynolds, John Hugh. *Arkansas from 1539 to 1836.* (From Vol. III, *The South in the Building of the Nation.* Richmond, the Southern Publication Society, 1909. pp. 270–287.) Arkansas under French, Spanish, and Territorial rule.

———. *Makers of Arkansas History.* Chicago, Silver, Burdette and Co., 1911. 353 p. il.

———, ed. *Publications of the Arkansas Historical Association.* Fayetteville, Arkansas Historical Association, 1906–17. 4 v. il. Competently written essays touching many important phases of Arkansas history.

Shinn, Josiah Hazen. *Pioneers and Makers of Arkansas.* Little Rock, Democrat Printing and Lithographing Co., 1908. 423 p. il.

Staples, Thomas S. *Reconstruction in Arkansas.* New York, Columbia University, 1923. 450 p.

Stockard, S. W. *The History of Lawrence, Jackson, Independence and Stone Counties.* Little Rock, Arkansas Democrat Publishing Co., 1904. 204 p. il.

Thomas, David Y., ed. *Arkansas and Its People.* New York, American Historical Society, 1930. 4 v. il. Vols. 1 and 2 contain essays on Arkansas history and institutions; 3 and 4 are biographical.

Williams, Harry Lee. *History of Craighead County.* Little Rock, Parke-Harper Co., 1930. 648 p. il., facsim.

GOVERNMENT

Blocher, S. J. *Civil Government of Arkansas and the United States.* Richmond, B. F. Johnson Publishing Co., 1907. 391 p.

Brannen, C. O. *Characteristics and Costs of County Government in Arkansas.* Fayetteville, 1937. 91 p. tables, diagr. (University of Arkansas. Agricultural Experiment Station. Bulletin 338.)

Donaghey, George W. *Autobiography.* Benton, Ark., L. B. White Printing Co., 1939. 315 p. il.

———. *Building a State Capitol.* Little Rock, Parke-Harper Co., 1937. 377 p. il. Under Governor Donaghey's administration (1909–13) Arkansas' present State capitol was completed.

Dunaway, L. S. *Jeff Davis, Governor and United States Senator.* Little Rock, Democrat Printing and Lithographing Co., 1913. 255 p. il.

Foote, Henry S. *The Bench and Bar of the South and Southwest.* St. Louis, Soule, Thomas, and Wentworth, 1876. 264 p.

Jacobson, Charles. *The Life Story of Jeff Davis.* Little Rock, Parke-Harper Co., 1925. 241 p. il.

McNutt, Walter Scott. *Government of Arkansas and the Nation.* Little Rock, Democrat Printing and Lithographing Co., 1933. 416 p. il.

PEOPLE AND FOLKWAYS

Allsopp, Fred W. *Folklore of Romantic Arkansas.* Kansas City, The Grolier Society, 1931. 2 v. il.

Clemens, Samuel L. *Life on the Mississippi.* New York, Harper & Brothers, 1927. 527 p. il.

Couch, W. T., ed. *Culture in the South.* Chapel Hill, University of North Carolina Press, 1934. 711 p.

Daniels, Jonathan. *A Southerner Discovers the South.* New York, The Macmillan Co., 1938. 346 p. A series of observations on agricultural and social conditions in the South, with several chapters relating to Arkansas.

Puckett, Newbell N. *Folk Beliefs of the Southern Negro.* Chapel Hill, University of North Carolina Press, 1926. 640 p. il.

Randolph, Vance, ed. *An Ozark Anthology.* Caldwell, Idaho, The Caxton Printers, Ltd., 1940. 374 p. Stories and sketches by Charles J. Finger, Charlie May Simon, Charles Morrow Wilson, Eleanor Risley, Rose O'Neill, Thomas Hart Benton, Rose Wilder Lane, and other Ozark writers.

———. *From an Ozark Holler.* New York, The Vanguard Press, 1933. 252 p. il. Ozark legends and folktales.

———. *The Ozarks.* New York, The Vanguard Press, 1931. 310 p. il. An outstanding authority on the Ozarks, Mr. Randolph supplies a sympathetic general view of hill country folklore and folk customs.

Read, Opie. *An Arkansas Planter.* Chicago, Rand, McNally and Co., 1896. 315 p. il. Fiction with an authentic Arkansas plantation background.

Street, James A. *Look Away: A Dixie Note Book.* New York, Viking Press, 1936. A collection of stories, usually with a sensational turn, derived from incidents in Arkansas and other Southern States.

Wilson, Charles Morrow. *Acres of Sky.* New York, Putnam, 1930. 340 p. il.

——. *Backwoods America.* Chapel Hill, University of North Carolina Press, 1934. 209 p. il.

RESOURCES AND CONSERVATION

Arkansas Forestry Commission. *Annual Report.* Little Rock, 1934–40.

Arkansas State Planning Board. *Arkansas Water Resources.* Little Rock, Arkansas State Planning Board, 1939. 92 p. il., tables, charts, maps.

——. *Progress Report: 1939.* Little Rock, Parke-Harper Co., 1936. 244 p. il., charts, tables, maps. A valuable and comprehensive source book regarding Arkansas' physical setting and natural resources.

——. *The Arkansas Plan for Flood Relief in Eastern Arkansas.* Little Rock, Arkansas State Planning Board, 1938. 35 p. il., charts, maps.

Branner, George C. *Outlines of Arkansas' Mineral Resources.* Little Rock, Bureau of Mines, Manufactures, and Agriculture in collaboration with Arkansas Geological Survey, 1927. 352 p. il., tables, charts, diagrs., maps.

Bruner, E. Murray. *Forestry and Forest Fires in Arkansas.* Little Rock, Agricultural Extension Service, 1930. 30 p. il., charts, tables, maps. (University of Arkansas. College of Agriculture. Extension Circular 281.)

Campbell, David. *Wooden Riches.* Little Rock, Arkansas Forestry Commission, 1938. 31 p. il., charts, tables, maps. (Bulletin 10.)

Collier, Arthur J. *The Arkansas Coal Field.* Washington, Govt. Printing Office, 1907. 158 p. il., tables, charts, maps. (U. S. Geological Survey. Bulletin 326.)

Harper, C. Armitage, and Henry, L. A. *Conservation in Arkansas.* Little Rock, Democrat Printing and Lithographing Co., 1939. 362 p. il., charts, maps. A school textbook with chapters on soils, water resources, minerals, forestry, wildlife, and parks.

Henry, James P. *Resources of the State of Arkansas.* Little Rock, Price and McClure, 1872. 2d ed. 164 p.

Simpich, Frederick. "The Great Mississippi Flood of 1927." *The National Geographic Magazine,* September 1927, v. 52: 243–89. With excellent photographs of inundated areas in Arkansas.

AGRICULTURE

McCormick, T. C. *Rural Social Organization in South-Central Arkansas.* Fayetteville, 1934. 39 p. tables. (University of Arkansas. Agricultural Experiment Station. Bulletin 313.) Factual study of farm social life.

Metzler, William H. *Population Trends and Adjustments in Arkansas.* Fayetteville, 1940. 59 p. tables, charts. (University of Arkansas.

Agricultural Experiment Station. Bulletin 388.) A view of population movements within the State with special reference to economic opportunities.

University of Arkansas College of Agriculture. *The Soils of Arkansas.* Fayetteville, 1923. 83 p. il., tables, maps. (Agricultural Experiment Station. Bulletin 187.) Competent analysis of Arkansas soil types.

——. *Types of Farming in Arkansas.* Little Rock, Agricultural Extension Service, 1936. 76 p. il., tables, maps. (Extension Circular 351.) A comprehensive survey, by regions, of farming in Arkansas.

Wilson, Isabella C., and Metzler, William H. *Sickness and Medical Care in an Ozark Area in Arkansas.* Fayetteville, 1938. 39 p. tables, charts. (University of Arkansas. Agricultural Experiment Station. Bulletin 353.)

——. *Sickness and Medical Care Among the Negro Population in a Delta Area of Arkansas.* Fayetteville, 1939. 36 p. tables. (University of Arkansas. Agricultural Experiment Station. Bulletin 372.) Includes material on Negro herb and home remedies and "charms."

Wilson, W. T., and Bryan, Stuart L. *Index Numbers of Prices Received for Arkansas Farm Products, 1910–1937.* Fayetteville, 1938. 46 p. tables, charts. (University of Arkansas. Agricultural Experiment Station. Bulletin 363.)

INDUSTRY AND TRANSPORTATION

Farris, Rev. J. K. *The Harrison Riot: The Reign of the Mob on the Missouri and North Arkansas Railroad.* Wynne, Ark., 1924. 195 p. il.

Gooden, Orville Thrasher. *The Missouri and North Arkansas Railroad Strike.* New York, Columbia University Press, 1926. 274 p. tables, maps. (*Studies in History, Economics, and Public Law.* Edited by the Faculty of Political Science of Columbia University. No. 275.) A carefully documented study of industrial strife in northern Arkansas in 1922–23.

Phillips, D. L. *The Early History of the Cairo and Fulton Railroad, and Its Successor Companies.* Little Rock, 1927. 840 p. il.

Steel, A. A. *Coal Mining in Arkansas.* Little Rock, Arkansas Geological Survey, 1910. 383 p. il., tables, charts, maps.

U. S. Department of Commerce, Bureau of the Census. *Manufactures: Arkansas.* Washington, Govt. Printing Office. (1860, 1870, 1880, 1899, 1904, 1909, 1914, 1919, 1921, 1923, 1925, 1927, 1929, 1931, 1933, 1935, 1937.)

Worthen, W. B. *Early Banking in Arkansas.* Little Rock, Democrat Printing and Lithographing Co., 1906. 129 p.

RELIGION

Anderson, James A. *Centennial History of Arkansas Methodism.* Benton, Ark., L. B. White Printing Co., 1935. 556 p. il.

Historical Commission of the Diocese of Little Rock. *The History of Catholicity in Arkansas.* Little Rock, The Guardian, 1925. Il.

Jewell, Horace. *History of Methodism in Arkansas.* Little Rock, Press Printing Co., 1892. 445 p.

Synod of Arkansas. *The History of Presbyterianism in Arkansas.* Little Rock, Arkansas Democrat Publishing Co., 1902. 199 p. il.

EDUCATION

Dawson, Howard A., and Little, Harry A. *Financial and Administrative Needs of the Public Schools of Arkansas.* v. I. Little Rock, State Department of Education, 1930. 100 p. tables, map.

Reynolds, John Hugh, and Thomas, David Y. *History of the University of Arkansas.* Fayetteville, University of Arkansas, 1910. 555 p. il.

Shinn, Josiah Hazen. *History of Education in Arkansas.* Washington, 1900. 121 p.

U. S. Department of the Interior. Office of Education. *Biennial Survey of Education: 1932–1934.* Washington, Govt. Printing Office, 1937. (U. S. Department of the Interior. Bulletin 2, 1935.) Collection of statistical reports covering the general field of education in the United States.

Weeks, Stephen B. *History of Public School Instruction in Arkansas.* Washington, Govt. Printing Office, 1912. 131 p. tables. (U. S. Bureau of Education. Bulletin 27, Whole No. 500.)

NEWSPAPERS

Allsopp, Fred W. *History of the Arkansas Press for a Hundred Years and More.* Little Rock, Parke-Harper Co., 1922. 684 p. il.

———. *Twenty Years in a Newspaper Office.* Little Rock, Central Printing Co., 1907. 266 p.

Arkansas Gazette. Centennial Edition: 1819–1919. Little Rock, Gazette Publishing Co., 1919. 240 p. il. Commemorates the 100th anniversary of the *Gazette.*

Harper, Clio. *History of the Arkansas Press Association.* Little Rock, Parke-Harper Co., 1930. 116 p. Contains a digest of the Association's annual meetings from 1873 to 1930.

Read, Opie. *Emmett Bonlore.* Chicago, Laird and Lee, 1891. An Arkansas newspaper editor is the principal character of this novel.

———. *I Remember.* New York, Richard R. Smith, Inc., 1930. 335 p. Includes memoirs of the author's newspaper days in Arkansas.

ARTS AND LETTERS

Allsopp, Fred W. *Albert Pike: A Biography.* Little Rock, Parke-Harper Co., 1928. 369 p. il.

———. *The Poets and Poetry of Arkansas.* Little Rock, Central Printing Co., 1933. 232 p.

Babcock, Bernie, and Ludwig, O. C., eds. *Pictures and Poems of Arkansas.* Little Rock, Sketch Book Publishing Co., 1908. 160 p. il.

Lewis, Troy W., ed. *The Scrapbook of Arkansas Literature.* Little Rock, printed for American Caxton Society Press by Central Printing Co., 1939. 432 p.

Matthews, Jim P., and Jones, Virgil L., comps. *Arkansas Books.* Fayetteville, 1931. 31 p. (University of Arkansas. General Extension Service. Bulletin, Vol. 25, No. 8.) A good, although incomplete, bibliography.

Van Deventer, Horace. *Albert Pike.* Jackson, Tenn., 1909. 83 p. front.

Wooten, Denham. "The History of the Theater in Arkansas." *Arkansas Gazette* Sunday Magazine, issues for Nov. 17 through Dec. 22, 1935. This work is the most complete and authoritative in its field.

List of Consultants

Allsopp, Fred W. Business Manager, *Arkansas Gazette.* Little Rock.
Arnold, W. H. Attorney. Texarkana.
Bankston, Marvin S. President, Arkansas Agricultural and Mechanical College. Monticello.
Baughman, Harold E. Fort Smith.
Betts, J. E. Assistant Engineer, U. S. Corps of Engineers. Little Rock.
Bishop, Mrs. Carroll. Executive Secretary, Arkansas State Library Commission. Little Rock.
Blackman, M. C. Little Rock.
Blackman, Mrs. Pearle. Draftsman, Pulaski County Planning Board. Little Rock.
Bone, S. M. Circuit Judge. Batesville.
Bonslagel, Miss Connie J. State Home Demonstration Agent. Little Rock.
Booth, H. D. Traffic Supervisor, Arkansas State Highway Commission. Little Rock.
Bowker, S. W. Secretary, Jonesboro Chamber of Commerce. Jonesboro.
Bragg, Zack. West Memphis.
Brannen, Claude O. Professor of Rural Economics and Sociology, University of Arkansas. Fayetteville.
Branner, George C. State Geologist. Little Rock.
Brashears, Vol. Berryville.
Brewer, Adrian L. Artist. Little Rock.
Brooks, J. Mell. Secretary, Blytheville Chamber of Commerce. Blytheville.
Brown, Dr. John E. President, John Brown University. Siloam Springs.
Bryan, Stuart L. Agricultural Statistician, U. S. Department of Agriculture. Little Rock.
Buckley, V. B. Engineer, Pulaski County Planning Board. Little Rock.
Burks, H. Ray. Architect. Little Rock.
Campbell, W. S. Secretary-Manager, Fayetteville Chamber of Commerce. Fayetteville.
Capel, Robert B. Director of Dramatics, Hendrix College. Conway.
Chambers, Miss Erle (Deceased, 1941). Executive Secretary, Arkansas Tuberculosis Association. Little Rock.
Cole, H. S. Meteorologist (Retired), U. S. Weather Bureau, Little Rock.
Crist, Marion L. Engineer, Little Rock Municipal Water Works. Little Rock.

Crowell, A. M. Director, Arkansas Oil and Gas Commission. El Dorado.

Davies, S. G. Director, Arkansas State Parks Commission. Little Rock.

Deane, E. C. Secretary, El Dorado Chamber of Commerce. El Dorado.

Delaney, Bill. Dealer in rare books. Fort Smith.

Dellinger, S. C. Professor of Zoology, University of Arkansas. Fayetteville.

Delony, Lawson L. Architect. Little Rock.

Deuster, Louis. Registrar, Subiaco College. Subiaco.

Dickinson, S. Dorris. Archeologist. Fayetteville.

Eichenbaum, Howard. Architect. Little Rock.

Eldridge, H. E. Registrar, Arkansas State College. Jonesboro.

Eno, Miss Clara B. Historian. Van Buren.

Epstein, Ben. *Arkansas Gazette*. Little Rock.

Erhart, Frank J. Architect. Little Rock.

Etter, W. H. Publisher, *Journal-Telegraph*. Washington.

Finger, Charles J. (Deceased, 1941). Author. Fayetteville.

Fordyce, Colonel John R. (Deceased, 1939). Vice Chairman, U. S. De Soto Expedition Commission, Little Rock.

Freund, H. Louis. Artist. Conway.

Frierson, Charles D. Attorney. Jonesboro.

Gaffney, Rt. Rev. Msgr. James P. St. John's Seminary, Little Rock.

Garrett, Mrs. Rufus N. El Dorado.

Garver, N. B. Bridge Engineer, Arkansas State Highway Commission. Little Rock.

Gazzolo, Joe. Texarkana.

Giles, Albert W. Professor of Geology, University of Arkansas. Fayetteville.

Graves, D. N. Secretary, Arkansas Game and Fish Commission. Little Rock.

Green, T. R. Secretary, Pine Bluff Chamber of Commerce. Pine Bluff.

Greene, Crawford. Arkansas State Department of Education. Little Rock.

Greene, Mrs. Vera Hardcastle. Librarian, Little Rock Junior College. Little Rock.

Gruver, F. A. Engineer, Operations Division, U. S. Corps of Engineers. Little Rock.

Guy, Francis Joseph. Historian, St. John's Seminary. Little Rock.

Hall, R. V. Civil Engineer. Texarkana.

Hall, Robert P. Secretary-Manager, Arkansas State Chamber of Commerce. Little Rock.

Halliburton, Arthur C. Art Director (1939-40), Arkansas State Publicity Department. Little Rock.

Hamilton, Scott D. Manager, Fort Smith Chamber of Commerce. Fort Smith.

Hanger, Mrs. Frederick. Little Rock.

Hardison, Dr. T. W. Chairman, Arkansas State Parks Commission. Morrilton.

Harris, Dr. M. Lafayette. President, Philander Smith College. Little Rock.

Henry, L. A. Engineer-Director, Arkansas State Planning Board. Little Rock.

Herndon, Dallas T. Executive Secretary, Arkansas History Commission. Little Rock.

Herring, Fred J. Engineer, Arkansas State Highway Commission. Little Rock.

Hickmon, Walter C. Meteorologist, U. S. Weather Bureau. Little Rock.

Hogan, Joe. Superintendent, State Fish Hatchery. Lonoke.

Hogue, Howard. Photographer. Nashville.

Holman, Miss Anna Jim. Agricultural Extension Service. Little Rock.

Horlacher, Walter R. Dean, College of Agriculture, University of Arkansas. Fayetteville.

Horton, Worth. Little Rock.

Hudson, Ralph M. Department of Art, University of Arkansas. Fayetteville.

Humphrey, L. M. Associate Agronomist, Cotton Branch Experiment Station. Marianna.

Huxtable, W. G. Chief Engineer, St. Francis Levee District. West Memphis.

Jackson, L. A. Manager, Little Rock Municipal Water Works. Little Rock.

Johnson, Earle. *Arkansas Democrat.* Little Rock.

Jones, Scipio A. Attorney. Little Rock.

King, Clifton. Artist. Mabelvale.

Koen, H. R. Forest Supervisor, Ozark National Forest. Russellville.

Lamb, W. E. Missouri Pacific R.R. Little Rock.

Large, Miss Sally E. Little Rock Public Library. Little Rock.

Lawson, Miss Willie A. Executive Secretary, Arkansas Education Association. Little Rock.

Leath, Sam A. Paragould.

Lemke, W. J. Department of Journalism, University of Arkansas. Fayetteville.

Lemley, Harry J. Judge, U. S. District Court. Hope.

Leonard, E. S. District Conservationist, Soil Conservation Service. Hope.

Livingston, Mrs. Ruby E. Russellville.

Loughborough, Mrs. J. F. Little Rock.

MacDuff, Mrs. Inez Hale. *Arkansas Gazette.* Little Rock.

Matthews, Miss Jim P. Fayetteville.

McAninch, A. N. Architect. Little Rock.

McComb, William. Director, Arkansas Automobile Club. Little Rock.

McKinley, E. I. State Labor Commissioner. Little Rock.

Mead, M. V. Judge, Jefferson County. Pine Bluff.

Melton, M. E. Secretary, Texarkana Chamber of Commerce. Texarkana.

Metzger, Ray. Secretary, Arkansas Field Trials Association. Little Rock.

Mikel, G. E. Secretary, District 21, United Mine Workers of America, Muskogee, Okla.

Miller, Fletcher. Artist. Little Rock.

Miller, Paul H. Arkansas State Plant Board. Little Rock.

Minton, Dr. H. L. Professor of Geography, Arkansas State Teachers' College. Conway.

Moore, David. Hartford Music Publishing Company. Hartford.

Moore, Dr. Dwight M. Professor of Botany, University of Arkansas. Fayetteville.

Nelson, A. L. Forest Supervisor, Ouachita National Forest. Hot Springs.

Noce, Major Daniel. District Engineer, U. S. Corps of Engineers. Memphis.

O'Shea, W. D. City Engineer. Fort Smith.

Parke, A. W. Secretary, Arkansas Centennial Commission. Little Rock.

Patterson, D. Palmer. Director, Arkansas State Employment Service. Little Rock.

Patton, Fred J. *Southwest Times-Record.* Fort Smith.

Pickins, Mrs. Burt. Chairman, Arkansas Federation of Garden Clubs. Little Rock.

Plemmons, L. R. City Engineer. Hot Springs.

Powell, Laurence. Director, Symphony Orchestra. Grand Rapids, Mich.

Presson, Bert. Adjutant, Arkansas Department, American Legion. Little Rock.

Pruniski, John. Editor, *North Little Rock Times.* North Little Rock.

Raff, Alfred. West Helena.

Reed, Smith. Industrial Engineer, Arkansas Agricultural and Industrial Commission. Little Rock.

Riddell, Glenn E. State Coordinator, Soil Conservation Service. Little Rock.

Riley, J. D. Superintendent, Arkansas Tuberculosis Sanatorium. Booneville.

Robins, Frank E. Editor, *Log Cabin Democrat.* Conway.

Robinson, Mrs. Bigelow. Director, Museum of Fine Arts. Little Rock.

Rodgers, W. C. Attorney. Nashville.

Rose, George B. Attorney. Little Rock.

Rudder, Hilary. City Engineer. Pine Bluff.

Sanders, Rabbi Ira E. Little Rock.

Scull, Miles, Jr. El Dorado.

Shiras, Tom. Editor, *Baxter Bulletin.* Mountain Home.

Shuffield, Dr. Joe F. President, Arkansas Fox Hunters Association. Little Rock.

Smith, Miss Alta. Hot Springs Chamber of Commerce. Hot Springs.

Snook, Miss Vera. Librarian, Little Rock Public Library. Little Rock.

Stephens, Oren. *Arkansas Democrat.* Little Rock.

Stuck, Miss Florence. Jonesboro.

Thackrey, H. M. Secretary-Treasurer, Arkansas State Federation of Labor. Little Rock.

Thatcher, H. K. Executive Director, Arkansas Agricultural and Industrial Commission. Little Rock.

Thomas, Dr. David Y. Professor of History and Political Science (Retired), University of Arkansas. Fayetteville.

Thomas, H. A. Chief Draftsman, Arkansas State Planning Board. Little Rock.

Thompson, Roy. President, Little Rock Baseball Association. Little Rock.

Vaughan, Mrs. Frank. Little Rock.

Vestal, C. H. Florist. Little Rock.

Watson, J. L. Superintendent, Pulaski County Rural School District. Little Rock.

Watson, Dr. John Brown. President, Arkansas Agricultural, Mechanical and Normal College. Pine Bluff.

Williams, Gene. Secretary, Helena Chamber of Commerce. Helena.

Wilson, B. N. Professor of Drawing and Architecture, University of Arkansas. Fayetteville.

Wilson, Charles Morrow. Author, Fayetteville.

Wilson, Isabella C. Professor of Home Economics, University of Arkansas. Fayetteville.

Wilson, L. A. El Dorado.

Wolf, George. Regional Director of Information, Farm Security Administration. Little Rock.

Zass, W. W. Chief Engineer, Arkansas State Highway Commission. Little Rock.

MAP OF
ARKANSAS
IN SIX SECTIONS

Index to Cities and Towns

Index to Points of Interest

LEGEND FOR STATE MAP

U.S. Highways .... ◁▭▭〔70〕▭▭▷

State Highways .... ◁▭▭[39]▭▭▷

Points of Interest (Symbol)............... ■

National Forests....................

U.S. Migratory
Bird Refuges

MAP SHOWING SECTIONAL DIVISION OF STATE MAP

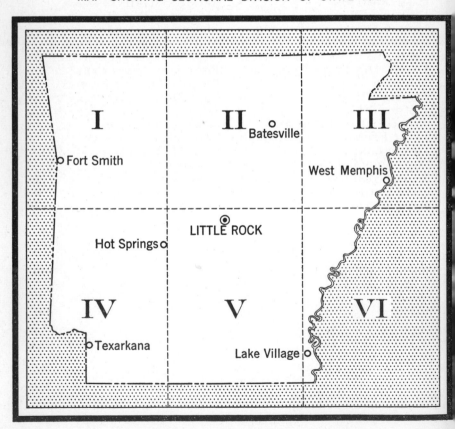

I

II
○ Batesville

III

○ Fort Smith

West Memphis ○

Hot Springs ○

● LITTLE ROCK

IV

V

VI

○ Texarkana

Lake Village ○

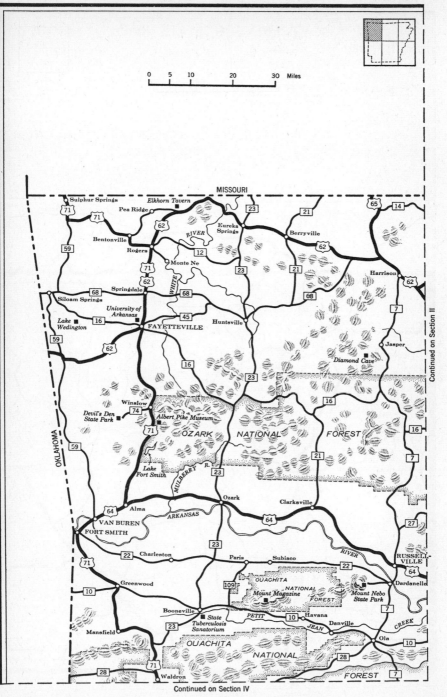

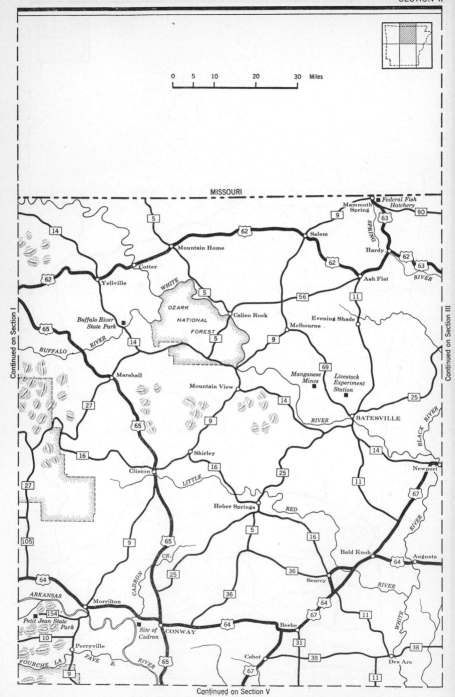

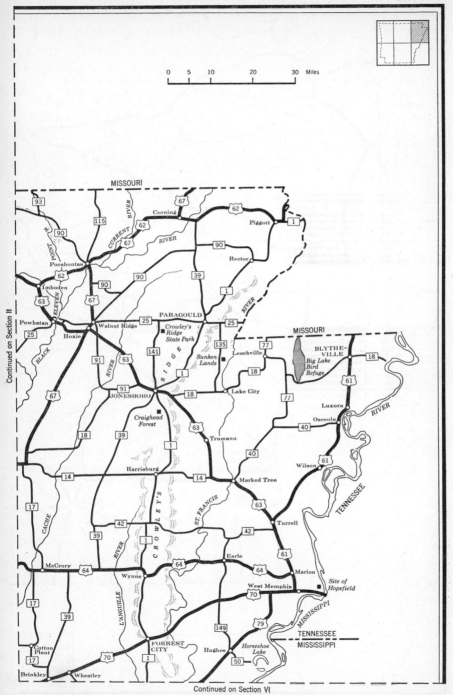

Continued on Section II

Continued on Section VI

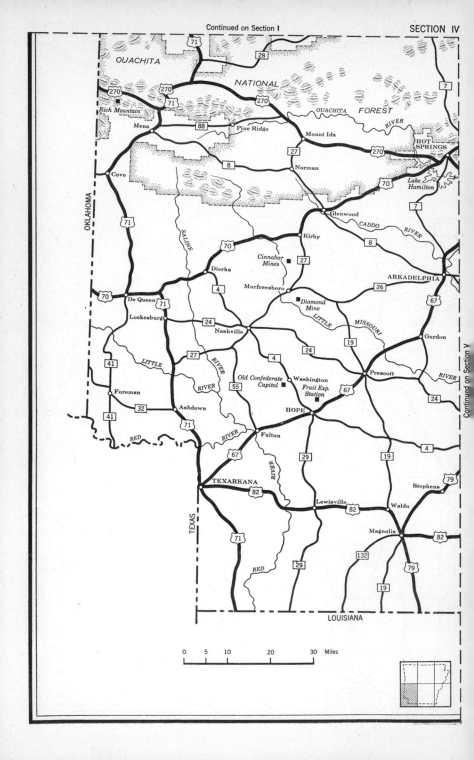

Continued on Section V

0   5   10   20   30   Miles

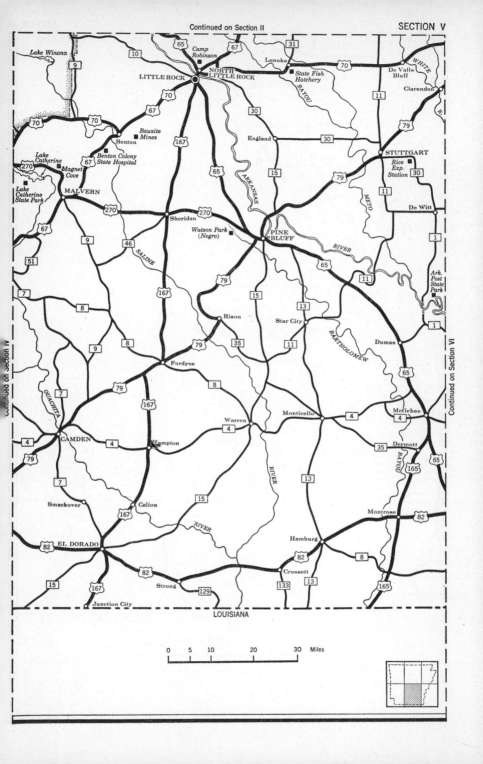

Continued on Section IV

Continued on Section VI

Lake Winona

9

10

65

67

Camp Robinson

31

Lonoke

70

De Valls Bluff

WHITE R.

LITTLE ROCK

NORTH LITTLE ROCK

State Fish Hatchery

11

Clarendon

70

70

67

70

167

30

BAYOU

30

England

30

79

Bauxite Mines

Benton

65

15

STUTTGART

Rice Exp. Station

30

Lake Catherine

270

67

Benton Colony State Hospital

ARKANSAS

79

METO

11

De Witt

Magnet Cove

MALVERN

270

270

Sheridan

PINE BLUFF

RIVER

1

Lake Catherine State Park

51

7

9

46

SALINE

Watson Park (Negro)

65

11

Ark. Post State Park

167

79

8

15

13

BARTHOLOMEW

1

9

8

Rison

35

Star City

11

Dumas

65

79

Fordyce

79

8

Monticello

4

McGehee

4

OUACHITA

7

167

Warren

4

35

Dermott

CAMDEN

4

Hampton

BAYOU

165

79

RIVER

13

65

7

15

Calion

167

Montrose

82

Smackover

El DORADO

82

Hamburg

8

15

167

82

Crossett

165

82

Strong

129

133

13

Junction City

LOUISIANA

0   5   10   20   30   Miles

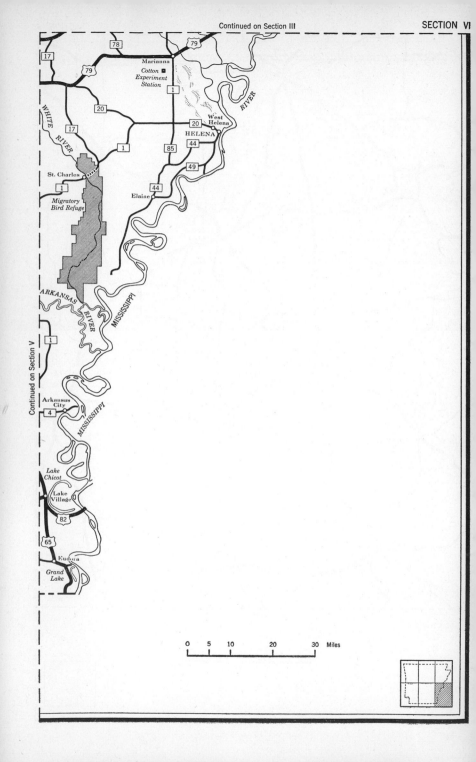

Continued on Section V

0   5   10   20   30   Miles

Index

425

Murrell, John, 282-283, 294
Museums: Aluminum, 231; Fairfield, 135, 325; Fine Arts, 128, 186; Geology and Ethnology, 154, 161; Harlan, 256; Henderson, 316; Hudson, 297; Indian, 161; Kimzey, 334; Koleta's Kurio Kabin, 386; Lemley, 28, 216; Natural History, 186; Phillips County, 353; Pike, 315-316; Pioneer, 260; Saunders, 263; State History, 181; Subiaco, 287
Music, 119-123
Mussel digging, 261
Mussels, 207, 291, 343
Myriophyllum moss, 290

Nance Motor Coaches, 196
Napoleon, 281
Narrows, The, 316
Nash, C. E., 352
Nashville, 234-235
Nation, Carry, 112, 263-264
National banks, 41
National Cemetery, 143, 148
National Forests, 19. *See also* Ouachita National Forest and Ozark National Forest
National Grange, 65-66
National Guard, 183
National Park Service, 155
Native plants, 12-14
Natural gas, 21
Natural resources, 18-24
Natural setting, 6-17
Natural Steps, 361
Negro Boys' Industrial School, 276
Negroes: Blytheville, 132; CCC camp, 382; churches, 85-86; education, 90, 182-183; Elaine riot, 354; El Dorado, 137; folkways, 100-102; FSA Colony, 354; Fort Smith, 143-144; Hot Springs, 156; Jonesboro, 165; Little Rock and North Little Rock, 171; music, 121, 327; Pine Bluff, 190; Texarkana, 198; Tin Cup, 313
Neighbors, The, 127
Nelson Packing plant, 310
Nettleton, 166, 293
Nevada County, 214
New Blaine, 286
New Gascony, 37, 190, 191
New Madrid earthquake, 10, 293
New South mill, 353
Newark, 386
Newport, 206-207
Newspapers, 93-95
Newton County, 297
Nickname, State, 20
Nighthawks, 170
Niloak Pottery plant, 71, 211

Noland, Charles Fenton Mercer, 5, 110, 385
Norfork, 259-260
Norman, 338
Norris Park, 136
North Fork, 259
North Little Rock, 168-188
North Mountain, 155, 161
Northeast Arkansas League, 164
Norton Co. plant, 231
Norton-Wheeler Stave mill, 194
Notrebe, Frederick, 281
Novaculite, 22, 335; quarry, 232; Uplift, 7, 9
Nuttall, Thomas, 108-109, 247, 344; Arkansas Post, 358; Dardanelle, 285; Fort Smith, 144; Hot Springs, 156; Little Rock, 173; Mount Magazine, 364

Oaklawn Jockey Club, 162-163
Oakland Park, 189, 194
Observation Tower (Hot Springs), 162
Oden, 339
O'Hara, William, 172
Oil, 21, 70, 304, 369-370; refineries, 70; tanks, 377-378. *See also* El Dorado
Oil, cottonseed, 70
Oil Painters and Sculptors Society, 128
Oil Trough, 386
Oklahoma Transportation Lines, 142
Ol' Man Adam an' His Chillun, 210
Ola, 363
Old Austin, 210
Old Mill (Lakewood), 229
Old Town Lake, 354
Omaha, 268
On a Slow Train Through Arkansaw, 111
Opera Bouffé Troupe, 117
Opera House (Fort Smith), 150
Opossums, 170, 319
Orchids, 12
Orr, Rev. David, 84-85
Osage Indians, 30, 31, 32, 306
Osage Orange, 314
Osceola (town), 325-326
Osceola, Chief, 325
Ostrich farm, 154
Otters, 226
Otto the Knight, 111
Ouachita College, 90, 213
Ouachita County, 302, 303
Ouachita Mountains, 6, 9
Ouachita National Forest, 19, 339, 364
Ouachita River, 8, 337, 339
Owen, David Dale, 9, 289
Owen, Ezra M., 230
"Owling," 77